A World
DIVIDED

HUMAN RIGHTS AND CRIMES
AGAINST HUMANITY

Series Editor: Eric D. Weitz

A list of titles in this series appears at the back of the book.

A World DIVIDED

The Global Struggle for Human Rights
in the Age of Nation-States

ERIC D. WEITZ

PRINCETON UNIVERSITY PRESS | PRINCETON AND OXFORD

Copyright © 2019 by Princeton University Press

Published by Princeton University Press
41 William Street, Princeton, New Jersey 08540
6 Oxford Street, Woodstock, Oxfordshire OX20 1TR

press.princeton.edu

All Rights Reserved

Library of Congress Control Number: 2019937950
ISBN 978-0-691-14544-0
ISBN (e-book) 978-0-691-18555-2

British Library Cataloging-in-Publication Data is available

Editorial: Brigitta van Rheinberg, Eric Crahan, Pamela Weidman and Thalia Leaf
Production Editorial: Jenny Wolkowicki
Text design: Leslie Flis
Jacket cover design: Faceout Studio
Production: Merli Guerra
Publicity: James Schneider and Kate Farquhar-Thomson
Copyeditor: Maia Vaswani

Jacket art: J. Thullen, *Execution of Dakota Indians, Mankato, Minnesota, 1884.*
Courtesy of the Minnesota Historical Society

This book has been composed in Arno Pro

Printed on acid-free paper. ∞

Printed in the United States of America

10 9 8 7 6 5 4 3 2 1

for Brigitta

In meinen Tagesträumen,
In meinem nächtlichen Wachen,
Stets klingt mir in der Seele
Dein allerliebstes Lachen

—Heinrich Heine, *Neue Gedichte* (1844)

CONTENTS

ILLUSTRATIONS

FIGURES

COLOR PLATES (following page 218)

MAPS

TABLES

ACKNOWLEDGMENTS

IT IS with great pleasure that I can finally acknowledge the many individuals and institutions that helped me formulate, research, and write *A World Divided*. First and foremost is Brigitta van Rheinberg, editor extraordinaire. This book, like my previous two, arose in conversation with her, both in its conceptual phase and in the many subsequent years of research and writing. Brigitta read the entire manuscript three times, individual chapters a number of additional times. Her superb, incisive commentaries have contributed greatly to whatever qualities the book has. She also ensured that I always kept the reader in mind. Along the way, Brigitta and I became more than editor and author, and it is to her that *A World Divided* is dedicated.

In the last stages, Eric Crahan took the manuscript in hand and saw it through to final publication. He also offered incisive commentary on the text and excellent guidance. I am grateful also to my superb production editor, Jenny Wolkowicki, and the entire production staff at Princeton University Press. I thank also Maia Vaswani for her excellent copyediting. Some historians move around to different publishers; I have always been thrilled to publish with PUP. Aside from the individuals mentioned here, the Press in general has always been wonderfully supportive—and efficient.

Since I arrived at the City College of New York in 2012, Rajan Menon has been a great friend. His commitment to intellectual life has made him, for me, a model scholar-teacher. He is a wonderful interlocutor on all things, from politics and history to college business, family life, and single malts. Raj also read the entire manuscript, and individual chapters more than once. His sharp criticism, on substance and style, has also contributed greatly to the final version of the book.

Hanna Schissler and I have been friends for twenty-five years. We have shared many experiences. She probably does not know it, but her comments over the years on articles I published and lectures I presented on the themes of this book helped convince me that I was on to something and should stay the course. She also read the entire manuscript, individual chapters more than once. As always, she too offered superb commentary and insightful criticisms.

Twenty-two friends and colleagues from the United States, Europe, and Australia agreed to read the entire manuscript and discuss it for one intense day at City College in November 2017. When I sent them the text, I thought I was just about done. They convinced me (quickly) that I still had some work to do. I am enormously grateful to all of them. I know the commitment of time and thought it takes to participate in this kind of workshop. So many thanks to Carlo Accetti, Omer Bartov, Jacqueline Bhabha, Sebastian Conrad, Eric Crahan, Bruce Cronin, Sheldon Garon, Fabian Klose, Sandrine Kott, Krishan Kumar, Rajan Menon, Dirk Moses, Samuel Moyn, Mary Nolan, Brigitta van Rheinberg, Hanna Schissler, Kathryn Sikkink, Jack Snyder, Ron Suny, John Torpey, Natasha Wheatley, and Danielle Zach. Michael Gordin and John Hall were unable to attend, but both graciously read the manuscript. Their extensive and insightful comments also pushed me to formulate my ideas as clearly as possible. Renee Philippi and her student staff, Yasmine El Gheur and Sophie Ziner, were indefatigable organizers of the workshop, always backed up by Moe Liu-D'Albero, the superb financial director of the Division of Humanities and Arts at City College.

The manuscript of *A World Divided* received two other vettings at forums, one at Università Bocconi in Milan, Italy, and another at the University of Newcastle in Australia. I thank León Castellanos-Jankiewicz, Andrea Colli, Giunia Gatta, Marco Percoco, and Graziella Romeo in Italy, and Nick Doumanis, Hans-Lukas Kieser, and Roger Marwick in Australia for their very helpful comments and criticisms.

Aside from all of these people, a number of friends and colleagues read specific chapters. I also benefitted greatly from their expertise and critical comments. Many thanks to Taner Akçam, Lucien Frary, and Yannis Kotsonis. In the last stages of writing, two anonymous readers for Princeton University Press pushed me to make my arguments as clearly and thoroughly as possible. I thank them as well.

The Human Rights Program at City College has been an excellent venue for me as I was writing *A World Divided*. There I encountered some of the best thinking on human rights from practitioners and scholars. I thank my co-founders, Rajan Menon, Juan Carlos Mercado, and Jeff Rosen, as well as Alessandra Benedicty and Danielle Zach. When we both served as deans, Jeff was also a wonderful mentor in the ways of City College and the City University of New York, and has since become a great friend. I began *A World Divided* while a faculty member at the University of Minnesota. My colleagues in History as well as the terrific human rights group in Political Science, Law, and Public Affairs were a great inspiration as I began to develop the arguments in this book.

I learned a huge amount from my participation in the Workshop on Turkish and Armenian Studies, and thank the founders, Fatma Müge Göçek, Gerard Libaridian, and Ron Suny. Borderlands: Ethnicity, Identity, and Violence in the Shatter-Zones of Empires, 1848–Present was a project founded by Omer Bartov that we then co-directed. The various forums, colloquia, lectures, and conferences that we organized at the Watson Institute at Brown University, the University of Minnesota, and the Herder Institute in Marburg, Germany, also proved immensely stimulating.

Over the years I have received generous financial support from my home institutions as well as numerous foundations and governmental agencies. These endowed chairs, grants, and fellowships have enabled me to travel to widely flung archives and libraries to conduct the research that underlies this book, and to universities and research institutes where I have presented numerous lectures and papers. I thank the Arsham and Charlotte Ohanessian Chair in the College of Liberal Arts and the Distinguished McKnight University Professorship at the University of Minnesota. I thank as well the City College of New York and the Research Foundation of the City University of New York. I am very grateful to the Harry Frank Guggenheim Foundation, the National Endowment for the Humanities, and the Remarque Institute at New York University. The periods I spent as visiting professor at the University of

Newcastle in Australia and Stanley Kelley Jr. visiting professor for distinguished teaching at Princeton University, as well as research fellow at the Shelby Collum Davis Center for Historical Studies, also at Princeton, were enormously productive. I thank Jeremy Adelman, Bill Jordan, and Dan Rodgers at Princeton; Phillip Dwyer and Hans-Lukas Kieser at Newcastle; and Giunia Gatta at Bocconi for arranging these vists.

I was fortunate to have three excellent research assistants during the latter stages of the research and writing of this book. Todd Leskinac located important sources for chapter 3 on American Indians. Daniela Traldi helped greatly with Portuguese-language materials for the Brazil chapter. She also provided information and materials on the Brazilian feminist Bertha Lutz. Yasmine El Gheur helped secure the images and maps. She was incredibly resourceful and efficient, an ideal research assistant. David Cox is a superb and gracious mapmaker.

Historians need libraries and archives. Invariably, the staff at the various institutions mentioned in the bibliography were friendly and helpful, often guiding me to little-known sources. I thank them as well.

Finally, I am pleased to thank the many institutions that offered me the opportunity to present aspects of this work at lectures and colloquia. *A World Divided* would be much diminished if I had not encountered the engaged and probing questions and comments from numerous audiences. They include: the Geschichtswissentschaftliches Zentrum Geschichte und Kultur Ostmitteleuropas an der Universität Leipzig, Strassler Family Center for Holocaust and Genocide Studies at Clark University, City College of New York, University of California San Diego, German Historical Institute Washington DC, Humboldt-Universität und Bundesstiftung zur Aufarbeitung der SED-Diktatur, Hamburger Institut für Sozialforschung, University of Newcastle (Australia), Università Bocconi, Graduate Center of the City University of New York, Freie-Universität zu Berlin (three times), Center for Holocaust and Genocide Studies at the University of Minnesota, Université libre de Bruxelles, Universität Konstanz, Watson Institute at Brown University, Eberhard Karls Universität Tübingen, University of Michigan, Institut für Zeitgeschichte Munich, Liechtenstein Center for

Self-Determination at Princeton University, Friedrich-Schiller-Universität Jena, Remarque Institute at New York University, University of Virginia, Davis Center for Historical Studies at Princeton University, Washington University, Mellon Foundation Sawyer Seminar at the University of Wisconsin at Madison, Center for European Studies at Harvard University, Georgetown University, Center for German and European Studies at the University of Wisconsin at Madison, Institute for Advanced Studies at Freiburg-Universität, University of Athens, Law and Public Affairs Program at Princeton University, International Seminar at Columbia University, Wissenschaftszentrum Berlin, University of Puerto Rico, University of California Berkeley, Westfälische Wilhelms-Universität Münster, Universität Koblenz-Landau, Ludwig-Maximilian-Universität Munich, Allen and Joan Bildner Center for the Study of Jewish Life at Rutgers University, Ramapo College, and the National University of Namibia.

Whatever errors remain in the book are my own.

Eric D. Weitz
Princeton, New Jersey

ABBREVIATIONS

ANC African National Congress

BAK Bundesarchiv Koblenz

CCP Chinese Communist Party

CEDAW Convention on the Elimination of All Forms of Discrimination against Women

CJH Center for Jewish History

CPSU Communist Party of the Soviet Union

CSP Conseil supérieur du pays (Rwanda)

CUP Committee of Union and Progress

EAM National Liberation Front (Greece)

FAO Food and Agriculture Organization

ICC International Criminal Court

ICTR International Criminal Tribunal for Rwanda

ICTY International Criminal Tribunal for the Former Yugoslavia

IDF Israel Defense Forces

IDPs Internally displaced persons

Ihud Unity Party

ILO International Labor Organization

KCP Korean Communist Party

KGB Committee for State Security

KWP Korean Workers' Party

MECW Karl Marx and Friedrich Engels, *Collected Works*

MEW Karl Marx and Friedrich Engels, *Werke*

MMA Manchurian Military Academy

NAN National Archives of Namibia

NEAJUA Northeast Anti-Japanese United Army

NGO	Non-governmental organization
PAAA	Politisches Archiv des Auswärtigen Amts
Parmehutu	Party of the Hutu Emancipation Movement
PMC	(League of Nations) Permanent Mandates Commission
RKA	(Bundesarchiv Berlin Lichterfelde) Reichskolonialamt
RPF	Rwandan Patriotic Front
SWAPO	Southwest Africa People's Organization
UDHR	Universal Declaration of Human Rights
UN	United Nations
UNA	United Nations Archives
UNESCO	United Nations Educational, Scientific and Cultural Organization
UNGA	United Nations General Assembly
UNHCR	United Nations High Commissioner for Refugees
UNIA	Universal Negro Improvement Association
UNRWA	United Nations Relief and Works Administration
UNSCOP	United Nations Special Committee on Palestine
Uprona	National Unity and Progress Party
USGSPA	Under-Secretary-General for Special Political Affairs
USSR	Union of Soviet Socialist Republics
WHO	World Health Organization
YMCA	Young Men's Christian Association

A World
DIVIDED

Introduction

❧

IN 2015, a young girl and her father crossed into the United States from the border with Mexico. Astrid and Arturo, K'iche' Indians from Guatemala, were fleeing the systematic discrimination and violence their people have suffered for decades. US officials detained Astrid and Arturo for only one day. They had applied for political asylum and were allowed to move on. They began to build a life in Pennsylvania as they awaited the decision on their asylum status. Three years later, in 2018, US immigration authorities raided their home in the middle of the night and arrested them. Human rights lawyers argued that Astrid and Arturo were unjustly detained. Amnesty International launched a campaign to free them. The authorities were deluged with nearly two thousand phone calls and tens of thousands of petitions demanding their release. The calls and petitions arrived from nearly every continent on the globe. Officials relented, and after a month set father and daughter free. For now. Their status as asylum seekers has, as of autumn 2018, still not been finally decided.[1]

One story from one family among the more than 68.5 million migrants, asylum seekers, and refugees in the world today (see plate 1).[2] Yet the experiences of Astrid and Arturo speak to the three questions that animate this book: Who has access to rights? What do we mean by human rights? And how do we obtain rights?

Human rights are never as simple as we might think from reading, say, the preamble and thirty articles of the Universal Declaration of Human Rights (UDHR). That is precisely the point of *A World Divided*. I aim not just to celebrate human rights (although I do most definitely support them), but to explore their complex origins, development, and meanings since the eighteenth century. I do so by examining the histories of various nation-states and one federation of nationalities (the

Soviet Union) and the human rights they proclaimed. I have chosen these particular cases, culled from around the globe over the past two and one-half centuries, because they encompass the variety of modern political and economic systems, from republic to empire, slavery to socialism, colonialism to communism.

Human rights offer people around the world the prospects of expansive, liberty-endowed, self-determining lives, despite the violations, deprivations, and atrocities we still witness on virtually every continent. Even where they exist only as promises and hopes, human rights stand as a triumph of the human spirit and intellect. Where implemented, they protect us from the arbitrary power of the state. They assure us that policemen cannot enter our homes unless granted a warrant, and no government agency can arbitrarily seize the property we own. Every time individuals around the globe go to a polling place to pull a lever or scratch an X to choose the representatives of their choice, wherever people raise their voices in meetings and rallies or in letters to their local newspaper, they are exercising rights of free speech that make them participants of the worlds they inhabit, whether it be their local village or town or country. Whenever people demand clean water or adequate healthcare, they are expressing their social rights. Through all these activities, they are no longer mere objects who are ordered about or moved around at someone's whim, nor subjects who, if fate treats them well, receive benefits from those above them. Rights give people power in the best sense of the term—the ability to shape their own lives and the societies in which they live. Rights enhance our capacity to be more fully human.

In our divided world of 193 sovereign nation-states, we have rights first and foremost as national citizens. But who, in fact, constitutes the nation and by what criteria? Were Arturo and Astrid, as Indians, national citizens and therefore able to exercise rights in Guatemala? Who has the "right to have rights"?—as Hannah Arendt, and the German Enlightenment philosopher Johann Gottlieb Fichte before her, asked.[3] Access to rights in the nation-state is the first major theme of this book. From Greek rebels in the early nineteenth century to anticolonial Africans in the twentieth, all had to face the questions: Who belongs to the nation? Who qualifies to be a rights-bearing citizen, and what kinds of rights may he or she possess? What happens to those who live within the territory of the new nation-state but are somehow different from the dominant group, whether by virtue of skin color, religion, language, or any other trait? This quandary remains with us today, as Arturo and Astrid know all too well.

A World Divided affirms the powerful and creative history of human rights from the late eighteenth century to the present. It also presents a critique of the *limitations* of rights, so long as they are based in the nation-state and national or racial citizenship.[4] In fact, the book takes the problem one step further: the great paradox of the history presented here is that nation-states create rights for some at the same time that they exclude others, at times quite brutally. The state is our protector; it is also our greatest threat.[5] This dilemma, that the state, at its best, enforces human rights, but at the same time limits the circle of those who can possess rights, is our history as well as our present and future. As far as anyone can imagine, we will continue to inhabit a world of 193 sovereign independent states (give or take one, two, or three).

Only since 1945 has the emergence of international human rights offered a model of universal rights beyond the nation-state. The UDHR, passed by the United Nations (UN) General Assembly on 10 December 1948, proclaims that rights inhere in everyone regardless of national citizenship. Scores of international treaties confirm the point that even the stateless possess human rights and therefore need to be protected by states and the international community.[6] Asylum seekers, like Arturo and Astrid, are especially protected, and they at least were released from detention after one month. Every step that moves the protection of human rights to the international level, however partial and limited, constitutes, I argue, a major advance, the best-laid path out of the quandaries and limitations of human rights based exclusively in national citizenship.[7]

Nonetheless, in the vast majority of cases we are still dependent on the nation-state to establish and enforce human rights, or are compelled to fight the nation-state as the supreme violator of rights. Activists around the globe appeal to international human rights standards. But their first station stop is their own state, which they call upon to ensure free speech, provide clean water, and rein in paramilitaries who wreak havoc on populations.[8]

One truth about human rights is incontrovertible (and it may be the only truth): they are dynamic. Their meaning has evolved over the past two and one-half centuries, and that is the second theme pursued in this book. Once reserved for some people—propertied men, white Europeans, loyal Soviets—they were quickly demanded by those who had been excluded. Activists turned the rhetoric and law of rights against those who reigned, and demanded a free and open, more inclusive society. We shall see this phenomenon at work time and again, in Brazil, the Soviet Union, South Korea, and Rwanda and Burundi, and in other histories explored in each of the chapters. We shall also see it at work internationally, notably in the movement for women's rights after 1945.

As the charmed circle of rights-bearing citizens expanded, so did the meaning of those rights. In the nineteenth century, new states were primarily liberal in character. They proclaimed political rights, like the right to free speech and assembly and protection from unwarranted search and seizure, but provided little to nothing in the way of social rights.[9] Yet already by the mid-nineteenth century, socialists, feminists, and some liberals raised the objection that rights conceived solely in political terms ignored the great needs and desires of the vast majority of the population.[10]

Today, most scholars and activists insist that the political rights derived from the great revolutions of the late eighteenth and nineteenth centuries must be complemented by social and economic rights. The UN said as much in 1966 by passing the International Covenant on Economic, Social and Cultural Rights (the United States, though a signatory, has never ratified the treaty). The Guatemalan Constitution, like so many others around the globe, conforms to this understanding.[11] Its section on "Human Rights," primarily political in orientation, is immediately followed by one on "Social Rights." Had the state come anywhere close to following its own prescriptions, Arturo and Astrid would have been able to speak out freely and express their cultural identity, and would have had access to healthcare and education—the full complement of human rights as understood today.

This expanded understanding of human rights, beyond the strictly political to social rights as well, implies that people must have the resources that enable them to make self-conscious, considered decisions about the lives they wish to lead. If people go hungry, if their life chances are so debilitated by the lack of access to healthcare and education, they hardly have the capacity to choose their life's course or to engage in politics. Instead, they are consumed by scouring urban and rural landscapes for the barest of provisions needed to sustain life in its most minimal and miserable fashion.[12] After 1945, the Soviet Union and the countries of the Global South forged a powerful alliance in support of social rights and national self-determination. However, social rights are meaningless if they are isolated from political rights, as we shall see in our histories of Korea and the Soviet Union.

The history of nation-states *is* the history of human rights, and vice versa. These histories cannot be disentangled precisely because human rights are embedded, first and foremost, in the proclamations, constitutions, and laws of nation-states as well as empires, like the Soviet Union, that were created as federations of nationalities. The origins of nation-states and human rights lie in the West, including the Americas, South and North. Over the course of the nineteenth and twentieth centuries, the nation-state became the predominant political model of the modern world. Virtually every one of them has a constitution that proclaims the rights of its citizens—even when those rights are only a veneer, below which the jailer, the torturer, the censor reign supreme. Still, something significant must be at work if even the most repressive dictators feel compelled to claim that they, too, are champions of human rights.

The nation-state and human rights have played a central role in the making of our global world, as much as have international commerce and communications revolutions from the telegraph to the internet.[13] No nation-state founding, no popular movement was ever completely autonomous. And that speaks to the third issue addressed in *A World Divided*: How do we obtain rights? Amnesty International's campaign in support of Astrid and Arturo is emblematic of the global reach of today's non-governmental organizations (NGOs). Lawyers also intervened on their behalf. Yet rarely does such activism suffice to create human rights advances. In every instance, the establishment of nation-states with their systems of rights—however imperfectly implemented—was the result not only of heroic actors or of the beneficence of leading statesmen. Popular struggles, state interests, and the workings of the international system came together in a highly fragile and fleeting consensus to found nation-states with their treaties, constitutions, and laws that enshrined—at least rhetorically—the principles of human rights.

Each history related in the individual chapters expounds on the three major themes of *A World Divided*. In various national settings, each chapter explores historically who possessed the right to have rights and who was excluded, the precise meaning of those rights, and how the nation-state and human rights actually came about. Some of the histories may seem, at first glance, to unfold in out-of-the-way geographies, distant from the capitals of the Great Powers or from today's global giants like India and China. These places, Greece in the Mediterranean, Minnesota in the American Upper Midwest, Korea in Northeast Asia, Namibia in Southwest Africa, Rwanda and Burundi in the Great Lakes region of Africa, Palestine and Israel, became focal points for the new politics of the nation-state and human rights—and its violations. The activism, for good and bad, of Greeks, Dakota Sioux Indians, Koreans, Herero and Nama of Namibia, Zionist Jews, and Hutus and Tutsis drew in central states and Great Powers, which were always unnerved by conditions of instability. These regions and countries, all small, some relatively isolated, decisively shaped the course of global politics and the intertwined history of nation-states and human rights.

I offer in this book no definitive answer to the ultimate question—the meaning of rights—that has occupied philosophers, theologians, and political theorists for centuries, as well as present-day scholars in a wide variety of fields. Rather, I explore the complexities of human rights and take an open-ended, capacious, and practical approach to the disputes regarding the philosophy and history of human rights. Human rights constitute in this book an angle of orientation, not a definitional end point.

Still, we need some working definitions and chronological perspective. Human rights have a long history. Traces of them are apparent as far back as the ancient and medieval worlds, in the great law codes starting with Hammurabi, in ideas of justice and humanitarianism evident in virtually all world religions, and in Saint Thomas Aquinas's meditations on the meaning of natural law. A breakthrough came with the "Machiavellian moment" of the sixteenth century, when political theory first emerged as a distinctive intellectual field.[14] Machiavelli's great contribution was soon followed by other towering intellects, notably Thomas Hobbes and John Locke in the seventeenth century, who began to elucidate the meaning of rights in a recognizably modern fashion.[15]

The deep historical traces of human rights are apparent not only in high theological and philosophic speculation. We see them also in society and politics. The charters of medieval European towns gave burghers the power to govern the politics of their commune. Even in nineteenth-century Russia, the most autocratic of European states, peasants appeared in court to claim that the law provided them some protection from the arbitrary power of their aristocratic overlords. Ottoman and Islamic property law gave tenants the right to dispose of the fruits of their labor and to occupy the land as long as they worked it productively.[16]

Many would dispute that these cases have anything to do with human rights. They would say that these examples and thousands of others we could summon are too fragmentary and episodic to constitute a full-blown program of *human* rights. These scholars would note that few people used the term "human rights" prior to the 1940s, and that its wide dissemination came only from the 1970s onward. Indeed, some would contend that we can talk about human rights only since the 1970s. Anything that appeared beforehand was partial, political, and national. Human rights, they argue, are a form of morality rather than politics, and reach beyond the nation-state and national identities.[17]

That is not the line of thought I follow in this book, though we do need some distinctions. Human rights are broader in conception than the political rights exercised by town citizens in Europe before the modern period, or the exclusively political rights of national citizens. But the border between the rights of man—*les droits de l'homme* or *Bürgerrechte*—and human rights is permeable, not hard and fast, something the drafters of the UDHR well understood.[18] They deliberately based their work on the great rights proclamations of the late eighteenth and early nineteenth centuries, like the American Declaration of Independence and Bill of Rights, the French Declaration of the Rights of Man and Citizen, and the Spanish Cadiz Constitution of 1812. Yet they believed that these principles had to be extended to encompass all people on the planet—not just citizens of particular nation-states—and required global methods of enforcement. Moreover, the term "human rights," while rare in the nineteenth century, was hardly unknown. Some American abolitionists explicitly spoke and wrote about human rights, as did pioneering feminists, many of whom were active in both the slavery abolition and the women's movements.[19]

I begin this book in the late eighteenth century because that is the moment when the ideas of the nation and rights, broached the century before by political theorists, became manifest in politics, notably in the American, French, and Latin American revolutions. The political model of the nation-state and human rights then spread across Europe and the Americas during the nineteenth century, and around the entire world in the twentieth.[20] In the process, other, non-Western ideas and traditions contributed to the broadening and deepening of the meaning of rights, notably in the realm of social and economic matters and national self-determination.[21]

Recognition of this deep history of rights, its long chronology and diverse geography, broadens the sight lines, enabling us to understand better the complex history and politics of human rights. This long history has constituted a fount of ideas and resources from which political actors drew very powerfully from the late eighteenth century onward. This longer perspective indicates that rights are *always* eminently political, not simply moral. Today, few human rights activists around the world would recognize themselves as post-national and post-political when they rally to transform their own country's political order, or suffer its tyrannies in jails and torture chambers.

In their most general sense, human rights are natural, inalienable, and universal. "Natural" means that rights inhere in us by virtue of being human, nothing more and nothing less. That understanding has its roots in Christian theology, notably as developed by Aquinas, but the writers and political activists of later centuries largely secularized the idea.[22] That is, "natural rights" no longer had to be grounded in the belief that humans were created in god's image and therefore must adhere to god-given natural law, which gives them the capacity to exercise rights. With god removed, the simple fact of being human, which meant the ability to reason, sufficed to grant people the "right to have rights."

Those rights, to be human rights, must also be "inalienable," as the UDHR preamble states. They cannot be removed from the person; no state or individual may strip a person of rights no matter what the circumstances. "Universal" means that human rights apply to everyone, or at least to all adults. Rights also mean that we have duties and obligations to others.[23] At minimum, we have to recognize that in order for us to enjoy rights, others must be able to exercise rights as well. Rights may be defined for individuals, but they can exist only in the social world of people thinking, arguing, and acting in relation to one another.[24]

Human rights as natural, inalienable, and universal, coupled with duties and obligations—that, to be sure, is an ideal and abstract definition. Still, it is essential as a standard by which we judge states and individuals and a goal to which people everywhere can aspire. Human rights enlarge the scope of human freedom and creativity—even when we know they can never be realized in their entirety, that utopia can never exist in the real world, that national citizenship, despite its contradictions and ambivalences, remains the bedrock for most human rights claims.

The historical cases that comprise this book are about nation-state foundings and reformations. However, *A World Divided* is also very much about empires, precisely because nation-states were almost always carved out of existing empires, and because even empires had to develop policies, some deadly, some humane, that responded to the allure of the nation.[25] These empires were of the most varied sort, yet there was one constant: empires by definition ruled (and rule) over diverse populations. No Ottoman sultan, Russian tsar, or Chinese emperor ever thought that all of his (or, occasionally, her) subjects had to be of one ethnicity or religious faith and speak one language. Empires blithely gathered in populations no matter what their particular characteristics. The only limiting factor was the expanse of territory imperial armies could conquer and tax collectors could traverse without getting killed or driven out by the local populace.

The modern era, in contrast, is defined by the triumph of the nation-state (although some empires still exist). The nation-state is, in most instances, a compact territory with clearly defined borders and a state that claims to represent one people. The allure of the nation-state is great.[26] It strikes deep emotional chords of shared language, homeland, religion, and great myths of lineal descent from heroic ancestors, a sense of blood kinship however fictitious in reality. Even when these states are federations or grant recognition to multiple ethnicities in some other fashion, the nation remains the overarching source of identification— all despite the intractable reality of human diversity.

Moreover, the nation-state proved its mettle in the American and French revolutions and the contemporaneous Industrial Revolution— it could mobilize human and productive resources far better than large, cumbersome, ineffective empires. When nation-states created their own colonial empires, forging a kind of national empire hybrid, as the British, French, Dutch, Japanese, and Americans did, they proved even more powerful. The nation-state became a model for activists around the globe, who typically blended in some of their own traditions. In that regard, the emergence of nationalism was by no means only a Western export to the rest of the world.[27]

The nation-state promised its citizens that they would be secure in their own person and property and could participate, should they so desire, in the political system in which they lived. Its appeal was still grander, because nationalists everywhere promised a bright, utopian future of prosperity and happiness once the shackles of foreign oppression had been destroyed. Such claims were shouted at rallies, broadcast over the radio, and printed on paper—the rivers of communication of the modern age that made possible the mass appeal of the nation-state and human rights. The promise of great things through the nation was often belied in reality, but that did little to diminish the nation-state's appeal.

The establishment and expansion of human rights have never been pure and straight. Paradoxes abound. The following chapters explore the mix of inclusions and exclusions, rights and their deprivation, accomplishments and disasters that accompanied nation-states and the establishment of human rights. The concluding section of each chapter draws the story into the present, since the impact of how rights-bearing citizens were defined historically resonates still in our modern world—and directly affects people like Arturo and Astrid and millions of others.

We begin with a *tour d'horizon* of the world around the late eighteenth and nineteenth centuries, when the idea and politics of the nation and rights had been initiated, but empires, small regional forms of governance, and tribes and clans still dominated the bulk of the earth's surface. Explicit hierarchies of power, not the promise of rights for all citizens, prevailed, and they were evident, as we shall see, in formal political structures, popular ceremonies, and everyday practices. At the same time, the great transformations of the nineteenth century, epic population movements as well as advances in economics, communications, and transport, opened up new possibilities and offered glimmers of the world to come, the world of nation-states and human rights.

Chapter 1

Empires and Rulers

THE EIGHTEENTH CENTURY AND BEYOND

ↄ

HOI AN is a lovely Vietnamese town, one that managed to survive, largely unscathed, the wars that ravaged the country in the twentieth century. Tourists flock to it today for its river views, old-style boats, and modern fashion shops that will turn out an expertly cut dress or suit, made of fine fabric, in twenty-four hours. In the warm weather— Vietnam is always warm—a visitor sits outside at a restaurant and watches the promenade of young and old, Vietnamese and foreigners, until late at night, the locals escaping their cramped, stuffy homes and apartments, everyone enjoying the sights of people and places.

Only remnants of Hoi An's earlier stature survive. But in the eighteenth century, it was a thriving, cosmopolitan trading port. Dutch, Portuguese, Chinese, Japanese, Indian, and many other merchants arrived, sometimes staying for months at a time until the trade winds could take them home. They bought silk, jade, porcelain, lacquer, buffalo horn, dried fish, and herbs. In turn, the merchants from overseas sold textiles, guns and tools, lead, and sulfur.

Hoi An was emblematic of a world globalized already in the late eighteenth and early nineteenth centuries. The links were commercial in nature. Goods came and went, merchants and seamen came and went, linking towns like Hoi An and the faraway Dutch entrepôt of Amsterdam, enabling both of them to flourish.

Other connections were more permanent. Since Columbus's voyages in the 1490s, Europeans had established transoceanic empires in the Americas, Southern Africa, slowly in the Antipodes, more quickly in India. Epic population movements, on a scale unheard of in prior human history, sent Europeans around the globe to establish permanent settlements, enslaved Africans to the New World, and Chinese laborers and merchants across the expanse of Southeast Asia and the Americas. Virtually every region of the world, already diverse, became much more so, a phenomenon that created grave problems for nationalists who believed that the state should represent one, homogeneous, population.

The webs of trade, empire, and migrations (free and coerced) created pathways for the exchange of ideas and political models. European scholars, publicists, and statesmen were forced to rethink their understandings of the human and natural world as they encountered different peoples, species, and environments around the globe. Sometimes they experienced these encounters personally, taking passage on merchant ships or government-sponsored explorations—as did, for example, the great naturalists Alexander von Humboldt and Charles Darwin. Others, like the French philosopher Montesquieu, rarely set foot outside their estates or villas. They sat in their libraries and read travel literature and scientific accounts, genres that became wildly popular in the eighteenth and nineteenth centuries, and reflected about what this wider world signified for Europeans and for the human condition generally.[1] Africans, Asians, and Middle Easterners did much the same. Confronted with Western power, products, and ideas, they reconsidered some of their own scientific, religious, and political beliefs. They did not just receive Western ideas; they developed their own syncretic reform movements that blended and adapted new models emanating from the West with their indigenous traditions. Fath 'Ali Shah, who ruled Persia from 1797 to 1834; Mehmet Ali, the effective leader and ultimately khedive of Egypt from 1805 to 1849; and a series of Ottoman sultans beginning with Selim III in 1789—all recognized the need for reform.[2]

Over the course of the nineteenth century, the webs created by economic relations, imperial power, and population movements became ever tighter. But in the late eighteenth and early nineteenth centuries, no one could have predicted that the outcome of a world increasingly linked together would also be a world divided into 193 sovereign states, virtually all of them trumpeting an ideology of human rights. The idea of rights was a mere glimmer in a few areas, the British North American colonies primarily. Then came the French Revolution and the expansion of French power throughout Europe, and the numerous Latin American revolutions. By 1815, however, the revolutionary surge in Europe had been beaten back, and its Latin American counterparts deeply contested. At the fabled Vienna Congress in 1815, the Great Powers reestablished dynastic legitimacy and fought every move toward national independence and rights proclamations. Surveying the world around 1815, one could see only vast inequalities and gross hierarchies of wealth and power. Those at the lower levels lived in states of abject submission with little claim on any kind of rights, let alone the resources necessary to sustain a full life. Slavery remained an accepted form of labor and life in virtually every region of the globe, including, of course, the United States.

The conditions could not have been more hostile for the establishment of nation-states and human rights. To be sure, human rights do not require complete social equality (if that were even possible). Gross disparities in wealth and vast differences in power are characteristic also of liberal societies that profess support for human rights. But to follow the German Enlightenment philosopher Johann Gottlieb Fichte (mentioned in the introduction) and his twentieth-century counterpart Emmanuel Levinas, human rights do require *recognition* of the other as a fellow human being who, by his or her very existence and nothing more, possesses the right to have rights. Even when nation-states limited recognition to fellow nationals or racial compatriots—as we shall see in the following chapters— that kind of citizenship at least marked an advance over hierarchies of power that left most people as subjects who had few, if any, rights.

The emergence of our modern world of rights and nation-states has to be *explained*, rather than assumed, as so many have been wont to do, as a natural, inevitable progression of the human condition. Beneath steep hierarchies of power and rampant injustices, the glimmers of a new form of politics are evident, at least in retrospect. First, we need to see just how radical a break is our own modern world from the preceding millennia marked by empires; small, regional forms of governance; and tribes and clans—all of them built on systems of inequality and *non-recognition* (at least in terms of rights) of other individuals. We will, with some help from travelers, explore the world of the late eighteenth and nineteenth centuries. We will see how these travelers reported on the societies and landscapes they witnessed and the people they observed (see map 1.1).

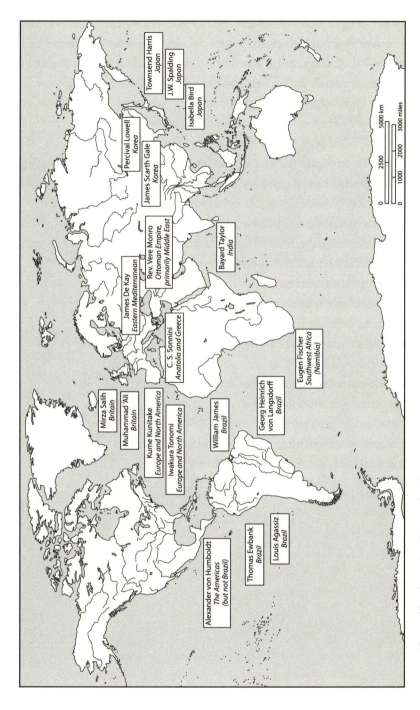

Townsend Harris
Japan

J.W. Spalding
Japan

Isabella Bird
Japan

Percival Lowell
Korea

James Scarth Gale
Korea

Rev. Vere Monro
*Ottoman Empire,
primarily Middle East*

Bayard Taylor
India

James De Kay
Eastern Mediterranean

C. S. Sonnini
Anatolia and Greece

Eugen Fischer
*Southwest Africa
(Namibia)*

Mirza Salih
Britain

Muhammad 'Ali
Britain

Kume Kunitake
Europe and North America

Iwakura Tonomi
Europe and North America

William James
Brazil

Georg Heinrich
von Langsdorff
Brazil

Alexander von Humboldt
*The Americas
(but not Brazil)*

Thomas Ewbank
Brazil

Louis Agassiz
Brazil

0   1000
0   2500
                2000   3000 miles
5000 km

MAP 1.1 The world with travelers discussed in the text.

All the while, they deepened the pathways of encounter and revealed, often unwittingly, the fractures in the old world. Both—pathways and fractures—would open the way for the global resonance of a political model developed first along the Atlantic Seaboard.

Hierarchies

In the early 1830s, an American, James De Kay, traveled through the Eastern Mediterranean, to Egypt, Syria, Greece, Anatolia, and many Ottoman and Greek islands. He observed a great deal, and managed to wrangle an invitation to an elaborate dinner party in Istanbul. Musicians played along as the guests sampled many courses of finely prepared foods. De Kay and his colleagues asked the musicians to perform a patriotic or national song. The musicians, apparently dumbfounded, replied through a translator that "none of this kind [of songs] are extant in Turkey."[3]

That was the world of empire—no "Star-Spangled Banner" or "Marseillaise," no national anthem of any kind. Loyalty might exist to the tsar, sultan, or emperor, but it was a personal loyalty infused with religious beliefs, not a patriotic connection with the nation shared by all citizens. Empires were (and are) by definition hierarchical. The emperor typically assumes an all-powerful, almost godly countenance. If he—or, occasionally, she—is seen at all, it is only from afar, the distance marking his unique status and separation from his subjects.

De Kay explored a great deal of Istanbul, but was not of high enough stature to be received at court. The palace and all its associated buildings, as well as the workings of the government, remained terra incognita to him—until a lucky stroke won him an invitation to an imperial ceremony.

Along with many thousands of Ottoman subjects, De Kay witnessed a coming-of-age ritual, the transfer of the young prince to his instructors. Whether the event also entailed the circumcision of the prince, as would have been typical in the Ottoman Empire, our author does not say, perhaps too discreet to mention it. In any case, De Kay depicted a ceremony that bore all the trappings of imperial power.

The sultan was seated on his throne, under a splendid pavilion, which far exceeded our ideas of oriental magnificence. The grand mufti, the chief ulemahs, and the professors of the seraglio [palace] stood on the right of the throne. On the left were arrayed all the great dignitaries of the empire; and in front were placed the general officers of the army and navy. The young prince was introduced, who, after embracing respectfully the feet of his father, took his seat on a cushion placed between the grand mufti and the sultan. After a short pause, a chapter from the Koran was read, and the grand mufti then pronounced a prayer suitable to the occasion. At every pause the children took up the responses of Ameen! which were shouted through the camp, and borne back in echo from the neighbouring hills. When the prayer was concluded, the prince arose, again embraced his father's feet, and after asking permission gracefully made an obeisance to the assembly and withdrew.[4]

Then the troops and state officials were offered a grand meal served with much "pomp and ceremony. . . . A long train of splendidly attired servants bore on their heads massy [massive] silver trays, loaded with every variety of food. The viands were covered with cloths of gold and silver tissue, and the procession moved solemnly to the various pavillions, to the music of a full military band."[5]

Here we have the display of power typical for empires around the globe, the blending of religion (the grand mufti and the ulemahs), military might (the generals), and state (the officials), all present, all honoring the greater power of the sultan, whose son offers up an act of subservience and obedience (see plate 2). Abundance and prosperity (the food) are on display as well, along with the merciful character of the sultan, whose ultimate power over life and death was revealed by his magnanimous pardon of fifteen criminals who had been condemned to death.

De Kay and his party, obviously Western, were noticed by the army commander (*seraskier*), who had them invited to tour the grounds of the palace and some of the buildings. But only after the sultan had retired— he could not be seen by such lowly guests. The painted columns and walls, ornamented with gold and silver; the rich and rare carpets; drapery fringed with gold; a throne made of rare woods, artfully carved and inlaid with gold and ivory, the back of which displayed a gold-sculptured sun—our American was deeply impressed, imperial splendor able to capture, in his day and ours, the swooning admiration of even the most ardent democrat.[6]

The ceremony and the tour that De Kay witnessed were expressions of imperial power. Not rights-bearing citizens but imperial subjects amassed before the emperor and other dignitaries. Religious authorities, state officials, common people—each stood in its particular place, each group subservient to the next, all up the hierarchy ultimately to the sultan.

Such systems of rank and displays of power and subservience were hardly an Ottoman specialty. In the late nineteenth century, after the United States had forced the "opening" of Japan, Western observers wrote about the country's great natural beauty and the industry of its population. The visitors also noted Japan's strict hierarchy and exclusiveness. They all remarked on the Japanese propensity for prostration, the complete body bow that even the highly ranked executed when in the presence of those above them. The corollary was a great reticence to take any initiative not approved by their superiors, even in the most personal interactions. A Russian emissary, for example, offered a Japanese official, his eyesight deficient, the use of a pair of glasses. The official would not accept the simple, humane proposition: "He must first," the emissary related, "ask permission of the governor."[7]

European subjects bowed rather than prostrated, but the displays of imperial power were just as vivid in Europe. The Vienna Congress in 1815, called to design the peace after twenty-five years of revolution and warfare, became as famed for its glittering balls and sumptuous dinners as for the negotiations among states great and minor, a circumstance that has inspired outrage and amusement from the commencement of the Congress in autumn 1814 down to the present day.[8]

As in the Ottoman Empire and Japan, the ceremonies were lavish and displayed strict attention to the order of rank. The grand processions, servants in livery, praetorian guards at arms, powdered wigs and corseted dresses, finely carved and painted carriages that brought statesmen and nobles to the negotiating table as well as to balls and dinners—all that impressed participants and spectators alike. Even well-placed nobles were bedazzled by the pageant Vienna had become.[9]

One such spectacle at the Imperial Riding School consisted of knights, bedecked in gold and silver, on horses, galloping at full speed with lances at the ready. Four of the twenty-four knights used their swords to lop off the heads of dummy Turks and Moors. Twenty-four honored princesses sat and watched, looking as if "all the riches of Vienna had been collected to adorn [their] heads, necks, and persons." The congerie of emperors, kings, and princes gathered in Vienna, in full formal dress and covered with medals of all kinds, also observed the display of equestrian prowess. Then followed a sumptuous meal. The entire spectacle "called to mind the days of ancient chivalry," as one English traveler reported.[10] And that, of course, was the point: Vienna affirmed the legitimacy of dynastic rule, on paper in the final treaty and in the many events that also served to amuse the luminaries of the time, and their accompanying wives and mistresses, after hours of wearying negotiations.

Prostration, bows, reticence—those are not the sentiments and actions of rights-bearing citizens.[11] Citizenship bestows upon its holders a certain confidence, a strongly held belief that they do, indeed, have the power to shape their own circumstances. Certainly, power inequities exist even in the most democratic society, and those at the top expect, at the very least, governmental policies that favor them and deference from those in lower ranks. Still, self-possession and determined action are the marks of rights-bearing citizens, and it is a far different sensibility from the subservience that prevailed in so much of the world prior to the modern age.

Our American traveler to the Ottoman Empire never did see Sultan Mahmoud II. Another American, Townsend Harris, did get to see the king of Siam and the emperor of Japan, but only after waiting for days, weeks, and months. Harris was an official US emissary, and when finally permitted to deliver to the Siamese king a letter from US president Franklin Pierce, the throne on which the king sat was so high that Harris could barely hand it to him.[12] Distance, vertical as well as horizontal, is one hallmark of power; another is time. Sultans, kings, and emperors kept waiting those below them, even those with official rank, and placed metaphorical moats between themselves and everyone else.

Harris was a businessman and merchant who had spent years in China, Siam, and other places in Asia. He had been the driving force behind the founding of the City College of New York (then known as the Free Academy), a great public initiative in which rich and poor men, the "children of the whole people," would be educated together.[13] In 1855, Harris was appointed the first American consul general to Japan, two years after Commodore Matthew C. Perry had "opened" the country to foreign trade and residency.

Harris was a notable representative of the American ethos, in which democracy, meritocracy, and business all ran together. He had recoiled from the sight in Siam of "each [person] crawl[ing] prone on his belly in the presences of some superior [as Harris had observed the nobles in the presence of the king], and in turn he strives to increase the number of *his* prostrate inferiors. The custom causes them to seek the company of those inferior to themselves"[14] (see plate 3). Japan's refusal to deal with foreigners and allow trade quite literally offended Harris; it was America's right and duty to open Japan, to bring to it American ideals and commerce from which all would benefit, as he had done in Siam.

Harris waited for a very long time. When he was finally allowed to enter the imperial chamber, the princes and other notables lay prostrate before the shogun.[15] At a meeting a few days later with the minister of foreign affairs and other leading figures, Harris elaborated on the American ethos. He explained that the world had changed with the introduction of the steam engine. Sooner or later, Japan would be forced to abandon her exclusive policy. Through trade, it could become great and powerful. Harris concluded by advising his Japanese interlocutors that they and Japan would be better opening the country voluntarily. In case they did not get the point, Harris threatened them with an attack.[16] The presence of American gunships made real Harris's threat, as they had Commodore Perry's supposedly peaceful opening of Japan five years earlier.

The treaty for which Harris longed was finally concluded on 29 July 1858, two years after his arrival. Japan opened the ports of Shimoda and Hakodate to American ships and permitted the establishment of a permanent US consul at Shimoda. The treaty also provided for extraterritoriality—that is, Americans in Japan lived under American laws and the supervision of the US consul.[17]

Japan would no longer be isolated, and it would soon launch its great modernization campaign, the Meiji Restoration. Certainly, commercial relationships did not mean recognition of rights-bearing citizens; they did mean, however, joining a "society of states," as the Austrian prince Klemens von Metternich had described it. "Politics," Metternich wrote, "is the science of the vital interests of States. . . . Since . . . an isolated State no longer exists . . . we must always view the *Society* of States as the essential condition of the modern world."[18] Metternich was thinking only of Europe. But the "opening" of China by the British in the 1840s and Japan by the Americans in the 1850s meant that they, too, would become members of the society of states. And that society would evolve from a collection of empires, kingdoms, and principalities into a society of *nation*-states, and from a European to a global phenomenon. In that sense, Japan indeed entered the modern world on the day it signed the treaty with the United States.

Elaborate court ceremonies and exacting diplomatic protocols express and reconfirm power relations in empires. But power is not only symbolic. It also entails military might and the extraction of resources from the empire's subjects. For the lower classes, the lived reality of hierarchy, which they experienced every day in countless interactions, could be painful indeed.

Imperial taxation systems constituted forms of exploitation pure and simple. A British traveler to the Ottoman Empire in the 1830s, the Reverend Vere Monro, when leaving Jerusalem, encountered a small cavalry detachment aiding in the collection of taxes. As empires had done since the origins of civilization, the ruling elite extracted wealth from the peasantry in the form of a poll tax. The chain of command descended from the "Pacha," as the reverend expressed it, on down. On the way up the chain, each official added his own bill to the tax the peasant, shop-keeper, and tradesman had to pay. The village sheikh, the official collector, the lowly secretary to the military commander, the provincial head, the regional governor, various officials in Istanbul—they all took their cut. The sheikh "never loses so favourable an opportunity of doing something for himself in the way of robbery; and the unhappy poor are thus compelled to pay double the just government tax, while no one is called to account for the abuse."[19] In other villages, taxation was even more onerous. Besides money, Monro noted that the villagers also had to give up horses, mules, and camels for the army, and lime and timber to help repair the port and fortifications of Acre (present-day Israel). They also were compelled to labor on roads and bridges.[20]

A system of pure extraction like this offered nothing in the way of economic incentives to improve production and productivity. For the Ottoman Empire and many others in the eighteenth and nineteenth centuries, modern economic thinking lay as distant as the next solar system. The nation-state, in contrast, promised something different: a world of prosperity for all members of the national community.

Emperors exploited their own populations. Western powers ex-ploited foreign lands and peoples. Bayard Taylor, an American traveler in India, excoriated the British East India Company, which was draining wealth from the country, so much so that it had created a "constant system of depletion."[21] He described a cascading system of exploitation, much like Ottoman taxation. The government, which is to say the Com-pany, held all the land in its domains and leased out parcels to tenant farmers or contractors who then sublet ever smaller parcels of land, re-sulting in "tyrannical extortions."[22] Rents increased in proportion to production, creating a disincentive toward improvements. The farmers lived on the barest margins of subsistence.[23]

Conditions were not much better in Europe for the great mass of people. The end to continent-wide warfare in 1815 eased the lot of peas-ants, who had seen their fields trampled and their produce robbed by crisscrossing armies. But the eruption of the Tambora volcano in far-away Indonesia resulted in extremely cold and wet winters in Europe from 1814 to 1817, which severely reduced the harvests. In Indonesia the volcano covered fields with ashes. The ensuing tsunami swamped rice paddies with seawater. Darkness covered the archipelago for three days as entire ecosystems were destroyed.[24] Natural events and environmental disasters, not only commerce and empires, linked the world together.

All over the globe, systems of production were largely archaic. Around 1815, the Industrial Revolution had only begun, its benefits for working people some decades away. The "industrious revolution," the more intensive and productive deployment of labor by households coupled with their ever-increasing demand for consumer goods, was concentrated in only a few areas of Europe, like the British Isles, the Low Countries, and parts of France and Germany, as well as in North America and Japan and a few other select regions of Asia.[25] The "great divergence" between China and the West, characterized by Western economic development and prosperity, was in its infancy in the last decades of the eighteenth century.[26] Only after 1825 did Western living standards begin to rise appreciably for large sections of the population, and the disparity between the West and the rest of the world become so notable.[27] Public health improvements in the West came even later, after 1850.[28]

Miserable is the most appropriate term for conditions in the factories of the early Industrial Revolution. It is no accident that the term "wage slavery" emerged in the nineteenth century. As Friedrich Engels observed in his famed book, *The Condition of the Working Class in England*, published in 1845, industrialization impoverished workers, destroyed their health, and subjected them to long hours of regimented and grueling labor. Engels drew on his own observations and parliamentary inquiry commissions, as well as other published reports. He documented child and adult workers whose limbs and spines had become deformed through factory labor. Their lungs filled with dust from the textile mills, resulting in severe bronchial problems like asthma and consumption. Water used in the spinning of linen yarn continually drenched young girls and children. Workers who were late were fined; those whose tools or machines broke were fined again. Any worker could be discharged at will.[29]

Poverty and prostration constituted one form of experiencing hierarchy, submissive work another. Upon arriving in Bombay, Taylor, our

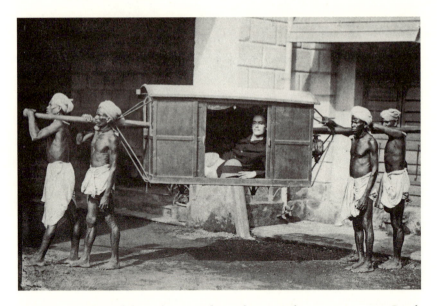

FIGURE 1.1 Wealthy English merchant carried in a palanquin, India, 1922. A prosperous British merchant in a palanquin is carried by four Indian bearers. Western travelers to Asia remarked on the ubiquity of the palanquin, but it was not unknown in Europe. The travelers occasionally expressed a sense of guilt at the burden they placed on poor, sometimes enslaved people, but that rarely stopped them from moving about in high fashion. (World History Archive/Alamy Stock Photo.)

American traveler, booked a palanquin, a taxi of sorts borne by four men (see figure 1.1).

> It was not a pleasant sensation to lie at full length in a cushioned box, and impose one's full weight (and I am by no means a feather) upon the shoulders of four men. It is a conveyance invented by Despotism, when men's necks were footstools, and men's heads playthings. I have never yet been able to get into it without a feeling of reluctance, as if I were inflicting an injury on my bearers. Why should they groan and stagger under my weight, when I have legs of my own?[30]

Taylor possessed enough of the American ethos of equality to be uncomfortable with the experience of a palanquin. That did not, however, stop him from traveling in it again and again, hoisted by four men. He rationalized his actions by claiming that his carriers would be displeased if he were to use his own legs.[31]

And then there was slavery, a common phenomenon around the globe and the greatest system of oppression, the absolute antithesis to rights-bearing citizenship. Slavery took many forms. In the Americas, plantation owners had an unceasing demand for cheap slave labor. Slaves mined silver and other minerals and planted, harvested, and processed sugar, tobacco, cotton, and coffee. The goods created by slave labor traveled all around the world, critical elements in the rise of the global economy. In the Muslim and African worlds, slavery was more often of the household variety. Slave armies were also common; in the Ottoman Empire, until the seventeenth century, they were largely comprised of men who as boys had been taken from their Christian families at a young age. They were then trained in the military arts and forcibly converted to Islam. A number of the slaves rose to high offices in the state and military.[32] A "dramatic resurgence" of slavery occurred in the Islamic world in the nineteenth century, a result of heightened global demand for export commodities.[33] In Africa, two eighteenth-century British writers claimed, slavery was "comparatively of a very mild character. The slave sits on the same mat with his master, and eats out of the same dish; he converses with him, in every respect, as an equal. . . . He [the native slave in Africa] is employed . . . as a domestic slave, sometimes as a guard and satellite; he is treated usually with indulgence, often with favour. Sometimes even the caprice of fortune raises him to the first rank under a despotic sovereign, to whom servile instruments are always agreeable."[34] Still, he (or she) was a slave, not a rights-bearing citizen.

Brazil, like the United States, was a slave society, meaning that slavery penetrated every aspect of life, including the economy, politics, society, and culture (as we shall see in more detail in chapter 4). Slaves were present everywhere in Brazil, in marketplaces, docks, households, workshops, farms, and plantations. Slaves fetched water, washed clothes, sewed lace, cooked, bought fruits and vegetables in the marketplace for their masters, loaded and unloaded ships, and labored on sugar and coffee plantations. Women were taken as concubines and prostitutes by their masters.

For the slightest infractions, slaves had to wear the tin mask, iron collar, and log and chain.[35] They endured repeated floggings. Labor itself could be deadly for slaves. The statistics alone demonstrate the point: Brazil's slave population did not reproduce sufficiently to meet the demand for slave labor, hence the continual importation of slaves from Africa despite the official ban. If not deadly, then labor was certainly onerous in the extreme. "Slaves are the beast of draught as well as of burden," wrote one traveler in 1856. "The loads they drag . . . are enough to kill both mules and horses."[36] And drag they did—a gang of six pushing a cart weighing up to a ton, men carrying on their heads and shoulders sacks of coffee weighing 160 pounds, back and forth to the warehouse or dock. Sometimes the slaves were chained to the cart they pushed; a girl not even sixteen with an iron collar around her neck; an old woman carrying an "enormous tub of swill" on her head, the tub secured with lock and chain to the iron collar around her neck.[37] Our traveler reported that the coffee haulers endured their labors on average ten years; "in that time, the work ruptures and kills them." While still alive, so many are "shockingly crippled in their lower limbs. They waddled before me, in a manner distressing to behold, a man whose thighs and legs curved so far outward that his trunk was not over fifteen inches from the ground. . . . I observed another whose knees crossed each other."[38]

Whether relatively benign or, as was mostly true, completely brutal, the condition of slavery signified the absence of all rights, the polar opposite of citizenship. Slaves were unfree by definition; they had been deprived of recognition—social death, in the words of Orlando Patterson.[39]

Encounters

Well over 140 million individuals moved from their places of origin to distant lands in the period from 1500 onward.[40] The greatest wave of migration occurred after 1815. Economics and politics drove these epic population movements. Irish and Sicilian peasants, Chinese tenant farmers, African peasants, East European Jews, Indian laborers—those who moved of their own volition were searching for a better life, those who were compelled were the victims of elites' determination to avoid labor and the descent into dark mines or the entrance into large fields under the blistering sun. Even free migrants did not make their wrenching decisions to uproot themselves and their families completely voluntarily, since poverty and persecution drove so many to seek better lives elsewhere.[41]

The figures are staggering. In 1820, the world's population stood at slightly over 1 billion, in 1920 at 1.8 billion.[42] Between 1815 and 1914, some 82 million people migrated of their own free will from their place of origin to a distant point.[43] Between 1820 and 1914 approximately 55 million people crossed the Atlantic voluntarily, 60 percent of them bound for the United States.[44] Around 12.5 million Africans were forcibly moved in the transatlantic slave trade from 1501 to 1867, nearly 1.9 million of them between 1801 and 1825, entwining the histories of Africa and the Americas. From 1501 to 1867, another almost 5 million Africans from south of the Sahara, the Horn, and the Swahili Coast were captured as slaves for the Islamic world in North Africa, Arabia, Persia, and India.[45]

Between 1831 and 1920 nearly 2 million indentured laborers, mostly South and East Asian replacements for slaves as abolition advanced, poured into plantations, mines, goldfields, and railroad beds all around the globe, including in the Caribbean, Southeast Asia, the Pacific Islands, East Africa, the United States, Peru, and Southern Africa.[46] Over 5 million "free" and nearly 1.5 million indentured Indians emigrated from South Asia in the period from 1834 to 1924,[47] one aspect of the Asian "mobility revolution" after 1850. Warfare, poverty, and environmental devastation spurred people to migrate; the new technologies of railroads and steamships greatly facilitated their movement.[48] The total Asian migration numbers, including indentured laborers, amount to 30 million from India to Sri Lanka, Burma, and Malaysia; 19 million from China to Southeast Asia; and more than 30 million Chinese from Northern China to the Northwestern region of Manchuria.

To these figures we can add around 4 million Muslims forcibly removed from the Crimea, Caucasus, and Balkans from the 1780s onward as Russian power advanced southward and new, Christian-dominated nation-states were established in Southeastern Europe. Most of those forced out settled in Anatolia, but others, like many Circassians, went farther afield to the Middle East. Of the circa 2 million people pushed out of the Caucasus by the Russian Empire between 1859 and 1879, most Circassian, probably one-quarter succumbed to the ravages of warfare and disease as they were on the move. Another 1.5 million left the Balkans for Ottoman lands after 1877.[49]

Quintessential merchant communities, like Indians, Lebanese, Jews, Greeks, and Armenians, migrated to various spots around the globe, as did the Chinese once the Qing Dynasty loosened restrictions on emigration following the Opium War in the 1840s. Over one-half million Chinese left just from the port of Hong Kong between 1854 and 1880, half of them bound for the United States.[50]

These figures do not even account for internal migrations from the countryside to the city, or when states or people themselves sought to develop new areas, as with the westward movement of Euroamericans, or Chinese, encouraged by the Qing state, who moved into highlands, Mongolia, and the Far Eastern frontiers in search of richer soil and available land.[51] The Russian and Chinese empires sent prisoners into exile in Siberia and Central Asia, and used them to develop the economy of these inhospitable areas. Nor do the figures account for the vast displacements of people by wars and rebellions, such as one-quarter of the population in many Chinese provinces forced out of their homes during the Taiping Rebellion in the 1850s and early 1860s, or the American Indians displaced by continual warfare on the frontier.[52]

These are the bare facts. They present a great historical irony. Precisely at the moment when virtually every region on the planet was becoming more diverse, nationalists began to advocate for sovereign nation-states, each of which would be the representative of one particular people. This great, unprecedented movement of peoples made even more pressing the question: Who belongs to the nation? Would Indians in the United States, ex-slaves in Brazil, Koreans in Japan, and Japanese in Korea be considered citizens able to exercise the full complement of rights? We shall see this history unfold in each of the subsequent chapters.

At the same time, migrant populations were rarely cut off completely from their home countries or regions. In the Irish, Jewish, Chinese, and

Indian diasporas, and in the European settler colonies, many people moved back and forth, migration not always a one-way ticket.[53] The ties among populations strewn far and wide opened up rivers of communication. No less than the telegraph and the printing press, people facilitated the flow of ideas, including the new political model of the nation-state and human rights.

Where did people go? To cities, frontiers, and plantations. Each form of settlement had existed for millennia. Each site took on new significance in the late eighteenth and nineteenth centuries, with profound consequences for the formation of nation-states and human rights—and their violations.

Frontiers are zones of interaction between empires or between indigenous and colonizing populations.[54] Almost invariably, great conflicts raged between natives and settlers. The hand of the state weighed lightly on many frontiers, if only because the state lay so far away. In the 1850s, it took months for British government orders to reach Tasmania from London, weeks for Siberian officials to receive directives from Saint Petersburg. Even when communications became easier, the state often lacked the resources to rule effectively.

By no means did that elemental fact of governance result in a better situation for indigenous peoples. European settlers often exercised greater brutality than regular armies; sometimes the state had to restrain its own citizens. The encroachments of European populations into areas crossed over by pastoral peoples necessarily meant bitter conflicts over land and property rights, as we shall see in chapter 3 on American Indians and chapter 6 on the Herero and Nama of Namibia. Almost none of the indigenous peoples—whether on the Eurasian steppe; the Kalahari Desert in Southern Africa; the forests, rivers, and plains of North America; or the Australian outback—had a concept of individual ownership of land. Yet security of private property constituted a central tenet of Western societies; indeed, it served as the original right from which security of life and many other basic rights descended. John Locke clearly articulated that position, and it was affirmed in the American Declaration of Independence, the French Declaration of the Rights of Man and Citizen, and the many Latin American constitutions written in the early nineteenth century. As European populations expanded around the world, they brought the concept of private property with them—creating a basis of rights for themselves, but with devastating consequences for indigenous peoples.[55] Entire ways of life were under attack by Euroamerican population movements around the globe.[56]

The decimation of indigenous communities was rarely total and could not obliterate the question of citizenship and rights, which would stalk the history of the United States and Southern Africa, for example, down to the present day—as we shall see in subsequent chapters. If Indians were members of sovereign nations, did that not suggest that they were also rights holders of some sort? And if, as later US policy dictated, they became assimilated, did that not also mean citizenship and rights?

Frontiers and sedentary agriculture were closely connected, large estates or family farms often established in the wake of settlers advancing on the frontier and pushing it farther out. While many indigenous communities suffered near elimination in the encounter on the frontier, plantations were the sites of brutal labor exploitation. Plantations flourished in East Africa, Southeast Asia, North and South America, and South and Southeast Asia. Indian indentured laborers went to Fiji, Sri Lanka, and various Caribbean islands, and enslaved Africans were transported to the New World. All these people produced cotton, rubber, tea, coffee, and sugar, the consumer goods and raw commodities critical to the development of modern capitalism. The labor force consisted of slaves and indentured workers, the latter technically free but totally impoverished and suffering conditions often as bad as under slavery. The most advanced forms of manufacturing depended on the oldest and most brutal forms of labor exploitation.[57]

And then there were cities, sites of state power, trade, production, and culture. While Euroamericans settled frontiers around the globe and most slaves and indentured laborers were compelled to work on plantations, many "voluntary" migrants settled in cities. Urbanization proceeded rapidly in the nineteenth century, a result only in part of industrialization.[58] Some cities flourished as administrative, commercial, or financial centers, Hoi An just one example. Already in 1800, Beijing had a population of over 1 million, London just under that figure. Istanbul had 570,000 inhabitants, Paris 550,000. Only three European cities—London, Paris, Naples—were among the top ten in terms of population, only six among the top twenty-five. Around 1800, China, India, and Japan had the largest urban centers. Chicago had fewer than 100 residents in 1830; in 1890 it had 1.1 million. Melbourne had no permanent residents in 1835; in 1891 it had 473,000.[59]

Cities served as key sites of population mixing. Port cities were particularly renowned—or notorious—for the diversity of their populations: black sailors in London and Hamburg; Malay, Dutch, and Japanese seamen and traders in Shanghai; Jewish, Greek, and Armenian merchants in Alexandria and Trieste; stevedores and sailors speaking multiple languages all around the globe. Nationalists around the world often denigrated cities precisely because of this mixing, making them sites of degradation and immorality. Instead, nationalists romanticized the rural landscape and idealized the peasantry as the "true" people of the nation.

At the same time, cities served as centers of agitation for the nation and liberty precisely because their density enabled political mobilization and communication. In cities news spread rapidly and printing presses churned out newspapers, leaflets, and books. The public sphere—an intermediate space of social communication between state and society—might have been most developed in Europe and the Americas, but something similar existed in the teahouses, schools, and madrasas of the Middle East and Asia, and it too became more pronounced over the course of the nineteenth century.[60] In the twentieth century, the first generation of anticolonial activists gathered in Paris and London, sites of great intellectual exchange between Europe and the Global South. Ho Chi Minh announced the independence of Vietnam in Hanoi; in Beijing Mao Tse-tung proclaimed the founding of the People's Republic of China. Only when rebel armies seized the capital could the leaders of nationalist revolts proclaim victory. Cities were the great prize. Without them, no nation-state and no human rights.

The coming and going of peoples in the modern era had, then, a profound impact on the history of the nation-state and human rights. The enhanced levels of population diversity and the encounters among different peoples could lead to brutal repressions, what we would now term human rights violations, especially ethnic cleansings and geno-cides on the frontiers of white settlement. The vision of the nation-state as the preserve of one race meant that Europeans and North American would be able to enjoy the full complement of rights available at the time, while indigenous people would be pushed to the margins. Rights for some and the exclusion of others were completely entwined.

At the same time, the sheer misery people experienced as slaves and indentured laborers on plantations; as workers, whether in traditional workshops or modern factories; or as laborers on the docks and in the warehouses of commerce created the possibility—only the possibility, not the inevitable occurrence—that they would respond to the siren call of the nation and liberty. Slave revolts, Indian uprisings, peasant rebellions, worker strikes, and the formation of trade unions and social-ist and communist parties were responses to the desperate conditions of life and would play a huge role in the emergence of human rights.

A great part of the global migration led people into cities, those con-centrated, sophisticated sites that, among many other things, were cen-ters of wealth and education and hothouses for the development of political ideas and political mobilizations. Cities served as critical nodes of communication created by population movements and new tech-nologies like the telegraph, railroad, and steamship. The public sphere expanded all around the globe. The political model of the nation-state and human rights achieved global domination only because of these new and rapid rivers of communication.

❧

What did people make of their encounters with others as world regions became more diverse, the globe more tightly linked by population movements and the growing ease of travel offered by steamships and railroads? Alongside mass population movements, individual travelers found their way around the globe. They were scientists, businessmen, missionaries, government emissaries, and adventurers. They wrote jour-nals, newspaper articles, memoirs, and books, some widely read. They created the pathways of communication that made the larger world known to literate publics in their home countries, and enabled the ideas of the nation-state and human rights, and of nationalism and racism, to spread around the globe.

Every traveler, Western or Eastern, Northern or Southern, was deeply attuned to human difference—between people in one's home country and those in the destination regions, and within those same lands. This was hardly a new phenomenon. The works of Thucydides and Herodotus ripple with descriptions, some quite fanciful, of different people in the known world, and the same is true of educated Chinese and Arab travelers in the medieval period.

Two factors, however, were different in the eighteenth- and nineteenth-century encounters. Europeans and North Americans who journeyed outward often—not always, but often—sought evidence for dividing the human species along racial lines. Classification of the natural world had been a defining characteristic of the Scientific Revolution and the Enlightenment. Many of the travelers in the first half of the nineteenth century were naturalists, like Humboldt and Darwin.[61] They observed closely rock formations, vegetation, and fish and animal species. Most could not refrain from commenting as well on society and politics. Like Carolus Linnaeus, the great eighteenth-century Swedish scientist and master of classification, they drew links from their analysis of the natural to the human world.[62] A racial understanding of human diversity became increasingly prominent after the mid-nineteenth century. All sorts of commentators drew on Darwinian ideas to promote "scientific" racism—even though much of the science was rank prejudice. In this sense, there existed in the West a "racial international," a way of thinking about human diversity that transcended national borders. In this view, the nation-state was (or should be) the representative of a nation defined in racial terms, the most exclusionary and potentially deadly form of categorizing populations. We will see this process at work in the United States, Brazil, Namibia, and Rwanda and Burundi.

No single generalization applies to Western views of Asians, Africans, Middle Easterners, or indigenous people generally. Western travelers, even if they opposed slavery and other forms of oppression, often let loose a litany of abusive epithets regarding other people. Our travelers wrote about "dirty Armenians, more dirty Jews, and chattering Greeks," and "Franciscan, Dominicans, and other monks . . . with their sanctimonious and dirty faces";[63] "fanatical" Eastern Christians;[64] Coptic Egyptians with "big, but empty [heads]" and "mean countenance[s] . . . and gloomy and melancholy [dispositions] . . . [with] no taste for the arts, no flight of curiosity . . . lazy and slovenly, clownish and ignorant, unfeeling and superstitious"[65]; Eurasians whose "love of stilted expressions . . . resemble our negroes";[66] Chinese as "the most debased people on the face of the earth," whose depths of "depravity [are] so shocking and horrible . . . Their touch is pollution."[67]

Encounters across difference often promoted a retreat to one's own identity and a riveting dismissal of the other. There are surprises as well. Western travelers often castigated Africans as barbaric. Sometimes, however, even writings on Africa rang with positive observations, though far more likely around 1800 than 1900. Two British writers, Leyden and Murray, surveying European knowledge of Africa in the late eighteenth century, recognized that Africans, too, had built kingdoms that displayed great accomplishments in art and civilization comparable to those of Europe.[68]

Travelers closely observed economies and technologies as well as populations. To many Western travelers, the nature of work and economy that they observed directly reflected the character of the people and marked the distinction between civilization and barbarism. Persian and Japanese travelers to the West were always impressed by the technology they witnessed; Westerners going east had the opposite reaction. They wrote page after page about primitive methods of labor and slovenly work habits. The director of a papermaking workshop characterized by "rude" methods and rough materials sat in front of the building, "complacently smoking his pipe under the cool shade of a tree, and evidently too magnificent and dignified a personage to attend to the details of the concern." Men like him, James De Kay concluded, "eat the bread of idleness, and consume a great part of the profits of the establishment."[69] Occasionally, however, well-cultivated fields in the Middle East or high-quality Japanese tools impressed Westerners.[70]

Two American travelers in the mid-nineteenth century reveal in stark terms the divergent reactions to human difference. Louis Agassiz, already a famed Swiss-American scientist, led an expedition to Brazil in 1865. Accompanying him was the young William James, just twenty-three years old at the time, who would later become a renowned philosopher and psychologist. Agassiz's goal was to collect and identify fish specimens as yet unknown in North America and Europe. As an unofficial representative of the United States, he also sought to open the Amazon to free navigation, an effort that succeeded when Emperor Pedro II issued just such a decree.[71]

Agassiz was a pioneer of scientific racism. With its highly diverse population and long history of race mixing, Brazil proved the perfect setting for his anthropological research. Here he sought evidence to support his anti-Darwinian, creationist theories and his racist views of human society. He understood the human species to be divided into a hierarchical order, with white Europeans inherently superior, darker-skinned people inherently inferior. Agassiz firmly supported racial segregation in the United States and viewed race mixing with utter horror. Miscegenation, he claimed, allowed inferior characteristics to triumph, leading to the degeneration of the dominant group, a view championed in the early twentieth century also by the German anthropologist Eugen Fischer, who carried out similar anthropological research in German Southwest Africa. Alongside his writings on the subject, Agassiz founded the Museum of Anthropology in Manaus in Brazil, dedicated to developing a photographic archive of indigenous and mulatto people that would demonstrate their inherent inferiority and the degenerative impact of race mixing.[72]

William James, still a student of Agassiz, had another view of human difference.[73] He surmounted the common prejudices of the day and wrote about indigenous and mestizo people with a sympathetic pen, the future author of *The Varieties of Religious Experience* seeing value in the varieties of human life. In so doing, he began to distance himself from his mentor Agassiz, a darling of the Boston and New England elite. James drew upon his family's abolitionist leanings, but went further.

James felt quite at ease in the company of his mixed-race host and guide and their Indian canoers as he traveled to the interior of the country. Yet he was not above a certain paternalism in regard to Africans and Indians, a "very nice people, of a beautiful brown color with fine black hair. Their skin is dry and clean looking, and they perspire very little so that on the whole I think they are better looking in that respect than either negroes or white men, who in this climate are always sweaty and greasy looking.... All the Indians I have seen are very christian and civilized."[74] But while "socially very agreeable," they were "mentally a most barren people."[75] When his party came across a group of Indian women who spoke Portuguese, he wrote in his diary: "I marveled, as I always do, at the quiet urbane polite tone of the conversation between my friends and the old lady. Is it race or is it circumstance that makes these people so refined and well bred? No gentleman of Europe has better manners and yet these are peasants."[76]

James wrote eloquently about the fish he found, the rivers and mountains, even the hordes of mosquitos. He extolled the absence of "our damned anglo saxon brutality and vulgarity either in masters or servants."[77] But he wrote virtually nothing about slavery, even though Rio was the most important disembarkation point for slaves in all of the Americas, and the institution of bonded labor would exist for another twenty-three years in Brazil.[78] For all his openness and empathy, it is doubtful that James would have gone so far as to include Indians and blacks in the circle of rights-bearing citizens of the Brazilian nation. As we shall see in chapter 4, many of the leading Brazilian abolitionists had the same limitations as James.

❧

Travelers moving east to west in the nineteenth century had their own encounters with human diversity. Five young Persians arrived in Great Britain in 1815, joining a sixth who had come a couple of years earlier.[79] They stayed until 1819. Their emperor, Fath 'Ali Shah (ruled 1797–1834), had suffered the loss of Persian territory to Russia. To his South and East, the British, via the British East India Company, were expanding their domination over India. Fath 'Ali Shah feared additional encroachments from both sides. But he knew he could use the British, who also worried about Russian expansion.

In 1815, Persia did not have a printing press. It had no newspapers; its scientific equipment was limited and antiquated.[80] Fath 'Ali Shah and his son, 'Abbas Mirza, were well aware of the great superiority of British science and technology, not least in military matters. 'Abbas Mirza initiated a modernization drive, one he labeled the Persian "New Order." He learned English and French and implemented reforms in the military and bureaucracy. He also accepted a small group of British military advisers, who came up from India.

So 'Abbas Mirza dispatched his young colleagues, sons of high officials in the Persian Empire, to Britain with the mission to learn as much as they could about British ways. They were not the first mission to Europe from the Middle East and Asia, but one of the most important, and one that would be replicated in far grander terms by Japanese and Koreans later in the century (as we shall see in chapter 7).

One of the Persians apprenticed in the blacksmith shop of James Wilkinson and Sons, "the Gunmaker to His Majesty." Two others worked with military engineers and artillerymen at the Royal Military Academy, while a fourth and fifth studied medicine at St. George's, one of London's most celebrated hospitals. The sixth (and author of a diary), Mirza Salih, studied languages, though in a rather improvised manner. Both Oxford and Cambridge required an oath of allegiance to the Church of England, not exactly welcoming to Irish Catholics, let alone to a Muslim from Persia.[81]

The Persian visitors, at first rather at sea in so foreign a land, seem to have quickly got their bearings. They soaked up as much as possible of the new technologies of the industrial revolution, from gunnery to printing to papermaking. Mirza Salih and one of his colleagues also observed textile mills, the engines of the early industrial revolution, and dockyards where some of the first steamships were being built.[82]

Mirza Salih was so taken with printing that he got himself apprenticed to a printer and literally got his hands dirty—quite unusual for a Persian of high birth and office. But he detected something of critical importance that went beyond the technology of printing.[83] He understood the powerful impact that printing had on the dissemination of ideas, all the while closely observing British society. Mirza Salih even became a Freemason. The secrecy and secularism of the Masons, which required no abandonment of Islam, attracted a number of elite Persians and Ottomans who traveled to Europe. It also served an important networking function that overlapped with official diplomatic missions. These Muslims may not have become supporters of human rights, but the rationalist, Enlightenment beliefs of Freemasonry, which were linked to ideas of liberty, did have an impact upon them. A few Persians, including those who had been abroad, founded a Freemason lodge at home in 1858. Meanwhile, another member of the Persian delegation, Muhammad 'Ali, was finding his way among radical artisans in the very lively London scene of coffeehouses and pubs.[84]

Mirza Salih was also impressed by his discovery that the Bodleian Library at Oxford contained books in Urdu, Persian, and Arabic; that the British East India Company presided over a thriving college for instruction in the languages he knew from home; and that the printer for whom he worked churned out the Bible in those same languages. Imperialism signified not just rule over others. It also provided another pathway for the dissemination of ideas. When he left Britain, Mirza Salih managed to bring a printing press home with him, though one had arrived a bit earlier via Saint Petersburg thanks to another enterprising Persian.[85]

Our Persian diary keeper had little to say about the conditions of life among early factory workers. He was too busy marveling at the technology and sociability of Britain to see what was right before him. As with William James failing to comment on slavery, our travelers wrote about what interested them. What they failed to see was no less important.

Fractures

In this world of dynastic and imperial power, of massive population movements, of rank poverty and deep-seated exploitation, of patterns of subservience and behaviors of submission—in this world, fractures existed that offered signals and glimmers, clear only in retrospect, of the world to come.

We have already mentioned one such fracture—Japan's opening, which set it on a course of modernization, one state among many in the "society of states." Other fractures and glimmers were evident even in the Vienna Treaty. Napoleon's imperial reign over Europe had directly challenged the distinctive European state system—that is, a continent with a multiplicity of sovereign, independent states. The Peace of Westphalia in 1648 had first enshrined that system; the Vienna Congress reinscribed it.

Dynastic legitimacy and territorial sovereignty constituted the main principles of the Vienna Treaty (see plate 4). But the ideas of the nation-state and human rights in Europe, unleashed by the French Revolution, could not be fully suppressed. Much as they wished to do so, Europe's princes, kings, and emperors could not turn the clock back to the 1760s, to the years prior to the American, French, and Latin American revolutions. As the force of nationalism grew over the course of the nineteenth and twentieth centuries, many of the dynastic states of Europe would be transformed into *nation*-states, as we shall see in subsequent chapters. Some provisions of the Vienna Treaty partly affirmed the principle of nationality—for example, by granting Poles national institutions if not their own state, and consolidating many of the small but previously sovereign German territories into larger states. The Vienna Treaty called for Jewish emancipation, thereby affirming one of the great achievements of the French Revolution.[86] Nations, constitutions, and rights now comprised an element of the European intellectual and political landscape, even when dynastic rulers held sway.[87]

⁊

The fractures of the old order and glimmers of the new were most evident not in great-power treaties and proclamations, but in movements from below. The great Haitian slave revolution, led by Toussaint Louverture, directly challenged an institution that had existed for millennia. Louverture understood the French Revolution's proclamations of liberty, equality, and fraternity. If such ideas and slogans applied to metropolitan France and to white people, why not to the colonies and black and mulatto populations? Haiti's revolution reverberated far and wide, inspiring slaves and abolitionists, raising immense fears among slaveholders and their supporters.[88] Throughout the Americas, countless other slaves engaged in individual and collective acts of resistance. They fled plantations and homesteads and formed maroon communities. By their actions, slave rebels and runaways demonstrated that conditions of oppression could be challenged. They expressed a longing for the rights that slavery had denied them so completely.

Their actions helped fuel the slavery abolition movement that emerged originally in Britain and North America in the late eighteenth and nineteenth centuries. Abolitionists forged the first great international humanitarian and human rights movement. Their political pressure led Britain to abolish the slave trade in 1807 and to promote the cause at the Vienna Congress. The Great Powers at Vienna condemned the slave trade as "repugnant to the principles of humanity and universal morality" and called on the signatories to end it, though they did not yet have the wherewithal to abolish the trade or slavery itself.[89] But many other countries soon followed Britain's lead, and Britain served as the international enforcer of the prohibition of the trade in human lives. Some abolitionists believed in hereditary black inferiority. Nonetheless, the drive to eliminate slavery—an institution that had existed for millennia—marked a revolution in moral and political practice, in the West as well as in the Islamic world, one with direct links to the development of human rights, as we shall see in chapter 4, on Brazil.[90]

Nor were other forms of extreme poverty and exploitation merely accepted. The idea of the "freeborn Englishman" resonated across Great Britain and its settler colonies (or ex-colony in the case of the United States). It ran through the countryside and cities of Great Britain and took many forms around 1815, including the destruction of industrial machinery, the first strikes, and mass demonstrations. The poetry of William Blake (among others) both captured the difficulties of the present and offered a vision of liberty and prosperity in the future. His 1810 poem "Jerusalem," infused with religious imagery, is a radical protest against the prevailing conditions in Britain—the "dark Satanic Mills"— and a call to arms. Blake holds open the possibility that people can indeed build a world of liberty in England's lush and fertile countryside.

And did those feet in ancient time
Walk upon Englands mountains green:
And was the holy Lamb of God,
On Englands pleasant pastures seen!

And did the Countenance Divine,
Shine forth upon our clouded hills?
And was Jerusalem builded here,
Among these dark Satanic Mills?

Bring me my Bow of burning gold:
Bring me my arrows of desire:
Bring me my Spear: O clouds unfold!
Bring me my Chariot of fire!

I will not cease from Mental Fight,
Nor shall my sword sleep in my hand:
Till we have built Jerusalem,
In Englands green & pleasant Land.[91]

Halfway across the world and a half century later, the Taiping Rebellion in China constituted a different form of resistance, yet one created in the context of a global economy and the global exchange of ideas. A vast, largely peasant uprising, the Taiping mixed Christian and Buddhist themes. No less than Blake, the leaders of the rebellion proclaimed a millenarian future in opposition to the oppressive conditions the peasants endured and to the Qing Dynasty's failure to uphold principles of just rule. While awaiting utopia, the Taiping rebels redistributed land and even emancipated women. After more than a decade of warfare, with both sides exercising brutalities on an unprecedented scale, provincial governors, local gentry, and the central government, frightened by the prospects of a Taiping-led China, recaptured the momentum and defeated the rebels. China's internal crisis enabled the Western powers to move in and exert ever-greater influence over the country, notably through the Second Opium War, 1856–60.[92]

The first glimmers of women's rights appeared in this period, not only in China in the Taiping Rebellion but in the West as well. Olympe de Gouges and Mary Wollstonecraft, in the 1790s, authored the first writings that explicitly demanded rights for women. This is an early example of how the granting of rights to some people—men in the French Revolution, in this case—inspired others to make similar claims, ever widening the circle of those deserving of rights-bearing citizenship. In Western Europe and North America, many women moved from the abolitionist movement to found the first organizations devoted to women's rights. They explicitly linked the two causes, typically blending religious sentiments and political ideology. It would be a long road, over two hundred years, from de Gouges and Wollstonecraft in the 1790s and the Taiping Rebellion in the mid-nineteenth century to the United Nations Convention on the Elimination of All Forms of Discrimination against Women, passed only in 1979. But the glimmers were apparent early on.

Another kind of fracture is visible through the lens of European imperial power. Colonial powers certainly exploited the "natives," reducing them to subjects. Our traveler Taylor was appalled at the "contemptuous manner" in which the English treated Indians of all classes.[93] At the same time, he asserted that the English had brought prosperity and British law and order to the subcontinent. Indians, he claimed, received more equitable treatment in British courts than in whatever kind of justice native rulers doled out.[94]

The expectation of just treatment was another important precondition for the establishment of human rights norms. Just as Toussaint Louverture turned French revolutionary ideas into demands for slave emancipation, the Indian national movement, founded later in the nineteenth century, would turn British ideas of justice against British domination.

Finally, yet other fractures and glimmers were evident within the very structures of empires. The French naturalist and traveler C. S. Sonnini, a prescient observer, had predicted already in the 1770s a Greek national revolution that would inspire others far and wide.[95] Beneath the surface calm of the Vienna System, people mobilized in democratic clubs and societies from Madrid to Moscow and all across Latin America. From the 1820s onward, intellectuals and publicists debated the ideas of democracy and revolution. The situation exploded (literally) in the European Revolutions of 1848. None except the Swiss succeeded, but every subsequent nation-state founding in Europe, every Western rights proclamation and constitution, can be traced back to the dramatic events of that year, also the year of publication of *The Communist Manifesto*. Over the subsequent decades and on virtually every continent, Marx and Engels won devoted followers with their clarion call for communism as the solution to all forms of injustice.

Many emperors were keenly aware of the challenges they faced from nationalist and reforming sentiments, as well as from the rise of Western power. Ottoman, Persian, and Chinese rulers had been engaged with the West for centuries. By the 1830s, they recognized that the West was newly dynamic. Western military, technological, and governmental superiority—the Western states' capacity to mobilize resources, including human capital—posed grave threats to their rule. They watched as the British, step by step, asserted their domination over India; the French moved into North Africa; and the Russians threatened Ottoman, Persian, and Chinese domains.

In response, empires initiated reform programs that responded both to internal dynamics and to the threat of European domination. Japan and the Ottoman Empire went the furthest down this road—the Japanese wildly successful, the Ottomans rather less so. As the Ottoman statesman Fuad Paşa said in the 1850s, "Islam was for centuries . . . a wonderful instrument of progress. Today it is a clock which is behind time and must be set."[96] Reforming empires expanded education, notably in engineering, the sciences, and languages, to make the bureaucracy and the army better able to contend with the growing power of the European states and to exercise greater control internally over their sprawling, diverse empires. The Ottoman Empire called upon religious communities to establish representative assemblies, and all subjects of the empire were promised just treatment and equality under the law. Most importantly, the Ottoman government promised security of life and property and an end to the oppressive system of tax farming, vividly depicted by our traveler, Reverend Vere Monro.[97] But how could the egalitarianism fundamental to citizenship be established when Islam was the religion of the state and all other religions considered inferior?

Japan demonstrated a different possibility. Townsend Harris had waited months on end to accomplish his mission and his movements were severely restricted. Twenty-five years later, an Englishwoman, Isabella Bird, moved rather effortlessly around Japan, and observed hordes of Europeans and Americans in government employ. The Japanese government, Bird noted, strove "to get all they can out of foreigners, and then to dispense with their service." The telegraph department had recently passed into Japanese hands, but the naval college had English instructors, the medical college Germans, the engineering college a British principal, and a French military commission instructed the Japanese army in European drill and tactics. Missionaries were translating the Bible into Japanese. A large Chinese community in Yokohama played a critical role in commerce.[98] This was all the result of the Japanese revolution from above, the Meiji Restoration, and a two-year trip around the world by an official delegation that brought home the knowledge of Western technology and governance.[99]

Conclusion

When Townsend Harris traveled from New York to Penang (in present-day Malaysia) on his way to Siam and Japan, his journey lasted three months. At every stop—and there were many—he waited expectantly for the mail. He lingered in Calcutta for a number of days, and was thrilled when the steamer from China arrived with newspapers and letters. Another traveler, J. W. Spalding, on board with Commodore Perry, rejoiced when, after eighty days, they put in at Singapore and found a mailbag waiting for them. "It was the first news we had gotten directly, since leaving the United States . . . and no one but he who has experienced it can appreciate fully the joy of getting a letter at such a time."[100]

While in Ceylon, Harris visited a "high priest," who "showed me a number of letters from the First King of Siam *written in English* by the King himself."[101] Harris was flummoxed by the king's fluency, just as Mirza Salih had been astonished to find Urdu, Persian, and Hindu speakers in Britain, and shelves full of books in his languages in the Bodleian Library. When Harris arrived in Menan in Siam, the king's retinue greeted him with a band playing the "Star-Spangled Banner."[102]

By the mid-nineteenth century, the world was alive with connections, sped along since 1815 by steamships, railroads, and, in the 1860s, telegraph cables lain across land and under oceans. Migrations, trade, travel, print: all facilitated communications, making possible something we can label a global public sphere.[103] Madrasas in Isfahan, coffeehouses in Boston, dockside taverns in Rio and London, and teahouses in Hoi An had their own particularities. But they were all places for the dissemination of ideas. By 1815, let alone 1850, none of these places was isolated; each was in some form of communication with the wider world.

Along the pathways of communication ran the ideas of the nation-state and human rights. They were in their infancy, barely implemented even in their locus of origin along the Atlantic Seaboard. The world remained dominated by empires and hierarchies of wealth and power that left most people subjects, not citizens, and subservience the prevalent mode of behavior. Slavery was only the most glaring example of the injustices that prevailed.

Yet fractures were evident in this world. The call for slavery abolition had resonated in many parts of the globe. Rebels in South America promoted the model of the nation-state and human rights. In Asia, leaders of the Taiping Rebellion advocated land reform and social equality. Marx and Engels formulated the idea of communism, which would reverberate around the world in the twentieth century. Women were writing, speaking, and demonstrating in a grand effort to broaden the circle of rights-bearing citizens. Reforming emperors, faced with dissension within and powerful adversaries abroad, began to adopt aspects of the new political model developed in the Atlantic revolutions. Even imperialism was never simply a system of oppression. When an imperial power like Great Britain established legal institutions and standards of fairness (however imperfectly implemented), it helped set in motion the ideas and practices that would lead to the eventual demise of its empire.

It is to these fractures, these glimmers and signals of a new global political order, that we now turn, starting with the Greek rebellion against the Ottoman Empire.

Chapter 2

Greece

LEAVING THE EMPIRE

❧

RIGAS VELESTINLIS (or Pheraeos) penned his "Patriotic Hymn" in 1797 while living in Vienna. A rousing cry against tyranny and an appeal to liberty and fraternity, it is known and performed to this day in Greece. "Patriotic Hymn" is the lyric song of all nationalisms. It proclaims love of the fatherland and mourns the debased present of slavery and servitude under foreign occupation. The future, however, holds great promise so long as men rally, break the chains of tyranny forged by the foreign overlord, and create the nation. Velestinlis's vision for Greece was capacious; it included "Bulgarians, Albanians, Armenians, and Greeks, blacks and whites," and even Muslims (or "Turks," as he wrote).[1] His "Political Statute" laid out his ideas for a Greek republic and the rights of its citizens. Sometimes word for word, he drew on the French Declaration of the Rights of Man and Citizen. "Sovereignty," he wrote, recalling article 3 of the French Declaration, "resides in the people; it is singular, indivisible, eternal, and inalienable."[2] All men are equal and all should be free and none a slave to others.[3]

In the "Political Statute," Velestinlis went on to reproduce the catalog of rights enshrined in the American, French, and Latin American revolutions and in virtually every other nation-state's constitution over the succeeding 250 years: the laws shall be freely chosen by the people, all citizens have the right to public employment, liberty is the freedom to do as one likes so long as no harm is inflicted on one's neighbors. Everyone has the right of free expression, Velestinlis wrote, and freedom of religion shall exist for all, including Christians, Muslims, and Jews.[4] Slavery was to be abolished, and education promoted for girls as well as boys.[5] All men who lived within the borders of Greece for at least one year would be recognized as citizens.[6]

Velestinlis offered a bracing, democratic vision for Greece. Inspired by the French Revolution, he directly challenged the hierarchies of power that prevailed in the Ottoman Empire and proposed that Greece enter the new world of nation-states and human rights. But life would not be so easy. In 1797, Velestinlis tried to launch an uprising to establish an independent Greece. Austrian officials got wind of the plans and turned him over to the Ottoman authorities. Later that year, they executed Velestinlis and twelve compatriots, and threw his body into the Danube.

Nor could there be a simple transition from a political pronouncement to the foundation of the nation-state—not in Greece, nor in any other of the histories discussed in this book. Instead, the road to an independent Greece and the proclamation of rights for its citizens would be marked by brutal warfare, diplomatic maneuvering, and uneasy compromises. Through all of these events and all the different political formations that governed the country over the next two and one-half centuries, the key questions remained: Who, in fact, was a Greek? Did the Greek nation include Jews, Muslims, Bulgarians, Vlachs, and a host of other groups? Would any Greek constitution match the breadth of Velestinlis's vision in 1797? And for those deemed Greek, what kind of rights would they exercise?

With all its accomplishments, limitations, and disasters, Greece became a touchstone for national independence movements in the entire Mediterranean region and beyond (see maps 2.1 and 2.2). The success of the Greek insurgency resonated in the Balkans, Anatolia, the Middle East, and as far afield as Latin America. For all these reasons—the partial character of every human rights advance; Greece as a model for other national movements; the central question of who constitutes the nation; the ongoing influence, for good and bad, of the Great Powers—we begin with the Greek story: the first nation-state founded in Europe after the Napoleonic era.[7]

&

The path to Greek independence began with a conspiratorial revolt in February 1821 in the Danubian provinces of Moldavia and Wallachia

MAP 2.1 Expansion and decline of the Ottoman Empire.

(part of present-day Romania), which were nominally Ottoman though under Russian protection.[8] Many Greeks, some of them wealthy merchants and high officials in Ottoman service, populated the two provinces. A few months later and with much greater force, brigands in the Peloponnese and the islands launched their own uprisings.

The two rebellions, in their beginnings, were hardly national in character and barely concerned with human rights in the sense of the American, French, and Latin American revolutions. Greece was a backward society. Literacy rates were exceedingly low, manufacturing archaic in nature. Orthodox Christianity provided one unifying force among the rebels. Beyond that, identities were primarily local. Political authority

MAP 2.2 Expansion of Greece.

lay ultimately in the hands of the sultan. In reality, in daily life, power was lodged more in local officials, landlords, and brigands, Muslim and Christian, than in faraway Istanbul. In such a setting, nationalism and human rights were improbable political ideologies.[9]

The revolts launched by Greeks in the 1820s stood in the long line of rebellions that sought an easing of Ottoman oppression. Greek insurgents wanted relief from taxes—recall our Reverend Munro who, in his travels to the Middle East, described the cascading tax system in which every Ottoman official all up the hierarchy took his cut, adding immeasurably to the burden on commoners and the wealthy alike. The rebels also desired the freedom to build and repair churches without having to appeal to the Ottoman authorities. In the Danubian provinces, merchants and officials wanted the autonomy and power to run things their own way without always having to answer to—and pay—Ottoman officials locally and in Istanbul. Along with religion, all these grievances united most Greeks, whatever their predominantly local identities.

The *klephts*, clan-based brigands on land and sea, played the most prominent role in the rebellion. They brought with them military experience, a sense of organization, and armed followers, sometimes including entire villages. The *klephts* rarely looked beyond their own locality and most had probably never heard of the Declaration of the Rights of Man and Citizen. Like the Danubian merchants, they sought an independent Greece that would leave them untrammeled authority in their own petty domains. To their family members and followers, the brigands provided protection and privileges, ensuring that "their people" could farm their land, move their herds, forge their products, and ply their fishing grounds in security. All this came at a price—unquestioned loyalty and some form of taxes delivered up the chain of command. Many of the brigands had long-standing relations with Ottoman officials and with Muslim brigands, and they dealt with them when there were advantages to be gained.[10]

For many centuries, Muslims and Christians had largely coexisted in the Eastern Mediterranean. Diverse populations often lived side by side. However, instances of intense communal violence punctuated the long periods of peace. Now, in the 1820s, the religious divide between Orthodox Christians and Muslims became even stronger as the Greek rebellion developed, over the course of the decade, into a national revolt with strong echoes of the rights of man. Religious identity took on newfound political meaning in the age of nationalism. The Ottoman Empire, like so many others, had accepted and tolerated diversity; the nation-state, much less so.

The Greek War of Independence, as it came to be known, unleashed ten years of intermittent warfare laced with astonishing brutalities on both sides. Into the fray of the rebellion entered more politically minded Greeks. Over the course of the decade of warfare, they provided intellectual resources and—no less important—ties to European society and European states. To governments and publics abroad, the activists made the case for a Greek nation, raised the funds needed to keep Greek armies in the field and Greek ships at sail, and prodded the European powers into action. Their task was not easy. The Great Powers never adopted fully the Greek national program, much to the disappointment of Greek activists, but instead looked after their own interests, as they always do (and as we shall see in other cases discussed in this book).

Many of the activists had been schooled abroad—in Paris, London, and some of the German cities. They were moved by the examples of the American, French, and Latin American revolutions, and by the writings and martyrdom of early national heroes like Velestinlis. In that regard, they already lived in a global world, where the events on one continent profoundly influenced those on another.

Velestinlis's ideas, drawn from the revolutions he observed in the 1790s, served as inspiration for the Philiki Etaireia (Friendly Society), the first recognizably modern organization in Greece. Founded in 1814 by the children of merchant families, it was a secret society with Masonic-influenced rituals. It had few members, yet its impact was great. The Friendly Society fostered the idea that Greece could be freed from Ottoman rule only by armed rebellion. It attracted intellectuals, teachers and clerics, merchants and shippers, all drawn to the ideas of the Enlightenment and the French Revolution. They joined forces with some landowners, and with brigands of various sorts. This diverse grouping, a cross section of society, made the Greek Revolution.[11] At least in the initial stages, the rebellion included various Balkan Christians—Russians, Bulgarians, Serbs, and Romanians—once again indicating the resonance of the events far beyond Greece.[12]

The Friendly Society members were, then, typical nationalist activists.[13] They drew on numerous Greek traditions—many of them, they discovered, more valued in Paris, London, Berlin, and Boston than in

Greece itself. Greece had a legendary past as the birthplace of classical civilization and democracy, the very foundation of Europe—as the Philhellenes, the foreign partisans of the Greek rebellion, never tired of repeating. It had a tradition of rebellion, honored in folktales that depicted heroic bandits who had protected home and hearth against infidel Turks. It was but a small step to turn these legends of local Robin Hoods into the forebears of national independence.

The activists also drew on and helped create something very new—a public sphere, that marker of the modern world, complete with presses, pamphlets, and coffeehouses, without which no *national* rebellion is possible. The expansion of Greek merchant activity throughout the Mediterranean and into Europe in the eighteenth century and during the Napoleonic wars had broadened the horizons of some Greeks. The public sphere, albeit in nascent form, emerged in the late eighteenth century alongside economic development, and it enabled the spread of national ideals. Wealthy merchants, especially in the Danubian provinces, endowed schools and supported the publication of works in Greek, all of which encouraged the formation of a Greek identity partly independent from religion. They also provided scholarships for young Greek men to study in Paris, London, or Berlin, where they came into contact with Enlightenment ideas, the legacy of the French Revolution, and the influence of ancient Greece on Western Europeans.[14]

The development of a Greek public sphere and Greek national thinking occurred at the precise moment when the sultan's writ had weakened as more-or-less independent governors and warlords emerged in many parts of the Ottoman Empire, notably—and this would prove decisive for the Greek events—in Albania and Egypt. The French occupation of the Ionian Islands in 1797 and then the invasion of Egypt in 1798 demonstrated very concretely that Ottoman domination could be challenged. These events also brought the ideas of the French Revolution into the Ottoman realm. The Serb revolt in 1804 provided something of a model, and the fact that the Vienna Treaty made the Ionian Islands a republic under British protection only confirmed the fragility of the Ottoman Empire. A heady brew of traditional Greek brigandage with more modern notions of national independence and the rights of man emerged in the Ionian Islands, something of a launching pad for the larger idea of an independent Greek state.

The nineteenth-century historian of the Greek rebellion, George Finlay, wrote that "the Greeks, from an insurgent populace, had . . . become an independent nation."[15] Finlay greatly exaggerated by dating this transformation as early as 1821, but he was not entirely wrong. The very traditional Greek rebellion became a popular revolution over the course of the 1820s. While kinship groups mobilized and proved effective military forces, agitators circulated through the country. They were typically Etaireia members. Sometimes they assumed the character of famous Greeks of the ancient past as they harangued crowds in villages and towns, stirring them up, often with rumors and stories of Ottoman atrocities and intended deportations of Christians to Africa.[16]

Brigands like Odysseus Androutsos could, at one moment, act like traditional rebels, and the next moment invoke the language of liberty and the nation.[17] Those words—"liberty" and the "nation"—connected Greek events to the revolutions of the eighteenth and early nineteenth centuries and to a host of similar movements across the expanse of Europe and the Americas, from the demise of the Napoleonic Empire in 1815 through the revolutions of 1848 and beyond. Greek rebels, at least the more politicized among them, were acutely conscious of the connection and used it to appeal for support. M. Rodios, the secretary of the Greek government, wrote to British Foreign Secretary George Canning reminding him that Great Britain had demonstrated a "philanthropic principle" toward the people of South America by supporting their struggles for independence from Spain. Therefore, one can hardly believe, Rodios continued, that Britain would allow Greece to be excluded like natives from the "catalog of civilized nations and left to the mercy of others, without having the right to constitute itself as a nation."[18] In another appeal, addressed to the "Citizens of the United States," Peter Mavromichalis, a brigand and head of the senate in Messenia, claimed that Greece was following in the footsteps of the Americans, those great promoters of freedom, who had been the very first to sound the bell of liberty. "In invoking her name [Liberty], we invoke yours at the same time. . . . In aiding us to purge Greece from the barbarians, you will crown the glory of America as the land of freedom."[19]

The initial revolt in the Danubian provinces fared poorly. The rebels had counted on Russian support, but Tsar Alexander I recoiled from a rebellion that threatened to unleash unknown furies. The tsar permitted Ottoman forces to enter the principalities and take their revenge, while crowds of Muslims in Istanbul and other Anatolian cities sacked churches and Christian homes and businesses. Hundreds, maybe thousands, were killed. Convinced that the Greek Orthodox patriarch had supported the rebellion, the Sublime Porte (the seat of the Ottoman government in Istanbul) had him executed by hanging—his body, along with those of other clerics, strung up for public display.

Matters were more difficult for the Ottomans in the Peloponnese and the islands. The brigands were politically unschooled, but they knew how to fight. They had learned to use their environment to their advantage. The many hills and mountains; the difficult passes; the long, craggy shorelines—all were congenial to guerrilla warfare on land and piracy at sea. The frontal assaults favored by the Ottoman army and navy were ill suited for such combat—except when massive force was put in play. Through 1821 and 1822 the Greek rebels had notable successes on the battlefield. But then the Ottomans put many more men into the field, and called upon Muhammad 'Ali's navy in Egypt. 'Ali had carved out Egypt as virtually autonomous within the Ottoman Empire.[20] He had trafficked with the Greek rebels. But in the end, he decided to throw in his lot with his sovereign. The insurgents now suffered notable reverses. The Ottoman forces exacted severe revenge for the rebellion, including the massacres at Chios and Missolonghi, which were immortalized by the great Romantic artist Eugène Delacroix (see plate 5).

By 1825, four years into the rebellion, the military situation was at a stalemate. But that did not mean any diminution in the violence. Year after year, Greek rebels and Ottoman armies slogged it out, inflicting great casualties on each other with neither able to turn the tide. To make matters worse, the Greek rebels had descended into civil war, the near-perfect expression of the local loyalties of the various brigands who led the fighting.

Two developments, both external to Greece, proved decisive, thought it would take another seven years of warfare and untold suffering until the various sides reached a political settlement. First was the emergence of the Philhellenes, the Romantic advocates of an independent Greece who were especially prominent in Britain, France, and the United States. Their unceasing public clamor in support of the Greeks had a significant (if often exaggerated) impact on British policy in particular. Second was the intervention of the Great Powers, in which Britain again, along with Russia, played the critical role. For both the Philhellenes and European governments, dogged Greek resistance coupled with Ottoman atrocities had created an untenable situation that aroused humanitarian sentiments and, more important for the Great Powers, threatened the Vienna settlement.

The European states wanted, above all else, stability in the Eastern Mediterranean. Russia proved a partial exception; it used the crisis caused by the Greek revolt to expand its territory and power into the Ottoman realm. The final outcome—a Greek state with a constitution (finally proclaimed in 1864) and a set of rights that enfranchised Greek men and excluded Muslims and Jews, all presided over by a Bavarian prince (of all things)—could hardly have been foreseen in 1821. The Great Powers had no desire, initially, for a semi-independent Greece. The nation-state and the rights of its citizens were created not just by heroic Greeks holding off the armies of a great empire, but also by the Great Powers' pursuit of their individual and collective interests.

First to the Philhellenes.

"The glory of the ancient Greeks," begins Thomas Gordon's *History of the Greek Revolution*, published in 1832, virtually in the heat of events.[21] Gordon, an English officer, acted on his devotion and became a general in the Greek army during the war. Another Philhellene and historian, the previously cited George Finlay, writing some thirty years after the Greek rebellion, extolled "the importance of the Greek race to the progress of European civilization." Though the Greeks became subjected to "the yoke of a foreign nation and a hostile religion" and lived in "abject servitude," they "never forgot that the land they inhabited was the land of their fathers. . . . The Greek Revolution . . . delivered a Christian nation from subjection to Mohammedanism, founded a new state in Europe, and extended the advantages of civil liberty to regions where despotism had for ages been indigenous."[22]

Here was the Philhellene manifesto, proclaimed by Gordon the same year the Greek state was founded, still alive in Finlay thirty years later despite the enervating experience of a hapless state ruled by an affable but semi-competent Bavarian king. Greece, the land of civilization; Greeks, the heroic fighters for liberty; Greece, the beacon of the past relit as a lodestar for the present.

Philhellenes like our two historians, the poets Lord Byron and Percy Bysshe Shelley, the philosopher Jeremy Bentham, and many others argued that the cause of national independence and the rights of man transcended borders. The Greek cause demanded action, whether actually fighting and dying in Greece, as did Byron, or canvassing for funds, publishing articles, and delivering speeches. In this way, the Philhellenes built a modern political movement, often taking their cues—and many of their supporters—from the slavery abolition campaigns. Down to the present day, our image of the Philhellenes is one of committed men and women devoted to a just cause.[23]

Byron, that mercurial poet and man-about-town, is the icon of philhellenism (see figure 2.1). He had been to Greece previously, and his great epic poem "Childe Harold's Pilgrimmage" vividly conveyed his fascination with classical Greece. His devotion was so great, his personal life so entangled with Greece, that he could hardly ignore the rebellion that seemed to herald Greece's rebirth. Shortly before his arrival in Greece in August 1823, he wrote in his journal:

The Dead have been awakened—shall I sleep?
The World's at war with tyrants—shall I crouch?
The harvest's ripe—and shall I pause to reap?
I slumber not—the thorn is in my Couch—
Each day a trumpet soundeth in Mine ear—
It's Echo in my heart—[24]

Byron died for his devotion to Greece, his "land of valour, of the arts, and of liberty throughout the ages."[25]

In this Greece, what place was there for Muslims, Jews, Vlachs, and others? Earlier, in his first travels to Greece and the Mediterranean, Byron had been enamored with the Ottomans he had met. He cherished

FIGURE 2.1 Lord Byron, 1814. Byron (1788–1824), Romantic par excellence, poet and political conspirator, was one of the most renowned Philhellenes. He had fallen for Greece on his first visit in 1810. In this engraving by William Finden, Byron fancies himself a Greek. (© National Portrait Gallery, London.)

their hospitality and friendliness, even when they were, in fact, despots. Byron prided himself on his encounters with people of all sorts, including Turks (as he called them) and Albanians.[26] He was received by Sultan Mahmoud II in Istanbul and by the Albanian leader Ali Pasha at his redoubt in Tepelene.[27] Nearly fifteen years later, during the war, Byron expressed empathy for Ottoman combatants. To the English consul in Preveza (in Epirus, Northwestern Greece), he wrote: "When the dictates of humanity are in question, I know no difference between Turks and Greeks."[28] Byron requested that the consul aid and protect twenty-four Turks he had happened upon, including women and children. He also prevailed upon Greek combatants to release their Ottoman prisoners, and took under his wing a Muslim mother and girl.[29]

Byron was more clear-headed than most Philhellenes. He had come to Greece, he declared, "not . . . to join a faction but a nation."[30] What he found, however, were Greeks divided among themselves; the worst of them (and not a small number, he claimed) "liars," "speculators," or "peculators."[31] To the Greek leader Alexander Mavrocordatos, Byron wrote of his dismay at the divisions among the Greeks. None of this, however, induced him to abandon his enduring affection for them or his commitment to their struggle for independence. In the terms that would also justify the exclusion of Muslims from the Greek state, he wrote that the Greeks had lived under "so long and so barbarous a tyranny," they fought not for political theories but "for their very existence" against "those Barbarians [and] oppressors" who were the enemies of "Enlightenment and Humanity."[32]

Such views were echoed by countless other Philhellenes. William Wilberforce, the great abolitionist, spoke fervently in favor of British intervention to aid the Greeks. He called on Britain to "rescu[e] the Greeks from bondage and destruction."[33] Wilberforce was responding to the terrible massacre of Greeks at Chios. Like many Philhellenes, he ignored the atrocities committed by Greeks against Muslims. The word and concept of genocide lay more than a century in the future. But both Greek activists and their philhellenic supporters used all the other terms we now associate with the most extreme crimes against humanity: "the annihilation of a whole people"; a "brutal war of extermination"; the extermination of "the most civilized, cultivated, and interesting people, the flower of Greece"; or the extermination of the "entire [Greek] race."[34]

Like Byron, Finlay was clear-eyed about the situation in Greece. With soaring rhetoric he depicted a Greece mired in corruption and incompetence, a nation that had established the veneer of representative institutions designed to impress Europe, but was incapable of forming the rational administration of a modern state. Instead, petty dictators dominated the land, all engaged in jealous wrangling over inconsequential issues. A chasm had opened between the lofty ideas of liberty and the political reality on the ground.

Finlay was unsparing and scathing about the atrocities Greeks had committed.[35] The brutalities of the war, he argued, were planned, promoted, and executed by the revolutionaries, and were designed to rid Greece permanently of Muslims. In the first months of the revolution, Finlay wrote,

> the Christian population . . . attacked and murdered the Mussulman population in every part of the peninsula. The towns and country houses of the Mussulmans were burned down, and their property was destroyed, in order to render the return of those who had escaped into fortresses hopeless. . . . Ten to fifteen thousand souls perished in cold blood, and . . . three thousand farmhouses or Turkish dwellings were laid waste. . . . The extermination of the Turks by the Greeks in the rural districts was the result of a premeditated design.[36]

The Etairists, he continued, were determined to "render peace impossibl[e] [and] inculcated the necessity of exterminating every Turk. . . . The slaughter of men, women, and children was therefore declared to be a necessary measure of wise policy, and popular songs spoke of the Turks as a race which ought to disappear from the face of the earth."[37] Even the massacre at Chios was a response to Greek cruelties, he claimed.[38]

Perhaps unwittingly, Finlay described the mix of modern and premodern elements in the violence of the Greek Revolution. The repression exercised by the Ottomans was traditional in character, a standard way of crushing unruly populations in the empire. But the Greek rebels, by seeking to make Greece unlivable for Muslims by killing them and by driving them out and reducing their homes to rubble, created facts on the ground that amounted to a form of ethnic cleansing before it had a name. Summing it all up, Finlay wrote: "The Greeks entertained the project of exterminating the Mussulmans in European Turkey; the sultan and the Turks believed that they could paralyse the movements of the Greeks by terrific cruelty. Both parties were partially successful."[39]

Finlay did not mention Jews, the other target of Greek hostility. As the Greek forces laid waste to Muslim villages and Muslim lives, they also devastated the Jewish population. Thousands were killed; many more thousands fled to areas that would remain Ottoman territory. Every time the borders of Greece expanded—as it did on numerous occasions between 1832 and 1913 (see map 2.2)—Jews fled or were expelled and found greater safety under Ottoman rule.[40]

For all their clear-eyed analyses, for all their humanitarian sensibilities, Byron and Finlay could not surmount the political contradictions of their positions. Both were in love with Greece, and it was a Greek state that they wanted, one in which other populations—most notably Muslims and Jews, but also Bulgarians, Vlachs, Catholics, and others—would, in fact, be rendered invisible. In the best of circumstances, they would be tolerated and protected. In point of fact, Byron, Finlay, and other Philhellenes wished they were not there at all. And that was the challenge that all nationalists faced (and still face): how to build a nationally defined state, complete with a constitution and rights, in a setting of great national and religious diversity. There was simply no accounting for Muslims, Jews, and others in Finlay's or Byron's philhellenic program for Greece.[41]

cs

Nor could the European states surmount the contradiction.

The Greek revolt could not succeed without European help. No nationalist movement, no human rights advance, succeeds solely by its own motor power (as we shall see also in the other cases discussed in this book). In the nineteenth and twentieth centuries, every attempt to found a nation-state and human rights principles drew on preceding models and, in turn, influenced others, most immediately in the surrounding areas but sometimes farther afield. These efforts also invoked great-power interests, especially if they occurred in areas of prime strategic importance, as was the case for Greece and the Ottoman, Russian, and British empires.

The Greek rebels knew all that. They used every rhetorical device they could muster, combining an old European rhetoric of hostility to Islam with the new language of *liberté, egalité, fraternité*. They castigated the sultan and the officials of the Sublime Porte one moment as infidel Muslims, the next as brutes and the destroyers of civilization. The Greek National Assembly in 1822, for example, invoked the glories of ancient Greece and the all-powerful god in its claim to national independence. It declared that the sultan ruled over an empire marked by "cowardice and baseness," an empire that exercised a "cruel yoke, despotic and capricious." After a "long slavery we have taken up arms to avenge ourselves and our Fatherland . . . against a tyranny . . . without compare."[42] The National Assembly claimed that Greece was waging "a national war, a sacred war, a war whose only goal is to reconquer the rights of individual liberty, our property and our honor, those rights enjoyed by our neighbors, the civilized peoples of Europe."[43]

The European powers would have none of it. Not at first, not even when the Greek rebels raised the specter of Islam.[44] Coming, in its first stage, just six years after the defeat of Napoleon, the Greek revolt portended instability and revolution, the two situations most abhorrent to the Great Powers. They trembled at its prospects, at the uncertainties that the Vienna System had been expressly designed to contain. To European statesmen, the Greeks were wild and dangerous rebels, especially when they pronounced the ideals of the French Revolution.

However, the European position evolved. The Greeks were persistent. They could not win alone against the Ottomans, nor would they give up. The fighting, month in, month out, with no end in sight, presented all sorts of possibilities, none of them good to the five Great Powers—Britain, Russia, France, Austria, and Prussia—determined to maintain the status quo. Perhaps the Greek rebels would win outright and establish a radical democracy in Europe, a new seat of contagion like France of the 1790s. Perhaps the Ottoman Empire would collapse, which could benefit only Russia, disturbing the balance among the five. Worse yet, the Ottoman Empire might win outright, and then expand its domains in Europe. Nothing looked good when statesmen in London, Paris, Vienna, Saint Petersburg, and Berlin gazed at the Eastern Mediterranean.[45]

Moreover, as the fighting dragged on and the Ottomans committed atrocities, both publics and statesmen in Europe (and across the ocean in North America) found their consciences aroused. Could they stand by when fellow Christians and liberty enthusiasts were being slaughtered? The philhellenic societies came to exercise a good deal of influence over public opinion in France and Britain and even in the United States.[46] In Russia, Pan-Slavists and an emergent public sphere exercised a similar pressure on the tsarist government to aid fellow Orthodox Christians.[47]

Precisely because the Ottomans proved unable swiftly to bring matters under control, the European states began to see the need for some kind of involvement in the events in the Eastern Mediterranean. None of them, at the outset, demanded a fully independent Greece. The European states were not advocates of liberty and national independence. Nor did they seek the dismemberment of the Ottoman Empire. Their overwhelming desire was for stability in the region. Not as a prescribed plan, but *only in the course of events*, did Greek determination, Ottoman excesses, and Russia's declaration of war against the Sublime Porte bring a Greek nation-state and human rights onto the table as a viable solution.[48] As we shall see in the other cases examined in this book, the emergence of a set of rights connected to the nation was not just the work of heroic liberators. Instead, within the context of the reigning international system, the Great Powers reluctantly came to accept the nation-state and rights because they provided the keys to stability—or such was the hope.[49]

Russia and Great Britain had the most at stake in the region. Russia sought to expand its influence southward and westward. Since the Treaty of Küçük-Kaynarca in 1774, which ended one of the many

Russian-Ottoman wars, Russia, on specious grounds, claimed the right of protection of all Christians under Ottoman rule. Great Britain's ever-expanding empire had turned the Mediterranean, linked to so many areas of British power, into a crucial site of its interests. France was still partly sidelined by the other states because of its unruly past. Prussia, the weakest of the five powers, had no direct interests in the region (at this point—matters would be different for a unified Germany at the end of the century). And the Habsburg Empire with Prince Metternich at the fore was unrelentingly hostile to the Greek revolt, hence incapable of acting with the flexibility and creativity that the situation demanded.

To the great chagrin of the Greek rebels, Tsar Alexander I, at the outset of the revolt, displayed no interest whatsoever in coming to their aid. He preferred to wage war against the Ottoman Empire at a time and place of his own choosing, not as a result of the actions of brigands and some hotheaded Greek conspirators inspired by French ideas. But Russia did demand that the Ottoman Empire guarantee the security of Christian lives. Baron Grigorii Stroganov, the Russian ambassador to the Porte, warned the Ottomans against excessive measures directed at Christians. Otherwise, he implied, Russia might be forced to take more serious action to defend its co-religionists.[50]

A string of plans and proposals emanated from Saint Petersburg, generally involving some autonomy for Greece coupled with the enhancement of Russian power.[51] The Russian government argued that unlike France and Britain, Russia had its most vital essential interests at stake when the Ottomans closed the straits to navigation.[52]

Soon after Baron Stroganov's missive to the Porte, Russia broke off relations. But Russian moves toward war met with sharp resistance from its allies. Indeed, they had held Russia back from the brink in 1821 and 1822 when the situation in Greece had first become threatening. Metternich was not only horrified by the Greek revolt, he was also furious at Russia's effort to expand its power via warfare against the Ottoman Empire. European statesmen of the post–French Revolution, post-Napoleonic period knew well that war unleashed unpredictable and uncontrollable demons.

Tsar Nicholas I, who had ascended the throne after Alexander's death in December 1825, sought a kind of new ideological legitimation. Autocratic rule, Orthodox Christianity, and Russian-ness comprised the so-called "official nationality" of his reign. Scarred by the Decembrist uprising, he would remain an arch-reactionary. While his elder brother Alexander had some sympathies for the Greeks' cause, though not for Greek rebels nor a fully sovereign Greek state, Nicholas saw nothing good in the entire situation.[53]

For the Ottomans, the uprising was simply banditry and rebellion, scourges that had long plagued the Greek peninsula, only now they were playing out on a larger scale. Since the latter part of the seventeenth century, when the Ottomans were defeated at the gates of Vienna, and certainly since the Treaty of Küçük-Kaynarca in 1774, the Ottoman Empire had become integrated into the European system. Its officials knew how to deploy the language of European statecraft. They rejected British (and the other powers') offers of mediation and claimed that the Greek affair was an internal matter. No other power would behave any differently, Ottoman statesmen argued in memoranda and manifestos. The empire, they asserted, acted in accordance with "the rights of governments and the laws of nations."[54] For the Ottomans, as for the European powers, state sovereignty had to be defended against all challengers, for upon it rested the divine order and the relations among nations. Using the categories that would become commonplace in subsequent decades and in the twentieth century, the Ottomans declared that they were dealing with mere brigands, a "perverse" lot, hardly another state. Mediation was only appropriate between recognized states, not between a pack of thieves and a glorious, divinely ordained empire.[55]

Not only had the Ottoman Empire learned European statecraft, it also deployed the language of the French Revolution, though in a highly selective manner. The empire had resolved to form a *"lever en masse"*—the famous appeal of the French revolutionary government—now reoriented for combat "in support of our religion and empire" and involving all the leaders of the religion and state, and, if necessary, all Muslims. "This war is a religious and a national war."[56]

In using the term "nation," Ottoman diplomats combined traditional understandings—as when Christians and Jews spoke of the "nation of Israel"—with the more modern understanding of a polity and society joined together. Two could play the game of the nation, even a five-centuries-old empire. For the Ottoman Empire, the war against Greeks was a war against brigands and thieves who had violated *imperial* sovereignty, and a war of religion, Islam against infidel Christians. It was also a war in defense of the Ottoman or Muslim nation, however undefined and illogical was that concept. The "Greek Nation," an entire people, had revolted against the beneficence and magnanimity of the Ottoman Empire, "provok[ing] the resolution of the entire Muslim nation [*la Nation Mahometane*]."[57]

Rather inconsistently with its invocation of the nation as a homogeneous people, the Porte reaffirmed the traditional practice of an empire that accepted diversity. It reminded Russia and its allies that Christians in the Ottoman Empire possessed the freedom to practice their religion. The Reis Effendi (essentially the Ottoman foreign minister) reminded Stroganov, the Russian ambassador, that many Greeks enjoyed great privileges, and some continued to serve in high positions in the empire—even while other Greeks had rebelled.[58] Greek insurgents killed with abandon, the Reis Effendi went on, leaving many Muslims dead and thousands more subject to "excesses and horrors."[59] The Porte noted with deep regret that the Orthodox patriarch himself had given support to the revolt. "Religion is one thing and crime another," the Reis Effendi wrote. "The proof is that those Greeks who have not dipped into revolution enjoy great tranquility and security."[60] Those who had rebelled, however, would suffer severe consequences.[61]

ᔆᔆ

By 1826, the British had decided that some kind of intervention was needed to restore stability to the Eastern Mediterranean. The Greek rebellion had begun when arch-conservative forces were holding sway in Great Britain—King George IV; Foreign Secretary Lord Castlereagh (who also became prime minister); and the hero of Waterloo, the Duke of Wellington. To all of them, the Greek rebellion was anathema, an action that threatened the peace and stability of Europe, the Greeks an unsavory lot. The British government steadfastly refused to do anything to help Greece; in fact, it gave tacit support to Sultan Mahmoud II and the Sublime Porte. And it became widely reviled at home for that stance, especially in the wake of the great publicity surrounding the massacres at Chios and Missolonghi. Even Castlereagh, the architect of the policy of neutrality, was outraged. Despite the hostility between George Canning, who would succeed Castlereagh, and Metternich—Canning despised Metternich's "Holy Alliance" of Russia, Austria, and Prussia—Britain and Austria were united by their common desire to restrain Russia.[62]

The British position evolved. The transition of foreign secretaries from Castlereagh, who committed suicide, to George Canning in 1822 signaled a shift toward a pro-Greek position. Canning had the philhellenic sentiments more typical of leading British statesmen. As foreign secretary and then prime minister (from February 1827 until his death six months later), Canning set the course of British policy.

As with the Philhellenes, an independent Greece evoked for Canning and other British statesmen the glories of the Hellenic past. They had imbibed a panoramic sense of history, as British statesmen would express a century later in regard to Zionism (as we shall see). Heroic Greek Christians versus corrupt and rapacious Muslim Turks—that was an inspiring vision for British statesmen brought up on the classics, the Bible, and tales of Christian martyrdom. More mundane matters played a role as well. An autonomous Greece—though not yet an independent state—would be a bulwark against Russian and Ottoman power, precisely at the moment when the Mediterranean figured ever more forcefully in British strategic calculations.[63]

That lofty vision partially collapsed when the British encountered real Greeks, whom many Britons condemned as mere shadows (at best) of their heroic ancestors, or as corrupt and degenerate despoilers of the great ancient heritage. Greeks lived literally on top of the emblems of past civilizational glory but failed to imbibe them as the British had done, many Britons claimed. Hence, the Parthenon Marbles, removed by Lord Elgin along with many other items of the classical heritage, can be viewed to this day in the British Museum in London, not in Greece. Moreover, Greek claims to ever-wider territory—what later in the century would be called the Megali, or "Great Idea"—went too far for British interests. Instead, the British had to rein in their erstwhile ally.

British statesmen had no interest in the destruction of the Ottoman Empire, which remained, in their eyes, a bastion of stability in the Eastern Mediterranean. Yet they also feared an expanded and overly powerful Ottoman Empire.[64] As a result, the British would support Greek territorial gains over the course of the century despite the initial preferences of British statesmen. That would be the pattern later on as well, as in Ireland, India/Pakistan, Palestine/Israel, and Kenya—the repulsion of nationalist claims, often with a great deal of violence exercised by the British, then reluctant acceptance of the nationalists' principal demands. Even the mighty British Empire could be brought low by determined nationalist movements and states that proved an unending source of difficulties from the early nineteenth well into the twentieth century.

Five years into the rebellion and its suppression, Canning and his successors, Lord Goderich and then the Duke of Wellington, in January 1828, had to calm the Philhellenes at home and contain Russian saber rattling. Something else had arisen: rumors swirled that Ibrahim Pasha, Muhammad 'Ali's son and the perpetrator of some of the worst atrocities of the war, intended to deport the entire Greek population of the Peloponnese to Africa and resettle Greece with Arab and African Muslims (see plate 6).

To this day, it is not totally clear whether Ibrahim or the Porte had truly planned to remove all Christians.[65] The Ottoman Empire had long dealt with unruly populations by moving them here and there. Yet this deportation would have occurred on a scale that even the Ottoman Empire in its heyday had never attempted or even imagined. The magnitude of the forced deportation and resettlement was a response to the *national* claims of the rebellion, which made virtually the entire Greek population of the Peloponnese suspect in Ottoman eyes. If the plan were true, it was something recognizably modern, an ethnic cleansing *avant la lettre*.

For the British government, the rumors of the planned deportation were a matter of the utmost importance. Such an act hit on all the issues central to British liberal thinking in the first half of the nineteenth century. Since 1807 Britain had committed itself to enforcing internationally the abolition of the slave trade; in 1838 it had ended slavery throughout its empire. Now came the specter of one million or more Christians transported to Africa, many of them to be sold in slave markets. The plan also raised the prospect of a new Muslim state in the very heart of classical civilization worshipped by Canning and virtually all educated Englishmen. Moreover, such a state would harbor pirates like those in the North African domains, nominally Ottoman but essentially independent, with which the British navy had so often come into conflict.

A Muslim state in the Peloponnese raised three horrors: Islam, slavery, and piracy. It could not be tolerated; on that, all British statesmen agreed. While the Russians deliberately fostered the rumors, British policy makers were uncertain and divided about the veracity of the story.[66] Wellington made clear that Britain would use force to prevent the deportation of Greeks and the importation of Muslims to the Peloponnese.[67] Lord Bathurst, conveying King George IV's views to the lords commissioners of the Admiralty, noted, with all the formal language of British governance, that the plans for the removal of the Greek population most decidedly went too far:

> [If] designs are avowed to extirpate systematically a whole community, to seize upon the women and children of the Morea [the Peloponnese], to Transport them to Egypt, and to re-people the Morea from Africa or Asia; to change, in fact, that part of Greece from an European State to one resembling in character the States of Barbary; his Majesty cannot ... hear of such an attempt without demanding of Ibrahim Pasha either an explicit disavowal of his ever having entertained such an intention, or a formal renunciation of it if ever entertained.[68]

Tsar Nicholas, in conversation with Wellington, the king's special envoy to Russia, expressed himself similarly: he was disinclined to go to war with the Ottoman Empire unless the Porte or Ali Pasha proceeded with plans to remove the Greeks from the Morea and populate it with Egyptians.[69]

George Canning, writing to Wellington, remarked that "a plan so monstrous and extravagant did, I confess, appear to me to be incredible. . . . Mr. Stratford Canning's despatch from Korfu, however, shows a prevalent belief in the existence of some such plan." If true, the Ottoman policy of deportations would justify war.[70] George Canning instructed his cousin Stratford Canning, the British ambassador to the Porte and the source of the initial reports on Ibrahim Pasha's supposed plan, to relay as much intelligence as he could garner, and to communicate to the Ottoman government that "Great Britain will not permit the execution of a system of depopulation which exceeds the permitted violences of war, and transgresses the conventional restraints of civilization."[71] In fact, military plans had already been sent to the British navy in the Levant to interdict any such deportations.

A British envoy and officer, Captain Robert Spencer, finally obtained an audience with Ibrahim Pasha. Spencer put the question very directly to the Pasha: Was the removal of the Greek population from the Morea and its resettlement with Africans part of his plan? Spencer made it clear that His Majesty could never allow such an operation. All Spencer got in reply were evasions. Ibrahim Pasha replied that only his superiors in Istanbul could answer the question, and that he, in Spencer's account, "had nothing to do with any cruelties, and that he thought it unjust his name should be coupled with any such acts." Despite repeated entreaties on Spencer's part, Ibrahim refused to make any clear disavowal of mass deportations.[72]

But Ibrahim Pasha was not the only one advocating ethnic cleansing. So were the Great Powers, and so were Greek leaders. In 1826, Britain, Russia, and France, attempting to mediate the conflict, proposed the complete removal of the Muslim population from an autonomous (though not fully independent) Greece. They then reaffirmed that principle in the first formal treaty regarding the Greek conflict that the Great Powers signed, in London on 6 July 1827: "In order to effect a complete separation between the individuals of the two Nations, and to prevent

the collisions which would be the inevitable consequence of so pro-
tracted a struggle, the Greeks shall become possessors of all Turkish
Property . . . on condition of indemnifying the former proprietors, either by an annual sum to be added to the tribute which they shall pay
to the Porte or by some other arrangement of the same nature."[73] This
was an astonishing step. Even though this plan did not actually come
to fruition, it indicated the Great Powers'—including liberal Great
Britain's!—endorsement of what we would now call ethnic cleansing.
In effect, the European powers proposed a mirror policy to Ibrahim
Pasha's supposed plan to deport all the Greeks from the Peloponnese.
Both sides had stumbled into that hallmark of the twentieth century,
the notion that societies should be homogeneous under the state.

The Great Powers also floated various plans for Greek autonomy
under official Ottoman control, and if not quite ethnic cleansing, at least
the complete separation of the two communities.[74] British and Russian
statesmen justified the proposals by recounting Ottoman atrocities
against Greece. As a result, they claimed, the two communities, Christians and Muslims, could never live together. "I think with [Alexander]
Mavrocordatos [the head of the provisional Greek government],"
George Canning wrote to Wellington, "that absolute separation of the
Turkish and Greek populations is the only security for the peaceable
continuance of any arrangement."[75]

Two years later, the three powers detailed the mechanism for the sale
of property. Mixed commissions of leading Muslims and Christians
would handle the transactions. In cases of dispute, an arbitration board
would make the ultimate decision.[76] Strikingly, these procedures were
not all that different from those adopted one hundred years later, after
World War I, in the Lausanne Treaty, which would implement the
forced deportations first broached in the 1820s. Already, the British pre-
sumed that Muslims and Christians could not live under the same political system. Already, they were staking out programs of recompense
for those removed, whether forcibly or voluntarily, from their homeland. Already in 1826, the possibility of population transfers, separations,
unmixings—ethnic cleansing, to use the colloquial term—had been

broached in a global region that would be the site of so many conflicts, and, not coincidentally, one of the birthplaces of modern politics of the nation-state, human rights, and population removals.

While the Ottomans threatened ethnic cleansing of Greeks and the Great Powers the same for Muslims, Greek activists had already excised Muslims and Jews from the circle of rights-bearing citizens. The National Assembly passed the first Greek constitution, labeled provisional, on 13 January 1822 in Epidaurus. It was revised in 1823, though the essential principles remained intact. The constitution was largely a fiction, an effort by Greek leaders to win European support by creating the appearance of a functioning, centralized state.[77] Still, like all good constitutions, it laid out the framework of governance and established individual rights. Article I proclaimed freedom of religion, but defined Orthodoxy as the state religion.[78] The constitution established civil rights and equality before the law, and guaranteed property, security, and honor for everyone. But it limited citizenship to those who lived in Greece and believed in Jesus Christ.[79]

Taking the matter even further, Mavrocordatos, in early 1826, told Stratford Canning that any settlement of the conflict required "a total separation from the Turks together with an adequate security against any encroachments on their newly acquired privileges."[80] And the third meeting of the Greek National Congress adopted a resolution that, in article 1, proclaimed that "no Turk shall be permitted to inhabit, or hold property in the territory of Greece, on account of it being impossible for the two nations to live together."[81] Meanwhile, Greek rebels slashed their way through the farms tilled by Muslims and the villages and neighborhoods inhabited by Muslims and Jews. Like so many other nationalists around the globe, the insurgents created facts on the ground, making Greece unlivable for anyone who was not Greek Orthodox.[82]

Subsequent constitutions—and there were many—also limited citizenship to Greek Orthodox men.[83] They were granted a catalog of rights, at least rhetorically, similar to what Velestinlis had sketched out three decades earlier, similar also to the constitutions proclaimed by every new nation-state in the nineteenth and twentieth centuries.

Unsurprisingly, none of these rights were extended to women. And the constitutions left no place for Muslims, Jews, or other minorities. Only by conversion would they have the ability to become Greeks, hence rights-bearing citizens in the new state. Velestinlis had frequently mentioned Muslims and Turks; not a word about them is present in the various constitutions.[84] Velestinlis had embraced all those who lived in the territory of Greece. Now only Greek Orthodox men could become rights-bearing citizens.[85]

ఆ

Meanwhile, the fighting went on, Greeks versus Turks, Greeks versus Greeks, the allied navies versus the Ottoman navy, and, the coup de grâce, Russia versus the Ottoman Empire. All the while, through 1827, 1828, 1829, and 1830, long, wearying negotiations went on among the three powers, and between them, individually and collectively, and the Porte. The borders of Greece had to be agreed upon, as well as the amount of tribute that Greece would have to pay to the Ottoman Empire. The powers contemplated a large loan to help the new Greece get on its feet, whatever its exact political configuration would be. A secret clause in the London Treaty committed the three allies to impose an armistice if Greece or Turkey refused to cease hostilities within a month. Russia's continual threat of war irritated the British no end, and British statesmen expended a great deal of effort to restrain their ally. The British argued strongly that any action against the Porte had to be mutually agreed upon and could not be a unilateral action. But the Russians paid no heed.[86]

The sultan had brought in help from the Egyptian army and navy under Muhammad 'Ali and his son Ibrahim. Ibrahim's forces had lain waste to great parts of the Peloponnese. The three allies, acting on the secret clause of imposing an armistice, blockaded the Ottoman fleet in the Bay of Navarino. It remains unclear who fired the first shot, but on 20 October 1827, a four-hour battle ensued. The British admiral faced subsequent criticism for acting beyond his orders, which were to maintain the blockade, not to fully engage the enemy. Nonetheless, the engagement was total. Separately, the British and French admirals used the same words: "The Turco-Egyptian Fleet is annihilated."[87] So was the sultan's and Muhammad 'Ali's conviction that Greece would remain Ottoman.

The destruction of the Ottoman-Egyptian fleet did not bring joy in all European capitals. Metternich was appalled at the enhancement of Russian power that the victory seemed to portend. Even Wellington feared that the Ottoman defeat was too great for the stability British statesmen always hoped to construct.

Russian troops crossed the Ottoman frontier on 20 April 1828, only adding to the dismay of Wellington (now prime minister) and Metternich, though their French and Prussian counterparts and some other Austrian diplomats looked forward to their own spoils of war as a result of this unsettling of the Vienna System.

Russia claimed to be acting in the interests of "Europe and humanity"—the latter a term that would become increasingly important in the diplomatic parlance of the nineteenth and twentieth centuries. Russia, its statesmen claimed, sought to protect its legitimate interests, notably freedom of navigation in the straits, and to defend Christians living under Muslim suzerainty.[88] Britain, meanwhile, feared the destabilizing effects of war, knowing only too well that its outcomes were unpredictable and could set in motion a train of events that the Vienna System was specifically designed to prevent.[89]

Russia did not have the blazing successes on the battlefield that its leaders had expected. Russian advances were slow and laborious, both in the Caucasus and in Southeastern Europe. The war ground down to slogging battles and winter encampments, giving Britain an opportunity to reassert its leadership role, which the Porte welcomed as a restraint on Russia. But Russia's military fortunes revived at the end of spring 1829. Russia seized Adrianople, within striking distance of Istanbul, in August 1829, forcing Turkey to sue for peace.

Now the specter of Ottoman collapse and great-power conflict over the pickings caused panic in the European capitals. A series of negotiations and agreements led ultimately to the final Treaty of London, signed on 7 May 1832 by the three powers. (Greek representatives had not been invited to the deliberations and Greece was not a signatory of the treaty.) The treaty confirmed Greece as an independent state (already proclaimed in 1830), a landmark decision that the Ottoman Empire, because of its defeat by Russia, was forced to accept. Greece's territory was not as grand as its leaders had hoped, but was more expansive than originally sketched by the Great Powers. Greece became a kingdom under the Bavarian House of Wittelsbach. With great fanfare, the three courts announced that they, acting on behalf of the Greek nation, had chosen Prince Otto of Bavaria as the Greek king, who would rule an independent monarchical state. No mention was made of a constitution. That would only come later, following another London treaty, this one in 1863.

The 1832 treaty said nothing on the matter of who precisely constituted the new Greek nation-state. But an earlier protocol in 1830, which the new treaty reaffirmed, had stipulated that both Greece and the Ottoman Empire had to issue immediate amnesties. Neither Greeks nor Muslims could be deprived of their property "or in any way disturbed." All Muslims "who may be desirous of continuing to inhabit the territories and islands allotted to Greece, shall preserve their properties therein, and invariably enjoy there, with their families, perfect security." All Greeks who wished to leave "Turkish territory" had a year to sell their property and depart freely; the same provision held for Muslims in Greece.[90]

The new Greek nation-state was not, then, fully sovereign, not with a Bavarian prince at its head and not with its independence guaranteed by Great Britain, France, and Russia. The plenipotentiaries of the three powers exercised supervisory rights over the country. Rarely has a treaty of such import been accompanied so thoroughly by the base issue of money. Article XII, the longest of the twenty-eight articles, defined the conditions of the loan that Greece would receive from the three powers. They were careful to stipulate that state revenues must *first of all* (italics in the original) be directed at the payment of the interest and principal of the loan.[91] Indebtedness would be the scourge of many empires and nation-states over the course of the succeeding two centuries, subjecting them to foreign control and interference—something that Greece has rarely been able to avoid in its modern history.

Ultimately, then, the Great Powers did not endorse ethnic cleansing, though the issue had been included in every previous agreement. In defeat the Sublime Porte had managed to negotiate firmly. It would not countenance so drastic a development as the removal of its Muslim compatriots from a newly established state carved out of its own domains. Moreover, the Porte, acting like most empires that accepted diversity, actually feared large-scale emigration from the empire of ethnic Greeks, who played a disproportionate role in international trade and artisanal production. The loss of Greeks (and Armenians, one might add) would harm the empire economically—something of no concern to the Young Turk successors nearly a century later when they annihilated Armenians and forcibly deported Greeks.

Finally, the Porte was decidedly concerned about the fate of Muslim property, notably that held by *waqfs*, the religious endowments connected to mosques. Ottoman representatives successfully argued that these were not state property, but communally or individually owned.[92] In so doing, the Porte, perhaps unwittingly, hit on two very sensitive aspects of rights that none of the powers dared to deny: the right to property and the right to religious liberty.

ജ

King Otto, our former Bavarian prince, arrived in Greece with a large German-speaking entourage, including 3,500 Bavarian troops. He disembarked from a British frigate at Nafplion on 6 February 1833, formally initiating the founding of independent Greece under a monarch protected by three European powers. Even had he been an adept ruler—and he most certainly was not—the tasks Otto faced were immense. Ten years of warfare had devastated the country and exacerbated, not diminished, divisions of clan, class, religion, and region. Moreover, the new nation was deeply indebted.

For many Greeks, however dire the situation, however restricted their sovereignty, the establishment of the nation-state constituted a grand achievement. The rebellion that had begun as a traditional-style revolt against Ottoman oppression had become a national uprising. The allure of the nation, of the mythic unity of the people who would revive the ancient glory of Athens in the modern world, proved a powerful force.

Yet History was not quite fulfilled in 1832. The borders of the new state were quite limited. Fully two-thirds of Greek speakers in the larger Mediterranean world lived outside the state, and some, especially prosperous merchants, were content to live under Ottoman or Russian rule.[93] For Greek nationalists, those outside the realm had to be brought within the national domain. The Megali Idea (as it came to be called from the mid-nineteenth century onward)—meaning a vastly expanded Greece, perhaps rivaling Alexander's Hellenistic Empire—served as the driving force of modern Greek history and the official ideology of the state. It gave to Greek nationalism a powerful, irredentist force—hardly unique in the world of nationalisms, but more potent in the Greek case precisely because the borders were so limited and because Greeks constituted one of the global diasporic peoples par excellence. King Otto also advocated an expanded Greece. As John Kolettis, one of the major clan leaders and a powerful supporter of Otto, expressed it:

> The Kingdom of Greece is not Greece. [Greece] constitutes only one part, the smallest and poorest. A Greek is not only a man who lives within this kingdom but also one who lives in Jannina, in Salonica, in Serres, in Adrianople, in Constantinople, in Smyrna, in Trebizond, in Crete, in Samos and in any land associated with Greek history or the Greek race.... There are two main centres of Hellenism: Athens, the capital of the Greek kingdom, [and] 'The City' [Constantinople], the dream and hope of all Greeks.[94]

Almost all politically conscious Greeks—and probably even those who were not—subscribed to this view, which would shape Greek politics for the remainder of the nineteenth and long into the twentieth century. The only division was a strategic one: whether to pursue the expansion of the country immediately, at all costs, because only an enlarged Greece would provide the economic and political bases for a flourishing society, or to move slowly, gradually, incrementally, so as not to threaten the support of the Great Powers, Britain in particular. Neither strategy would totally work. But it did mean that the Eastern Mediterranean would be a locus of conflict for decades to come. The stability for which the Great Powers yearned proved elusive.

Conclusion

"Better one hour of free life than forty years of slavery and captivity," wrote Rigas Velestinlis, the first great advocate of Greek independence and human rights for all men, in 1797. And so began, in 1942, a pamphlet distributed surreptitiously by the National Liberation Front (EAM).[95] As Greece suffered under Nazi occupation, EAM quoted Velestinlis in its drive to rally the population to active resistance. From 1941 to 1944 the Nazis utterly devastated Greece. They robbed the country of vital foodstuffs and other resources, ordered the execution of fifty Greeks for every German soldier killed by the resistance, and deported Greek Jews to Auschwitz.[96] Famine ruled the land, its ravages a direct consequence of Nazi policies. Only the Ukrainian famine of 1932, a result of Stalin's forced collectivization program, bears any comparison in twentieth-century Europe. In that same pamphlet, EAM, specifically invoking 1821, called on Greeks to join a national uprising that would liberate their country just as their forefathers had freed their country from Ottoman domination. By creating, once again, an independent nation-state, EAM and its followers would restore "all the people's freedoms," including the rights of free speech, security of property, and suffrage.[97]

Some thirty years later, in November 1973, students at Athens Polytechnic shouted, "We are the Free Besieged!" The phrase referred to the Greeks surrounded at Missolonghi by the Ottoman army in 1825 and 1826. The Ottomans then carried out the massacre of Greeks memorialized in Delacroix's painting *Greece Expiring on the Ruins of Missolonghi*, and in the poem "The Free Besieged," parts of which were penned virtually in the heat of the Greek rebellion in the 1820s by Dionysios Solomos.[98] The students had gone on strike and occupied their campus. They demanded an end to the military junta that had ruled Greece since 1967, and the restoration of democracy and all the rights that went with it.

Around the polytechnic thousands of demonstrators gathered in support, including many high school students. The junta sent a tank crashing through the university gate, the signal for a full-scale repression.

Nearly twenty-four people were killed in and around the polytechnic, most of them students. But the dictatorship did not last much longer. Within a year it was gone. The precipitous event was the junta's inept response to the Turkish invasion of Cyprus, but the stage had been set by the student rebellion—and the popular revulsion at its repression.

Almost immediately after the fall of the junta, the great Greek composer Mikis Theodorakis and the equally great songstress, Maria Farantouri, both of whom had lived as exiles during the dictatorship, held a concert in Athens. The featured song, "The Laughing Boy," was a reworking of a poem originally penned in 1922 by the Irish writer Brendan Behan. Behan wrote it as a paean to Michael Collins, the Irish Republican Army leader assassinated by his former comrades because he sought an agreement with the British rather than continued warfare. The Greek poet Vassilis Rotas had first reworked the poem to apply to Greek events. Theodorakis set it to music, Farantouri adapted it further.[99] When Farantouri changed "August" in the original to "November," the month of the polytechnic uprising, and "curse the time . . . an Irish son, with a rebel gun, shot down my Laughing Boy" to:

I see a girl crying
"The Laughing Boy has been murdered"
Cursed be the hour when the fascists murdered him

the crowd erupted in wild applause, which kept up all through her performance. She concluded the song with:

My dearest love, I will forever tell
What you did
Because you wanted to oust the fascists.
Fame and honor to the unforgettable Laughing Boy![100]

These three vignettes—the Greek resistance in World War II, the student rebellion against the dictatorship in 1973, and the concert to celebrate the fall of the junta in 1974—demonstrate the powerful legacy of nation-state foundings and human rights. Greeks in the twentieth century drew directly on the language of rights first expressed by Velestinlis in the 1790s, disseminated by the Friendly Society in the early decades of the nineteenth century, and implemented, however partially, in the various constitutions and regimes that followed the War of Independence in the 1820s.

These rights were limited to men who adhered to the Greek Orthodox religion. But rights are never static. Especially after 1945, they broadened significantly. In 1952, women finally won the right to vote. The socialist government that took power in 1981 greatly expanded social rights and brought many more people into the political realm, even while it vastly extended the system of clientelism that sapped the economy of resources.[101]

Greek men, and finally women as well, benefitted from the rights granted them by the various constitutions—eight in all since 1822. Others were not so fortunate.[102] The Greek rebels of the 1820s killed and drove out large numbers of Muslims and Jews. As the country expanded in the late nineteenth and twentieth centuries, bringing Crete, Thrace, and other areas into its domain, its population would again become more diverse, provoking the issue, yet again, of who, precisely, had the right to have rights. Virtually all the constitutions defined citizenship in terms of adherence to the Greek Orthodox Church.

The 1974 constitution, written in the wake of the overthrow of the junta, was more democratic than those that came before. It proclaimed the equality of all citizens and the rights of all men, including the freedom of religious worship to "all known religions." At the same time, it recognized Eastern Orthodoxy as the dominant religion.[103] For naturalization purposes, the Greek legal code places a heavy emphasis on ethnicity, with continual references to people of "Greek descent," even if it does not formally exclude Muslims, Jews, or others.[104] Muslims are the only officially recognized minority, and they constitute around 1 percent of the population; Jews, only 0.3 percent.[105] Fully 97 percent of Greeks identify themselves as Orthodox, the result of a century and a half—counting from the 1820s to the early 1960s—of nation-state formation, violent ethnic cleansing, gradual assimilation of other Christian groups, and Nazi occupation and the Holocaust.

Why, then, did Greece become a nation-state with rights, however limited in practice, available to Greek men? The outcome was by no means a foregone conclusion. Determined Greek resistance was decisive. Greek rebels could not win on their own, nor would they give up. The Ottomans, meanwhile, were unable to repress the uprising and swiftly bring the Peloponnese under control. That provided an opening for the Great Powers. Very reluctant at first, they ultimately intervened, partly pressured by Philhellenes at home and the moral and political outrage they mobilized. Perceived interests of state were more decisive. For Great Britain, that meant stability in the Eastern Mediterranean, a key site of British interests. For Russia, the Greek events provided an opportunity to expand its influence in the Black Sea region and beyond.

In Greece and in many other instances around the globe, the Great Powers and the fabled international systems that they built—Vienna, Paris, Washington-Moscow—were often brought low by determined actors on the ground. They would be forced to find solutions to conflicts they had not wanted, to crises foisted upon them (as we shall see in regard to Palestine/Israel and Rwanda and Burundi). In the desperate search for solutions, they would often consent to the establishment of independent states with constitutions and sets of rights that sometimes went far beyond what they granted their own populations. At the same time, foreign powers decisively limited the scope of human rights in Greece, from the imposition of a Bavarian prince, and then a Danish one, whose family ruled Greece until 1974. British and American interventions in the civil war of the 1940s and American support for the Greek dictatorship in the 1960s and 1970s drastically curtailed the scope of rights, to the extent of US collaboration in the imprisonment, torture, and killing of Greek citizens.

From Velestinlis and Androutsos to Byron and Delacroix and many others, the ideas of the European Enlightenment and Romanticism, wound up with the French Revolution, moved to the near abroad, to Greece and the Eastern Mediterranean. That movement made a European and trans-European world, a global world, since the Greek events would echo throughout the nineteenth and twentieth centuries all across the Ottoman realm, including the Balkans, Anatolia, and the Middle East.

In 1827 the National Assembly extolled the accomplishments of the Greek rebellion. "Thousands of Muslims have disappeared from the sacred soil of the Fatherland. We can annihilate [*aneantir*] thousands of others, if we know how to love one another and have but one will, the salvation of the Fatherland of fellow citizens! The freedom of the country is the well-being of all today!"[106] Freedom for some, annihilation for others—that is the paradox that accompanied the foundation of Greece. That same paradox played out an ocean and continent away, in the American North Country, as an expanding republic confronted its Indian population.

Chapter 3

America

INDIAN REMOVALS IN THE NORTH COUNTRY

❧

ON 21 August 1862, Minnesota governor Alexander Ramsey sent a terse telegram to the War Department in Washington. "The Sioux Indians on our western border have risen," he wrote, "and are murdering men, women, and children."[1] Telegraph lines did not yet extend beyond the state capital Saint Paul to the rest of Minnesota. Ramsey's information came from a few couriers who had managed to make their way through Indian lines. The governor's words were few, but they reflected the deep unease and fear along American outposts in the North Country. That same day, Ramsey wrote a more extensive letter to Secretary of War Edwin Stanton. He noted that he had ordered a party of soldiers under Colonel Henry Hastings Sibley to proceed as rapidly as possible to the scenes of attack, "for the purpose of giving protection to the settlers [and] of arresting the cruel barbarities of the savages.... There [is] also trouble with the Chippewas."[2] Ramsey called for additional United States Army forces to aid the beleaguered Minnesotans.

Amid the crisis of the Civil War, when the very fate of the Union stood in the balance—and the summer and fall of 1862 marked the nadir for the North, suffering as it had one military defeat after another—no less important was securing white settlement in the North Country around the source of the Mississippi River. The scale of the hostilities on the Minnesota frontier paled in comparison with the large-scale combat between North and South. The political significance, nonetheless, was clear to all involved. The fate of the Union as a transcontinental nation settled by Europeans lay in the balance not just at Antietam, Bull Run, and Gettysburg, but also at New Ulm, Fort Ridgely, and Saint Paul (see maps 3.1 and 3.2).

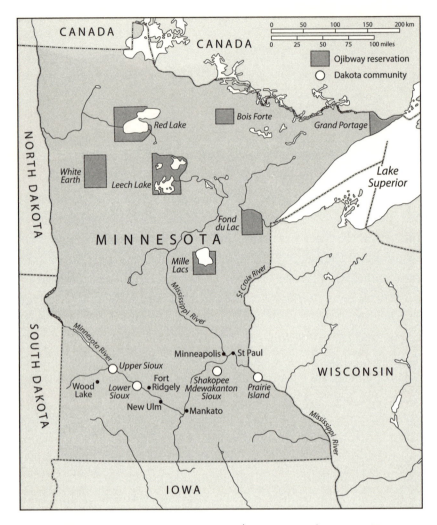

MAP 3.1 Minnesota with important Indian places. (Map courtesy of Minnesota Humanities Center, "Why Treaties Matter," by permission.)

The War Department ordered the dispatch of the Third Minnesota Volunteers and, after some deliberation, established a military department of the Northwest, a sign of the deep concern of federal officials. Stanton appointed Major General John Pope—who had fared so poorly as head of the Union Army at the Second Battle of Bull Run—as commander of the department, with wide-ranging responsibilities to deploy

MAP 3.2 Minnesota in the United States.

whatever force was necessary to suppress the uprising. Stanton underscored the significance of the charge given to Pope: "You cannot too highly estimate the importance of the duty now intrusted to you."[3]

In the middle of the Civil War, a relatively small-scale conflict on the Minnesota frontier quickly took on national significance. The Sioux uprising threatened the American political union, and Minnesota's and America's burgeoning place in the world economy. Around 1840, the area that would become the Minnesota Territory had all of about 700 white and mixed-race people.[4] But by 1849, 4,000 white settlers were sprinkled through the area, and in 1855 the total population had reached 40,000, and 150,000 in 1857.[5] From the first European explorations in the 1600s, furs from what would become the Northwest Territory, which included Minnesota, were transported to the East and from there to Europe. Soon, red winter wheat, the source of that prized, hard, high-gluten flour; corn and soybeans; and timber and iron ore would integrate

Minnesota fully into the American and world economies. Minnesota iron would move through the Great Lakes to Chicago and on to the steel mills that came to line the American Midwest. Minnesota would ship out flour to Europe and other destinations around the globe. In short order, from around 1870 to 1920, the voracious national and international demand for wheat, lumber, and paper would devastate Minnesota's lush forests.

Greece is emblematic of the human rights achievements and disasters that accompanied nation-state foundings out of empires in the nineteenth and twentieth centuries. The history of Sioux Indians in the American North Country is emblematic of another global process of this era: the displacement of indigenous peoples and the clash of very different understandings of rights—especially in regard to land and property—as Europeans and Americans extended their power all over the world. In North America, South America, Australia, New Zealand, and South Africa, native populations were removed from areas of white settlement. Each place has its particular history; all were bound together in a common global pattern. White settler colonies fought drawn-out wars for control of territory and people, bringing with them the notion that the right to individual property underpins all other rights. Native peoples, in contrast, almost invariably had a communal understanding of land ownership. Ultimately, superior Western technology proved decisive. Direct violence as well as communicable disease and the disruptions of their environments decimated indigenous populations.[6] Sometimes the state ordered the violence. At other times, local settlers acted more or less on their own and brutalized native peoples. Often, the two—state and settlers—worked hand in glove.[7]

In this epic movement of peoples, European and American settlers obtained the right to have the rights that had been spelled out in the revolutions of the late eighteenth and early nineteenth centuries. At the same time, indigenous peoples suffered violence, the loss of their lands, and the deprivation of rights. Nation-states and human rights developed together.

Removals and killings did not, however, put an end to the issue of how to live with the natives. The natives remained a "problem," however

reduced in number they were. What was to be their fate in the new society? If not citizens with the full panoply of rights enjoyed by Euroamericans, would they be some kind of second-, third-, or fourth-class
citizens? And if granted rights, would Indians hold them as individuals
or as members of the Indian nation? Whether Minnesota (and other
American) Indians would be rights-bearing citizens in a nation that
claimed to be a democracy of the first order—that question proved enormously complex and, to this day, has been continually in flux.

❦

Minnesota had been populated primarily by two groups of Indians, the
Ojibway and the Dakota (or Chippewa and Sioux, the latter also called
Santee Sioux). In the nineteenth century, the federal government settled
a small number of Winnebago in Minnesota from points farther east.[8]
The United States hoped the Winnebago would serve as a buffer between the warring Dakota and Ojibway. That policy failed, though the
Winnebago remained on the reservations to which they had been
moved. The Ojibway lived predominantly in the forested Northeast of
the state, where they pursued sedentary agriculture and fishing and
hunting, a way of life that drew productively on the rich resources of the
region. The seminomadic Dakota traveled through the forests, lakes,
and rivers of the North Country and sometimes into the vast plain that
stretches west of the Mississippi River to the Rocky Mountains and
extends north into Canada and south to the Gulf of Mexico. The Dakota
lived by farming as well as fishing, hunting, and gathering in the bountiful land of Minnesota.[9]

In the early 1600s a few French hunters and traders penetrated the
area. The French explorer and priest Louis Hennepin, in the 1680s, was
the first person to map the region. One hundred and twenty years later,
few white people had settled in the land that became Minnesota. The
only Europeans were a few trappers and traders, mostly French or Canadian. As they moved West and South in search of more furs and
other resources, they encountered the Dakota and Ojibway.[10] Many of
these first Europeans became partly assimilated into Indian life. They

lived with the Indians for months on end. Some learned the language, many fathered children with Indian women and were taken up into Dakota kinship networks.[11] For the Dakota, these kin groups were of cardinal importance; the moral responsibility for support and protection extended well beyond the immediate family to the larger group. But in the nineteenth century, the press of white settlers and the demand for land would become too great, sundering the equanimity that had been established in the North Country between Indians and Euroamericans.

Minnesota became American, rather than French, with the Louisiana Purchase in 1803. Now the United States made a more determined effort to map and master the region, but it had to deal with the Dakota and Ojibway, who farmed and roamed the area. The young United States concluded its first formal agreement with the Dakota on 23 September 1805 near the confluence of the Mississippi and Minnesota rivers, a sacred site for the Dakota still today, the place of their creation story, although the locale is now a part of metropolitan Minneapolis–Saint Paul. The Dakota ceded to the United States small tracts of land near the rivers and also near the Saint Croix River for military outposts. They were granted $2,000 and the right to cross and hunt on the lands.[12] The gradual extension of US authority over the territory led to additional treaties in 1837, 1851, and 1858. Typically, the Indians ceded land to the United States, usually in return for provisions and the payment of annuities. In 1851, in the Treaty of Traverse des Sioux, the Dakota tribes ceded all land east of the Mississippi and all land west of the Mississippi in Minnesota Territory, which included the fertile Minnesota Valley. The federal government moved the Dakota Sioux to reservations farther north on the Minnesota River.[13]

The Dakota chiefs made strategic choices by signing the treaties with the US government. Certainly by the 1850s they were well aware of the armed power of the United States, yet could hardly imagine that in the "vast domain" of North America their lands would ever be so terribly diminished to the reservations on which they were to be consigned.[14] Instead, they stood to gain guns, ammunition, blankets, foodstuffs, and other goods that would help them survive the long, harsh winters in the

North Country. They had known Europeans for almost two hundred years; little did they expect that white migrants would flood the region beginning in the 1850s. Nor did they expect the deceptions and fraud that went along with so many treaties. Traders usually handled the annuity payments for the government; despite federal prohibitions, they typically deducted the debts Indians owed them before disbursing the agreed-upon funds to the tribes.[15]

The federal government dispatched Indian agents, as they were called, and army detachments to Minnesota. Presbyterian missionaries followed and established permanent representations to the Dakota and Ojibway beginning in 1829—one small example of the global impact of Protestant missionaries, which we shall also see in chapter 6 on Namibia and chapter 7 on Korea.[16] The missionaries had some successes, including giving written form to the indigenous languages. They faced regular attacks by Indians, as did the European-born and descended settlers who slowly began to populate the region, especially after it was established as the Minnesota Territory in 1849 and became a state in 1858. The 1851 treaty in particular stimulated a rush of white settlers, many of whom simply staked out claims, including on land not ceded by the Indians.[17] Most were English, Scottish, German, Scandinavian, and Irish. These pioneers "had no troublesome scruples" and "swarm[ed]" over the territory, wrote an early historian of Minnesota.[18] Individuals took land; timbermen sent crews into the forests to cut down pine trees for what seemed like an endless supply of lumber.

Governor Ramsey sought a "preemption" from Congress, which would retroactively grant title to those who had arbitrarily taken land that, legally, resided in the hands of either the Indians or the federal government. Ramsey wrote: "These hardy pioneers . . . constitute the rank and file of that great army of peaceful progress, which has shed . . . lustre on our name. . . . They bring with them to the wilderness . . . maxims of civil liberty . . . inscribe[d] in their hearts . . . as living principles and practical rules of conduct." They cost the government nothing, he went on. Instead, "they make the country, its history and its glory."[19] In 1854, these early settlers had their land claims confirmed, despite their blatant violation of the treaties with the Dakota.

The steamship and railroad made the Minnesota Territory more accessible. In 1855 a "flood of immigration" began. It would not stop, not for decades. Mostly the settlers came from the mid-Atlantic states, New England, and the Midwest, very few from the South. Only from the 1870s onward would people come directly from Europe to the state. By 1865 the state's total population stood at 250,000, a 45 percent increase over 1860. In five short years, the population had almost doubled again, to 439,706 in 1870. Of that number, 279,009 were native-born, 160,697 foreign born. Of those, the largest group hailed from Scandinavia, followed by Germans, British, and Irish. Among the native-born, less than half had been born in Minnesota.[20]

Already in the 1850s skirmishes had erupted in Minnesota between Indians and whites. The settlers lived in isolated villages or dispersed cabins. The battles, such as they were, had all the characteristics of frontier warfare typical of many places around the globe. Small groups of Dakota Indians, sixty at most, usually far fewer, descended on the settlers with great brutality. They sometimes took a few women captive, but tended to kill all the men. The combat, small-scale that it was, had a ferocious character and spread great fear among the settlers. "Barbarous acts"—the term of the day for scalpings, decapitations, amputated limbs—were common on both sides, though lynchings were a specialty practiced by Euroamericans. All these actions contributed to a sense of fear on both sides.

❧

"The whites were always trying to make the Indians give up their life and live like white men—go to farming, work hard and do as they did.... The Indians wanted to live as they [the Indians] did ... go where they pleased and when they pleased; hunt game wherever they could find it, sell their furs to the traders and live as they could," related Big Eagle, a Dakota chief, many years later.[21]

But Indians could no longer "go where they pleased." At the basis of all the conflict was the land, the relentless white drive for land that could be fenced and farmed. The Dakota, like most Indians, did not have a sense of individual private ownership. They did, though, believe in a collective right over the land where they could roam, trap, hunt, fish, gather, and farm. For this reason they had fought the Ojibway, each of them contesting control over territory, and for this reason they fought white settlers and the US government. These two radically opposed conceptions of property rights clashed on the Minnesota frontier (and similarly, as we shall see, in Namibia).[22]

There was more. "The Indians kept no books," Big Eagle said, "[so] they could not deny their accounts but had to pay them. . . . The Indians could not go to the law [to contest the accounts], but there was always trouble over their credits."[23] Perhaps more importantly, Indians and whites had very different cultural norms regarding debtor-creditor relations. Indians believed a debtor should pay when he had the resources, not just on a particular date.[24] A traditional Indian moral economy, based on the dense relationship—familial, tribal—between creditor and debtor clashed with a burgeoning American capitalism that guaranteed the rights of the creditor above all else.

To add to the difficulties, many traders deceived the Indians, while the US government deducted the costs of "civilization"—construction of schools, platting of individual holdings, building of workshops and churches—from the annuities, and often failed to deliver promptly what was left. Long delays in the payment of annuities, indebtedness, and crop failures in 1860 and 1861, followed by a severe winter in 1862, added to the burdens on the Dakota. Without the annuities, Indians could not buy flour and other necessities from traders. By the spring of 1862, many Indians were living in desperate circumstances, their families near starvation.[25]

To the Dakota, the violations of the 1858 treaty were especially egregious. The provisions of the treaty constituted a direct assault on Indian ways of life. The treaty promised greater rewards to Indians who took up individual allotments of land and other manifestations of "civilization"; namely, Western clothes, cut hair for men, and Christianity. Some 125 families among seven thousand Dakota had declined the "blanket," as the phrase went for Indians who kept up their customary lifestyle. Those Indians who had gone for "civilization" were often lonely and isolated and subject to ridicule, thefts, and attacks from their compatriots who kept up traditional ways of life.[26]

Misunderstandings and deceptions ran together. In addition, two large, general issues aggrieved Indians. According to Big Eagle, white men thought that they were better than the Indians, and sometimes abused Indian women. "The Dakotas did not believe that there were better men in the world than they. . . . All these things made many Indians dislike the whites."[27]

Overall, Indians received little from the treaties, and many tribe members had no understanding of the provisions to which their chiefs had agreed. All sorts of divides opened up among the Dakota, young versus old, traditional versus "civilized," band against band. Many younger men hated the land concessions agreed to by their chiefs. The authority of chiefs and elders began to dissipate. In the highly constrained circumstances of white encroachments, Indians made various choices for their bare physical as well as their cultural survival. Those who chose the path of farming individual plots knew that the alternative was moving farther west, to the Great Plains, where they would face cold and starvation and the hostility of other tribes.[28]

Amid the internal conflicts among the Dakota, virtually all of them protested that whites had reneged on the treaties in which the Indians had been promised, at least orally, all the things they wanted, including blankets, guns, ammunition, coffee, tea, tobacco, pork, flour, and sugar "in plenty." Such promises, whether or not they had in fact been made, were burned into Dakota consciousness and reiterated by them time and again. "It was not strange," wrote a prominent Minnesotan and early historian of the state, "that the Sioux harbored a lurking suspicion that [their land] tenure [from the treaties] might at any time be revoked by the insidious white man," given the constant encroachments even on land granted to them through the treaties.[29]

ᏆᎧ

"If you strike at them they will all turn on you and devour you and your women and little children. . . . You are fools. . . . You will die like rabbits when the hungry wolves hunt them in the Hard Moon."[30] So responded the Dakota chief Little Crow to a small group of his followers who had attacked trading outposts and warehouses (see plates 7 and 8). The desperate Indians seized flour, meat, and other vital items. They also killed four whites, unleashing a flood of fear on all sides. Little Crow knew that the authorities would make the entire tribe responsible for the actions of a few. The Dakota would be deprived of the annuities and would be forced to make other concessions, not least turning over the responsible parties to be imprisoned, tried, and no doubt hanged. They also knew that the whites were preoccupied with the Civil War, that the war was going badly for the North, and that many Minnesotan men, including mixed-race ones, had enlisted or been drafted into the Union Army. Those Dakota inclined to fight thought that the time, summer 1862, was propitious.[31]

Little Crow's hotheaded followers accused him of cowardice. He reacted furiously to the charge. Nonetheless, Little Crow threw in his lot with his more rebellious followers, turning a skirmish into a full-fledged war.

As the Dakota battled settlers and the army in attacks, they also circulated among other tribes and bands in a vain attempt to unify their forces. Some joined. Others, however, were as cautious as Little Crow had been before he joined his more radical, risk-taking followers. The rebels never won total support from the Dakota, let alone other Indians in the North Country. Many Indians feared losing ever more land and resources if they engaged the US government in an all-out war. Often, the focal point of dissension among the Indians involved the hundreds of white and mixed-race people they had captured as hostages, who were forced to move along with the rebels. The Dakota knew only too well the value of their hostages in negotiations. Beyond that, the Dakota understanding of kinship meant they had to protect those mixed-race and white people to whom they were related, however distantly.

Both the war and peace parties among the Dakota ("hostile" and "friendly" in the nineteenth-century sources), around a thousand all told, as well as hundreds of whites and mixed-race captives, gathered at Little Crow's village. Tensions ran high: the captives fearful of being killed, Indians on both sides ready to take up the fight against one another.[32] Paul Mazakutemani, a Christian convert, stood up between both parties, despite the ever-present threat to his life. He pleaded with

Little Crow to give up the fight. "The Americans are a great people," he said. "They have much lead, powder, guns, and provisions. Stop fighting, and now gather up all the captives and give them to me. No one who fights with the white people ever becomes rich, or remains two days in one place, but is always fleeing and starving."[33] At a later council, Maza-kutemani again chastised Little Crow and his followers, wondering whether they were "asleep or crazy. In fighting the whites, you are fighting the thunder and lightning. You will all be killed off. You might as well try to bail out the waters of the Mississippi."[34]

After nearly two centuries of interactions on the frontier, of rapidly accelerating numbers of Euroamerican settlers and ever-greater seizures of Indian lands, Mazakutemani understood the power of white people. He knew that behind the settlers stood the Minnesota militia and the United States Army. He understood, if only implicitly, that the US government would never let Indians triumph by force, even when the United States was fighting for its survival against a Southern insurgency. Little Crow, however, was undeterred, even though he probably understood the hopelessness of the cause. "I tell you we must fight and perish together. A man is a fool and a coward who thinks otherwise, and who will desert his nation at such a time. Disgrace not yourselves by a surrender to those who will hang you up like dogs, but die, if die you must, with arms in your hands, like warriors and braves of the Dakota."[35]

All along the fertile Minnesota Valley, Dakota warriors descended on settlers and Indian Agency outposts. The attacks followed well-worn patterns—brutal killings of the men and sometimes of women and children, though Little Crow had ordered that they be spared. More typically, women and children were taken into captivity. Sometimes Indians killed deliberately: a particularly hated trader, known for supposedly saying the Indians could eat grass if they were starving, was found beaten to death with grass stuffed in his mouth.[36] At other times, the killings were indiscriminate. Indians also spared many whites, especially those with whom they shared kinship ties.[37] However, settlers became particularly irate when Indians they thought they knew well turned against them.

Despite the protection that some received, "wild panic"—"wide, universal, and uncontrollable"—set in among white residents.[38] Thousands of "frantic refugees" made their way to larger settlements like Minneapolis and Saint Paul and to US Army forts. Some never returned to their homes and farms. For around two hundred miles the Minnesota Valley was "devastated or depopulated."[39] John G. Nicolay, President Abraham Lincoln's secretary, writing some months later to the president, contended that "there has hardly been an outbreak so treacherous, so sudden, so bitter, and so bloody, as that which filled the State of Minnesota with sorrow and lamentation."[40]

"Like a destructive storm, the war struck suddenly and spread rapidly," wrote one Dakota woman many years later. "It was difficult to know who was friend and who was foe."[41] She expressed the fear and panic that traveled through the Sioux as well.[42] The divisions among them, already noted, became graver still amid the armed conflict. Some Dakota clamored for war, spurred on by the exploitations committed by white people and by a culture that prized male warriors. Others echoed Little Crow in their sentiments. They knew that war with the United States would bring disaster upon them, but found themselves going along out of a sense of solidarity with the men in their bands or just to prove, once again, their own capabilities as fighters.[43]

All told, around 1,500 Dakota out of a population of 7,000 had taken up arms.[44] Rumors swirled that the entire Sioux Nation to the Missouri River, some 25,000, might be on the march, and the same of the Ojibway and Winnebago to the North.[45] None of this was true, but the rumors contributed to the sense of panic among white settlers and the Minnesota and federal authorities.

Yet the simple divide between whites and Indians fails to capture the complexity of life. The frontier was a zone of conflict, oftentimes violently so; it was also a zone of interaction.[46] Hundreds, if not thousands, of mixed-race people lived among Indians and among whites. They were Franco-Dakota and Anglo-Dakota, the result of almost two hundred years of sexual relations on the frontier. Sometimes, a "mixed-blood" was able to save the family, as Samuel J. Brown, the son of a famous frontiersman and Indian agent, related. When news came of the Indian attacks, his family fled their home, and soon found themselves surrounded by a band of Indians stained with blood, the result of a killing episode just shortly before. Brown's mother started yelling in Dakota to the crowd of Indians. She shouted she was Sisseton (one of the Dakota bands) and demanded protection for her, her family, and other white people who were fleeing with them. One of the Indians remembered that Brown's mother had taken him in one winter when he was near freezing, and had let him warm up by the fire and had fed him. He demanded that the other Indians leave the group of white and mixed-race people in peace. The Indians responded that they had pledged to kill every white person and were going to make good on their oath. The friendly Indian demanded again the security of the group. The Indians, around twenty-five in all, held two councils, and ultimately let the group move to Little Crow's settlement, where they found protection, despite numerous scares along the way.[47]

❧

"Attend to the Indians," President Lincoln wired Governor Ramsey.[48] His admonition accorded with the views of Pope, the US commander, who was convinced of the seriousness of the rebellion as soon as he set foot in Minnesota. Pope had graduated West Point and served in the Mexican War and in other Indian campaigns. Governor Ramsey now had a high-ranking officer as his adviser, one disgraced in Washington but not on the frontier. With a direct line to the War Department, Pope had greater ability to obtain reinforcements and war matériel—and spare Minnesota even further siphoning of men and resources to the Civil War. President Lincoln himself overruled his secretary of war and suspended the military draft in Minnesota—another sign of how securing the frontier was as vital to the federal government as suppressing the Southern rebellion. Quickly, Ramsey and Pope nationalized the state militias and incorporated them into the United States Army.

Pope sent a force of nearly 1,400 men up the Minnesota Valley (see map 3.1). It relieved the garrison and refugees besieged at Fort Ridgely, which the Dakota had tried twice to seize, each time failing. The US forces then turned toward New Ulm, where a pitched battle occurred between the army, supported by settlers, and the Dakota. Despite losses of people and materials as buildings in this prosperous frontier town lit up in flames, the white settlers were able to hold off the attackers.[49]

Meanwhile, Colonel Sibley gathered a considerable force to meet the Indians near the location of the Upper Indian Agency (see figure 3.1). It was a ragtag group consisting of many white refugees and soldiers with little experience. Sibley and some Indians sought to negotiate, all to no avail. Sibley promised Indians protection so long as they were not involved in murders. But he was coming under heavy criticism from the newspapers and local white citizens for not staging a full attack at once. As so often and in so many places around the globe, the settlers wanted blood and outright revenge and opposed any negotiations.[50] Sibley found support from missionaries who were allied with those Indians who had converted to Christianity. He advanced slowly and again attempted negotiations, not least because he hoped to get the nearly 250 white and mixed-race ("half-breeds" in the sources) prisoners released. He wrote to his wife that he would exercise full justice against the Indians, but that he did "not propose to murder any man, even a savage, who is shown to be innocent."[51]

Others, however, quite freely called for the Indians' extermination. As in Greece in the 1820s, nationalists could not abide those who stood in the way of the unified nation. Nicolay, Lincoln's secretary, cabled Secretary of War Stanton: "As against the Sioux, it must be a war of extermination."[52] Governor Ramsey, too, invoked the word on numerous occasions.[53] After the Dakota had been defeated, Pope wrote Sibley:

> The horrible massacres of women and children and the outrageous abuse of female prisoners, still alive, call for punishment beyond human power to inflict. There will be no peace in this region by virtue of treaties and Indian faith. It is my purpose utterly to exterminate the Sioux. . . . Destroy everything belonging to them and force them out to the plains. . . . They are to be treated as maniacs or wild beasts, and by no means as people with whom treaties or compromises can be made.[54]

The words were not all that different from the infamous "extermination order" that the German general Lothar von Trotha issued in 1904 in regard to the Herero and Nama of Southwest Africa, as we shall see in

FIGURE 3.1 Henry Hastings Sibley, 1862. Sibley (1811–91) came to the Northwest Territory as a fur trapper. He lived with Indians for extended periods and fathered a child with an Indian woman. Sibley became the first governor when Minnesota achieved statehood in 1858. He was then appointed to lead the Minnesota State Militia against the Sioux rebellion in 1862 and in the pursuit campaigns of 1863 and 1864. His slow and deliberate military tactics and relatively moderate political position, believing that only Indians who had killed whites should be executed, generated a great deal of hostility from Euroamericans. For many Minnesotans he remains a revered figure. (Minnesota Historical Society, from Whitney's Gallery.)

chapter 6. The rules of warfare were yet to be codified as international law. The US Army's Lieber Code, the model for many efforts to limit the brutalities of warfare, would be written one year later; the first Geneva Convention would be held in 1864. Nonetheless, the rules of warfare existed as tradition. However, Pope and others never considered that they might apply to war against Indians.

If the Dakota had been able to take Fort Ridgely and New Ulm, they would have had open access all down the Minnesota Valley to the state capital of Saint Paul and the Mississippi River. Probably their successes would have inspired other Indian revolts. But they failed, and in that failure lay the seeds of a still greater defeat. Now, the full force of the United States—again, even though the Civil War raged—would be deployed against them. Not only would the rebellion be crushed and some held responsible for the depredations of white settlers, but the Dakota would be removed entirely from Minnesota, opening the way for the full exercise of rights by Euroamerican settlers.

The United States Army went into the field and played a central role in securing white settlement. So did volunteers, settlers who brought their own rifles and their own determination and were commissioned more or less on the spot into the state militia. They fought the Indians and staffed the forts when regular troops went into combat, serving anywhere from a few days to a few months. They gave themselves glorified names like the Frontier Avengers, Le Seur Tigers, Red Wing Cavalry, or Scandinavian Guards, and they were sometimes formed into larger, more regular (if temporary) companies. They received pay and compensation for their losses from the state and federal governments.[55]

As volunteers and militiamen, they stood in that strong, democratic American tradition of a people-at-arms—the Second Amendment's right to bear arms—and of hostility to a professional, standing army. Yet this was a racially defined democratic tradition, a white-people-at-arms against the uprising of the Dakota. Some of the soldiers were professionals, but many of them had little more experience than the farmers and tradesmen who took their rifles, left their homesteads, and joined the Frontier Avengers and the like.

In this sense, the character of the frontier conflict was no different from that in other settler colonies like Australia, New Zealand, South

Africa, and German Southwest Africa.[56] In all these cases, indigenous peoples granted land to settlers and states via treaties, then settlers seized more land in arbitrary fashion. Typically, indigenous peoples had no concept of the private right to land ownership. Their conception of collective rights, of tribal ownership of the land, clashed directly with white settlers who sought to define the boundaries and fence in the land each pioneer family acquired, sometimes by sheer will and force irrespective of any treaties. Typically also, agreements struck by chiefs, often to their own benefit, were not acknowledged and often not even known of by their followers, as we shall see also in the case of Namibia. Eventually, white encroachments became too onerous, leading to rebellions. Native peoples' conception of collective rights fell to defeat.

❧

Unlike Sibley, Pope refused all negotiations.[57] Finally, on 18 September 1862, Sibley, at the head of an army of about 1,500 men, moved up the Minnesota Valley. Many white hostages had been protected by friendly Indians; others had been raped and had seen family members killed.[58] On 23 September, in what is known as the Battle of Wood Lake (though the hostilities actually took place at another nearby lake), Sibley and his forces engaged Little Crow and his Dakota warriors, who may have numbered as many as one thousand.[59] "The whole prairie seemed to be alive with [Indians]," wrote one veteran of the campaign.[60] Some Indians wanted to kill all the hostages outright; others thought the captives could be used as leverage in negotiations. The Dakota decided to wait. As a result, somewhat more than seven hundred Dakota, others having been left behind to guard the white and mixed-race captives, descended on Sibley's forces. They attacked from three sides, but suffered heavy losses and retreated. Accustomed to attacking isolated settlers, they now faced an organized, well-armed, and experienced military force in the form of the United States Army. As in the earlier battles, cannons fired by the US Army made all the difference. Little Crow and some 150 to 200 warriors fled to the Dakota Territory and into Canada. Others remained, even though they knew they would face some form of retaliation.

The retaliation came quickly, severely, and for the most part indiscriminately. Some thirty thousand white settlers had become refugees, crowded into the forts and larger towns in desperate circumstances. Somewhere between five hundred and one thousand had been killed, some in quite brutal circumstances, their bodies mutilated.[61] The atrocities committed by Indians had inflamed the settlers and authorities and fueled a drive for revenge. They were determined to brook no further rebellion, to ensure that the Indian threat would be finally and totally eliminated and that the Upper Midwest would be secure and open to white settlement for eternity.

Those who were determined to have rebelled were to be executed or imprisoned. Even Sibley (now promoted to brigadier general)—who, as a fur trader, had lived among Indians, fathered a child with an Indian woman, and sought negotiations—firmly held to the conviction that Indians who had killed whites were to be executed. "My heart is steeled against them," he wrote Governor Ramsey, "having seen the mutilated bodies of their victims. . . . Unless we can now, and very effectually, crush this rising, the state is ruined, and some of its fairest portions will revert for years into the possession of these miserable wretches, who, among all devils in human shape, are among the most cruel and ferocious. . . . I will sweep them with the besom of death."[62] Fierce words from the man who had been the first governor of Minnesota when the territory became a state in 1858.

Sibley set up a military commission to try 16 Indians so accused. In fact, 20 Indians had already been hanged. He was ordered to send prisoners to Fort Snelling; in mid-October 1862, 101 shackled Indians, with over 2,000 more to come, were dispatched on a forced march to the fort.[63] Several hundred died there over the winter of 1862–63.[64]

Witnesses were called, evidence heard. The trials ran fast, sometimes forty prisoners convicted after a single day of testimony. Some dissenting voices were heard, missionaries among them, who decried the mangled judicial procedures. In Minnesota, the hostile sentiment reached epic levels, with demands for the execution of all the Indians interned and the removal of all other Indians from the state.[65] Public opinion was especially incensed that so many "civilized" Indians had taken part in the massacres. The US district attorney in Saint Paul, George A. Morse, conveyed to President Lincoln some of this sentiment:

> Nor will even the most rigorous punishment give perfect security against these Indians so long as any of them are left among, or in the vicinity of, our border settlements. The Indian's nature can no more be trusted than the wolf's. Tame him, cultivate him, strive to Christianize him as you will, and the sight of blood will in an instant call out the savage, wolfish, devilish instincts of the race. It is notorious that among the earliest and most murderous of the Sioux, in perpetrating their late massacre, were many of the "civilized Indians" . . . with their hair cut short, wearing white men's clothes, and dwelling in brick houses built for them by the Government.[66]

Of the 393 Indians brought to trial, 65 were acquitted, the case against a few others not proved, and 16 sentenced to imprisonment. But 309 were sentenced to death.[67] The decision was sent to President Lincoln, who requested the full trial records. Governor Ramsey wrote to Lincoln advising that the decisions be carried out; otherwise, he feared, "private revenge"—that is, vigilante mobs—would take matters into their own hands.[68] Indeed, mobs had already threatened the imprisoned Indians, and the authorities worried about their ability to maintain the rule of law and to control crowds determined to kill any Indians they encountered, especially those already imprisoned.[69] However, Lincoln and a number of his advisers were skeptical of the bellicose rhetoric emanating from Minnesota. More than anything else, Lincoln believed in the rule of law. Determined to make his own assessment and not be swayed by Pope's hysterical fulminations, he put the executions on hold as he read carefully the trial transcripts and decisions. Minnesota officials and settlers were incensed. They wanted the executions to take place, all of them and immediately.

Ultimately, Lincoln reduced the execution number to thirty-nine, saving the lives of those who had joined in the uprising but whose participation in murders had not been proven. Two days before the scheduled execution, the military commander at Mankato imposed martial law on the region and forbade the sale of alcohol, fearful of ever-threatening mob actions.

At a very large gallows in Mankato, one of the largest ever constructed, thirty-eight Indians (one sentence having been commuted) were legally murdered, all at the same moment, on 26 December 1862 (see plate 9).[70] This was the largest single execution in American history. Crowds flooded the fields and trees around the gallows. Over one thousand soldiers were positioned at full attention. The executioner had lost three children to the rebellion, and his wife and two remaining children were still held by Little Crow.[71] On 27 December 1862 Sibley wired Lincoln that the executions had been carried out. "Everything went off quietly, and the other prisoners are well secured."[72] Lincoln himself had written the execution order, at the same time ordering that the other prisoners remain in captivity and that they be protected from "unlawful violence."[73] All along the routes that the Indians traversed, those condemned to execution as well as those to prison terms, the US Army escorts faced vigilante crowds who threatened to massacre all the Indians. The local press only exacerbated the situation with its virulent calls for "death to the barbarians!"[74]

Total, mass killings of Indians did not, in fact, take place. There was no genocide, as California Indians endured.[75] Instead, expulsion became the policy of choice, and included the Ojibway and Winnebago, although those tribes had launched only a few minor skirmishes.

The real decisions were made at the federal level. On 16 February 1863 Congress abrogated all treaties with the Dakota, eliminating the annuities and all Sioux claims on lands within Minnesota. Portions of the revenue forfeited were used to compensate white settlers for their losses. Another law on 3 March exempted from deportation those Dakota who had aided whites, and allotted eighty-acre homesteads, carved out of the old reservations, to "meritorious individuals."[76]

Their new homes, however, lay in what would become South Dakota, not in Minnesota. Indians were scattered to the Dakota Territory, Iowa, and Nebraska. Many ended up on Crow Creek Reservation in present-day South Dakota or on Fort Totten (now Spirit Lake) in present-day

North Dakota.[77] Some Dakota remained on the Canadian side of the border; others wandered farther west and would join with their Lakota brethren for yet another chapter of Indian resistance. A few families managed to settle in dispersed communities in Saint Paul and Faribault on eighty-acre allotments, but faced the intense hostility of neighboring whites.[78]

All those whose death sentences Lincoln reversed were sent to prison at Davenport, Iowa. Missionaries aided many of those in detention and kept up their education efforts. The Dakota endured horrendous conditions in prison. Some literally starved, others froze during the winter. They grieved over the separation from family members and their inability to take care of them. A good portion of the hundreds imprisoned there died, as had those held initially at Fort Snelling.[79]

Many of those who had converted to Christianity, either before or during their sentence, wrote to the well-known missionary Reverend Stephen R. Riggs with plaintive pleas for information about relatives or for help in securing their own release from prison. They attested to their belief in the "Great Spirit," and assured Riggs that they had given up alcohol and "Indian ways."[80] They asked him to pray for them and their families. As one prisoner, Ruban His Sacred Nest, wrote to Riggs: "A lot of young men who learned to write are always dying. I am saddened.... Since we have come here, forty-five and more have died, and a lot will die.... The women are pitiful and frightened, and some have not eaten, they flee, and several have not remembered the Holy Spirit. They are getting scattered and separated."[81] Another prisoner, Robert Hopkins, responded to a letter from Riggs, who had inquired about their conditions. Hopkins wrote that many were sick and some would die, especially in the winter when they would freeze to death. "If you free one [of my relatives] from prison, you will make me glad."[82]

Little Crow, as mentioned, had fled with an ever-diminishing band of followers around Minnesota and into the Dakotas and Canada. On 3 July 1863, about one year after the Battle of Wood Lake, Little Crow and his son came upon two settlers. They exchanged shots. One bullet killed Little Crow. His body would later be mutilated, the scalp and other body parts put on display for the Fourth of July celebration in 1863, then sold off as souvenirs.

All these forced removals had wrenching consequences for the survivors. They became impoverished and were often persecuted. And they were severed from the Minnesota land that nourished them, and that had such deep spiritual and cultural significance in Indian life.[83]

☙

By the end of 1863, most Minnesota Dakota were dead or deported. Small-scale Indian raids continued, which invariably gave rise to rumors of much larger Indian forces in the waiting. Both the Minnesota state government and the federal War Department authorized the formation of irregular forces—scouts—with the goal of killing Indian raiding parties. They were paid $25 per scalp, which eventually rose to $200. Clearly, the government promoted a form of vigilante justice. In the end few Indians were found and only four scalps were returned for payment.[84]

Still, the few Indian raids against settlers and, more importantly, widespread fears of renewed, full-scale attacks, led state and federal authorities to extend the war into the Dakota Territory. Expeditions sent out in 1863, 1864, and 1865 in pursuit of the Dakota sometimes crossed over into Canada, despite Lincoln's express prohibition.

In these expeditions, the army massacred men, women, and children. When the soldiers encountered Indian encampments, they destroyed whatever provisions they could not consume or cart away. Winters were harsh in the North Country. Fierce winds blew down from the Arctic, sheer across Canada and the United States, and the snow fell two and three feet deep, sometimes higher. Food could scarcely be found in those circumstances, except by ice fishing. The Indians could only survive by killing and drying buffalo or other game meat, which they mixed with dried berries and fat to make the famed pemmican that had also kept trappers and explorers going since the early days of European arrivals. In one encounter near what is now Ellendale, North Dakota, General Sully refused desperate Dakota attempts at negotiation.

Instead, he ordered the massacre of all the Indians, and then had his men burn four to five hundred thousand pounds of buffalo meat as well as the lodges and anything else of value, including dried berries, animal skins, utensils, and saddles and poles, as well as horses and dogs.[85]

So the pattern continued, the Indians overwhelmed by the superior firepower of the US Army, which then deliberately destroyed the resources on which Indian survival depended. No less than Greek rebels burning Muslim villages and farms, the American soldiers made life unsustainable for their adversaries. Only a few individuals, mostly missionaries, contested the ill treatment of the Dakota at the hands of the federal and state governments and the settlers.[86]

❧

The Dakota had been driven from their bountiful and sacred lands of the Minnesota Valley. Those who had joined their Lakota brethren would also be displaced from the Black Hills of the Dakota Territory once gold was discovered there in 1874. The defeat of the Dakota, the killings and forced deportations to reservations, the destruction of the resources on which their lives depended, was one chapter in the relentless European settlement of the North American continent.

Once defeated, once Minnesota and then the Dakotas were incorporated as federal states into the United States, what could be the legal and political status of Indians? Would the Fourteenth Amendment's equal protection clause, passed in the wake of the Civil War, apply to Indians? And if so, in reality as well as theory? Were Indians citizens, individuals who had the "right to have rights"? Or were they members of separate nations within the United States, sovereign nations as defined by the treaties between the United States and various bands of Indians? Or both? The complexity of the issue goes to the heart of the conundrum of nation-state formation and human rights.

Most of the battles in the Dakota wars were small by the standards of the mid-nineteenth century, including the American Civil War, the Franco-Prussian War, and the Taiping Rebellion in China, let alone the total wars of the twentieth century. But the unrelenting character of the Indian Wars marks their global historical significance. Skirmish after skirmish, scores and hundreds of Indians were killed. The tribes were pushed back and back and back, clearing the way for commercial agriculture and industrial development tied into international markets on a scale never before seen. Soon Minnesota wheat, corn, lumber, and iron would be shipped to Chicago, Saint Louis, New Orleans, and New York, and westward to California once the transcontinental railroad was built, and from these ports and entrepots on to Europe and Asia.

The men who did the fighting against the Indians had come from Europe, representatives of the epic population movements described in chapter 1. Women worked the farms and maintained the households. Along with men who farmed, trapped, manufactured, mined, and lumberjacked, they extracted, sowed, plowed, and forged the goods that filled American and global markets and sustained an ever-increasing population in the United States. As they removed Indians through killings and deportations, they also destroyed Minnesota's rich forests.[87]

Most of the settlers were immigrants or first- or second-generation-born Americans. Many had moved to Minnesota from points East; only around 1870 would they immigrate directly to Minnesota from Europe (as mentioned previously). They came from England, Scotland, Germany, the Scandinavian countries, and Ireland.[88] They left their home countries for the same reasons that all white immigrants came to the United States: religious and political persecution, oppressive economic conditions, and the search for new opportunities. Some of them extolled the "glorious new Scandinavia" and the productivity of its land, with the "milk and cream richer than in Norway."[89]

As white settlers, they enjoyed the rights proclaimed in the US Constitution—not least, property rights, which the federal and state governments went to great lengths to protect. They also feared Indian attacks, and went around always with loaded weapons; the fear became very real and immediate when the Dakota rebelled.[90] It required the power of the state to destroy Indian power and secure Minnesota for white settlement and for Euroamericans as rights-bearing citizens. One kind of population movement, from Europe to America, led to another, the displacement of Indians by Euroamericans in the North Country.

In this epic historical drama, the displacement of indigenous peoples by Euroamericans and the creation of the United States as the absolute, sovereign state from the Atlantic to the Pacific, a dizzying array of actors came to define the status of Indians as Americans. The list includes the Constitution (if we can call a parchment an actor); the Supreme Court; Congress; the federal government's Bureau of Indian Affairs; lower level federal courts; state courts, legislatures, and governments; and settlers— as well as, of course, the Indians who resisted the overwhelming force deployed against them. Constitutionally, only the federal government should have been involved in Indian policy. In actuality, individual states exercised a great deal of power that the federal government only rarely challenged.[91]

To add to the complexity, Indian policy shifted over the years, often dramatically so.[92] Perhaps the only general comment that can be made in regard to Indians and human rights is that American policy oscillated between granting rights to surviving Indians, on the one hand, as collectives, as particular nations within the United States, and, on the other, as individuals, so long as they subscribed to "American" customs and values. Both options, the collective and the individual, were premised on the suppression of Indians, their reduction in numbers through killings and the removal of survivors to reservations, all marking their demise as powerful nations that, by their very being, had challenged the emergence of the United States as a unified nation-state that dominated the continent from coast to coast.[93]

However much policy shifted over the years and the driving forces oscillated among various governmental institutions as well as other actors, like missionaries and reformers, certain constants undergirded the suppression of American Indians and the assertion of US domination in North America. Those constants are captured in keywords like civilization, discovery, sovereignty, and rights. They were expressed by settlers and local authorities in Minnesota and by national bodies like the Supreme Court.

"Civilization" was the dominant ideology—and it was an ideology— of virtually all white people, including missionaries, government officials, army officers, farmers, tradesmen, and merchants. Civilization contained within it both humanitarian and exterminatory possibilities. It promoted a policy of assimilation, granting Indians inclusion and citizenship so long as they gave up their tribal affiliations, converted to Christianity, and, not least, became individual property owners and pursued a sedentary lifestyle. Living by "the chase," as Euroamericans called it, meaning the hunt, signaled barbarism, the very antithesis of civilization. For Indian women, a sedentary life meant sewing and weaving, while the men pursued the "masculine" task of working the fields, a gender reversal from traditional Indian farming culture. Alongside the Bible, "Protestant missions carry with them the plough and the loom," wrote missionary Riggs.[94] Should Indians reject the opportunities offered them by white citizens, then the only recourse would be killings and removals.

Charles S. Bryant, for example, author of one of the first histories of the Dakota-US War, wrote that "the inferior race must either recede before the superior, or sink into the common mass, and, like the raindrops falling upon the bosom of the ocean, lose all traces of distinction." Linking Minnesota and global developments, he continued:

> This warfare takes place the world over, on the principle of mental and material progress. . . . The superior, sooner or later, overwhelms the inferior. . . . The white race stood upon this undeveloped continent ready and willing to execute the Divine injunction, to replenish the earth and *subdue* it. . . . The result could not be evaded by any human device. . . . The Indian races were in the wrongful possession of a continent required by the superior right of the white man.[95]

Bryant came to the grim conclusion that the "attempt to civilize these Dakota Indians, the forty years . . . of missionary and other efforts, have been measurably lost, and the money spent in that direction, if not wasted, sadly misapplied."[96]

Civilization in both its guises, peaceable and murderous, meant that Indian as a way of life, as a culture, would disappear. For virtually all the newcomers to Minnesota around the mid-nineteenth century, that perspective was unquestioned, the Indians' fate preordained. In one of its early volumes devoted to the history of the state, the Minnesota

Historical Society, in 1880, vibrantly expressed that sense of history and destiny. Regarding the "Indian period" of Minnesota history, the authors wrote that the Indians constituted a "rapidly disappearing race," as if this were some sort of natural process. They would become "nearly extinct, or so changed in customs and religion, that the primitive Indian . . . will be only a matter of history." Once they were gone, once they were no longer a threat, Indians could be mythologized and romanticized. The Minnesota Historical Society's mission was to "collect and record all valuable and interesting facts regarding [Indians]. . . . The Indian period of our Northwestern history will be the most romantic and thrilling chapter in the records of its discovery and settlement, and the history of the Red Race is so interwoven with that of our State, that it cannot be omitted."[97] The entwining of civilization and extermination could not be more clearly expressed.[98]

Civilization defined federal policy as well as the practice of missionaries and Minnesota state authorities. In 1819, Congress passed a law that called for the government actively to promote "the habits and arts of civilization" among the Indians, including instruction in the "mode of agriculture suited to their situation."[99] About the best that can be said is that Congress did not authorize a policy of extermination. It did, however, seek an end to Indianness as a way of life.[100] The costs of such civilizing efforts were, once again, offset against the annuities agreed upon in the treaties, meaning that Indians paid for the drive to abolish their culture.[101]

Yet the division between civilized and barbarian, American and Indian, was never clear and simple. Some of the Dakota Sioux had become partially assimilated. Even Little Crow had settled into village life with farms around him, though he himself did not farm. He attended church, though he was never baptized. He sometime wore Euroamerican clothing, and he had been to Washington twice to negotiate the treaties between the federal government and the Dakota. He married Indian women, but he lived among many mixed-race people. Missionaries generally frowned upon intermarriage, yet they stopped shy of demanding its outright eradication.[102] Reverend Riggs admitted that those in such relationships learned Dakota life and language better even than the missionaries, which was a great advantage in missionary work—and Riggs himself had mastered Dakota and had given it written form.

Every entity of the US government and, most notably, the Supreme Court deployed the ideology of civilization. Thirty and forty years prior to the suppression of the Dakota Sioux, the Supreme Court handed down three critical decisions. Together they are known as the "Marshall Trilogy," named for Chief Justice John Marshall, whose majority decisions, delivered with soaring rhetoric and sweeping historical vision, marked US Indian policy for the next 150 years.

The Marshall Court first rested its decisions on the US Constitution, which mentions Indians in two places.[103] One is of dramatic import. It states that Congress has the power "to regulate Commerce with foreign Nations, and among the several states, and with the Indian Tribes," a provision that forms the basis of all the legislative, administrative, and judicial measures regulating Indian life.[104] The provision suggests that tribes were sovereign nations whose origins preexisted the formation of the United States.[105] As such, Indians could negotiate and make treaties with other states, a situation that continually worried American officials as they struggled to secure the country's existence and territorial ambitions on a continent where the French, English, and Spanish also had claims.

The Marshall decisions drew on these basic principles and supported Indian self-government, independence, and collective land ownership. But only in part. The Court also authorized the dispossession of Indians, though by legal means; namely, treaties and purchases. Most importantly, the Marshall Court asserted the supremacy of the federal government in regard to Indian policy. However, even the Supreme Court could be overruled in practice by the executive and legislative branches, settlers, and state governments, all of them consumed with zeal to take Indian lands and remove Indians from their presence.

In *Johnson's Lessee v. M'Intosh* (1823), the Court proclaimed the principle that only the federal government, not the states and not individuals, could negotiate with Indians and purchase their land.[106] The text of the decision is blunt: the United States possesses the "exclusive right . . . to extinguish their [Indians'] title and to grant the soil."[107] The decision also invoked the claim that would be expressed in more developed terms in subsequent cases: the right of the "discoverers," the "civilized inhabitants [who] now hold this country" to "alienate" the land from Indians, though only in proper circumstances of negotiations and treaties since the Indians were recognized as sovereign nations.[108] "Conquest gives a title which the Courts of the conqueror cannot deny."[109] At the same time, the "conquered shall not be wantonly oppressed . . . [and] the rights of the conquered to property should remain unimpaired."[110]

Indians possessed rights, of that there was no question in the Court's decision. These were collective rights, of Indians as nations over the lands their tribes possessed. No Bill of Rights was granted to Indians; individual rights like these were light-years removed from the Court's imagination. In a move of dramatic historical significance, the Court also limited Indians' property rights. Indians had rights of occupancy, not of absolute title.[111] So long as they hunted, fished, and farmed on areas clearly delineated as theirs, so long as they had not ceded land to whites through treaties, Indians possessed their lands. But the "absolute ultimate title" lay with the "discoverer," the Europeans and their descendants who had come to these distant shores.[112] Invoking the civilizational argument, the Court argued that Indians were "fierce savages" who lived from the forest. "To leave them in possession of the country was to leave the country a wilderness"; in other words, to leave it uncivilized.[113]

Despite the semi-protection afforded Indians by the Court's decision in *Johnson's Lessee v. M'Intosh*, individuals and states continued to encroach upon Indian lands. Georgia pursued a particularly egregious policy. The federal government had promised Georgia that it would aid the state in purchasing Indian territory. It had done little; hence, Georgia took matters into its own hands, seizing Indian lands, daring the federal government to act against it. On one of the first occasions in which Indians made use of the courts to defend their lands and their way of life, the Cherokee sued the State of Georgia in federal court. They also faced Congress and President Andrew Jackson, advocates of the Indian Removal Act of 1830 that resulted in the Trail of Tears, the forced removal of the Cherokee and other tribes from their homelands in

Georgia, North and South Carolina, and Florida to territories west of the Mississippi, primarily Oklahoma.

In *Cherokee Nation v. State of Georgia* (1831), the Court reaffirmed the sole and exclusive power of the United States over Indian lands. Moreover, the Court maintained that the Cherokee constituted a state; they had been treated as such by the first colonists and by the United States. Otherwise, no treaties would have been made with them.[114]

As quickly as the Court delivered this far-reaching decision, it just as quickly retreated. Were they a "foreign state"? Marshall asked. "The condition of the Indians in relation to the United States is perhaps unlike that of any two people in existence," he opined.[115] In the decision, Marshall coined a phrase that would echo through the decades: Indians constituted "domestic dependent nations," whose relation to the United States "resembles that of a ward to his guardian."[116] In other words, they were sovereign, but not completely so, foreign, though not a foreign *state*. They lived within the jurisdictional boundaries of the United States, whose writ was absolute.[117]

It was left to a dissenter, Justice Smith Thompson, to make a full defense of Indian rights. He argued that the Cherokee possessed all the criteria of a sovereign state. They governed themselves by their own laws and customs and exercised "exclusive dominion" over their lands. To be sure, they had given up some of their land by treaty, but in so doing they had not ceded their sovereignty. Indeed, weaker states often allied themselves with stronger ones, seeking the protection of the more powerful. That, too, did not signify that they had abandoned their sovereignty.[118] With grand rhetoric and a sense of moral revulsion, Justice Thompson condemned the State of Georgia for its violations of Indian sovereignty. Indeed, Georgia's acts were "repugnant" and showed a "direct, and palpable infringement of the rights of property."[119] The "injuries" to the complainants—that is, the Cherokee Nation—"go to the total destruction of the whole right of the [Cherokees]. The mischief threatened is great and irreparable."[120] Few other individuals in American history holding such elevated positions would articulate such a thorough defense of Indian rights as did Justice Thompson and his "brother," as he called Justice Joseph Story, who joined him in the dissent.

In the last of the Marshall Trilogy, *Worcester v. Georgia* (1832), the Supreme Court reaffirmed the point that the Cherokee Nation constituted a "distinct community" on its own territory. Therefore, the laws of the State of Georgia did not apply. Only the United States possessed the power to address the Cherokee Nation.[121] This time, Marshall penned a long, eloquent historical discourse to underpin the Court's decision and to provide the rationale for the combination of Indian sovereignty and, at the same time, dependence upon the United States. "After lying concealed for a series of ages," Marshall wrote, "the enterprise of Europe, guided by nautical science, conducted some of her adventurous sons into this Western world. They found it in possession of a people who had made small progress in agriculture or manufactures, and whose general employment was war, hunting, and fishing."[122] By what right, Marshall asked, did these people claim rights over the native inhabitants? The answer was simple. "Power, war, conquest, give rights." In North America, those attributes proceeded from discovery. "Discovery gave title."[123] But what of the native populations that were already present on that soil? The discoverer had the sole right to purchase land from them "as the natives were willing to sell."[124]

The Indians constituted sovereign nations, ones with whom Great Britain and its successor, the United States, entered into treaties. In so doing, the Cherokee acknowledged that they were under the protection of the United States. "Protection," Marshall wrote in powerful words, "does not imply destruction of the protected," nor did it mean that Indians "divested themselves of the right of self-government."[125] Georgia's encroachments on the Cherokee Nation, its lands and its rights to self-government, were "repugnant to the constitution, laws, and treaties of the United States."[126]

Justice Marshall struck an "uneasy middle ground" in the Court's decisions, one that recognized and limited Indian sovereignty, defined their particular status in the United States yet also allowed for continued dispossession of Indian lands as long as this was done in a legal fashion.[127]

The Marshall Trilogy cases demonstrate that sovereignty and rights are layered; they are not absolute, nor do rights or sovereignty amount to a singular thing. Even the grand power of the United States had its sovereignty limited on Indian lands. The cases are also notable for their powerful emphasis on property possession as the substratum of all rights claims. Sovereignty and rights derived from property. Without it, Indians would be almost as unprotected as the stateless peoples of the twentieth and twenty-first centuries.

⁊⁊

Later in the nineteenth century the Supreme Court whittled away at the Marshall Court's assertion of Indian rights and limits on the ability of white people simply to seize native lands, while the federal and state governments ignored the admonitions of Chief Justice Marshall. The actions of Georgia and the federal government under President Jackson were only the most blatant examples of violations of the writ of the Court. Then, in 1871, Congress legislated that no additional treaties would be concluded with the Indians. The Supreme Court ruled that treaties could be unilaterally abrogated by the United States, and that Congress possessed "plenary powers" in regard to Indians, underscoring Congress's ability to pass legislation directly affecting Indians, a position the courts have consistently upheld.[128]

From sovereign nations that exercised collective rights on behalf of their members, Indians had become "wards" of the federal government—the term used in judicial decisions, legislation, and reforming tracts from the 1840s onward. Never were the fiduciary and legal obligations of the ward's "trustee" fully and concretely defined.[129]

At the same time, Protestant missionaries and other liberal reformers had a profound impact on federal Indian policy after the Civil War. The "friends of the Indians," as they were dubbed, sympathized with the plight of American Indians and believed in the importance of the rule of law. But they also believed in Manifest Destiny and the civilization ethos, which meant that Indians could only become worthy of citizenship when they had abandoned their errant ways and adopted white customs, including Christianity, monogamous family relations, and, not least, individual property.[130] Their orientation led directly to the so-called "allotment era," on the basis of the Dawes Act of 1887, named for Senator Henry L. Dawes of Massachusetts. Indian communal property, Dawes claimed, amounted to nothing less than socialism. Upon its basis there exists "no enterprise to make your home any better than that of your neighbor's. There is no selfishness, which is at the bottom of civilization. Till this people will consent to give up their lands, and divide them among their citizens so that each can own the land he cultivates, they will not make much more progress."[131] One reformer, Merrill E. Gates, in 1900 called the Dawes Act a "mighty pulverizing engine for breaking up the tribal mass."[132]

And so it was. The Dawes Act promoted the individuation of property among Indians as the path to citizenship. Indians who pursued this course, and adopted "American" ways, then had access to citizenship. The law, in effect until 1934, had a devastating impact on Indian social and cultural life. It also resulted in another massive loss of land: Nationally, Indians had held 137 million acres in 1887; only 47 million in 1934.[133]

Even the promise of Indian citizenship via individual land ownership and property rights was rarely fulfilled. To return to Minnesota: Prior to statehood in 1858, Minnesotans had debated whether Indians should be granted voting rights. Ultimately, the state constitutional convention and subsequent legislatures decided that "mixed-blood" Indians could vote if they had adopted the "customs and habits of civilization." "Full-blood" Indians had to do the same, but required a certificate of attestation by a local court. White foreigners could vote so long as they declared their intention to become citizens; blacks barely figured in the debates, their exclusion from voting rights assumed by nearly all involved, as was the case with women.[134]

However, the wounds of the Dakota-US War remained raw, and Minnesotans went to great lengths to deny Indians the vote. A Minnesota Supreme Court decision in 1917 affirmed that Indians who remained tied to their tribes were uncivilized even if they lived in houses, dressed like whites, and attended church. As tribal members they were wards of the federal government, hence incapable of exercising the full independence expected of citizens.[135] Even as the federal government, in 1924, granted citizenship to all Indians—perhaps the ultimate effort at Indian assimilation—Minnesota and many other states kept up a host of discriminatory measures that deprived Indians of that basic democratic right, the right to vote.[136]

In the 1920s and 1930s, governmental officials and reformers finally recognized the disasters that had resulted from the Dawes Act. As part of the New Deal, federal officials sought to ameliorate the poverty and poor health and educational standards among Indians. The federal government now sought to strengthen the tribes, a policy led by John Collier, the new commissioner of Indian affairs, through the Indian Reorganization Act (1934). Whatever the shortcomings—and they were many—the result of the new policy was a "rejuvenation" of tribal government "after a century of oppression," and an increase in tribal landholdings.[137]

The new policy did not last long. Between 1953 and 1968 the federal government pursued a policy of "termination" of the United States's trust relationship with Indian tribes. The emphasis shifted once again to assimilation and divestment by the federal government of its responsibilities—and financial commitments—to Indian tribes, including many health and welfare benefits.[138] The federal government abolished more than one hundred tribes, distributed their lands to individual members, and discontinued federal aid. Some states were given powers over the tribes, a radical departure from the constitutional provision of Indian sovereignty. Government policy encouraged Indians to move to urban areas, where they were promised jobs and housing, promises that were rarely fulfilled.

The final period emerged in 1968 as Indian policies became part of broader shifts in American politics and society. Termination had proved to be one more disastrous federal policy. President Lyndon Johnson declared in 1968: "We must affirm the rights of the first Americans to remain Indians while exercising their rights as Americans. We must affirm their rights to freedom of choice and self-determination."[139] Republican presidents Richard Nixon and Ronald Reagan echoed these sentiments.

A new wave of Indian activism, influenced by the civil rights movement, spurred these changes. Indians took to the streets and the courts, and organized new groups like the American Indian Movement, founded in Minneapolis in 1968. They occupied sacred lands, like Alcatraz in San

Francisco Bay and Wounded Knee in South Dakota. On some occasions, occupations and demonstrations turned deadly in shootouts with law-enforcement agents. Activists demanded adherence to existing treaties, compensation and reparations for past abuses, and an end to discrimination against Indians. The Indian Studies program founded in 1969 at the University of Minnesota was the first of many that emerged at that time.

In 1968 Congress granted federal status to nearly all the tribes that had been terminated, a stark reversal of previous policy. Federal aid again began to flow to the reservations. The new policy reached something of a culmination with the Indian Bill of Rights (1968) and Indian Self-Determination and Educational Assistance Act (1975). The first law granted Indians most of the constitutional rights that other Americans had long taken for granted; the second gave tribes the right to administer various federal programs on their lands. Other laws also protected Indian rights from incursions by local, state, and federal officials. The government settled numerous compensation claims, some of which had been languishing in the courts for over forty years.

A new era seemed to have dawned after the depths of Indian defeats and removals, and disastrous federal policies like allotment and termination. Despite the drastic reduction in their numbers, Indians remained across the United States. In Minnesota, they were (and are) Dakota, Ojibway, and Winnebago—Indians who had managed to avoid the expulsions or had later trickled back to the state. Among the 560 recognized tribes in the United States, 11 are in Minnesota; many live on the four reservations in the state.[140]

But the issue of how, precisely, Indians possessed rights, and what kind of rights, remained as ambivalent as ever.

Conclusion

In 1898, at Leech Lake in Minnesota, the Ojibway and the United States Army fought the last battle of the long-running Indian Wars. The Ojibway lost, of course. Six US soldiers were killed, ten wounded.[141] Small stuff compared to other engagements in the Northern forests and plains of the United States, and as far as casualties go, a mere grain of sand compared with the losses in the Civil War. The symbolic significance of the battle far outweighed its military character. Coming right at the end of the nineteenth century, the desperate nature of the Ojibway attack and the desultory character of the battle demonstrated the triumph of European settlement and the removal of Indians. Only five years before, Frederick Jackson Turner, in his famous speech to the American Historical Association, had spoken with foreboding about the closing of the frontier, that social and geographic phenomenon that, he claimed, had shaped the American character.

The Euroamericans who settled in Minnesota quickly assumed all the rights, privileges, and protections that the American nation-state had to offer. If newly arrived from Europe, they only had to declare their intent to become citizens and they could vote, speak out, and find redress in the courts. These rights were—and still are—highly individualistic with little attentiveness to social rights like economic well-being or access to healthcare. In the collection of rights that these Americans exercised, security of private property was perhaps preeminent. As hard as life was on the farms and in the lumber camps, paper mills, and mines, the prospect of a better life than they had known in Europe or elsewhere in the United States was always present and, for most, became a reality.

For Indians, the story has been far more complex and much less inspiring. To the extent that Indians possessed any rights, it was as "wards," as members of the collective Indian nation, not as individuals.[142] At different points in American history, Indians as individuals could, at least theoretically, become citizens with all the rights that status signified, especially if they managed to assimilate into white Christian society. After 1924, all Indians possessed American citizenship. Yet the Dakota, like many others, suffered from discrimination and persecution such that they rarely were able to act even on the theoretical rights granted to them, at least not until later in the twentieth century when Indian activism opened up new possibilities.

The ultimate dilemma of Indian rights—collective or individual— has never been resolved. And it has made for a series of ironies that complicate the meaning of rights. When Congress debated the Indian Civil

Rights Act in 1968, even legislators expressed astonishment that Indians had never possessed those basic individual rights enshrined in the US Constitution, including the Bill of Rights, when they were resident on the reservations. Yet this act, full of democratic principles that other Americans had enjoyed for generations, signified a potential attack on Indian sovereignty and self-government precisely because it granted rights to Indians as individuals, not as members of a collective.

Indians were deeply divided about the act because of the threat to Indian self-government, however limited it had been.[143] Tribal sovereignty and, more generally, indigenous rights are highly regarded among both Indian and human rights activists and scholars.[144] They applauded when the UN General Assembly passed in 2007 the Declaration on the Rights of Indigenous Peoples, which affirmed native peoples' full enjoyment of human rights and self-determination.[145] However, tribal sovereignty offers almost no protection to individual Indians, especially women who have been subject to abuse. Human rights violations committed on tribal territory cannot be prosecuted in federal courts. The only avenue for redress is tribal courts, where victims may face the same people who committed the abuse in the first place. On Indian reservations, an eighteenth- and nineteenth-century understanding of sovereignty is vigorously defended—with sometimes dire consequences for individual Indians.[146]

The history of Dakota-white interactions in the North Country shows just how complex is the history of rights. To this day, no single standard of rights has existed for Indians. For whites in Minnesota, the advantages of citizenship were based upon the opening up of Indian lands to settlement and the establishment of individual property rights. Only with the vast reduction of the Indian population through killings and removals could these rights be secured. The American nation-state claimed to be the bastion of rights for all. As it created a republic that stretched from the Atlantic to the Pacific, it proved, in reality, to be highly selective in choosing those deemed worthy of its protection.

However oppressed they were, Indians were not slaves. In the New World, that benighted condition was reserved for Africans and their descendants. Slavery signified the complete opposite of rights-bearing citizenship; the abolition of slavery, one of the great human rights advances of the modern era. Just as the legacy of the Indians' defeat reverberated through the subsequent decades, so too the legacy of race-based slavery remained profound, limiting the life prospects of freed men and women. We shall see all these tragedies and achievements, the paradoxes associated with nation-state and human rights foundings, as we move to Brazil.

Chapter 4

Brazil

SLAVERY AND EMANCIPATION

ℰↄ

BRAZIL CAPTIVATED every traveler who arrived on its shores. They were enchanted by its natural beauty and fertility; the great variety of enticing fruits and vegetables; its abundant, inexpensive, and luscious meats and fish. The bay of Rio de Janeiro, the windswept plains, the tropical Amazon, endless miles of coastline, countless species of flora and fauna—the spectacle was dazzling (see plate 10). "Bountiful nature," wrote one German traveler, Georg Heinrich von Langsdorff, in 1817, "who here far exceeds all ideas ever conceived of her fertility, of the brilliance of colouring and beauty of form among her productions, of her delights and riches, has animated these forests with an endless variety of living creatures."[1] (See map 4.1.)

A century later, another visitor, also enraptured with the beauty and liveliness of Brazil, believed he had entered a world in which people of the most diverse backgrounds lived together peacefully. Writing as a refugee from Nazi Germany, the Austrian-born novelist and playwright Stefan Zweig swooned over "one of the most magnificent landscapes in the world . . . a unique combination of sea and mountain, city and tropical scenery—but quite a new kind of civilization."[2] He was impressed by the diversity of Brazil's population; surprised, given (as he said) his European background and the raging war in Europe, that all of Brazil's "different races . . . live in harmony with one another."[3] Contrasting a Europe enmeshed in the "insane attempt to breed people racially pure, like race-horses and dogs," he described Brazil as "built upon the principle of a free and unsuppressed miscegenation, the complete equalization of black and white, brown and yellow. . . . There is no colour-bar, no segregation, no arrogant classification."[4]

MAP 4.1 Brazil in the nineteenth century.

Brazil was not just beautiful. It was also, until 1888, a slave society. The human misery of bondage abounded in towns and cities as well as in the countryside. Some travelers, like William James (whom we met in chapter 1), buried in their studies of Brazil's flora and fauna, seemed to take no notice at all of slavery.[5] Yet, of the estimated 12.5 million Africans transported as slaves to the New World between 1501 and 1867, nearly 5 million, approximately 40 percent, were sent to Brazil.[6] Rio de Janeiro was the single largest port of the transatlantic slave trade, outpacing even New Orleans. Some 1,839,000 slaves landed in Rio after the perilous, disease- and death-causing Atlantic crossing.[7]

Something rings a little hollow, then, when European and North American travelers, as well as Brazilians themselves, in the past and the present, write rhapsodically about Brazil as a racial democracy, a society without discrimination.[8]

Slavery is the most benighted human condition. Those individuals owned by another are utterly deprived of rights; they endure "social death," to quote again Orlando Patterson's powerful phrase.[9] Indeed, Brazil in the nineteenth century retained the Portuguese law (itself derived from Roman law) that defined a slave as a "thing" and therefore "legally *dead*, deprived of every *right* and possessing *no representation whatsoever*. . . . Therefore, he cannot claim political rights," as the nineteenth-century legal scholar Agostinho Marques Perdigão Malheiro wrote. Only free men, if they are Brazilian citizens, "enjoy certain political rights and can exercise political responsibilities."[10]

Slaves, then, are the complete opposite of rights-bearing citizens. The abolition of slavery, an institution that had existed for millennia on virtually every continent, marks one of the greatest human rights advances of the modern era. Brazil's history demonstrates both critical points. The condition of slavery highlights the bracing significance of human rights. Only in retrospect does slavery's end seem predetermined or natural. Instead, we shall see how abolition, like every other human rights achievement discussed in this book, came about through a fragile confluence of factors—slave resistance; the activism of some liberal politicians, including their links to the international abolitionist movement; and economic developments that made the slave economy unprofitable in large parts of the country. Yet just as in the United States, slavery left a powerful legacy, contributing to the vast inequalities that define Brazil to this day.

❧

The great majority of Africans taken to the New World, some 95 percent, were enslaved in Brazil and the Caribbean.[11] The United States had the distinction, after the abolition of the slave trade in 1807, of having a slave population that grew by its own reproduction. Not so Brazil, where high mortality rates and the huge preponderance of men over women forestalled that possibility.[12] Instead, slave cargoes arrived continually on the shores of Brazil. By best estimates, Brazil (as mentioned earlier) took 41 percent of all African slaves, and the other sugar-producing colonies—those of the British, French, Dutch, and Spanish Caribbean—about 48 percent. North America, in contrast, took only 5 to 6 percent of the Africans transported by force to the New World.[13] In 1864, there were 1,715,000 slaves in Brazil, 16.7 percent of the population.[14] That was still very substantial, but less proportionately than in the 1820s, when 2.8 million free Brazilians lived alongside around 1.2 million slaves.[15] In 1872, the first national census revealed that Brazil's total population numbered 9.9 million, of which nearly 60 percent were African, African-descended, or mixed.[16] In the 1870s in some areas, like the coffee-producing provinces, slaves constituted a majority of the population.[17] All the while, race mixing proceeded apace. It was often violent, Portuguese men taking at will African or Indian women, resulting in a society with many gradations of black, brown, and white.

The Portuguese, as far back as the fifteenth century, had garnered extensive experience with slave labor on sugar plantations on their Mediterranean and Atlantic islands. Sugar was a highly prized commodity in Europe, still rare in the early sixteenth century when most of the production came from the Portuguese Madeira and São Tomé and the Spanish Canary Islands. By the late 1500s, the Portuguese had established extensive sugar plantations and mills in Northeastern Brazil, notably in Bahia and Pernambuco. These, along with the Caribbean sugar plantations, became phenomenally productive and profitable, the global demand for sugar essentially unlimited.[18]

Slavery flourished through successive crops and minerals. The slave economy began with sugar and mining, then tobacco and cotton. The coffee boom of the nineteenth century gave a new lease on life to slavery. By the 1880s, the four major coffee-producing provinces in the Southeast possessed 65 percent of Brazil's slaves.[19] Slavery also flourished in the cities, in workshops and on the docks, in well- and not-so-well-appointed households, in highly skilled trades and the most low-level, back-breaking, unskilled labor.

The forms of labor were age-old, but they established Brazil's complete integration into the modern global economy. Brazil took slaves as commodities from Africa and sent out goods extracted from the mines and the soil. Sugar, silver, cotton, tobacco, and coffee went not only to Europe and North America, but also around the world, to China, Russia, and the Middle East. Brazilian commodities slaked the desire for sweetness (sugar) and light (cotton textiles), for smoke (tobacco), bitterness (coffee), and wealth (everything, including silver). In the colonial era, Portuguese merchants, protected by the state and the prevailing mercantilist system, dominated the trade and grew rich. Everything went first to Lisbon and from there to other markets. In the first third of the nineteenth century, Brazilians themselves, after three centuries of Portuguese domination, sought to wrest the trade from Portuguese merchant houses, which they did—with British help. In return, the British received privileged entry into Brazilian markets, another source of profit in the nineteenth century for the wealthiest country in the world.

Meanwhile, slave traders from a host of maritime countries—Portugal itself, as well as the Netherlands, Britain, France, the British American colonies and the United States, and Spain—moved up and down the African coasts, east as well as west, gathering and hauling slaves to Brazil to work the plantations and mines. Brazilian slaves came from Senegambia and Angola and everyplace in between, and as far away from Brazil as Africa's East coast, notably the areas that today are Tanzania, Kenya (around Mombasa), Mozambique, Zambia, and Malawi.[20]

New World slavery was black African slavery, the first and only time in world history that this demeaning condition became identified with people of one phenotype. In Brazil, as elsewhere in the Americas, the Indian population had been decimated. The Spanish and Portuguese crowns believed that those Indians who remained could be Christianized and therefore should not be enslaved. Planters and colonial authorities believed Indians were unsuited for regular, harsh labor in mines and plantations (though they did enslave Indians in the first century of colonization). Moreover, Indians resisted. They fought and fled, the vast topography of Brazil offering them refuge.

Another great barrier existed: no Spanish or Portuguese impoverished nobleman or merchant who went out to the Americas to make his fortune had any intention of laboring in the hot sun or in the deep, dark, and dank mines. He was there to become wealthy and to exploit (in the literal sense of the word) the resources, human and natural, of the land, not to work. If Indians and Portuguese could or would not work, then labor, always in great demand in Brazil, could only be secured from Africa.[21]

୧୨

In 1719, Count Pedro de Almeida, the captain general of the province Minas Gerais, wrote to King João V, lauding the successful suppression of a slave revolt. However, worrying signs remained: "Since we cannot prevent the remaining blacks from thinking, and cannot deprive them of their natural desire for freedom; and since we cannot, merely because of this desire, eliminate all of them, they being necessary for our existence here, it must be concluded that this country will always be subjected to [the] problem [of slave rebellions]."[22] The count went on to note that the sheer numerical domination of slaves gave them the courage to rebel, while the geography offered them countless places to hide.[23]

One hundred years later, little had changed. Masters and their slaves in Brazil exist in a "a state of domestic war," wrote one government official in 1818.[24] Another five decades on and the situation was no better. Slave rebellions were an ever-present danger, a "volcano that constantly threatens society, a bomb ready to explode with the first spark," wrote Perdigao Malheiro, the Brazilian legal scholar, in 1866.[25] In 1835, Brazil had indeed experienced a major slave rebellion, the Bahia revolt, the second largest in the Americas (pride of place going, of course, to Haiti in the 1790s) and only the most dramatic of many in Brazil.[26] Thousands more slaves fled the plantations, workshops, and homes in which they labored and established *quilombos*, maroon communities, some of which proved long-lasting.

Rebellion and flight were the two major forms of slave resistance, and they shaped Brazil as much as the sheer economics of slavery. Without slave resistance, it is hard to imagine abolition—that great human rights advance—ever coming to pass despite the near total absence of a democratic ideology and a commitment to rights on the part of the rebels.

Slaves had good cause to resist and owners good reason to fear their slaves. The horrendous conditions under which slaves lived began with the conditions on board ship from Africa to Brazil. Even worse than labor in the fields, households, or workshops, life—if it can be called that—on the Atlantic crossing was sheer horror. In the slave society, Africans had some possibilities of relief and pleasure in family and community and of recourse through rebellion and flight. Not on board a slave-trading ship. Thrown together into the ship's hulls, stacked in three tiers, unable to stand or move about, slaves could only lie on their sides, the better to pack in more people. They endured temperatures that reached 120–130 degrees Fahrenheit, with barely one cup of water to drink every three days. The passage from Africa to Brazil lasted twenty days to two months. Mortality rates sometimes reached more than one-half of the slaves on board. Those who survived the voyage emerged emaciated and covered with bruises and sores, their bones virtually protruding from the skin. Deprived of standing for up to two months, many were unable to walk and had to be helped when they first disembarked the slave ship. Before being placed on the slave market to be sold, most were held in barracks for up to three months until their strength was restored and they recovered from communicable diseases.[27]

On the occasions when slaves revolted aboard ship, the repression was severe. In one case on an American flag ship with a Brazilian crew, slaves rebelled while still in irons. Around forty-six were then executed by slow hanging, sometimes thrown overboard while still alive. When the slaves were chained together but only one was slated for execution, his legs were cut off and left in the irons while he was then hanged. Others were flogged by two men at a time. The women who were flogged all died; the men endured the rest of the voyage in still greater pain, able to lie only on their stomachs while the flesh on their buttocks rotted off. The Brazilian crew made "all kinds of sport" disposing of the bodies that were hanged, according to the testimony of a British sailor.[28]

A British physician described the condition of the slaves on a ship the Royal Navy had seized. He is worth quoting at length:

> Although somewhat prepared . . . to encounter a scene of disease and wretchedness, still my experience . . . fell short of the loathsome spectacle which met my eyes. . . . Huddled closely together on deck . . . cowered, or rather squatted, three hundred and sixty-two negroes, with disease, want, and misery stamped upon them with such painful intensity as utterly beggars all powers of description. In one corner . . . a group of wretched beings lays stretched . . . in the last stage of exhaustion . . . all covered with the pustules of small-pox. . . . On every side, squalid and sunken visages were rendered still more hideous by the swollen eyelids and the puriform discharge of a virulent opthalmia . . . with which the majority appeared to be afflicted; added to this were figures shrivelled to absolute skin and bone, and doubled up in a posture which originally want of space had compelled them to adopt, and which debility and stiffness of the joints compelled them to retain. . . .
>
> The stench on board was nearly overwhelming. The odour of the negroes themselves, rendered still stronger by their filthy and crowded condition, the sickening smell of the suppurative stage of small-pox, and the far more disgusting effluvium of dysentric discharge, combined with bilge water, putrid jerked beef, and numerous other matters to form a stench, it required no little exertion of fortitude to withstand. To all this, hunger and thirst lent their aid to finish the scene, and so poignant were they, that the struggles to obtain the means of satisfying them were occasionally so great as to require the interference of the prize crew.[29]

These slaves, rescued by the British, were the lucky ones. Britain enforced the international ban on slave trading. Its navy seized slave ships and its government established courts composed of local and British officials, the first international tribunals dedicated to the enforcement of rights.[30] Slaves freed by the British navy had the chance of living their lives as legally free men and women. Others who had survived the transatlantic journey and the recovery period in Brazilian barracks then found themselves on Rio's infamous Valongo Street, the center of the

FIGURE 4.1 Slave Market at Rio de Janeiro, circa 1820. Belying its beauty, Rio was also the largest slave trading port in the Americas. After some recuperation from the horrendous conditions on board ship, slaves were offered for sale at the slave markets along Rio's infamous Valongo Street. This drawing by the renowned travel artist Augustus Earle is one of a number he completed depicting slavery in Brazil. (JCB Archive of Early American Images. ©John Carter Brown Library, Brown University.)

city's slave trade (see figure 4.1). There they were, yet again, huddled tightly together, only in warehouses rather than in ship hulls. As one British visitor, a clergyman, wrote:

> These ware-rooms stand at each side of the street, and the poor crea-
> tures are exposed for sale like any other commodity. When a customer
> comes in, they are turned up before him, such as he wishes are handled
> by the purchaser in different parts, exactly as I have seen butchers feel-
> ing a calf. . . . I have frequently seen Brazilian ladies . . . shopping for
> slaves, exactly as I have seen English ladies amusing themselves at our
> bazaars.[31]

The touch, the searching looks, the sport of it all—a perfect description of the status of slaves as commodities.

Once sold, it was off to labor in extreme conditions.[32] To be sure, some slave owners provided adequate food and medical care for their slaves, allowed pregnant women to not work beyond the fifth month, and demanded only light labor from them in the twelve months after childbirth. Benevolent slave owners gave their possessions a day off on Sundays, and provided them with small plots of land that they could work for their own and their masters' sustenance. They prohibited their overseers from exercising corporal punishment, though would do so themselves. Even in those instances when slaveholders were relatively humane, the fact remains: a slave was a slave, a non-person because he or she was the possession of another and deprived of virtually all rights.

Benevolent slaveholders sometimes liberated their slaves, far more so than in other slave societies in the Americas.[33] Slave owners tended to manumit their own children, the result of their liaisons with black or mulatto slave women. Brazil's substantial number of free blacks were to a significant degree manumitted former slaves and their successor generations. According to the 1872 census, fully 74 percent of people of African descent, blacks as well as mixed race, were free, not enslaved.[34] Brazilian law, though often violated, protected free blacks and mulattos from being reduced to slavery.[35]

Other slave owners were brutal in the extreme, working their slaves twenty hours a day, at a whim chopping off their limbs and other body parts, whipping and otherwise torturing them.[36] Overseers flogged and shoved slaves to plant, weed, and harvest at an unbreakable pace (see figure 4.2). In the sugar mills, slaves labored in excessive heat and with primitive, dangerous machinery that resulted in severed arms and other bodily injuries. Slaves labored sunup to sundown in fields with no protection from the blazing rays.[37]

Most slaves suffered from an exceedingly poor and monotonous diet—manioc flour or corn cooked into a paste, beans, perhaps a little fat and dried beef, occasionally yams, pumpkins, or sweet potatoes. On some plantations slaves were fed rancid meat or were "numb with hunger," as one Brazilian physician reported.[38]

FIGURE 4.2 Slaves on a coffee plantation in São Paulo, 1882. Brazilian slaves were put to work in a variety of settings, rural and urban. Plantation slavery spanned sugar, cotton, tobacco, and, finally, coffee production. Here slaves, mostly women, are drying the coffee beans. They are at work just a few years before emancipation. An overseer can be seen on the left. The Brazilian Marc Ferrez (1843–1923), who produced this image, spent a lifetime photographing his country, leaving one of the best documentary records we have of Brazil in the throes of modernization. (© Instituto Moreira Salles.)

Violence was endemic to the system, and the brutalities and tortures that slaves suffered—fifty, one hundred, and even two hundred lashes; logs and chains around the neck and feet; the tin mask; deliberate maimings; hangings and exposure to swarms of ants or mosquitos—can barely be described. Slave owners held concubines and profited from slave women's prostitution. Even a slaveholder who had raped a twelve-year-old slave girl was exonerated by the courts.[39]

All these conditions contributed to the extremely high mortality rate among Brazilian slaves. In 1872, the life expectancy for male slaves was eighteen years, versus twenty-seven for the entire population (in the United States around 1859, the figures were thirty-six for slaves and forty for the entire population).[40] In one district, a Brazilian senator reported that only 25–30 percent of slave children survived to the age of eight.[41] The high mortality rate is one reason Brazilian slave owners resisted so fiercely the abolition of the slave trade, let alone slavery itself.

Given these oppressive and horrendous conditions, it is no surprise that some slaves resisted. They ran away, deceived their masters where and when they could, and rebelled. Bahia in the Northeast experienced a series of rebellions, including one of the largest in the Americas. Many Bahian slaves were literate because they were Muslim. In Brazil, fully 86 percent of the entire population in the 1870s, whatever the skin color or legal status, could not read. The unvarnished fact of literate slaves had a powerful, unnerving impact on white people.[42] The rebellion that these Koran- and other-text-reading slaves led challenged the liberal, pro-slavery political order of Brazil—and sparked the deepest fears of the regime's protagonists and the white population generally.[43]

The Bahian revolt, perhaps unique among slave rebellions, took place in an urban area. In Salvador, the provincial capital, thousands upon thousands of slaves labored in haulage, carrying the endless piles of sugar sacks to the docks and ships. They transported well-heeled locals and visitors in the infamous palanquin and worked in artisanal shops and household service. Women labored as laundresses, cooks, street vendors, concubines, and prostitutes (see figure 4.3).

The masters expected slaves to earn a certain amount each day from their labors, from which their owners took the major portion. Blacks constituted a majority of the population of Bahia, slaves a plurality. White people lived the reality of the "domestic war" and the "volcano," anxiously existing in a sea of dark faces.

Muslim slaves in Bahia had managed to keep their communities relatively intact despite the horrors of the ocean passage from what are today Nigeria and Benin to Brazil. They shared a common belief system and language. Most belonged to a particular ethnic group, the Nagôs, a Yoruba-speaking population. Literacy facilitated communications and the conspiratorial organization of the revolt. The Bahian rebels had other resources to draw upon—namely, safe spaces where they were able to meet and plot in nearby maroon communities, as well as in living quarters, rooms, and buildings owned by free black sympathizers.

The Bahian rebels were mostly first-generation slaves. They viewed black Brazilians of longer standing with a degree of contempt despite the help some free blacks had provided them. The rebels hailed from a region in West Africa that had been beset by ethnic, religious, and

FIGURE 4.3 Slaves at the market in Rio de Janeiro, 1875. Urban slavery was quite pronounced in Brazil. Here, female slaves bring produce to the market, which might have been grown on plots granted them by their owners. Typically slaves had to turn over the bulk of their earnings to their masters. Still, some slaves did manage to save enough to purchase their emancipation. This image, also by Marc Ferrez, is one of many he produced on slavery. (© Instituto Moreira Salles.)

political conflicts. They were experienced with conspiratorial organization and armed conflict. And they drew locally on a tradition of slave rebellions—at least eleven slave revolts just in Bahia between 1807 and 1835.

Like the Sioux uprising in Minnesota and, as we shall see, the rebellion of the Herero and Nama against German colonialism, the slave rebels were never able to win the support of all their brethren. Some were too frightened to take up arms; others had managed to live a life that, although unfree, had a modicum of security. The adherence to Islam gave the rebels a sense of superiority that undermined black unity. Race, religion, and region further divided Brazilians and undermined the possibilities of a revolt on the dramatic scale of Haiti in the 1790s. By best estimates, only six hundred people rebelled—but the effects were far-reaching.

"Death to Whites! Long live Blacks!" the rebels cried out, in Bahia and in many other places of revolt, sometimes extending their killing slogans to mulattos as well.[44] Slave rebellions were never pretty, and the Bahian revolt played to form. Intense and often gratuitous violence extended far beyond what was strategically necessary for the slaves to win. The Bahian rebels had few rifles and pistols. But they had machetes, swords, clubs, and knives, and they smashed and slashed their way through almost anyone they encountered, including blacks who had not joined the rebellion or whom they disregarded and disrespected because they were not fellow Muslims.

The Bahian rebels wanted to end *their* enslavement, not slavery in its entirety. After their expected victory, they envisaged enslaving other blacks and mulattos.[45] The political ideology of the French Revolution had greatly influenced the Haitian revolutionaries. Not in Bahia, where Islam dominated the worldview of the rebels. Nonetheless, knowledge about the Haitian Revolution loomed large in Brazil. Haiti was the country in which black slaves had revolted and taken control. The very act of rebellion, if not its governing ideology, served as a bright shining star for Brazilian slaves.[46]

Learned Muslims and other religious figures comprised the leadership of the conspiracy in Bahia. They hardly embodied a commitment to democracy or human rights. After all, slavery had long been a recognized feature of Muslim societies. Many of the rebels wore loose-fitting white dress and carried amulets and shreds of Arabic text. Their celebrations, like their clothing and accessories, often blended Muslim and West African traditions. Not coincidentally, the conspirators planned the revolt for the days right after Ramadan.

Still, the Bahian rebels rose in powerful movement against their enslavement, the condition that defined the polar opposite of rights-bearing citizenship. They rebelled against the horrendous conditions into which they had been thrown and took a stand for the human dignity that was constantly violated by Brazil's liberal order. Yet the rebels' activism did not bode well for others—one other irony along the march of human rights.

The rebellion failed. No surprise. Nor was it a surprise that its repression came swiftly, violently, and indiscriminately, catching in its whirlwind any black person, slave or free, rebel or pacifist. The police entered at will any dwelling where blacks resided, wrecking and beating as they moved.

The chief of police, Francisco Gonçalves Martins, wrote ominously in regard to blacks who had previously been freed from slavery: "None of them has the rights of a Citizen, nor the privileges of Foreigners."[47] Had this "most horrible of plans" succeeded, the district attorney argued, it would have meant the "extinction of whites or mullatos, the destruction of the National Constitution, the loss of our property, the burning of public edifices, the profaning of our altars, the burning of our Temples, and of all monuments of our splendor and glory."[48] Clearly, the "splendor and glory" of Brazil were reserved for those on one side of the color line.

The province of Bahia brought the rebels to trial. It was an odd move, since slaves had no rights, but a trial no doubt represented yet another attempt to be modern and liberal: "civilized," in a word.[49] The repression was brutal in the extreme, with one leader sentenced to one thousand lashes; others, to twelve hundred. Between five and one thousand was common—fifty lashes a day until the sentence was fulfilled. The floggings were held in public, making the ritual of punishment even more degrading and humiliating to the victims. A significant number of free blacks, even men who had accumulated some wealth, were actually deported back to West Africa. Some masters, in an effort to break up the community of rebels, sold their rebel slaves to other slaveholders in the South.[50]

Slave resisters did not seek a fulfillment of liberalism's universalist promise, of citizenship rights for all, as their more politically conscious counterparts in Haiti had done in the 1790s. Not when they imagined enslaving others following their victory. Nonetheless, slave rebels in Bahia in 1835—and in many other, smaller rebellions that permeated the Brazilian landscape—by their actions, demanded at the very least to be treated as human beings. They claimed for themselves the dignity that comes with the recognition of the other, the basis of all human rights claims.

"They live in absolute liberty," wrote one exasperated official describing a quilombo, a runaway-slave community. He found the slaves "dancing, wearing extravagant dress, phoney amulets, uttering fanatical prayers and blessings. They lay around eating and indulging themselves, violating all privilege, law, order, public demeanor."[51] The quilombos had existed since the beginning of slavery in Brazil and were found all over the country—hundreds, maybe even a few thousand of them.[52]

Brazil's vast and sometimes forbidding geography facilitated the flight of slaves, which constituted a more common form of slave resistance than outright rebellion. Newspapers were awash in advertisements promising rewards for the return of runaways.

Some quilombos became more or less regular towns, and at least one, Palmares in the seventeenth century, had a recognized legal status and a political and social organization based on African traditions—Angolan in particular, fused with Indian and Portuguese elements.[53] Indeed, the word "quilombo" seems to derive from Angolan military societies and the ceremonies of circumcision that initiated boys into adulthood.[54] Alas, Palmares was eventually crushed, but its memory lived on in the popular culture of the region, where an annual festival commemorating it lasted at least until the mid-twentieth century. The revelers sang, "Black man rejoice. White man won't come here."[55]

Most maroon communities were smaller and not legally recognized, many highly unstable. But others became more or less normal, functioning communities. The inhabitants engaged in agriculture and craft production and sold their goods in nearby towns. In these communities the ex-slaves performed African rites complete with the songs and dances they had carried with them across the Atlantic. Some blacks, especially urban slaves, moved back and forth to the quilombos, using them for periods of respite and recovery from their daily oppressions.[56] Sometimes the quilombos served as a staging place for attacks on storehouses. The ex-slaves secured guns, ammunition, and food, or planned for rebellion.[57]

"Trails full of traps, ruses, and defenses"—that is what the Rio police found when they went out on one expedition to destroy a chain of quilombos. They discovered eight huts and burned them, and confiscated a cache of firearms, swords, scythes, axes, fishing gear, carpentry tools, and many bundles of good firewood. "These *quilombos*," the police noted in their report, "are very old [and] were located in a vast mangrove forest, with an outlet to the sea on one side which allowed easy communication with the city of Rio de Janeiro, from where many people came to supply themselves with firewood." In exchange, the quilombo inhabitants received food and rum. They were, in short, well integrated into the popular economy, so much so that locals often warned the run-away slaves of imminent police raids.[58]

These communities lived always in peril because the authorities and slaveholders considered them—rightly so—magnets for more run-aways and, by their very existence, a challenge to the system of bonded labor. Slave rebels and runaways made Brazil continually unstable. By their actions, however inchoate in formal ideological and political terms, they posited a world in which rights would not be reserved for the privileged few.

ഌ

"God! O God! Where are you that you do not answer!" begins the great abolitionist poem, "Voice of Africa," by Antônio de Castro Alves.[59] He did not live to see emancipation. Castro Alves died young, only twenty-four, of tuberculosis, in 1871. But this son of a well-placed, Portuguese-descended family gave voice to the lament of slaves, abandoned by all, even god. His poems, many published posthumously, would be read at rallies and meetings, helping to spread anti-slavery sentiment.

> Today my blood feeds America.
> . . . .
> Enough, Lord! Send forth your potent
> Arm, across the stars of space
> Forgiveness for my crimes!
> For two thousand years I have had one cry . . .
> Listen to my protest from your everlasting throne,
> My God! Lord, My God!!![60]

Like many abolitionists, Castro Alves did not necessarily believe in equality. The "crime" that he mentions is the Curse of Ham, one of the myths that slaveholders deployed to justify the enslavement of Africans. In the biblical story, Ham, one of Noah's three sons, supposedly revealed his father's nakedness. Noah flew into a rage, and the curse he levelled on his son reverberated through the ages on all of Ham's descendants, black Africans. Castro Alves appeals for the curse to be lifted. More than that: he knows—and tells others—that a world without slavery is within reach. "Enough, Lord!" Enough of slavery, let the wrathful god "send forth" his "potent arm" to free those who have suffered so long.

Castro Alves and many others challenged the liberal order infused with race thinking, a liberalism that proclaimed the rights of man yet enslaved a major proportion of the population. He and other abolitionists desperately wanted Brazil to be recognized by the European powers, Britain and France in particular, as modern and progressive. They knew that could only come with the abolition of slavery, which proved a moral, political, and, finally, economic weight on society. They sought to make Brazil more consistently liberal, yet they could never fully expunge the power of race from liberalism.

In Brazil, as in Greece and many other places in Europe and the Americas, the American and French revolutions and the Napoleonic conquests resonated loudly. Napoleon's invasion of Iberia in 1808 demonstrated that the worlds of the Spanish and Portuguese empires were no longer fixed and stable. All across Latin America, colonies declared their independence, unleashing decades of political conflict.[61] For all intents and purposes, Brazil became independent after 1808, formally so on 1 December 1822 when the scion to the Portuguese crown became Emperor Pedro I of Brazil.[62]

Pedro ruled the Brazilian Empire, as it was called, until an army coup in 1889 created the republic (as we shall see). Whatever its moniker, Brazil was in essence a nation-state with a liberal political order—fragile to be sure, with great regional differences, social and political conflicts galore, and a prevalent aristocratic ethos.[63] In that regard, it was quite similar to liberal European nation-states in the nineteenth century, almost all of which had crown heads of state and still-powerful nobles alongside constitutions, representative government, and rights proclamations.[64]

Liberal, independent Brazil had a constitution, granted by the emperor in 1824, that provided for the separation of powers, representative institutions, political rights for citizens, equality before the law, and security of property—all eminently liberal principles. The constitution even incorporated the French Declaration of the Rights of Man, albeit with a couple of notable revisions.[65]

Yet this liberalism coexisted quite easily with slavery, as was true also of the United States.[66] The association of work with slavery devalued labor, while the elite prized the ostentatious display of wealth, a kind of aristocratic style.[67] Our American traveler, Thomas Ewbank, whom we met in chapter 1, and many other travelers remarked that slavery produced a society of torpor, all sustained by the Catholic Church and the state.[68] These were hardly the typical bourgeois values of sobriety, prudence, hard work, and accomplishment through merit.

At the same time, elite Brazilians were schooled in the Enlightenment. On their library shelves lay works by Montesquieu, Voltaire, and Rousseau; Adam Smith and Jean-Baptiste Say. And also Carolus Linnaeus, Johann Friedrich Blumenbach, and Immanuel Kant—Enlightenment thinkers who explained the human population as a hierarchical order of races. Each differed in his count of races; all agreed that white people stood at the top of the hierarchy, blacks at the bottom. New World slavery, precisely because it was only black slavery, created race; these Enlightenment thinkers added philosophy and science to the mix, making race a most powerful way to understand human difference.[69]

For the first three-quarters of the nineteenth century the vast majority of Brazil's elite had no interest in abolishing slavery. If need be, they could pick and choose among their Enlightenment mentors to defend slavery or, at the very least, the inherited inferiority of black people. More fundamentally, the elite believed that the economy—indeed, their very existence—depended on slave labor. It was a life-and-death question for them. Haiti always echoed in their imagination: the ultimate horror, one that conjured up existential fears for their very lives. And for good reason, because the Haitian slave revolt, like the Bahian rebellion, was not a pretty affair. Abolitionists argued that if slaves were not emancipated, Brazilians would experience a second Haiti, an event in which no white life, and perhaps no mulatto life, would be secure. Slaveholders and their supporters argued that only the utmost control and regulation, the deepest repression, of slaves would prevent a second Haiti in the Americas. This liberal state followed their fears and desires and did its utmost to enforce slavery.

For whites and light-skinned mulattos, and even a few blacks, the possession of slaves was a marker of wealth and status. And that included the clergy. The further up the hierarchy, the more slaves a priest, bishop, or cardinal owned.[70] Household servants, wet nurses, haulers, carriage carriers—the four men who carried elite men and women as they sat in a finely appointed sedan, much like our American traveler in India in the 1850s, whom we saw in chapter 1—all that marked the immense social distance in nineteenth-century Brazil and continued well beyond emancipation. As one Brazilian reformer, José Verissimo, wrote: "The habit of giving commands [to blacks] from earliest childhood, far from strengthening character, demeans it, not only because it perverts the concept of authority, making it arbitrary and basing it upon privilege alone, but also because it suppresses the inclination to act independently."[71] The Maranhão writer and politician João Dunshee de Abranches described in his memoir strident efforts to "maintain a clear distance between the two races. In São Luis ladies of good families desperately struggled to avoid bastard offspring and to preserve pure blood among the children." Their efforts were constantly undermined by their husbands, who were attracted to slave and mestizo women. The men typically kept a "second house" where their lovers or concubines lived and the children they had with them were raised. Often the "legitimate" and "illegitimate" children played and went to school together.[72]

Social distance and race mixing, the striving for purity and the reality of miscegenation—the two ran together, elite Brazilian men able to exercise their ownership and patriarchal control over black and mixed-race women. For all their commitment to the idea of race purity, their actions created the great diversity of Brazilian society.

❦

"Tragedy at Sea: The Slave Ship," another of Castro Alves's great poems, begins with a lyrical description of the wide open sea, the blue sky, the "high-sailed ship" piercing the waves. He writes about noble, sunbaked sailors, from the ancient Greeks to the Spanish and British who found their way to the New World. The beautiful imagery suddenly turns threatening: this is a slave ship, packed with men in "clanking irons," suffering the "crack of a whip"; "listless children" who "hang at their mothers' exhausted breasts / Spattered with blood." But an end to the horror is possible.

> Constellations! nights' storms!
> Set loose destruction from your hands,
> Typhoons, sweep the seas!
> . . . .
>
> Blot out this filthy brig
> From the trail opened by Columbus
> Like a rainbow on the uncharted seas—
> Against this infamy
> Rise up, heroes of the New World!
> Andrada, tear this flag from the wind!
> Columbus, close the doors of your seas![73]

Like William Blake's "Jerusalem," quoted in chapter 1, Castro Alves's poems not only lament the present condition. He calls men to arms, to rebellion if need be, to transform the corrupted world—the slave world in his case—they inhabit.

Slave resistance made Brazil inherently unstable, but slaves were unable to win their emancipation by their actions alone. Only rarely, if ever, are popular movements and heroic activists alone able to win human rights advances. In Brazil, another mobilization was necessary—of members of the elite who had come to believe that the modern, liberal Brazil they desired and the slave society in which they lived stood in stark contradiction to each other. Only by emancipating slaves could Brazil progress and take its rightful place among the civilized nations of the world, they believed.

The abolitionist movement in Brazil developed late, almost a century after its emergence in Britain. In making their case, the abolitionists countered the world of liberty and rights to the benighted, regressive condition of slavery. Joaquim Nabuco, André Rebouças, José do Patrocínio, and Luís Gama were among the most renowned protagonists of abolition.[74] They drew on their own experiences, and also on British, French, and American anti-slavery ideas, bringing to life abolition as the first truly global social movement.

Gama was an ex-slave and, like Frederick Douglass and Sojourner Truth in the United States, used his personal experiences of bondage to great rhetorical and political effect. He, Rebouças, and Patrocínio were mixed race; they lived between both worlds, black and white, slave and free, and could see a flourishing future of liberty and opportunity for themselves and their country only if Brazil abandoned slavery.

Nabuco and Castro Alves were classmates, and Nabuco was also the scion of a well-established Brazilian family. Not even one generation removed from his slaveholding ancestors, Nabuco gave eloquent voice to the cruelties of slavery and Brazil's wide-open future should it finally move toward emancipation. He became the most influential and well-known Brazilian abolitionist, spending years abroad, in London especially, where he became the key contact between abolitionists in his home country and the international movement (see figure 4.4). Most importantly, he was in close communication with the British and Foreign Anti-Slavery Society, the preeminent abolitionist organization.[75]

In his great work, *O Abolicionismo*, and in hundreds of other writings and speeches, Nabuco gave powerful voice to the long-standing criticism that the slave system had created in Brazil "demoralization and inertia . . . servility and irresponsibility . . . despotism, superstition, and ignorance" among masters as well as slaves.[76] The population has to learn freedom to counter slavery's debilitating effects and create a future political order infused with "justice and moral rectitude." Otherwise, the country will continue on a downward spiral, a process of degradation that will affect each and every person and the institutions of the nation. Abolition, Nabuco claimed, is designed to free slave *and master* and to unleash their talents to create a free and prosperous society. Like other major abolitionists, Nabuco commanded great rhetorical powers to depict the lash on the back, the mere drops of milk left to a slave child

FIGURE 4.4 Joaquim Nabuco, 1870. Nabuco (1849–1910) was Brazil's preeminent abolitionist. He spent extensive periods of time abroad in France, Britain, and the United States (where he was later Brazil's ambassador). He forged close ties with the international anti-slavery movement headquartered in London. After many dead ends and partial successes, slavery abolition finally triumphed in 1888, the result of black resistance, organizing efforts of abolitionists like Nabuco, and the decline of the sugar economy. The photograph is by Alfredo Ducasble, who left an important collection of images of Brazil in the late nineteenth century. (The History Collection/Alamy Stock Photo.)

after the mother has nursed the master's children, the endless agony and sorrow of slavery.[77]

Nabuco recognized the contribution of African and African-descended people to the country. They literally built Brazil: black hands cultivated or constructed everything. Moreover, the black population was so large that blacks "gave us a people." Hence, the "black race . . . is an integral part of the Brazilian nation."[78]

Yet a wistful tone runs through Nabuco's writing, as if he wished that Brazil could have been created without blacks.[79] That sentiment signaled the limits of Nabuco's liberalism. His was not a celebration of Brazil's multiculturalism (as we would now call it), but a grim coming to terms with reality. As slaves produced mixed-race children for the master, they multiplied, and the "vices of African blood came into widespread circulation throughout the nation." The major result was the "mixing of the servile degradation of the one [blacks] with the brutal arrogance of the other [whites]."[80]

Nabuco, deeply influenced by British and North American liberalism and by his long residencies in Paris, London, and Washington, sought no revolution, but moral and political redemption through legislative reform and education. Indeed, he feared nothing so much as a slave rebellion. It would be the height of irresponsibility were abolitionists to foster rebellion. He showed his hand when he also argued, like so many European and North American abolitionists, that the "slaves, kept until now at the level of animals, with passions broken and bridled by fear, would seek limitless retribution."[81]

One hears, sotto voce, Haiti and Bahia in Nabuco's writings. Self-liberation by slaves would lead to a cycle of violence that would be disastrous for the nation and its entire population, bonded and free. Nabuco summoned the great eighteenth- and nineteenth-century abolitionists—Wilberforce (British), Lamartine (French), and Garrison (American)—against the terrifying specter of those who had led rebellions—the Romans Catiline and Spartacus, and, in living memory, the American John Brown.[82] As he wrote to Charles Harris Allen, the secretary of the British and Foreign Anti-Slavery Society: "Emancipation cannot be done through a revolution, which would be to destroy everything—it will only be carried by a Parliamentary majority."[83]

Nabuco upheld the Brazilian mythology in one regard: unlike in the United States, he claimed (rather in contradiction to his other statements), "slavery never poisoned the mind of the slave toward the master . . . nor did it arouse between the two races that two-way loathing which naturally exists between oppressor and oppressed. . . . The contact between the two races outside slavery was never bitter, and the man of color found every avenue open before him."[84] Upon this basis—of friendship, even love, between blacks and whites and everyone in between—a great and flourishing Brazil could be built. Human labor would no longer be degraded but honored. Industry, so long stifled by the economy of slave labor, would develop.[85] Social unity would open unlimited vistas for the nation.[86]

Other abolitionists were more radical than Nabuco. Rebouças, Gama, and Patrocínio envisaged a social revolution in Brazil. The abolition of slavery would be accompanied, they hoped, by land reform, especially the breakup of the great estates, universal education, and broadening of suffrage. In the 1870s and 1880s, they trumpeted the slogan, "Democratization of the soil."[87]

Abolitionists wrote and campaigned, demonstrated and celebrated. They held great meetings in local theaters, read poetry, and performed plays. They placed slaves who had survived hangings with an iron collar at the head of processions (with all the religious symbolism) and displayed various instruments of oppression and torture to arouse the public's revulsion at slavery.[88] The message was always the same—the inhumanity of slavery, its dire economic effects, all of which held Brazil in a state of moral and economic backwardness. To be great and modern, Brazil had to abolish slavery. Some abolitionists, at great risk, engaged in direct action. They interfered with slave traders; circulated on plantations, convincing slaves to flee; and faced down armed militias. They created a mass movement, which started in the 1860s, experienced a lull in the 1870s, but gathered momentum in the 1880s.

❧

Slave resistance via rebellion and flight, a significant abolitionist movement with major support abroad—these two powerful factors were, by themselves, not enough to force the abolition of slavery in Brazil. The third factor was mundane in comparison, but no less important: in major parts of the country, slavery was no longer economically viable.[89]

Brazil's great resources had drawn it into the world economy since the sixteenth century. Commodities markets are, however, harsh taskmasters. Brazilian tobacco and cotton production in the Northeast had been in decline at least since the turn of the nineteenth century, battered by cheaper cotton produced in the United States and higher quality cotton exported from Egypt and other countries to European and North American textiles manufacturers. Even Brazilian tobacco could not keep up. Then the sugar plantations also went into decline, unable to compete with the vast productivity of the Caribbean and new sugar-beet cultivation in Europe and North America. In all three areas, planters had more capital and invested more thoroughly in mechanization. Many Brazilian sugar-plantation owners could no longer afford slaves. The government sought to stimulate improvements in the sugar economy. It issued pamphlets, held seminars, granted subsidies, awarded prizes. All to no avail. Neither the capital nor the will for the necessary investments existed.[90]

Only the coffee-producing regions in the Southeast remained profitable and wholly committed to slavery. Many slaveholders in the North sold their slaves to the coffee barons, a last-ditch effort at recouping some of their investments. Efforts to find alternative sources of labor, like Chinese or European immigrants, and to extend the sharecropping system had all failed. Many Brazilians opposed Chinese immigration on racial grounds, and few European immigrants had any desire to labor as dependents of planters in the sharecropping system. Only later, after emancipation, did large-scale immigration, primarily from Italy and Portugal, succeed as a new form of labor, legally free if poorly paid.

Technological changes, which finally began to reach Brazil after 1850, also made slavery less economical.[91] Railroads vastly improved on the disastrous state of Brazilian transportation. Even some sugar plantations were able to survive, and sometimes thrive, if situated near rail lines. Coffee producers especially benefitted from the railroads. Slaves, urban and rural, still hauled huge weights of sugar and coffee, but they were also being replaced by machines. On enterprising plantations, machinery hulled, sorted, and bagged the precious crop.

The slave trade was the first to go, banned ineffectively in 1831 and more thoroughly in 1850, largely owing to intense British pressure, including the threat to invade Brazilian ports. Between 1845 and 1850, the British seized almost four hundred slave ships.[92] As late as the 1870s, the British were still issuing irate warnings to vessels carrying slaves, who were often disguised as servants. British flag ships that took part in transporting slaves for the internal trade were warned that the crew and shipping companies were liable for prosecution, the ship for seizure, under British law.[93] Appeals to other European consuls to bring their flag carriers in line with international treaties seem to have had success.[94]

The momentum was developing, fueled by a combination of liberal abolitionist sentiment, slave resistance, fear of slave rebellions, and the declining economics of slavery itself. A series of partial emancipation measures adopted in the 1870s freed newborns and slaves over sixty, but these made barely a dent in Brazil as a slave society. The legislation was so limited in scope that children remained more or less enslaved, and the high mortality rates among slaves meant that few survived to sixty.

The five-year war with Paraguay, from 1865 to 1870, took a deep toll on Brazil despite its final victory. The fact that a small, weak, and unstable country like Paraguay could tie down Brazil for five years caused many Brazilians to question the direction of their own country. The undermanned and ill-equipped army triumphed only because the government promised slaves their freedom if they enlisted. Many did, and the organizational and military skills they acquired would aid the abolitionist movement in the coming years.

In the 1880s, abolitionists intensified their campaigns.[95] In 1881 in the Northern province of Ceará, they blocked ships from transporting slaves south. Crowds surged onto the beach and port, convincing sailors not to take the slaves. The police looked on, unwilling to intervene. The next year, some six thousand Brazilians demonstrated on the beach, again to prevent a ship from taking on slaves for the domestic market. The campaign continued in 1884, abolitionists facing down troops despite the government's more intense effort to take hold of public order.[96]

Sensing the shifting tide in the 1880s, smallholders in the province began to emancipate their slaves, starting a trend that was followed in the Amazonas region (where there were few slaves). Ceará became the first province to declare itself free of slavery. Other provinces and towns soon followed, even in the coffee-producing regions of the Southeast.

Then slaves took matters into their own hands. Not by rebellion, but in massive flight, a runaway slave movement with few parallels in the sordid history of slavery. It was an extraordinary development, akin to a general strike.[97] Slaves simply fled the coffee plantations, first in small numbers, then in droves. Some flights turned bloody. When police confronted a group of 150 runaways, the well-armed slaves proceeded to overwhelm the authorities, stripping and beating them. News of the event spread rapidly, kindling great fears. Army units hunted down some of the runaways, others found safety and were celebrated at banquets hosted by abolitionists.[98]

Meanwhile, a Brazilian version of the underground railway offered runaways shelter and protection. Planters established private militias to bring back runaways, but army and police units refused to fire on them, a development as extraordinary as Russian troops refusing to fire on demonstrators in Petrograd in February 1917. Some slave owners, desperate to retain something of their power and a continual source of labor, began freeing their slaves in exchange for service contracts.[99] Even in São Paulo, the center of the coffee-producing region, some slaveholders began to accept the inevitable and started emancipating their slaves.

Finally, on 13 May 1888, parliament passed an emancipatory act, simple and clear: "From the date of this law slavery is declared extinct in Brazil. . . . All provisions to the contrary are revoked."[100] Slaveholders received no compensation. Princess Imperial Regent Isabel signed the law because her father, Dom Pedro II, was in Portugal.

"The victory was so sweeping and unexpected that the enthusiasm of the people overflowed all bounds," wrote the abolitionist A. J. Lamoureux. "The streets [of Rio] have been continually crowded, business almost wholly suspended . . . over a hundred thousand people in the streets on Sunday . . . nothing but enthusiastic joy, good temper, and good order."[101] In the Northern city of São Luis, newly liberated slaves swarmed the streets for a week, covered in flowers and palms, singing and dancing.[102] Music echoed through the cities; crowds surged in parades. In Rio, four days after the passage of the law, Princess Isabel led the cabinet and other notables to a high mass. Horse races, theatrical productions, and more parades united people of all classes.

ᴄ⁄ᴐ

The abolition of Brazilian slavery was an extraordinary human rights advance. The Americas were now free of the scourge of slavery. Abolition and emancipation were not the inevitable working out of history. To the bitter end, large segments of Brazilian society lived off the slave economy, and hundreds of thousands of Brazilians derived their status, their very sense of being, from the fact that they were not black. The move to abolition required constant slave resistance, enough to create perpetual unease among the elite; an explicit abolitionist movement that created great mobilizations; and the more or less blind workings of the market that eviscerated the support for bonded labor among those who could no longer afford to buy and keep slaves. In addition, the American Civil War and Emancipation Proclamation reverberated loudly. Brazil was left as the last slave society in the Americas; even those other holdouts, the Spanish colonies of Puerto Rico and Cuba, had emancipated their slaves in 1873 and 1886. If Brazil were to be a modern and civilized nation-state, as its elites wanted, then, they finally understood, they had to give up slavery.

Slaves only rarely articulated a political program consonant with democracy and rights. Violence was endemic to both slavery and slave resistance. Had slaves ever come to power, even in one region if not the entire country, it would most likely have been a bloody affair with little attention given to the niceties of parliamentary debate and due process. Few would have enjoyed the state's protection of their rights, and some, if the example of Bahia is taken, would have been newly enslaved by recently emancipated slaves.

Nonetheless, by their resistance, Brazilian slaves helped defeat the institution that, until the twentieth century, was the most consistent and brutal violator of rights, that so thoroughly assaulted the dignity of the individual that nothing was left except a commodity: bought, sold, exchanged, and brutalized at will. Until the totalitarian and genocidal states of the twentieth century, nothing stood in such absolute contradiction to the principles of citizenship and rights as slavery.

Abolitionists, for all their shortcomings—and they had many—in effect linked their cause to slave resistance and together helped topple the institution. They understood that the dignity of the individual had to be recognized for Brazil to be a truly modern nation-state. To go back to Johann Gottlieb Fichte and Hannah Arendt, as well as the Brazilian legal scholar Agostinho Marques Perdiagão Malheiro, human rights are underpinned by the recognition of the other. Slaves were unrecognized; they were only commodities. As free men and women after 1888, they were now recognized, at least in law.[103]

ⁱⁿⁿ

In 1889, a military coup overthrew the dynasty and established a republic. There was no revolution, no mass uprising. Doubts regarding the virtue of the monarchy had long circulated among the elite. Discontent had been rife in the army for many years. Patronage played a critical role—one segment of the army moved to establish its predominance before another. The imperial family and entourage boarded a ship bound for Portugal, and that was that.

What did all this mean for newly emancipated slaves, only eighteen months out of bondage? And for Brazil as a highly heterogeneous society? In the last two decades of the nineteenth century, Brazil developed pulsing cities, the beginnings of industrialization, and an expanding middle class, which chafed under the domination of the planter and merchant elite. The foundation of the republic was a response to these developments, another signal of Brazil's move toward modernity, one more effort to align the country with Europe. Liberalism's paradoxes remained, however. The power of race could not be lain to rest, not by the abolition of slavery and not by the establishment of an explicitly liberal republic.[104]

The establishment of the republic gave men, including new immigrants from Europe, political rights, much like those of the Euroamericans who settled in the Minnesota. A new constitution, proclaimed in 1891, had all the rhetorical trappings of the Enlightenment ideals of the American, French, and Latin American revolutions. Brazil was now a land of liberty and equality, the constitution asserted. It established literacy and maleness, but not property or race, as the prerequisites for voting. The Church lost its legally protected position, and new aristocratic titles were forbidden. Foreigners had only to reside in Brazil for two years to obtain citizenship. Once naturalized they enjoyed "all the civic and political rights of natural-born citizens."[105] However, the liberal constitutional order coexisted with the long-standing patronage system, which received a new lease on life in the late nineteenth century, aided by a federal system that left a great deal of power to local elites.[106]

Men had access to political rights in the Brazilian republic. Women, however, still were deprived of the most basic rights, like suffrage. Liberal reformers argued that women should concern themselves with home and family. They should have enough—but no more—education to enable them to raise upstanding (white male) Brazilian citizens.[107]

For most blacks and mixed-race citizens, the situation was much worse. Brazil had no formal system of discrimination and segregation like Jim Crow in the United States or apartheid in post-1948 South Africa. But it had discrimination aplenty. Under freedom as under slavery, individual blacks and mulattos could rise in Brazilian society. In the interior more than in the major cities, some of them held local offices and owned land. But those who rose high were, in fact, rare birds whose flights to the near heights of society were exceptional in the extreme.

For most blacks and mulattos, conditions remained dire despite the great achievement of slavery abolition and the establishment of a republic. The call for "democratization of the soil" had failed: the abolition law made no provisions whatsoever for land reform. Ex-slaves would have to find their own way to support themselves, which more often than not meant wage labor on the plantations in which they had formerly been enslaved.[108] Left to their own devices, ex-slaves now also had to compete with the sudden influx of European immigrants, primarily from Portugal and Italy. Few blacks were able to exercise suffrage rights because of the literacy requirement. In fact, electoral participation plummeted from 10 percent of the total population in 1872 to less than 1 percent in 1886, and was not much improved under emancipation.[109]

Brazil remained intensely race conscious, perhaps even more so after the legal category of slavery had been abolished. The Brazilian elite, always receptive to trends from Europe, had already found attractive positivism and social Darwinism. Now race science was added to the mix.[110] One of Brazil's leading lights, João Baptiste de Lacerda, the director of the National Museum of Rio de Janeiro, attended the First (and only) Universal Races Congress, held in London in 1911. He joined numerous renowned scientists, intellectuals, and political figures, W.E.B. Du Bois and Franz Boas among them.

Lacerda addressed the Congress on the problem of *metis*, or, as the English translation went, half-breeds.[111] It was a strange presentation, mixing racist and egalitarian views, but one that reflected Brazilian ideas both popular and scientific—and demonstrated that slave abolition hardly signified a commitment to racial equality. Lacerda lauded the mixing of races in Brazil—but only because it would eventually whiten the entire population and lead to the elimination of blacks as a group. The disappearance of the mixed-race population will "coincide with the parallel extinction of the black race in our midst."[112]

Lacerda was hardly unique. Nabuco and many others wrote similarly.[113] Brazil's great tragedy, they argued, was that slavery left behind so many black and mixed-race people. Unlike most European and North American intellectual racists of the day, they did not believe that race mixing led to the degeneration of the race. Mixing science (or pseudoscience) and hope, they believed that the whitening of the population would be an inevitable occurrence. It might take a century, but it would happen, and then Brazil would finally take its place among the great nations of the world. Hedging their bets on nature taking its course, the Brazilian elite, almost to a person, promoted restrictive immigration policies that barred additional people of African descent from entering the country, while promoting immigration from Europe.[114] A prosperous and creative Brazil, a Brazil where all would enjoy the rights of man—and they did mean man—would be a white Brazil.

Conclusion

"One day Le Corbusier said to me: When you design, you have the mountains of Rio in your eyes," spoke the great Brazilian architect Oscar Niemeyer to an interviewer shortly after the turn of the millennium.[115] Le Corbusier was right. Niemeyer's many buildings expressed in concrete, glass, and steel the captivating beauty that so many people, like Georg Heinrich von Langsdorff and Stefan Zweig, whom we encountered at the beginning of this chapter, found in the Brazilian landscape. But not only mountains. Niemeyer offered a more rounded description of his aesthetics: "I am not attracted to straight angles or to the straight line hard and inflexible, created by man. I am attracted to free-flowing, sensual curves. The curves that I find in the mountains of my country, in the sinuousness of its rivers, in the waves of the ocean, and on the body of the beloved woman. Curves make up the entire Universe, the curved Universe of Einstein."[116]

Niemeyer collaborated with Le Corbusier on the design for the UN building in New York, though he bowed to the wishes of his senior colleague and mentor. The result was a beautiful building that has become an icon of mid-twentieth-century modernism, but a rectilinear one. In the new city of Brasília, however, Niemeyer was able to let loose all his prodigious talents. He produced buildings with soaring curves, dramatically open interiors, and broad sheets of glass that let the Brazilian sun pour inside (see plates 11 and 12). The best of his buildings appear to defy gravity; massive in form, they seem to float above the ground.

> I visualized [the Palace of the Three Powers] rich in forms, dreams, and poetry . . . new forms, startling visitors by their lightness and creative liberty, forms that were not anchored to the earth rigidly and statically, but that uplifted the Palaces as though to suspend them, white and ethereal in the endless night of the highlands. Forms full of surprise and emotion, which delivered the visitor, if only momentarily, from the insurmountable difficulties with which life burdens man.[117]

Brasília was built from scratch, in the savanna, 750 miles from Rio with its beaches, bars, art galleries, and theaters, 600 miles from the industrial might of São Paulo. The idea to make a capital city in the interior had been around since the 1820s; President Juscelino Kubitschek made it so in just four years, from 1956 to 1960. He enlisted Niemeyer's other mentor, Lúcio Costa, to draft the overall plan for the city, Niemeyer to design the buildings.

Brasília, with its ministries, congress, and presidential residency, became the governing seat of the country. It was also a dramatic statement of Brazil as a modern country with an industrial economy, a vibrant culture, and a political system defined by citizenship and human rights. Niemeyer gave architectural form to the desires of Nabuco and so many other elite Brazilians from the nineteenth century onward—that their country be recognized as modern and progressive. "We wanted a world without borders; an open world, open for the exchange of thoughts and products. The UN building and Brasilia stood for this world," Niemeyer told his interviewer.[118]

Very soon, the world that Niemeyer adored would crash around him. Just four years after the opening of Brasília, the army carried out a coup. The military, with US support, established a dictatorship—Brazil's second in the twentieth century—justifying its actions with the standard anticommunist rhetoric of the Cold War. Niemeyer, a long-standing member of the Brazilian Communist Party, fled into exile. For almost twenty years he lived in Paris, until democracy, finally, was restored to Brazil. Great mobilizations, by members of the elite as well as the popular classes, akin to the abolitionist movement, ultimately brought down the dictatorship.

In 1988, a new constitution was promulgated. With amendments it remains in force to this day. It is strongly democratic. The preamble proclaims Brazil as a country with "social and individual rights, liberty, security, well-being, development, equality and justice as supreme values of a fraternal, pluralist and unprejudiced society."[119] The list of social rights is extensive, including, for example, 120 days' paid maternity leave. Children of foreigners born in Brazil are Brazilian citizens; foreigners resident for fifteen years can easily acquire citizenship.[120]

The legacy of slavery, however, is not so easily discarded by the great human rights provisions of the constitution. Brazil has one of the highest indices of social inequality in the world. Between 1960 and 1990, the top 10 percent of the population enjoyed an 8.1 percent increase in income; the bottom 50 percent a decrease of 3.2 percent. In 1990 the top 10 percent of the population possessed nearly half the income of the country, an increase of 10 percent since 1960. Black mean income in 1960 was less than half that of whites; mixed-race people closer to the black than the white level. In 1950 over half the black population but only one-quarter of the white population was illiterate. Careful analyses have demonstrated that the low mean income of blacks is not only related to poor education or dead-end jobs; sheer discrimination provides much of the reason.[121] Despite some narrowing of the spread of wealthy and poor over the past twenty-five years, Brazil sits at place 19 of 150 countries on the scale of unequal income distributions.[122]

Social inequality in Brazil largely aligns with race. Those at the top are disproportionately white—radically so; those at the bottom largely black. Around 2000, Afro-Brazilians constituted 44 percent of the population. At the University of São Paulo, the most prestigious institution of higher education, the student body numbering in the thousands included fewer than twelve Afro-Brazilians; the faculty even fewer.[123] Rio's favelas have grown dramatically since 1960 as poorer, black Brazilians pour into the city from the countryside.

All of this in a country that had no formal, legal racial discrimination or segregation, as did the United States and South Africa.[124] Yet an intense race consciousness prevails in Brazil. When a government agency in 1976 asked Brazilians to identify their skin color, 134 different classifications came up, including pure white, bronzed tan, cashew-like, orange, black, greenish, high pink, and many others.[125] One scholarly study identified 500 categories.[126] For many years, the slogan and ideology of Brazil as a "racial democracy" masked, at least in public discourse, the severe inequalities that defined the lives of black and mixed-race people, and limited the appeal of black-identity mobilizations. Left-wing parties, like Lula's (Luiz Inácio Lula da Silva) Workers' Party, have emphasized class issues and have been loath to discuss race or to develop policies of redress that are oriented specifically toward the black and mixed-race population.

❧

The emancipation of Brazilian slaves marked a huge advance. Like the other human rights achievements discussed in this book, it came about through popular activism—in this case, slave resistance and flight. Slaves posed a constant threat to liberal Brazil, but slaves could not liberate themselves. They needed support. That came from well-placed abolitionists, who built a parallel movement, one that tapped into international anti-slavery activism. The final blow came when slavery proved no longer economical in major areas of the country. However partial were the rights that blacks received in 1888, they at least received the most basic right—to be recognized as free persons.

More than anything else, the ideology and practice of race—slavery, systemic discrimination—in Brazil and many other places around the globe, shattered the universalist claims of liberalism, sharply delimiting those who had the right to have rights. The belief in inherited black inferiority, strengthened by so-called racial science, long outlasted the abolition of slavery. The close identity of race and class left many blacks and mulattos subject to deep-seated prejudices and a market economy that sometimes proved nearly as harsh as slavery itself, especially when, in the nineteenth and early twentieth centuries, and more recently with the rise of neoliberalism, a classical liberal perspective refused to adopt any kind of social policies that would have mitigated the workings of the market.

Abolition was a great achievement, but the line between slavery and freedom was not always as clear and firm as abolitionists, and slaves themselves, had hoped. And the legacy of slavery remains. Formal, legally enshrined rights are of fundamental importance. But they also require social capacities—to return to the argument of Martha Nussbaum and Amartya Sen discussed in the introduction—and a socially egalitarian order for people fully to exercise the rights laid out for them in constitutions and laws. The case of American Indians demonstrates the complexity of human rights, particularly the dilemma of collective rights—sovereignty on the reservations—and the protection of individuals. Brazil demonstrates the importance of social alongside political rights.

Brazil has no minorities. The population is too diverse, the classification categories so numerous as to be almost uncountable, the myth of racial democracy too strong. In other places in the late nineteenth century and still today—perhaps even more so today—many minorities believe their recognition as a group is the path to a life of rights-bearing citizenship. But identification as a minority can have highly ambivalent, and sometimes disastrous consequences, as we shall see with Armenians and Jews in Eurasia.

Chapter 5

Armenians and Jews

THE CREATION OF MINORITIES

༄

ON 27 June 1878, Catholicos Mkrtich Khrimian of the Armenian Apostolic Church wrote to the German chancellor, Otto von Bismarck. He and his colleague, Archbishop Khorine de Nar Bey, had been charged with expressing the "voices and aspiration of Armenians in Turkey" to the congress of European states that Bismarck had convened. The catholicos included with his letter a cache of documents that explained the "rights of Armenians," the same rights that have been accorded other Christian populations of Europe. The documents also supported the Armenian claim for wide-ranging autonomy within the Ottoman Empire. Khrimian then called on Bismarck to "invoke your protection in favor of [the Armenian] nation."[1]

The catholicos's submission to Bismarck and the Berlin Congress marked the debut of Armenians on the global political stage. Never before had they been represented at a congress of the European powers. Never before had their concerns and interests been so clearly expressed to an international audience.

Two weeks prior to the catholicos's letter, two representatives of the Alliance Israélite universelle had also written to Bismarck. The condition of Jews, especially in Romania and Serbia, was dire, Charles Netter and his colleague Kann explained. Despite pledges and agreements in the past, Jews throughout the region lived under continual persecution. Kann and Netter argued that only upon the principles of international law, the equality of all men, and religious liberty could peace be secured in Europe. The two representatives enclosed a memorandum signed by twenty-four Jewish organizations and individuals that called on the Berlin Congress to secure the rights of Jews, and thereby the peace of Europe.[2]

Unlike the Armenians, Jewish representatives had been present at earlier European conferences, at 1815 in Vienna and 1856 in Paris (to resolve the Crimean War). That representation had been limited to a few notables, the grand, wealthy men like the Rothschild brothers, Moses Montefiore, and Adolphe Crémieux who had entrée to European princes, prime ministers, and kings.[3] Their type was present in 1878 as well, notably in the person of the German-Jewish banker and Bismarck confidant Gerson von Bleichröder. But now, far more extensively than ever before, Jewish representatives mobilized public opinion and arrived in significant numbers in the host city of an international congress.[4]

Armenians and Jews *became* the quintessential minorities in 1878 as nation-state foundings and empire flounderings in the face of nationalist movements moved to the very center of European and global politics. Armenian and Jewish representatives believed that great-power recognition would provide them a lifeline of support and the rights their people deserved. Backed by the major European states, Armenians and Jews would be able to live in peace and prosper all across Eurasia. Yet the recognition of minority status, so often promoted down to our present day as the path to rights-bearing citizenship and full equality, contains within it all sorts of ambivalencies, one other fragile pane in the multistoried glass house of human rights. The lifeline for which Armenians and Jews desperately lunged carried a tag—"minority"—that would lead, ultimately, to the greatest tragedies in the histories of both groups.[5]

ℰℬ

In the last quarter of the nineteenth century, diplomacy could no longer occur exclusively behind closed doors. In a world linked ever more tightly by the revolutions in communications and transportation, news of battles and atrocities moved swiftly by telegraph to be rapidly published in newspapers with burgeoning circulations. The public sphere expanded notably in Asia, the Middle East, and parts of Africa, as well as in Europe and the Americas. Availing themselves of the new modes of communication and transport, Serbian officials, American Quakers and missionaries, British abolitionists, Armenians and Jews, Muslim villagers in Greece, and many others traveled to Berlin or sent letters and petitions that raised their concerns to the most important European congress between Vienna in 1815 and Paris in 1919.[6] They (or their letters) boarded steamships up the Danube and across the Mediterranean and the Atlantic; when they reached sea or inland ports, they continued their journey by rail to Berlin.

They addressed their missives to Bismarck, the congress convener and president. As a result, the German Foreign Office was deluged with letters and petitions; Berlin hotels were filled with visitors from as far away as Istanbul and Philadelphia. Bismarck no doubt never expected the outpouring that arrived in Berlin. Powerful and imposing as he was, Bismarck, at this moment, was only an expression of the larger global transformations of the nineteenth century.

The Berlin Congress convened during one of the high tides of nation-state building (the others would come after the two world wars of the twentieth century, as we shall see). German and Italian unification in 1871, the second founding of the United States through the Civil War and Reconstruction, the British Reform Act of 1867 that enfranchised most men, and the Meiji Restoration in Japan in 1876 are the most notable signs of the era. The Ottoman *Tanzimat* (reorganization), Russian reforms, and Austro-Hungarian *Ausgleich* (compromise) in the same era were more about empire renovation than nation-state formation, but the policies that the rulers implemented, even halfheartedly— constitutions, citizenship, representative organs, reformed legal codes, the abolition of serfdom (in Russia)—marked the somewhat desperate response of empires as they were pushed into the modern era of nation-states and human rights.

The Vienna Treaty in 1815 centered on dynastic legitimacy and state sovereignty within clearly defined borders. "His Highness [the King of Prussia] shall add to his titles [that] of Duke of Saxony" (among others); "His Highness the Duke of Saxe-Weimar shall assume the title of the Grand Duke of Saxe-Weimar"[7]—so ran much of the text of the Vienna Treaty, reflecting an earlier era of empires dominated by kings and emperors, dukes and princes. In sharp contrast, the Berlin Treaty in 1878 and even more so the Paris Peace Conference treaties after World War I were primarily about nation-states and the liberal principles that undergirded them—rights, constitutions, representation, and the rule of law. The transition from the Vienna to the Paris System marked the full-blown emergence of nation-states and human rights as the locus of global politics—and made ever more contested who, precisely, was a member of a nation and had the right to have rights.[8]

The Berlin Congress reflected these principles by adding four new nation-states to the map of Europe. It also marked the moment when minorities were created, Armenians and Jews the pacesetters. While the term itself was used only occasionally in 1878, the concern with the fate of these two populations in the new nation-states and one old empire, the Ottoman, marked the onset of an entirely new phase of European and global politics. By 1900, the words and phrases "minority," "minority problem," and "minority rights" had become commonplace. In 1919 at the Paris Peace Conference after World War I, they moved to the very center of domestic and international politics, and there they have remained down to our present day.

Minorities are an invention of the nation-state.[9] Under empires, all inhabitants were subjects, not citizens. In the hierarchical order typical of imperial rule, certain groups, defined by their religion, dominated the political and social order, like Muslims in the Ottoman Empire or Russian Orthodox Christians under the tsars. Those who did not belong to the dominant group—Jews and Muslims under the Romanovs, Jews and Christians under the Ottomans—were subjects of a lesser order. They had to pay special taxes and plea for approval to build and maintain their religious buildings. In public they had to display respect for the dominant religion. With some exceptions, like Spain in the late fifteenth century, no one denied their place in the imperial order, no one labeled them minorities, just subjects of a different (and lesser) religion. In some cases, as for a time under the Muslim Mughal emperors of India, the imperial regime actually promoted and celebrated the diversity of religions within the realm. In their own communities, people were allowed a wide range of self-government and the autonomy to practice their own religion.

The concept of minorities, in contrast, only truly developed in the modern era, when the nation-state was understood to be the representative of one particular population, and religious identities became politicized in national terms. "Bulgaria for Bulgarians" meant Bulgarian Orthodox Christians, and all others—Jews, Muslims, Greeks, Macedonians—were now minorities living in someone else's nation-state. A minority, once so classified, was always a visible disruption of the unity of the nation, and therefore a "problem."[10]

ço

Bismarck convened the Berlin Congress to resolve the many issues that had arisen from peasant and national revolts in the Balkans, starting in 1876, and the Russo-Turkish War of 1877–78. He was determined to bring the wars and rebellions to a conclusion that suited the interests of all the major states, Germany, of course, included. Convened just seven years after he had engineered the unification of the German nation-state, the Berlin Congress signaled Bismarck's determination to elevate Germany's international role—as he would also do in 1884–85 at the Berlin Conference on Africa (as we shall see in the next chapter).

Much like Greeks fifty years earlier, Bulgarian activists, brigands, and peasants had rebelled against oppressive Ottoman taxes and the unjust and arbitrary exercise of power by local officials. The Ottoman government responded in its typical fashion—that is, with astonishing brutality that crushed the uprising. Ottoman officials should have known better, given the Western response during the Greek rebellion. They missed the fact or did not care that in an age of mass communication, their misdeeds would become widely known. Indeed, the incident became a cause célèbre when the four-time British prime minister William Gladstone, summoning all his great rhetorical powers, published a pamphlet, *Bulgarian Horrors*, in which he described "crimes and outrages, so vast in scale as to exceed all modern examples, and so unutterably vile as well as fierce in character."[11] These horrors, according to Gladstone, had been perpetrated by the "Turkish race . . . [that] one great anti-human specimen of humanity." Wherever they go, he continued, they leave behind tracks of blood; they destroy civilization and rule by force, not law.[12] Like the Philhellenes a generation earlier during the Greek revolt, Gladstone levelled a blistering attack on the passivity of the British government. He called on his country to defend humanity and civilization by protecting the oppressed Christians living under Ottoman suzerainty. He rejected any claim that Balkan Christians might have also engaged in atrocities against Muslims or, indeed, against one another.

The instability in the Balkans gave Russia an opening to expand its influence. Under the pretext of doing just what Gladstone had prescribed—protecting fellow Christians—the Russian government declared war on the Ottoman Empire on 24 April 1877. The attack marked the eighth Russo-Turkish war in little over a century. The Russians had a more difficult time than they had anticipated, but they were able to seize large swaths of Ottoman land. In the Treaty of San Stefano, signed on 3 March 1878, Russia won significant territory from the Ottoman Empire in the Balkans and Eastern Anatolia and created a large Bulgaria. As in the 1820s, the other European states, now with Germany (not just Prussia) among them, thought Russia had gotten rather too powerful. Bismarck convened the Berlin Congress precisely to roll back these Russian gains. Unwittingly, he also inspired wide-ranging political mobilizations, most of them in support of nation-states and human rights.

Armenians came to Berlin not quite ready to demand their own nation-state. Such a claim would have been highly dangerous to the protagonists once they returned home to Istanbul and anywhere else in the Ottoman realm. Nor were the European powers prepared to support an independent Armenia. It would take another decade until Armenian political parties with explicit nationalist agendas emerged. In 1878, traditionally minded priests served as the spokesmen for the Armenian community. In their representation to the Berlin Congress, Catholicos Khrimian and Archbishop de Nar Bey carefully affirmed the loyalty of Armenians to the Ottoman Empire and rejected any demand for "political liberty"—that is, a separate nation-state. They characterized Armenians not as a national group, but as an ancient people who had preserved their historical memories, traditions, language, and religion.

At the same time, Catholicos Khrimian represented a new type of cleric, one who was an outspoken political activist with views bordering on nationalism. He was willing to work within the structures of the Ottoman Empire so long as the Western powers protected Armenians and supported their demand for autonomy. His proposal called for an international commission to oversee the implementation of the reforms that would ease the plight of Armenians.[13] The Sublime Porte and the palace, the two sites of imperial governance, responded with fury. They viewed these measures as a severe attack on Ottoman sovereignty and one more effort to dislodge still more Christians and Christian territory from Ottoman rule.

The Armenian effort to forge a formal link with the Great Powers added an entirely new dynamic to Armenian-Ottoman relations. Without using the term, both sides had begun to define Armenians as a minority—Armenians because they were seeking autonomy, a model that would reemerge globally with the minority protection treaties in 1919, the Ottomans because they increasingly came to see every Armenian as a member of an inherently disloyal subset of the Ottoman population. In 1878, Armenian representatives and Ottoman officials set out on a dangerous path.

For Jews, the Congress of Berlin presented an opportunity to reaffirm the principles of equality and religious liberty first established on a wide scale by the great revolutions of the late eighteenth and early nineteenth centuries.[14] Romania was the burning point because its treatment of Jews had been so discriminatory and its governments had resisted all external pressure to establish equality for Jews.[15] Sensing a once-in-a-lifetime chance to establish the "final regulation of the Jewish Question in the Balkan lands" that would put an end to discrimination and persecution, Jewish organizations all across Europe and North America met, argued, passed resolutions, wrote appeals to their governments, and publicized in newspapers the desperate condition of Romanian and other Eastern European Jews.[16]

The various national Jewish organizations coordinated their efforts, going far beyond the personal missives and conversations in which the Rothschilds and Montefiore had engaged with eminent leaders at previous international congresses. Jewish activists flooded Berlin with telegrams, letters, and petitions, all expressing grave concern for the condition of Jews in Eastern Europe, all calling for the emancipation of Jews.[17] As the opening of the Congress approached, Jewish community leaders from all around Europe and the United States arrived in Berlin. More sophisticated politically than the Armenians, more attuned to moving in high circles, they had meetings virtually every day with leading statesmen.[18] In so doing, Jews established in 1878 an innovative model of effective lobbying by an ethnic community.

Bleichröder, Bismarck's banker and a leading figure in the German Jewish community, lent his great influence to the effort. Bismarck, always quick to take advantage of a situation, used the convolutions of German private and public investments in Romanian railroads to exercise pressure on Romania. He happily used the demand for Jewish equality as one of his hammers.[19] For his part, Bleichröder advised his coreligionists to direct petitions to the German chancellor. To Bismarck, Bleichröder wrote: "For twenty-two years I have faithfully served your excellency without demanding any kind of remuneration. Now is the time for my payment: equal rights [*Gleichberechtigung*] for Romanian Jews."[20] Jewish lobbying was so effective that Jovan Ristić, the Serbian minister of foreign affairs, felt compelled to assure Bismarck that his country was completely tolerant and that Jews had "perfect equality" with their fellow citizens.[21]

The Alliance Israélite universelle and other Jewish organizations referred constantly to "equality under the law," "equal rights," "political rights," and "civil rights," all under the mantel of the nation-state.[22] Those who wrote in support of Jewish claims did the same. They included the American ambassadors to Austria and Germany, the latter none other than Bayard Taylor, whom we met in chapter 1 as one of our travelers to Asia and Africa. Taylor arrived in Berlin to take up his post just days before the opening of the Congress.[23]

Another innovation emerged at Berlin. For the first time in an international forum, Jewish leaders, more nimble than their Armenian counterparts, explicitly used the term "minority." Already gathered in Berlin, they penned yet another memo to Bismarck in which they appealed to him to ensure that the Congress address "the concern for the weak and oppressed minorities of every nationality and every confession" and ensure equal rights of all races and religions.[24]

Like Armenian and Jewish representatives, petitioners from all over Ottoman Europe, Muslims, Christians, and Jews, also invoked the language of equality and rights. No doubt Ottoman authorities organized many of these efforts. Nonetheless, they show how widely modern ideas of rights had disseminated and how political mobilizations had become a fixed feature of European politics, West and East, North and South. Muslims, Christians, and Jews, separately and occasionally together, combined traditional, religious-based appeals for redress with the modern language of the nation, equal rights, liberties, and minorities and majorities.

These words, phrases, and ideas could also be used as weapons in communal and national warfare. Muslims, Jews, Bulgarians, Greeks, and others—each group placed itself on the side of civilization and progress, and castigated its opponents as barbarians and savages who violated the principles of liberty and rights and conducted policies of extermination. Each group deployed identical terms. In so doing, they created unbridgeable political and social chasms.

A group of Muslim notables from Rumeli (Thrace), for example, wrote to Bismarck that Muslims stood for "justice . . . humanity, and civilization. . . . and our sacred rights," all of which were now gravely threatened by Bulgarians. They warned him that guaranteeing Bulgarians "exclusive rights . . . without any respect for the basic rights of others and especially Muslims" would violate the very principles that Bismarck and the Congress represented.[25] They charged that Bulgarians could not be trusted to uphold the values of civilization and humanity, and pleaded with Bismarck and the Congress not to allow an "ignorant minority that is consumed by blood and vengeance" to preside over a people "superior in administrative competence and religious tolerance." Bulgarians were trying to expel Muslims from Rumeli, the notables claimed. "Can humanitarian Europe, civilized Europe . . . remain passive when [such an action] would be an eternal stain on this century of enlightenment and progress?"[26]

Meanwhile, the Serb foreign minister Ristić denied any place for Muslims or even other Christians in the Serb nation-state. He wrote to Bismarck that Serbia for centuries had upheld "civilization" against the onslaught of the Ottomans. The Serbs were the only Christians "animated by a spirit of independence . . . [who] have not ceased to protest against the Ottoman exploitation." That struggle, extending over centuries, established the "right of the [Serb] nation to an independent political existence."[27] "Justice mandates," he claimed, a Serbian state with a homogeneous population and very extensive borders.[28] The Turks, according to Ristić, represented a grave threat to humanity. They prosecuted the war "against all the ideas of civilization but also against the general principles of modern international law."[29]

Occasionally, Muslims, Christians, and Jews petitioned together and claimed that their communities had long lived together peacefully under the Ottoman sultans, each respecting the rights of the others.[30] However much such appeals might have been orchestrated by the Ottoman authorities, they illuminate the fragile possibility of unity across religious and national lines against the new world order of exclusive nation-states with their dominant majorities and endangered minorities.

∾

The Berlin Treaty was signed on 13 July 1878. It confirmed the independence and sovereignty of Serbia, Bulgaria, Romania, and Montenegro out of Ottoman territory.[31] The four new countries in Europe's Southeast had to pay a price for their independence, and it came in the currency of constitutions, citizenship, and rights. To their dismay (Romania especially), the Great Powers forced them to establish civil and political rights for all people—and that meant preeminently Jews—and religious liberty.[32] Muslim property holders who left the countries still retained rights of ownership.[33]

The new countries were *nation*-states. Bulgaria meant the state of Bulgarians, Montenegro the state of Montenegrins, and so on. However, the population of each country remained highly diverse. Now Jews, Muslims, Vlachs, Bulgarians in Greece, Greeks in Bulgaria, and so on became *minorities*, even if the statesmen at Berlin did not yet use that term.

The Berlin Treaty also rolled back some of Russia's territorial gains in the Russo-Turkish War of 1877–78. Russia kept Ardahan, Kars, and Batum in Eastern Anatolia and parts of Bessarabia along the Black Sea, but was forced to renounce most of its other territorial gains from the initial Treaty of San Stefano. Bulgaria also lost a great deal of land.

The Ottomans had to pay a price for the rollback of Russia's most expansive territorial ambitions, and it came in the currency of minority protection. The Ottoman Empire, like the four new countries, had to implement civil and political rights and religious freedom for all peoples in the empire. Under duress, the Ottomans, according to article 61, agreed to undertake immediate "improvements and reforms" in the condition of Armenians and "periodically make known the steps taken to this effect to the powers, who will superintend their application."[34] The "Armenian Question" had become international; it also opened yet another pathway for great-power intervention in the Ottoman Empire, a source of grave concern to Ottoman officials and the general public.

Jews were ecstatic; Armenians left Berlin with mixed emotions. Armenians had not achieved autonomy, their major goal. Still, their appeal for redress and recognition had been recognized by the Great Powers. Article 61 gave them the lifeline for which they yearned, the protection of the West and Russia.[35] Now, they believed, the persecution and discrimination Armenians had suffered would be alleviated. Similarly, Jews believed that the provisions for equal citizenship and religious liberty would now become reality. Jewish leaders profusely praised and thanked Bismarck, and trumpeted that theirs was a victory for all humanity and the principle of justice.[36]

The text of the Berlin Treaty did not employ the term "minority," nor "citizens" or "nationalities." It defined populations by "religious creeds and confessions." In that sense, the Congress and the Treaty harkened back to the world of empires and religious identities, not nation-states and rights-bearing citizens. Still, by creating new states that everyone recognized as the expressions of particular populations and by trying to guarantee the rights of all groups within these nationally and religiously exclusive nation-states, the Berlin Treaty went a long way toward introducing the concept of minority and majority into policy making at the domestic and international levels in Eurasia. When the Great Powers denoted Bulgarians, Romanians, Serbs, and Montenegrins, they were clearly thinking of them as *nations* or even *races* (to use common nineteenth-century parlance), not as religious communities. They were admissible to the community of civilized nations, but only if they adopted its practices—namely, the prevailing liberal principles of civil and political rights, the rule of law, and religious liberty.

ℭℭ

Despite their high hopes, the conditions for Armenians in the Ottoman Empire and Jews in Eastern Europe only worsened over the next few decades.[37] Their recognition as minorities—whether or not the word itself was used—proved to be no panacea. Just the opposite. Both groups came to be seen as the ever-present irritant, the minority that by its very existence threatened the coherence, the very life, of the four new nation-states and the Ottoman Empire.

Armenians suffered land seizures by Kurdish bands and Ottoman officials and pogroms on a massive scale, often carried out with the connivance of the central government (see map 5.1 on Armenian populations in the Ottoman Empire).[38] The assaults on Armenians in the 1890s and in 1909 resulted in thousands of deaths. Across Europe and North America, missionaries, reformers, women and peace activists, and many others organized relief efforts on a scale rarely seen before.[39] Thousands more Armenians left their homeland in search of a more secure and better life. They fled to France, the United States, Latin America, and many other places around the globe, a constituent element of the epic population movements of the nineteenth and early twentieth centuries described in chapter 1.

Jews fared no better. Discrimination and pogroms, especially in the Russian Empire and Romania, fueled the great Jewish migration across the Atlantic and to Western Europe—2.5 million people—another portion of the global population movements in this period.[40] Romania maintained its unsavory reputation, leading to protests by Jewish

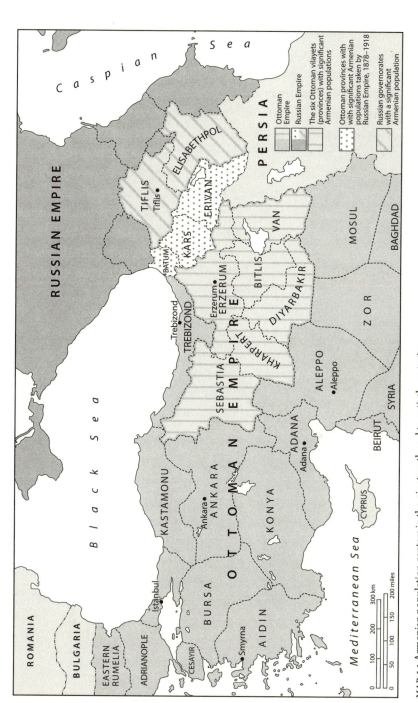

MAP 5.1 Armenian population centers in the nineteenth and twentieth centuries.

communal organizations and some governmental leaders all across the Western world.[41] Conditions were so bad that Jewish organizations promoted and organized Jewish emigration from Romania.

Muslims also found their situation highly fragile in the new Christian-dominated states. Like Jews and Armenians, they migrated or were expelled. Balkan Muslims had a nearby place to go: the Ottoman Empire, Anatolia in particular. They left in droves because they saw their life prospects drastically diminished in the nation-states defined by their majority Christian populations.[42] Moreover, beginning in 1862 and 1863, the Russian and Ottoman empires agreed on a series of population exchanges of Christians and Muslims in the Caucasus, probably the first bilateral agreements of this sort. These actions were not total in character, the way the deportations of the twentieth century would be, and were not yet geared toward creating ethnic, national, or racial homogeneity as an intrinsic aspect of state and nation building.[43] In that sense, they bear all the hallmarks of traditional politics. But the fact that the Ottoman and Russian empires concluded treaties legitimizing the compulsory removal of populations was a harbinger of things to come.

The Great Powers proved to be fickle benefactors of the two minorities. Certainly, no country was going to risk war to protect Armenians or Jews. The Great Powers offered little more than occasional rhetorical protests over their treatment, sometimes not even that. In the era of Weltpolitik under Kaiser Wilhelm II, beginning in the 1890s, Germany defined the Ottoman Empire as a key site of imperial interest. Germany sought not colonies, but political influence and markets for German goods, opportunities for German investments, and a place to contest British, French, and Russian primacy. Like Britain, though for different reasons, Germany sought to maintain the integrity of the Ottoman Empire. For many German officials and imperialist entrepreneurs, Armenians counted not as brother Christians who had to be protected, but as a disruptive minority that constantly threatened the stability of the empire.[44]

❧

The Balkan Wars marked a fearsome and politically powerful interlude between the Congress of Berlin and the outbreak of World War I. The wars entrenched more deeply into global politics the model of exclusive nation-states with unwanted minorities, and political rights reserved for the majority. The impact of the Balkan Wars reverberated far beyond the limited geography of Southeastern Europe.

The two wars, 8 October to 3 December 1912 and 29 June to 30 July 1913, were extraordinarily brutal precisely because nationalist sentiment imbued the Balkan states. The Ottoman Empire, now under the Young Turks, fought desperately to maintain the integrity of its domains against the threat of nationalism. Bulgaria, Romania, Greece, and Serbia launched the war to drive the Ottomans out of Europe. Within this larger war, each of the four countries turned on the minorities within its own borders.[45]

Jews and Muslims everywhere suffered violent pogroms, as did Greeks in Bulgaria and Bulgarians and Albanians in Serbia. The Balkan states sought to destroy two essential principles, one old, one new: the legacy of the Ottoman Empire, in which peoples of diverse ethnicities and religions mostly coexisted despite the absence of equality among them, and the most far-ranging liberal conception of a polity in which all male inhabitants could be rights-bearing citizens.

Bulgaria was the major victor in the first war, which then led the others to join together and push back against the very substantial expansion of its territory. The Great Powers, fearing a spiral of instability and the demise of the Ottoman Empire, reluctantly intervened, forcing a settlement that resulted in a larger Greece, a chastened Bulgaria, and an Ottoman Empire with only the barest sliver in Europe, a huge blow to an empire whose European domains had once stretched almost to Vienna.

The human costs of the two Balkan wars were immense, in direct killings and in new waves of expulsions and migrations. Following the wars, treaties among Greece, Bulgaria, and the Ottoman Empire led to mass deportations, each of the Balkan countries determined to rid itself of minorities who by their very presence disrupted the drive toward homogeneity on the part of the nation-states.[46] Even the long-lived Ottoman Empire, as we shall see shortly in more detail, once renowned for its diversity and relative tolerance, sought to become more clearly Turkic and Muslim in character. Tens of thousands of Muslims were forced out of their homelands by their Christian neighbors or the Bulgarian, Greek, Serb, or Montenegrin authorities. The Ottomans deported some hundred thousand Aegean Greeks to Greece in 1913. By one scholarly estimate, on the eve of World War I, refugees from the Balkans and Caucasus comprised fully 13 percent of Anatolia's population.[47] Salonika, an Ottoman city in which Sephardic and Romiot Jews had flourished for centuries, now came under Greek control. Jews could expect only a deterioration in their living circumstances.[48] In a repeat of 1878, Western Jews lobbied their governments, requesting their intervention with the Balkan states to guarantee the security and equality of Jews.[49] But all the pronouncements and memos by Western statesmen did little to stave off the disasters that befell minorities in each of the states.

World War I began only thirteen months after the end of the Balkan Wars. A war among states, it too swiftly became a war among peoples, and thereby opened up all the issues of nation-state creations; majorities and minorities; and who, precisely, would have the right to have rights.[50] The war shattered much in its four years, first and foremost soldiers' lives: over seventeen million dead in total, more than twenty million physically wounded, many more who suffered psychologically from the experience of battle. Women endured exploitative conditions in war factories, severe food shortages at home, and fractured families. Three empires, the Ottoman, Russian, and Habsburg, collapsed. Britain and France drew on their colonial subjects as combatants and support personnel, adding new elements of instability to imperial relations. Sexual and other social and cultural mores underwent a sea change. Mahatma Gandhi's famous riposte when queried about his thoughts regarding Western civilization—"it would be a good idea," he said—was never truer than at the war's end. In tatters lay the West's claim to represent progress, civilization, justice, humanity itself.

❧

Amid all these upheavals, the Ottoman Empire under the Young Turks carried out the second genocide of the twentieth century—the unfortunate distinction of being the first victims of genocide after 1900 goes to the Herero and Nama in Namibia (to be discussed in the next chapter). In the nineteenth century, slavery represented the greatest opposition to human rights, as we saw in chapter 4, on Brazil. In the twentieth century, genocide served as the ultimate challenge to a world of rights-bearing citizens.

The Committee of Union and Progress (CUP, Unionist, or, colloquially, Young Turks) had first come to power through a revolution in 1908 and then more thoroughly in a coup d'état in 1913.[51] Its leaders—the triumvirate of Talaat, Enver, and Djemal, pashas all—presided over a great, long-lasting empire, yet one suffering disasters of all sorts. Just in the last years before World War I, the Ottomans had lost territory in North Africa, among the islands of the Eastern Mediterranean, and in the Balkans. The losses in the Balkans included the birthplaces of many leading Young Turks, who hailed from places like Albania and Salonika or the Caucasus.[52]

Initially, the Young Turks sought to preserve the multiethnic and multireligious character of the empire.[53] Quite quickly, however, their political goals became more exclusively Turkic in character, propelled especially by the military and diplomatic catastrophes and their own schooling in Western nationalist ideas. The Young Turks moved increasingly toward a conception of a national empire, a hybrid political entity that would preserve the vastness and diversity of the Ottoman realm and, at the same time, greatly enhance the preeminence of Muslim Turks.[54] The precise ideological boundaries were often blurred, but already in the last decade of the nineteenth century young Ottoman reformers articulated a new ideology of Turkish nationalism.[55] On the verge of World War I, the Young Turks' nationalism—however entwined it remained with their desire to revive the empire—targeted Armenians, Assyrians, and Greeks as threatening and disloyal minorities.

When the Young Turks took the Ottoman Empire into World War I on the side of the Central Powers, they tied their fate to Germany's.[56] The war quickly proved to be yet another catastrophe, especially with the Russian advance through the Caucasus and into Eastern Anatolia, precisely where the Armenian population was concentrated. The specter of defeat and the extreme circumstances of total war offered the Young Turks the possibility for radically revamping the demography of the empire, making its core regions more decisively Muslim and Turkic.

They turned on those they deemed enemies who threatened the very existence of the empire.

That was the setting in which the deportations and killings of the Armenians and Assyrians unfolded, beginning in February 1915 and accelerating through the spring and summer and into 1916 in their most concentrated phase (see maps 5.2 and 5.3). Pontic and Aegean Greeks endured on-again, off-again deportations to Greece.[57] The statistics are imprecise, but the Young Turk regime killed circa one million Armenians, around 60 percent of the prewar population, in a deliberate process designed to rid Anatolia of those whom the Young Turks considered the major threat to the Turkic character of the empire they sought to maintain and expand.

"We must create a Turkish bloc that is free from foreign elements so that the European powers will never again be given the opportunity to intervene in the internal affairs of Turkey," said Talaat Pasha—interior minister, later grand vezier as well, and the chief architect of the genocide—to Konstantin von Neurath, the undersecretary in the German embassy.[58] Minister of War Enver Pasha justified the annihilation of the Armenians to the mercurial journalist, foreign-policy meddler, and Turcophile Ernst Jäckh by arguing that the Turkish Empire had had to secure itself against an Armenian revolution that had broken out in the rear of its troops. Talaat made clear, according to Jäckh, "that he greeted the annihilation of the Armenians as a political relief."[59] In a memorandum, Talaat wrote, "the work that is to be done must be done *now*; after the war it will be too late," obviously referring to the deportations and killings.[60] In this way, Young Turk leaders openly and vividly articulated their goals to their German allies.

Together, the Central Powers and the Ottoman Empire went down to disastrous defeat. From the once-great empire that had stretched across Europe, Anatolia, and the Middle East, only parts of Anatolia remained under the control of the various successor Ottoman and Turkish governments.

American president Woodrow Wilson had proclaimed that the war had been fought to make the world safe for democracy. Now he, the other Allied victors—David Lloyd George, Georges Clémenceau, and

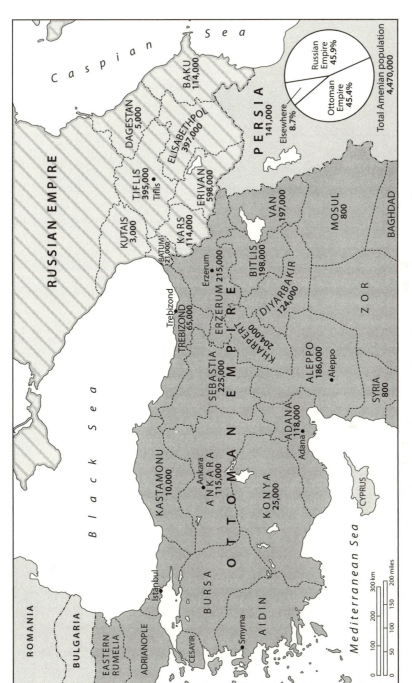

MAP 5.2 Armenian population around 1914. (Map adapted from original by Andrew Anderson, by permission.)

Caspian Sea

RUSSIAN EMPIRE

BAKU 114,000

DAGESTAN 5,000

ELISABETHPOL 397,000

PERSIA 141,000

Total Armenian population 4,470,000

Russian Empire 45.9%

Elsewhere 8.7%

Ottoman Empire 45.4%

TIFLIS 395,000
Tiflis

ERIVAN 598,000

KUTAIS 3,000

KARS 114,000

BATUMI 21,000

VAN 197,000

MOSUL 800

BAGHDAD

BITLIS 198,000

Erzerum

ERZERUM 215,000

DIYARBAKIR 124,000

Trebizond

TREBIZOND 65,000

KHARPERT 204,000

ZOR

SEBASTIA 225,000

OTTOMAN EMPIRE

ALEPPO 186,000
Aleppo

SYRIA 800

Black Sea

KASTAMONU 10,000

ADANA 118,000
Adana

ANKARA 115,000
Ankara

KONYA 25,000

CYPRUS

Istanbul

BURSA

AIDIN

Smyrna

Mediterranean Sea

ROMANIA

BULGARIA

EASTERN RUMELIA

ADRIANOPLE

CESAYIR

0   100   200   300 km
0   50 100 150 200 miles

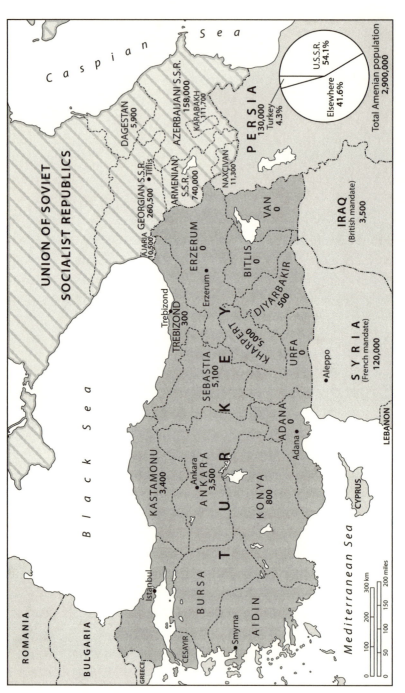

MAP 5.3 Armenian population around 1926. (Map adapted from original by Andrew Anderson, by permission.)

Vittorio Orlando—and a host of lesser figures had to make good on that promise. They had to construct a global peace for the first global war of the twentieth century. The leaders convened in Paris in January 1919. French crowds feted Wilson, the first US president to travel abroad while in office, all along the route from ship's dock in Cherbourg to Paris.

The Paris System was the outcome: a postwar world defined by nation-states and human rights; the protection of minorities within those states; and the civilizing mission for those deemed not yet fully mature politically—namely, the new Eastern European states (a reprise, more radically so, of the decisions of the Berlin Congress), the former German colonies in Africa and the Pacific, and Ottoman territories in the Middle East.[61] All the tendencies at work in the nineteenth century, all the particular problems of nation-state foundings and the question of who, in fact, had the right to have rights—evident in Greek independence, Indian removals, slave emancipations, colonial practices—emerged in concentrated form at the Paris Peace Conference.

The Paris System made more robust the link between national citizenship and the right to have rights, and made minorities and colonized populations ongoing "problems." It also masked the fact that Britain, France, Italy, the United States, and Japan were, at one and the same time, nation-states and empires that presided over colonial populations in Africa, the Middle East, and Asia.

President Wilson had established the Commission of Inquiry in 1917 to plan the peace. Its legion of experts, men armed with maps, statistics, and historical studies, accompanied the president to Paris. The British and French also had their specialists on hand. All these men (nary a woman among them) sought to define exactly which nation fit into what borders. By this point, the concept of majorities and minorities had become second nature to all these people. But the Americans especially were flummoxed by the great diversity of populations all across Eurasia and the Middle East. Their desire to create homogeneous nations under the state could not be fully implemented. Instead, they tried to figure out how to protect minorities in the new national states, and how to educate natives and Eastern Europeans for civilization. The Commission of Inquiry wrote about the need for "safeguarding . . . minorities or weak [i.e., colonized] peoples" and ran together widely strewn geographic areas including Russia, the Balkans, Anatolia, Pacific islands, and Africa, indicating how closely the planners linked Eastern Europe with Africa and other imperial zones.[62] These populations needed protection, while new states had to be forced to abide by liberal standards in order to be admitted into the family of "civilized nations."[63]

The logic of self-determination, posed implicitly at the Berlin Congress, became explicit and took on even greater urgency at Paris. Both Wilson and the Bolshevik leader Vladimir Lenin had trumpeted the concept, which echoed around the globe, much to Wilson's chagrin.[64] How could new sovereign, self-determining nation-states be founded out of the wreckage of the Ottoman, Habsburg, and Russian empires when every attempt to draw boundaries left substantial minorities in place? Two solutions emerged: minority populations could be either protected or removed. They would be the recipients of rights or the objects of deportations, a dual-track policy that would reverberate all through the twentieth and into the twenty-first century.

Even more so than in Berlin in 1878, representatives of civic and religious organizations deluged Paris and knocked on the door, desperate to get a hearing and have some influence on the final treaty. Pacifists, women's groups, trade unionists, Africans, Middle Easterners, Vietnamese, clerics, missionaries—they all filled Parisian hotels and boarding houses, wrote up memoranda and petitions, and sought meetings with the major statesmen and their advisers. Steamships and railroads were more powerful and spacious than in 1878. They crossed the oceans, seas, and land more quickly, and the telephone complemented the telegraph. On the periphery of Europe, from America and revolutionary Russia, rang the calls for liberty, freedom, rights, and self-determination.

Among those who came to Paris were Armenians and Jews, the quintessential minorities. They returned to an international congress more thoroughly prepared than they had been in 1878. Jews wanted protection; Armenians wanted a state. The one would be successful, the other not. Both efforts signified that in the Paris System era, rights were attainable only through national belonging.

All across Europe and North America and places as far afield as South Africa, Jews mobilized. They met in local, regional, and national settings, as socialists, Zionists, assimilationists, businessmen, politicians, rabbis, and any other category one can imagine. They drafted petitions and pronouncements, sent them on to national bodies and to the self-constituted Jewish leadership in Paris. Jewish activists published pamphlets and newspaper articles. They worked at the popular level and in the old-fashioned way of diplomacy, meeting prominent persons and their assistants in offices and conference rooms over tea, sherry, whiskey, or cognac.

It was an extraordinary effort, marked by a mixture of fear and foreboding at the fate of Eastern European Jews, and great optimism and hope for the future.[65] The entire movement drew on Jewish self-organizing going back to the Berlin Congress; at Paris, the efforts were even more extensive and visible.

Yet Jews were divided by an East-West border, a geographic frontier representing deeper social and political differences. The divide, not surprisingly, turned on the nationalities question. Eastern European Jews, Zionists and socialists, wanted Jews defined as a nationality. Leo Motzkin, the secretary-general of the Comité des délégations juives, the major representative organ of Eastern European Jews at Paris, wrote that Jews had to be treated as a "national organism," not as a "religious community."[66] Only if Jews were recognized as a nation, Eastern European Jews argued, could the "rights of Jews be protected"—the latter an idea spurred along by the British government's Balfour Declaration of 1917, which promised British support for a Jewish homeland.[67] For the Westerners, Jews should live as equal citizens of their respective states. Jews, they argued, were simply Americans, or British, or French "citizens of Jewish faith," and that model needed to be extended to Eastern Europe.

The French Alliance Israélite, Joint Foreign Committee of the Board of Deputies of British Jews and the Anglo-Jewish Association, and the American Jewish Committee closely coordinated their activities and won access to the major statesmen at the Peace Conference (see figure 5.1). Western European Jews, more assimilated into their liberal societies,

FIGURE 5.1 Lucien Wolf, 1907. Wolf (1857–1930) was the leader of the major British Jewish organizations. Looking for all the world like an English aristocrat, Wolf moved easily in high governmental and diplomatic circles. Along with American and French Jewish leaders, with whom he often sparred, Wolf helped ensure that the peace treaties included minority protection. Jewish leaders were convinced that they had won a great victory at the Paris Peace Conference. However, the rise of antisemitism and the Nazi seizure of power destroyed the minority protection system. (© National Portrait Gallery, London.)

more experienced and successful, were also more attuned to the Allied position and managed to thoroughly sideline their more radical Eastern European brethren.[68]

Whatever the national, ideological, and religious differences among Jews, the personal animosities and national jealousies that lingered long after Paris, all parties understood that rights were defined not in terms of autonomous individuals, but by membership in a national collective. Even when the term "human rights" surfaced, as it did occasionally, its advocates never departed from the idea that rights were encased within the nation-state.[69] Either way, it was Jews as national beings, not autonomous individuals, who would be rights-bearing citizens.

Most major Allied statesmen recognized the necessity of minority rights, but did not go down that road happily. They worried that the new states would be inherently unstable if minorities as such were granted legal status.[70] Yet the Allied powers also recognized that Eastern European Jews needed special protection given the long history of discrimination and outright violence they had suffered. The Eastern European states could not yet be trusted to ensure equality of all religions, and their societies were not yet fully civilized.[71] They had to be supervised, more thoroughly than had been the case after 1878. Hence, Jews and others should be granted special recognition as minorities and protected by the League of Nations through a new mechanism—the minority protection treaties.

The target states, Poland especially, put up fierce resistance, just as the Balkan states had in 1878. The Poles charged that explicit minority protection clauses signified unwarranted interference in their internal affairs. They worried that any kind of recognition of Jews as a community, religious or national, would lead to constant instability, a concern the Allies shared. They raised the telling critique that Britain, France, the United States, and Italy did not have to sign such provisions for their own countries.[72]

All the protestations from Poland and the other Eastern European states amounted to naught. Too much was at stake. The Bolsheviks were in power in Russia, multiple wars raged in Anatolia, the Habsburg Empire had unraveled, and Central and Eastern Europe seemed adrift in revolutions, pogroms, and civil wars. The Poles, Czechs, and others would get their respective states only if they signed on to the minority protection treaties—as they all did, just as their Balkan forebears in 1878 had agreed, rhetorically, to establish political and civil rights for all citizens in order to get their independence and sovereignty.

The treaty with Poland, signed at Versailles on 28 June 1919, the same day that Germany reluctantly signed its treaty, served as the model for the other agreements: seven more in 1919 with Czechoslovakia, Yugoslavia, Romania, Greece, Austria, Bulgaria, and Hungary. An additional ten followed: Lithuania, Latvia, Estonia, Albania, Turkey, Iraq, Upper Silesia, the Free City of Danzig, the Free Port of Memel, and Finland for its Aaland Islands.[73] The minority protection provisions explicitly built on the Berlin Treaty of 1878. Typically, the Polish treaty did not deploy the word; it simply called people "inhabitants of Poland who differ from the majority of the population in race, language, or religion."[74] But the treaty did afford minorities—and in Poland that meant preeminently Jews—civil and political rights and a significant degree of autonomy over education and religious affairs.

The Versailles Treaty also contained the founding document of the League of Nations, Wilson's cherished creation. It defined the League as the guarantor of minority protection with supervisory and interventionist powers (unlike the Berlin Treaty, in which the Great Powers granted themselves supervisory rights). On that basis, the League built an elaborate mechanism for protecting minorities. Over the span of its life until 1939, the Minorities Commission investigated stacks of petitions concerning violations of minority rights and issued hundreds of reports.[75] Sometimes, in very specific cases of discrimination, the Minorities Commission actually had an impact, even though the overall conditions of life for many minorities deteriorated drastically in the interwar period—with the notable exception of the Soviet Union in the 1920s and 1930s, which promoted the cultural and economic development of many (though certainly not all) nationalities (as we shall see in chapter 9).

The Paris Peace Conference and the League of Nations brought the concept of minority rights and protection into the very center of the international system. As in 1878, Jews relished their victory. The Alliance

Israélite wrote that the treaty "consecrate[s] the principle of the equality of rights among all the subjects of the new Polish state."[76] The Board of Deputies of British Jews trumpeted its accomplishments, proclaiming the treaties not only satisfactory for Jews, but also a standard of "political liberty and social justice" for all peoples.[77]

The victory would prove short-lived. The very same principle that defined populations as minorities, placed them under protection, and granted them rights also served to underpin forced removals of minority populations.

ℰℐ

The successful Turkish nationalist movement of Mustafa Kemal (later Atatürk) completely undermined the Treaty of Sèvres, one of the five original Paris Peace Conference treaties, this one between the Allies and the successor state of the Ottoman Empire. His armies defeated the Greek invasion of Anatolia, launched in 1919 with the support of Britain, France, and Italy, and assumed control over a significantly larger region than Sèvres had envisioned. In the process, the Turkish nationalist army destroyed the *Megali* (Great Idea) of a revived Greek Mediterranean empire and the hopes of both Armenians and Kurds for the states that each had been promised by the Allies in the Treaty of Sèvres. The Allies convened the Lausanne Conference in November 1922 to formulate a new treaty with Turkey. They had a long list of critical issues to resolve: they had to fix Turkey's borders; come to a new agreement on ship traffic through the Straits; determine various restitution and reparations claims; decide on the capitulations (the privileges that Europeans had been granted in the Ottoman Empire); and settle the fate of the oil-rich city and region of Mosul, whether it would become part of British-dominated Iraq or of Turkey.

Most significantly, Lausanne took the meaning of the five Paris treaties to their logical conclusion by authorizing the deportations of over one million Christians from Anatolia to Greece and around 350,000 Muslims from Greece to Turkey. The treaty made minorities out of Greeks in Turkey and Turks in Greece, thereby affirming the principle of homogeneity under the state and the understanding of rights as rooted in national citizenship. The Lausanne population exchange was no violation but an intrinsic element of the principles enunciated at Paris.[78]

The initial idea for the Greek-Turkish exchange came either from Eleutherios Venizelos, the Greek prime minister, or from Fridtjof Nansen, the League of Nations' first High Commissioner for Refugees.[79] Venizelos was enraptured with the notion of moving around hundreds of thousands of people to create homogeneous states (see figure 5.2).[80] He had proposed the idea in London in 1913 at the conference to settle the Balkan Wars, and afterward in negotiations with the Ottoman Empire and Bulgaria.[81] To Venizelos, Greek rights could only be secured in a Greek nation-state that was cleansed of substantial minority populations. In this way, he was a reincarnation one hundred years later of the Greek rebels of the 1820s.

However, the victory of Kemal's Turkish nationalist army convinced a devastated Venizelos that the dream of a revived Greek Mediterranean empire had turned into the "Asia Minor catastrophe," typified symbolically by the burning of Izmir (Smyrna) in September 1922 and the hasty and chaotic evacuation of Greeks and Armenians as the Turkish forces took the city. Venizelos proposed the exchange to Mustafa Kemal, who responded to the idea with alacrity. By this time, hundreds of thousands of Greeks had already fled Anatolia for Greece, so the convention concluded on 30 January 1923 partly legitimated in international law the facts on the ground. The agreement was then attached—and thereby received international sanction—to the Lausanne Treaty, which was signed on 24 July 1923. Article 1 of the convention mandated "a compulsory exchange of Turkish nationals of the Greek Orthodox religion established in Turkish territory, and of Greek nationals of the Moslem religion established in Greek territory. These persons shall not return to live in Turkey or Greece respectively without the authorisation of the Turkish Government or of the Greek Government respectively."[82]

The obligatory and sweeping character of the exchange could not have been more clearly and forcefully stated. Lausanne enshrined the

FIGURE 5.2 Eleutherios Venizelos, 1919. Venizelos (1864–1936) was the leading political figure in Greece in the first part of the twentieth century. He was a major advocate of an expanded Greece and of population exchanges to create homogeneous states in the Balkans. He served as the prime minister of Greece from 1910 to 1920 and from 1928 to 1933. (Photograph by Harris and Ewing, Library of Congress, Prints and Photographs Division, LC-USZ62–85047.)

overarching principle of national homogeneity and the notion that minorities everywhere were a "problem." The price to pay was the forced removal of over 1.5 million people.[83]

As with the minority protection provisions, the major powers were not enthusiastic about the population exchange; many international legal experts strongly objected to it.[84] According to the stenographer's report, Lord Curzon, British foreign secretary and the major figure at Lausanne, claimed that compulsory exchange of populations was a "solution extremely vicious and for which the world will bear a heavy price for a hundred years to come. He is repulsed by it."[85] Later on, toward the close of the first round of the negotiations, Curzon asserted that "all of the delegations, and particularly those of the two powers especially interested—Turkey and Greece—view with horror and almost consternation the principle of obligatory exchange." He asserted that the conference had only agreed to it because "the greater homogeneity of the population [will result in] the disappearance of the causes of ancient and deep-rooted conflicts."[86] Venizelos claimed that Greece viewed the compulsory exchange with "particular antipathy."[87]

The leaders shed crocodile tears. If these sentiments rang at all true—most unlikely in the case of Venizelos; Lord Curzon; and İsmet İnönü, the lead Turkish delegate and later president of the Republic of Turkey—they did little to impede the flow of events (see figure 5.3). Venizelos, as we have just seen, time and again had called for population exchanges. İnönü was a major figure in the Turkish nationalist movement, whose armies had carried out all sorts of depredations against Greeks and remaining Armenians in Anatolia in an effort to finish the work of the Armenian Genocide. Curzon had spent years administering the British Empire, including as viceroy of India, where he had sought to engineer the partition of Bengal, reputedly for administrative purposes. But an ethno-religious dimension fueled this effort, because Curzon's plan would have entailed a partial separation of Muslim and Hindu populations.[88] As for the other powers, their delegates raised only a few scruples.

Two terms entered diplomatic parlance at Lausanne—"population exchange" and "population unmixing." Both pallid phrases, they masked the sheer misery and desperation of Muslims and Christians as they

FIGURE 5.3 Turkish delegation at Lausanne, 15 July 1923. The Lausanne Treaty marked the first international legitimation of forced deportations. Many Greek refugees had already fled Anatolia, but the treaty made compulsory the removal of the remaining Greeks, as well as Muslims from Greece. In total, nearly 1.5 million people were displaced. İsmet İnönü, foreign minister and leader of the Turkish delegation and later president of the Republic of Turkey, is seated fourth from left. (Ullstein-bild.)

were forced out of their ancestral homes, leaving Anatolia, for the first time in two millennia, mostly devoid of a Greek population, and a good part of Greece without Muslims for the first time in nearly six hundred years. For each group, the integration into the Greek or Turkish nation-state and society proved a wrenching experience that continued over generations, traces of which can still be found today. Fully one-quarter of Greece's population after 1923 was composed of refugees from Turkey, an astounding figure. In Turkey the exiled numbers were smaller, forming about 4 percent of the total population, but these individuals joined an almost continual stream of Muslim refugees produced since the 1860s.[89] Neither reality is in the least captured by the term "population exchange," the phrase used in the official documents of the Lausanne Treaty, nor the even more egregious term invented by Lord Curzon, "unmixing of peoples," as if there were something unnatural in the fact that people of different identities lived side by side and interwoven.

For the first time in a prime arena of international politics, forced population movements were not the result of the exclusive actions of a victorious state or, as in the 1860s and in the wake of the Balkan Wars, bilateral agreements, but of a multilateral treaty. Statesmen and diplomats remembered. For decades afterward they considered Lausanne a great accomplishment, a model way of establishing nation-states, securing the rights of national citizens, and managing ethnic and national conflicts—as we shall see in chapter 9 on Palestine/Israel.

⁊

Armenians also found their way to Paris (see figure 5.4). As at Berlin in 1878, they lagged behind Jews in terms of organizational prowess and influence. Now they also represented a devastated community. More than one million Armenians had been killed, along with some tens of thousands of Assyrians. Armenian survivors, numbering in the hundreds of thousands, eked out a life in refugee camps, neighborhoods, and orphanages across the Middle East, Russia, and Western Europe. Some would soon find their way across the Atlantic. In the last year of war, an Armenian Republic had been founded in Transcaucasia. It was a fragile thing, buffeted on all sides. Russian revolutionaries, Bolsheviks and Mensheviks; Russian counterrevolutionaries; various nationalist groups and armies in the Caucasus, notably Georgian, Azeri, and Armenian; the emergent Turkish nationalist army; Germans for as long as World War I continued; and the British and French, who had occupied Istanbul and other key strategic locations in Anatolia and the Caucasus—all contested for power in the region.[90]

Armenians evoked great sympathy at Paris. They were the fellow Christians who had been slaughtered by a Muslim power that had fought with the Allies' enemies during World War I. Perhaps the Allies

FIGURE 5.4 Armenian delegation at the Paris Peace Conference, 1919. Armenians first made their entrance on the global political stage at the Berlin Congress in 1878. They were better prepared in 1919, although the Paris Peace Conference came hard on the heels of the Armenian Genocide and while conflicts were still raging in the Caucasus. The Armenians along with the Kurds were the great losers at Paris. Each had been promised a state, perhaps under an American mandate. The victory of the Turkish nationalist forces under Mustapha Kemal (later Atatürk), Western fears of Bolshevik power, and revival of American isolationism put an end to such plans. (ARF Archives, Watertown, MA.)

even felt a tinge of guilt at their inability to prevent the extermination of Armenians despite all the proclamations of support, all the diplomatic maneuvering, in 1878 and the decades afterward.

American missionaries in particular had had a strong presence in Anatolia, dating back to the 1830s. Their initial efforts to convert Muslims had met with virtually no success. Instead, they had turned their attention to one of the most ancient Christian communities and had sought to make Protestants out of the Armenians, who were overwhelmingly Gregorian Christians. That effort had more success. As they did elsewhere around the world, American missionaries established schools, hospitals, and colleges. At home in the United States, their co-religionists had organized support and relief campaigns during the pogroms of Armenians in the 1890s and 1909, and even more so during the genocide.[91] All around the United States local newspapers published accounts of the genocide as it unfolded. "Armenians Will Be Exterminated," "Children Hurled into River by Frantic Mothers: Prefer Death Rather Than Have Babies Suffer at Hands of Turks" ran just two headlines in Minnesota newspapers.[92] The United States never declared war on the Ottoman Empire, so missionary reports on the fate of Armenians continued to stream out of Anatolia and the Middle East.

That kind of sympathy helped ensure that American missionaries, like Jewish representatives, had entrée to the offices of government. Wilson, after all, was a strict Presbyterian, and Protestantism defined the American elite. The British and French also expressed great sympathy for Armenians. France, throughout the nineteenth century, had been the place of choice for wealthy Armenians who sent their sons abroad to be educated and acculturated in Western ways. Even before the genocide, Armenians had settled in France, and the country would accept many more refugees in the 1920s.

The representatives of the newly founded Armenian Republic arrived in Paris on 4 February 1919, and merged their efforts with Armenian notables already present in the city.[93] Neither group had been recognized by the major powers as an official delegation. But Armenian hopes had been raised by the decision of the Supreme Allied Council on 29 January 1919—just days after the Paris Peace Conference had convened—that Armenia should be separated from the Ottoman Empire.

In the late winter and spring of 1919, when the Paris Peace Conference convened, the entire region stretching over the Caucasus, Anatolia, and the Middle East remained mired in conflict. The Republic of Armenia attempted to rule an area and a population in the Caucasus devastated by war and genocide. Around three hundred thousand Armenians had fled Ottoman persecutions for Russian Armenia. The World War I armistices brought no peace to the area. The weak government did not even rule over the main centers of Armenian history and population: the six provinces of Eastern Anatolia, including the symbolically important Mount Ararat, and Cilicia.[94] The winter of 1918–19 was especially harsh; the condition of the population, dire in the extreme. Famine and disease ravaged Armenians, all made dramatically worse by the presence of refugees. Entire villages perished, a brutal and tragic postscript to the genocide.[95]

Given these conditions, Armenians and their sympathizers argued that Armenia needed great-power protection. They lobbied in particular for an American mandate over an Armenian nation-state. The supporters of that position mobilized far and wide. Like Jews, Armenians and their supporters published newspaper articles, wrote petitions, gathered in rallies. As just one example, the American diplomat James W. Gerard, a former American ambassador to Germany, wrote in the *New York Times* that America should take up the mandate out of humanitarian concerns, and because the American ideal entailed helping others move toward freedom. For its own security, Gerard wrote, the United States could not retreat into isolationism. The world was too entwined. A stable, prosperous Armenia would ensure a peaceful Middle East. "It is the duty of Christian America to respond to the call of Christian Armenia—the world's first Christian nation," he wrote. An American mandate would make Armenia "an outpost of American civilization in the east."[96] Armenia would also become a bastion against Bolshevism, wrote another pro-mandate American.[97]

In one sense only was the Armenian delegation at Paris more politically "advanced" than Jews—the solution for survivors would have to be, it seemed, an Armenian nation-state, the same argument that Jews would make after World War II. Only in their own state—run by Armenians, populated by Armenians, defined by Armenian-ness—could this population rebuild its society and surmount the tragedy of the genocide perpetrated by the Young Turks. Minorities—Turks, Georgians, Tatars, Persians—would have to be induced to leave, yet another drive at homogeneity, this time by a population that had paid so dearly for that same principle.[98]

On 26 February 1919, the Allies finally allowed the unified Armenian delegation to present its case to the Peace Conference.[99] The delegates called for a large, independent Armenian nation-state running from the Mediterranean into the Caucasus, with a good part of Anatolia in between. Turks, Tatars, "and others"; "lawless nomadic tribes" (the Kurds); and Muhajirs (Muslims who had migrated into the country from the Balkans and Caucasus since the 1860s), would be induced to leave.[100] The representatives argued that a homogeneous Armenia was a necessary precondition for "universal peace." To fulfill that goal, they proposed an exchange of populations with Turkey.[101] Armenians, the delegation continued, were productive and creative. The Turkish conquerors, in contrast, "have created absolutely nothing"; they are among the hordes who "since the Assyrians, have conquered and ravaged our country."[102]

An independent Armenia never came to be. Armenians and Kurds were the great losers in the post–World War I settlement. The Great Powers pursued their own interests—as we see in so many of the histories discussed in this book—despite all the sympathy for Armenians. The United States returned to its isolationist stance, proven by Wilson's inability to prevail upon the Senate to ratify the Versailles Treaty. In June 1920, months after the American withdrawal from the Peace Conference, both the Senate and the House of Representatives rejected a resolution in favor of an American mandate for Armenia. Meanwhile, the French and British populations were clamoring for the return of their troops from Turkey. World War I had ended. What were Johnny and Jean-Paul still doing under arms in a foreign land?

Most importantly, the Turkish nationalist army quickly emerged as the dominant force in the region. In Western eyes, a modern, secular Turkey would be more of a stabilizing factor, more of a bulwark against Bolshevism, than a small, insecure Armenia. Once again, the great-power lifeline to which Armenians had clung so desperately had proven quite frayed—in fact, barely existent.

Squeezed on all sides, under constant attack from the Red Army, Azerbaijan, Georgia, and the Kemalist forces, in a country whose population lived in misery with virtually no economic production, the Armenian Republic could not survive. It soon became the Soviet Republic of Armenia, while the Kemalist forces drove out of Anatolia Greek and other Allied forces. The Lausanne Treaty, as we have seen, authorized a new Republic of Turkey, the last of the new states forged under the

Paris System. It, too, had to sign a minority protection treaty, but that was rather after the fact: the Armenians had been largely killed or driven out. As one German observer paraphrased his conversation with a Young Turk official in the last year of the war, "the Armenian question as it has been will certainly no longer exist because there are no more Armenians."[103]

✧

Yet rarely are genocides or expulsions complete. Survivors remain, as does the legacy of a population that had once lived and flourished in the lands from which they had been expelled. Despite best efforts on the part of the state, the past of a people cannot be simply erased. The Republic of Turkey is one kind of a model for how successor states and societies create rights for the dominant group while suppressing the remnants and legacies of their minority populations.

The new Turkish state, hardly a democracy, nonetheless secured for Muslim Turks property and citizenship rights. For the remnants of the Christian minorities, Armenians, Greeks, and Assyrians, the state offered only rampant discrimination and insecurity. A national line ran right through the population, dividing it between the proud members of the new state and those who existed only on its sufferance.

On the basis of the Lausanne Treaty, the Republic of Turkey was founded on 29 October 1923. In both personnel and policies, strong lines of continuity marked the Young Turk and Kemalist regimes.[104] The national empire strategy pursued by the Young Turks had failed, destroyed in the ashes of the Ottoman defeat in World War I. But the demographic engineering pursued by the Young Turks had largely succeeded. Anatolia, about 80 percent Muslim before World War I, by 1923 had become about 98 percent Muslim.[105]

Nothing inspired fear and loathing on the part of the nationalist movement and the Republic as much as the prospect of tens and hundreds of thousands of survivors coming back, reclaiming their properties, and reigniting the "Armenian question." To summarize a highly complex and technical matter: the republic never legally expropriated

Christian property.[106] To do so would have put it too blatantly in violation of its own founding principles and various international agreements regarding the sanctity of private property. These principles were encoded in the republic's constitution, Islamic and Ottoman legal traditions, the Swiss-based civil code adopted in 1926, and the Lausanne Treaty. The republic claimed only to administer property in the name of owners who for one reason or another had fled Turkey. It even promised an orderly process to arrange compensation for those who did not regain their property.[107]

In fact, through a Kafkaesque cascade of legal and bureaucratic measures and wild, chaotic seizures by villagers and urban residents, the republic, with very few exceptions, prevented survivors from regaining their property or receiving compensation. In essence, the republic fulfilled the expropriation of Christian property holders that had begun in the late nineteenth century and drastically intensified during the genocide.[108]

This was plunder on a vast scale, comparable to the seizure of Jewish property all across Germany and Europe under Nazi rule. And it continued. During World War II, the state imposed a capital tax, supposedly to inhibit speculation and black-market activity. In fact, the tax was applied primarily to Jews, Christians, and other non-Muslims. Minorities had to pay rates ten times those of Muslims and had to deliver their payments immediately. Many had to sell their businesses; others, especially Jews, were deported to forced labor camps.[109] The anti-Greek riots of 1955, orchestrated by the state, caused many thousands of remaining Orthodox Christians to flee to Greece. They left behind their shops, businesses, and apartments, something of a culmination of a forty-year process of creating a society and state in which only Muslim Turks possessed property rights.[110]

The expropriated assets fueled a long line of beneficiaries, first among them CUP and Kemalist loyalists, including the families of former CUP leaders who had been assassinated after the war by Armenian hit squads.[111] Second were the hundreds of thousands of Muslim refugees from the Caucasus and Balkans, many of whom were resettled in now-vacant villages in Eastern Anatolia.[112] The state used much of the expropriated assets to support the development of a Muslim bourgeoisie, which stepped into the shoes of the old Greek and Armenian commercial elite, 90 percent of whom had been eliminated through deportations and killings.[113] These efforts would come to fruition only after World War II as a result of Kemalist etatism, launched in the early 1930s, coupled with wartime economic stimulation.[114] As the state intervened more directly in the economy, it became an engine of mobility for Turks.[115]

Property was one key hinge on which rights and repressions turned. So was citizenship. The constitution of 1924 technically made citizens of all those resident within the borders of Turkey. In that way, it conformed with the Paris System treaties, including Lausanne, that guaranteed minorities equal protection under the law and the right to practice their religion and establish communal organizations. It also conformed with Ottoman legal codes since the 1830s that had established equality of citizenship, although those provisions were hardly realized in practice and stood in direct contradiction to the religious organization of Ottoman society.[116] Atatürk and many other leaders of the republic pronounced the equality of all Turks no matter what their religion or ethnicity.

Yet the republic's formal political and territorial definition of citizenship masked an ethnic and even racial understanding that it applied through a maze of laws and decrees. The republic never revoked in a blanket fashion the citizenship of Armenians or other Christians who had been expelled or had fled, just as it never legally expropriated their property. At the Lausanne negotiations, Turkish diplomats successfully resisted all efforts to place into the treaty the right of return for former Ottoman citizens. The republic followed that "achievement" with a series of legal and administrative measures that made it nearly impossible for Armenians who had fled abroad to return to Anatolia. The state also deprived others of citizenship—for example, if they had not fought in the war of independence.[117]

Those minorities who remained in Turkey endured the strong assimilationist drive that Kemalism applied to non-Turks (and not just non-Muslims).[118] "The foreign cultures must melt into this homogeneous nation," said Prime Minister (later, president) İsmet İnönü in 1925.[119] The Kemalist assimilation program reached into virtually every aspect of social life, including language, religion, education, history, and architecture. By force of law and the reality of instruction in the schools, everyone had to adopt the Turkish language in the public sphere. A 1926 law permitted only Turks—and not the broader category of citizens—to be employed in the civil service. The "race name law" of 1934 required all citizens to adopt Turkish surnames. Administrative measures created, at best, second-class status for Jews and Christians and defined out of existence Kurds and other non-Turkish Muslims as distinct ethnic groups. Kurdish was banned in public and its teaching forbidden. Furthermore, the 1934 Law on Settlement restricted the possibility of immigration and naturalization to those "of Turkish descent and culture," while the communal institutions of non-Turks were subject to highly restrictive regulations.[120] A variety of laws and administrative decrees favored Turks for entry into education and the professions, and obtaining licenses for founding businesses.

In fact, if not in theory, the republic instituted an ethnically based form of nationalism that deprived minorities of virtually all rights.[121] The Ottoman Empire under the Young Turks had killed and deported around two million Ottoman Christians. Its successor, the Republic of Turkey, ensured that the survivors would never regain or receive recompense for their property and would be deprived of the rights attendant with citizenship. They would be either assimilated into Turkish society and culture or excluded altogether. The republic created a nation-state that made the "right to have rights" possible only for those on one side of the national line.

❧

The experience of Jews after the Paris Peace Conference ran partly in parallel with that of Armenians. As the chief advocates of the minority protection treaties, Jews watched with fear as extreme nationalist and fascist movements, virtually all of them antisemitic, rose to prominence all over Central and Eastern Europe in the 1920s and 1930s. They made short shrift of the League of Nations' minority protection system. In Poland, Hungary, and other states, antisemitic legislation and other discriminatory

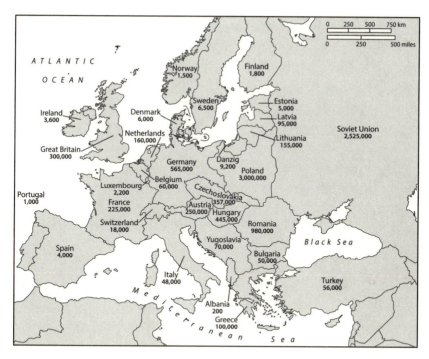

MAP 5.4 European Jewish population around 1933. (Map adapted from original, United States Holocaust Memorial Museum, by permission.)

measures drastically worsened the situation of Jews.[122] Germany, already some years before the Nazi seizure of power, made a mockery of the League by using the Minorities Commission to protest the condition of ethnic Germans under the rule of the new states in Eastern Europe.

Even without the blunt racist force of the Third Reich, the situation, by the 1930s, had turned bleak for the Jews of Central and Eastern Europe. The quintessential minority, Jews could not prevail against the larger forces of extreme nationalism, made worse by the onset of the Great Depression in 1929. With the Nazi conquest of Europe, the threats to them turned murderous and genocidal. The rights that were supposed to protect Jews were completely obliterated.

The history of the Holocaust is so well known that it hardly needs repeating here (see maps 5.4 and 5.5). Genocide, the physical annihilation of a group, signifies the utter and complete deprivation of rights, the absolute, deadly antithesis of even the possibility of a more fruitful

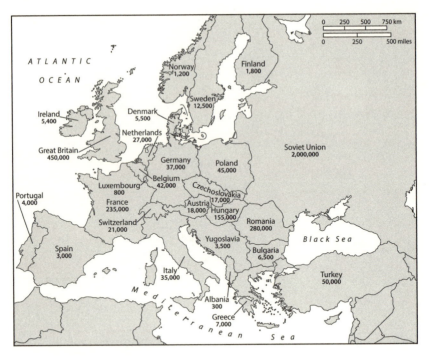

MAP 5.5 European Jewish population around 1950. (Map adapted from original, United States Holocaust Memorial Museum, by permission.)

life that human rights affords people. Genocide also signifies the destruction of the first right, the right to property, which in many instances preceded the actual killing of Jews. All across Germany and occupied Europe, the German state listed, registered, cataloged, and confiscated Jewish assets. "Wild" property seizures certainly occurred, acts of popular complicity in the exclusion and murder of European Jews. But overall, the Nazi state drove the theft of Jewish assets, which resulted in a massive shift of property ownership that extended from the Atlantic coast nearly to the Urals.[123]

And yet, as with Armenians, not all Jews had been exterminated, nor could the memory of their lives and communities in Central and Eastern Europe be totally obliterated. What could come next? For Jewish survivors there was no single answer.

One solution seemed self-evident to Jews as well as the victorious Allies: a Jewish nation-state. Since the Paris Peace Conference, the nation-state had become the predominant political model in Europe; anticolonial movements would take that model to the global level. Only within the Jewish version of that model—a state organized, defined, and run by Jews, a state that would put an end to the supposedly exceptional status of Jews as a minority—it seemed, could the rights and the very lives of Jews be secured. Yet that development would create grave consequences for others who lived on the territory that would become Israel (as we shall see in chapter 9).

The European states all had to deal with the legacy of the Holocaust and the Jewish presence. West Germany and then unified Germany went furthest down the road of recognition, offering a model diametrically opposed to the Republic of Turkey and its treatment of the Armenian legacy. In the Federal Republic of Germany (founded in 1949), the government of Konrad Adenauer sought integration into the Western alliance, and that required some kind of coming to terms with the past.[124] In addition, Adenauer's own deeply conservative Catholic and anti-Nazi beliefs led him to support some kind of moral reckoning with the crimes of the Third Reich.

Even before the end of the war, the Allies demanded the restitution of property seized by Germany in the occupied areas. Under their writ, some significant progress was made for Jews and others, though in the Soviet occupation areas restituted property went to the state rather than to individuals. Then, in 1952, the Federal Republic signed a reparations agreement with Israel. Adenauer faced down great hostility to the act among many Germans, including his fellow Christian Democrats, who continued to deny the vast crimes of the Holocaust. In Israel as well there was substantial opposition to "blood money" from Germany. Adenauer prevailed, also with a 1957 law authorizing restitution to individuals.

For years, the Finance Ministry and other government entities blocked and limited payments to Jewish survivors.[125] Still, the Federal Republic's status as a constituent member of the Western liberal political order meant that its cardinal principle—the sanctity of property rights—could not be completely ignored. Moreover, the growth of "Holocaust consciousness" beginning in the 1960s, meaning the recognition of the murder of the Jews as the defining character of the Third Reich and as a universal moral touchstone, provided more power to demands for reparations and compensation. A series of amendments to the restitution law over the course of the 1950s and 1960s broadened and made more generous the terms of settlement.

The matter was rather different in Eastern Europe. At the war's end, Polish citizens and the state seized Jewish property. A kind of mass hysteria accompanied rumors of Jews returning and taking back their apartments, homes, and factories, leading to a few pogroms.[126] The process was similar in other countries. As the Soviets step by step locked down their control over Eastern Europe, they buried the entire issue of individual restitution. At least in this regard, the communists had great popular support. In yet another irony of history, communism, by nationalizing most property, completed the expropriation of Jewish assets initiated by the Nazis.

In West Germany, at each step of the restitution process, officials thought that they had put the issue behind them, only to see it reemerge, as it did again in the 1990s. With the fall of communism, new archives became available that provided many more details on the European-wide robbery of Jews that the Nazis had committed. If not evident earlier, it became crystal clear in the 1990s that virtually all of Germany's esteemed companies, countless individuals, and most European states had been involved in the theft of Jewish assets. Under immense international pressure, mostly from the United States, as well as demands from civil society in Germany and other Western countries, numerous historical commissions were established that investigated both private companies and German and other European ministries and other state agencies. Historians with knowledge of finance were kept busy as consultants. The details do not need to detain us; the results, overall, led to another round of restitution and compensation payments both to individuals and charitable institutions. Jews were the primary recipients, but so were thousands of Eastern Europeans who had been forced into slave labor under the Nazis.

To this day, numerous cases, especially involving artworks, remain open. The entire process of restitution confronted Jewish survivors and their heirs with all sorts of bureaucratic and political hurdles. Almost all Jewish claimants suffered under a mountain of paperwork, arcane bureaucratic procedures, and wearying legal battles. Often they received a mere fraction of the worth of their former assets. Ultimately, nothing could compensate for the years they had lost as slave laborers and concentration-camp inmates, for their many loved ones who had perished in the Holocaust.

Still, restitution and reparations meant they were now recognized as rights bearers, whether in Germany or elsewhere in Europe, who had been unjustly deprived of that most basic right after life itself, the security of their property. Unlike Armenian survivors in Turkey and the diaspora, Jews in Europe at least achieved the status of former citizens based on the recognition of their property rights. Germany's moral reckoning with its past, evident in the Memorial to the Murdered Jews of Europe in the heart of Berlin as well as thousands of local memorial sites in towns and cities around the country, is worlds removed from Turkey's adamant refusal to acknowledge the Armenian Genocide. Armenians are still waiting for recognition.

Conclusion

To every "civilized" population a state, then the world would be at peace: so ran the Wilsonian ideal proclaimed in the nineteen months of American belligerence in World War I. Rights in this understanding were not those of the individual abstracted from society, but of the national or racial being who was anchored in his (and it was most often his) community. Human rights did not at all wane in the nineteenth or first half of the twentieth century, as some historians claim. Instead, they were widely proclaimed (even if the term itself was not used) from the Berlin Congress to the Paris Peace Conference and beyond. Statesmen and movement activists alike understood that these rights had to be based in national citizenship, and that the nation, to the extent possible, should be homogeneous in character.

Nation-state foundings in the Balkans, elsewhere in Eastern Europe, and Turkey signified a human rights advance for the members of the dominant group. They were able to exercise whatever rights were available, as limited as they may have been, and reveled in the sense of belonging that accompanies national citizenship. They were the proud partisans of the Bulgarian, Greek, Turkish, Polish, or other nation.

This enthusiasm for the nation-state inevitably created problems for those who did not share the nationality or race in whose name the state governed. What was to be the fate of Slovaks in Hungary, Ukrainians in Poland, Turkomans in Iraq, let alone of the two quintessential minorities—Armenians and Jews?

The concept of minorities was created from 1878 to 1919 and remains with us today. It is a category of the nation-state. As the concept defines, it also divides. Populations may be the entitled members of the majority, or they might be cast into the "problem" category of minority. Never are people only individuals; their national and racial identities, sometimes freely chosen, sometimes imposed by state and society, follow them everywhere, and especially into that most critical arena, the right to have rights.

From 1878 until the demise of the League of Nations in 1939, Western statesmen and movement activists devised a variety of mechanisms to protect minorities. At the Berlin Congress the Great Powers imposed liberal principles, including the all-important equality of rights, security of property, and freedom of religion, on the new states. At Paris in 1919 they went further, forcing new states to agree to minority protection treaties and clauses and establishing an elaborate system with the Minorities Commission. Ultimately that system failed miserably, and not only because of the rise of the Nazi Party. The very definition of populations as minorities carried within it dangerous seeds. The Lausanne Treaty demonstrated that the exact same understanding that linked rights with the nation-state could lead to minority protection or forced deportations, as around 1.5 million Greeks and Turks experienced.

In the end, the logic of the nation-state prevailed, as we have seen in previous chapters. The nation-state granted Orthodox Christians in Greece, Euroamericans in the United States, and light-skinned males in Brazil the privileges and responsibilities that came with rights. They possessed the benefits of full citizenship, including security of property and person and the ability to participate politically, that human rights offer. For those who did not fit the dominant category, it was a different matter, even more so with the rise of the explicit category of minority. Those who were unable to achieve their own independent state languished as non- or partial citizens, like Armenians in the nation-state defined by Turkishness. Only in the diaspora and, somewhat, in the Soviet Socialist Republic of Armenia, could Armenians flourish, always casting a tearful eye toward Mount Ararat.

Eurasian societies were creating minorities at roughly the same time the European powers and Japan were colonizing populations around the globe. Essentially no region of the world lived untouched by the long arm of imperial power. In nation-states governed by constitutions, the rule of law, and systems of rights, however imperfect, what would be the status of colonial subjects? What kind of rights, if any, could they exercise? We shall explore the issues through the history of German colonialism in Namibia.

Chapter 6

Namibia

THE RIGHTS OF WHITES

❦

"WHOSE LAND is Hereroland? Hereroland belongs to us!" sang Herero women as their men went into battle against German colonial troops and attacked German farms in Southwest Africa (present-day Namibia).[1] Soldiers and settlers were unnerved as the women's voices soared over the sound of gun and cannon fire. So were German officials and the broader public at home when, on 14 January 1904, a district judge in Windhoek, the capital of German Southwest Africa, telegraphed his superiors at the Foreign Office in Berlin: "All farms in the vicinity of Windhuk plundered by Herero. Whites living on isolated farms murdered. Situation very grave."[2]

Southwest Africa had been a German colony since 1884.[3] Germans had great hopes for Southwest, as it was called colloquially (see maps 6.1 and 6.2). It was to become a German Australia, South Africa, or America, a place where solid and enterprising people from home would come and prosper. They would work the soil and raise livestock in a country where, supposedly, the land was free and open, the indigenous people sparse, primitive, and uncivilized. While creating a blooming colony, Germans would exercise all the rights they had at home while they also carried civilization to the natives and extended their country's global power.

Or so they thought. Now all that was threatened by the Herero uprising, an embittered and forceful response to German land seizures and the violence executed by German settlers and officials against Africans. The Herero rebellion would soon turn into a full-fledged war that also involved the Nama people in the Center and South of the colony and the Ovambo in the far North. In its initial phase, the rebels had great military successes against the rather undermanned Schutztruppe, the German colonial army. From Berlin the military command poured

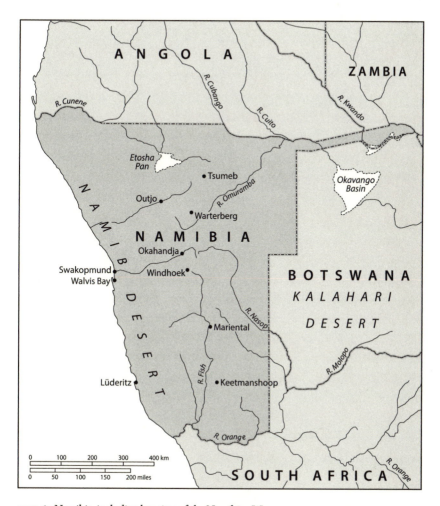

MAP 6.1 Namibia, including key sites of the Namibian War.

reinforcements into Southwest, ultimately around thirteen thousand troops. Under the command of Lieutenant General Lothar von Trotha, the army finally suppressed the rebellion. In the process, it also committed a genocide, the first of the twentieth century. Somewhere between 60 and 80 percent of the Herero and 40 to 60 percent of the Nama were deliberately killed by direct shootings, starvation and thirst in the Omaheke desert, and the dire conditions of internment in concentration camps.[4]

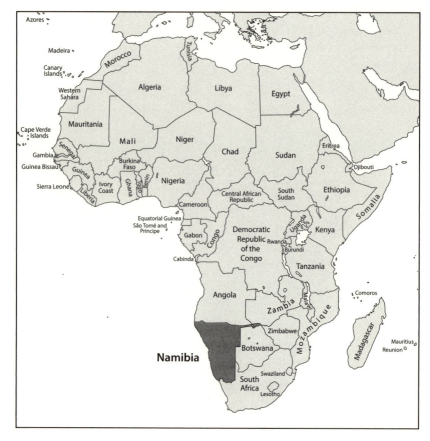

MAP 6.2 Namibia in Africa.

Why a chapter on genocide in a book devoted to human rights? For multiple reasons. Genocide not only leaves in its wake countless corpses and traumatized survivors—it is also an act of political creation, as we saw also in the previous chapter on Armenians and Jews. Deliberate mass killings and repressions radically reshape the social landscape. In the aftermath of genocide, elites have new possibilities for structuring the political and economic order. In Southwest Africa, genocide opened the path for German colonial authorities to establish apartheid and racial capitalism. South Africa continued these policies when it took control of the colony in 1915 during World War I, and then under a League of Nations mandate and a UN trusteeship (until 1966). In this setting, white people had their rights secured. They might not have had *human* rights in the full sense of the term today, but they certainly possessed rights to property and political representation. Blacks became subjects of an oppressive regime—hardly rights-bearing citizens—until they won independence for Namibia in 1990. The history of genocide, then, is not separate from the history of nation-states and human rights.

Genocide, apartheid, racial capitalism—these policies were created by a semi-liberal state, Imperial Germany. In the previous cases we have discussed—Greece, the United States, Brazil, Armenians and Jews—states and the international community enacted policies that reflected the prevalent liberalism in the West—namely, the formation of nation-states with constitutions and representative government and human rights based on national citizenship. This liberalism, for all its progressive, forward-looking politics, was also highly restrictive. For most nineteenth-century liberals, as we have seen, no contradiction existed between their commitment to rights and their belief that the access to rights had to be limited to propertied men of particular nations and races. Support for imperial conquests also went hand in hand with liberalism.[5] Liberalism's advocates also saw no contradiction between their progressive politics and the establishment of colonial empires in which "lesser races" became subjects with few, if any, rights.

As W.E.B. Du Bois famously wrote in *The Souls of Black Folk* (1903): "The problem of the twentieth century is the problem of the color-line." Du Bois was writing about the creation of rigid racial segregation in the United States. However, even at this early stage of his career, he was an internationalist, and his coinage of the term "color-line" also took into account "the relation of the darker to the lighter races of men" around the globe, and especially in colonial societies. In Du Bois's characterization, the color line was never innocent. It signified a global hierarchical order defined by both rights and repressions. In the Americas, Africa, Asia, and the Antipodes, white people exercised rights, while black and other darker-skinned populations experienced brutal discrimination and exploitation.[6]

The events in Namibia constitute one chapter in this global history of the twentieth-century color line and its meaning for nation-states and human rights. In the ocean seaboard states and regions of the United States, Canada, Southern Africa, Australia, and New Zealand, white settlers drove out indigenous peoples, as we have already seen in Minnesota.[7] Germany, determined to be recognized as a global power, joined the crowd of nation-states with an overseas empire. It became an imperial nation-state—a clumsy locution perhaps (as is "national empire"), but a revealing one—like Britain, France, the Netherlands, and others.[8]

In the twentieth century, two new elements came to define this global history: the application in politics of a more systematic, supposedly scientific, conception of race, joined to the belief that a worldwide racial struggle was under way. After 1945, its reverse took hold: the mobilization of the international community through the UN and NGOs in support of global human rights, including, as central features, decolonization and racial equality. Namibia's history is emblematic of these twentieth-century trends: the deep, agonizing, race-based repression of the Herero and Nama and the surprising revival, after 1920, of their society concomitant with the long struggle for Namibian independence. For most of the twentieth century, the "right to have rights" in Namibia ran on one side of the color line. The story, however (and thankfully), does not end there.

✌

"Wherever my cattle graze, that is Herero land!"[9] So goes another Herero adage that reaches back to the nineteenth century. It expresses their long tradition as pastoralists who moved large herds of cattle across vast stretches of territory. The Herero comprised part of the Great Bantu migration from Central Africa. In the eighteenth century they moved farther south, from present-day Angola into Namibia, always in search of grasslands so their cattle could feed. As they migrated south they encountered the Ovambo, Khoikhoi, Nama (one group among the Khoikhoi), Reheboth Bastar (the offspring of Dutch men and Nama women), San, and other peoples who, together, made up the complex ethnic diversity of Southwest Africa.[10] The Nama were also cattle herders, though both groups hunted and gathered as needed. The Nama moved up from the South, also searching for grasslands. For a good part of the nineteenth century, warfare raged between the Herero and Nama (and other Khoikhoi) over land and cattle. The Nama had guns and horses that they had obtained through trade with the Dutch and other Europeans. As a result, the wars initially went badly for the Herero. Not for long. The Herero too began to obtain rifles and horses from Europeans in return for live cattle and animal hides. Over the course of the nineteenth century, the Herero prospered as their herds grew. In the 1870s and 1890s, peace agreements with the Nama, brokered by German missionaries and colonial authorities, reduced the violent toll on cattle and people.

Like the Dakota and Ojibway in Minnesota, the Herero and Nama had a sense of collective rights to land ownership, but nothing in the way of individual title to private property. They knew how to move herds of livestock across the bush and desert, and where watering holes could be found. The San knew how to hunt and gather even in the harshest of terrains, the Kalahari Desert. Never was Southwest quite as devoid of population, never was the land as free and open, as German colonizers liked to believe.

German and Finnish Protestant missionaries came to Southwest in the 1840s. Earlier, a few isolated traders and adventurers had moved up from the Dutch Cape Colony or disembarked from Portuguese ships as they headed around the continent. The missionaries were the first Europeans to establish permanent settlements in Southwest Africa. As in Minnesota and as we will see in the next chapter, on Korea, missionaries brought with them the Bible, and also schools, healthcare, and European customs; they even established their own trading companies, which provided the first impulse to economic development in Southwest Africa and to increased encounters with indigenous peoples. Missionaries sought to Christianize and civilize the natives—much the same thing in their eyes. After German unification in 1871, the missionaries increasingly saw themselves as the agents of German nationalism in addition to Christianity.[11]

Missionaries had few successes initially, the Herero particularly resistant to the siren song of Christianity. Slowly, however, missionaries were able to convert some leading tribesmen of the Herero and Nama, who sent their children to mission schools. By the late nineteenth century, Samuel Maharero, the paramount chief of the Herero, spoke and wrote German, while his Nama counterpart, Hendrik Witbooi, knew Afrikaans. Both had been educated by missionaries and became devout Christians. Other native leaders knew English as a result of the British presence in the nearby Cape Colony.[12]

In 1884, a German merchant, Adolf Lüderitz, literally planted the flag and proclaimed a German colony. Its borders were undefined, its future unclear. Back home, Chancellor Otto von Bismarck had long asserted that Germany had no interest in obtaining overseas colonies. But Bismarck was very interested in making Germany a Great Power. By the 1880s, along with industrial might (Britain) or the governance of a huge land mass (Russia) and a powerful, well-armed military, great-power stature meant colonial possessions. Germany could not be left behind, in the eyes of Bismarck and many other elite Germans. If not the lead actors, colonies could play important supporting roles in Germany's drive to become a powerful nation-state amid its European competitors.[13]

So Germany joined the ranks, albeit briefly, of European nation-states with overseas colonial empires. Germany gained five colonies in all—Southwest, German East Africa (more or less Tanzania today), Togo, and Cameroon in Africa, and German Samoa in the Pacific, along with participation in the European concessions in China. Bismarck also brokered the Berlin Conference of 1884–85 that adjudicated the "scramble for Africa." In the Final Act of the Conference, the European powers, including the Ottoman Empire, established the criteria for securing colonial claims, defined the borders of colonial possessions, and loftily proclaimed Europeans' common goal of bringing civilization and prosperity to the continent, all the while protecting "native" traditions.[14] The reality could be quite different, as the Herero and Nama would soon discover.

❧

Southwest conjured up the classic colonial vision of open lands and vanishing peoples, a place where Germans could escape from the stifling conditions at home, prosper, and live free as rights-bearing citizens while contributing to Germany's economic development and global power.[15] Paul Rohrbach, an imperialist entrepreneur who served the German government in Southwest, East Africa, and the Ottoman Empire, came to the colony for a second time, now accompanied by his wife, Clara, amid the Namibian War. Despite the violence all around him, he wrote home elegiacally about the money it was possible to save, the lovely house one could build for little expense, the freedom the children had to run around unhindered, the servants one employed. "In Europe, only notably wealthy people can live this way." He and his wife Clara had "complete freedom of space . . . something very lovely." And he could work independently. "The freedom of work, with a good salary and a halfway independent character, is much greater here in Africa than at home."[16] So wrote and sang German farmers as well, proud to be a part of a pioneering enterprise that gave them independence and spread German might around the globe. As one of their songs went:

> Southwest, sweet land of sun and stars,
> You land of endless blue horizon, open spaces, and wild field deer,
> You land of the Kudus and range animals;
> I'll build on your sunbaked earth happily,
> Stone by stone in the native soil.[17]

Yet Southwest was not an easy place. "This is not Africa," noted another German visitor to the colony, a marine who disembarked his transport ship in Swakopmund.[18] His mood was rather different from Rohrbach's. The marine expected a lush tropical jungle and all sorts of wild animals. Instead, he found a desert with little of the wildlife he longed to see. Colonial enthusiasts like Rohrbach tended to ignore the fact that about one-third of Southwest Africa was desert, and another third semiarid. Only in the far North, on the border with Portuguese Angola, was extensive, cultivated agriculture possible. A lush, fertile land this was not, and it never quite became a booming, bustling colony.

On the eve of the Namibian War, Southwest had attracted only about four thousand settlers and some hundreds of German colonial administrators, from lowly police officers to the governor, who was appointed by the chancellor.[19] Still, for some thirty years, from 1884 to 1915, South-west Africa was German territory, until South African troops defeated the German forces in a sideshow battle of World War I. For even longer, down to the 1950s, Southwest loomed large in the German imagination. Until that decade, many Germans dreamed of regaining the colony; to this day, a significant German population resides in Namibia.

Bismarck expected the colony to be ruled with little expense and even less bother. For quite a number of years following 1884, the German presence was rather thin. The authorities ruled indirectly through agreements with local chieftains and left the leadership and internal structure of the groups intact. Germans had things to offer—guns, horses, ammunition, household manufactures, provisions. All these items were important for pastoralists whose very existence could be threatened by a single drought or warfare with a neighboring tribe. Or by an epidemic, like the rinderpest, which devastated cattle herds in Southwest in 1897.

The Herero were especially affected. Cattle and land provided the essential life resources, and the very bases of their culture and society. The Herero venerated their cattle; status in the community depended on how big was a man's herd, which in some cases could run into the thousands. A newborn Herero was made to touch the head of a calf; at a Herero's grave, his favorite animal was slaughtered to follow his owner, the rest of his herd drawn together so that the spirit of the deceased would draw pleasure from his animals.[20] The epidemic left the people weakened physically and culturally, the authority of the chiefs and elders threatened. Many desperate Herero wandered north to Ovambo country or east to Bechuanaland, or became laborers on farms now owned by settlers.[21]

Even before the epidemic, Maharero and Witbooi had begun to cede land to the German authorities in exchange for the goods Germans had on offer and "supreme protection" (*Allerhöchster Schutz*) against external enemies. Maharero and Witbooi were clever strategists, not desperate supplicants (see figure 6.1). Both proved particularly adept at dealing with the German authorities. Witbooi wrote to Governor Theodor Leutwein, shortly after the latter's arrival in the colony: "Von François [the

FIGURE 6.1 Samuel Maharero, circa 1900. Maharero (1856–1923) was the paramount chief of the Herero. He had been educated in missionary schools and was fluent in German. He spent years meeting and corresponding with the German governor of Southwest Africa, Theodor Leutwein. Nonetheless, he led his people in revolt against German colonization. The ensuing genocide decimated the population. Maharero survived in exile in Bechuanaland. After his death in 1923, the South African authorities permitted the return of his body to Namibia. The burial became a great event that marked the revival of Herero culture. In this photograph, Maharero is wearing the uniform of the German colonial troops. After his death, his followers did the same, turning the tables on their German oppressors. (Bundesarchiv.)

preceding German head of the colony] demanded from me what is mine, and I refused: for I alone have the right to dispose of what is mine. If someone wants it, I may give it, or I may not, as I please."[22]

Those are the words of a proud, powerful leader. Even the German military had to admit that both the Herero and Nama had a strong sense of freedom and independence, and were not inclined simply to give in to German power without a fight.[23] "Whoever wants to colonize this land," wrote the historians of the general staff during the Namibian War, "must grab the sword and lead the war—not with measured and half-hearted steps, but with strong, imposing power until the total destruction [*Niederwerfung*] of the natives. . . . No kind of clever policies could . . . avoid . . . this race struggle [*Rassenkampf*]."[24]

As rivals, Maharero and Witbooi each hoped to use German "protection" against the other, and both established effective working relations with Governor Leutwein. Maharero used Leutwein to support his claim, against internal rivals, to paramountcy among the Herero, while the governor used Maharero to gain land for German garrisons and German settlers. In turn, the Herero and Nama chiefs promised that land would only be transferred with the agreement of the German government; no treaties would be concluded with other powers, and only Germans were given the right to conduct trade.[25]

Now, with the rinderpest raging among the cattle herds, Maharero and Witbooi concluded additional agreements, ceding ever more land to the German authorities. At the same time, German traders deliberately promoted the indebtedness of Africans (echoes of the Minnesota frontier!), including Samuel Maharero, who paid his debts by selling off even more land and allowing his followers to be forcibly expelled. Unscrupulous traders generally resolved debts by seizing cattle, including sacred ones. They often acted with blatant disrespect and violence against tribal elders.[26]

Land, that precious resource that nourished cattle, the very life source of the Herero and Nama, was slipping from their control. Younger men grew increasingly incensed at the actions of their elders (again, echoes of Minnesota). German settlers began to carve up the land into individual holdings. They believed they had bought the land legally (typically at very low prices) from German concessions or the German government. Sometimes settlers simply seized land. They built fences, which further impeded the free flow of cattle and people that had defined Herero and Nama life for centuries.

There was something else. German colonists and officials displayed a penchant for violence against Africans. Later, in 1918, Africans spoke bitterly about the quick and often arbitrary brutalities they suffered. In one testimony after another given to British officers, they described traders who flogged them if they refused to purchase goods, farmers who on a whim shot and killed Herero women and men. Adding to their bitterness was the knowledge that no white people, even murderers, were ever punished for mistreating Africans.[27] As the Nama Adam Pienaar told his interviewers, describing the years before the war:

> The law gave us no protection; the German soldiers did just what they pleased. We were helpless and powerless. . . . Many of our people died in prison through starvation, floggings, and general ill-treatment. . . . The evidence of one white man . . . was quite sufficient to secure a conviction for almost anything. Our people were literally flogged to death. . . . A white man could do as he pleased to us. White men were not punished. Our word was never taken in a court. . . . [Because of our mistreatment] we lost all respect for the Germans.[28]

Discord and discontent were on the rise in Herero and Nama country. In 1903, at meetings called by Herero chiefs, young men and women of all ages, deeply aggrieved by the loss of land and German violence, demanded action. Word had leaked out that the government planned to build new railroad lines, which would further impinge on Herero land, and move the Herero to reservations.[29]

Much like Little Crow, Samuel Maharero threw in his lot with his younger, more radical followers, despite his years of good relations with Leutwein.[30] He also sought to rally other Africans, notably the Nama and Reheboth Bastar, to the cause of rebellion. On the very day the Herero launched the revolt, Maharero wrote to his Nama counterpart, Hendrik Witbooi, who had previously resisted the idea of a war: "My brother, do not let your last word stand, do not keep your distance from the uprising. Fight with all Africa against the Germans. Better that we die together and not die from mistreatment, prison, or any other thing."[31]

The Nama would enter the war, but only later, after the Herero had been defeated, while the Reheboth Bastar largely remained loyal to the Germans. Many Herero, numbering at least in the hundreds, served as auxiliaries to the Schutztruppe, even during the war. As in Minnesota, the native combatants were never able to rally all their people against the colonial power.[32]

☙

Some Nama had already attacked settlers in autumn 1903. The Schutztruppe, with Governor Leutwein at the helm, headed south to protect Germans and assert German authority. Officially, though, the war began on 11/12 January 1904 as Christian and non-Christian Herero united and attacked German farms in the Okahandja district, the center of Herero land, and areas to the north.[33] They killed white farmers, often with gruesome mutilations, but generally followed Maharero's orders and spared women, children, and missionaries.

To the surprise, amazement, and horror of Germans in the colony and at home, the initial military campaign went badly for Germany. Leutwein now moved his troops north, from Nama to Herero country. With only one, rickety, railroad line located in another part of the country (between Swakopmund and Windhoek) and not much in the way of roads, moving troops and equipment was an arduous undertaking that lasted for weeks. Moreover, the German army, even the colonial Schutztruppe, had been trained for pitched battles. It did not know how to fight a guerrilla war. The German forces were weighed down by their heavy artillery and provisions; the Herero and Nama moved lightly and stealthily across the countryside they knew so well. The Herero attacked, then melted away—a tactic that defeated German troops in battle and allowed the Herero to continue plundering German farms—taking cattle, provisions, and whatever else attracted them.

PLATE 1. A rally in support of asylum seekers in central Sydney, 2013. After Australia announced it would seek to impose stricter regulations to limit the increase of refugees entering the country via boat, two women participate in a rally supporting asylum seekers. (Daniel Munoz/Reuters Pictures.)

PLATE 2. Ottoman imperial ceremony, 1789. Sultan Selim III (1761–1808) holding an audience in front of the Gate of Felicity. All of the courtiers are lined up by rank, a powerful symbol of the hierarchy of empires. (Topkapı Sarayı Müzesi, Istanbul. Bridgeman-Giraudon/Art Resource, New York.)

PLATE 3. Reception of the ambassadors of Siam by Napoleon III and Empress Eugénie at the dance hall of Henri II at Fontainebleau castle, 27 June 1861. The ultimate symbol of hierarchy was the full-body prostration. Typical of Asian empires especially, the practice is here brought by the ambassadors from Siam to the court of Napoleon III in France. (Painting by Jean-Léon Gérome, 1864. Musée de Château de Versailles. © RMN-Grand Palais/Art Resource, New York.)

PLATE 4. Vienna Congress, 1815. Watercolor by August Friedrich Andreas Campe (1777–1846) depicting Europe's emperors and kings. They are reestablishing empires by drawing the borders on the map, but they have not forgotten the larger world as depicted by the globe. (State Borodino War and History Museum, Moscow/Bridgeman Images.)

PLATE 5. The Massacre at Chios, Eugène Delacroix, 1824. The masterpiece by Delacroix (1798–1863) depicts the massacre of Greeks carried out by Ottoman forces in 1822 on the island of Chios. The Greeks are suffering and are being rounded up for execution or enslavement. The painting helped rally the support of Philhellenes in Europe. Nothing comparable or as powerful exists for the massacres that Greek rebels conducted against Muslims and Jews. (Musée du Louvre. Scala/Art Resource, New York.)

PLATE 6. Ibrahim Pasha, 1846. The portrait by Charles-Philippe Auguste Larivière depicts Ibrahim Pasha (1789–1848), the eldest son of Muhammad 'Ali of Egypt, who had made Egypt virtually autonomous within the Ottoman Empire. 'Ali nonetheless remained loyal to the Ottoman sultan during the Greek rebellion. Ibrahim's troops bore much of the fighting against the Greek rebels, and were responsible for the massacre at Missolonghi. He inherited his father's position as khedive of Egypt and Sudan, but died four months later. (Musée de Château de Versailles. © RMN-Grand Palais/Art Resource, New York.)

PLATE 7. Little Crow (Taoyate Duta) at the Treaty of Traverse des Sioux, 1851. Little Crow (1810–63) was the leader of the Mdewakanton band of the Dakota Sioux. Here he is depicted at the signing of the Treaty of Traverse des Sioux, which ceded major portions of Sioux lands to the US government. A decade later, the land cessions would be a major cause of the Sioux rebellion under Little Crow's leadership. In this painting by Frank Blackwell Mayer, Little Crow is depicted in traditional Indian garb. (Painting by Frank Blackwell Mayer; Minnesota Historical Society.)

PLATE 8. Little Crow (Taoyate Duta), 1862. Little Crow moved between two worlds. In contrast to plate 7, here he is wearing mostly Western clothing. Little Crow traveled to Washington to negotiate with the federal authorities, yet led the Sioux rebellion. He lived a settled life in a village, though he did not farm. He attended church, but refused to be baptized. (Photo by John H. Gravenslund; Minnesota Historical Society.)

PLATE 9. Execution of Dakota Indians, Mankato, Minnesota, 1862. In the largest mass execution in American history, thirty-eight Dakota Sioux were executed on 26 December 1862. The gallows were specially built to accommodate so many individuals at once. Federal soldiers, evident in the sea of blue, were deployed en masse to keep vengeful crowds at bay. (Painting by J. Thullen, 1884; Minnesota Historical Society.)

PLATE 10. Rio de Janeiro bay, 1869. Travelers were enchanted by the beauty of Brazil, starting with Rio de Janeiro. The calm waters reflected the hills around the protected harbor, as shown in this painting by Nicolau Facchinetti (Treviso, Italy, 1824–Rio de Janeiro, Brazil, 1900) from 1869, titled Botafogo Bay. (Oil on canvas, São Paulo Museum of Art. Gift: Drault Ernanny de Mello e Silva, 1947, Inv. MASP.00237. Collection Museu de Arte de São Paulo Assis Chateaubriand. Photo by João Musa.)

PLATE 11. Oscar Niemeyer's Alvorada Palace, Brasília, 1956–60. Niemeyer (1907–2012) was Brazil's great modernist architect. He designed the buildings for Brasília, the capital created from scratch in the middle of the country between 1956 and 1960. The Alvorada Palace, the presidential residency, is built of steel, glass, and concrete, the materials beloved by modern architects. The building has an open feel to it because of the large glass panes; the curves soften the harsh lines more typical of modernism. The pool adds dramatic color by playing off the white of the building and reflecting Brazil's blue sky. All of Niemeyer's Brasília buildings are designed to symbolize the modern and progressive character of the Brazilian nation-state. (Studio Leonardo Finotti.)

PLATE 12. Oscar Niemeyer's Planalto Palace, Brasília, 1956–60. Another example of Niemeyer's striking modernist style, the Planalto is the presidential workplace. The horizontal construction plays off the surrounding savannah, the many windows flood the interior with natural light and symbolize openness and progress—the nation-state on the move. (Studio Leonardo Finotti.)

Panic spread among the settlers. And among the natives. Many Herero had no desire for a military conflict with little chance of ultimate success. They knew the Germans would exact vengeance; they had no idea how bad that would be.

News of the events traveled rapidly, now that undersea telegraph cables connected most parts of the world. Governor Leutwein sought a negotiated end to the war. Kaiser Wilhelm II and the general staff, the real centers of power in Germany, had other ideas. They wanted total and complete victory, the signature piece of German military strategy and culture. On 9 February 1904, one month after the start of the war, the general staff in Berlin assumed control over the military campaign and soon dispatched to the colony General Lothar von Trotha. The kaiser, never a paragon of cool thinking and moderation, felt personally affronted by the rebellion of his African subjects. He would now demonstrate to them what German power signified. "Destroy the rebellion!" he ordered Trotha, who effectively assumed civilian and military power upon his arrival in Southwest on 11 June 1904, six months into the war.[34]

Meanwhile, the press riled up the population at home by publishing lurid accounts and drawings of beast-like Africans rampaging through German farms, burning buildings, killing men, and raping German women, even though Herero combatants generally followed Maharero's orders to spare women and children. In the color-line era, it was not difficult to arouse the public to fever pitch against dark-skinned people.

Leutwein, in title still governor, continued to correspond with Maharero despite orders that he could undertake negotiations only with the express approval of the kaiser. Maharero forcefully laid the blame for the uprising on white settlers and traders. "The war did not begin because of me," he wrote, "but because of the whites. As you know, the whites and especially the traders have killed many Herero, by guns and by lock-up in the prisons. . . . The traders have even tried to push their own debts on my people . . . and robbed [our cattle]."[35]

Trotha's name is indelibly linked to genocide, but he hardly acted alone (see figure 6.2). For six months he had the full support of the kaiser, general staff, and colonial lobby. All of them rejected

FIGURE 6.2 Lothar von Trotha, 1904. Trotha (1848–1920) came from a prominent noble family. As a military officer he was known for his ruthless actions in China and East Africa, all in service of German imperialism. As a lieutenant general he was assigned to crush the Herero rebellion. Trotha issued two extermination orders, one against the Herero and another against the Nama, one of the only times that a genocidal campaign was publicly announced. (Photograph by M. Batz. bpk Bildagentur/Art Resource, New York.)

negotiations with the rebels. Only total victory would suffice. Following Leutwein's initial plan, Trotha decided on an encirclement campaign around Warterberg, where some six thousand Herero combatants, along with their families and cattle, had gathered (see map 6.1). German troops launched the attack in mid-August 1904. The battle, which afterward would be feted in colonial memoirs and novels as well as the general staff's own history of the war, actually failed. The German troops could not close the circle around the Herero, though the battle did mark the latter's military defeat. The Herero, entire families and cattle, fled eastward into the Omaheke Desert.

Trotha followed standard German military doctrine—once the annihilation battle had failed, pursuit was the next step.[36] It was not so easy. Germans had no experience fighting in desert conditions and were unfamiliar with the terrain, unlike the Herero, who knew where to find the few watering holes. German soldiers were racked by thirst and typhus. Units were sent out one after another to search for water, only to come back empty-handed—until a Herero attached to the German army led them to a watering hole.[37]

All along the pursuit route, the troops encountered human and animal bodies, Herero and cattle that had been shot or died of thirst or starvation. Jan Kubas, an African who served with the German troops, told British officers in 1918:

> The Germans took no prisoners. They killed thousands and thousands of women and children along the roadsides. They bayoneted them and hit them [with rifle butts]. Words cannot be found to relate what happened; it was too terrible. . . . Mothers holding babies at their breasts, little boys and girls, old people too old to fight and old grandmothers . . . they were killed, all of them, and left to lie and rot on the veld for the vultures and wild animals to eat.[38]

Even for some hardened soldiers the spectacle was gruesome. One of them, Ludwig von Estorff, later wrote that Trotha was a "terrible statesman, not fit to be a leader in war. . . . To destroy [zertrümmern] the people was a brutal and misguided policy. We could have saved many of them and their wealth, their cattle. . . . They had been punished enough. I proposed that to General von Trotha, but he wanted their complete annihilation."[39]

Trotha continued the pursuit. The military's policy of relentless killing came to something of a culmination with Trotha's infamous and publicly circulated "annihilation order" (*Vernichtungsbefehl*), issued on 2 October 1904: "The Herero people must leave this land. If they do not, I will force them to do so by using the great gun. Within the German border every male Herero, armed or unarmed, with or without cattle, will be shot to death. I will no longer receive women or children but will drive them back to their people or have them shot at."[40] News of the proclamation traveled quickly. Trotha had it widely disseminated among the Schutztruppe and the Herero and other Africans. Journalists in South Africa picked it up and wired the text to newspapers in Britain and Germany. The public outcry was great. In an era of heightened European tensions, Germany appeared as a particularly brutal colonizer. The British loftily claimed they brought civilization to the natives, the Germans extermination.

In an attempt to quell the outrage, the kaiser, on 8 December 1904, countermanded Trotha's order by granting clemency to those Herero who had not participated in killings. He also ordered Trotha to use the pastors of the Rhenish Mission—deeply opposed to the extermination campaign—as mediators.[41]

Nonetheless, the extreme policies of the German military continued, as Nama in the South and Ovambo in the North also entered the conflict. A guerrilla campaign launched by the Nama in autumn 1904 tied down German troops. Trotha issued a second annihilation order, this time directed against the Nama.[42] Leutwein, technically still the governor though powerless against Trotha, tried to prevail on the Nama leader, Hendrik Witbooi, to give up the fight.[43] Witbooi rejected Leutwein's entreaties and turned the tables on him: "You accuse me of murdering helpless White people. I beg you, when you have read this letter sit down quietly and reflect. Count up the souls which have perished in this country in the ten years since you arrived."[44] To Karl Schmidt, a German official in Keetmanshoop, Witbooi wrote that he had kept the peace for ten years, yet had "come to see in it nothing but the destruction of all our people."[45] Witbooi always wrote of god and the afterlife in his letters. Still a combatant at age eighty, he died shortly after this last letter from wounds received in the Nama war against German domination.

ↄ

"They died in droves," wrote one missionary about the fate of Africans in the concentration camps.[46] Alongside the killings, German authorities set up a string of camps, including in the port towns of Lüderitzbucht and Swakopmund (see figure 6.3). The Shark Island camp by Lüderitzbucht was particularly brutal. Fifteen miles inland the terrain is semi-arid, the climate hot and dry. Between that point and the coast the temperature can drop forty degrees Fahrenheit. The Namib Desert along the coast is often dry as well—except that the Benguela Current moves up the Atlantic from Antarctica. The current has the opposite effect of the Gulf Stream, which warms the East Coast of the United States before it heads across the Atlantic and has the same impact as far as Greenland. The Benguela, in contrast, dumps wet fog and cold winds on the coast. The Herero and Nama were accustomed to the arid conditions inland where they roamed with their cattle. They suffered terribly from the wet, cold environs of the concentration camp, with hardly any blankets or clothes and completely inadequate prison food. Women were subjected to a huge incidence of sexual assault.[47] Fritz Isaac, who later testified about the conditions on Shark Island, was one of 193 Nama inmates who survived—out of 3,500.[48] Only the intervention of missionaries helped to alleviate somewhat the conditions. Still, the overall mortality rates in the camps ran to 45 percent—according to official German statistics.[49]

The colonial administration also placed prisoners on settler farms, where Africans were used as convict labor, and on railroad construction gangs. In addition, the army ran its own prisoner-of-war camps and also used convict labor. In essence, a whole series of camps run under a variety of administrations dotted the land. In all of them, women and children were put to work, including the starving and ill. A few hundred were exiled to the German colonies of Togo and Cameroon, whose

FIGURE 6.3 Seven Herero men in chains, German Southwest Africa, circa 1907. Approximately 60 percent of the Herero and 40 percent of the Nama died between 1904 and 1907 in fixed battles, from starvation and thirst in the desert into which they had been driven by the German forces, and from internment in concentration camps. These chained prisoners are probably on their way to a camp or to forced labor on German farms or on infrastructure projects. The Swakopmund camp was particularly notorious for its horrendous conditions. (Chronicle/Alamy Stock Photo.)

tropical conditions, poor provisions, and excessive labor demands shattered the health of the Herero and Nama no less than the Shark Island concentration camp.[50]

Trotha had become a liability because of the public outrage he inspired. He was removed from power in Southwest Africa in November 1905—but only after he had waged the campaign of destruction against the Nama as well as the Herero. Fourteen months later, on 27 January 1907, the kaiser's birthday, the German government officially declared the war over. As an act of clemency on that same day, a testament to the supposed merciful and benevolent character of Wilhelm II, the government also abolished prisoner-of-war status and released the last Herero and Nama from the official concentration camps. These acts of munificence came only after 60–80 percent of the Herero population and 40–60 percent of the Nama had died in battle, in the desert, or from internment in concentration camps.

∾

In some ways, the Namibian War was little different from scores of colonial conflicts around the world. California Indians suffered a terrible genocide in the mid-nineteenth century. The brutalities exercised by Belgians in the Congo perhaps surpassed even those Germans implemented in Namibia.[51] In this context of extensive colonial violence on a global scale, the widely touted argument that the annihilation of the Herero and Nama opened the pathway to the Holocaust remains unconvincing.[52]

Rather, Namibia is notable—not unique, but notable—for two other reasons. First, German military strategy and culture were built around the goal of total victory, the complete annihilation of the enemy.[53] The strategy had been developed in the nineteenth century; it came to fruition in the twentieth, first in Namibia and then in the two world wars. The consequences for populations, civilians and combatants, were devastating. The unrelenting drive for the complete defeat of the enemy opened the way to massive human rights violations, as we would now call them.

The second reason is no less important. The limitless character of the Namibian War was also fueled by an explicit racial ideology. Racist sentiments certainly existed in regard to Indians in Minnesota and black slaves in Brazil. However, by the turn of the twentieth century, racial ideology had become far more systematic and was underpinned—so its advocates thought—by science. Many of Germany's protagonists in the Namibian War believed they were involved in a global racial conflict, a fight to the death, if need be, between the superior white race and inferior dark-skinned peoples. This belief in racial war was one other way, one very disconcerting way, that the global world was made in the nineteenth and twentieth centuries—not through a belief in the equality of peoples and human rights, but in their rigid, racially defined difference in a hierarchical order. For many in the Western world, including in Germany, the United States, and many other countries, racial conflict was a historical and political necessity.

As well as anyone, Trotha articulated these views. The campaign against the Herero and Nama, he claimed, was part of a global "race struggle" (*Rassenkampf*), which could only be decided by the "annihilation" (*Vernichtung*) of the lower races when they dared challenge white domination. "The [Herero] nation as such must be annihilated," he wrote.[54] The war in Southwest Africa was only one battle in the larger race struggle with which all the European colonial powers would have to contend. Any concessions on the German side would only fuel the idea that Africa belongs only to its black population.[55] Colonial wars were not to be fought by the laws of the Geneva Convention. Instead, he opined, the race struggle had to be fought with "blunt terrorism and even with brutality. I will annihilate [*ich vernichte*] the rebellious tribes with streams of blood and money."[56] He warned against the overestimation of the economic value of natives. "Where the labor of the white man is possible . . . philanthropical sentiments will not drive out from the world Darwin's law, 'Survival of the Fittest.'"[57] In response to the missionary August Kuhlmann, who pleaded that the Herero be allowed to keep their cattle and that only those who actually committed murder be pursued, Trotha claimed to have studied African people. He wrote that the Herero "are the same presumptuous, treacherous, and barbarian people as are all Bantus."[58] No concessions, certainly no rights, should be granted them.

Trotha's unbridled racism and blazing fury knew no bounds. The postwar repression had to be systematic and far-reaching. A large contingent of troops had to remain in the colony and any natives still at large who had participated in the uprising, along with their entire families, had to be expelled.[59] Even loyal tribes had to be closely watched. In regard to "our 'comrades,' the Bastar, whose arrogance knows no bounds, we shall settle accounts with them at a later date," Trotha wrote ominously.[60] The natives were destined to die out, Trotha believed, a common enough sentiment that we have also seen in play at Minnesota.[61]

Trotha hardly acted alone. Even after his annihilation order had been revoked he retained significant support among the army command and the colonial lobby.[62] The army's official history of the war lauded Trotha's campaign against the Herero, and concluded: "No efforts, no deprivations were avoided to rob the enemy of the last bit of his capacity to resist. Like an animal hunted half to death, he was forced from watering hole to watering hole, until finally, left without any will, he became a victim of the nature of his own land. The arid Omaheke would fulfill what German arms had begun: the annihilation of the Herero [*die Vernichtung des Hererovolkes*]."[63] For the general staff, history had taken its course, the extinction of an uncivilized race, almost as if it were a natural occurrence rather than a brutal event carried out as a systematic policy executed by some human beings against others.

❧

Trotha's views did not go unchallenged. Almost no one, not even Social Democrats, thought of Africans as equals. But they did advocate a more humane policy, one that might, after generations or centuries, lead some Africans to civilization and rights-bearing citizenship. For the time being, however, the colony needed labor, especially as Germans imagined a blossoming Namibia integrated into the global economy through the export of diamonds (discovered in 1907) and meat. As Chancellor Bernhard von Bülow, Rohrbach, the new colonial secretary Bernhard Dernburg, missionaries, and many others pointed out, where was labor to be obtained if the natives were annihilated?[64] And if they were totally deprived of their cattle and land, as Trotha also advocated, they would become the wards of the German state, a drain on the German treasury rather than a source of riches.[65] The reformers envisaged not "streams of blood," as Trotha wrote, but subordinate yet "civilized" Africans who practiced Christianity, respected German discipline, and followed German customs. Bülow also worried about "Germany's reputation among the civilized nations."[66] Leading intellectuals warned that if Trotha's policies were not contested, they could be implemented in other places.[67]

The reformers won the argument.[68] Trotha had been too open and public with his extremist views, his ideas too much in opposition to the economic policies required if Southwest were ever to fulfill its promise as the blooming, prosperous German colony.

The kinder, gentler racial order—at least in comparison with what Trotha advocated—advanced by men like Rohrbach and Dernburg signified the establishment of a rigid color line: on one side, whites with all the rights and privileges of property and citizenship; on the other, blacks who labored on white-owned farms or diamond mines with almost no access to rights except those minimally granted as part of the civilizing process. It also meant the wrenching economic, social, and cultural transformation of the Herero and Nama from pastoralists to proletarians and the endurance of systematic violence, if not quite of the murderous sort. In essence, Southwest was to be a prime exemplar of racial capitalism and of apartheid before it had a name.[69]

Three imperial decrees in 1907 established the bedrock of the new order. First, the remaining land and cattle were confiscated from the Herero and Nama, a huge transfer of real and movable (literally—cattle) assets to German settlers. With their life resources expropriated, the Herero and Nama had no choice except to seek wage labor. Second, virtually all Africans were required to wear identity badges around their necks so they could be tracked all the time. Third, marriages between whites and blacks were banned, even retroactively. The color line, then, would be drawn around land and labor, property and citizenship rights, sex and marriage.[70]

This was, in many ways, a maniacal, impossible-to-implement vision of total control. As the authorities and settlers quickly discovered, the Herero, much like Brazilian slaves, engaged in all sorts of actions that contested the new order, from flight to theft to land occupations. Their tenacity ensured the reconstruction of their society (as we shall see) and the ongoing instability of the color-line order—though it would take until the end of the century before it was finally dismantled.

To live "free and independently"—that was the ideal for German settlers, and it meant, first and foremost, that they had to possess land and feel secure in their property rights.[71] The authorities quickly opened the newly expropriated lands for colonization. German officials sold off land to white settlers at low prices, and sometimes for nothing, provided the settlers lived on their parcel and worked the land.[72] For their part, the colonial societies at home strove to find more Germans willing to stake out a claim in Africa. Colonial officials wanted Germans with some capital to establish farms, and sought to recruit German farmers from South Africa.[73] The archives are full of appeals by German settlers, including farmers, innkeepers, bakers, and others, to colonial officials. Settlers sought permission to bring over their relatives, typically sisters or wives, or they wanted a servant, farm maid, or tutor for their children "from a good family." The officials vetted the requests and then passed them along to the German Colonial Society, which screened the applicants. If they passed, they signed contracts with the Colonial Society at home, which paid third-class steerage to the colony.[74]

Settlers who had suffered great losses during the war received compensation from the German government, another sign of the property rights white people exercised in the colony. Rohrbach, as head of the Compensation Commission, traveled the land on horseback, assessing the damages and determining the amounts to be paid.[75] Some native people also received compensation, though more as an act of beneficence than a recognition of any kind of rights they might have had. As Dernburg stated, it was "politically necessary" to compensate some natives in order to maintain the loyalty they had already expressed during the uprising.[76] This measure applied to the Reheboth Bastar, who had largely supported Germany in the war, and "loyal natives" from a variety of groups. The compensation they received was set at a lower rate than for Germans.[77] Those who received funds were also to be granted cattle from which they could live; however, not so many that they no longer needed or wanted to work, a development that would worsen the already dire labor shortage in the colony.[78] For Africans who had typically moved their herds over large distances and for whom cattle were the major repository of wealth, the requirement for German permission to own even a couple of animals must have been intensely grating.[79]

German colonial rule obliterated the Herero and Nama conception of collective property rights, the pastoralist understanding of open lands and free movement. In its place emerged a system of individual, private property rights, one available only to German settlers and other white people.

Some Herero and Nama seized cattle from German or Reheboth farms, a mark of African resistance and a constant headache for German officials. The thieves typically disappeared into the bush; the police went in pursuit, sometimes successfully, sometimes not. The unfortunate Jakobus van Wyk, a Reheboth Bastar and aide to the German police, seemed always to be losing his animals, especially when he was out on patrol. In one instance, there was certainly no getting them back: the thieves had already slaughtered his animals. Poor van Wyk complained that he did not even get a share of the meat![80] A sympathetic official asserted that van Wyk was a special target for "thieving natives," who exercised revenge against him because he cooperated with the Germans. Therefore, he was awarded compensation.[81] In some cases, missionaries intervened, as when one pleaded for the compensation of a horse to three African children. The children's original horse had been commandeered by the military during the war, but then the horse was stolen from the soldiers.[82] Apparently, not even the Schutztruppe could keep their hands on everything they had seized from Africans.

The freedom to move around a country is a fundamental right, actual mobility a highly symbolic and powerful assertion of rights. Whites could move around the colony at will, free and unhindered. Not Africans. The German authorities tried to track every African, all the time—a relentless, hopeless effort at total control. The imposition of identity badges in 1907 marked the first step in this direction. Africans needed a different document, an internal passport, if they wanted to move within the colony. Any white person could stop a native and demand to see the identity badge. If the native did not have it, he or she was to be brought to the closest police station.[83] Africans who traveled around the land without fixed abode were also subject to prosecution, a measure clearly designed to ensure that no Herero or Nama "reverted" to the pastoral life.[84]

Africans were constantly running away and "losing" their identity badges, one of the few forms of resistance left to them since the deep repression of the Namibian War.[85] Farmers complained that officials lacked the required vigilance to catch natives who had fled, and thought that the punishments meted out were much too mild. A farmer by the name of Bayha complained that during the rainy season the natives, even hard-working ones, ran away into the bush, only to return when the dry season came. The official to whom Bayha expressed his lament agreed: much greater punishment had to be meted out to natives who ran away.[86]

Up and down the colony officials sent out inquiries for missing Africans, setting off streams of paper and investigations.[87] The governor demanded that the police not just announce that someone had disappeared. They had to detail how the person had run away and what measures they had taken to apprehend the individual. In one instance, the "*Mischling*" (mixed-race) Fritz, P.M. 208—that is his identity badge number—around ten years old, Christian, "without service [employment]," gave the following plaintive testimony, as transcribed by the police:

> I ran away from Okahandja with the intention of going to my mother. My mother, the Hottentot woman Anna, had often gone to Herr Uhlemann and has requested to be able to take me in, but my mother was not allowed to take me. I said to Herr Uhlemann that I wanted to go to Windhuk to my mother, that I had nobody in Okahandja and my father has gone to Germany. Herr Uhlemann promised me that I could go to Okahandja to my mother, but he hasn't kept the promise, and since my pleas didn't work, and since I had no money I walked to Windhuk [about forty-five miles].
>
> I ask to be allowed to remain with my mother in Windhuk, since I asked correctly to be allowed to go but my efforts were in vain.[88]

Fritz ran away with a friend of his, and they were caught together. Then the police brought in the two women, both of whom testified that they were, indeed, the mothers. The resolution of the case is not clear, but it is highly unlikely that the boys were allowed to stay with their mothers.

The construction of *Eingeborenenwerften*, native housing settlements, played a major role in the German drive to establish an extensive apartheid and surveillance system. Each settlement was restricted to a particular tribe—as the authorities defined them—and each was overseen by an elder responsible to the officials.[89] A registry was kept of the residents, which was also to be posted on the outer wall next to the hut number. Alongside the registry of the huts, officials tried to maintain a complete card catalog of every one of the residents. No doubt this great expenditure of bureaucratic energy proved hopeless, especially since Africans were accustomed to moving around just in order to survive. Nor were the German officials sent to Southwest the pride of the civil service. They had to be instructed in the strictures of alphabetization. Among the bureaucratic instructions for maintaining the identity cards, one finds this critical explanation: "If for example one is looking for a native by the name of Jakob, his personal card should be found under the letter 'J.' "[90]

Violence served as the most powerful sign of a system of rights built on the color line. Whites were free from the exercise of violence by state officials, secure in the integrity of their bodies—a fundamental, core element of rights systems since the eighteenth century.[91] Not Africans. The violence practiced against them on a widespread and arbitrary scale had been one of the causes of the Namibian War. In its aftermath, violence did not cease, but now it was supposed to be rational and regularized rather than arbitrary, one lever among the many techniques of the civilizing process.

Africans suffered ubiquitous and severe violence—slaps in the face, kicks, floggings with a stick or whip.[92] Colonial Secretary Dernburg advised that a more limited exercise of corporal punishment would promote the "progressive cultural and moral uplifting of the native population."[93] Governor Friedrich von Lindequist issued an order detailing the size and material of the *Schambock*, a whip. For official use, it was to be round and smooth, one centimeter in diameter; settlers sometimes studded it with pieces of iron.[94] Seven years later, his successor, Oskar Hintrager, warned that the victims' faces and heads were to be protected, and that fifteen blows should suffice. Moreover, children and nursing mothers who were in custody had to be shielded from excessive labor and had to be provided with adequate nourishment. "It is the special responsibility of all officials to ensure, in every way, that no natives die in prison."[95] One governor protested that with floggings, "natives receive serious wounds that have a long-term negative effect on their health. This is not the purpose of the law and is not permitted."[96]

German officials often came into conflict with settlers about excessive and arbitrary punishment, which had already caused scandals at home.[97] They threatened such farmers that they would no longer send them workers from the official labor office. Yet at the very same time, officials ordered that "energetic measures" had to be taken against native cattle thieves and vagabonds and warned against the "excessive moderation of officials against natives."[98]

The result: "legitimate" violence and a stream of reports from the various police stations to Windhoek detailing the charges against individuals and the number of floggings delivered. Usually fifteen blows were given, but sometimes the victims endured twenty-five and, occasionally, even fifty lashes. These reports were reviewed on a quarterly basis by officials in the governor's office, who sometimes reprimanded lower officials for excessive violence.[99]

To give just a few examples of "legitimate" violence against Africans from an archive bursting with such reports: A Herero named Jonas had supposedly neglected his work as a herder. The livestock he watched often ran loose. He had left his herd, allegedly to find some missing animals but really just to "relax" in the bush. He received twenty blows.[100] In another instance, a hotel proprietor requested that the authorities punish his servant (*Kaffer*) Heckelbey because of freshness and lying. He received fifteen blows.[101]

In another case, a Herero by the name of Ludwig was convicted of a "deadly attack on a white [man]." The officials condemned Ludwig to four months' imprisonment, during which he was to be chained, and to receive fifty blows in two sessions. The severity of the punishment was further justified by Ludwig's "fresh behavior" toward his employer, who had displayed an "admirable patience."[102] The "Herero Schlappe passport Nr. 1719" received for "freshness and laziness" seven blows.[103] Another African also received seven blows for "disobedience and indolence."[104]

Only a few settlers shied away from violence, even of the "rational" sort. Clara Rohrbach, for example, placed great store in teaching her servants how to work well, as opposed to the many natives who, she mocked, moved at an exceedingly slow pace wherever they were going. Beatings were not her method: she claimed to treat her natives—the best in the entire colony—with care, and even visited those who had become ill in their native settlements. "To drag [a native] man into the kitchen to beat him, to me that would be dreadful," she wrote.[105]

But of course the color line meant that natives were to be kept in their place as well. Too much education was not a good thing. When Clara Rohrbach visited one of her servants who had fallen sick, she encountered an African teacher. "His home is a large, nicely [*hübsch*] built, clean hut [*Pontok*]. He himself goes about in clean khakis like the whites. He speaks virtually flawless German and has, oddly, educated viewpoints. The missionaries have educated him much too far and have let him go way beyond his station. A native should never speak as he does."[106] Clearly, there were limits to the civilizing process. In fact, the civilizing project and the deep-seated repression of Africans were inextricably entwined.[107]

In only a few, highly restricted realms could Africans claim any rights. If the authorities agreed to let them own a few cattle, then those animals became their property. The sanctity of private property, that most basic right of all, could not be violated, not by white farmers and not by the authorities, who believed firmly in the *Rechtsstaat* (legal state), even though that state was shot through by the color line.

And there was the matter of free labor. Africans were supposedly at liberty to enter into and withdraw from labor contracts, a matter not just of economic development, but of civilization itself.[108] The German constitution of 1871 and the subsequent civil code enshrined the free mobility of labor and the sanctity of contracts that two (or more) parties freely joined. Such provisions were, of course, essential elements of capitalist economies. They also affirmed individuals as rights-bearing citizens who could freely dispose of their property, including their own labor power.

However, the racially determined repressions of the color line immediately undermined the apparent equality of contracts. The vast asymmetry of power relations meant that Africans had little choice but to enter the labor market, and the acute labor shortage meant that the authorities and settlers did everything possible to keep Africans tied to their employers. Although Africans supposedly had free choice to decide with whom they would enter into a service contract (*Dienstvertrag*), an African seeking another position had to have a signed release from his current employer. Any farmer who hired an individual bound to another settler could be fined the considerable sum of six hundred marks.[109]

Despite the repressions that went along with the color line and a whites-only system of rights, the German legal order still left open to blacks two paths toward citizenship—at least theoretically. Although Germany had banned marriages between German settlers and indigenous people, mixed-race children were a part of the reality of the colony. If the fathers were German (as was almost invariably the case), the children could claim citizenship in Germany since citizenship rights ran through the paternal line. Moreover, blacks who had served in the Schutztruppe, the German colonial army, could also claim citizenship, military service a well-recognized path to citizenship. The authorities were loath to tamper with these essential features of the German *Rechtsstaat*. Only the Nazis closed off altogether those options for black veterans and mixed-race children.[110]

Meanwhile, settlers demanded that they be granted the same rights as people had back home (as would Japanese colonists in Korea, as we shall see in the next chapter), even though a somewhat different legal order reigned in the colony. The authorities responded, not least because they were in many ways dependent on the settlers and always sought to make Southwest Africa hospitable to Germans. After long discussions and negotiations, the authorities instituted in 1909 communal representative organs on the German model at home.[111] Secure in their property rights, German settlers were now on the verge of obtaining greater citizenship rights. Only the outbreak of World War I short-circuited this development.

Marriage constituted another arena of contestation around the drawing of the color line and the nature of citizenship rights. As mentioned, the decrees of 1907 had banned interracial marriages, even retroactively.

A number of Germans who had married African women contested this ban. One settler, Carl Becker, had married a Reheboth Bastar. As a result of the new laws and decrees he lost the right to vote, and his children, two of whom had been born in Germany, would not be recognized as German citizens. Becker used both racial and legal arguments to press his case, noting that his wife was "almost white" and that they lived in a "moral and spiritual" relationship. He argued that his family deserved its "citizenship rights" (*bürgerliche Rechte*). Should these not be granted, he concluded in a petition to the authorities, "then my joy and interest in this country [Southwest Africa], to which I have given all my strength, will be extinguished." The authorities nonetheless rejected his appeal.[112] For German officials, the maintenance of the color-line determinants of citizenship proved more important than any argument Becker was able to summon.

The racial society and color-line rights meant drawing not just one color line between whites and blacks, but also a variety of other lines between the races and tribes—Africans as well as Europeans—in the highly complex demographic order of Southwest Africa. German authorities and settlers had varying and mobile evaluations of the various African groups. The Reheboth Bastar were generally more privileged than other indigenous peoples because of their "mixed-race" character. But, to some Germans, that same trait marked the Bastar as the chief carriers of racial degeneracy.[113] The Herero were both admired and feared because of their independence and military prowess.[114] The Bergdamara, because they had been enslaved by the Ovambo and the Nama in the eighteenth and nineteenth centuries, fell to the bottom of the ladder in German eyes.[115]

Among Europeans, the Boers, the descendants of the seventeenth-century Dutch settlers in South Africa, occupied the lowest rank of the white population. The German administration allowed Boers to settle, but was wary about the establishment of closed Boer communities that might undermine German influence.[116] "The Boers have a stubborn character," wrote one German official. "The greatest caution is required in dealing with them. At the same time, we must never lose sight that they are gradually to be subordinated to our culture."[117] Boer settlements "were to be sprinkled with strong and numerous German-national elements."[118] Yet, as whites, the path of citizenship lay open to them. They were allowed to establish their own churches and to use their own language in the service, though their children were obligated to attend schools in which German was the language of instruction.[119] In short, Boers could achieve citizenship, but only as a result of assimilation.

However, not every white person was an asset. "This land needs arms-bearing men, who can establish families and produce many children," wrote Deputy Governor Hintrager in 1909.[120] It was especially important to recruit German girls and young women. Officials worried about German men's attraction to African women, which more than anything else threatened to undermine the strict racial boundaries that were critical to the apartheid society. Governor Lindequist wrote: "As experience has shown and because of the lack of white girls, many young [German] men are inclined to enter into marital relations with natives, especially [Rehoboth] Bastar girls . . . [who] bring a herd of cattle, a wagon, and not rarely a farm into the marriage."[121] Paul Rohrbach wrote that already a pack of half-white children were running around. Astonishingly quickly, he wrote, "every sentiment for morality, culture, social order, and national well-being is lost. The people go native [*verkaffern*], as one says here . . . [the men] sink into a swarm of wild, ill-bred, dirty bastard children."[122]

Conclusion

In the summer of 1923, thousands of Herero streamed toward Okahandja, the center of Herero land. They traveled from all over Southwest Africa, and from Bechuanaland, Angola, and the Cape Colony. They came to honor the legacy of their paramount chief, Samuel Maharero. Since 1915, when British South African troops had defeated the Germans in a side-show battle of World War I, Namibia had been effectively under South African control. In 1920, the League of Nations made it official by granting South Africa a mandate over the country.

Maharero had died in exile in Bechuanaland. Now, with the permission of the South African authorities, his coffin was allowed back into Southwest, to be buried with honor in Okahandja. An honor guard of thousands of Herero soldiers, decked out in German military uniforms, accompanied the casket. Many of them had fought with South Africa against the German army in World War I; some had fought with the Germans during the Namibian War. Two of Maharero's sons and other prominent Herero led the procession. They were met in Okahandja by thousands of their compatriots and by missionaries and South African officials. On 23 August 1923, Maharero was buried in Okahandja. The German missionary pastor Heinrich Vedder performed the service in Otjiherero.[123]

The burial of Maharero beside his father and grandfather in Oka-handja was the most powerful symbol of the revival of Herero society after the devastation of the genocide. Herero had survived in exile and in the colony. They rebuilt their community, establishing new institutions and revitalizing older ones. Amid life in captivity, in the concentration camps, and even at large, thousands more had converted to Christianity—as had the Dakota in Minnesota after their defeat—which gave them solace in a wrenching period, and some modicum of material support and education.[124] A militaristic society since the nineteenth century, Herero men, with exquisite irony, established *otruppe*, communal organizations in which they adopted German uniforms, ranks, and, occasionally, names, the ultimate expression of the colonized absorbing but also manipulating to their own benefit the customs of the colonizer. And in the 1920s, Herero and other Africans flocked to Marcus Garvey's Universal Negro Improvement Association (UNIA), with its Pan-Africanism and call for the liberation of black people around the world. Garvey's movement attracted a great number of followers in North America, the Caribbean, Europe, and Africa. In Namibia, the UNIA had even greater success, at least in regard to membership and organization.[125]

In spite of the genocide and the deep repression that followed, the Herero and Nama had managed to reconstitute their societies. They had great hopes when South African troops overthrew German colonial rule, expecting to get their land back and to be able to graze their herds. Herero flooded back into their country from Bechuanaland, Angola, and other parts of Southwest Africa. They expanded their herds and took land in a somewhat chaotic, disorganized mass movement.

It would not last. South Africa, with the legitimacy of the League of Nations mandate, was not about to let the Herero dominate the country.

In the 1920s, officials removed many Herero and other Africans to native reserves and restricted their herds. White South Africans bought or seized land, much like the Germans before them. After World War II, the mandate revolved into a UN Trusteeship. South Africa was supposed to move the territory toward autonomy and independence. It never did. The Afrikaner nationalist victory in 1948 signified the establishment of total apartheid in the country—including in Southwest Africa, which the Nationalist Party essentially annexed and incorporated into South Africa.

In the 1960s, black Namibians, with a preponderance of Ovambo people, organized the Southwest Africa People's Organization (SWAPO). Decolonization and national liberation struggles, from Africa to Asia and the Middle East, were at their high point in that decade. SWAPO joined the surge, also influenced by the larger and more dynamic African National Congress (ANC) in South Africa. The UN actively promoted human rights, decolonization, and racial equality (as we shall see in chapter 10, on Rwanda and Burundi). In 1966, it revoked the trusteeship, South Africa so obviously in violation of all these principles. However, South Africa flouted the decision, as it did so many others, in a desperate and increasingly violent and repressive effort to maintain apartheid and hold on to Southwest Africa. But in the 1990s, under the pressure of the armed struggle led by SWAPO and the ANC (at great personal cost to the militants and their families) and almost universal international condemnation, apartheid and white rule crumbled in South Africa. Namibia led the way. It became independent in 1990, four years before Nelson Mandela's election as president of South Africa (see figure 6.4).

Some years later, on a drive north from Windhoek to the Etosha National Park, I watched mile upon mile of bush country go by, nary a person or animal in sight. I asked the guide: "Who owns all this land?" He laughed, then replied, "Germans." He was not totally accurate. The heirs of German settlers do still own a substantial portion of the land, but so do the descendants of white South Africans who came in the 1920s and in the subsequent decades.

Since independence, Namibia has a democratic constitution that proclaims the full equality of all citizens. The land issue remains, and

FIGURE 6.4 Sam Nujoma and Javier Perez de Cuellar celebrate Namibian independence in 1990. The League of Nations granted South Africa a mandate over Namibia in 1920, which was continued after 1945 as a UN trusteeship. The UN revoked the trusteeship in 1966 because of South Africa's policy of apartheid and refusal to move Namibia toward independence. That did little to change South African policies. As a result, SWAPO launched an armed struggle in the 1960s, parallel to the efforts of the ANC in South Africa. Namibia led the way toward independence in 1990, followed by South Africa in 1994. The UN played a major role in both efforts. Here, UN secretary-general Javier Perez de Cuellar congratulates SWAPO'S leader and Namibia's first president, Sam Nujoma, at the celebration of Namibian independence in Windhoek on 21 March 1990. (UN Photo/John Isaac.)

the vast disproportion between white and black ownership contributes mightily to the poverty and inequality that mark Namibian society today. Still, black citizens, like their white counterparts, exercise voting rights, have security of property ownership, move around the country at will, and possess a significant degree of freedom of expression. The rights so long denied them became reality with independence. Namibians surmounted the tragedy of genocide and its brutal legacy.

Herero and Nama have joined the post-1945 human rights world in another way: with demands for recognition of the genocide and reparations payments from Germany.[126] Appeals heard in German and

American courts have, as of this writing, been unsuccessful. The appellants are, however, acutely aware of the reparations and restitution that Jews have won from Germany over the decades (as discussed in the previous chapter). They have a simple explanation for their own lack of success: "We are black," said Barnabas Veraa Katuuo, a founder of the New York–based Association of Ovaherero Genocide.[127]

The genocide in Southwest Africa was a foundational act that created a new political and economic order emblematic of a global trend: the drawing of the color line in the first half of the twentieth century. The annihilation of the Herero and Nama deeply etched the new political economy that emerged in genocide's wake. The huge expropriation of wealth—land and cattle—allowed the development of the white settler class. The systems of rights that emerged enfranchised the color elect— whites in Southwest Africa—and excluded and repressed the survivors. Although Southwest Africa could not remotely be called a democratic society, whites certainly exercised rights in an array of arenas, not least over property, and benefitted from the forms of representation available to them.

The history of repression, then, is also the history of the claim and cry for rights. As Du Bois well knew, rights regimes are never stable. The fact that some categories of people possess the "right to have rights" inevitably provides an opening to those excluded from the pantheon of rights-bearing citizens. They, too, can demand those same rights. The long struggle for Namibian independence from South Africa ultimately proved successful. However great the social inequalities today in Namibia, apartheid has been abolished and blacks, since 1990, exercise full citizenship rights. The promise of rights is always present, even when the exclusions seem most pronounced.

Imperialism was not only a European and American venture. In the late nineteenth century, Japan also began to create a colonial empire. The same questions we have explored in Europe, North America, Asia Minor, Latin America, and Africa emerged in an Asia under Japanese domination: Who would be able to exercise rights? What kind of rights? And how did a system of human rights finally come to be? We shall explore these issues through the history of Korea.

Chapter 7

Korea

COLONIAL LEGACIES AND HUMAN RIGHTS IN A DIVIDED COUNTRY

෴

PERCIVAL LOWELL, scion of the storied Lowell family of Massachusetts and renowned scientist, traveled widely in Japan and Korea in the late nineteenth century. He described Korea as a land of great, if sometimes harsh, beauty, with lovely blooming trees and flowers, fertile rice paddies, striking mountains, dramatically rocky coasts; a land where even the Bengal tiger, used to warmer climes, roams. The people, garbed in white, presented a no less wondrous spectacle. Yet this beautiful country was cut off from the rest of the world.

> Go with me to a land whose life for ages has been a mystery,—a land which from time unknown has kept aloof, apart. . . . For cycles on cycles she has been in the world, but not of it. Her people have been born, have lived, have died, oblivious to all that was passing around them. They might have been denizens of another planet for aught they knew of the history of this. And the years glided into centuries, and the centuries grew to be numbered by tens, and still the veil remained as tightly drawn as at the beginning. It was but last year that Korea stepped as a *débutante* into the society of the world.[1]

Orientalist? To be sure, with its evocation of a timeless, mysterious, never-changing people and country. Yet Lowell captured something about the relative isolation of Korea over many centuries. Beginning in 1876 with a treaty forced upon it by Japan, it most certainly became "of the world"—in crashing, thunderous fashion. Korea, for the next eighty years—until 1953 and the end of the Korean War—experienced devastating wars, civil conflicts, and Japanese colonialism, only to end up with two states divided by the most highly militarized border in the world.

A people that had, by and large, been as rooted and sedentary, as ethnically homogeneous as is possible in this world of great diversity and mobility, suddenly found itself jostled around Northeast Asia. Nearly one million Japanese settled in Korea in this period, crossing the mere 120 miles of sea between the two, disrupting the relative uniformity of the population.[2] Then, at the end of World War II, they found themselves forcibly repatriated to Japan. About the same number of Koreans had migrated to Manchuria and Japan, many of them also to be repatriated—back to Korea in their case—in 1945.[3] (See maps 7.1 and 7.2.)

Korea and Koreans were battered about by more powerful countries near and far, while they also underwent, as a Japanese colony, rapid economic development and modernization. An oppressive overseer, Japan also offered some Koreans great opportunities for advancement.[4] All the while, Japan competed with Russia, China, and the United States for preponderant power in East Asia, and with American missionaries and Russian and Chinese communists for predominant influence over Koreans and their future.

From the 1890s onward, while many Koreans benefitted from Japanese rule, others took to the lectern and the streets, the pulpit and the mountain hideouts of guerrilla warfare, all in the name of democracy; liberty and rights; and the independent, self-determining Korean nation. It was a popular mobilization of extraordinary depth that waxed and waned, but went on even in the face of the most severe repression and the devastation of total war.

Along the way, however, Korean nationalists, left and right, North and South, came to idolize the state as the expression of the nation and gave short shrift to individual liberties. Both Koreas developed a militarized, authoritarian nationalism that sundered the link between the nation-state and human rights—a common twentieth-century phenomenon and a striking departure from the prevalent liberalism of the nineteenth century, which defined the nation-state through constitutions, representative government, security of person and property, and political rights.

Yet the course of Korean history, like every other case considered in this book, also shows that human rights are nearly always present in

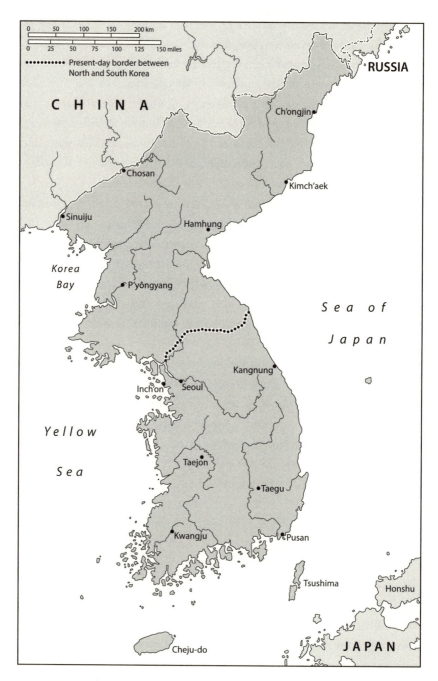

MAP 7.1 Korea in the twentieth century.

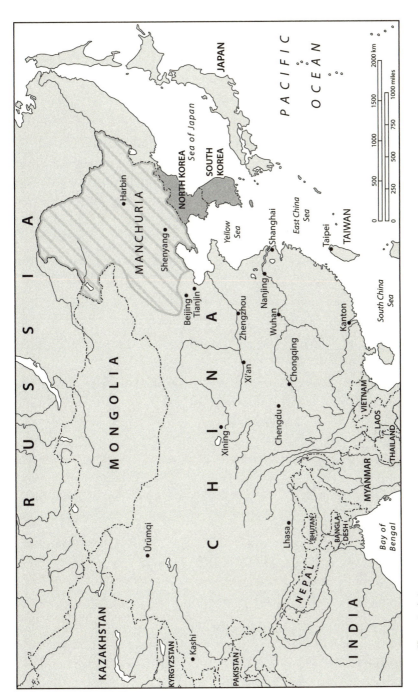

MAP 7.2 Korea in Asia.

modern nation-states. Even when brutally suppressed, human rights live on as dreams and aspirations. South Koreans in the latter part of the twentieth century drew upon the pre-1945 popular movements to forge powerful mobilizations. They succeeded in toppling two dictatorial regimes and creating, in the late twentieth century, a far more democratic, rights-respecting political order. In the North, the severe repression exercised by the party-state left no space for popular movements. North Korea did proclaim and, to a degree, implement social programs that have, at times, benefitted its populace. As we shall see, however, the provisioning of the population, a policy known to dictatorships far and wide, is not quite the same thing as social rights rooted in rights-bearing citizenship.

Korean history, then, moves us more fully into the twentieth century. It enables us to explore the meaning of social as well as political rights, and the power of popular movements against authoritarian dictatorships, both Japanese and home-grown variants. In the modern era, however, Koreans could never make their own history. The unrelenting force of Great Powers—Japan, China, Russia and the Soviet Union, and the United States—was ever present. We shall explore these developments through the persons of Syngman Rhee and Park Chung-hee, South Korea's preeminent leaders from 1945 to 1977, and Kim Il-sŏng, the founding dictator of North Korea, whose family has reigned over the country ever since.

ↁↁ

But, first, a foray into the worlds of Japanese imperialists; American missionaries; Russian, Chinese, and Japanese communists—and Koreans.

Korea had the makings of a nation from the fourteenth century. It had a unified kingdom; a population about as homogeneous as possible, however diverse its origins in the ancient past; and a common language (although Chinese served as the language of state and high culture). Koreans expressed something like a national consciousness, though certainly not the nationalism of a nation-state—that is, a state built on some form of popular sovereignty, whether real or imagined, and a set of rights attendant to its citizens, however circumscribed those rights might be in reality. Instead, old Korea was defined by a strict hierarchical order undergirded by a conservative Confucianism. Presiding over it all was the Chosŏn Dynasty, which lasted from 1392 to 1910, about as long as the Ottoman reign.[5]

Scholar-officials stood at the apex of Korean society. The *yangban* (as they were called) had become, by and large, a hereditary class defined by their possession of office, education, and landed property, and their freedom from taxation. Only occasionally was a particularly adept commoner able to scale the heights via education and the exam system and enter the top ranks of the office-holder hierarchy. Below them sat the vast majority of commoners, slaves, merchants, peasants (the largest group), and tradesmen—including those deemed "unclean," like butchers.

The palace, office holders, and landed elite lived by extracting wealth from the peasantry. And extract they did, massively so. Korean reformers as well as Western travelers in the latter part of the nineteenth century described a peasant class ground down by harsh taxation and forced labor. The hereditary elite lived very well, the *yangban* justifying to themselves that they alone embodied and upheld Korean culture and civilization across the centuries. Dissenters there were, and even royal efforts at reform, usually prodded by periodic peasant revolts. Reformers wrote clear-eyed tracts, describing the dire condition of the peasantry and the abuse of power by officials and landholders (usually one and the same). They argued that family origin by no means translated into ability.[6] However, the *yangban* managed to subvert even the mild reform measures proffered by kings.

The signs of hierarchy were everywhere. When Lowell was to be presented to King Kojong, our American arrived in a palanquin—the infamous sedan chair we have seen in India and Brazil. It was borne not by slaves, as in Rio de Janeiro, but by "coolies." Lowell and the American minister who accompanied him were of course kept waiting, and then were finally brought into the king's presence by a high official, Hong Yŏng-Sik. "No sooner had we reached the top of the steps," wrote Lowell, "than Hong fell nearly flat on his face,—the usual Korean prostration

before royalty,—while we began the first of our series of three bows."
When they left, everything ran in reverse: the two Americans bowing
three times, Hong prostrating himself.[7]

The act of prostration, even of bowing, characterized the world of
hierarchy, not the world inspired by the revolutions of the eighteenth
and nineteenth centuries with their clarion calls for equality under the
law, security of property, political representation, and individual
rights—the world, that is, of nation-states and human rights.

In old Korea, the Chosŏn Dynasty had to worry about China and
Japan. It worked out a fine arrangement with China. Three times a year
a delegation went to Beijing and delivered tribute. So long as the flow
into Chinese coffers continued unabated, Korea was allowed its autonomy. Japan, in the early seventeenth century, retreated behind its seas,
never to bother Korea again—until it arrived first in 1876, and then with
devastating force in the 1890s. Korea, a small, once-isolated country,
came to stand at the crossroads of all the great streams of politics of the
twentieth century—an emblem of the global world, for good and bad.

Japanese imperialists and American missionaries provided the earliest and most powerful modernizing influences.[8] They made for odd
(and unacknowledged) bedfellows, but so they were.[9] Then came communists. Each in its own way fostered the development of Korean nationalism, both its militarist elements and the claim for human rights
within a Korean nation-state.

Decades after the events discussed here, an elderly Korean living in
the United States, Hong Ŭlsu, recalled a life that traversed all the possibilities and disappointments, all the political streams, all the influences—
American, Japanese, Chinese, Russian—of Korea's twentieth century.
Hong Ŭlsu was a poor villager. In his youth he thought the world was
comprised of Korea and the only other countries he had ever heard
about: Russia, China, and Japan. At the ripe age of sixteen, he had still
never seen the local town, eight miles away. His Japanese schoolteacher
showed him and a few other students a globe. He and his classmates
could not identify Korea. "How ignorant can I be?" he thought. "I resolved to broaden my knowledge and get an education."[10]

Japan opened the world to him, and off to Osaka and Tokyo he went, despite the disapproval of his family. On the journey, he encountered trains and toilets for the first time. He described the clothes he wore that the Japanese would rail against.

> My clothes at the time were the Korean traditional clothes (*hanbok*). In those days, the poor farm people changed into a set of winter clothes at the end of September and wore them day and night until the following April. All during that time, they did not wash their clothes or take baths. You know that the *hanbok* is white, so by spring it was almost black because of the accumulated dirt, and that is what I had on. It was January, so I had been in the same clothes for more than three months.
>
> On my feet I wore straw sandals; I did not even know about leather shoes. So here I was, in the middle of Osaka, Japan, with dirty, smelly Korean clothes and straw sandals. No wonder people in the train would not sit next to me.[11]

In Japan he encountered both modernizing forces: Japan itself and American missionaries. He worked for a benevolent bookseller in Tokyo and managed to get an education at the same time. He attained entrance to the Aoyama Christian University, operated by American missionaries, and decided to become an English teacher.

Then he encountered something else: communism. While a student, he joined a communist study group with about thirty Japanese students. Hong was the sole Korean. "We got along just fine. They would hold my hand and say, 'We will all work together to drive the Japanese out of your country.'"[12] That was communist internationalism in action—an internationalism fundamentally committed to the nation-state as a stepping-stone on the way to the glorious future (as we shall see in more detail in the next chapter, on the Soviet Union). "Most of the Korean students in Japan became infatuated with communism. The Russian revolution was only a few years back, and communism was the new force. It was well organized, systematic, logically reasoned out, or so I thought, and also the Communist Party in Japan had as one of its slogans, 'Independence for Korea.'"[13]

In his second year at the university, Hong became a communist activist, leading the study group and secretly distributing communist literature. His organizing activity among Korean students in Japan swiftly landed him in jail, where he was interrogated and severely beaten. With plenty of time on his hands—the inmates were not allowed to talk to one another—he began to rethink his communist commitments. The Confucian mandate to take care of one's parents came roaring back to him. So he abandoned communism, returned to his studies, and completed his degree as an English teacher while also becoming fluent in Japanese.

Christianity, Japan, and communism—the three major modernizing influences, all combined in one individual.

Missionaries had few successes initially. In 1900, probably only about 1 percent of the population—113,000 out of about 11,310,000—had converted to Christianity. By 1930, the numbers had risen significantly, even though the great surge would come only after 1945. In 1930, out of approximately 21,058,000 Koreans, around 320,000, 1.5 percent of the population, were Christian.[14]

Despite their small numbers, Christians played an outsized role in the politics and culture of Korea from the 1890s onward. For those who chose to convert, Christianity provided a path into the modern world. Missionaries built schools and hospitals as they spread the gospel. They promoted an ethic of cleanliness as a celebration of god, and a life of work and worship. American missionaries also promoted global trade and economic development, which they viewed as vehicles for "civilization."[15]

With its theology, Christianity gave Korean converts a language of humanism, of equality—indeed, of rights. Korean Christians no longer had to suffer the old, oppressive hierarchy of traditional Korea, nor the widespread poverty it had created. There could be more justice in the world. In their drive to disseminate Christianity, such as we have already seen among Indians on the American frontier and the Herero and Nama in semi-arid Namibia, missionaries linked Europe and North America with the Middle East, Africa, and Asia—including Korea.[16]

Japan would prove to be a more powerful influence. "The countries in Europe shine with the light of civilization and abound in wealth and power," wrote Kume Kunitake, the chief secretary to nobleman Iwakura

Tonomi and the official chronicler of the famed Iwakura Mission.[17] Just three years into the Meiji Restoration of 1868, Iwakura led a delegation, comprising half the state leadership and fifty students, that traveled through Europe and the United States. They were abroad for two years. Much like our Persians in Britain in the second decade of the nineteenth century, whom we encountered in chapter 1, though on a much larger scale, the members of the Iwakura Mission looked, observed, marveled, and came back to Japan transformed, anxious to make their country a Great Power on par with the Western states—and to secure and protect Japan from their imperial designs. A rapid modernization program directed by the state was the answer. It entailed a change in cultural values as well as the absorption of the West's technical knowledge. Japan, the reformers argued, had to place much greater emphasis on accomplishment than lineage, on the rule of law rather than the arbitrary exercise of power, and on the mobilization of the population for national goals through education, labor, political participation, and military service.[18]

Within just a few years of the Meiji Restoration and the Iwakura Mission, Japan had a well-functioning central state, a representative system of governance, an industrial economy, and a lively public sphere. It also had a powerful, well-armed and well-disciplined army eager to expand Japan's might throughout Asia. In two wars, against China in 1894–95 and against Russia in 1904–5, Japan created its supremacy in East Asia. Chinese and Russian officials and merchants were largely driven out of Korea. The Russo-Japanese War had particular resonance, because it was the first time an Asian power triumphed over one of the great European states.[19] (Ethiopia, another non-Western state, had defeated Italy in 1896, but Italy was not quite a Great Power, so the Ethiopian victory did not resonate as loudly as the Japanese one.[20]) In the final settlement in 1905, brokered by the United States, Korea became a Japanese protectorate. Five years later, Japan threw out all the pretenses and deceptions and annexed Korea as a colony.

For Korea, so close geographically, Japan's rise could spell only danger. One can easily transpose (and slightly modify) Porfirio Díaz's contemporaneous comment on Mexico and the United States to Asia: "Poor Korea, so far from Heaven and so close to Japan." Even more dangerously, Korea bordered on two other large and powerful—or potentially powerful—countries: China and Russia.

Yet the Díaz-like statement carries only one part of the truth. Japan was a danger; it was also a magnet. Its rapid and highly successful modernization drive won it the admiration of many Koreans as well as other Asians, Africans, and Middle Easterners. Like the United States but in much greater dimensions, the Japanese magnet pulled in thousands upon thousands of ambitious students, intellectuals, businessmen, and military officers, as well as impoverished Koreans desperately seeking a way out of their continual existential crisis.[21] With its vision of a trans-Asian economic, political, and cultural realm, culminating in the Greater East Asia Co-Prosperity Sphere of World War II, Japan stimulated development on the peninsula, creating the foundations of Korea's industrial economy. Like American missionaries, the Japanese built hospitals and schools, and also roads, railroads, bridges, ports, telegraph lines, and much else besides, creating the infrastructure for a modern economy.[22] They also, inadvertently, stimulated the emergence of mass political mobilizations among Koreans, both those who admired Japan and those who fought against its power in Korea.

Korea's many and disparate streams of reform and rebellion came together in 1919 in the March First Movement, the great uprising that served as the touchstone for every Korean political movement in the twentieth century and is celebrated still today in North and South Korea. Unexpectedly, hundreds of thousands of Koreans took to the streets in March 1919 to protest Japanese control. Official Japanese figures counted 3,200 demonstrations and more than one million participants overall, who rallied to the cry, "*Manse*" (long live Korean independence).[23] They were moved, most immediately, by the slogans of self-determination emanating from Washington and Petrograd, by the death and funeral of the ex-emperor Kojong, and by similar movements in China that had led to the overthrow of the emperor and establishment of a republic in 1912. Koreans abroad lent whatever support they could provide to their co-nationals.[24]

"We hereby declare that Korea is an independent state and that Koreans are a self-governing people."[25] So begins the Korean Declaration of Independence, proclaimed on 1 March 1919 to a large crowd in Seoul's Pagoda Park. It was written in traditional, flowery literary style, yet has all the hallmarks of the national independence declarations from the American, French, and Latin American revolutions of the eighteenth and nineteenth centuries to the anticolonial movements of the twentieth.[26] It invoked history—five thousand years of it, somehow adding a millennium onto the usual proclamations—and connected Korean specifics to the "great movement of world reform based upon the awakening conscience of mankind." The "clear command of heaven" dictates the "right of all nations to coexist and live in harmony." Yet Koreans suffer under the "agony of alien suppression." An independent Korea will be a light in the East, leading Japan to correct its ways and China to fulfill its destiny. Writing in lyrical fashion, the authors proclaimed that "a new world is before our eyes. . . . A new spring has arrived prompting the myriad forms of life to come to life again. . . . The present is a time of mild breezes and warm sunshine, reinvigorating the spirit." Independence will mean a new era of creativity in which the "national essence" blossoms.[27]

Korean activists went on to write a provisional constitution and establish a provisional government, which existed in exile, mostly in Shanghai, down to 1945. The constitution of the Korean Republic, as it was called, like so many constitutions since the eighteenth century, proclaimed the equality of citizens and their basic rights, and called for membership in that new international body, the League of Nations.

Koreans had entered the world of nation-states and human rights. Why did a very traditional society and culture like Korea develop these hallmarks of the modern world? It is hard to imagine any other path forward for Korea in the global age of the nineteenth and twentieth centuries. Korea could not survive as an isolated country amid the compulsions of capitalist trade and imperialism. Korea had never been an empire, despite the fact that King Kojong, in 1894, proclaimed Korea an empire and gave himself the glorified title of emperor in a vain effort to place the country on par with China and Japan. In the modern world, Korea's resistance could only be in the nationalist mode. Traditionalists, liberals, socialists—all advocated Korean nationalism. If it were ever to survive as an independent country, Korea required a nation-state with all that signified—its own government, army, educational system, myths, language, and, not least, a constitution that proclaimed human rights. Korea's long history of isolation coupled with a highly developed state and literary culture provided the substratum that a modern nationalist movement could build upon and, at the same time, radically transform through popular mobilizations, including armed rebellions.[28]

The March First Movement unnerved the Japanese authorities. They repressed it, destroying for the moment the possibility of creating an independent Korea. Much like Britain, France, and the Netherlands, Japan had become an imperial nation-state—that is, a compact nation-state with clearly defined borders plus an overseas colonial empire.[29] The Japanese invented in the 1930s a new term, *kōmin*, or "imperial subject," to define the status of Koreans and Taiwanese (Taiwan was also a Japanese colony).[30] In its most progressive form, the status of imperial subject opened paths of advancement for Koreans (as we saw with Hong Ŭlsu and shall shortly see in the case of Park Chung-hee). They had new opportunities in the economy and society, and in intellectual and political life. Many Koreans went to Japan to study and pursue careers, as did Hong Ŭlsu.

The favored status of some Koreans did not, however, come for free. The Japanese demanded displays of loyalty to the empire and changes in Korean customs as officials proudly trumpeted the "one-race" idea—Koreans and Japanese as Asian brothers and sisters.[31] Much like American Indians, Korean males who attended a Japanese school or sought a job in a Japanese company had to cut off their long braids. They had to abandon traditional Korean clothing. The Japanese promoted soap and baths.[32] In the 1930s and 1940s the Japanese forced Koreans to practice Shinto rituals under the slogan "One Body, One Spirit," meaning not just individuals but the union of Asian races.

For every advance some Koreans enjoyed, others suffered greatly. "Though we studied side by side," recalled Kang Pyŏngju, another elderly Korean immigrant to the United States, "we never socialized together. The separation between Japanese and Korean students remained thorough and complete."[33] Those who engaged in anti-Japanese activities experienced imprisonment and torture. If released, the police monitored their every move.[34] Many Koreans reported systematic discrimination by the Japanese, officials and settlers—lower pay for the same work, failure to get promoted, inability to receive permits to open a shop or obtain a driver's license, arbitrary harassment by the police.[35] By the workings of the market as well as official policy, many Koreans were forced off the land and out of urban neighborhoods.[36] As far back as the 1880s Japanese rice merchants had penetrated the Korean countryside by lending money to Korean farmers, who often were unable to pay their debts and lost the land that they had put up as collateral.[37] In shops, Koreans were sometimes treated to verbal abuse; on buses, they were sometimes forced to give up their seats to Japanese. Japanese-owned public baths often barred Koreans. Overall, "Japanese and Koreans were living 'together' as if 'water and oil,'" remarked one visitor to Seoul in the late colonial period.[38]

The worst came during World War II as the human and material demands of Japan's great imperial ambitions strained resources to the utmost and war brought its terrible destruction to Korean lives. The war began in Asia in 1937 with the Japanese invasion of Southern China, and went on to develop into a vast conflict throughout Asia and the Pacific. The Japanese uprooted hundreds of thousands of Koreans and other Asians as soldiers, workers, prostitutes, and forced laborers.[39] Beginning in 1942, the Imperial Japanese Army drafted tens of thousands of Korean men. Perhaps as many as two hundred thousand Korean women (among many of other nationalities) were forced into sex slavery for Japanese soldiers.[40] Japanese-sponsored industrial development in Korea and Manchuria intensified the brute exploitation of Korean workers. In the Korean countryside the Japanese requisitioned the rice crop, though some farmers and merchants managed to evade the regulations.[41] Overall, the population entered a downward spiral of impoverishment and famine. The vast exploitation brought on by total war rendered hollow all the sunny phrases of the Greater East Asia Co-Prosperity Sphere and imperial citizenship, even as individual Koreans continued to thrive under Japanese sponsorship in business, the bureaucracy, and, not least, the army.

Japan, of course, lost the war. Its forces in Korea awaited instructions as the imperial government and the emperor convened following the

American nuclear attacks on Hiroshima and Nagasaki and the Soviet declaration of war against Japan on 8 August 1945. Japan's leaders finally accepted the fact that their grand imperial ambitions had been ground to dust. In Manchuria and Korea the situation descended into utter chaos.[42] Japanese troops waited to board transport ships home, harassed and brutalized by Korean irregulars and common citizens. Some Japanese settlers whose families had been in Korea for nearly seventy-five years also waited to be sent back to Japan, a country many barely knew. They, too, experienced the revenge of Koreans, some of whom had been happy to be friendly and cooperative when Japan was on the ascendancy. Meanwhile, most Koreans in Japan, over one million of them, as well as those in farther-flung parts of the former empire, like the Philippines, were also forcibly repatriated home to Korea.[43]

The end of the war only sharpened the political rifts that had defined Korean politics since the 1890s. Communists, socialists, liberals, conservatives—all contended for the decisive role in shaping the future nation-state. Numerous efforts at compromise and cooperation quickly fell apart. As had been Korea's fate since its first treaty with Japan in 1876, Koreans could hardly define for themselves their political future. On the basis of their "trusteeship" agreement, the Soviet Union and the United States, in December 1945, divided the country at the thirty-eighth parallel.[44] At the time, both the Soviet Union and the United States expected the arrangement to be temporary. Both envisaged for the long term a unified nation-state on the peninsula. The step-by-step emergence of the Cold War dashed such visions and hopes, solidifying the division of the peninsula for decades to come.

Social mobility and brutal exploitation; university education and professional employment; communism, Christianity, and the "one-race" ideology—through all of Koreans' diverse encounters and experiences under Japanese colonialism, one aspect was common: the intensification of the feeling of being Korean, of being different from the Japanese occupiers. More than most populations around the globe that experienced colonization, Koreans already had a highly developed national sense. The Japanese occupation only intensified that sentiment. And politicized it. The status of imperial subjects, with all its contradictions, made only greater the desire for an independent, self-determining Korean nation-state. Whether its political form would be supportive of human rights would be another matter.

ۏ

Three postwar leaders epitomized Korea's political divisions and its decoupling of the nation-state from human rights: Syngman Rhee and Park Chung-hee in South Korea and Kim Il-sŏng in North Korea. Rhee, the US-backed first president of the Republic of Korea (South Korea), spoke fluent English. After early schooling in traditional Confucian academies, he was educated in American missionary schools and universities, including Princeton University, where he received his doctorate in political science. Park spoke fluent Japanese and was educated at the Japanese-run Manchurian Military Academy (MMA). He went on to serve in the Imperial Japanese Army and then the US-constituted army of the Republic of Korea. Kim spoke Russian and Chinese. He had some formal Confucian schooling as a child. His real education came as a guerrilla leader in the anti-Japanese struggle and as an advanced student at the Soviet military training school in Khabarovsk, Siberia. The three typify the worlds—American Protestant, Japanese imperialist, and Soviet and Chinese communist—that shaped the Korean nation-state(s) in the twentieth and into the twenty-first century.

Syngman Rhee converted fully to Christianity while serving a life prison sentence under Emperor Kojong.[45] Rhee had been involved in reform and anti-Japanese activities. He was a distant relation of the emperor, a scion of the impoverished *yangban* class—Rhee's father was convinced that the family's poor financial circumstances were a result of deficient ancestor worship, and he spent much time researching the family genealogy—but that did not save Rhee from imprisonment. For at least six months he had to wear constantly a twenty-pound weight around his neck, a punishment akin to the terrible exactions imposed on rebellious or disrespectful Brazilian slaves.

Already familiar with Christianity, Rhee had an epiphany in prison and became a true believer. He went on to convert forty inmates and prison guards, an early sign of his great rhetorical skills and charisma. Fortunately for Rhee, the king commuted his sentence after five years. Korean officials released him in 1904, just as the Japanese hold on Korea was tightening. Rhee was fully and totally committed to two causes— Korean nationalism and Christianity—and the two, for him and many others, were inextricably entwined. He understood that he could pursue these commitments only abroad. Otherwise he would languish in prison, the Japanese authorities fulfilling what Emperor Kojong had started.

Rhee left Korea for what would turn into a nearly forty-year exile, interrupted by only a few brief, mostly incognito visits to his homeland (see figure 7.1). He went first to Hawai'i, since 1898 an American territory, and then to the mainland United States. At every step of his long life and career past the age of twenty, Protestant missionaries aided his efforts. They helped him secure admission to George Washington, Harvard, and Princeton universities. They supported his energetic efforts to educate Koreans, including girls. Missionaries aided his ceaseless, almost fanatical organization of Koreans abroad and within the country for the eventual independence of Korea.

Rhee imbued all his activities—educational, political, diplomatic— with a fervent Christianity. Rhee's self-confidence, even imperiousness, were legendary. He made many enemies, the infighting among various Korean organizations rivaling that of Trotskyists. Yet he displayed charisma, commitment, and intelligence. American Protestants stood by him, the prominent as well as those well-meaning though not possessed of wealth or fine connections.[46] Rhee's correspondence in English is replete with letters containing small donations—five, twenty, sixty dollars—to help him attend a Christian meeting here, speak before a gathering of the Young Men's Christian Association (YMCA) there, to provide tuition for one of his students, or to help him found a Korean girls' school in Hawai'i. Contributions also flowed into the slew of Korean national organizations that he founded.

His Protestant friends and colleagues offered advice on pursuing his studies, and afterward found him positions at the YMCA in Seoul and then as a principal of a school in Hawai'i. They arranged meetings for him with high-ranking American officials, including presidents

FIGURE 7.1 Dr. Syngman Rhee, 1942. Rhee (1876–1965) received both a traditional Confucian and a Western education. He converted to Christianity, and throughout his career American Protestant missionaries lent him support. For a brief period after 1919, Rhee became the head of state of the provisional government of Korea, which operated largely out of Shanghai. Rhee then went into exile to the United States, where he proved to be an indefatigable organizer. Despite State Department hostility, he won the backing of the United States, thanks largely to his fluent English, Protestant support, and fervent anti-communism. His presidency, 1948–60, became increasingly dictatorial. Pro-democracy demonstrations drove him from office. (Underwood Archives/Getty Images.)

Theodore Roosevelt and Warren G. Harding. Some of the interlocutors addressed him as "Brother Rhee," or signed their letters, "Your brother in Christ."[47] Rhee, in short, moved completely in the Christian missionary world—the American Protestant world that, until the 1960s, fully dominated American life in virtually every arena.

In his correspondence, Rhee and his Protestant interlocutors wrote a great deal about Christ, little about rights. To the extent that rights played a role, they meant, first and foremost, national rights, the independence of Korea from Japan. A fully sovereign Korea, they all believed, would be a Christian nation in Asia, Korea the vanguard of the second coming, at least when it appeared in the East.

Rhee himself organized or represented a host of organizations. In 1919, he was chosen as the president of the provisional Korean government in exile, which spent most of its years in Shanghai. The position did not last. Rhee had a falling out with almost everyone with whom he worked. His imperious attitude and practice grated on many others who were no less committed to Korean independence. One low point came in 1925, when the other members of the government-in-exile impeached him. But he was not to be sidelined: he was too committed to the Korean cause (as he understood it), too enmeshed in the interlocked, influential worlds of Protestant America's missionaries, educators, journalists, and businessmen, all with entrée into government circles.

Nonetheless, Rhee's relationship with American officials was always rocky. The State Department in particular often found him annoying and rather too big for his small-country breeches. After all, he claimed to represent Korea. What was Korea? The United States had to worry about Germany, Japan, China, the Soviet Union. But the dynamics of World War II and the Cold War forced it to take seriously the fate of Korea. Reluctantly though inevitably, American officials came back to the most prominent Korean they knew, one with the most impressive Protestant connections and anticommunist credentials, the result of decades of writing, lecturing, organizing, and lobbying on behalf of an independent, Christian Korea. Rhee represented the fruits of the labors of James Scarth Gale and all the other missionaries who had first come to Korea in the 1880s.

Rhee returned to Korea in October 1945 aboard a US military transport at the personal disposal of General Douglas MacArthur. He arrived in Seoul to great acclaim. His wife, the Austrian-born Francesca Donner, had all along shared his views and offered him stalwart support. She joined him in Korea six months later. Their correspondence reveals a devoted couple united by a deep commitment to Christianity and Korea, the Korean nation-state as a Christian bastion, coupled with a deep suspicion of US officials, especially those in the State Department.

In 1945–46, American diplomats still believed they could proceed in Korea with, not against, the Soviets. For Francesca Rhee, Dean Acheson, soon to be one of the architects of the Cold War, would "have to go—he is the arch pinko who is . . . muddling our Asian policy." There is, she reassured her husband, great popular support for an independent Korea and a strong anti-Russian policy.

> Your action against trusteeship and getting Russia out of the North will have the fullest support of the people. Dear God I thank you that at least justice has caught up with the gang in the State Dept. It is too humiliating to think how they have treated you all these years. . . . These men . . . have worked against their own country [and] are getting the punishment they deserve. God's eternal justice has brought them to the judge and I pray that men are not making judgments against God.[48]

Like her husband, Francesca Rhee was politically adept and knew how to cultivate friends. For Christmas 1945 she sent presents of solid gold pen-and-pencil sets to the top American occupation officers in Korea, along with a series of lesser gifts (black billfold with chain, $15.00; blue Morocco billfold, $4.20; and so on) for lesser officers.[49] From Lieutenant General John R. Hodge, the commanding general of the US occupation forces, on down, they all replied with heartfelt thanks.[50]

Despite many hesitations and discomforts, the American authorities backed Rhee and then helped him win the election for Korea's first president, leading to the declaration of the Republic of Korea on 15 August 1948. The United States stood by him in the Korean War, and then all through the 1950s. Rhee spoke a language the United States understood— not just English, though his fluent command of the language was vitally important, but, just as significant, a fervent anti-communism laced with Christian idioms. As Rhee set up a vicious dictatorship, a police state in which any individuals, not just communists, who articulated opposition found themselves in prison and often the victims of torture, the United States stood by him, both the American government and the deep networks of Protestants.[51] Americans had already created, in December 1945, the nucleus of the army of the Republic of Korea, staffed by many officers and soldiers who had served in the Imperial Japanese Army, Park Chung-hee among them (as we shall soon see). In the wake of the Korean War, the United States then supported the buildup of all the security forces of the state—regular army, police, paramilitary forces, secret services—that spent as much time regulating, harassing, and repressing their own population as they did guarding against the enemy to the North.

In the process, South Korea became a sham democracy. The powerful industrialists and landlords whom the United States left largely intact backed the Rhee regime, as they would Park's government. The realities of the police state of the 1950s undermined the human rights articles in the Republic of Korea's constitution. South Korea became a constituent member of the anticommunist Cold War international. Many Protestants, like Rhee and his supporters, were so fervently anti-communist that they abandoned their commitment to democracy and human rights.

All rulers of small states count on the support of their great-power benefactors. But Great Powers are fickle, as we saw also in regard to Armenians and Jews. When the ruler no longer serves their interests, he can easily be discarded. As often as it has happened, such rulers, possessed of immense and sometimes monomaniacal self-confidence, are shocked when the denouement comes. Big brother abandons them and leaves them to their own devices, or, if they are lucky, finds them a nice estate somewhere backed up by a very large bank account. So it was with Rhee. When student demonstrations in favor of democracy erupted in 1960, American authorities decided that the stability of the country was more important than the person of Syngman Rhee. They abandoned him, as they would soon Ngo Dinh Diem in Vietnam, Riza Shah Pahlevi in Iran, and Manuel Noriega in Panama. Rhee was forced to resign and spirited to exile in Honolulu, where he lived out the last five years of his life, his legacy deeply ambivalent.

❦

Student demonstrators thought they had won a great victory in spring 1960. They had carried banners inscribed with demands for democracy and human rights. It was not to be, not yet. General Park Chung-hee, the second of our figures, led a military coup one year later. The American authorities were not totally pleased, nor were they really opposed to the establishment of another dictatorship in South Korea, which Park quickly went about constructing.

Park Chung-hee was born into a poor peasant family. He managed to get some education and to qualify as a schoolteacher, but his real love was the army. The Japanese had sent some Koreans to the Imperial Military Academy; the ever-expanding ambitions for territory and power and the demands of total war led them to found a new outpost, the MMA. Park, in 1940, was admitted to the academy's second class. Throughout his military and political career, his fellow students from the MMA would be at his side.

The MMA that Park attended was the epitome of the militaristic ethos, a training ground for order and discipline, not for the sometimes raucous and undisciplined character of popular democracy.[52] It was a closed-off, masculine environment in which the cadets all dressed alike, lived together, moved in unison, and were subject to the most severe disciplinary measures. From day one individualism was repressed. The cadets all had their heads shaved in the same manner, their civilian clothes locked and stored away. They learned to speak in a loud, commanding manner, which went along with the erect posture of the military man. They had to show deference to the officers above them, and demanded subservience from those below them, which included virtually all civilians. Discipline and perseverance, tested in the extreme weather conditions of Manchuria, the rudimentary facilities at the academy, and the daily, strenuous military exercises, were the hallmarks of the good cadet. Park excelled at all of it.[53]

Confession for infractions of the rules or poor performance was another part of the discipline of the academy. Confession was always public—before one's peers, before the supervising officers. It was a ritual of shaming and control, one practiced also in the communist parties of the twentieth century, taken to extremes in China and Cambodia, but no less a feature of Park's upbringing and of the South Korea he would rule for almost twenty years.[54]

The cadets were instilled with a special sense of mission, a devotion to the cause of the Japanese Empire in the 1930s and 1940s. They absorbed the Japanese idolization of the samurai, the Meiji Restoration, and Japanese military victories over China in 1894–95 and Russia in 1904–5, and then the invasion and occupation of Manchuria in 1931–32.[55] On a state visit to Japan in 1961, Park, speaking in excellent Japanese, told his interlocutors that he and his comrades were studying Meiji history and acting "in the spirit of the men of high purpose of the Meiji Restoration."[56]

Despite all the repressive features of Japanese colonialism, those Koreans who, in the 1930s and 1940s, entered into the Japanese-dominated worlds of the military, business, or governance knowingly served the emperor and the empire. It was, for them, a path of upward mobility, at least for as long as Japan was ascendant.

Yet Japan lost the war, leaving stranded in Manchuria Park and his Korean officer friends. It took Park about six months, moving through the chaotic conditions of Manchuria and China at the end of the war, to find his way back to Seoul. It must have been a trying experience. His former classmates and comrades recalled him as the most self-controlled and most skilled cadet at the MMA, characteristics that no doubt helped sustain him as he wandered around for months.

The Americans resurrected him. As mentioned, he quickly found his way to the constabulary established by American occupation officers, which became the nucleus of the army of the Republic of Korea. Park served in the Korean War and through all the years of the Rhee government. With the support of his MMA comrades, he launched a coup in March 1961 against Rhee's rather hapless, short-term successor.

Park's speeches and writings after he took power show his absolute commitment to the idea of the nation-state (see figure 7.2). For Rhee, the nation-state and Christianity were inextricably entwined. For Park, the army epitomized the nation-state. The militaristic values he lived and enjoyed as a cadet became the ethos of his rule—order, discipline, service, nary a word about rights.

"There is absolutely no other means to save the state and nation," said Park in 1961, justifying the military coup he had engineered.[57] The army, with its "unshakeable sense of national mission," expressed the state and nation better than anyone or anything else.[58] Park's policies launched

FIGURE 7.2 Park Chung-hee, 1963. Park (1917–79) received his military training from the Japanese at the MMA. After the Japanese defeat he found his way to the constabulary force established by the Americans, which would develop into the army of the Republic of Korea. Park rose in the ranks and carried out a coup in 1961. He ruled until his assassination (in still-mysterious circumstances) in 1979. Under Park the South Korean economy boomed, but the government became ever more dictatorial. The Korean Central Intelligence Agency had free rein to imprison and torture political dissidents. (Bride Lane Library/Popperfoto/Getty Images.)

the South Korean economic miracle, which in twenty years lifted the country out of poverty into the ranks of thriving, industrialized nations. His program, however, lay far from neoliberalism with its undying faith in the market. Instead, Park promoted state-directed development. Unfettered capitalism, he wrote, breeds selfishness and only material gain, while the state, or, better, the army-run state, cares for the nation as a whole. Under the Rhee regime, business fostered "a mean and base attitude of frivolity and consumption, [it] created an economy of unearned income, extreme egoism, and money worship."[59] American, Japanese, and Western products had replaced Korean ones, resulting in a "spiritual laxity and enervation of the people. . . . I could hardly suppress my wrath," wrote Park.[60] All these "alien things" sapped the "dignity, . . . worth, . . . and self-respect" of the people.[61]

Park's views aligned completely with the total-war thinking expressed by his Japanese instructors at the academy, and also with the very traditional critique of trade articulated by Korean conservatives in the nineteenth century.[62] In his ultimate tirade, Park charged that the Rhee regime had unleashed "spiritual degradation, apostate imitation of foreign customs, . . . corruption, . . . vanity, luxury and indolence."[63] Yi Hangno, King Kojong's adviser in the 1860s, could not have expressed it any better: he had called on the king to burn all his Western clothes, food, and any other items, and thereby establish a model of discipline, rectitude, and virtue.[64]

"We are an ancient homogeneous society," wrote Park, two years after the coup he led.[65] He lauded that fact and Korea's five-thousand-year continuous history, and lamented the divisions and conflicts that constantly ravaged the country, endangering its very existence. Like nationalists everywhere, he bemoaned the fallen, degraded state of the present, and promised great things for the future, labelling his military coup a "revolution" that would transform the country. The revolution's "resolve must remain the salvation of the nation, selfless public dedication, correct and honest judgment and unyielding will and determination."[66] Ominously, he wrote that he had resolved to "uproot all the existent germs . . . [and] institute . . . a strong disinfection program, and at the same time, to plant grains to feed the families on the point of despair and starvation."[67]

These are the biological metaphors deployed by twentieth-century authoritarian regimes around the world when they set out to extirpate specific populations. Stalin, Hitler, Mao, Pol Pot, Kim Il-sŏng—all could have spoken or written lines like these. All of them also continually invoked grave threats to the nation to justify their rule and to mobilize their parties and populations. "As if camped on a battlefield with the river behind us, our backs are to the wall, and there is now no retreat. Our future lies only in advance," Park wrote.[68] The solution was a voluntarism that knew no bounds, also reminiscent of the communist dictatorships of the twentieth century. "We can do [anything] if we try," he wrote.[69]

Park claimed to be a supporter of democracy. In reality, he advocated national solidarity, the millennia-long Korean concept of *jaju*, which means, he said, being the "master of our own house."[70] Harmony, discipline, the union of state and individual—these were the Korean values, he claimed, that his revolution and government were making real. On the basis of the "harmonious order between the individual and the state, a stable democratic society can take root in Korea."[71]

"Diligence, self-help, and cooperation" were other slogans of the Park era.[72] One looks in vain for any mention of rights in Park's myriad speeches and writings. Instead, freedom had come to mean the progress of the army-led state as the expression of the Korean nation, and economic development, both coupled with an intense anti-communism, not support for rights-bearing citizenship.[73]

❧

Missionary Protestantism and military authoritarianism were two major political trends of Korea's post-1945 history. Neither contributed to the development of human rights. Nor did communism, the third of Korea's major political streams.

In the wake of World War I and the Russian revolutions, Koreans, like so many other people around the globe, organized a communist party.[74] In fact, they founded four of them in the 1920s—an extreme version of the factionalism typical of communist parties at the time. The Korean factions fought bitterly with one another, even to the point of armed conflict. The Communist International seemed bewildered by it all, and did little more than issue the usual admonitions for better organization, better work among the masses, and better understanding of Marxism-Leninism.[75] Korean Communist Party (KCP) organizations existed in Japan and China, including Manchuria (under both Chinese and Japanese rule), and the Soviet Union, notably in Siberia and the Eastern Maritime Province. Seoul, Irkutsk, and Shanghai were the major KCP centers in the 1920s, with additional groups in Tokyo, Harbin, and other sites.

The places with significant communist party organizations were the exact same places with major Korean populations. By 1919 some 200,000 Koreans were living in Siberia, and 430,000 in Manchuria. The

Manchurian number rose to 600,000 by 1930.[76] Some Koreans had populated these regions for generations and were, essentially, Russianized or Sinicized Koreans; others were relatively new arrivals with deeper attachments to the homeland. Japanese authorities in 1930 estimated that one-tenth of the Koreans in Manchuria were communists, or at least communist sympathizers.[77]

By the 1930s, Japanese repression had become so severe that it had largely eliminated the organizational presence of the KCP in the peninsula. As a result, numerous party groups simply dissolved themselves.[78] Those acts, however, by no means signified the end of Korean communism. Instead, Koreans joined the communist parties of Japan, China, and the Soviet Union, another example of communist internationalism in action.

Korean communists, in short, forged a transnational movement within global communism. No less than capitalism, nationalism, Christianity, and, indeed, human rights, communism produced the global world as we know it.

What did Korean communists, however small in number, actually do? The same things that communists all around the world did in the 1920s, 1930s, and 1940s. They wrote pamphlets and newspapers and smuggled them into Korea from their places of exile in China and the Soviet Union. They tried to organize trade unions and associations of impoverished peasants. Strikes and agrarian unrest, quite significant in the 1930s, offered them opportunities to organize and assume leadership roles. In the 1920s, when Japanese rule was relatively more open, they went on lecture tours, speaking against Japanese control, homegrown and foreign capitalists, and missionaries—the tripartite enemies of the people.[79] The most dedicated—or most lucky—among them survived prison and torture. And they participated in the armed struggle against Japan in cooperation with Russian and Chinese communists, with profound consequences for the character of Korea after 1945. Moving in the communist world in Siberia, Moscow, Yenan, and Shanghai, they learned the ideology and discipline of Marxist-Leninist parties.[80]

No less than Protestants (Rhee) and militarists (Park), Korean communists were deeply nationalist—and had the theory to support their commitment. "Our national emancipation movement is merely a step to the ultimate purpose of social revolution," wrote Korean communists in the very first manifesto of the KCP.[81] "We are the great Korean people. We have heroically struggled for the past thirty years despite the severe oppression of Japanese imperialism," communists wrote some twenty years later, reprising the point that the nation and its people stood in the forefront of the communist program.[82] Marxism-Leninism provided the theory, developed by none other than Joseph Stalin (as we shall see in the next chapter): the sovereign nation-state was a necessary step on the road to the communist future.

The link drawn between national liberation and social revolution is precisely what made communism appealing to some Koreans. Those settled in the Russian East had eked out a living off the land and in forests and fisheries. It was a hard life that barely enabled them to survive. Much the same was true of Koreans in Manchuria and on the peninsula itself. The first news of the Bolshevik Revolution and the Bolshevik program excited many of these people, as well as Korean students at home and abroad, especially in Japan. When the Bolshevik and subsequent Korean communist programs announced the dawn of the new era, land to the people, an eight-hour day for factory workers, and unemployment insurance, all coupled with the independent, self-determining Korean nation-state—all that played like ancient Korean music to the ears of those who lived under landlord and capitalist domination entwined with Japanese control.

Had communism been about only class struggle, it probably never would have attracted much support. But it was also about the *nation*, and that also meant it was about a certain idea of rights. In all their propaganda, Korean communists called for political and civic rights, echoing virtually every grand proclamation from the American constitution forward. Universal suffrage, democratic government, freedom of speech, equality of the sexes—all these classic elements were present. To that bundle of political rights Korean communists added a very twentieth-century emphasis on social rights: compulsory and universal education, the eight-hour day, land reform, nationalization of large enterprises that cooperated with the Japanese. In the pièce de résistance, they called for "human rights."[83] All of this proved inspiring to many Koreans.

However, Korean communists also expressed an uncompromising and often brutal rhetoric about the oppressors—the Japanese and their Korean collaborators. They were the "blood suckers" who "slaughter[ed] the masses," "engulf[ed] the cities of China in flames from land, sea and air"; they had "plundered Manchuria" and instituted the "extreme barbarity of white terror" against workers and peasants. "They have intensified the exploitation of the proletariat by transforming all industrial organizations to military use and war industries; they have produced an army of unemployed by depriving the peasants of their land; and they exploited the people to the last drop of blood and sweat."[84] However justified the charges may have been, it was a fearsome rhetoric that allowed for no compromise, no half measures, and could easily spill over to other individuals and groups.

Communism was never something simply imposed on Korea by outside forces; it spoke to the concerns, interests, and aspirations of a segment of Korean society.[85] For some, the armed struggle against Japan provided the only path to achieve their aspirations. Among them was Kim Il-sŏng. Like Park Chung-hee, Kim came from a modest peasant family. His father moved the family around, as did many Koreans, between Korea and Manchuria. He received some education in Chinese schools, and had already become involved in communist activities as a teenager. Barely twenty, he made his way to the guerrilla struggle and joined the Chinese Communist Party (CCP).[86] In 1938, the Japanese authorities made mention of him in one of their reports on communist "banditry" in Manchuria.[87] Kim was a formidable fighter, his venue the Chinese communist-organized Northeast Anti-Japanese United Army (NEAJUA). In the nature of guerrilla warfare, much was left to the discretion of individual units. The CCP could not exercise tight control of the NEAJUA. Talented commanders like Kim had the leeway and opportunity to distinguish themselves.

Kim led a band of a few hundred men who harassed the Japanese forces (see figure 7.3). But they could not sustain themselves against the greater power of the Japanese army. In April 1941, Kim retreated from Manchuria into the Soviet Far East with around two hundred men, seasoned fighters all.[88] Kim had spent nine years, from 1932 to 1941, engaged in guerrilla warfare. He had had no contact with the Korean

FIGURE 7.3 Kim Il-sŏng, 1940s. Kim (1912–94), like Park, was born into a modest peasant family. He became a renowned communist guerrilla leader against the Japanese in Manchuria, receiving some support from both Chinese and Soviet communists. Constantly harassed by the Japanese army, he retreated with a couple hundred men into the Soviet Union, where they received advanced military training. Some of them, including Kim, were granted commissions in the Soviet army. Kim returned with the Soviet forces to Korea in 1945. He and his comrades from the guerrilla campaign came to constitute the core leadership of North Korea, sidelining other communists. Kim ruled from the founding of North Korea in 1948 until his death in 1994; he has since been succeeded by his son and grandson, a communist family dynasty. (© CORBIS/Corbis via Getty Images.)

communists of the 1920s and 1930s. He did, however, receive military training at the Soviet camp—not quite an academy—in Khabarovsk (Siberia) and received a commission as an officer in the Red Army. Other Koreans, probably around thirty-five thousand, fought with the Chinese Communist People's Liberation Army.[89]

The Soviets, as mentioned, declared war on Japan on 8 August 1945. Their troops entered Korea and Manchuria, a front some nine hundred miles long. With the Soviet forces was Kim Il-sŏng, along with around three hundred other Koreans, many of whom had also been at Khabarovsk.[90] Some were Soviet citizens; others were guerrillas, like Kim, who had found refuge in the Soviet Union. They would become the dominant force in North Korea, much like the German communists who returned to their country from Moscow in the company of the Red Army and established the German Democratic Republic. They were Kim's close comrades from the NEAJUA. Step by step, Kim purged communists who came to the North from China and from Korea itself. He remade the KCP into a more cohesive, more disciplined, Sovietized party, ultimately named the Korean Workers' Party (KWP), founded in August 1946. On 9 September 1948, the party established the Democratic People's Republic of Korea.

Guerrilla warfare, the communist party, and, certainly not least, Korean nationalism—these were the defining features of Kim Il-sŏng's background, and that of thousands of other Korean communists. Their advanced training took place not at Princeton or the MMA, but in the Chinese and Soviet communist parties and their armed forces. Nothing, absolutely nothing, in these experiences served as a training ground for a commitment to democracy and human rights. Quite the opposite. No less than his South Korean counterpart Park Chung-hee, Kim absorbed the hierarchy and discipline of the military, even if his battle experience was as a guerrilla rather than in a field army with its elaborate hierarchy. Kim had one additional resource that Park lacked—the communist party, which, by the 1940s in its Stalinized version, also emphasized discipline and hierarchy and implemented brutal procedures against anyone perceived to be in opposition to the standard party line.

Kim's training also placed him firmly in line with the anticolonial struggles all around the globe from the 1940s into the 1960s (and, in a few cases, like East Timor, into the later decades of the twentieth century) and the absolute priority they gave to the nation-state. Kim, like all other Korean communist leaders, including those he purged and those of whom he knew nothing and cared less, were united around one theme: the national struggle and the social revolution were one and the same. "Korea is for the Koreans," ran one KCP slogan in 1925, a line that would be repeated again and again.[91] Underlying the slogan was a sense, so widely understood that it did not have to be expressed, that Koreans comprised a homogeneous nation.

Very quickly, the KWP launched a social revolution in the North.[92] The state confiscated large landholdings and distributed plots to the peasantry. It nationalized major industries and built public-education and public-health facilities. Despite the ravages of war, the Northern part of the country began an economic revival and the population began to see some improvements in their living conditions. The North Korean constitution, adopted on 8 September 1948, proclaimed all the standard political rights, and even, in article 2, reprised the famous principle enunciated in the French Declaration of the Rights of Man and Citizen: "Sovereignty . . . resides in the people."[93] It also included all sorts of social rights, like the confiscation and nationalization of all Japanese-owned property and the right to education and health. Following Soviet nationalities doctrine, it also granted minorities—few as they may have been in Korea—the right to develop their own culture. Meanwhile, the KWP increasingly dominated all aspects of life in North Korea. Kim instituted an almost continual round of purges, setting the stage for a one-man (and after his demise, one-family) dictatorship within a communist system. All along, his closest supporters were his comrades from the NEAJUA.

And then came the Korean War. Virulent disagreements continue to rage among both scholars and political figures about its origins. North and South had been engaging in cross-border raids and other provocations for nearly a year preceding the North Korean attack on 25 June 1950. It seems today, with the advantage of more or less open Soviet and even some Chinese archives, that Kim Il-sŏng launched the war with Soviet support and Chinese acquiescence, grudgingly given in both cases.[94] The initial victory came quickly; the retreat and then advance again, with Soviet matériel and Chinese troops, also happened quickly. After one year, the front stabilized where it had been and where it still remains, along the thirty-eighth parallel. But it took another two years until the two sides could agree on a cease-fire. During that time, the

United States utterly devastated North Korea. US bombing raids, including with napalm, destroyed 90 percent of the country, leaving no city or factory, no human lives, untouched.[95]

Despite the vast destruction, the drive to rebuild the country in the 1950s and 1960s proved quite successful. Economic growth far outpaced that in the South. In his self-proclaimed slogan *juche*, or self-reliance, Kim reprised both the standard nationalist line going back to the nineteenth century and the Stalinist slogan of "socialism in one country."[96] In touting these achievements, Kim conveniently ignored the fact that North Korea received vast amounts of aid from the Soviet Union, the Soviet-bloc countries, and China. Kim, much like Park one and two decades later, created a potent mixture of the nation, self-reliance, and economic development, on which basis he was able to win some significant support among Koreans. All of this was overlaid with a powerful militarism. "All Youth! Let us become honor bodyguards and death-defying fighters defending the party and the leader and executing the orders of the leader with our lives on behalf of unification of the Fatherland and the Revolution!"[97] "Shock brigades" of labor were another typical communist formulation with militaristic overtones.[98]

Missing was only any effort to make real the political rights proclaimed in the North Korean constitution.

☙

Kim Chi Ha is the poet laureate of the South Korean democracy and human rights movement.[99] Like so many activists, he suffered long prison terms and torture under the military dictatorship of Park Chung-hee and his successors. His poems, many written in jail, evince a sense of despair and loneliness, and outrage at the inhumanity purveyed by the state. Yet he also conveys a certain hopefulness despite the oppressions he and his fellow citizens experienced every single day. The poetry is lyrical, and, at times, comical and sardonic. In one of his most famous poems, "The Story of a Sound," the powerful worker Ando is blocked at every single stage. No money, no title, no degree, no connections, manipulated and deceived by "shake-down artists . . . [and] rake-off operators," he cannot even commit suicide because he has no rafter from which to hang himself and lives in a room full of broken windows that let the oven gas escape. He tries everything to survive—every low-level, dirt-poor-paying, brutal-laboring job that South Korea's booming economy has to offer. "Agh! What a dog's life this is."[100]

That cry of despair is enough to get him handcuffed and thrown into jail. Every possible charge is hurled at him: being "idle," "weak-willed," "impertinent," and, perhaps worst of all, neglecting the policies of incessant production for export and "insufficient veneration for the fatherland." His body is hacked to pieces while the harsh sound of the prison walls and slamming doors, "K'ung K'ung," reverberates.[101]

Yet even in this gruesome, oppressive setting, hope triumphs.

Dear mother, I shall return home;
    return, even though I die.
Though my dead body be torn
    in a thousand, ten thousand pieces,
    I shall return.
Through this wall,
    over the next,
even as a spirit
    I shall pierce and vault
    these brick walls.

I shall return, mother;
even in death I shall return.[102]

Under Park, South Korea indeed experienced an economic boom that transformed the country. In the 1950s and early 1960s, the North, despite the devastation of the Korean War, managed a powerful economic revival and expansion. In the 1970s, its economy began a long stagnation and decline, while the South became a model of industrial development, the "Miracle on the Han," proudly proclaimed by development experts, businessmen, American officials, and, of course, the Park government itself and those that followed. Hundreds of thousands of Koreans left the countryside for the new factories. They labored for a pittance in unsafe and unhealthy conditions, while the state suppressed every effort at independent union organization.[103] Kim Chi Ha gave voice to these workers as well, many of them women, as in his poem "The Road to Seoul":

> I am going.
> Do not cry;
> I am going,
> Over the white hills, the black, and the parched hills,
> down the long and dusty road to Seoul
> I am going to sell my body.[104]

The oppressive dictatorship and the brutal labor conditions fueled the writings of Kim Chi Ha and the incessant political activities of Kim Dae Jung, who would finally become president of South Korea in 1998, and many others. Kim Dae Jung also endured (and survived) prison, house arrest, at least two assassination attempts, one formal judicial order of execution, and forced exile to the United States. Kim Dae Jung and many other democracy and human rights advocates engaged in a wide range of actions. They went on strike and marched in demonstrations, staged theater plays, and wrote songs and poetry. Despite all the repressions, they created an active, pro-democracy public sphere that ultimately felled two dictatorships—those of Syngman Rhee in 1960 and of Park's successors into the early 1990s. But not without sacrifice on the part of those struggling for democracy and human rights. In April 1960, more than one hundred thousand students and young people converged on the presidential palace. The guards opened fire, killing more than one hundred and injuring nearly one thousand.[105] More demonstrations followed, forcing Rhee's resignation; though, as noted, Park's military coup one year later stole the victory from the democratic forces.

All through the 1960s and 1970s the state exercised severe repression while the economy grew and some Koreans prospered. Still, workers and students organized, and an underground public sphere expanded dramatically. A wave of strikes ensued in the Southwest, one of South Korea's most impoverished areas and a center of activism and rebellion throughout the country's modern history. At Kwangju, the capital of

South Chŏlla province, in May 1980, the South Korean military, with the backing of the US army command, carried out a massacre of demonstrators even worse than that in Tiananmen Square in 1989. To this day, the exact figures are unknown, but at a minimum five hundred and more likely up to three thousand people were killed and many thousands more wounded.[106]

Tiananmen is, of course, renowned and infamous because it displayed in brutal and open fashion the oppressiveness of the Chinese communist state. Kwangju is unknown, except to Koreans, because it was an action carried out by an American ally with American support. Yet Korean activists kept alive the memory of Kwangju, which helped spark yet another wave of protests ten years later. In this region, Kim Dae Jung's homeland, he consistently attracted overwhelming support—when he was able to run for office.[107]

By the late 1980s, the South Korean military could no longer exercise unlimited power. Koreans kept up the pressure for democratization by persistent demonstrations, strikes, union organizing, and an active public sphere. They were now aided by a global human rights movement, the same combination—domestic activism and international support—that would lead to the fall of Latin American military dictatorships, the Soviet Union and its allies, and the South African apartheid regime. The United States wanted, above all else, a stable South Korea. It had bid goodbye to Syngman Rhee when his continued tenure in office threatened its own overall strategic goals, and it did the same, though quite belatedly, with Park Chung-hee's military successors.

Kim Chi Ha and Kim Dae Jung, to use just two prominent examples, understood the importance of international support. Both often referred to the inspiration they received from great thinkers and activists of the past, including Mahatma Gandhi, Leo Tolstoy, Thomas Aquinas, Dietrich Bonhoeffer, and many other philosophical, literary, and ethical luminaries far beyond the limits of Korea. Both also drew on domestic protest movements, from the Tonghak in the 1890s to the March First Movement of 1919 and the April Revolution of 1960. And both were fervently Catholic. Their faith no doubt sustained them through the many trials each endured. It also fueled their commitment to democracy and human rights. Christianity is protean. The faith led many Western missionaries to such a pronounced anti-communism that they supported Rhee, Park, and Park's successor generals who exercised power with blatant brutality and complete disregard for individual human rights. For Kim Chi Ha, Kim Dae Jung, and many others, Christianity led them to a profound commitment to democracy and human rights. As every chapter in this book has shown, many streams lead to human rights, and Christianity is one of them.[108]

And what of the North? The various constitutions proclaimed political and social rights for all citizens. On paper, the constitutions read like great paeans to democracy. The reality has been rather different. Political rights have been non-existent; party and family domination of society has been complete. As in most communist states, one might see a degree of social rights prevailing in provisions like the eight-hour workday, the right to education, paid vacations, universal health coverage, and so on. Until around 1970, living standards did improve for most Koreans.

However, any dictatorship with a halfway functioning economy, whether the regime is fascist, capitalist, or communist, can improve the material well-being of its citizenry. The policy is as old as Rome's bread and circuses. The regime *provisions* its population, but those actions are worlds removed from recognizing the *social rights* of the citizenry. Rights of all sorts, whatever the modifying adjective, give people a sense of power. They come not as supplicants, happy that the king, emperor, or dictator grants them another bowl of soup. Social rights mean that people expect and demand what is theirs simply by virtue of their humanity—a decent living, adequate food, clean water, a decent environment, and also participation in how the economy and society are ordered.

Social rights, to be worthy of the title, are inextricably entwined with political rights. More than that: social rights are political rights directed at the economy and society. Otherwise they are mere provisions that the regime in all its glory grants, and just as easily rescinds, whether out of sheer caprice or in moments of crisis. That is precisely what occurred in North Korea in the late 1990s, when floods and droughts and the loss of support following the collapse of the communist bloc in Europe sent the economy into a tailspin. Famine stalked the land. Perhaps two million North Koreans died.[109] The Kim family continued to live in fine circumstances, as did other members of the elite, while scarce resources were channeled to the military, including a nuclear weapons program.[110] A regime so willing to sacrifice its citizens can hardly be declared one that respects social rights. North Korea's policies make the vital point: without political rights, social rights are meaningless.

Conclusion

"Korea is being used as a pivot-point for the whole hemisphere," wrote the Protestant missionary James Scarth Gale early in the twentieth century.[111] He was right. Dragged out of its isolation, the country was crisscrossed by armies, buffeted about, an imperial plaything of the Great Powers, Japan preeminently. Korea was a testing ground for the greater Japanese empire, and a groundswell for nationalism, whether liberal, conservative, communist, or socialist. Suddenly, all the ideologies of the modern world swirled inside Korea, all the features of industrial development sprang into action, all the characteristics of state building emerged in concentrated, and ultimately divided, form. Like Greece earlier in the nineteenth century, Korea was another small country that could not escape the interest of the Great Powers. Koreans would never be able to make their history solely on their own, certainly not in the globalized world of the nineteenth and twentieth centuries. The reverse would also be true: Korean developments would reverberate far beyond the peninsula and its people.

Korean reformers and revolutionaries had one thing in common with the old scholar-officials—an abiding, unquestioned commitment to the Korean nation. Indeed, Korean nationalists drew upon long-standing traditions that they then remolded into a modern movement. Around the turn into the twentieth century, many of the reformers and rebels advocated democracy and human rights. By the 1920s, another strain had appeared, and it would become dominant: a militarized nationalism that viewed militant Christianity, the army, or the party as the embodiment of national values and the savior of the nation. The result would be a nationalism and two nation-states devoid of commitment to individual human rights—a classic twentieth-century model that linked the Koreas to countries in Africa, the Middle East, Latin America, and Europe. Where once nationalism had been joined with human rights, the autonomy and power of the nation-state became the single overwhelming right promoted by dictatorships major and minor around the globe, helped along, after World War II, by their sponsors, Soviet, Chinese, and American.

Syngman Rhee, Park Chung-hee, and Kim Il-sŏng embodied these currents that crossed Korea in the twentieth century—America and American missionaries, Japanese imperialists, and Russian and Chinese communists. They laid out the forms of citizenship and rights that Koreans enjoyed and, perhaps most importantly, those from which they were barred. North and South, the state became the primary, rights-bearing entity, making a mockery of human rights despite the lofty phrases in the constitutions of both Koreas.

But that is not the end of the story. Mass, popular activism has been a driving force in the democratization of South Korea, aided since the 1970s by the international human rights movement. In 1998, finally, Koreans elected as president the long-struggling campaigner Kim Dae Jung. He served until 2003, and in this time transformed the political order of the South while also dealing with a massive economic crisis. In 2000 he was awarded the Nobel Peace Prize for his efforts to open up dialogue with the North and resolve the partition of the country. For all its problems, South Korea is now a democracy that champions many aspects of human rights. Only North Korea seems, for the moment, impervious to popular demands and international pressure. That too could change in the most unexpected ways—as we shall see through the history of the original communist country, the Soviet Union.

Chapter 8

The Soviet Union

COMMUNISM AND THE BIRTH OF THE MODERN HUMAN RIGHTS MOVEMENT

ℰᏬ

IN 1936, the Soviet Union proclaimed a new constitution. Socialism had been achieved, asserted Josef Stalin, a result of the Bolshevik Revolution, the guiding spirit of Vladimir Ilyich Lenin, and the grand successes of the five-year plans. The land had been collectivized, and the country was moving into the front ranks of industrialized countries. A new era of prosperity and freedom awaited Soviet citizens, even while dangers lurked from traitors at home and enemies abroad. The accomplishments of the Communist Party of the Soviet Union (CPSU) and the array of peoples who comprised the Union of Soviet Socialist Republics (USSR) had to be registered in a new constitution.[1]

The constitution reaffirmed the country as a federation of culturally distinct nationalities represented by their own republics, each also including a vast number of other ethnicities within its borders (see map 8.1). The strength of the Soviet Union, so the official ideology went, came precisely from its multinational character, each national and ethnic group contributing its particular cultural characteristics to the totality, all of them committed to communism. As Stalin proclaimed, the old hostilities among the nations of the Russian Empire had been vanquished by the Bolshevik Revolution and Soviet rule. The "feeling of mutual distrust has disappeared, a feeling of mutual friendship has developed among them, and thus real fraternal co-operation among the peoples has been established within the system of a single federated state."[2]

The constitution also laid out a set of rights for Soviet citizens that—on paper—equaled and even surpassed those of democratic, capitalist states. In the political realm, the Soviet constitution sounded every bit like the liberal ones proclaimed in the French, American, and

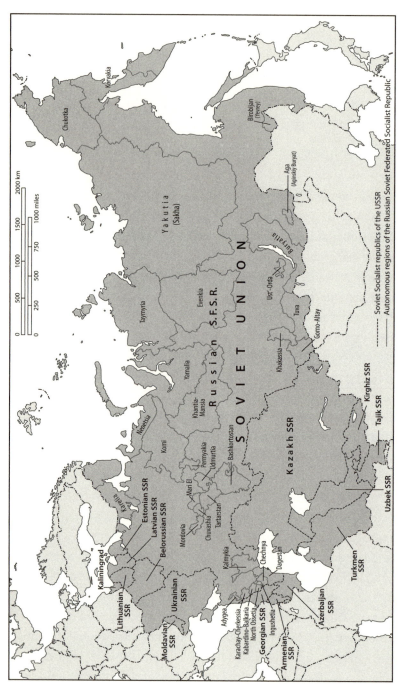

MAP 8.1 USSR as a federation of nationalities. Map shows both the republics of the USSR and the autonomous regions of the Russian republic. SSR, Soviet Socialist Republic; SFSR, Soviet Federated Socialist Republic.

Latin American revolutions; in the foundation of Greece in 1830; and in the new nation-states established by the Berlin Congress in 1878 and the Paris Peace Conference in 1919. Soviet citizens were guaranteed rights of free speech and assembly, and participation in the political order. In the social realm the constitution, presaging the UDHR of 1948, went much further than liberal ones by proclaiming for all Soviet citizens rights to education, employment, leisure, and healthcare. It seemed as though a socialist paradise was at hand.

The USSR announced its bracingly democratic, rights-oriented constitution for all the diverse peoples of this vast, sprawling empire just at the moment that the Stalin terror was at its height, when millions of people were experiencing denunciations, deportations, internments in labor camps, torture, and execution. Sheer hypocrisy? Mere deception? Can we even talk about human rights in a system that was bloodily repressive, that killed, tortured, and deported millions of its own citizens? That allowed over six million of them to starve to death in 1932 during the collectivization of agriculture campaign?

Yes, we can talk, in one and the same breath, about rights in the Soviet Union while also recognizing the deeply repressive and murderous character of the system. No country considered in this book has a pristine record on human rights, and certainly not the USSR. Soviet history does, though, add many new angles and panes to the multistoried, fragile glass house of human rights.

Communists, including Stalin and his successors, Nikita Khrushchev and Leonid Brezhnev, were steeped in the long ideological tradition of socialism and communism. They believed that their movement would finally complete the rights revolution begun by the French in 1789. They also viewed nation-states under capitalism and national republics in the Soviet Union as essential steps toward the communist future. After all, Marx and Engels in the 1860s and 1870s and the socialist Second International in 1896 had expressed their support for the self-determination of nations. Soviet citizens would be the living fulfillment of the socialist tradition and its commitment to political, social, economic, and, not least, national rights. The new Soviet man and woman, as they were called, members of the most diverse nationalities and ethnicities, would live joyous, prosperous, and free lives.

As in all the other histories explored in this book, not every inhabitant of the country could enter the charmed circle of rights-bearing citizens. The USSR drew the line between those included and those excluded not fundamentally by distinctions of nation and race, as we have seen in the previous cases, although these factors certainly came into play. The Soviets, instead, drew primarily a political line between those deemed loyal Soviet citizens and others marked as traitors and conspirators. These tags—"loyal," "traitor," "conspirator"—were (and are in today's Russia) ominous, dangerous, and highly mobile. Under Stalin especially, the CPSU's leaders and functionaries applied the term in an arbitrary fashion, pulling into the whirlwind of repression all sorts of people who had done nothing illegal or disloyal, including entire nationalities.

At the same time, the proclamation of rights proved meaningful to millions of Soviet citizens, who were able to take advantage of the programs implemented by a regime that took seriously its identification as a workers' and peasants' state and a federation of distinct nationalities. After 1945, those defining elements of Soviet communism proved immensely attractive to the movements and nations of the Global South (as we would now term it), many of them just emerging out of colonial empires into independent sovereign states. On the international plane, the USSR became a firm advocate of human rights, especially in regard to decolonization, self-determination, social rights, and women's rights (the latter a topic we will address more centrally in the conclusion). Strange but true: a country that on its home turf was deeply repressive, that denied large segments of its populace basic rights, and at times murdered and terrorized its own citizens on a vast scale, this same country promoted human rights at the international level.

There is something curious, though, about human rights. As we have seen in the other histories examined in this book, once pronounced, the genie's bottle is open. The escaping scents cannot be easily recaptured, the bottle resealed. Haitian slaves took up the cry of the French Revolution as they fought for their own liberation, and influenced, in turn, Brazilian slave rebels. After their defeat, American Indians began demanding the rights that other Americans possessed. Pioneering feminists all around the world rallied around the idea that women, too, deserved rights. In many instances protesters and activists called not for revolution, but for adherence to existing laws and principles. They demanded that the political order make real the rights promises written into cherished founding documents like constitutions and declarations of independence.

So it was in the Soviet Union. When a human rights movement emerged in the mid-1960s, its members—in its origins overwhelmingly from the intelligentsia; that is, intellectuals committed to critical inquiry and an ethical form of politics, often in opposition to the reigning system—called not for the overthrow of the Soviet Union, but for the fulfillment of Soviet law. The language of rights, proclaimed with such flourish in the 1936 constitution and its successor in 1977, served as the weapon hurled by dissidents as they called on the Soviet government to respect freedom of speech and assembly and the right to emigrate (among other rights). Activists demanded a halt to the extrajudicial, inhumane repressions of individuals who had dared to speak out, many of whom languished in prisons, psychiatric hospitals, and labor camps. Soon enough, activists would also draw upon the UDHR, thereby internationalizing their movement. In turn, foreign support for these Soviet dissidents helped create the modern human rights movement— Amnesty International and Human Rights Watch two prominent examples.

National and social rights within the country, the USSR as a major actor in the creation of the postwar human rights system, and the emergence of a domestic dissident and human rights movement from the 1960s onward—these topics make the Soviet experience critical to any history of human rights. We turn first to the issue of national rights.

❧

In 1912, Lenin dispatched his comrade Stalin to Vienna to write a tract on the "national question," as it was called in the nineteenth and early twentieth centuries. The two future Soviet dictators had already established a rapport and were thinking alike on this matter. Both had become acutely aware that national sentiments could not be ignored if Bolshevism were ever going to attract mass support. Both understood that workers, too, were animated by their national identity. And Stalin was, of course, Georgian. He lived the reality of an oppressed nationality within the Russian Empire, but also knew the opportunities that membership in a much larger entity, a Eurasian Great Power, afforded to energetic individuals from small and relatively backward nations.[3]

Stalin went on to write the most important book (actually a booklet, or long essay) on Soviet nationalities policies, a work that would shape communist thinking and communist policies around the globe, from East Berlin to P'yôngyang to Havana, as well as Leningrad and Moscow. Stalin was not the first communist to ponder the problem of the nation. The great progenitors of communism, Marx and Engels, had bravely declared that the proletariat has no country. But even they, within a decade of the revolutions of 1848 and the publication, that same year, of the *Communist Manifesto*, had to become reconciled to the great power of the nation and nationalism in the modern era.[4] As much as Marx and Engels and their successors proclaimed the force of class as the determining element of history, and the new class of the nineteenth century—the proletariat—as the one that carried the future of liberty and progress in its very being, they could not ignore the political realities around them. After all, they were living in the great era of nation-state foundings (a number of which were recounted in the previous chapters): the establishment of Italy and Germany in 1871 and Bulgaria, Montenegro, Serbia, and Romania at the Congress of Berlin in 1878; the Meiji Restoration in Japan; and the re-founding of the United States through the Civil War, Reconstruction, and westward expansion. Not individual rights but national rights became the primary focus of state founders and political activists.

As Marx and Engels moved toward a more "scientific" effort to describe the workings of the capitalist economy and the political conflicts of the day, they began also to write about nations, not in the great theoretical works like *Capital*, but in their journalistic articles and political correspondence.[5] Always scouring the landscape for any glimmer of revolution, Marx and Engels leapt with enthusiasm at the signs of burgeoning national movements—Irish against the English, Poles against the Russians, Italians against the Habsburg Empire. They deployed the term "self-determination" for those nations-in-the-making that had demonstrated the capacity for self-defense and economic progress. About others, like Slavs with the exception of Poles, they were scathing.[6] None of them constituted a "viable people"; they were, at best, semi-civilized and therefore incapable of forming nation-states.[7]

Like Marx and Engels, second-generation Marxists were always on the hunt for signs of progress and revolution. They, too, responded to the political events around them. However reactionary in practice were many of the newly founded countries, the nation-state was a sign of History making its way, surmounting decrepit, autocratic empires, and a major new step on the path to socialism. A precious few exceptions, like Rosa Luxemburg and her comrade and sometime lover Leo Jogiches, adhered to a rigorous internationalist position. But most socialists heard the siren song of the nation and believed that the individual could only be the bearer of rights as a national citizen.

From Marx's and Engels's writings, the nation and self-determination entered easily into the language and politics of the socialist movement. In 1896, the Socialist International included in its program an article on "self-determination for all peoples"—a decisive way station on the path to self-determination becoming a human right.

For socialists in the multinational Habsburg Empire, the problem was especially acute. How could democracy and socialism be built amid the great ethnic and national diversity of the empire? Who, precisely, constituted the nation when so many nationalities were present? Who had the right to have rights in the new nation-states or in a federal system? The most determined and forthright effort to address this problem came from the Austro-Marxists, a group of socialist activists and intellectuals. Otto Bauer, one of their main theorists, argued that in a multinational setting, a powerful central state inevitably becomes a battleground of nations, each one striving to capture it. Bauer pleaded, instead, for a decentralized state and widespread national autonomy within the empire. In that way, the "self-determination of the nations" would become the program of the working class of all nations and the pathway to socialism.[8]

The Austro-Marxist program never went beyond conjecture. The shattering of the Habsburg Empire in World War I put an end to its political possibilities. But, in a different way, it exercised profound influence on a global scale throughout the twentieth and into the twenty-first century. Precisely because of the Austro-Marxists, Lenin suggested to Stalin that he go to Vienna. There Stalin could study and write immersed in the environment of the most developed socialist thinking on the nation. Stalin had only a "smattering" of German, but some of Bauer's and Karl Renner's (another prominent Austro-Marxist) writings had been translated into Russian.[9] A significant number of Bolshevik exiles from Russia lived in Vienna, and they knew German and could help Stalin with the language. And they did, including none other than Nikolai Bukharin, who would go on to be Stalin's supporter in the factional struggles of the 1920s and then Stalin's victim in the Great Terror of the 1930s.

In Vienna Stalin wrote *Marxism and the National Question*. It was published shortly after his return to Russia at the beginning of 1913. Right afterward he was caught by the tsarist police and, once again, exiled to Siberia.[10]

As a good Marxist, Stalin argued that the nation is a form of political organization specific to the period of capitalism. Yet he also drew on the Austro-Marxists by positing that the nation had a certain stability over time. Writing in the catechism-like style he preferred, Stalin's ultimate, oft-cited definition was: "A nation is a historically constituted, stable community of people, formed on the basis of a common language, territory, economic life, and psychological make-up manifested in a common culture."[11] " 'National character,' " Stalin claimed, is not fixed for eternity and is "modified by changes in the conditions of life; but since it exists at every given moment, it leaves its impress on the physiognomy of the nation."[12]

Stalin's argument—lauded by Lenin—signified that the nation is a historical reality that cannot simply be wished away. It evolves historically, yet has a certain stability that is reproduced among its members through culture. As he wrote later, in 1930, proletarian power would contribute to the "blossoming" of national cultures. Once they were fully developed, then the preconditions would exist for their ultimate "fusion into a single, common, socialist (both in form and content) culture, with a single, common language, when the proletariat is victorious throughout the world and socialism becomes an everyday matter."[13] Yet even after the worldwide victory of the proletarian revolution, national differences "are bound to remain for a long time."[14] Despite ritualistic criticisms of Austrian moderate socialists like Bauer, Stalin's writings clearly contain the traces of Bauer's definition of the nation as a "community of destiny" and a "community of shared character."[15]

Stalin's writings were not arcane, theoretical flights. They determined Soviet policy toward the many nationalities and ethnicities within the Soviet Union, and, as we shall see, Soviet support of decolonization, nation-state foundings, and international human rights after 1945. These positions would win the Soviets sympathy in the Global South, which the USSR actively cultivated through support for guerrilla movements and national liberation struggles as well as cultural exchanges and economic development programs with newly emergent countries in Africa, the Middle East, and Asia.

❧

The Bolsheviks assumed power in an empire with a dizzying array of nationalities and ethnicities. From the very beginning, they proclaimed the right of all nations to self-determination, even to the point of secession—not exactly a promise that would be honored, but one that reflected their utopian beliefs in autumn 1917. What nationality would really be so foolish as to want to separate from the country that embodied the great socialist future? (Many, as it turned out.) The proclamation was soon followed by the establishment of the Commissariat of Nationalities, led by none other than our author, Josef Stalin, the recognized communist authority on the national question.

The Bolsheviks prevailed despite the extremely difficult years following 1917, marked by civil war, foreign intervention, and the near-total collapse of the economy—all on top of the disruption and misery of World War I. By 1921, the Bolsheviks had defeated their enemies on the battlefield and had launched the New Economic Policy, which allowed for some elements of a market economy. It was a desperate, innovative effort by Lenin to revive agricultural and industrial production and relieve the desperate circumstances of the population. It worked. Peasants sowed, factories reopened, intellectual and cultural life flourished. The time seemed right, then, to formalize the nature of the very large country that the Bolsheviks ruled.

The USSR was formally created on 28 December 1922 as a federation of nationalities, a structure that would be reconfirmed in the constitutions of 1936 and 1977. On that basis, the Soviets actively promoted national rights. Soviet policy meant that "socialist content was only accessible to nationals in national form."[16] The hallmark of this approach was *korenizatsiia*, or indigenization—a program that fostered national languages and national elites. The Soviet system granted members of the nationalities preference for governmental positions within the republics; established quotas for them in higher education; and founded newspapers, theater companies, and publishing houses in the particular language. Soviets (or councils) were established for all the nationalities.[17]

Like Japanese imperialists and Protestant missionaries, the Soviets pursued their version of national rights and the civilizing mission. For some of the more underdeveloped peoples of the Soviet Union, *korenizatsiia* entailed receiving young communist activists, who were sent out to teach the natives to brush their teeth, bathe, and read, just as the Japanese had to teach Koreans to dye their white clothes so the dirt would not always show.[18] The Soviets even promoted small-nation—indeed, small-tribe—nationalism within the republics. Soviet scholars developed written languages for populations that numbered fewer than one thousand, and consolidated some groups and handed them one common language. Through the use of native languages, the various peoples would also learn to "speak Bolshevik."[19] At the same time, the national republics and their citizens partook of the great industrialization, literacy, and public health campaigns launched by the USSR.

FIGURE 8.1 Jewish children in Minsk, 1930s. The Soviet Union was formed as a federation of nationalities. Throughout its history the USSR celebrated its diverse nationalities and ethnicities, even while some groups suffered the most severe repressions. Here, Jewish children in the Soviet youth movement carry banners in Yiddish that read, "We are all proletarian children." Only after World War II would Jews be subject to state-directed antisemitic attacks. (Lebrecht Music and Arts/Alamy Stock Photo.)

For many members of the former subject nations of the tsarist empire, these policies felt like a huge breath, a windstorm, of fresh air. Theaters and publishing houses in Yiddish and Kazakh, celebrations of Georgian folk culture, Ukrainian orchestras—these gave many people a sense of being a part of the great communist project, of creating a freer and better world for themselves and their children, one in which they could develop their national culture to new heights (see figures 8.1 and 8.2). Some of their co-nationals played leading roles in the republics and the central state, a source of great pride. After all, Stalin was Georgian by background, Lazar Kaganovich Jewish, and Anastas Mikoyan Armenian. Why not also a Kazakh or Korean in the leading organs of the Soviet Union? National rights, many citizens of the USSR felt, constituted one of the great achievements of the Soviet system.

But what the state gives, the state can take away, as we saw with North Korea in the previous chapter.

FIGURE 8.2 Sportswomen from the Azerbaijan SSR join the All-Union parade of athletes, USSR, 1939. Another celebration of national cultures, as well as of women's emancipation, Soviet-style. Here, Azeri women march in the All-Union parade of Soviet athletes. The Soviet Union always trumpeted women's achievements at work, in education, and in cultural activities like sports and music. Home life, however, remained resolutely traditional. (soviet-art.ru.)

With the new constitution in 1936, Soviet leaders touted the triumph of socialism in the USSR.[20] The nobility, then the bourgeoisie and the *kulaks* (wealthy peasants), had been vanquished. No internal class enemies existed any longer. But enemies still lurked about. Some were real, like Nazi Germany. Many others were fictive, mere imaginings on the part of an increasingly paranoid Stalin and a system built on popular mobilizations. The domestic policies of the 1930s had resulted in enormous instabilities and discontents. In some areas, like Ukraine, famine had killed around six million people. Blame had to be fixed somewhere, and certainly not on Stalin himself.

Among the wreckers and saboteurs—choice Soviet words of the 1930s—were certain nations.[21] The very importance granted to the nationalities principle through *korenizatsiia* now also underpinned the attack on "suspect" nations. Over the course of the 1930s the objects of persecution shifted from class enemies to "enemies of the people," which slid easily into "enemy nations." Along with many other victims of the Stalin Terror, they would be purged out of the circle of rights-bearing citizens.

Beginning in the mid-1930s, then, the state limited the proliferation of nationalities without abandoning the nationalities principle. Some nations continued to flourish, and their members enjoyed all the benefits associated with national rights. Russians in particular became privileged—the state asserting Russia's cultural and political superiority within the USSR. The consolidation process deprived many diaspora nationalities of their institutions, such as their national soviets, publishing houses, and theater groups in their own languages. Cultural Russification, marked especially by the mandatory teaching of Russian, became the watchword. The party's theoretical journal and school textbooks trumpeted the achievements of the Great Russian people and their history of heroic battles for independence and freedom against countless enemies.[22] In World War II, this kind of rhetoric only intensified, as the Soviet state articulated the war as virtually a racial battle between Slavs and Germans, and explained the ultimate victory as a result of the inherent superiority of Russians and their Slavic brethren.[23]

Alongside the elevation of Russia came the escalation of ethnic and national purges.[24] In the Western border regions in the 1930s, the regime deemed Poles, Germans, Estonians, and Finns "unreliable" and forcibly removed them to points eastward.[25] Although they were not deprived of their civil rights, nor labeled counterrevolutionary, the compulsory resettlements signified the assignment of collective guilt to entire nationalities, no matter what any individuals among them did or did not do. Along the border in the Soviet Far East, where the USSR feared war with Japan (now ensconced in Korea and Manchuria), the regime, in 1937, deported Koreans. The state identified all Soviet Koreans as real or potential Japanese spies and carried out the first total purge of a nationality.[26] Koreans endured inhumane conditions, including a month spent in barely heated freight cars. Then they were deposited into open areas in Uzbekistan, Turkmenistan, Kazakhstan, or Kyrgyzstan without any shelter or food. Many died from epidemics and hunger.

Worse was still to come. During the war years, the purges escalated further as the Soviet Union reeled from the massive force of the German invasion and the leadership feared betrayal from within. The regime deported Germans, Chechens, Ingush, Crimean Tatars, Karachai, Balkars, Kalmyks, and Meshkhites to Kazakhstan, Uzbekistan, or Kyrgyzstan. In the Crimea and Caucasus the Soviets charged Greeks, Bulgarians, Armenians, Meshkhites, Kurds, and Khemchines with harboring "anti-Soviet elements," and they too faced deportations.[27] As late as 1948 the regime forcibly removed Turks, Armenians, and Greeks in the Black Sea region.[28] After the war, yet another round of purges affected populations in the Western borderlands, especially in the re-annexed Baltic republics. One count based on Soviet archives opened in the 1990s yielded fifty-eight peoples, three to three and one-half million individuals, deported on national grounds.[29] At the outset of the 1950s, more than 90 percent of those classified as "special deportees" represented members of nationally defined populations.[30] For some groups, the mortality rates during the deportations reached 25 percent.[31]

The Soviet government charged that these people had collaborated with the Germans and had resisted the policies of the socialist offensive of the 1930s, forced collectivization in particular. Following the population removals, the regime changed place names, destroyed buildings, and bulldozed cemeteries in an effort to erase the visible signs of a once extant people and culture—all the same practices that occurred in Greece and Turkey following the Lausanne exchange and in Israel following the removal of Palestinians.[32]

It is grimly appropriate that the very last Stalinist attack on a national group, an attack imbued with racial elements, was directed against Jews.[33] All the repressive measures and charges, symptomatic of the worst excesses of the Stalinist imagination, were, in all probability, the steps toward a revival of terror on a grand, societal scale, which would certainly have extended beyond Jews. The charge of "cosmopolitanism," leveled throughout Stalin's last years, reverberated with Nazi-style anti-semitism. Moreover, in the weeks just before Stalin's death, reports circulated of a plan to deport eastward the entire Jewish population.[34] Less than ten years after the end of World War II, the scheme raised the specter of the worst actions of both the Nazi and Soviet regimes.

The deportations carried out by the Soviet Union were hardly unique. As almost every chapter in this book has demonstrated, the removals and repressions of some population groups while others were elevated into rights-bearing citizens is a central feature of the history of human rights. The difference in the Soviet case is the criteria on which those decisions were made. The regime drew a political line, though one that became imbued with national and even racial elements. The Soviets applied the charge of disloyalty, of supporting "anti-Soviet elements," to entire national groups, a form of collective guilt that violates any conception of human rights. National identity in the Soviet Union cut both ways, a source of progress and development and the basis of forced removals, the foundation of rights claims and of their deprivation.

ℝ

Whatever the reality in the country, the USSR's express commitment to national rights, self-determination, and social rights also gave it an opening to play a major role in the creation of the post-1945 human rights system.[35] That system was never simply a liberal creation. Indeed, liberal states like the United States, Great Britain, and France opposed many of the elements that we now take as fixed features of international human rights. In contrast, the Soviet Union became a driving force behind many of the postwar UN human rights resolutions and conventions, especially as UN membership expanded to include the newly independent, decolonized countries. The Soviet magnet attracted them. The USSR was, after all, a Great Power, and it had resources and influence to deploy as well as an ideological commitment to national and social rights.

As early as 1947, at nothing less than the UN debate on Palestine—a topic we will address in more detail in the next chapter—Andrei Gromyko, the Soviet ambassador to the UN and later foreign minister (and many other things besides), gave an acute and moving speech in support of the foundation of a Jewish state (see figure 8.3). Before the UN, Gromyko spoke with great sympathy about the "indescribable" Jewish suffering and "almost complete physical annihilation" of Jews under the

FIGURE 8.3 Andrei Gromyko, 1947. Gromyko (1909–89) came from a working-class and peasant family in Belarus and was one of the longest serving high-level Soviet officials. He was the USSR's first permanent representative to the UN and then became foreign minister. In 1947 he gave a moving speech to the General Assembly supporting the foundation of a Jewish state. Here, Gromyko (in the center) is shown with the first UN secretary-general Trygve Lie (on the left) and Alfred Fiderkiewicz (on the right), the Polish representative to the UN. (UN Photo/MB.)

Nazis.[36] Gromyko went on to lament the sorrowful state of Jewish survivors: many of them homeless or living in displaced-persons camps, all of them impoverished. If the UN ignored their plight, he argued, it would violate "the high principles proclaimed in [the UN] Charter, which provide for the defense of human rights, irrespective of race, religion, or sex. The time has come to help these people, not by words, but by deeds."[37]

Gromyko used the desperate situation of Jews to attack the Western powers, who had utterly failed the Jews, he charged. None had been able to protect them from Nazi violence; none had helped Jews defend their rights. Hence, the Jews aspire to their own state, and the UN should not deny them this right. Gromyko went on to call for a single state in which the rights of both peoples, Arabs and Jews, would be protected. If that proved impossible, then the Soviet Union would support partition.[38]

The USSR's position in favor of a Jewish state should not be reduced to an early campaign in the vitriolic competition of the Cold War. Gromyko's recognition of the Holocaust—as it would later be called—and the necessity of a Jewish state were not one-show wonders, singular and temporary exceptions to the overall thrust of Soviet foreign policy. Rather, they had deep roots in the ideology and politics of the USSR. The path to communism, as we have seen, lay through the nation, whether nation-states under capitalism or national republics within the USSR.

Through all the human rights debates within the councils of the UN from the 1940s onward, the USSR pursued this stance, advocating decolonization, national independence, and self-determination, as well as economic and social rights. And the Soviets and their allies prevailed, making these items central features of the postwar human rights system.

At the time of its drafting from 1946 to 1948, the UDHR was broadly understood as only the first step in a new world order in which human rights would be fully guaranteed by both the UN and its constituent members. Quickly, it was thought, the UDHR would be followed by an international criminal court and by an international treaty that would deepen and make legally binding the rights principles enunciated in 1948. It was not to be, not any time soon, as the Cold War burgeoned and affected virtually every arena of political life, including human rights.

Years of intense wrangling marked the creation of the international human rights system. The conflicts began on day one, at the UN's founding conference, which convened in San Francisco from 25 April to 26 June 1945.[39] The Soviet Union, loyal to the position laid out by Lenin and Stalin, forcefully pushed for the inclusion of decolonization, national liberation, and self-determination in the founding documents of the organization. On these issues they had one American ally—namely, Ralph Bunche, a member of the US negotiating team. Bunche would go on to a long and illustrious career at the UN. (We will encounter him again in chapter 9 on Palestine/Israel and chapter 10 on Rwanda and Burundi.) At the time, Bunche was one of the most prominent

African-Americans in the United States. He was a firm advocate of civil rights at home and of decolonization abroad. Despite sharp opposition from the State Department and other US agencies, Bunche managed to win the American delegation's acceptance of—or at least acquiescence to—article 1 of the UN Charter, which calls for the promotion of "equal rights and self-determination of peoples," and article 7, which established the Trusteeship Council, the UN body charged with guiding colonized countries toward independence.[40]

These were positions long advocated by the Soviet Union and its allies. Now the young UN espoused them as well, as did representatives of countries like India, Afghanistan, Saudi Arabia, Syria, and Ethiopia. All of them argued that self-determination constituted a self-evident human right, and any human rights instrument worthy of the name had to include the concept.[41] The Uruguayan representative in 1951 stated the point most simply and clearly, and in a way that would be repeated through all the debates from the 1940s into the 1960s: "any limitation of . . . the right [of self-determination] would deprive the other rights of reality."[42] The Czech representative, reflecting the Soviet position, echoed the sentiment: the "implementation of the right to self-determination is an essential condition without which no people can achieve . . . the genuine implementation of other human rights."[43] National rights came first; individual rights would follow.

Meanwhile, the Soviet Union and its allies had an easy time lambasting the United States and other Western powers for their deficiencies in the realm of human rights. In 1952, the delegate from the Ukrainian Soviet Socialist Republic charged that in the United States, twenty states had legislation that discriminated against African-Americans, and Britain subjected its colonial populations to corporal punishment.[44] A decade later, the difficulties for the United States accentuated when television news displayed images of policemen in Birmingham, Alabama, turning high-pressure water hoses and clubs on African-American children and young adults.[45] The British also had little to say when the Soviets and their allies raised the issue of concentration camps where British soldiers killed and tortured Kenyans fighting for their freedom, and the same was true of the French when reports circulated that they tortured at will members of the Algerian National Liberation Front. The Soviets could point to their own constitution and laws to claim adherence to the principles of the UDHR and their open support for civil rights demonstrators and anticolonial fighters.

The proposed clauses and resolutions in favor of self-determination caused great consternation, especially for Britain, Belgium, and Portugal, and the United States as well. For good reason. The principle threatened their empires and gave the USSR a powerful propaganda weapon. The British and their allies claimed to be defending state sovereignty, another founding principle of the UN. They raised the fearsome specter of continual instability in the global order if every self-proclaimed people demanded its own state.

As the debates continued through the 1940s and 1950s, the Western powers reverted to the old imperial line that only "mature" populations had the capacity to exercise self-determination. The Belgian representative, expressing his country's continued resistance to decolonization, set off a firestorm in the UN in 1951 when he argued that the right to self-determination had to be "conditional on the degree of political maturity prevailing in the country concerned."[46] René Cassin, one of the twentieth century's great advocates of human rights, a Nobel Peace Prize recipient for his work on the UDHR, also opposed self-determination, though for different reasons. He argued that human rights are "purely individual rights"—a position echoed by Eleanor Roosevelt, the head of the UN Human Rights Commission.[47] By the end of the 1950s, the United States was sounding much like the old colonial powers when its representative warned that self-determination could lead to excessive "political fragmentation," and that "emerging peoples" first had to have "adequate preparation for self-government."[48]

Cassin and the United States prevailed in 1948. Social rights but not self-determination made it into the UDHR. In the years afterward, however, the Soviet and Global South position won the day.[49] On 5 February 1952, concluding the debate on the drafting of a human rights convention, the General Assembly directed its Third Committee—the drafting body—to include in the treaty an article on self-determination. Reflecting the Cold War divide, it also decided that the Third Committee should prepare two treaties, one on political and civil rights and the other on economic, social, and cultural rights. The vote was forty-two to seven with five abstentions. The United States, Great Britain, France, Belgium, and three other countries voted against the resolution, a reflection of their hostility to both self-determination and social and economic rights.[50]

From that point onward, every resolution, every declaration, every covenant on human rights affirmed the "right of all peoples to self-determination." By 1960, the anticolonial tide had become unstoppable, and many more newly independent countries gained admission to the UN. Ghana was one of the first to join. With soaring rhetoric, its president, Kwame Nkrumah, expressed the views of many Africans:

> The great tide of history flows. . . . One cardinal fact of our time is the momentous impact of Africa's awakening upon the modern world. . . . Our voice booms across the oceans and mountains, over the hills and valleys, in the desert places and through the vast expanse of mankind's habitation, and it calls out for the freedom of Africa; Africa wants her freedom; Africa must be free.[51]

That meant self-determination.

Khrushchev, with rhetoric that soared not quite as high as Nkrumah's, made the same point:

> Africa is seething and bubbling like a volcano. For some six years now the Algerian people have been waging a heroic and selfless struggle for their national liberation. . . . No force . . . can halt this struggle of the peoples for their liberation. . . . Colonial slavery is giving place to freedom. We must have done with colonialism. . . . It is the UN's duty to reaffirm faith in human rights, in the dignity and worth of the human person, in the equal rights of nations large and small. . . . [We must] make an end of this infamy [colonialism], this barbarism, this savagery.[52]

Khrushchev went on to present the Soviet Union as a model for the rest of the world. Echoing Soviet policies since 1917, he argued that nationalities that had been oppressed and impoverished under the tsars now lived freely in the Soviet Union. On the basis of communist self-determination, they had been able to develop their individual cultures and their living standards had improved greatly.[53]

Khrushchev's claims were rather far-fetched, given the fact that so many nationalities had been oppressed, not liberated, by the Soviets. At the same time, the Soviet Union could point to real economic and social advances among those nations that had been deemed loyal. Soviet rhetoric echoed like music in the ears of Nkrumah and the hundreds of thousands of anticolonial activists around the globe. In this way, Stalin's tract on nationalities achieved worldwide resonance, while the British, like the Americans, warned about the dangers of granting self-determination to peoples not yet mature enough to exercise the right responsibly.[54] In 1960, the Soviets sponsored a resolution on decolonization, with article 2 affirming that "all peoples have the right to self-determination." It passed eighty-nine to nil with nine abstentions, among them Belgium, France, Britain, and the United States.[55] Ghana, needless to say, voted in the affirmative.

Six years later, "after two decades of laborious, indeed epic endeavor," as the delegate from the Dominican Republic phrased it, the UN took up the two covenants, one on civil and political rights and the other on economic, social, and cultural rights, plus an additional resolution in support of self-determination.[56] The half-baked compromise of two covenants pleased almost no one, but reflected the ideological and political stalemate of the Cold War. To the Soviet bloc and Global South representatives, political and civil rights were meaningless if people did not have adequate food and clothing, shelter, means of employment, and healthcare.[57] The United States and its allies ferociously resisted the articulation of these issues as rights, while the colonial die-hards, Portugal and Britain, were about the only ones to oppose publicly the rhetoric of self-determination.

At its 1966 meeting, the UN General Assembly passed the resolution on self-determination and, unanimously, the two human rights covenants, both of which, as article 1, inscribed into international law the "right of self-determination" of "all peoples."[58] The rapporteur of the Third Committee, Ponce de Leon of Columbia, expressed the prevailing sentiment of two decades of debate: "The right of self-determination is one of the most important human rights, since it is a prerequisite for the full enjoyment of other fundamental freedoms and rights . . . [including] the equal rights of women and men in all fields of human rights. . . . With the adoption of these instruments [the two covenants] every imaginable aspect of the life of the individual is covered."[59]

The passing of the two covenants represented a landmark in the development of the international human rights system. The promise of 1948 and the UDHR had, it seemed, been fulfilled. A great deal of the credit rests with the countries of the Soviet bloc and the Global South. The United States, in contrast, has still not ratified the covenant on economic, social, and cultural rights.

In the subsequent decades and down to our present day, almost every other human rights instrument and document reaffirms social and economic rights as part of the mix of human rights, and repeats, virtually word for word, the same phrases regarding self-determination. Whether the primacy given to national over individual rights is truly a victory for human rights is a matter to which we shall return in the conclusion.

☙

On 5 December 1965, a small group of Soviet citizens ventured to Pushkin Square in Moscow. Fifty or so people appeared, along with about two hundred observers, quite a number of them incognito Committee for State Security (KGB) agents. Two writers, Andrei Sinyavsky and Yuli Daniel, had been seized by the KGB and placed on trial. The charges were trumped-up; the event echoing the worst of the Stalin years. "Socialist legality," the term Khrushchev had touted in his famed 1956 speech denouncing Stalin, was nowhere in evidence. The mathematician Alexander Esenin-Volpin organized the demonstration (see figure 8.4). He had chosen the date and place carefully. Pushkin Square honored the great Russian literary figure; it faced the house of *Isvestiia*, the government's newspaper. And 5 December was Constitution Day, the anniversary of the promulgation of the 1936 constitution. The participants unfurled signs, "Respect the Constitution," and "The Sinyavsky-Daniel

FIGURE 8.4 Alexander Esenin-Volpin, 1974. Esenin-Volpin (1924–2016) was a mathematician and poet, and one of the founders of the dissident and human rights movements in the Soviet Union. He argued that the Soviet constitution and Soviet laws proclaimed human rights, so the movement should simply demand that the country live by its laws. In 1965 he organized the first human rights demonstration in the USSR. The authorities confined him to psychiatric hospitals multiple times. He emigrated to the United States in 1972, where he died at the ripe age of ninety-one. (© Rosemary Winckley/Archive of the Research Center for East European Studies at the University of Bremen.)

Trial Should Be Open to the Public."[60] The police quickly moved in, tore down the signs, and shut down the demonstration.

The Soviet Union had parades and rallies galore, all orchestrated by the government. Rare indeed were independent demonstrations. Esenin-Volpin had broken through the long, cold winter of the Stalin years and the timidity of his successors to organize a civil society action, one not sanctioned by the state. There were, or course, precedents. In the late 1950s, members of some of the nationalities that had been deported collected petitions and staged demonstrations. Crimean Tatars launched petition drives requesting the right to return to their homelands. In total, they gathered three million signatures.[61] The famed *samizdat* (self-publishing)—individually typed and surreptitiously distributed literature—began in the 1950s, first with poetry, then longer literary works, and, finally, political tracts. Long before personal computers, when even copying machines were a tightly controlled rarity in the USSR, those who typed and disseminated *samizdat* displayed enormous courage and determination. Despite the severe repression that so many participants suffered, *samizdat* became a broad-based phenomenon all across the Soviet bloc, as did its cousin, *tamizdat*, works published "over there"—that is, abroad in the West.[62]

Whatever the precedents, the demonstration organized by Volpin marked a decisive civil society initiative and the birth of the Soviet human rights movement.[63] The activists failed to win the release of Sinyavsky and Daniel. But in broad daylight in a central Moscow plaza, they had demanded the implementation of socialist legality. The genie had been released from the bottle.

Khrushchev and other Soviet leaders had helped uncork the bottle. The vocabulary of human rights entered Soviet discourse, even though the USSR had abstained in 1948 on the vote on the UDHR. Khrushchev used the phrase "human rights" in his address to the General Assembly in 1960, as had Gromyko before him in 1948 (as we have just seen). The USSR and its Soviet-bloc allies retained their seats on the UN's Commission on Human Rights, a powerful perch from which they influenced international proclamations and treaties. By the late 1950s, the Soviet Union was speaking and acting as if it had actually signed the UDHR.[64]

And then, of course, there was Khrushchev's famed secret speech condemning the crimes of Stalin, delivered in February 1956 to the Communist Party congress. The secrecy lasted barely a few days, if that.[65] Hardly a call for human rights, the speech nonetheless lay down a grand red-carpet opening for the entire Soviet bloc.

The "thaw" that ensued entailed the broadest range of cultural freedom since the Soviet 1920s. The publication in 1962 of Alexander Solzhenitsyn's *One Day in the Life of Ivan Denisovich*, a bristling condemnation of the Soviet gulag, provided one bracing signal of the great, though temporary, transformation. Academics and officials hoped that the renowned and lamented inefficiencies of the centrally planned economy would be corrected by the introduction of market mechanisms. Many Soviet citizens hoped that under the continued aegis of the Communist Party, the political system would become more open. Some even ventured to imagine that the two systems, capitalism and communism, were moving toward some sort of convergence that would join together the best of both.

"Socialist legality" was the stock phrase used by Khrushchev. Stalin had violated that sacred principle of the socialist society. He had ruled as a one-man dictator, exercising at will his whims and proclivities. The Soviet Union would become "normal," Khrushchev suggested, still communist, to be sure, but functioning according to its own rules and regulations and principles—including the 1936 constitution with all its human rights provisions and the international agreements that the Soviet Union would soon promote and sign.

Soviet human rights activists like Volpin, Andrei Sakharov, Valery Chalidze, the brothers Roy and Zhores Medvedev, Lyudmila Alexeyeva, and many others quickly traversed the red carpet, all the while writing and talking about "socialist legality." Never in the 1960s and 1970s did they demand an end to Soviet communism or to the leading role of the CPSU. Instead, they called for the fulfillment—in deed as well as rhetoric—of the Soviet constitution and Soviet laws.

Volpin, a mercurial mathematician, and Chalidze, a scientist turned legal scholar, were the major advocates of this approach. Volpin came at the notion through a logician's adherence to strict, formal rules, which he derived from his discipline as well as from cybernetics, a popular philosophy and methodology across the Western world, including the USSR, in the 1950s and 1960s. He also drew on his study of Ludwig Wittgenstein's linguistics.[66] Volpin distinguished himself from other intellectuals by applying "exact methods," the approach touted by cybernetics, not to the planned economy or scientific research, but to official Soviet ideology.[67] He argued that Soviet citizens already had rights; all they had to do was act on them. It was a wild and fanciful notion; some people thought Volpin was literally crazy. "Have you forgotten where you live?" was one common response to his call for the demonstration on Constitution Day in 1965.[68] Vladimir Bukovsky, another important human rights campaigner, remarked that Volpin's ideas were:

> both inspired and insane. The suggestion was that citizens who were fed up with terror and coercion should simply refuse to acknowledge them. . . . The inspiration of this idea consisted in eliminating the split in our personalities by shattering the internal excuses with which we justified our complicity in all the crimes. It presupposed a small core of freedom in each individual . . . [and] a consciousness of his personal responsibility. Which meant, in effect, inner freedom.[69]

The strategy proved effective in stimulating others, however small in number, to take a stand in support of human rights. Volpin believed in all the social and political provisions of the constitution. Soviet citizens already possessed the rights to education, healthcare, and social security, and to freedom of speech and assembly, fair and open trials, and the development of one's own national culture.[70] They just had to make the state be true to its own commitments.

When the Soviet Union signed on to the 1966 UN covenants on human rights, Volpin added another arrow to his quiver. He managed to obtain the text of the treaties and circulated them as *samizdat* documents. Now he and others demanded that the Soviet Union not only follow its own laws; it also had to adhere to the international treaties it had signed.[71]

By the time of the 1965 demonstration, the promise of the Khrushchev thaw had faded badly. The cultural lake had refrozen; the red carpet had been rolled up and thrown into deep storage. While in power, Khrushchev himself had zigzagged—sometimes espousing a more open policy; at other times, faced with demonstrations at home and outright rebellion abroad (Hungary and Poland), reasserting the achievements of Stalin and the Soviet state's powerful mechanisms of repression. Other Soviet leaders feared that Khrushchev's reforms, however halfhearted they were, as well as his mercurial temperament and policies, threatened the stability of the entire Soviet system and, of course, their own powers and privileges. The twenty-second congress of the CPSU in 1962 marked the high point of the reform period; soon thereafter Khrushchev was ousted by his colleagues, though not killed—one sign of the difference between the 1960s and 1930s.

FIGURE 8.5 Larisa Bogoraz, 1983. Bogoraz (1929–2004) was an early and steadfast Soviet human rights activist. She organized a demonstration in Red Square against the Soviet Union's 1968 invasion of Czechoslovakia, which put a brutal stop to the efforts there to create "communism with a human face." She was quickly arrested and dispatched to internal exile in Siberia. Bogoraz wrote many appeals, petitions, and longer works, and contributed regularly to the major underground publication *Chronicle of Current Events*. As the Soviet Union dissolved, she chaired the Moscow Helsinki Group and called for the release of all political prisoners. She kept up her human rights activism in Russia until her death. (Archive of the Research Center for East European Studies at the University of Bremen.)

Within a couple of years, Leonid Brezhnev had emerged as the new leader. He sealed shut the cultural opening. The efforts by Czech reformers in 1968 to create "socialism with a human face" proved a turning point. News of the Czech events aroused great hopes among Soviet opposition figures, and stimulated more intense repression by the state, both within the Soviet bloc and at home. For many activists, the sight of Soviet tanks on the streets of Prague dashed their hopes for peaceful, incremental change. Nonetheless, Larisa Bogoraz, another pioneering human rights campaigner, organized a small demonstration in Red Square against the Soviet invasion of Czechoslovakia (see figure 8.5). In the typical pattern, she was quickly arrested and dispatched to internal exile.

Yet the human rights movement continued to expand, one sign being the formation in 1970 of the Human Rights Committee, founded by three prominent scientists: Sakharov, Chalidze, and Andrei Tverdokhlebov.[72] They and many others continued their efforts despite the fact that Brezhnev unleashed all the repressive measures the state had at its disposal, including prison, exile, confinement in psychiatric hospitals, and beatings, let alone shattered careers with dire financial consequences. The regime did not spare family members, putting another form of pressure on activists.

Soviet human rights activists, much like their counterparts around the world, wrote pamphlets, articles, and books exposing the repressiveness, and the deceptions, of the system under which they lived and suffered.[73] They printed and distributed their writings as *samizdat*. They took up the cases of individuals persecuted by the authorities, demanding their freedom from imprisonment and other forms of internment and, at the very least, fair and open trials. They wrote appeals to the authorities, to their fellow citizens, and, finally, to supporters in the West. And they wrote and spoke in clear, direct, and honest language. As Chalidze argued, that kind of language was itself a statement of protest against the lies, deceptions, and mystifications of official propaganda, and proved influential in the West.[74] The major venue for publication in the USSR, the *Chronicle of Current Events*, was founded in 1968 and lasted until 1982, a remarkable fifteen-year run. Its US-based analogue, the *Chronicle of Human Rights in the USSR*, founded in 1973 by Chalidze, ran until 1983. Both chronicles provide an inestimable resource that details the repression, in all its minutiae, of individuals and the efforts of activists.

Human rights activists demanded the rights of free speech and assembly. They called for freedom of movement, within the country and abroad, including the right to emigrate. Activists publicized the fate of some of the Soviet Union's most marginalized groups, like religious believers and the deportees of the 1930s and 1940s, Crimean Tatars in particular. All along the way, most of the human rights advocates, at least in the 1960s and 1970s, asserted their commitment to social and economic rights, those areas where the Soviets could proudly claim some achievements, and demanded the simple adherence to Soviet law so that people could exercise their political and civil rights.

The Helsinki Accords in 1975 marked a critical advance in human rights. Major issues left over from World War II had never been fully decided by the Allies. The USSR had long sought confirmation of the borders in Eastern Europe and, in general, recognition as the Great Power it had become. This was the era of détente—the effort to reduce the tensions and conflicts between the two camps, and especially between the United States and the USSR. The United States took little interest in the negotiations leading up to Helsinki. Nor had it any desire to insert human rights norms into international diplomacy, certainly not under National Security Adviser and Secretary of State Henry Kissinger and presidents Richard Nixon and Gerald Ford. The Europeans, however, were determined to do just that: in return for the recognition of the borders established by the Red Army at the end of World War II, they wanted an agreement that included human rights provisions. Long negotiations ensued under the auspices of the Organization for Security and Co-operation in Europe, during which the Europeans literally forced the United States and the USSR to accept their position.[75]

The result was the Helsinki Final Act, signed by thirty-five countries on 1 August 1975, with its explicit statement in support of human rights:

> The participating States will respect human rights and fundamental freedoms, including the freedom of thought, conscience, religion or belief, for all without distinction as to race, sex, language or religion.
>
> They will promote and encourage the effective exercise of civil, political, economic, social, cultural and other rights and freedoms all of which derive from the inherent dignity of the human person and are essential for his free and full development.[76]

The signatories also agreed to respect the rights of minorities.

But why, pray tell, did the USSR sign an international agreement that stood in such direct opposition to its own practice? For multiple reasons. The diplomatic gains were simply too enticing, first and foremost the formal recognition of the borders in the regions of Europe presided over by the USSR since the defeat of Nazi Germany. That agreement also signified an informal recognition of the USSR as a Great Power, something always important to the Soviet leadership. Moreover, the Soviets, as we have seen, had already adopted the rhetoric of the UDHR. They probably believed that the Helsinki Final Act expressed nothing that contradicted the principles laid out in the Stalin constitution and in Soviet law, and soon to be embedded again in the Brezhnev constitution of 1977. Like all dictators, the Soviet leaders had the hubris to believe that they could contain any opposition that emerged, that demanded the implementation in fact and not just in rhetoric of human rights principles. Indeed, after ten years of active repression, the KGB probably assumed it had been successful in crushing all independent, oppositional groups.[77]

In August 1975, the government even published in newspapers the Helsinki Final Act, touting it as a great Soviet achievement. The text had a lightning effect on the human rights movement. Soviet readers "were stunned" by its humanitarian and human rights provisions.[78] Quickly, some activists recognized the potential, just as Volpin had seen the potential in the Soviet affirmation of the two 1966 human rights covenants. Even more forcefully with the Helsinki Final Act, dissidents demanded that the USSR follow the international treaties it had signed as well as its own laws and constitution. Within a year, another scientist turned dissident, Yuri Orlov, spearheaded the foundation of the Moscow Helsinki Watch Group. It was a brilliant stroke, soon followed by analogues in a variety of cities.[79] As Soviet activists had done before, the members of the Helsinki Watch groups gathered precise information about human rights violations and wrote letters, pamphlets, and appeals that they directed at all thirty-four other Helsinki signatories as well as at their own government.[80] In essence, the Soviet human rights movement merged the domestic emphasis on social and economic rights based in the Soviet constitution with the international human rights movement.[81]

The Soviet authorities thought they had successfully repressed the dissident and human rights movement. Instead, they gave it new life by signing the Helsinki Final Act. The ties became tighter among the specifically human rights and national and religious dissenter groups. The movement became more diverse sociologically; it developed beyond its purely intelligentsia roots.[82] Helsinki was a banner that activists of all stripes held high together.[83]

The inspiring stories of Soviet dissidents and human rights campaigners had a galvanizing impact in the West. Helsinki support networks emerged at both the governmental and popular levels. In the United States, the election of Jimmy Carter as president in 1976 signified a profound shift in direction. Despite his earlier criticisms of the negotiations sponsored by the Organization for Security and Co-operation in Europe, Carter quickly recognized the human rights potential of Helsinki. A strong movement had emerged in Congress, pioneered by Representative Millicent Fenwick of New Jersey, to monitor compliance with the human rights provisions of the Final Act. President Gerald Ford reluctantly signed a bill establishing the US Commission on Security and Cooperation in Europe; President Carter embraced it.[84] Similar developments occurred in the European countries.

Within just a few years of the act's signing, a Helsinki network had emerged.[85] It included both governmental bodies and NGOs, and linked East and West. More than that: the human rights movement in the Soviet Union had a profound influence on activists in the West, who set out to establish their own Helsinki Watch groups. In the United States, the original group was funded by the Ford Foundation, and it soon developed into one of the most important of all NGOs, Human Rights Watch.[86]

The thirty-five Helsinki signatories met in Belgrade in 1977–78 and in Madrid from 1980 to 1983 in follow-up conferences designed to ensure implementation of the agreements. Both meetings accomplished little in formal terms. Cold War divisions were still too great. At Belgrade especially, US representatives berated their Soviet colleagues for violations of human rights, a negotiating tactic that left even some Westerners bewildered and concerned. Perhaps more importantly, both meetings provided venues for activists to submit their concerns. As at the Berlin Congress in 1878 and the Paris Peace Conference in 1919, statesmen were deluged with petitions, letters, and appeals, many of them smuggled out from the Soviet Union and other communist countries. Despite the best efforts of diplomats to keep their deliberations confined to closed-door negotiations, Belgrade and Madrid opened up avenues of political mobilization for dissidents and human rights activists East and West.[87]

❧

The Soviet human rights movement produced many determined and courageous individuals, all of whom paid dearly for their commitments. Volpin was one of them and Bogoraz another, as was Chalidze. Andrei Sakharov was still another (see figure 8.6). A brilliant physicist who became a member of the prestigious Soviet Academy of Sciences at the very young age of thirty-two, Sakharov had played a key role in the development of the Soviet Union's nuclear capabilities—the "father," as he was sometimes called in the West, of the hydrogen bomb. For fifteen years he labored at the secret Soviet nuclear facility. He had the highest security clearance and was rewarded with the privileges accorded the system's most loyal and deserving citizens: awards, medals, high salary, large and lovely apartment, limousine and driver.

Sakharov first ventured into opposition with a polite letter to Khrushchev and other Soviet leaders questioning the usefulness of an underground nuclear test. The health and environmental costs were too great, Sakharov wrote, and the test itself was unnecessary. His letter went unanswered, his objections were brushed aside. Sakharov kept at it as the Soviets carried out additional tests. Khrushchev, when he finally responded, did so in patronizing fashion: scientists should do their science; we will make policy.

Word of Sakharov's efforts circulated. For all the USSR's two hundred million people, its universities and academies and state and party agencies stocked full of people, the circle of the intelligentsia in Moscow and Leningrad was rather small. "Everyone knew everyone else," as the saying goes.

Like Albert Einstein and J. Robert Oppenheimer, Sakharov had helped create the weapons of ultimate human destruction and then recoiled from what he had done. In "Progress, Coexistence, and Intellectual Freedom," an article, virtually a manifesto, that appeared in 1968 and quickly gained renown within the USSR and abroad, Sakharov

FIGURE 8.6 Andrei Sakharov, 1970. Sakharov (1921–89) was a renowned Soviet physicist and the Soviet Union's most prominent human rights activist. For more than fifteen years he worked at a top-secret military research facility, where he became a major contributor to the design of the Soviet hydrogen bomb. Sakharov began his dissident activity with respectful letters to Soviet leader Nikita Khrushchev protesting continued underground nuclear tests. Sakharov became increasingly engaged in human rights activism. His writings provided acute analyses of the Soviet and world situation, and displayed a commitment to peace, democracy, environmental protection, and internationalism. He and his family suffered greatly from Soviet repression. Sakharov died soon after his release from internal exile in Gorky. (Archive of the Research Center for East European Studies at the University of Bremen.)

wrote: "The division of mankind threatens it with destruction. Civilization is imperiled by: a universal thermonuclear war, catastrophic hunger for most of mankind, stupefaction from the narcotic of 'mass culture,' and bureaucratized dogmatism."[88] Intellectual freedom—the ability to think, write, speak, and debate about the conditions facing all humanity, not just the inhabitants of the Soviet Union—provided the only road out of the existential crisis of humankind.

As a first step, the Soviet system had to be opened up, had to allow its citizens a clear-eyed view of the issues they faced; and from there, to consider, discuss, and debate the path forward. Freedom of thought requires the defense of all thinking and honest people.[89] The violation of intellectual freedom poses a threat to the "independence and worth of the human personality, a threat to the meaning of human life."[90]

A more powerful defense of the meaning of human rights would be hard to find.

In posing a direct challenge to Soviet reality, Sakharov moved beyond socialist legality to embrace the UDHR, which he cited.[91] In this sense, he was a pioneering advocate for the international as well as the Soviet human rights movement. He welcomed the involvement of various Western-based human rights organizations—notably, Amnesty International, whose Soviet affiliate was founded in 1973. At the same time, the support for Soviet dissidents gave Western human rights organizations a notable cause that enabled them to recruit many more members and donations. In fact, two campaigns in the late twentieth century largely created the international human rights movement: in support of Soviet dissidents and against South African apartheid.[92]

Sakharov was always an internationalist. He understood the connections between the Soviet human rights movement and the larger struggle for a peaceful, more humane world. His broad and powerful sense of the interconnectedness of human beings, no matter what their origins or skin color, his opposition to racism and nationalism, charted the path toward the future of human rights.[93] Sakharov wrote about developing countries, the plight of African-Americans, and environmental degradation. If not everything he wrote was exactly about human rights, his perspective most certainly involved recognition of the other, of our common humanity, the fundamental prerequisite for human rights.

"The basic aim of the state is the protection and safeguarding of the basic rights of its citizens. The defense of human rights is the loftiest of all aims," wrote Saharov,[94] directly challenging Soviet practice. He called for a reduction in the militarization of the economy and a loosening of the intense bureaucratism that prevailed in the Soviet Union.[95] Sakharov summed up his views: "My ideal is an open pluralistic society which safeguards fundamental civil and political rights, a society with a mixed economy which would permit scientifically regulated, balanced progress. . . . Such a society ought to come about as a result of the peaceful convergence of the socialist and capitalist systems . . . [which is] the main condition for saving the world from thermonuclear catastrophe."[96]

As a high-ranking, well-regarded Soviet citizen, Sakharov had appealed to the Soviet leadership, to no avail. Then he had joined a citizens' movement that he would never abandon, at great personal cost to him and his family. In 1980 the Soviet state exiled Sakharov to Gorky and forbade him from traveling in the Soviet Union, let alone outside its borders. Security personnel tracked his every movement. They raided his home and seized his manuscripts. The KGB set up jamming equipment so that Sakharov could not get radio reception. He could not even use the telephone. His maltreatment inspired a worldwide campaign that demanded his release. After nearly ten years, the new, reform-minded Soviet leader Mikhail Gorbachev granted Sakharov's release at the end of 1987, two years before his death.

Other activists suffered far worse: internment in prisons, labor camps, and psychiatric hospitals, in the latter case sometimes subject to forced medication.[97] Some died in captivity; others had their health permanently ruined. Under Brezhnev the repression was particularly severe and the regime broke up most human rights organizations. Still, activists, if only a tiny minority of the Soviet population, persisted and the human rights and dissident movement proliferated.

Like all movements, its expansion brought new problems. Some activists resisted what they saw as the excessive legalism of Volpin and Chalidze. Jealousies arose, especially when luminaries like Sakharov garnered a great deal of attention in the West, while others who suffered far worse were barely noticed. Ideological differences also emerged. Some dissidents like Roy Medvedev retained a fundamental loyalty to the idea of communism. By the 1980s, other dissidents were finding that position much harder to maintain.[98] Many of them had gone back to Lenin, as Medvedev advocated, read his works in depth—and came away profoundly disillusioned. Lenin, they discovered, was narrow-minded, severe, and dogmatic, and had willingly advocated the exercise of terror. The problems with Soviet communism could no longer be pinned solely on Stalin.

Moreover, the purged and repressed nationalities and ethnicities also became active. Crimean Tatars, Volga Germans, Chechen and Ingush, and many others still, in the 1960s and 1970s, languished in their places of deportation, far from their historic homelands. Not all of them were committed to a broad program of human rights; they wanted the right to return to their homelands or to emigrate. Jews were especially active, and could count on support in the West and in Israel.[99] Ultimately, the USSR allowed three hundred thousand to emigrate, though here too the Brezhnev regime became more repressive as the years went on, granting ever fewer exit visas and harassing family members left behind. An agreement with West Germany also provided for the emigration of a substantial number of ethnic Germans, many of whose ancestors had lived in Russia since the time of Catherine the Great.

Religious dissenters—evangelical Baptists, Seventh-Day Adventists, Pentecostals—faced similar dilemmas. Despite the tensions between a broad human rights movement and those focused on their own national, ethnic, or religious concerns, a rough working relationship developed among them. Sakharov, for one, whenever he spoke and wrote for reform in the Soviet Union, always pointed to injustices the Crimean Tatars had suffered.[100]

Conclusion

"The regime conquered the majority," wrote Valery Chalidze.[101] My great-aunt said much the same thing, if not so dramatically, when I met her in Moscow in 1978: most of our countrymen support Brezhnev, she said. Amid all the repressions and the terror, the Soviet system had accomplished the aspirations of many twentieth-century dictatorships: it had won the loyalty of a significant segment of the population. It did so by providing avenues of upward mobility for many common people and improving their living conditions, at least until the 1980s. Those nationalities not categorized as enemies continued to enjoy some cultural freedoms. And the USSR had fought off the massive Nazi invasion, a point of great pride for Soviet citizens, not one of whose families was left untouched by the atrocities and disasters the Third Reich wrought on Soviet soil.

The Soviet Union never ruled by terror alone. The loyalty of the general population went so far that many of them viewed human rights activists and dissidents as troublemakers, unpatriotic and perhaps in reality Western agents, the charge trumpeted endlessly by the Soviet media. Maybe they even deserved the prison sentences and exiles they suffered.

The small number of human rights activists who first emerged in the 1960s were, however, anything but disloyal Soviet citizens. They were firmly rooted in Soviet soil, knew its laws and constitutions better than anyone else, sometimes better than the prosecutors who hounded them. They demanded the fulfillment of the rights provisions that the Soviet state itself had pronounced.

In their origins, Soviet human rights were not an import from the liberal West. The socialist tradition provided their basis, and that included the large mix of political, social and economic, and national rights, a more robust understanding of rights than the strictly liberal conception that is concerned exclusively with political rights. Human rights have many diverse roots, and one of them is most certainly the socialist one that came to the fore, even if only in rhetorical form, in the Soviet state.

The rhetoric of human rights Soviet-style certainly won the Soviets support in the Global South. Together, the Soviet-bloc governments and the states of the Global South, many of them newly independent in the 1950s and 1960s, shaped in profound ways the postwar international human rights system, often to the chagrin of the United States, Great Britain, and other liberal states. Self-determination and social and economic rights are central aspects of human rights as we now know them because of the Soviet bloc–Global South alliance.

Chalidze, in the 1980s, had been living in exile in the United States for more than fifteen years. He observed from afar Mikhail Gorbachev's efforts to reform Soviet communism. Chalidze ranted against the insufficiencies of the system. He lambasted the shoddy construction of Soviet apartments, the many families crowded into small spaces, sometimes without even an indoor toilet, the interminable waiting lists for better apartments. New automobiles quickly fell to pieces. Soviet citizens spent endless hours searching for basic goods. The quality of services, including in such vital areas as healthcare, was absolutely dismal.[102]

What kind of social rights are these? Chalidze asked. What can they mean when the level of social life is so abysmally low? He went further. In international fora the USSR always touted its achievements in the social and economic arena. No one went hungry in the Soviet Union, its officials claimed. Everyone had an apartment and a job. Chalidze argued that the Soviet claim of the "primacy of social and economic rights" was an utter fallacy and deception, a way the Soviet Union and other dictatorial systems diverted attention from their consistent violation of civil and political rights.[103] When people suffer from lack of food and shelter, that is when they most need the freedom to speak out, Chalidze argued. They require political rights to enable them to publicize the conditions under which they live and to make claims on their government.[104]

Chalidze was right. As we saw in the case of North Korea, social and economic rights—to which we might add national rights—are meaningless without political rights. What the state gives, the state can also take away. Rights cannot simply be granted by the state. They have to mean an active citizenry that can protest, that can place demands on its government to ensure that it provides a reasonable condition of life for all its citizens and protects their rights. Yet the prevailing notion in the Soviet Union was not that rights inhere in persons simply by virtue of their being human, but that the socialist or communist state bestowed rights on deserving citizens.[105]

The USSR, like every other country discussed in this book, drew a boundary between those included and those excluded from rights-bearing citizenship, however constricted were those rights. Those on the wrong side of the line suffered terribly. Many died, either directly by execution or because of the dire conditions in exile and confinement. Lives were shattered across generations. Ultimately, the line could not hold and the system collapsed. However hounded and repressed were the dissidents and human rights campaigners, their efforts contributed to the demise of the Soviet Union. Whether what followed has met any of their dreams is another question.

We turn now to another way the founding of a nation-state resulted in human rights for one part of the population and the exclusion of another. In Palestine/Israel, Zionist Jews, Arabs, and the international community drew a nearly impermeable line between two communities.

Chapter 9

Palestine and Israel

TRAUMA AND TRIUMPH

❧

AFTER 380 pages and twenty-one chapters, the Palestine Royal Commission of His Majesty's Government came, in 1937, to its conclusion: "A Plan for Partition." Not only partition (see maps 9.1, 9.2, 9.3, and 9.4). Ten pages later, with nary a hint of self-doubt nor any indication that the consequences could be life-wrenching, especially for Arabs, it drew the corollary conclusion: population exchange. Its historical reference point was the Lausanne Treaty of 1923, an "instructive precedent," the Royal Commission (commonly known as the Peel Commission after its chairman, William Robert Peel, 1st Earl Peel) stated. It noted the high numbers involved, some 1,300,000 Greeks and 400,000 Turks. "But so vigorously and effectively was the task accomplished that within about eighteen months . . . the whole exchange was completed." Although Fridtjof Nansen (the League of Nations high commissioner for refugees, whom we met briefly in chapter 5) had been subject to great criticism because of the supposed inhumanity of the program, "the courage of the Greek and Turkish statesmen . . . has been justified by the result. Before the operation the Greek and Turkish minorities had been a constant irritant. Now the ulcer has been clean cut out, and Greco-Turkish relations . . . are friendlier than they have ever been before."[1] A clearer statement in support of homogeneous populations under the state would be hard to find.

The Peel Commission report was extraordinary. For the very first time, partition and ethnic cleansing came into the public domain as a solution to the ever-burgeoning Arab-Jewish conflict in Palestine. The report offered public recognition of the failure of the British Mandate for Palestine, granted to Great Britain in 1922 by the League of Nations. Under its terms, Britain was supposed to guide Palestine toward

MAP 9.1 Peel Commission partition plan, 1937.

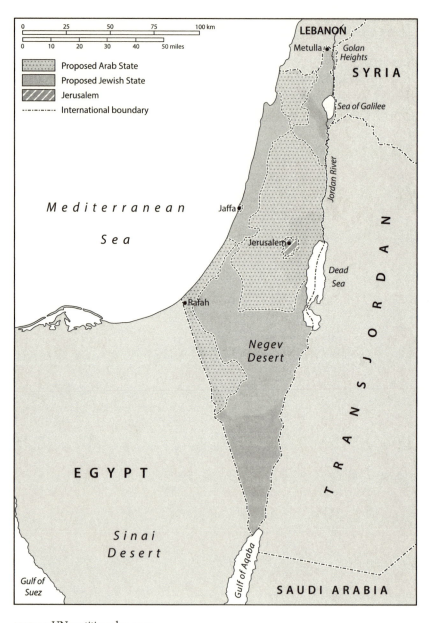

MAP 9.2 UN partition plan, 1947.

MAP 9.3 Partition borders after the First Arab-Israeli War, 1948.

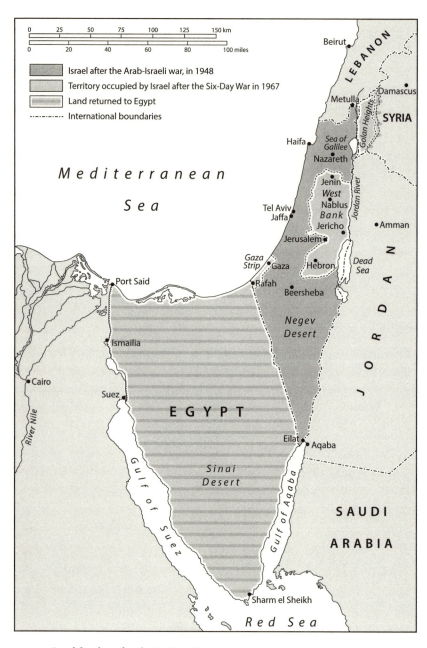

MAP 9.4 Israeli borders after the Six-Day War, 1967.

independence. The mandate agreement incorporated the Balfour Declaration of 1917, in which Great Britain had declared its support for the establishment of a Jewish homeland in Palestine, so long as the rights of other groups—they were not specified by name—were not violated.

The Peel Commission report not only reaffirmed the Balfour Declaration, it also recognized the success of the Zionist movement in establishing the economic, social, and cultural bases for a nation-state. Jews had reclaimed lands, developed schools, founded a university, and formed political organizations that could be turned into representative bodies—all the elements of a modern society. But the hostility between the two communities, Arabs and Jews, the report claimed, citing reams of historical and political evidence, could not be bridged. Hence, the only solution was partition and population exchange.

Like Greeks and Koreans and many others discussed in the preceding chapters, Jews and Arabs could not make their history on their own. Sometimes reluctantly, more often enthusiastically, the Great Powers rushed into Palestine and Israel. Too much was at stake. Strategic, economic, political, and, not least, religious interests all came into play, only intensifying the heat of the Middle Eastern cauldron.

Perhaps more powerfully than any other case discussed in this book, the history of Palestine/Israel demonstrates the tight intertwining of nation-states and human rights. By the time of the Peel Commission report, both Jews and Arabs had developed national movements. The wrenching reality of the Nazi annihilation of six million European Jews made the foundation of a Jewish state an urgent matter. Only in a state established, run, and dominated by Jews, it seemed, could Jews from around the world be certain of that most basic right, the security of life. Upon that basis, Israel would be created as a democratic socialist state in which Jewish citizens would exercise the full panoply of political and social rights.

And what about Arabs? Zionist leaders made clear that the Jewish state could only flourish with, at most, a small Arab minority. Everything in Jewish history, and especially the Holocaust, made the prospect of a multinational state or Jews as a minority in the land they claimed as their own anathema to Zionist leaders. The consequence was the Nakba, the Palestinian catastrophe, the forced removal of around seven hundred thousand Arabs concomitant with the founding of Israel. In a world in which the nation-state seemed to be the only viable political model, human rights for one group meant the exclusion of others from rights-bearing citizenship. Two tragedies, the Holocaust and the Nakba, were intertwined and have shaped the history of the Middle East and international politics down to the present day.[2]

☙

Zionism had been founded as a political movement by Theodor Herzl in 1897. It was a latecomer to the ranks of European nationalist movements, reflective of the dispersal of Jews—the diasporic community par excellence—throughout Europe. Zionism had to contend and compete with a wide variety of political and religious movements among Jews, including liberalism, socialism, communism, Hasidism, and other religious orthodoxies.

Zionists engaged in quiet diplomacy and active publicity—writing, speaking, rallying for the cause of a Jewish state. They built on Jewish efforts at the Berlin Congress in 1878 and the Paris Peace Conference in 1919 (as we saw in chapter 5). The defeat of Germany and the Ottoman Empire in World War I intensified the westward shift of Zionists, who moved their search for a great-power protector to Britain and the United States. Major Jewish organizations, however, had decidedly mixed views regarding the idea of a Jewish state. They worried that their ongoing efforts to improve the lot of Jews within their own liberal countries, in France, Britain, and the United States, would be undermined by the Zionist drive. They feared accusations of dual loyalties. Only as a consequence of the Holocaust did Zionists win majority support of European and North American Jews.

In 1916 and 1917, Britain engaged in secret diplomacy with Arab representatives and its own allies to decide the fate of the Middle East after the expected defeat of the Ottoman Empire. The Ottomans still reigned over vast territories. In the correspondence between Hussein bin Ali, sharif of Mecca, and Lieutenant Colonel Sir Henry McMahon, the British high commissioner in Egypt, Britain promised independence to the Arabs in exchange for an Arab uprising against the Ottomans. The British, in desperate military straits in 1916, hoped to win at least one victory, even if it were a sideshow to the trench warfare on the Western front. At roughly the same time, the Sykes-Picot Agreement between France and Britain divided up the Middle East between the two imperial powers. Meanwhile, British statesmen also believed that worldwide Jewish support would add a decisive morale boost to the population at home and soldiers in the field, and keep major loans and war matériel flowing to Britain from the United States. Those interests led to the Balfour Declaration in 1917, the British promise to support a Jewish homeland in the Middle East.[3]

All three documents and agreements—Balfour, Hussein-McMahon, Sykes-Picot—have stamped the history of the Middle East down to the present day. The British made contradictory promises, one to Jews, one to Arabs, and yet another to their French ally. They applied the nation-state orientation, the political model that had achieved primacy in Europe, to the heartland of the Middle East. Britons, as well as Jews and Arabs, promised, in their varying endeavors, that whatever happened, the rights of minorities would be respected. But who, really, would have the right to have rights if sovereign nation-states were founded in the Middle East?

British forces conquered Jerusalem in 1917, sealing British domination over large swaths of the Middle East. In 1922, the League of Nations granted Britain the mandate over Palestine. Under its terms, Britain was expected to guide the region toward self-rule and ultimate independence, but it could never act alone. The League's Permanent Mandates Commission (PMC) exercised a supervisory role. The League of Nations in essence internationalized the Palestinian issue at the same time that Britain became the target of competing Arab and Jewish claims. In the modern world of nation-states and human rights, those claims only had resonance when Arabs and Jews asserted their status as *nations*. Each proclaimed its millennia-long history as a nation and derided the other as a mere assemblage of individuals with no legitimate right to a nation-state. Great-power statesmen, steeped in the Hebrew Bible, had no trouble recognizing Jews as a nation. About Arabs they were always uncertain.

The Peel Commission report, for one prominent example, contained an extraordinarily thorough historical exposition that defined Jews for millennia as a nation. The report went back to the Bible and the story of Abraham's migration from Ur to Palestine, the formation of the Jewish people, and on through Christianity and the emergence of Islam. With their profound sense of history, British policy makers believed that they were righting a great historical injustice, as Foreign Secretary Arthur Balfour himself had written in 1917: "The destruction of Judea that occurred nineteen centuries ago was one of the great wrongs which the Allied Powers were trying to redress. This destruction was a national tragedy."[4] Lord Peel, in the parliamentary debates on the commission report, remarked how easy it was for the English to understand the "Jewish passion for a return to Zion." Invoking the span of History, he noted: "After all, we have all been brought up on the Bible; the judges and the Prophets and the Kings are as familiar to us as Richard Coeur de Lion and Queen Elizabeth. We know as well as the Jews about the history of the Temple, its building and its rebuilding and its destruction."[5]

This panoramic sense of history, going back to the ancient world and the Israel of Saul and David, united present and past to make the ultimate, modern point: to each people its state. The Peel Commission also depicted Jews as a modern, enterprising, accomplished "race," who were also able to command resources from the international Jewish community. Jews had developed the land in productive and significant ways, another characteristic that made them worthy of the moniker "nation" in a world increasingly comprised of nation-states.

Zionists, of course, fully agreed. The Zionist Organization proudly declared that the Balfour Declaration was not a promise to individual Jews, but to the "Jewish people as a whole." Jews were not "alien" to Palestine, but a "people returning to the soil from which it sprang, there to rebuild the fabric of its national life." This was a homecoming, not a colonization.[6] Indeed, the condition of non-nationality was "abnormal," a "maladjustment in the world."[7] In that way, Zionists completely entwined the Jewish cause with the world of nation-states.

But what about Arabs? Did they constitute a nation also worthy of a state? The British, and the Americans after World War II, could never quite decide. The Peel Commission report referred to the glories of medieval Arab civilization and Islam as one of the three great monotheistic religions. The Arabs view Palestine "as part of a new renascent Arab world," long dominated by the Turks but "now a young nation . . . with one object in view: to revive once again the glories of Arab medieval civilization," as Colonial Secretary William Ormsby-Gore stated.[8] The Peel Commission expressed concern for Arabs who saw themselves crowded out by a more modern, more enterprising population that had seemingly appeared out of nowhere.

Yet the British (and later the Americans) were not quite sure that the Arabs constituted "a nation" with all that implies in the modern world—a people in a delimited territory that forms a sovereign and independent country with a rights-bearing citizenry. Although the heirs to a great civilization, they were living in past time, with retrograde land tenure that made it difficult for the British to enter their worldview.[9] They possessed a glorious past that extended over a large and amorphous territory, but that was not quite the same thing as a nation and certainly not a nation-state. Arabs, the report argued, were, with some few exceptions, backward economically and culturally. The implication was clearly that they were not, or at least not yet, worthy of a nation-state.

Zionist leaders made the point even more sharply. "There is no such thing as Palestinians. They did not exist."[10] So spoke Golda Meir years later. Meir, longtime Zionist leader and prime minister of Israel from 1969 to 1974, expressed pointedly what most Zionists had articulated since around 1900. In its long memorandum to the Peel Commission in 1937, for example, the Jewish Agency, the formal representative body of Jews in Palestine, argued that Arabs constituted an amorphous collection of individuals; hence, they had no claims on statehood, no possibility of being rights-bearing citizens. David Ben-Gurion, who became the leader of the *yishuv* (the Jewish community in Palestine) in the 1930s and later Israel's first prime minister, claimed that Arabs would have equal rights in a Jewish Palestine. Jews would civilize Arabs, offer them economic and cultural advances. But never would Palestinians rise so high that they would be worthy of being rights-bearing citizens in their own or in a binational state.[11]

Arab leaders, in contrast, defined Arabs as a people worthy of a nation-state. They drew, of course, on Islamic traditions, Muhammad's delivery of god's message in Arabic to the Arab people. But Islam was only one part of the ideological assemblage that constituted a specifically Palestinian-Arab identity.[12] Already by the turn into the twentieth century, a Palestinian national consciousness had begun to emerge. It overlapped with pan-Arab, religious, local, and Ottoman identities—but that only made it typical, hardly unique, in the annals of nationalism. Virtually all nationalist movements drew on local and religious identities. Jerusalem, the third holy city in Islam, the site of Muhammad's ascension to heaven, constituted another piece in the assemblage. Palestinians looked on Jerusalem with pride and concern; it was important for all Muslims, but perhaps especially for those who lived in its environs. Palestinian nationalism, also like others throughout the nineteenth and twentieth centuries, developed in concordance with the modern public sphere. Nationalist ideas spread through newspapers, libraries, reading clubs, and coffee houses, and by steamship and railroad. A series of congresses between 1918 and 1923, organized by notables, affirmed Palestine as a distinct political entity, Arab in character.

The conflict between two national claims, Jewish and Arab, came to a head in 1936. Jewish life in Europe had become desperate. The Nazi regime was the worst, of course, but in the 1930s Jews also faced increasing hostility and discrimination in Poland, Hungary, and Romania.[13] Palestine became one destination for Jews thrown to the winds by European antisemitism.

Jewish land purchases and Jewish immigration constituted the central features of the Zionist program. The land had mystical connotations for Jews. Their possession of it would erase two millennia of dispersion from the place that god had promised to Abraham. But Zionism was a modern nationalist movement largely secular in orientation. Ownership of the land would also erase the deformities of Jewish life in Europe, defined by ghettos, money lending, petty trading, and poverty. A new economy of productive Jews, working the soil, would flourish, providing the basis for a Jewish revival that would extend to all spheres of life. The new Jewish man and woman would be the result. The socialist influence is manifest: labor, production, and "newness" all wrapped together. The Soviets could not have expressed it any better.

Jewish land purchases and immigration inspired great unease among Arabs. By the 1930s, their fears of displacement had reached crisis levels. Arabs resisted and, in the process, deepened the national movement. Peasants occupied land to resist Zionist encroachments; notables wrote articles in newspapers and gave speeches. A mélange of political ideas came to the fore. Some activists called for an independent Palestine, others for Palestine as part of a greater Syria or a larger, pan-Arab federation. All of them decisively rejected Jewish settlement and any hints of a Jewish state, and called for recognition of Arabs' or Palestinians' "national rights."[14]

The British tried to work through local notables, as they had elsewhere in their empire. In 1921, Herbert Samuel, the first British high commissioner for Palestine, promoted the establishment of the Supreme Muslim Council. It would contribute to the development of self-rule for Palestinians—as the strictures of the mandate demanded—and serve as a consultative body to the British authorities. Its president, Hajj Muhammad Amin al-Husaini, who later became infamous for his pro-Nazi stance, was a keen politician as well as a religious leader. The British also appointed him mufti, the leader of the Muslim religious community. From these two positions, Hajj al-Husaini built a powerful patronage network and also brought together leading Muslim figures from the Middle East and South Asia to consider the problem of Palestine.[15] He moved Palestinian politics far beyond the narrow course that the British intended.

Younger Palestinians, meanwhile, chafed not only under British rule and Zionist advances. They were impatient with the diplomatic niceties that typified the politics of Palestine's elite families, even though many of them were the sons of those same families. They criticized their elders for being too close to the British and began to forge a more active, popular politics against both the British and the Zionists.[16] The League of Nations PMC provided another venue for political mobilizations.

Individuals and groups could petition their grievances to the PMC in Geneva; sometimes, as during the Peel Commission hearings, the PMC actively solicited petitions.[17] In 1929, a few young men organized the Istiqlal (Independence) party. As a formal organization, the Independence Party did not last long, but its legacy ran deep. Many of its leading figures would find other venues for their Palestine-oriented politics.

Fearful of the ever-growing Jewish presence and, to their eyes, Britain's Zionist sympathies, Palestinian Arabs in 1936 went on strike, then boycotted Jewish businesses. The Arab Revolt, as it came to be called, involved the entire palette of popular politics, including demonstrations, riots, and armed attacks on Jews.[18] The British repressed the revolt with the virulence that they used throughout their empire, leaving over one thousand people dead and hundreds locked up or imprisoned abroad. The British permitted arms to flow to Jewish self-defense units, some of which also engaged in violent actions against Palestinians.

The British government empaneled the Peel Commission midway through the Arab Revolt, when it thought it had calmed the situation. British policy had zigzagged, leaving everyone, including the British, confused about the country's intentions. The Peel Commission report, issued after countless other investigations and studies, was supposed to resolve the situation in Palestine once and for all. Instead, both Jews and Arabs turned their anger on Britain, each one charging it with favoring the other.

The Peel Commission proposed, in effect, a three-way partition of Palestine, since Britain would retain oversight of the holy cities of Jerusalem, Bethlehem, and Nazareth, as well as corridors linking the sacred sites with the coastal cities of Tel Aviv and Haifa (see map 9.1). The British government quickly accepted the findings of the Peel Commission report, but it faced a storm of opposition in parliament and in the country at large. As the mandatory, not the colonial, power, Britain could not decide the issue on its own. The government needed cover for its radical plan to partition Palestine. It tossed the entire issue to the League of Nations, as it would later do to the UN. Both the British parliament and the League of Nations became the sites of vociferous debate, exposing all the issues, all the problems, of nation-state formation and human rights in a conflicted Middle East.

During the parliamentary debates, Colonial Secretary Ormsby-Gore remarked: "In that little country [Palestine], there is a keen, vivid Jewish nationalism and a keen, vivid Arab nationalism, both of which have rights and are in acute controversy." The only way to resolve the conflict in the mandate, Ormsby-Gore contended, was to give "Jews and Arabs sovereign independence and self-government . . . each over a part of it [Palestine]. . . . Only by partition can the ideals of both be realised, only by partition can peace be restored to these two nationalities, so that they will be able in the future one to help the other without fear of domination by either."[19]

Ormsby-Gore went on to note that partition might have to be compulsory, and that minorities would exist in both states. Jews and Arabs would need two things to reassure them: the "presence of a neutral and friendly Power, friendly to them both," meaning Britain, of course, and "specific guarantees" in line with the League of Nations minority treaties.[20] He made another point: inquiries were required to discover how many Arabs from Palestine could be settled in Transjordan and in the Arab part of the partition, and Jews resettled in the Jewish section. "A scheme of transfer is most desirable," he responded to questioning from Lloyd George.[21]

Ormsby-Gore seemed oblivious to just how ominous was his comment. The British diplomat, with his tidy remarks and neat policy statements, soared unconcerned over the devastating effects on the ground—on real people and their lives and families and communities— that population transfers always entail. That was the history of expulsions and exchanges since the 1860s and with the 1923 Lausanne Treaty (as we saw in chapter 5).[22] The uprooting of hundreds of thousands of people had become normal, one item in the palette of policies that statesmen and nationalist movements deployed in the era of nation-states and human rights. The bland terminology—"transfer" or "exchange"—covered up the human devastations and tragedies that such policies always bring, just like Lord Curzon's coinage of "population unmixing" at Lausanne.

Ormsby-Gore made still another point, one critical to British statesmen as they peered around the globe at their far-flung empire. Arabs were watching the advance of independent nations in the Middle East.

Britain had relinquished its Iraq mandate in 1932; the French were planning to do the same in Syria (and retain essential powers, as Britain had done in Iraq). Egypt, too, had become more self-governing.[23] And in India—always the place of Britain's greatest concern and commitment—Muslims were watching how events transpired in Palestine, deeply worried about the future of their religious brethren. In these circumstances, asked Ormsby-Gore rhetorically, how long could Britain go on as the supreme power in Palestine?[24]

The opposition to the report, in parliament, among the British public, and at the League of Nations, was fierce.[25] The League's PMC met for nearly three weeks in August 1937 to consider the Palestinian issue. It heard testimony from Ormsby-Gore and scores of others. It took Britain to task for its inconsistent policy in Palestine, which had only worsened the situation. Rather lamely, it advocated yet another compromise: the continued development of separate self-governing institutions of Arabs and of Jews, with a common central council, presided over by Britain, for foreign and defense matters. Like a father chiding his errant children, it decried the impatience of both Arabs and Jews and said they should be thankful to a magnanimous Great Britain, which had fostered the national emancipation of both groups.[26] Most importantly, the PMC declared itself open to the idea of partition.

Arabs completely rejected the Peel Commission report. Partition signified recognition of a Jewish right to a state, something that no Arab leader could countenance. They wrote reports, sent letters and telegrams and petitions to the PMC and to the British government.[27] Always they asserted that Arabs, too, were a grand historical people who deserved a state; always they denied Jewish claims to a state.

On one issue, the Peel Commission was correct: Jews were more resourceful. They had behind them a seventy-five-year history of political mobilization. Despite the state interests of Britain and the United States that sometimes aligned them with the Arab cause, despite the genteel (and sometimes not so genteel) antisemitism that often ruled the Foreign Office and the State Department, Jewish representatives had more experience moving in the halls of Western power than did their Arab counterparts.

Among Jews, the Peel Commission report inspired dismay and apprehension. Only a calculation of political realities led the majority of the Zionist representatives to accept the notion of partition, though with many qualifications. If Jews were to reap only a portion of the land of Palestine, they argued, then there had to be population transfers. Partition and deportations, whether forced or voluntary, went hand in hand.[28]

The ever-circumspect Chaim Weizmann, the president of the Zionist Organization and future first president of Israel, an anglophile to his very bones, responded with white-hot anger to the Peel Commission report. Publicly, in a speech to the Zionist Congress, Weizmann gave full vent to his fury—so much so that he had to sit down and take a break midway into his remarks. The attempt to limit immigration in conjunction with the partition plan

> spell[s] the destruction of the National Home. We shall resist these proposals . . . with every means at our disposal. . . . This is breach of the promise made to us in a solemn hour, at an hour of crisis for the British Empire. . . .
>
> I say to the Mandatory Power: You shall not outrage the Jewish nation. You shall not play fast and loose with the Jewish people. Say to us frankly that the National Home is closed, and we shall know where we stand. But this trifling with a nation bleeding from a thousand wounds must not be done by the British whose Empire is built on moral principles—that mighty Empire must not commit this sin against the People of the Book.[29]

History, religion, nation—it was all there in Weizmann's speech. At the same time, he hinted that partition was not out of the question, so long as such a plan enabled Jewish life to flourish and contributed to the "solution of the Jewish problem" worldwide.[30] The possibility of some kind of Jewish state was simply too enticing for moderates like Weizmann, and also for Ben-Gurion.[31] The prospects of a smaller Jewish state made the demographic issue even more critical, as the Peel Commission implicitly realized. Hence, Weizmann wrote to the South African leader Jan Smuts, the "gradual transfer of its Arab population [was] absolutely essential." This would be a "difficult and delicate process." It would have to be conducted in association with Great Britain and the future Arab state.[32] But transfer there would be.

Zionist leaders were fearful of discussing population transfers openly, not least because such a stance placed them uncomfortably close to Nazi policies in the 1930s, which had resulted in refugee flows of thousands upon thousands of Jews. Yet even before the Peel Commission presented its partition proposal, Ben-Gurion had suggested it to the Mapai (Labor) party's central committee. After the report was released, he extolled the transfer plan, which went even further than he had earlier imagined because it would remove Arabs from the Jezreel Valley, the Western Jordan Valley, and the coastal plain. He wrote to his son Amos:

> This would mean that the Jews would receive these valleys completely empty of Arab villages, and could settle more Jews there. This proposal has a tremendous advantage. . . .
>
> We cannot and are not entitled to propose [transfer], because we have never wanted to dislodge the Arabs. But as Britain is giving part of the country which was promised to us to the Arabs for their state, it is only right that the Arabs in our state should be transferred to the Arab part.[33]

To the Jewish Agency Executive Ben-Gurion spoke even more bluntly: "I am for compulsory transfer; I do not see anything immoral in it."[34] His views were echoed by many others, notably Yosef Weitz, the head of the Land Department of the Jewish National Fund. Weitz wrote in his diary in 1940: "It must be clear that there is no room in the country for both peoples. . . . The only solution is a Land of Israel . . . without Arabs. . . . Not one village must be left. . . . And only after this transfer will the country be able to absorb millions of our brothers and the Jewish problem will cease to exist. There is no other solution."[35]

The Arab Revolt and the Peel Commission report were watershed moments for all concerned. For the British, it showed the limits of their effort to govern Palestine peacefully. It was in this context that the government empaneled the Peel Commission and proposed partition. For Zionists, the uprising indicated the depth of Arab antagonism, and dispelled many illusions that Jewish immigration and land purchases could proceed peacefully without any impact on Arab society—precisely at the moment when so many Jewish immigrants to Palestine were fleeing violence directed at them in Europe. Arabs realized that both local and international forces were arrayed against them. Only hard political struggle, if necessary with arms, would give them a chance to flourish in their homeland.

Britain, in the Commission's view, was the great innocent, the noble, impartial peacemaker that played no role (it claimed) in exacerbating the conflict. In reality, the British managed to antagonize both Arabs and Jews. The British decided to appease Arab concerns by issuing, in 1939, a White Paper that severely restricted Jewish immigration and land purchases in Palestine. It could not have come at a worse time. Jews had already endured the severe discriminatory practices of the Third Reich; soon they would face extermination. Never again would Zionists put their full faith in the British government.

క్రు

The removal of Arabs from the prospective Jewish homeland was, then, an idea broadly discussed and widely accepted in the Zionist movement even before the White Paper and the onset of World War II and the Holocaust.[36] Such views were soft-pedaled in public.[37] In 1942, Ben-Gurion gathered six hundred leading Zionists at the Biltmore Hotel in New York City. By this point, he was the acknowledged leader of the Zionists in Palestine, a stature affirmed by the many formal positions he held: three chairmanships, including the Jewish Agency Executive, the Zionist Organization Executive, and Histadrut, as well as the leadership of the Mapai party. The Jewish Agency had been founded in 1929 as more or less the governing body of the Jewish community in Palestine and was recognized as such by Great Britain and the League of Nations. Histadrut was officially the Jewish labor union in Palestine, but its writ went far beyond the formal representation of workers. Along with the Jewish National Fund, Histadrut essentially organized and administered the Jewish economy of Palestine. For Ben-Gurion and other Eastern European immigrants, Histadrut served as the nascent socialist economy of a socialist Jewish state. The Mapai party that Ben-Gurion led dominated all these organizations, though not without intense political struggle within the Zionist movement. It would go on to dominate Israeli politics until the 1977 electoral victory of Menachem Begin and the Likud party.

When Zionists met in New York in 1942, they had already heard first reports of the Nazi annihilation of Jews. A great pall hung over the proceedings, and it inspired a radical leap forward. In the program that emerged from the conference, Zionists called for the establishment of a Jewish "commonwealth" in Palestine, escalating their demands beyond the "homeland" idea to an explicit state. They also called for unrestricted Jewish immigration to Palestine. They made no mention of the removal of Arabs, but the idea had become prevalent and perhaps predominant among Zionists by the late 1930s and 1940s. After all, as both Ben-Gurion and the Peel Commission stated, the Lausanne Treaty that formalized the so-called population exchange of Greeks and Turks had been a great success. Why not reproduce it in Palestine?

Was there ever an alternative to a state that governed exclusively in the name of one people, Jews or Arabs, with only one or the other worthy of human rights? A plenitude of political plans and dreams existed on the margins, but they lacked sufficient power to weaken and displace the furious force of nationalism. In the 1920s and 1930s, a small group of intellectuals organized Brit Shalom, which advocated Arab-Jewish cooperation. Its successor, the Ihud (Unity) party, actively promoted a binational state and opposed partition and the establishment of the Jewish state. Even in the wake of the terrible events of the World War II era, Ihud challenged the recourse to arms by Jews and the fight for a separate Jewish state. Its members feared that the great moral purpose of Zionism would be sapped by Jews who shot British soldiers and terrorized Arabs. The day Jews defeat Arabs in battle, Judah Magnes, the founding president of the Hebrew University, wrote, is the day "when we shall be sowing the seed of an eternal hatred of such dimensions that Jews will not be able to live in that part of the world for centuries to come."[38] Magnes and his colleagues felt Jewish youth slipping away from them. They drew sustenance from any slight shard of comity they could find, such as Arab and Jewish citrus growers or municipal laborers working in common.[39]

FIGURE 9.1 Chaim Weizmann and Emir Faisal, 1919. Weizmann (1874–1952) and Faisal I bin Hussein bin Ali al-Hashemi (1885–1933) signed an agreement in Paris in which they called for peace, recognition of the Balfour Declaration, support for Jewish immigration to Palestine, and defense of the rights of Arabs. Faisal cited the close historical relations of Jews and Arabs and expressed support for Zionism. Weizmann was a renowned chemist and the leader of the Zionist Organization. Faisal, the third son of Hussein bin Ali, the grand sharif of Mecca, played a leading role in the Arab Revolt against the Ottoman Empire in World War I. Little would come of their 1919 agreement. Faisal went on to become the British-installed ruler of Iraq; Weizmann would become Israel's first president. (Universal History Archive/UIG via Getty Images.)

The organ of those advocating a binational solution, *Ba'ayoth*, wrote that "the Zionist movement has again and again declared . . . that its goal can be fully achieved without a single Arab being ousted from his lands."[40] Magnes and the philosopher Martin Buber had founded Ihud; its motto, "Neither a Jewish nor an Arab State," was unlikely to find much support from either side—certainly not in the wake of the Holocaust, nor amid Arab fears of displacement.[41]

A few voices of reconciliation sounded on the Arab side. In 1919 at Paris, Emir Faisal had met with Chaim Weizmann (see figure 9.1). Together they issued an appeal for peace, recognition of the Balfour Declaration, support for Jewish immigration, and defense of the rights of Arabs. They asserted, in essence, that room enough existed in Palestine for Arabs and Jews. On numerous occasions, Faisal cited the close relations of Jews and Arabs and support for Zionism. "We are demanding Arab freedom, and we should show ourselves unworthy of it if we did not now say to the Jews: welcome back home. Dr. Weizmann's ideals are ours."[42] To Felix Frankfurter, a leading member of the American Zionist delegation to the Paris Peace Conference, Faisal wrote:

> We feel that the Arabs and Jews are cousins in race, have suffered similar oppressions at the hands of Powers stronger than themselves, and by a happy coincidence have been able to take the first steps toward the attainment of their national ideals together.
>
> The Arabs, especially the educated among us, look with the deepest sympathy on the Zionist Movement. . . . [Jews and Arabs] are working together for a reformed and revived Near East, and our two Movements complete one another. The Jewish Movement is national and not imperialist. Our Movement is national and not imperialist, and there is room in Syria [meaning Greater Syria, including Palestine] for us both.[43]

Such sentiments did not long prevail, battered as they were by existential fears on both sides. Faisal, like Little Crow, like Samuel Maharero, had to contend with younger, more radical family members and followers, who would come to rule the day—not necessarily to their own ultimate advantage.

On the ground in Palestine, a few Arabs and Jews also sought reconciliation. In the winter of 1947–48, after the UN had approved the partition plan (as we shall shortly see), as both sides prepared for war, activists from both sides pursued various local peace initiatives.[44] These, too, could not prevail. Already in the 1930s, those Arabs who countenanced cooperation with Zionists lived under severe political pressure, including the threat of violence, from the major Arab political forces.

On the diplomatic front, in the run-up to the partition resolution and the foundation of Israel, various proposals were floated. All of them entailed some kind of federal solution or a bicultural state and society—a Switzerland or a Belgium relocated to the Middle East. These proposals ran against the entire thrust of international politics in the 1930s and 1940s. The minority treaties were already seen as grand failures given the persecution of the Jews in Germany and elsewhere in Europe, Belgium and Switzerland quaint relics of earlier political solutions. The national or racial state prevailed as the dominant political model.

ᐧᑫᐧ

"We hate them and they hate us," said Ben-Gurion in May 1947.[45] He was referring not to Arabs, but to the British (or English, as he said). His eyes were fixed on the lodestar of a Jewish state, and that meant that the British had to be expunged from Palestine and the Arabs reduced to a manageable minority. "We cannot afford to live under a foreign government any more," he said to a meeting of Zionists in New York. "We can't. . . . To live under a goyish [non-Jewish] state now is absolutely impossible."[46]

The "now" meant, of course, in the wake of the Nazi annihilation of the Jews. It also meant in the wake of the highly restrictive British immigration policies that were still largely in effect in 1947. Ben-Gurion's frustration with the British was palpable. But he had no trust in the Arabs either. "The only thing which I want as a Zionist is to get rid of the British. . . . Simply they should leave. . . . Either we will sit down with the Arabs and come to an agreement or we will fight it out."[47] Ben-Gurion also made clear the sequencing that he had in mind: first a Jewish majority, then a democracy.[48] Jews could not live under a "goyish state," nor could they live as a minority in their own country. Four days before the UN partition resolution on 29 November 1947, Ben-Gurion spoke to his Mapai party supporters and reiterated his earlier views. "There can be no stable and strong Jewish state so long as it has a Jewish majority of only 60%." Ominously, he continued, "we must think like a state."[49] Earlier, he had said "What was done in Greece"—meaning the Lausanne Treaty and citing a slew of other examples—"can certainly be done in a Jewish State."[50]

Quite quickly after the end of the war, Great Britain and the United States came under great political pressure over the Palestine issue. The realization that the Nazis had gone a long way toward exterminating Jews in total, coupled with the searing images of concentration camp survivors in Buchenwald and Dachau, led to a wave of sympathy around the world for Jews. In Europe, Jewish survivors languished in displaced persons camps that, on the surface, seemed little different from the Nazi concentration camps they had just managed to survive. In the summer of 1945, US president Harry S. Truman sent the former commissioner of immigration and naturalization services, Earl G. Harrison, to Europe to investigate the conditions. Harrison issued a scathing report, which quickly acquired renown. Its oft-quoted paragraph: "As matters now stand, we appear to be treating the Jews as the Nazis treated them except that we do not exterminate them. They are in concentration camps in large number under our military guard instead of S.S. troops. One is led to wonder whether the German people . . . are not supposing that we are following or at least condoning Nazi policy."[51] How was it possible, months after the defeat of Nazi Germany, that Europe's Jews lived in such miserable conditions, impoverished and stateless, while under the protection of the liberator countries? Harrison proposed the immediate immigration of one hundred thousand Jews to Palestine, a figure that had already been broached by the Jewish Agency. President Truman supported the proposal. Jewish organizations in Britain and the United States kept up the drumbeat of pressure in support of very substantial Jewish immigration, leading to the establishment of the Jewish state.

The US State Department and the British Foreign Office, however, recoiled from any measures that would antagonize Arabs. A floodtide of diplomatic communiqués flowed into the State Department, the White House, and Whitehall. Strategic and economic interests came to the fore, laced with not-so-subtle antisemitic comments from British and American officials, all part of a backlash against intense Jewish lobbying. Even Truman grew impatient with the pressure from Jews. Oil and military power ruled the day. All the communiqués decried the damage to American interests caused by Truman's support for Jewish immigration.[52]

The British watched the American back-and-forth on these matters with the gravest concern. They referred continually, uncharitably, and with great exaggeration to the strength of Jewish influence in America, and were particularly piqued that the United States offered all sorts of proposals while taking no responsibility for developments in the Middle East.[53]

The British had other concerns as well—India, to name the gravest of them all (as Ormsby-Gore had stated earlier). The Labor Party had come to power in 1945 in the first postwar election. The Labor prime minister, Clement Attlee, responded with chagrin to the Harrison report. He wrote to Truman with the genteel antisemitism typical of many British statesmen. Not only Jews, he argued, had suffered in the war and afterward. Europe was awash with the uprooted. No one should be treated "on a racial basis. . . . If our officers had placed the Jews in a special racial category at the head of the queue, my strong view is that the effect of this would have been disastrous for the Jews and therefore their attempt to treat them alike was a right one." Attlee pleaded for time and rejected outright Harrison's recommendation that the British allow one hundred thousand Jews to enter Palestine. "We have the Arabs to consider as well," he reminded Truman. Attlee lectured Truman that India was home to "ninety million Moslems, who are easily inflamed." And inflamed they would be, he claimed, by major Jewish immigration to Palestine.[54]

Thus ensued a series of commissions of inquiry, visits to the troubled land of Palestine, and reports. To read the first of these, the Anglo-American Enquiry report of 1946, is to enter a world of different possibilities. It is, to be sure, a world that never came to be in the Middle East, one of many discarded visions on the road to the Jewish state and the Palestinian disaster. The report asserted forcefully Christian interests in Palestine, reminding all concerned that all three monotheistic faiths revered the Holy Land. The Anglo-American Enquiry rejected the idea of separate Jewish and Arab states. It called for the conversion of the mandate into a UN trusteeship, presumably for a long transition during which the seeds of a state of Palestine, home to Jews and Arabs as well as many others, would flower, where each religious community could freely practice its beliefs and its holy sites would be protected, and all would live in harmony.[55]

Zionists and Arabs quickly disparaged the report; observers since 1946 have dismissed it as yet another harebrained scheme quickly and deservedly consigned to the dustbin. Ben-Gurion expressed the Zionist view perfectly: "There was no possible solution to the world Jewish problem but a Jewish State." Ben-Gurion even rejected items in the report that were beneficial to Jews. It was still not clear, he complained, when the hundred thousand immigrants would be allowed to enter Palestine. Moreover, that figure foreclosed the possibility of even more Jews arriving in the nascent Jewish state. The report envisaged a trusteeship lasting many years and possibly, sometime in the future, a state based on the "Brotherhood of Man, whatever that might be," as Ben-Gurion sarcastically expressed it.[56]

The British response was desultory. The foreign secretary, colonial secretary, and prime minister raised all the same arguments. Palestine could not possibly absorb one hundred thousand Jewish immigrants; Arab reaction would be intensely hostile to Jewish immigration and to the lifting of prohibitions on the sale of land to Jews. Other countries needed to join in and address the problem of stateless Jews. The United States freely offered opinions without taking on any of the burdens of responsibility. Britain's position in the Middle East was of critical strategic and economic importance and its interests would be severely threatened by Arab hostility if the report's recommendations were adopted.[57]

Between the dry lines of a cabinet committee meeting's minutes, one senses the anxiety, frustration, and outright fear of British policy makers as they pondered the seemingly intractable conflict in Palestine and the slow, steady collapse of the British Empire. Prime Minister Attlee and Foreign Secretary Ernest Bevin were presiding over the greatest permanent retreat of British power since the loss of the American colonies. The pride of victory over Germany and Japan was being undermined by recalcitrant Jews and restless Arabs, and the Americans were more hindrance than help.

After much dithering about how and when to publish the Anglo-American Enquiry report, and numerous leaks about it in any case, the British and Americans finally, on 1 May 1946, let it see the full light of day. The storm broke. The British high commissioner for Palestine, Sir Alan Cunningham, wrote to the colonial secretary that the publication of the report "plunged the country into a ferment of racial polemics which on the Arab side, reached a degree of bitterness unequaled since 1939." Jews had "exploited" various comments "to their maximum propagandist value." Cunningham touted, once again, the fine intentions of the British government and expressed dismay that the *yishuv* was suspicious of it.[58]

The British quickly backed away from the report. The colonial secretary lambasted it as unrealistic and uninformed; in only a few weeks since its conclusions had become known, it had managed to inflame Arabs and Jews, rendering the situation in the Middle East even more precarious. The adoption of the policy recommendations would have "disastrous effects on Great Britain's position in the Middle East and might have unfortunate repercussions in India." Arabs would lose their faith in Great Britain and would become open to Russian influence.[59]

Finis. Yet another investigatory committee, yet another report, failed completely. It would not be the last. A rapid succession of other plans followed over the next year and a half, from April 1946, when the Anglo-American report was completed, to the UN partition resolution of November 1947. Some of these plans essentially revised the conclusions of the Anglo-American Enquiry; others proposed autonomy or partition or federation or a unitary state. None would have any traction under the existing configuration of forces, based as they were upon separate and exclusive nationalisms that both Jews and Arabs advocated.

Meanwhile, the British faced intense security concerns. They were losing soldiers and policemen in Palestine to Jewish armed actions and terrorist attacks, while Arabs stepped up their assaults, more on Jews than on British officials. Pounds flowed like water to support the security services stationed in Palestine. Internal British documents are replete with worries about how many troops and what kinds of arms would be required to maintain order. "Disorder," "rebellion," "uprising," "terrorism," and "bloodshed" are words that appear continually in British deliberations.[60]

Every potential political settlement risked even greater armed resistance from one or the other side, or from both combined. The prospects of mass shootings of Jews, coming so soon after all the reports of Jewish suffering under Nazi domination, after the Harrison Report, must have caused many a sleepless night for many a British statesman. Mass shootings of Arabs risked completely eviscerating whatever goodwill and support Britain had in the Arab and Muslim worlds. Meanwhile, the Joint

Chiefs and the civilian cabinet worried about how Britain would be able to protect its larger global interests if it lost Palestine as a military base.

⌘

For three hours on 29 January 1947, eleven members of the British government sat cloistered with ten leading Zionists. The Labor government was composed of men with decades of experience in the British trade union movement and in British politics. Most were not lords, and at least one key person, Foreign Secretary Bevin, had been a dockworker and longtime trade-union official. Still, they had all absorbed the mannerisms of the British aristocracy. Their Jewish interlocutors had decades of political experience in the often raucous and divisive Zionist movement. Most if not all of them stemmed from Eastern Europe. They spoke fluent though accented English, and had none of the mannerisms of the British upper class (unlike Chaim Weizmann, who was not present).

Two worlds clashed on that day (and on many other days)—the political chasm between the two sides accentuated by vast differences of culture and experience. It was a testy meeting, one more discussion that failed to bring any progress to the conflict. Foreign Secretary Bevin and Colonial Secretary Arthur Creech-Jones presided. Neither was very sympathetic toward Jews, and it showed. They must have been near the end of their tether. Ben-Gurion led the Zionist delegation, and his intransigence did much to arouse the ire of the normally circumspect British statesmen.

Creech-Jones launched the meeting with a lament about the intolerable state of affairs in Palestine. His Majesty's Government had tried numerous times to reach a settlement with the interested parties. Was it so impossible for the two communities to come together? Creech-Jones asked. Was reconciliation impossible?[61] A plaintive plea, but one that elicited little sympathy from the Zionists sitting opposite the British officials.

Ben-Gurion referred continually to Palestine as "their [the Jews'] country." The Zionist goal was "to be able to return their people to their country," he declaimed. All 1.2 million of them in Europe and the

Oriental countries, should they so desire.[62] Palestine, he declared, could absorb them all and no harm would be done to Arabs. Since the Jews had departed Palestine two millennia ago, the countryside had become desolate. In two generations, Zionists had regenerated the land, and still more was possible, including in the Negev Desert. Jews had succeeded in "creating a new civilization and striking social achievements" that benefitted the entire Middle East.[63]

One can imagine what Bevin, Creech-Jones, and the other British statesmen were thinking. The British government had already rejected the American proposal that one hundred thousand Jews be immediately admitted to Palestine. Now Ben-Gurion was talking about over one million? Zionists, among themselves, had spoken of that number; no one previously had ventured to place it right in front of the British government. Had we a film of the meeting, no doubt we would have seen the look of shock register on the British faces, their minds quickly racing to the same conclusion—these Jews are preposterous, their proposals ridiculous, the negotiations pointless. (Can we quickly bring this useless meeting to a close and adjourn to our beloved sherry and whiskey?)

Ben-Gurion went on that Jews wanted "national freedom and independence. They were convinced that the Jews could never enjoy equality of treatment until they enjoyed the same independence as other peoples—that is to say, a Jewish State."[64] Meanwhile, in their own country, Jews were subject to racial discrimination by the British, who had banned Jewish land purchases, while their people in Europe were "confined in concentration camps" because of the severe limitations on immigration.[65] The Arabs were "a great race," but they had land in plenitude. In comparison, Jews needed only a small sliver, in Palestine, in "their only country."[66]

Creech-Jones replied with more pleas for reconciliation between the two communities. Ben-Gurion made some halfhearted efforts to describe instances of cooperation between Jews and Arabs. Bevin, completely frustrated, let loose a barrage of insinuations. "What guarantees could the Jews offer that they would not use their wealth in America to buy up the Arabs and create a landless proletariat? The Jews should be frank and keep no cards up their sleeves."[67] Bevin complained that it was "most unfortunate that the American Government had never committed itself to anything. At the same time, American nationals were finding money which was being used to make the British Government's position impossible.... The United States upset things every time he [Bevin] was beginning to make progress."[68]

One can imagine what must have been going through the minds of Ben-Gurion; Moshe Shertok (later Sharett), the political secretary of the Jewish Agency and later foreign minister of Israel; and the other Zionist leaders while Bevin was on his tirade: Here we see the true colors of the British government, the old antisemitic insinuations never die, not just Nazis but British officials believe the lie of duplicitous yet powerful Jews with endless resources at their disposal.

Later and publicly, Bevin would be even more insidious. Referring to the Jewish electorate in New York, he told parliament: "In international affairs I cannot settle things if my problem is made the subject of local elections. I hope I am not saying anything to cause bad feeling with the United States, but I feel so intensely about this."[69] He might not have caused bad feeling all across the United States, but he certainly did among American Jews, who, like the Zionist leaders, grew increasingly distrustful of the British.

All along, Ben-Gurion and other Zionist leaders argued that a Jewish majority had to be created in Palestine. Continually, unhesitatingly, they repeated that line. "There could not be a Jewish State until the Jews were in a majority," Ben-Gurion told the British government at yet another meeting of British officials and Zionist leaders. One thing Jews could not contemplate, he continued, "was that the Jews would remain a permanent minority in Palestine."[70] Hence, the persistence of the demand for unrestricted Jewish immigration to Palestine. Hence, its consequence: the drive to remove Arabs from Palestine.

And so it went, back and forth, a zero-sum game about rights and national belonging. Bevin no doubt tired of it all. For the Zionists, even the hint of "minority" immediately evoked trains of images, of exile and pogroms and ghettos and, ultimately, of Nazi death camps. It was the word and the status that could not be countenanced given the burdens of Jewish history, given the biographies of Zionist leaders who had spent their whole lives trying to erase the minority status of Jews.

Arabs, meanwhile, offered Jews representation in a state, but one in which offices, the legislative body, and the electorate would all be legally and constitutionally dominated by Arabs.[71] That was hardly a formula designed to appease Zionist concerns. However, it is not clear whether any proposals would have moved Zionists from their commitment to massive Jewish immigration, leading to Jewish demographic domination and a Jewish state. The Arab Higher Committee charged that Jews were the enemies of democracy because they, a minority, were seeking to impose their will upon the majority population. They were the embodiment of Nazism.[72]

Later, in 1947, the Arab Higher Committee wrote that "Palestine has been an Arab country for the last fourteen centuries."[73] In the years after World War I, Arabs had believed that their national aspirations would soon be realized. Britain in its various commitments to the Arabs and US president Wilson and his call for self-determination had inspired these hopes. But Arabs, the Higher Committee wrote, had been betrayed by the British and the United States had not followed through on its promises. Arab hopes had been dashed.[74]

To be a nation meant to be on the side of progress, civilization, and economic development. Palestine was not backward, Arab representatives claimed, not "desolate," not impoverished, not unpopulated. Throughout the Arab world, including Palestine, "the Arabs have made great strides of progress in culture, industry, art and life generally because of their modern awakening, in keeping with the march of time."[75]

In a mirror image of Zionist arguments, Arabs denied Jews the status of a people. Judaism, the Arab Higher Committee proclaimed, was only a creed; Judaism itself "no longer possesses the characteristics of a nation or a race." Jews did not even have a common language. Hebrew has to be learned, it is not a mother tongue but the language of religious books.[76] Nor did Jews have historic claims on the land. The early Jews were "mere intruders," who occupied only a part of the land for a brief period. "The Jews were driven from Palestine leaving behind them no traces worthy of mention either from the religious point of view or that of civilization."[77]

৩৩

Competing national claims, neither side conceding the political status of the other, endless negotiations that went nowhere. That was the situation in 1946–47. After the failure of the Anglo-American Enquiry and many others like it, British statesmen, convinced that American Jews exercised inordinate influence on American policy, came to the conclusion that they could never come to a common stance with the United States. Britain could not master conflicting Arab and Israeli interests as Palestine descended into rounds of violence over the course of 1946 and 1947, let alone its own interests in the region. Britain essentially gave up and threw the matter into the lap of the UN.

And so began yet another inquiry into the situation in Palestine, now presided over by the still-young and inexperienced UN. The United Nations Special Committee on Palestine (UNSCOP) in effect returned to the Peel Commission report of 1937 and resurrected partition, though now on terms more favorable to Jews.

The UN had appointed Count Folke Bernadotte, an experienced Swedish diplomat, as its chief mediator for Palestine. His top assistant was Ralph Bunche, whom we met briefly in the previous chapter. Bunche was a recognized expert on Africa based on his 1937 Harvard doctorate on the French colonies of Dahomey (today Benin) and Gabon, which led to his recruitment to the State Department to head up the Africa desk—of which he was probably the one and only member. He served on the US negotiating team at Dumbarton Oaks and San Francisco, the two international meetings that laid the foundation for the UN. Bunche was committed to the independence of colonial countries, and fought hard—within the US government and among the various delegations—to get that principle included in the founding documents and institutions of the UN. The formation of the UN trusteeship system, the successor to the old League of Nations mandate system, was largely his accomplishment (as mentioned in the previous chapter).

After the negotiations, in 1946, Bunche moved to the UN, where he had a long and illustrious career.[78]

Around mid-century, Bunche was one of the most prominent African-Americans in American life. He understood American civil rights in global terms and connected the struggle for racial equality in the United States with international human rights and decolonization. And he was a firm believer in the nation-state as the agent of progress.

Bunche's sympathy for the Zionist cause grew out of his deep awareness of the persecution of Jews, which he associated with the injustices suffered by African-Americans and colonized Africans. It was also based on the promise of Israel as a developing country par excellence, a country where human rights; self-determination; and economic, social, and cultural progress would unfold together. For Bunche, the domination of Jews in the state would not be a problem so long as the rights of minorities, as individuals, were respected. Arabs could and should build their own development paradise, so long as they, too, respected the rights of the minorities in their midst. Neither an Arab state (or states) nor a Jewish state should be forced to endure large and potentially destabilizing minorities. The promise of progress could best be implemented by nationally defined states, even when that meant the acceptance of forced deportations and streams of refugees.

It was Bunche who drafted, in late summer and autumn 1947, the partition plan for Palestine amid endless negotiations within UNSCOP.[79] The plan inspired a floodtide of political mobilization. Jews reprised 1878 (Berlin Congress) and 1919 (Paris Peace Conference) in far more intense form. The shadow of the Holocaust hung over every Jewish writing, every Jewish gathering and mass meeting in support of a Jewish state in Palestine. Partition, rather than all of Palestine, was a bitter pill, but Jews swallowed it, determined to have a state even on a truncated territory. Jews rallied support wherever they could find it. American Jews were most crucial to the effort, and for numerous reasons. The UN was headquartered in the United States (though the iconic building had yet to be constructed), giving American Jews more immediate access to the statesmen gathered at Flushing Meadows and Lake Success in New York (the latter a name redounding with great irony given the subsequent history of the Arab-Israeli conflict). American Jewish organizations, with the good fortune of geography, had remained intact, unlike those of the shattered European Jewish communities. And America was the ascendant power in the postwar world, a fact Ben-Gurion quickly appreciated. American Jews now outpaced the British, French, and German Jewish communities that had been so prominent in 1878 and 1919. It was a new world.

The partition resolution came before the UN General Assembly in autumn 1947. Jewish lobbying reached a feverish pitch. The resolution affirmed "human rights" and "fundamental freedoms," and access to citizenship for all peoples, whatever side of the partition line they found themselves.[80] All these rights were linked, as always, to the nation-state—in this case, two nation-states. The resolution provided excruciating detail on the border between the two envisaged states (see map 9.2). It also called for an economic union between the two countries, a step on the way, it was hoped, to eventual union. About 43 percent of mandatory Palestine would constitute the Arab state. Jerusalem and its various access roads would be under international control. The British would evacuate Palestine no later than 1 August 1948; the two states would be founded no later than 1 October. It was a rapid timetable, but by November 1947 the British longed to be on board ship and airplane home as soon as possible, leaving Palestine to the Jews and Arabs (and the Americans) to fight it out.

UN committees and subcommittees deliberated, delivered resolutions, suggested amendments. Jews, especially in the United States, raised their lobbying efforts to even greater heights. Arabs rejected the resolution in total. Passage required a two-thirds majority. No one was certain how the vote would go. Everyone watched nervously on 29 November 1947 until the final tally was delivered—thirty-three in favor of the amended partition plan, thirteen opposed, ten abstentions, and one (Thailand) absent. The United Kingdom abstained; Greece and Turkey voted against the resolution. Virtually all of the other European countries, including the Soviet Union and its allies, the United States and Canada and other dominions, and most of Latin America voted in favor of partition. Countries from what we now call the Global

South—India, Afghanistan, Iran, and those of the Middle East—either opposed the resolution or abstained. It was a momentous decision, but few could have imagined that the state designed to protect Jews and secure their human rights would also be at the center of decades of unceasing conflict, including at least four major wars, the displacement of over seven hundred thousand Arabs from Palestine and around the same number of Jews from the Arab Middle East, and countless thousands of terrorist incidents.

In winter 1947–48, the months following the UN partition resolution, Jews and Arabs positioned themselves to achieve the maximum advantage before the end of the mandate. Ben-Gurion, along with other Zionists, talked about democracy and cooperation with Arabs as necessary steps in this transition period. At the same time, he reiterated his belief that the Jewish state would only be secure when one and one-half million Jews had immigrated and settled in the country.[81] He called for the expansion of Jewish settlements in three areas that the partition plan assigned to the Arab state.[82] It was a classic policy: change the reality on the ground before the new authority—in this case, the Jewish state—was consecrated.

All through these tense months, Zionist leaders feared that the United States and the UN would backtrack on the partition resolution. The composition of the Security Council became somewhat less favorable to Zionism, while the Americans seemed to have serious second thoughts about partition. Britain flailed about. The Zionist project began to lose support among journalists and public opinion in the West. The violence practiced by the various Jewish armed groups—Palmach, Haganah, Irgun, Lehi—against the British and Arabs threatened to dissipate whatever goodwill Zionism had among the member states of the UN. Arab attacks against Jews intensified, and the British proved unable or unwilling to protect Jewish lives. As if all that were not enough, the logistical tasks ahead were mind-boggling. As much as Zionism had successfully built up an infrastructure of state and society under the Jewish Agency in Palestine, hundreds of items had to be transferred from Great Britain as the mandatory power to the new state, including posts, telegraphs, land registries, and state bank accounts.[83]

The Zionist response to the tense situation was: more Jews, more arms, more military training. The Zionist leadership knew international support could be unstable and uncertain. Most of the leaders, like Ben-Gurion and Shertok, had been personally dealing with the British for two decades; some like Weizmann, for over thirty years. They had been through many ups and downs. Always, the shadow of the Nazi annihilation of Jews hung over Jewish leaders. Zionism needed the international community, but with victory close at hand, Zionists were not about to leave things to chance and throw themselves on the mercy of fickle Great Powers. From New York especially, but also Washington, London, and Paris, Zionist leaders coordinated their efforts to influence this or that government official, major figure, or the public at large.[84] Arab intransigence only heightened the Zionist inclination to rely on arms and people, or, to put it more precisely, on armed Jews.

Despite their worst fears, the pro-Israel coalition held, with the United States the decisive actor. David Ben-Gurion proclaimed the State of Israel on 14 May 1948 (see figure 9.2). Jews around the world were jubilant. Minutes later, the United States telegrammed its recognition of the state, the speed of the action belying the intense conflicts within the American government and President Truman's wavering stance over the preceding months.[85] The Soviets soon followed with a statement of recognition. While the position of the Soviet Union would before long change, in 1947 and 1948 it was a strong advocate of a Jewish state.[86]

Why did both the United States and the Soviet Union, in the end, support partition and recognize the new State of Israel, with Britain following one year later?

The simple answer is because they could not deny the claims of Jewish statehood in a world where nation-states had become the predominant political form. With the major exception of Arabs, no one challenged the fact that Jews constituted a people. British and American statesmen who knew their Bible—and they all did—believed that Jews had been a people since the original covenant between god and Abraham. Amid the genteel antisemitism that characterized the State Department and the Foreign Office, amid all the concerns about economic and strategic

FIGURE 9.2 David Ben-Gurion reading Israel's Declaration of Independence, 1948. Ben-Gurion (1886–1973) was born in Poland. He immigrated to Palestine in 1906 and became the leading figure of the Zionist movement. He often came into conflict with Chaim Weizmann, but Ben-Gurion established his preeminence in the 1930s. He held multiple posts as leader of the Jewish Agency; of Histadrut, the Jewish labor union; and of Mapai, the Labor Party. Ben-Gurion was unrelenting in his commitment to a Jewish state with a Jewish majority population. He fostered the removal of Palestinian Arabs in 1947 and 1948. Here, he is reading the declaration that established Israel as a Jewish state on 14 May 1948. (Bettmann/Getty Images.)

interests that powerfully pulled American and British officials toward Arabs, the logic of a people constituted as a nation, deserving of a state within which rights would be proclaimed, could not be denied. The Soviets, as we saw in the previous chapter, also believed that the nation-state constituted an inexorable stage of human development.

Moreover, between the lines of the generally harsh attitudes toward Zionism and Jews that one encounters in the diplomatic documents, one senses another sentiment—guilt. Guilt at the Allied failure to save

European Jews, guilt at the dismal conditions in which Jewish survivors existed in the camps of the liberators in the months right after the defeat of Nazi Germany. The 1939 White Paper restrictions on immigration remained in force. The charge that British policy, by refusing to allow Jews to immigrate to Palestine, vastly accentuated the Jewish death toll—that charge cut deeply. Similarly, Earl Harrison's acute and sharply worded report on the status of displaced persons in US-run camps aroused the ire and guilt not only of President Truman but also of substantial segments of the American public. On its own, guilt could never determine policy. But it was palpably present and a factor to reckon with.

☙

The joy among Jews in May 1948 was tempered by the fragility of Israel's position. On 15 May, one day after the Israeli declaration of independence, Egypt, Syria, and Jordan, along with Iraqi units, attacked Israel. The war went on for ten months. At the end, Israel triumphed and emerged with significantly more territory than the partition plan had envisaged (see map 9.3).

Amid the fighting, an ethnic cleansing of Arabs took place—a combination of flight, expulsion, and terror (see figure 9.3). The implementation of Arab removals followed a zigzag, on-again, off-again policy that depended on a multitude of factors.[87] A central, all-encompassing order for the expulsion of Arabs never existed. In fact, at one point the army received orders to the contrary—not to remove Arabs and not to destroy Arab homes and villages.[88] The army and the civilian government were sometimes at loggerheads. Some left-wing Zionists and other groups raised continual objections to the forced deportations of Arabs. The government, acutely aware of international opinion and, especially, the hostility of the UN and the United States to the displacement of Palestinians, tacked this way and that depending on its reading of the external political circumstances. Hundreds of thousands of Arabs fled in panic at the behest of their leaders or because they saw no future for themselves in a state so clearly dominated by Jews. They also fled from assaults and terror actions launched by Israeli settlers and the security

FIGURE 9.3 Palestinians fleeing their homeland, 1948. The Nakba (catastrophe) accompanied the founding of the Jewish state. Over seven hundred thousand Palestinians left their homeland through a combination of forced removals by the Israeli security forces and Palestinians' fears for their future in a Jewish-dominated state. The UN established its Relief and Works Administration to provide support for Palestinians. The refugee camps still exist, making Palestinians the longest-lasting, most multigenerational population still under UN protection. (AP Photo/Jim Pringle.)

forces. Sometimes the army, government, or Jewish National Fund ordered the removals of Arabs from particular areas.[89] At other times, army units or Jewish settlers took the initiative.

Certainly, Arab attacks—both unplanned, on-the-ground violence and the war launched by the surrounding Arab states—threatened the lives of Jews and the very possibility of the Jewish state, which only intensified the support for Arab removals. Over 1947 and 1948, Jews in Palestine lived in a state of existential threat—all this, it always bears repeating, just three years after the defeat of Nazism and the enormous tragedy of the Holocaust.

No Jewish settlers, soldiers, or government officials required a central order for the expulsion of Palestinians. An overarching consensus, reaching back to the 1930s, existed that Israel, as a Jewish state in which Jewish rights would be protected, had to be populated by Jews. A large Arab minority would necessarily be a threat, in this view. To the extent that reprimands or cease-and-desist orders were rare and inconsistent, rank-and-file soldiers, lower-level officers, and settlers no doubt believed they were enacting a commonly supported policy by terrorizing and expelling Arabs.

Moreover, both the army and the civilian leadership were constantly worried about security—legitimately so, given the attacks on Jews and Israel from local Arabs and the Arab states, and their unbending refusal to grant Israel legitimacy. The Israeli leadership constantly pleaded "military necessity" in its drive to clear out Arabs from the border regions and from other areas deemed security interests (and what would not be a security interest in so small a country?). But the concept of "military necessity," so often invoked by general staffs and civilian governments in conflict situations worldwide, does not exist in isolation from forms of political thinking. When a state is conceived as the representative of one particular group, it almost inevitably identifies others as dangerous minorities, particularly when they have cross-border ties of language, family, religion, and ethnicity.

All through 1948 and into 1949, the Israeli position hardened. The Israeli security forces destroyed countless Arab villages or repopulated them with Jews.[90] In autumn 1948, the Israel Defense Forces (IDF), which had been founded within days of the establishment of the state the previous May, undertook offensives in which a series of atrocities occurred, all too typical of forced deportations in other places and times—massacres, rapes, beatings, lootings. The events caused a political storm within the government, military, and the political parties. Any number of times, internal critics raised the specter that "Nazi atrocities" were being committed by Jews against Arabs. In response, Ben-Gurion and the army launched a number of internal investigations, leading to another set of orders demanding humane behavior by soldiers. A few officers faced disciplinary sanctions.[91]

None of this changed the overall policy. As in so many cases of forced deportations, the homes and farms of the removed became the settlement sites for the immigrants, the numbers of whom soared in the first years of the state—some from Europe, others forced out of the Middle Eastern countries that had been their home for generations, even millennia. In the rural areas, an "agrarian revolution" unfolded.[92] The removal of Arabs opened vast amounts of new land. The Jewish National Fund, the beneficiary, then leased plots to Jewish cultivators and settlements. In cities, the density of the Jewish population increased as the state placed immigrants in the apartments of Arabs who had departed, whether forcibly or voluntarily. Often, Jews were settled in areas to secure critical military points, like the approach to Jerusalem. The prospects were dizzying, a fulfillment of the Zionist dream (even if in a truncated territory) of a Jewish—not a multinational—state and society, and it inspired a wave of enthusiasm among Zionist leaders, Jewish settlers, and Jews worldwide.[93]

This was, to a large degree, a socialist-Zionist vision. Ben-Gurion and the Mapai party dominated the political realm. Many of the commanders of the Palmach, the elite strike force of the Haganah, were even more radical leftists. Mapai envisaged a socialist Israel, with only the barest differences in income between workers and the elite. The state would direct the economy and ensure that equality reigned; the educational system would offer opportunities for advancement to all Israelis.[94] This socialism was inextricably entwined with the vision of an exclusive Jewish state. The unfortunate truth about ethnic cleansings is that their protagonists range all across the political spectrum, from right to left and those in the middle.

Meanwhile, the international community, beginning in late 1948, desperately sought a resolution of the refugee crisis. The UN General Assembly passed on 11 December 1948—one day after approving the UDHR; two days after accepting the Genocide Convention—resolution 194 (III) asserting the right of Palestinian refugees to return to their homes in Israel. It established a Palestine Conciliation

Commission and sponsored negotiations in Lausanne. Western diplomats pressured Israel on the refugee problem. Over the winter of
1948–49, the United States, committed to stability in the Middle East and
worried about Soviet influence, took a harder line with the Israelis, demanding some concessions on the refugee problem. The United States
advised Foreign Minister Sharett that Israel should take back 250,000 refugees. The US representative on the Palestine Conciliation Commission,
Mark Ethridge, had personally witnessed refugee columns fleeing to
Lebanon. He was appalled that Israeli officials refused to take any responsibility for the refugee problem that they themselves had created.[95]

Ben-Gurion resisted all entreaties from Ethridge and even from Secretary of State Dean Acheson and President Truman. The Arabs were
also unmovable and refused to integrate Palestinian refugees. Israel
implemented a minor family reunification scheme and floated a proposal for the repatriation of one hundred thousand Arabs. But this was
mere window dressing designed to keep international pressure at bay.
Within Israel, the offer "caused a major political explosion."[96] Meier
Grabovsky, the head of Mapai's parliamentary delegation, said that the
events of the war had resulted in a "more or less homogeneous [Jewish]
state, and now to double the number of Arabs without any certain
recompense ... [should be seen] as one of the fatal mistakes destroying
the security of the state.... We will face a Fifth Column [and a minority
problem like that] in the Balkans."[97] Sharett's deputy, Leo Kohn, in a
note on 22 April 1949, invoked another forced population movement to
defend Israel's position: "Now that the exodus of the Arabs from our
country has taken place, what moral right have those [i.e., the Allied
powers] who fully endorsed the expulsion of the Sudeten Germans
from Czechoslovakia to demand that we readmit these Arabs?"[98] Indeed, what moral right did they have?

Israeli leaders were neither sad nor surprised when the hundred-
thousand offer was rejected by the Arab side. As the US embassy wrote,
no Israeli "from the Prime Minister down wishes [to] see a single Arab
brought back if can possibly be avoided."[99] William Burdett, the US
consul in Jerusalem, captured the developments best: "Since the U.S.

has supported the establishment of a Jewish State, it should insist on a homogeneous one which will have the best possible chance of stability. Return of the refugees would create a continuing 'minority problem' and form a constant temptation both for uprisings and intervention by neighboring Arab states."[100] Shades of the Lausanne Treaty! For Burdett and many other diplomats, domestic and international stability would best be anchored by a rights-based state that promoted development. And that state would be most successful if it presided over a population as homogeneous as possible.

The UN stance was similarly mixed. Even more than the Americans, the UN mediator, Count Bernadotte, sharply condemned Israel's policy and called on it to allow the return of the refugees. That position fed the perception among radical Zionists that Bernadotte was anti-Israel and even antisemitic. For that reason the Lehi, the most uncompromising of the armed Jewish organizations, assassinated Bernadotte on 17 September 1948, an action that made the domestic and international situations even more tense and uncertain. But the Lehi won in one regard: Bunche, Bernadotte's successor, was far less inclined to pressure Israel to take back Palestinian refugees.

Bunche went on to mediate the cease-fire agreements between the Arab states and Israel. For that, he was awarded the Nobel Peace Prize in 1950, the first person of African descent to win a Nobel. His image then graced the cover of *Time*, the legendary American magazine.

For Jews, the foundation of Israel was a great triumph. With their own nation-state, many believed, they could live in security and develop a flourishing society complete with human rights. For Palestinian Arabs, the events signified the near total destruction of their society. Over 350 Arab villages were destroyed. Jaffa's population fell from seventy to eighty thousand Palestinians to three to four thousand.[101] The old notable families were drastically weakened by the loss of lands, the de-urbanization of the Arab population, and the ethnic cleansing of so many Palestinians, let alone the establishment of a new political order in which they had no place whatsoever. The Nakba—catastrophe— was more than just the forced removal of a population, as searing as was that event. It also meant the destruction and decomposition of an entire society.

❧

"The landscape is . . . beautiful—I enjoy it, especially when traveling between Haifa and Tel Aviv, and there is not a single Arab to be seen," said Z. Onn at a meeting of the Mapai secretariat. He expressed a commonly held view among the Zionist leadership, but one laced with anxiety. While over 700,000 Arabs had fled or been expelled, the circa 150,000 who remained in the Jewish state, whom Onn professed not to see, appeared to many as a real or potential fifth column. "There are too many Arabs in this country," said Itzhak Ben-Tzvi, the future president of Israel, after the 700,000 had already been removed.[102]

The Israeli Declaration of Independence that Ben-Gurion read publicly in 1948 is sprinkled with the lofty language of rights for all, including the inherent dignity of all men and women. (Israel has no written constitution, but a series of basic laws that possess constitutional status.) One would expect nothing less from a socialist labor government whose members had long expressed their commitment to democracy.

However, Israel, like every other state founded as the purported representative of one particular nationality, now faced its own minority problem. Some advocated assimilation and integration, others expulsion of the remaining Arabs. One inescapable fact remained—Arabs, as well as Druze, Bedouins, and other minorities, were the "problem" that stalked the Jewish state. The occupation of the West Bank and Gaza as a consequence of the Six-Day War in 1967 vastly expanded the number of Arabs under Israel's writ, which only exacerbated the dilemma (see map 9.4).

The Palestinian Arabs who had been resident in mandate Palestine and remained within the 1949 armistice lines of Israel received citizenship in 1952. They can vote, have access to the educational system, and receive social welfare benefits like Jewish Israeli citizens. Palestinian Arabs sit in the Knesset (parliament); a few are university professors or run their own businesses. But Palestinian Arabs cannot serve in the army—in so many countries, the ticket to full citizenship rights, a complement of veterans' benefits, and, not least important, the moral claim to have served the nation. Druze and Christians serve in the IDF, but only in separate battalions and not in combat. Social prejudices remain acute, even for high-ranking Palestinian Arabs in Israel. For those Arabs living under Israeli occupation in the West Bank or control in Gaza (Israeli forces withdrew in 2005), the conditions are much worse, life-threatening in many circumstances, while Jewish Israelis live in a state of constant uncertainty and tension. Hardly a whiff of possibility exists that Arabs displaced in 1948 or their descendants will be able to return to their homes and villages. In sharp contrast, the Law of Return grants Jews anywhere in the world the right to come to Israel and receive immediate citizenship.

Moreover, for twenty years after the founding of the state, areas with high concentrations of Palestinian Arabs were subject to martial law.[103] The Military Government, as it was called, controlled the movements of Arabs. It enforced curfews and relocated Arabs at will. The Military Government determined the degree of services like schooling and healthcare available to the communities and continued the confiscation of Arab lands. Palestinians suffered constant raids of their homes and businesses. The laws were drawn directly from British emergency regulations during the mandate; the young Jewish state expanded them.[104] Virtually everything critical to the daily lives of Palestinians required the approval of the Military Government, including work permits, travel requests, and contracts. The Israeli authorities retained the right to appoint village leaders. Even that precious life resource, water, became a means of control over the Palestinian population.[105]

All told, during the period of military rule the state confiscated over half the land owned by Palestinian Israelis.[106] The rural Arab population was transformed from peasant-cultivators to agricultural laborers on Jewish settlements, a transformation akin to that of the Herero and Nama in Namibia. A maze of bureaucratic and judicial measures—something familiar to Armenians after the founding of the Republic of Turkey—blocked any effort by Palestinians to regain their old houses or villages or, at the very least, compensation.[107]

The policies were contested, to be sure. Israel's raucous democracy provided many openings for some left-wing Jews in the parliament, army, and political parties to demand the abolition of the Military Government. Arab Israelis used whatever mechanisms they could, including the courts, passive resistance, and demonstrations, to contest the inequalities and discrimination under which they lived. They engaged in constant negotiations over issues like the release of political prisoners, the provisioning of water, unemployment, and curfews.[108]

Jews who supported full, equal citizenship for Palestinian Arabs in Israel could not surmount the contradiction. Israel was defined as a Jewish state. What role could there be for Arabs? And what if Arab Israelis resisted the siren song of membership in a national community defined by Jewishness? True equality between Arabs and Jews, said Meir Ya'ari, a left-wing member of the Knesset, is a necessity for security, which would lead to the "deepening and strengthening of the Arab sector's bond and loyalty to the State of Israel."[109] What could that mean, however, when the state represented only Jews? Others, like the 1948 war hero and later prominent political figure Yigal Allon, opposed the Military Government on the grounds that the blatant discrimination it exercised only fed Palestinian national consciousness, the exact opposite of what Israel needed to create ongoing security.[110] Both observations exemplify the contradictions at the heart of basing citizenship and human rights on the nation-state when it is conceived in exclusive, national terms.

Conclusion

In 2007, a group of Palestinian Arabs in Israel—intellectuals, activists, political figures—issued the *Haifa Declaration*. Two other documents, *Future Vision* and the *Democratic Constitution*, were published around the same time.[111] All three reflected the disillusionment and despair with the Oslo peace process that had begun in the 1990s. The two-state solution that Israel, the Palestine Liberation Organization, and the international community had recognized in the Oslo Accords in 1993 and 1995 seemed dead. The deeper context for the documents lay in the ongoing discrimination that Palestinian Arabs in Israel endured and the far more dire straits of Arabs in the Gaza Strip and the West Bank.

The *Haifa Declaration*, like the others, affirmed the unity of the Palestinian people whether they are citizens of Israel, live in the occupied territories, or have moved abroad. It revisited the history of Zionist settlement, the Palestinian catastrophe, and continued repression by the Israeli state of Arabs within and beyond the borders of Israel. It invoked international human rights as a standard often violated in the case of Palestinians and promoted the rights of women.

> As we are a homeland minority whose people was driven out of their homeland, and who has suffered historical injustice, the principle of equality—the bedrock of democratic citizenship—must be based on justice and the righting of wrongs, and on the recognition of our narrative and our history in this homeland. This democratic citizenship that we seek is the only arrangement that guarantees individual and collective equality for the Palestinians in Israel.[112]

The most dramatic lines of the *Declaration* entailed the recognition of the Holocaust and the rights of Jews to live in peace in Israel.

> This historic reconciliation also requires us, Palestinians and Arabs, to recognize the right of the Israeli Jewish people to self-determination and to life in peace, dignity, and security with the Palestinian and the other peoples of the region. We are aware of the tragic history of the Jews in Europe, which reached its peak in one of the most horrific human crimes in the Holocaust perpetrated by the Nazis against the Jews, and we are fully cognizant of the tragedies that the survivors have lived through. We sympathize with the victims of the Holocaust, those who perished and those who survived.[113]

Most importantly, the *Haifa Declaration* called for a "democratic state founded on equality between the two national groups."[114] Only on that basis could human rights be secured for all. The *Democratic Constitution* declared that Israel would be a bilingual state with both Arabic and Hebrew as official languages. It also affirmed the right of return for Palestinians displaced from their lands since 1948.

The *Haifa Declaration* spelled out the consequences: Israel would no longer be the Jewish state. For virtually all Jewish Israelis and Jews abroad, that position was akin to sacrilege. A storm of criticism, laced with charges of disloyalty, spewed forth from the Israeli media and government. Over ten years later, on 19 July 2018, the Israeli Knesset passed a new basic law defining Israel as the "nation-state of the Jewish people." The law abolished all pretenses of equality between Jews and Palestinians, and even demoted Arabic from its status as one of Israel's official languages to "special status" (whatever that means).[115]

Arabs and left-wing Israelis raised a storm of protest. But in many ways, the law only confirmed in words what Israel has been since its founding—the state of Jews. It is hard to see any other political option in the 1940s for the shattered Jewish community than the founding of the Jewish state. Jews had endured discrimination and vicious pogroms in Europe, all culminating in the Nazi extermination campaign. In their own state Jews would be rights-bearing citizens, their lives secure. The establishment of Israel represented a great triumph for Jews, and one kind of culmination of the global political model of the nation-state and human rights.

Only the support of the international community enabled Jews to achieve that goal. They knew that, of course, and mobilized successfully everyone and everything within reach, expanding the successful political campaigns Jews had launched at the Berlin Congress in 1878 and the Paris Peace Conference in 1919. As in the other histories discussed in this book, nation-state foundings and human rights advances—such as they are—emerge from a confluence of forces, including popular activism, the interests of particular states, and decisions by the international community. In the case of Palestine and Israel, the Great Powers and the UN have remained embedded in the Middle East, sometimes a force for peace and reconciliation, more often contributing to the ongoing violence.

The consequences for Palestinians were traumatic as they were driven into exile. Even as Israeli citizens, they have suffered discrimination. The *Haifa Declaration*, the *Democratic Constitution*, and the *Future Vision* documents all firmly draw upon international human rights laws and principles established since 1945. As radical as are the statements, especially in the Israeli context, they, too, are unable to get beyond the nation-state as the basis of citizenship rights. Mostly, they envisage one state, not the two states of the Oslo Accords.[116] Whether in one or two, Arabs and Jews would each have their representative bodies; each would be self-determining within the strictures of democracy.

Palestine and Israel reveal in stark terms the conundrum that has marked the history of nation-states and human rights. Only membership in the nation gives an individual full access to rights. Recognition and protection as a minority may improve one's lot. But minority status in a nation-state always carries a stigma. We shall see the conundrum play out also in our last case, Rwanda and Burundi.

Chapter 10

Rwanda and Burundi

DECOLONIZATION AND THE
POWER OF RACE

❦

ON 24 March 1957, nine Hutu intellectuals issued the *Hutu Manifesto*. It was a response to the *Statement of Views* issued a month earlier by the Tutsi-dominated Conseil supérieur du pays (CSP). Rwanda and its sister country Burundi were Belgian trusteeships under the UN. The two territories were veering unsteadily toward independence—the 1950s the great decade of decolonization (see maps 10.1 and 10.2). The *Statement of Views* appeared like a Tutsi grab for power. The *Hutu Manifesto*, more expansive than the CSP document, was remarkable in many ways. The *Manifesto* invoked the language of the French, American, and Latin American revolutions by calling for democracy, freedom of expression, and equality under the law. All the communities of Rwanda, including Europeans, should have representation in the administrative and political institutions of the country. The authors of the document also advocated social and economic policies to move the Hutu majority out of poverty, like land reform and the abolition of "feudalism" in the country. They placed great hopes on the expansion of education for all citizens, including girls. The *Manifesto*, a powerful assertion of self-determination and human rights, rejected the notion that Hutus required "tutelage" under the Belgian trusteeship.[1]

The subtitle of the *Hutu Manifesto*, however, indicated that it would not be a typical, ringing call for liberty and national independence, the tone of so many nationalist proclamations from those issued by the Greek rebels in the 1820s to the Israeli Declaration of Independence in 1948. The subtitle ran, "Note on the social aspect of the indigenous racial problem in Rwanda." True to the title, the document forcefully brought forth the issue of race, which entailed not just a problem of white against

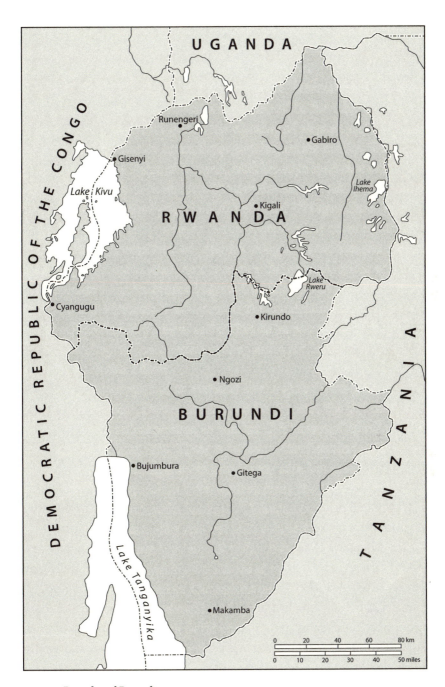

MAP 10.1 Rwanda and Burundi.

MAP 10.2 Rwanda and Burundi in Africa.

black—the Belgian colonizers against Africans. Even more profoundly, the *Manifesto* charged, race was a matter of Tutsis against Hutus.

The *Manifesto* claimed that only one "caste," the Tutsis, who comprised a mere 14 percent of the population, had benefitted from Belgian efforts at "civilization." The Tutsis' long-standing "political monopoly," supported by Belgium, had been parlayed into an "economic and social monopoly," a feudal system that had condemned Hutus to an "eternal subaltern" position. The Hutu intellectuals went on to demand a complete transformation of society and politics. Belgium, as the trustee power, had to abandon the idea that the Rwandese elite was composed only of those of the "Hamitic" rank (that is, Tutsis, the supposed descendants of the biblical Ham). Immediate action was required for the "economic and political emancipation of the Hutu from the yoke of the Hamite tradition."[2]

The position laid out in the *Hutu Manifesto* would be carried into the establishment, later that year, of the Party of the Hutu Emancipation Movement (Parmehutu), the Hutu "Social Revolution" of 1959, and the founding of two separate states, Rwanda and Burundi, in 1962. Alongside the invocation of the eighteenth- and nineteenth-century revolutionary concepts of the nation, liberty, and rights, the *Manifesto* signaled that in both countries, the circle of those who would have the right to have rights would always be severely circumscribed by the ideology and practice of race.

The making of the global world in the nineteenth and twentieth centuries entailed not only the emancipatory promise of nation-states and human rights. It also included race, the most rigid, hierarchical, and oppressive way of defining human difference, and one of the most powerful, most widely diffused ideologies of the modern world. We have seen race at work in other chapters—in the United States, Brazil, Namibia, and Japan and Korea. Race reached into the farthest places of the globe, even into Africa among Africans where one would have expected (and hoped for) an anti-race politics, since Africans and African-descended populations were among the prime victims of racial politics. But in Rwanda and Burundi, racial politics would infuse the anticolonial movements, offering elites—with a few notable and ultimately unsuccessful exceptions—an easy strategy for mobilizing populations and securing their own power base. The construction of two nation-states sharply delimited and at times obliterated the promise of rights, even though both sides invoked the postwar language of human rights. Each nation-state became defined in racial terms—Rwanda for Hutus, Burundi for Tutsis—and each would descend into the most violent forms of racial politics against the other in its midst. The Rwandan Genocide of 1994, an event that evoked shock and horror around the world, did not suddenly emerge out of the blue sky. It had roots that went back to the 1950s and 1960s when racially minded nationalist movements first emerged in the territories, and even earlier to the period of Belgian colonization.

In Korea, we saw how extreme nationalist and authoritarian states undermined the promise of human rights. In Rwanda and Burundi, racial politics had much the same effect. Nonetheless, we shall also see how a few brave and committed individuals in the territories and among the UN staff, at the time of independence and today, have sought to counter the divisiveness of race and establish human rights.

ↀ

Long before Europeans came in the late nineteenth century, clientelist systems defined Rwandan and Burundian societies. Every group paid tribute to those above in a hierarchical order, ultimately leading upward to the king. Peasants and low-level cattle herders owed labor, loyalty, and tribute to their superiors, in return for which they received land, protection, and other resources. These relations partly—but only partly—mapped onto ethnic differences between Hutus and Tutsis. Tutsis were largely pastoralists who some centuries previously had migrated south, into the lands that Hutus, part of the earlier Bantu migration from Central Africa, cultivated. But some Hutus were also pastoralists or practiced a mixture of herding and farming, as did some Tutsis. The Twa, only 1 percent of the population, had resided in the territory the longest and also pursued a mixed economy. By the late eighteenth century, Tutsis had largely established their political and social domination, but they did not comprise a closed caste. A significant degree of intermarriage occurred, and some Hutus also established clans over which they predominated. Both societies were patrilineal, meaning ethnicity was passed on from the father to the children.[3]

As in the rest of Africa, European colonizers came in the late nineteenth century. Germans arrived first, in the mid-1880s, spilling over from their possession, German East Africa (today Tanzania). They never established much of a presence, and they lost the colony—along with all their others, like Namibia—when the Allies forced the Versailles Treaty on Germany in June 1919. The League of Nations then granted Rwanda and Burundi to Belgium as a mandate.

German and Belgian colonizers drew on the differences between the two groups and propounded a much simplified, racial conception of the division between Tutsis and Hutus. In keeping with the race thinking that was predominant in the West around the turn of the twentieth century, they argued that the Tutsis were the superior race in the colonies, a characteristic purportedly demonstrated by their greater physical beauty.[4]

Germans and Belgians also elaborated the "Hamitic myth," which existed, though in a different form, in the Americas. In the Americas' version of the biblical story, Noah's son Ham removed his father's loincloth, displaying Noah's nakedness. Noah cursed his son, and the reproach lay upon all of Ham's progeny, black Africans, all through the ages. Blackness was the sign of their accursed state and inferiority, thereby justifying their enslavement. In the East African version of the myth, the descendants of Ham were the noble Africans, Egyptian or Ethiopian in origin, who then migrated south toward the Great Lakes region. Their superiority was supposedly evident physically in their height and beauty, making them—the Tutsis—the ideal allies of the colonizers, while the Hutus and Twa were consigned to the bottom of the racial hierarchy as low-level peasants and laborers. The White Fathers, Belgian Catholic missionaries, sometimes even propagated the idea that Tutsis were descended from Coptic Christians. The Tutsis' Christianity still lay within them, the White Fathers claimed, and could easily be activated by the intercession of missionaries.[5]

The Hamitic story resounds to this day, a powerful myth that shapes politics, especially the deadly, multiple forms of violence in the Great Lakes region, which includes Rwanda, Burundi, and parts of Congo, Uganda, and Tanzania. The Hamitic myth echoed Tutsi origins stories; the mingling of the two—Tutsi traditional beliefs with the racial myths brought by the colonizers—provided strong ideological sustenance for Tutsi domination across the colonial and independence periods. Hutu leaders turned the Hamitic myth on its head, as they did in the *Hutu Manifesto*. Tutsis were, indeed, a race, they argued, but an alien, exploitative one that had invaded Hutu lands and brutally oppressed the hardworking, upright Hutus.

Belgium administered the region as two separate territories, as they had been in the eighteenth and nineteenth centuries, each presided over by a royal dynasty. In the 1930s the Belgians instituted a passport system.

As in Namibia, the authorities sought to keep track of every African, all the time. Passports were also the prime symbol of the age-old policy of divide and rule. On each document the authorities stamped "Hutu," "Tutsi," or "Twa," a racial categorization that the authorities determined simply by looking at individuals. Belgian authorities ignored the mixing that had long existed among the population. Instead, they counted the population for each territory as 84 percent Hutu, 15 percent Tutsi, and 1 percent Twa. Mysteriously, these figures have been repeated in every source for every period. Somehow, the proportional division of the population has remained constant, an improbability in any situation and completely unrealistic given the millions of refugees and excess deaths (to use the demographic term) produced since 1959.

Under the Belgium mandate, later converted into a UN trusteeship, Tutsis received better education and greater economic opportunities. In fact, the Belgians established two entirely separate educational systems—a more advanced one, in French, for Tutsis, who were then slated for the colonial administration, and a rudimentary education for Hutus. In that way, Belgian policy granted some Tutsis an additional layer of power atop their more traditional forms of domination. The colonial rulers also weakened the complex, clientelist society by removing local chiefs, many of them Hutu. In their place, they instituted a "rational," European-style administrative structure. In essence, German and Belgian policies simplified and hardened, made more rigid, the ethnic and social differences among the population, turning them into racial divisions.[6]

In a more or less official Belgian publication at the end of the 1950s, on the eve of independence, a group of scholars analyzed the political, social, and economic situation in the trusteeships. The studies brimmed with optimism. Among the authors was the soon-to-be eminent, Belgian-born Africanist Jan Vansina, who would go on to train two generations of Africa specialists in the United States.[7] According to the analyses, urbanization, the cultivation of cash crops, and a European administrative and legal order had already weakened the feudal system in Rwanda and Burundi. A greater degree of individualism had become evident, a sure sign of progress. Even the family as the primary social institution had declined, the ties of blood no longer as significant. Land as a source of individual capital and of individual control had taken on greater importance. This process of individuation provided the substratum for democracy and rights, which would flourish once independence from Belgian domination had been achieved. With grand historical sweep, the authors claimed: "Liberated . . . from fear, from servility, from passivity, [from] the [entire] climate of the ancien régime . . . the individual becomes conscious of himself and takes the first steps on the road to the principles of the rights of man."[8]

Belgian scholars and many others deceived themselves. The diminution of clientelism did not necessarily lead to individualism associated with human rights. The process was also accompanied by a profound enhancement of racial identification. The links in the chain of individuation—liberty, rights, development: the whole complex of modernization—were, in Rwanda and Burundi, composed of discrete races, Hutu and Tutsi. Hence, individuation cum nation building formed the foundation of systems of rights for one group exclusively, a severely limiting example of the right to have rights. The consequences were dire for the population categorized as the "other." The blazing optimism of the Belgian scholars was amazingly blind in this regard.

Nor were the Rwandan and Burundian anticolonial movements on par with developments elsewhere on the continent. In most other parts of Africa, anticolonial movements had first emerged in the interwar period. London and Paris in the 1920s and 1930s were the great intellectual centers of anticolonialism as a global movement, the cities where Africans from across the continent, Caribbeans, and Americans met, debated, and organized amid the crosscurrents of Pan-Africanism, communism, and nationalism. No Rwandans or Burundians were among them. The few who did travel to Europe went mostly to Catholic seminaries in Belgium. The Belgian territories produced none of the great anticolonial intellectuals and activists, like Léopold Senghor, Aimé Césaire, Julius Nyerere, C.L.R. James, or Frantz Fanon.[9]

There would be a price to pay for this political backwardness. London and Paris were places of intellectual and political ferment. Catholic seminaries in Belgium and the two capital cities, Kigali and Bujumbura, were not. The narrowness of vision, the reflexive reversion to race as the essential political category that came to define the Rwandan and the Burundian political parties, had much to do with this lack of experience in the larger anticolonial movement of the interwar and postwar periods. The most apt comparison is not with Kenyan or Ghanaian or Algerian activists, but with Cambodia, also a relatively backward country that, in economic and political terms, lagged far behind neighboring Vietnam. As in Rwanda and Burundi, the anticolonial movement in Cambodia developed late. Only a handful of Cambodians went abroad to France in the late 1940s and 1950s, and there they stayed encased in the intellectual world of the Stalinist-infused French Communist Party, not quite a breeding ground for democracy and human rights.

Nonetheless, a powerful domestic mobilization began in Rwanda and Burundi around 1950. The much larger, resource-rich Congo, also under Belgian domination, preoccupied international attention. Rwanda and Burundi could hardly remain isolated given the ferment close at hand in neighboring Congo, Tanganyika, and Kenya, and the general human rights and anticolonial surge of the postwar years. The activism—and activism is the right word—of the UN provided an international venue for Hutu and Tutsi elites, who protested the inequities they suffered under Belgian domination. However, the nationalist movements that emerged in both territories in the 1950s had a powerful racial dimension to them. Only a handful of individuals had the intellectual and political wherewithal to move beyond race. These few—including, notably, the Burundian prince Louis Rwagasore—posited a political program of human rights and development for all the people living in the trusteeships. But the prince and his supporters could not ultimately surmount the power of race, as we shall soon see.

❧

The *Hutu Manifesto* provided the most dramatic display of anticolonial political mobilization. Its signatories included Grégoire Kayibanda, who would go on to become Rwanda's first president (see figure 10.1). He and his associates constituted a small but cohesive generation that had studied at seminaries run by the White Fathers. Despite the overt

FIGURE 10.1 Grégoire Kayibanda, 1961. Kayibanda (1924–76) was Parmehutu's leader and first president of Rwanda, ruling from 1962 to 1973, when he was overthrown in a coup led by Major General Juvénal Habyarimana. Parmehutu dominated politics in Rwanda as the Belgian trustee- ship moved toward independence. It carried out its Social Revolution in 1959, which displaced Tutsis from leading political and social positions and installed Hutus in their stead. (Musée royal de l'Afrique centrale. HP.2007.17.16, collection RMCA Tervuren; photo Inforcongo, © RMCA Tervuren.)

preference given by Belgium to the Tutsis in schools and universities, a number of Hutus had become educated, enough to constitute an intelligentsia, however small in numbers. Once graduated, these young intellectuals entered the Belgian administration or worked as schoolteachers. Some of them, like Kayibanda, also found a career—and a mission—in journalism.[10]

Hutu activists, the Catholic Church, and Belgium were all on board when Parmehutu launched a revolution in autumn 1959. The party gave its achievement a grand name—the Social Revolution. Its results were, in fact, highly limited. The revolution's signal achievement was that Hutus replaced Tutsis in the key political institutions, traditional ones dominated by chieftains as well as those Belgium had established.[11]

As revolutions go in the modern era—French, Russian, Chinese, Cuban—this was not much. But it gave Hutu activists, and probably much of the population, a great sense of accomplishment and bright hopes for the future. Now, at long last, Hutu leaders would run the state and the Hutu population would enjoy the full complement of rights that accompany the founding of the nation-state in the modern era.

Belgian support proved crucial in Parmehutu's victory.[12] Suddenly and very late in the game, Belgium switched course. It abandoned its Tutsi allies and threw its backing to the majority Hutus in a desperate effort to retain a significant presence in the territories even after independence. In so doing, Belgium dramatically enhanced the tensions and conflicts as the territories moved toward independence. Almost immediately upon the proclamation of the *Hutu Manifesto*, mass killings of Tutsis in Rwanda occurred. In Burundi, Belgian authorities, UN officials, and local activists eyed nervously the events across the border, all the while trying to keep in check revenge killings of Hutus.

Tens of thousands of Tutsis fled Rwanda, the first of many refugee streams in the Great Lakes region that have continued down to the present day. Most of these early refugees journeyed to the Kivu province of Congo. Tutsi communities had lived there for centuries, long before colonial powers drew tight borders.[13] In the 1930s, the colonial authorities had moved Hutu laborers into the province to work on Belgian plantations, and then placed Tutsis as chieftains over them. Tutsi refugees in 1959 were able to acquire significant landholdings, often through political connections in Kinshasa, the capital of Congo, where a number of Tutsis had risen in the ranks of the government. "Native" Congolese came to resent the presence of both Tutsis and Hutus. Tutsis of long-standing and recent refugees became commingled in the eyes of many political forces; Tutsi radicals seeing them as potential allies, Congolese and Hutus seeing them as deadly dangers. Within one year of the Social Revolution, the tensions extended outward, beyond Rwanda and Burundi to Congo, Uganda, and Tanzania, wherever refugees fled.[14]

Belgium could not decide matters on its own (as we have seen in other places, like Greece, Korea, and Palestine/Israel). Not in its colony Congo, and certainly not in the territories it held under UN trusteeship— Rwanda and Burundi. Enter the international community.

Today, when the UN is such a bedraggled institution, it may be hard to remember its great stature in the 1950s and early 1960s. Its founding most certainly expressed the state interests of the victorious Allied powers in World War II.[15] Yet the UN was never a static, one-dimensional institution. It inspired great hopes for peace, progress, and, not least, human rights. All around the United States, for example, the United Nations Association, a civic organization, had community affiliates, often led by local notables. They staged lectures, discussions, and celebrations, all promoting the ethos and mission of the UN.[16] Around the world, UN development agencies like the International Labor Organization (ILO), the Food and Agriculture Organization (FAO), and the World Health Organization (WHO) played major roles in alleviating poverty and generally improving the health and welfare of people. As a force in global politics, the UN was unprecedented. Its reach was much broader, its institutional elaboration much thicker, than anything that had previously existed. Europeans had created international systems at the Vienna Congress in 1815, at the Berlin Congress in 1878, and at the Paris Peace Conference in 1919. The last had established the League of Nations. But none of these creations matched the post-1945 international system and its institutional body, the UN.

Nor did these earlier international systems have a membership anything approaching the global character of the UN in its origins, and even more so after 1960 amid the decolonization surge. The UN had 51 founding members in 1945. Ghana joined the organization in 1957 as the first sub-Saharan, ex-colonial African nation (South Africa was a founding member). In 1960, 18 newly independent countries were admitted to the UN, 15 of them from Africa. (Today the UN has 193 members.) It would be a new era. Virtually all the new states joined earlier members from what we now call the Global South—India, Haiti, Indonesia—along with the Soviet-bloc countries. They formed a powerful group that placed decolonization and human rights front and center on the UN agenda (the Soviets, as discussed in chapter 8, promoted human rights at the international level, though certainly not domestically).[17]

In these matters the UN staff, in particular Ralph Bunche, whom we met in previous chapters, played a central role (see figure 10.2). In the 1950s and 1960s, the staff was as important as the Security Council and the General Assembly in shaping UN activities. Bunche, while he mediated the conflict over Palestine, was already director of the Trusteeship Council. He then became under-secretary-general for special political affairs, meaning that he served directly under the UN secretaries-general Dag Hammarskjöld and his successor U Thant.

Bunche forged around him a coterie of high-level, highly capable international civil servants. The group included C. V. Narasimhan, the chef de cabinet in the Office of the Secretary-General; Dragan Protitch, executive assistant to the secretary-general; and Under-Secretary-General for Trustee Affairs Godfrey K. J. Amachree; and extended into the wider circle of staff at UN agencies, notably the United Nations High Commissioner for Refugees (UNHCR) and the ILO, as well as the World Health Organization (WHO); the FAO; and the United Nations Educational, Scientific and Cultural Organization (UNESCO). As a group the staff was committed to decolonization, nation-state foundings, social and economic development, and human rights—all together the classic development ideology of the 1950s and 1960s. Development in their minds meant not just economics—enhancing agricultural production in poor countries, for example. Although often overlooked, human rights were a fundamental component of the development ideology. Bunche and his staff forcefully advocated that program.[18] They expected that

FIGURE 10.2 Ralph Bunche, 1950. Bunche (1904–71), a member of the US negotiating team for the founding of the UN, played the key role in ensuring that the UN Charter contained a commitment to decolonization. Bunche went on to an illustrious career at the UN, first as director of the Trusteeship Council and then as under-secretary-general for special political affairs. He forged a tight group of high-level UN staff committed to decolonization, human rights, and development. Bunche negotiated the ceasefire of the First Arab-Israeli War, for which he won the Nobel Peace Prize. In the 1950s and 1960s he was centrally involved in UN support for decolonization, including in the Congo, Rwanda, and Burundi. (UN Photo.)

decolonization would lead almost naturally to the institutionalization of human rights in the newly independent countries, defined by nationality but with the rights of minorities respected.[19]

The top UN staff around Bunche was remarkable in its cohesion and commitment. Together, they applied their program in many places around the globe, including Rwanda and Burundi. They had staff on the ground in the territories who communicated regularly to UN headquarters in New York and UN agencies in Geneva. UN staff believed that on the foundation of independence and partition, Rwanda and Burundi would become sites of stability, democracy, human rights, and development.[20] They channeled as much aid and technical assistance— administrative, military, economic—as they could muster, and involved other UN organizations. For all that the UN, even in this period, had an infamous, agonizingly slow-churning bureaucracy, Bunche and his colleagues managed to mobilize successfully the wide-ranging and scattered agencies into a cohesive political development and aid program for Rwanda and Burundi. The program included UNESCO, headquartered in Paris; WHO, UNHCR, and ILO in Geneva; and the Rome-based FAO.

Bunche and his staff would fail, terribly so. They would prove unable to surmount the blunt force of racial mobilizations in both territories as UN trusteeships and then, from 1962, independent countries. But it is worth recounting and recognizing their efforts and pondering the possibilities of the roads not taken.

❦

Rightly suspicious of Belgium's slow and hesitant efforts to move Rwanda and Burundi toward independence, the General Assembly and the UN staff, with Bunche in the lead, exercised enormous pressure on Belgium. Throughout the 1950s, UN commissions visited the territories. Their investigations, their very presence, accentuated the politicization process, as in Palestine just a decade before. Hutu and Tutsi activists understood that they could use the UN, with its stated commitment to decolonization and human rights, to support the transformation of the two territories into sovereign, independent countries.

Frustrated with Belgium, the General Assembly went further and established a UN Commission for Ruanda-Urundi (the French spelling adopted by the UN) to oversee the transition, and appointed to it Max Dorsinville of Haiti (the chair), Majid Rahnema of Iran, and Ernest Gasson of Togo. All the important cable traffic from the Commission and, later, UN representatives circulated among Bunche and his close associates in New York and Geneva.

The pressure on Belgium mounted as the General Assembly convened for its fifteenth session in 1960–61, just as the UN was about to admit nearly twenty newly independent countries. Belgium was battered, both in public on the floor of the General Assembly and from UN staffers on the ground in Rwanda and Burundi and in the headquarters in New York and Geneva.

On 14 December 1960, the General Assembly passed the Soviet-initiated Declaration on the Granting of Independence to Colonial Countries and Peoples, a ringing call for the "speedy and unconditional end to colonialism," which would lead to the establishment of human rights, including self-determination. Many delegates no doubt thought of Belgium when they affirmatively proclaimed that "inadequacy of political, economic, social or educational preparedness should never serve as a pretext for delaying independence." And Belgium was certainly among those targeted by article 5: "Immediate steps shall be taken, in Trust and Non-Self-Governing Territories or all other territories which have not yet attained independence, to transfer all powers to the people of those territories without any conditions or reservations . . . without any distinction as to race, creed or colour, in order to enable them to enjoy complete independence and freedom."[21]

Less than one week later, on 20 December 1960, the General Assembly passed another resolution that ordered Belgium to prepare its trusteeships for independence and mandated elections on the basis of universal adult suffrage. The resolution specifically called for the establishment of a unitary state.[22] On 21 April 1961 yet another resolution sharply condemned Belgium for moving slowly and seeking to manipulate the situation so it could maintain its influence.[23]

Belgium tried to undermine the UN, but it could not frontally resist its directives, another sign of the power of the international organization in those days. Responding to UN pressure, Belgium authorized elections in Rwanda and Burundi, which finally took place in September 1961. In Rwanda, the major Tutsi party obtained only 16.8 percent of the vote, while Parmehutu won 77.7 percent. In a referendum, the electorate chose a republic over a constitutional monarchy. Parmehutu felt justified in taking complete power, while Tutsi anxieties became ever deeper. In Burundi, the National Unity and Progress Party (Uprona) won over 80 percent of the vote. Prince Rwagasore, the eldest son of the king and an advocate for unity among Hutus and Tutsis, led Uprona. For the time being, Burundi was to remain a monarchy, albeit one in which the king's powers would be sharply limited.

In January 1962, just a few months after the elections, Belgium's foreign minister (and deputy prime minister) Paul-Henri Spaak appeared before the General Assembly. Spaak had a long career in Belgian politics—foreign minister for eighteen years, from 1939 when the government was in exile to 1966—and in the international socialist movement. He played a major role in the formation of what ultimately became the European Union. For all of these activities, Spaak remains a revered figure in Belgium today and is honored by the EU as one of its founders, a Belgian counterpart to the Frenchman Jean Monnet. Spaak was, nonetheless, a colonialist, as was virtually every other major Belgian politician. When he could no longer prevent the independence of Rwanda and Burundi, he sought various ways to maintain Belgian influence in the region.

Spaak claimed that Belgium was committed to leaving Rwanda and Burundi "in good conditions" and to providing substantial economic, financial, and technical assistance as its trustees became independent.[24] Much like Lord Peel's rendering of the British situation in Palestine, Spaak portrayed Belgium as the great innocent, the honest broker who was powerless in the face of the antipathy between the two communities.[25] He claimed to support the unity of Rwanda and Burundi, even though Belgium had quite deliberately administered the two as separate territories and had fostered racial identifications. The reality of Belgium's role was still more nefarious, as we shall soon see.

It is no surprise that Spaak felt very much on the defensive. Just one week prior to his speech, Majid Rahnema, the UN commissioner for

Ruanda-Urundi, had presented a devastating attack on Belgium on the floor of the General Assembly. He charged Belgium with trying to undermine the resolution that called for its withdrawal from the territories. He argued that a composite feudal-colonial exploitation of the country existed, but it did not run along ethnic or racial lines. A small group of "feudal" Tutsis allied with Belgian colonizers exploited the masses, Hutu, Tutsi, and Twa alike.[26] He suggested that Belgium deliberately fostered ethnic conflict. "The great majority of Tutsi," Rahnema argued, "in spite of their impressive height and aristocratic past, were in the same unfavourable situation as the great mass of the Hutu." All Hutus and Tutsis, with the exception of a very small minority who benefitted from their power positions, aspired to a better life and wished to rid themselves of the double yoke of feudalism and colonialism.[27]

Rahnema did not spare Parmehutu. He charged that Belgium's sudden decision to give every possible support to the leaders of Parmehutu resulted in its "rapid strengthening" and "the systematic elimination of all opposition claiming to be nationalist, all this accompanied by an increasingly hostile policy towards the Tutsi."[28] Keeping up the attack, Rahnema claimed that Parmehutu, with Belgian collusion, exercised near-dictatorial powers. It intimidated the opposition, often with violence, and made Tutsis en masse, rather than the feudal-colonial system, the enemy.[29]

Rahnema was much closer to the mark than Spaak with his hapless assertion of Belgian innocence and its supposed lack of power. Rahnema was also chillingly prescient: "The real problems created by the present tension are much more serious. . . . [They] may result either in the gradual extermination of the majority of the Tutsi population, or it may at any moment degenerate into violence and, possibly, civil war."[30]

৵৩

"Never will we say to the people elect this Tutsi because he is Tutsi, or elect this Hutu because he is Hutu!" declaimed Louis Rwagasore. He called for the emancipation of the masses, a mass that is "neither Tutsi nor Hutu: it is Burundian [*murundi*]."[31]

Rwagasore was the one leading political figure who offered a bracing alternative to the racial politics that had emerged and would define the situation in the two countries down to the present day (see figure 10.3). As in Palestine under the British mandate, moderates there were among Hutus and Tutsis in Rwanda and Burundi—people who advocated domestic unity and a single state. In Rwanda they could gain no traction. Kayibanda and other Parmehutu leaders knew that by invoking race, they had a powerful mobilizing tool. In Burundi the situation was, at first, more hopeful. The political divides initially were not so much about race but factional struggles between royal clans. Uprona, Rwagasore's party, had triumphed at the polls in September 1961 on the basis of a program that espoused unity among Hutus and Tutsis and a regional confederation with Tanganyika.

In Prince Rwagasore, Uprona had a powerful, charismatic leader.[32] He was of royal lineage and a Tutsi, yet his politics went far beyond the defense of privilege. As a young man in the early 1950s, Rwagasore had been sent to Belgium for advanced education. In various interviews around this time, he evinced a moderate and respectful, often obsequious tone toward the Belgian authorities, even claiming that they treated blacks the same as Europeans.[33]

As the decade advanced, Rwagasore became far more radical, far more impatient with the Belgian authorities. Within three years, he accused them of a "lack of honesty" in their dealings with Burundians, which threatened to result in a profound, destructive schism in the country.[34] In accordance with Bunche and others at the UN, Rwagasore began to berate Belgium for its achingly slow response to the demands for decolonization. He accused the authorities of meddling in the internal politics of both countries in a desire to maintain their influence after independence. Rwagasore charged that the Belgian switch to support of the Hutus marked a typical divide-and-rule policy. Belgium, he argued, wants to maintain the population "under a painful and socially unjust yoke" that "paralyzes the economic, social, and cultural life of the nation."[35]

Rwagasore joined Julius Nyerere, the leader of Tanganyika and his mentor, in advocating independence, Pan-Africanism, and socialism. The Belgians grew alarmed. Even more so when Rwagasore spearheaded the establishment of cooperatives, his version of socialism, and sought

FIGURE 10.3 Prince Louis Rwagasore, circa 1960. Rwagasore (1932–61) was the eldest son of the Burundian *mwami* (king) Mwambutsa IV. The family was Tutsi. Educated partly in Belgium, Rwagasore became increasingly radical over the course of the 1950s. He advocated unity among Tutsis and Hutus, national independence, socialism, and Pan-Africanism. He led Uprona, the National Union and Progress Party, which triumphed resoundingly in the first elections held in Burundi. On that basis he became Burundi's prime-minister-designate in advance of national independence. Three weeks later, he was assassinated, almost certainly with the connivance of Belgian security forces. (Musée royal de l'Afrique centrale. HP.2001.20.18–18, collection RMCA Tervuren; unknown photographer, s.d.)

support and financing for them from nationalist leaders elsewhere in Africa and the Middle East.[36] The Belgians went on endlessly about the dangers of Soviet influence in Africa, although scant evidence existed of Soviet involvement in Rwanda and Burundi.[37] This was, however, the era of the Cold War, and Belgian charges won the country support from the United States.

Belgium, if it could not actually hold on to its overseas possessions, at least sought to retain preponderant influence in Congo, Rwanda, and Burundi. Rwagasore's cooperatives were most certainly an effort to diminish if not completely abolish the power of Belgian and other Western companies that operated in the country. Cooperatives, Rwagasore claimed, would promote economic and social development in a humane, equitable, and just fashion.[38] They would lie at the basis of the entire East African economy, a Common-Market-type system, but one based in socialist rather than capitalist production.

In his speeches and writings in the early years, Rwagasore mentioned only rarely the different ethnic groups in Rwanda and Burundi. When he did, it was only to reject the substance of the labels "Hutus" and "Tutsis" in favor of national unity.[39] No doubt the force of politics, the racial mobilizations under way in both countries, compelled him to face the issue more directly. The problems in the country, poverty and injustice, he proclaimed another time, are most certainly not those of race. Burundi only needs the opportunity that other nations have had, independence, self-determination, and human rights. Any regime that refuses the essential rights of all the peoples of Burundi will disappear, for "that is the march of history."[40] With sweeping rhetoric, he claimed that Burundi had embarked on the path of a true revolution. With its victory, the Burundian *mwami* (king) will be able to cry out like the Persian king Cyrus, "I am king of a country with numerous races. I have entered Babylon without spilling blood, without pillage, without killing, and to all *I have given security and joy.*"[41] Another time Rwagasore proclaimed that "all the citizens of the country should have the same rights and the same duties."[42] In Rwanda and Burundi around 1960, these were radical statements indeed—and oceans removed from the overt racialism of the *Hutu Manifesto*.

On the basis of Uprona's sweeping electoral victory in September 1961, Rwagasore became Burundi's prime-minister-designate under a constitutional monarchy. He began moving the country toward independence. Three weeks later, on 13 October 1961, he was assassinated. A Greek national working for the rival Christian Democratic Party pulled the trigger. There is little doubt that Belgian officials collaborated in and perhaps ordered the killing.[43]

Rwagasore's death came nine months after the execution of another, independent-minded African leader, Patrice Lumumba, and one month after the plane crash that killed UN Secretary-General Dag Hammarskjöld in what was most likely another assassination. Lumumba and Rwagasore were trying to move their countries in a Pan-African and somewhat socialist direction. They would have sharply curtailed the activities and profits of Western companies. Each also sought to create a unified national movement that included all of the various ethnic groups in the respective countries. Hammarskjöld was trying to negotiate a settlement of the internal conflict in Congo that would have kept some of Lumumba's allies in power.

One can only speculate whether the crises that have bedeviled the Congo, Rwanda, and Burundi ever since could have been surmounted or at least moderated had Lumumba, Rwagasore, and Hammarskjöld lived. Perhaps surrounded by two countries with more inclusive rather than radically exclusive politics and a socialist-based economy, Grégoire Kayibanda, the Rwandan leader, might have been compelled to moderate his pro-Hutu position. Perhaps.

In any case, the assassination of Prince Rwagasore was a huge blow. It is rare that one individual—or three if one counts Lumumba and Hammarskjöld—can shift the course of history. But in this very tense, highly conflictual situation in the run-up to independence, Rwagasore was the one leading person advocating unity, the single figure who had a large following among Hutus and Tutsis. He strove to protect Burundi from the descent into racial violence that already marked Rwanda. Moreover, he advocated a real social revolution, not a sham one like Parmehutu's in Rwanda, which simply replaced one elite with another.

And that was precisely the problem. Serious social reform or revolution, unity rather than racial division—neither Parmehutu nor many Tutsis nor the Belgians nor the American Central Intelligence Agency (CIA), with whom the Belgians worked closely in Congo, could tolerate this vision. So Rwagasore was killed. His Uprona party remained in power, but, without the much-beloved prince in the leadership, it lacked the ability to move the country forward in a democratic manner. One of Rwagasore's Uprona successors, the Hutu Pierre Ngendandumwe, tried. He began a second term as prime minister in early 1965. Then he too was assassinated, probably again with the complicity of Belgium. From that point began the racialization of politics in Burundi, including the evolution of Uprona into an authoritarian, Tutsi-exclusive party.[44] Although Tutsis comprised a numerical minority, as in Rwanda, they held on to the institutions of power, especially the army, which soon became an agent for the worst kind of violence against those defined as outside the national and racial community.

Amid all these conflicts, the UN strove valiantly to maintain the peace and protect endangered communities. Despite the brave face they put on developments, UN staffers were overwhelmed by the recurring cycles of violence and the huge refugee flows. Publicly, the UN proudly proclaimed its efforts to support and resettle refugees. Privately, staff members were anguished about the situation. Even before independence, one UN staffer on the ground reported back to UN headquarters: "Government as well as opposition have reported to Commission that they wish withdrawal of Belgian troops and do not want any foreign troops nor United Nations forces in territory. I cannot help thinking that they want absence of any kind of troops in order to be able to exterminate each other, both sides hoping to be winners."[45]

Battered on all sides, the UN abandoned the hope for a unitary state and caved in to the reality of racial politics. An independent, Hutu-dominated, Rwanda and an independent, Tutsi-dominated, Burundi came into being on 1 July 1962.

Nearly two months later, at the very end of August, a simple, sober telegram from Taghi Nasr, the major UN official on the ground, belied the momentous nature of the event and the intense political wrangling that had preceded it. "DC-3 departed 29 August. This completes with-drawal and evacuation of all Belgian military forces from Rwanda and Burundi."[46]

Belgium was gone. But independence hardly marked the end of the story. Belgium scurried around in an effort to retain influence, while UN officials in 1963 and 1964, shortly after the founding of the states, and in subsequent years scrambled to contain a very dangerous situation involving cross-border incursions, war between the two countries, and additional refugee streams.[47] Well-informed UN staff members monitored carefully the various political parties and developments, always on the lookout for the "constructive elements" with whom they could work.[48] The tone of their reports was sometimes naively optimistic (at least in hindsight), but more often quite sober in their assessment of the difficulties ahead.[49]

Burundi and Rwanda traded charges, each accusing the other of provoking war and carrying out large-scale atrocities; each claiming that spies ran free while pretending to be refugees. Each state claimed to be acting on the basis of the UN Charter and the UDHR; each charged the other with colluding with imperialists and neocolonialists with the goal of undermining, dividing, and ruling the country.[50]

In a 1964 report to UN Secretary-General U Thant, the Rwandan government, dominated by Parmehutu, condemned the "terrorism" of the Tutsi paramilitaries, whom it labeled "*inyenzi*," or cockroaches. The "racist and feudal" system that had prevailed in Rwanda went back four hundred years to the Tutsi invasion and put the Hutu population in a "heavy yoke, cruel and without hope."[51] The "feudal race" was another term for Tutsis in the twenty-five-page document, along with other choice words and phrases that condemned Tutsis in toto for their "cruelty," "duplicity," and "absence of scruples." The government proclaimed that "the instruments of domination and imperialism" deployed by Tutsis were only rivaled by Caligula and Nero, and described Tutsi actions as "the most savage terrorism."[52] The Rwandan government issued a few rhetorical concessions concerning loyal Tutsis, but generally applied Belgian-derived racial categories to attack Tutsis in toto.

Here was the worst kind of political rhetoric, an absolute denial of any wrongdoing on the part of the government and the identification of an entire people as the enemy, the precise opposite of the recognition of the other that underpins every human rights claim. Another generation of Hutu extremists, in 1994, would revive the same, highly exclusive language.

The UN could not escape the dire situation. Pressure mounted on it to intervene, in part from officials in its own agencies like UNESCO. Bunche, however, maintained that the Security Council could only act on request from a member state, and none had been received from Burundi or Rwanda.[53]

A. J. Lucas, the major UN official stationed in Bujumbura and generally an informed observer, doubted that the violence against Hutus in Burundi had been ordered by the government. But he thought that the major Tutsi political party might be operating under its own rules. "The hills have returned to their secrets and no foreigner has access to them," he wrote to Bunche.[54]

The UN confronted a huge refugee problem. Officials estimated in 1964 that over the previous five years, some sixty thousand Tutsis had fled Rwanda just for the Kivu province in the Congo, and there were at least twenty-five thousand more in Burundi.[55] The official UNHCR refugee camps were overwhelmed, even though many Rwandans tried to settle with family or friends. Refugees provided a source of discontent and of recruits for rebel armies. Ongoing political instability in the capitals, Kigali and Bujumbura, only worsened the situation.[56] UN officials recognized that some refugees had taken up arms, but more often they were victims of the crisscrossing armed political movements. Many were "living in pitiful conditions."[57] Somewhat desperately, the UN air-dropped leaflets, calling on the refugees to stay neutral and avoid all political involvement, the condition for their asylum status in the Congo.[58] The Congolese government tried to expel the refugees, but UNHCR managed to negotiate a pause. UN officials worried about how they would resettle refugees back home in Rwanda—repatriation the stated goal of UNHCR—when, in fact, people were still fleeing the country.[59]

The UN hoped that its program of resettlement would be the "final chapter" in its efforts to support Rwandan refugees in Burundi. UNHCR involved the ILO and the Lutheran World Federation in its efforts.[60] Together, they hoped to find homes for ten thousand refugees in Tanganyika from the Congo, in addition to the ten thousand they had already moved there from Burundi.[61] But the Burundian government claimed that under its international obligations it could not forcibly remove people, and reports were coming in about the difficulties of transporting refugees. Congo had agreed to expel only those involved in rebellion, while Rwanda placed on trial and executed as rebels those extradited from Tanganyika—making repatriation ever more improbable.[62]

In some regions the refugees matched or outnumbered the indigenous population. Hence, any efforts to relieve the refugees' conditions had to involve the locals as well in projects that were typical of the development ethos of the day.[63] UNHCR noted in regard to Tutsis under its protection in Burundi:

> Although [the refugees] have an understandable nostalgia for their native land [Rwanda], they appear to be realising more and more clearly that their best hope lies in settling in Burundi and that, as a result, they must do all they can to make the plan succeed. The setbacks recently suffered by those who tried to fight their way back into Rwanda will probably have an effect on their attitudes as well. . . .
>
> Furthermore, it is obvious that the economic and social development of the area where refugees are living must, in no circumstances, aim at creating small, isolated, self-sufficient units. On the contrary, the objective must be to make the development centres inter-dependent so that they are forced to rely on each other. This in turn will help to create a lasting community spirit.[64]

But that "community spirit" would only be of Tutsis. In that way, the UN, reluctantly, tragically, became party to the ethnic cleansing that both countries pursued.

Publicly, once again, the UN touted the success of its resettlement efforts. Internal correspondence reveals that UN officials often felt inundated and overburdened by the depth of the crisis and recognized how difficult it was to isolate humanitarian efforts from ongoing political conflicts, a huge problem that would become only greater in the subsequent decades.[65]

All through the 1960s, UNHCR struggled unsuccessfully to contain the refugee situation.[66] Felix Schnyder, the high commissioner for refugees, wrote in December 1964 that despite some success in consolidating the settlement of Rwandan refugees, he remained seriously worried about another twenty-five thousand who were unsettled and eking out an existence in the border region. He argued that it was a serious mistake to settle any refugees near boundary lines, where they became easy targets for agitators.[67] Other UN officials chimed in, worried about the "persecution" of Tutsis and the progressive disintegration of the economy in Rwanda.[68] While the overt attacks on Tutsis might have stopped, "they are submitted to threats and persecutions and practically live in a state of terror (this is even true of Tutsi employees working in Kigali)."[69] Kayibanda accused UN officials of acting as spies.[70] *Le Monde* headlined "Extermination of the Tutsis: The Massacres in Rwanda are the Manifestation of a Carefully Cultivated Racial Hatred."[71] Under the headline ran a long letter from a Belgian teacher employed by UNESCO. The teacher had resigned his position, saying he could no longer work for a government "responsible for and complicit with a genocide." He charged the international community in the country with "indifference and passivity." Some of his own students had been killed solely because they were Tutsi. He would not be the last to write such a plaintive plea.

UN staffer Osorio-Tafall wrote in even more explicit terms. In a telegram to Bunche about Rwandan refugees in the Congo, he stated that the displaced Tutsis were considered

> a dangerous fifth column by provincial authorities and there are many good reasons to support belief that some at least actively support and fight on behalf of rebels. Situation in Central Kivu is so serious that presence of Tutsi refugees, particularly in areas near Rwanda border, constitutes a source of peril that provincial authorities and security forces can hardly ignore when future of governments both provincial and central are at stake. Government in these circumstances would have to take very strict measures to control refugees.[72]

He argued that it was unfeasible to integrate the Rwandan Tutsis in Congo with the local population because of the general hostility toward refugees. He reiterated Schnyder's point that it was a mistake to settle refugees along the border, and advocated moving them farther afield to Uganda, Burundi, and Tanganyika.[73]

All the problems were exacerbated by the emergence in Burundi of an extremist Hutu party that echoed Rwanda's Parmehutu. In October 1965 Hutu officers attempted to carry out a coup. The Tutsi-led army responded ferociously, killing virtually all the Hutu political and military elite in Burundi. Across the country, radical Hutus carried out massacres of Tutsis. Ultimately, the army proved able to stabilize the situation, typically with the use of excessive force.[74]

Then, in 1972, in another effort at total domination, the Tutsi-led government carried out a genocide of Hutus in Burundi. The army, with the collaboration of some Tutsi citizens, killed about two hundred thousand Hutus. Another three hundred thousand fled to Tanzania, Rwanda, and elsewhere. Both the killings and the new round of forced removals are little known outside the country, at the time and ever since. Factional and regional conflicts among Tutsis, with various groups vying for domination, made the killings still more virulent. For years afterward, the state completely barred Hutus from governmental administration, higher education, and the military.[75]

Twenty-two years later, in 1994, an even greater disaster erupted in Rwanda. Journalists rushed to the scene. Many first had to learn who were the Hutus and Tutsis, and even where the country was located. The photos and articles they dispatched evoked shock and horror, and rightly so. Within three months, Hutu Power, in many ways Parmehutu's successor, had caused the killings of eight hundred thousand Tutsis and moderate Hutus. Had journalists and other observers known just a little history, they would have understood that the horrific events of 1994 were by no means the first in the Great Lakes region.

And they might have realized that massacres, if not quite genocide, were already under way in neighboring Burundi. Most accounts of the Rwandan Genocide begin with the assassination of Rwanda's President Juvénal Habyarimana—his plane shot down on the night of 6 April 1994. Rarely mentioned is that Burundi's President Cyprien Ntaryamira was also on board and he too was killed. The two countries' destinies have always been linked, as they were once again on that fateful night.

Responsibility for the assassination remains disputed, despite a series of official inquiries and journalistic investigations. It might have been Hutu extremists, or members of Paul Kagame's Tutsi-dominated Rwandan Patriotic Front (RPF). Each group sought to derail international negotiations and establish its own primacy.[76]

In any case, Burundi had already entered a phase of genocidal violence the preceding fall, when the Tutsi-led army carried out a coup against the country's first democratically elected (in June 1993) and first Hutu president, Melchior Ndadaye. Ndadaye and two colleagues, one Tutsi, the other Hutu, were executed, the first victims in yet another tidal wave of violence. Ndadaye had taken steps to bring other Hutus into the leadership ranks of the state and army. His government held out the promise of cooperation between Hutu and Tutsi moderates, which is precisely why those committed to exclusive Tutsi domination eliminated him. Following his execution, Hutus in many parts of the country took their vengeance against Tutsi civilians in brutal pogroms, the memories of 1972 still strongly held and cultivated by Hutu political leaders. Tutsi-led army units responded in kind. The country plunged into a sixteen-year civil war that left some three hundred thousand dead.[77] As Human Rights Watch reported, "the civil war in Burundi is above all else a war against civilians."[78]

The specific events leading to the Rwandan Genocide began in October 1990 when the RPF invaded the country from neighboring Uganda.[79] Its leader, Paul Kagame, is the perfect exemplar of the troubled history of the Great Lakes region. He had grown up among other Tutsis in a refugee camp in Uganda and had achieved a high position in the Ugandan army. Uganda's government, in an effort to extend its influence, decided to support Tutsi forces seeking to reclaim a position of dominance in their homeland. Kagame's closest colleagues and many of the rank and file in the RPF had also grown up in refugee camps. Many, also like Kagame, had served in the Ugandan army. Violence, not human rights, was their way of life from an early age.

The RPF's invasion of Rwanda unleashed a civil war. The ensuing instability, marked by killings; renewed refugee streams; and all sorts of violent conflicts within and among Uganda, Congo, and Tanzania worried the international community. As in other histories discussed in this book, from Greece to Korea, local conflicts drew in outside states, great and minor. France, the United States, and the Organization of African Unity convened negotiations in Arusha, Tanzania. The Arusha Accords, signed on 4 August 1993, provided for a ceasefire; power sharing among the different Rwandan parties; and a commitment from all sides to abide by the rule of law, repatriate refugees, and hold free and fair elections. The Accords also provided for a UN peacekeeping force, staffed mainly by Belgians.

President Habyarimana had been in office since 1973, when he led a coup against Rwanda's first president, the Parmehutu founder Grégoire Kayibanda. In an effort to hold on to exclusive power, Habyarimana blocked implementation of the Arusha Accords, which necessitated further negotiations. For that reason he traveled again to Arusha in April 1994, when he was assassinated. Whoever launched the missiles that shot down the plane, Hutu Power immediately made use of the crisis to launch a genocide. The UN peacekeeping force was completely overwhelmed, even though its commander, the Canadian general Roméo Dallaire, had wired back to the UN headquarters in New York warning of an impending genocide and pleading for more troops and arms. His pleas went unheeded.[80] Some eight hundred thousand Tutsis and moderate Hutus were killed in three months.

Kagame's RPF resumed the fighting. By July 1994 his forces had taken control of virtually the entire country. By seizing power in Rwanda, the RPF halted the genocide. And it set off another huge refugee stream. Around two million Hutus, fearing their fate in a Tutsi-led Rwanda, fled across the borders to Tanzania, Uganda, and Congo. Fate did, however, catch up to many of them. In the ensuing years the RPF crossed the borders, entered the refugee camps, and slaughtered hundreds of thousands of Hutus. Many of the UN refugee camps were, in fact, run by remnants of Hutu Power and the Hutu government that had carried out the genocide. They were armed and carried out military incursions in Rwanda, providing Kagame with justification for the involvement of the Rwandan military forces in the neighboring countries, all the while engaging in war crimes and crimes against humanity.[81]

Since these events of the early 1990s, the politics of the Great Lakes region have become only more complex.[82] Political alignments come and go. Heavily armed paramilitaries operate at will. Countless efforts at negotiations have failed. The level of sexual violence against women has been of horrendous, almost indescribable proportions. Competition for diamonds and precious metals in Congo has elevated conflicts even beyond the violent state in which they previously existed. Rwanda under Kagame is an island of stability and a darling of international development agencies. But Kagame presides over a dictatorial regime that has achieved economic growth and human development at the cost of major human rights violations within the country and wherever the Rwandan army has ventured in the neighboring states.

Burundi, meanwhile, is still emerging from the effects of its sixteen-year civil war. The recourse to violence as a political strategy emerged once again in 2015 when the president, Pierre Nkurunziza, reversed his previous stand and announced he would run for a third term. Street fighting broke out and security forces engaged in widespread human rights violations, leading the UN Human Rights Council to assert that there were "reasonable grounds" to believe that the government was engaged in crimes against humanity.[83]

The overall figures for the Great Lakes region are staggering (see tables 10.1 and 10.2): nearly three million refugees just up to 1994, and somewhere over five million deaths by 2006. And these figures are probably low. Certainly, many more refugees have been created since 1994 as the Great Lakes region has descended into unending warfare. Nor do these figures account for the staggering incidence of sexual violence against women. The chasms between populations along with a dizzying array of parties, armies, and paramilitaries across the five countries of the Great Lakes region has resulted in the greatest humanitarian and human rights catastrophe of the late twentieth and twenty-first centuries.

TABLE 10.1 Refugees in the Great Lakes Region, 1959–95

Year	Number	Group	Country of Origin	Explanation
1959–63	150–200,000	Tutsi	Rwanda	Parmehutu victory
1972	300,000	Hutu	Burundi	Tutsi military coup
1993	400,000	Hutu	Burundi	Assassination of first Hutu president of Burundi, Melchior Ndadaye
1994	2,000,000	Hutu	Rwanda	RPF victory
1995	200,000	Hutu	Rwanda	RPF victory

Source: Lemarchand, *Dynamics of Violence*, 36–37.

TABLE 10.2 Excess Deaths in the Great Lakes Region, 1963–2006

Year	Number	Group	Country of Origin	Explanation
1963–66	14,000	Hutus and Tutsis	Congo, Rwanda, Burundi	Congolese nationalism
1972	100–200,000	Hutus	Burundi	Genocide perpetrated by Burundi government
1993	40,000	Hutus and Tutsis	Burundi	Assassination of first Hutu president of Burundi, Melchior Ndadaye
1994	600–800,000	Tutsis	Rwanda	Genocide perpetrated by Rwandan government
1994	25–45,000	Hutus	Rwanda	Killings by RPF
1998–2006	4,000,000	Various	Congo	Multiple wars and killings

Sources: Lemarchand, *Dynamics of Violence*, 14, 31–32, 71–72, and Human Rights Watch, "The Rwandan Patriotic Front," Human Rights Watch, report, 1999, last modified 19 July 2017, https://www.hrw.org/reports/1999/rwanda/Geno15-8-03.htm.

Conclusion

For some young Burundians, 1972 marked the first time that they encountered their own identity. Samson Gahungu, a Hutu who had just finished his teacher training at the time, later remarked: "I discovered I was of a certain ethnic group because they started taking people to prison." Jean-Marie Nibizi, of a mixed family, was even more direct: "I did not know about the existence of ethnic groups till 1972 when they killed people."[84] Some Tutsis who gave shelter to Hutus in 1972 were later saved, during another round of persecutions in 1993, by the families they earlier had protected.[85] Many Rwandans offered similar stories. Only when they were older did they hear the terms Hutu, Tutsi, and Twa; many Hutu and Tutsi intermarried; others became friends. As one Hutu told an interviewer: "Since 1959 there were Hutu who made blood pacts [drinking one another's blood, an act that sealed friendship] with Tutsi. . . . They did everything to protect their Tutsi friends and their belongings. . . . My father had a Tutsi friend whom he had made a blood pact with and at the time of events, he hid him with his entire family and their belongings, including the cows."[86] Many more Hutu participated in killings than saved their friends; many turned on their neighbors, even on their Tutsi wives. Still, these stories warn us from presuming that everyone in a group marched in lockstep when intercommunal racial killings destroyed so many lives.

The commune of Rumonge in Rwanda experienced terrible violence in 1972. In 1993 and 1994, local leaders and regular people, Hutus and Tutsis, worked together and maintained the peace—for a while. They did so not because of human rights as a set of worked-out ideas, but out of fear that violence would consume all of them if one or another group initiated attacks. Nonetheless, their actions demonstrated a commitment to the values that characterize human rights. Hutu elders, priests, and political officials held meetings counseling peace and brought the two communities together in markets and at parties. Local Hutus even established productive working relations with Tutsi army commanders. Sometimes the locals intervened when others of their group were on the march to attack Tutsi families. One local political leader faced down fifty armed Hutus on their way to kill Tutsis.

> I asked if they had confidence in me. They said yes. So I said, "Then don't kill the Tutsis. The Tutsis who killed the president were in Bujumbura. The Tutsis here stayed here. They didn't kill the president, so you shouldn't kill them." Afterwards, they went home. . . . If I had been indifferent, if I had let those Hutus kill the Tutsis—okay, the Tutsis would have been killed, but then the Hutus would also [subsequently] have been killed.[87]

Similarly in Rwanda some local leaders were able, at least for a time, to maintain cohesion among the different communities. These local efforts bought a reprieve. But the flood-tide of violence emanating from the center of politics and roaming military bands soon overwhelmed Rumonge and other areas in Rwanda. Hutu rebels from outside the commune disrupted the fragile peace that the local populace had constructed.

Still, these local initiatives and memories demonstrate that race is *learned*. Similarly, human rights can be *learned*. Race as a basis for political mobilization is an option, not a predetermined outcome. As a way of understanding human difference, race is one of a range of possibilities. For political elites, the easiest and oftentimes most successful strategy is to mobilize populations on the basis of racial or national identities. It is a simple matter, one that resonates loudly, to claim that those who share the same language, culture, and appearance partake of the same destiny, while the outsider is the source of all the woes to which the individual and group have been subjected. The proponents of race are radical simplifiers; they reduce the complexities of human experiences and identities to one, supposedly inheritable marker that bears all the characteristics of either virtue or debasement. When those views are ensconced in the state, then life gets truly dangerous for those considered beyond the pale, and even those members of the dominant group who advocate a more moderate course or have chosen to intermarry.[88] Not only do they lose the right to have rights; in the most extreme cases, they lose the right to their very lives.

None of this violence—the creation of huge refugee streams; the killings from genocides, near genocides, and warfare; deliberate maimings; and sexual exploitation—was inevitable. But by depicting every single member of a group as an existential threat, racial politics as practiced by both Rwanda and Burundi increased the likelihood of mass atrocities.[89] The impact of the killings at certain moments—Rwanda in 1959–61, 1963–64, 1973, and 1994; Burundi in 1965, 1972, 1988, 1993–2009—deeply etched people's memories, shaping their anxieties for the future, defining their friendships and those whom they feared to encounter. Very often, killers and survivors lived side by side, thinking thoughts that could not be spoken.[90]

The Belgian colonizers, by racializing identities, helped create the disasters that have ensued since 1959. But Hutu and Tutsi elites in both countries absorbed and radicalized their Belgian inheritance.[91] Almost any time a leading figure advocated cooperation across the Hutu-Tutsi divide, he was eliminated, in the early years with Belgian complicity, as in the case of Louis Rwagasore. The UN made great efforts to ensure a peaceful and humane transition, but the driving force of racial politics overpowered its efforts.

Rwanda and Burundi present the picture of a decolonization and development policy gone sadly awry. Bunche and his associates expected that the path they promoted would lead almost naturally to the institutionalization of human rights in the newly independent countries. But their hopes were countered by the same problem that has stalked the advocates of nation-states and human rights all over the world: Who constitutes the people? Who, in reality, can become rights-bearing citizens? With a few exceptions like Prince Rwagasore, Hutu and Tutsi activists built on Belgian practices and gave an exclusive, racial answer to that question. They were able to counter the international community's initial commitment to a unitary state and instead promoted each state as an expression of one race, Hutu or Tutsi, in the process creating millions of refugees and unnecessary deaths. These refugee camps, with so many people living in dire straits, barely existing, while paramilitaries exercised great power, were anything but training grounds for democracy and human rights.

The community leaders who staved off the violence in Rumonge and the Burundians who protected their neighbors did not recite the UDHR. Their actions, nonetheless, were consonant with the meaning of human rights. At their very least, human rights mean that no one should be deprived of the resources of existence, of their very lives, simply by virtue of their national or racial identity. And they also mean that those who violate these norms should be held accountable. Racial politics as practiced in Rwanda and Burundi underscore the bracing importance of human rights. However imperfectly implemented, human rights at least demand a world in which millions of people do not have to suffer extreme violence and displacement.

After World War II, activists, individual states, and the international community sought to create such a world, one in which everyone—no matter his or her nationality, race, or gender—can exercise human rights, while those who violate these norms are subject to accountability. These are the themes to which we turn in the conclusion.

Conclusion

Nation-States and Human Rights

THE TWENTY-FIRST CENTURY AND BEYOND

℘

IN 1941, a young Nelson Mandela was finding his way toward a life of political commitment. "I had no epiphany," he wrote years later in his memoir, "no single revelation no moment of truth, but a steady accumulation of a thousand slights a thousand indignities . . . produced in me an anger, a rebelliousness, a desire to fight the system that imprisoned my people." He would devote himself to the "liberation of my people" (see figure Concl.1).[1]

One moment of revelation came when Mandela heard the news of the Atlantic Charter. In August 1941, Prime Minister Winston Churchill and President Franklin Delano Roosevelt met on board ship off Newfoundland. The United States was not yet a belligerent in World War II (though all that would change four months later with the Japanese attack on Pearl Harbor). Nonetheless, the two leaders were already envisaging a post-Nazi, post–Imperial Japanese world. The Atlantic Charter that they signed promised a future of self-determination and democracy for all peoples. "[Great Britain and the United States] respect the right of all peoples to choose the form of government under which they will live; and they wish to see sovereign rights and self government restored to those who have been forcibly deprived of them."[2]

Mandela believed that Churchill and Roosevelt were talking to him. "Some in the West saw the charter as empty promises, but not those of us in Africa."[3] They were, instead, inspired. In response, the ANC issued its own charter, which called for full citizenship for all Africans, the right to purchase land, and the revocation of discriminatory laws. A democratic South Africa, freed from white domination and with human rights available to all, would be the future—and it would not be far away, Mandela believed. All South Africans, whatever their skin color and

FIGURE CONCL.1 Nelson Mandela, circa 1950. Mandela (1918–2013) was born into a royal Xhosa family and became an icon of democracy and human rights. Trained as a lawyer, he joined the anti-apartheid movement while still a young man. For decades he led the ANC, despite his twenty-seven-year confinement in prison. Continued resistance by black Africans and international isolation eventually caused the destruction of apartheid. Mandela became the first president of a newly free South Africa and served from 1994 to 1999. Here, he is shown as a young man in traditional garb. (Photo by Eli Weinberg/Apic/Getty Images.)

background, would soon share in a postwar world of liberty and prosperity.[4]

A few years later, having just returned from negotiating the armistice to the First Arab-Israeli War, Ralph Bunche spoke informally to UN staff in New York. After regaling the audience with harrowing stories of the UN negotiating team dodging bullets, passing up sleep, scraping together the bare provisions that kept body (if not soul) together, he lauded the effort to bring peace to the Middle East.

> This was a United Nations effort all the way. . . . We were able to bring together a completely heterogeneous secretariat, for the most part recruited haphazardly . . . involving many nationalities, and practically all of the people . . . had done no work on Palestine, and had certainly never expected to see Palestine. Yet, they were plumped down in this area, and under very unpleasant conditions. They were certainly not cordially received. . . . Within this situation, these people welded themselves together into as fine a team as the United Nations has ever had and . . . will ever have. . . . If this operation had produced results thus far—and it has produced results—it was because of this fine spirit.[5]

Bunche, already a veteran of the American civil rights movement, heralded the work of the UN as an agency for peace and human rights, the creator of a new world order that would surmount the injustices of the past.

In 1945, as a delegate from Brazil, Bertha Lutz participated in the founding conference of the UN in San Francisco (see figure Concl.2). She had behind her more than two decades of political experience as a pioneering Brazilian feminist. Now she was one of four women who would sign the UN Charter. Just as Bunche spearheaded the inclusion of decolonization in the mission of the UN, so Lutz led the drive to include the equality of women as a founding principle of the organization. The phrase in the preamble to the Charter that commits the UN to women's rights, to "faith in fundamental human rights, in the dignity of the human person, in the equal rights of men and women and of nations large and small," is a result of the pressure she exerted on the negotiations at San Francisco.[6]

FIGURE CONCL.2 Bertha Lutz, 1945. Lutz (1894–1976) was a pioneering Brazilian scientist and feminist. She founded in 1919 the Liga para a Emancipação Intelectual da Mulher (League for the Intellectual Emancipation of Woman). As a member of the Brazilian delegation to the founding conference of the UN, held in San Francisco in spring of 1945, she was one of only three women to sign the UN Charter. Lutz led the drive to include in the Charter language committing the UN to the equal rights of men and women. (UN Photo/Mili.)

The period since 1945, represented by these three activists, is the grand era of nation-states and human rights. It stands in sharp contrast to the world of empires and rulers around the eighteenth century with which this book began. Human rights were mere glimmers then, established first in the French, American, and Latin American revolutions. Many of those victories were short-lived. Napoleon and then the European empires defeated the French revolutionary claims for liberty. At Vienna in 1815, the Great Powers reestablished dynastic legitimacy as the reigning political principle. Latin American countries won their independence from Spain and Portugal, but became mired in deep-seated internal conflicts that did little to promote the cause of liberty. Brazil and the United States remained slave societies long into the nineteenth century, drastically compromising their espousal of liberalism and liberty. Empires and principalities dominated Asia; many of Africa's kingdoms had lost much of their luster even before the wave of European colonization in the late nineteenth century. Sub-Saharan Africa had largely fractured politically. Traditional understandings of a just order may have reigned in all these places, but nothing like a system of rights existed.

Over the course of the nineteenth and twentieth centuries, nation-states became the predominant political form around the globe. All their founders and advocates, in declarations of independence and constitutions, trumpeted their new countries as bastions of rights. The idea of human rights had arrived. Yet every chapter of this book has explored the cracks and fissures, the partiality of the human rights advances these states proclaimed. Every achievement, from slavery abolition to minority protection, from liberty for white settlers to independence from colonial rulers, had its underside in which some people, defined by their nationality or race, were denied or granted only very limited rights. Even with the greatest leaps out of oppression, like the emancipation from slavery, women were accorded, at best, second-class status or denied altogether the rights that men possessed.

Yet achievements there were, and they paved the way for the postwar era of nation-states and human rights. Mandela, Bunche, and Lutz expressed precisely the hopes and optimism of the era. All three had experienced in their lives great injustices and tragedies. They lived the reality of oppression in their own countries. They witnessed the monumental crimes committed by Nazi Germany and Imperial Japan, and, closer to home, the violence and humiliation of apartheid, lynchings, and military dictatorship. Yet Mandela, Lutz, and Bunche were buoyed by the prospect of creating a new world in which human rights would reign. Legal scholars, theologians, political leaders, resistance fighters in Asia and Europe, and local activists around the globe joined them. All clamored for a new world order that guaranteed democracy and human rights. They wrote treatises and issued proclamations, gathered in meetings and demonstrations, sent petitions to the centers of power. In a surge of activity that ran from around 1945 to 1952, people from the most diverse backgrounds and political orientations contributed to making human rights a predominant way of thinking and of structuring society and politics.[7]

None of this came easily. Mandela endured twenty-seven years in South African prisons because of his opposition to apartheid. Bunche's health and family life suffered greatly under the strains and pressures of his work as he sought to resolve endless crises from Palestine to Congo to Rwanda and Burundi. Despite his revered status within the UN and his decades-long activism for the civil rights of African-Americans, he found himself, toward the end of his life, castigated as an "Uncle Tom"—as I heard the Black Power activist Stokely Carmichael charge at an anti–Vietnam War demonstration in 1967. Lutz, an indefatigable organizer, could do little on behalf of women within her own country under Brazil's two dictatorships—of Getúlio Vargas, which ran from 1937 to 1945, and then under the military, which began in 1964 and lasted until 1985, three years after her death.

Mandela, Bunche, and Lutz, like so many others, operated at multiple levels. Each was a highly skilled diplomat able to move in the corridors of power. But each also retained close ties to popular organizations like the ANC; Southern Christian Leadership Conference; or Liga para a Emancipação Intelectual da Mulher (League for the Intellectual Emancipation of Woman), the organization founded by Lutz in 1919. They joined others in demonstrations, rallies, and court cases, and, in the case of Mandela, armed struggle. Bunche early in his life had some ties to communism, not all that extraordinary for an African-American activist in the 1930s; Mandela's ANC always had close links to the South African Communist Party. The legacies of socialism and communism as mass movements for justice remained strong in many parts of the world. They shaped and influenced the human rights movement despite the authoritarian and sometimes murderous policies of the Soviet-bloc states and the People's Republic of China.

The activism of these three underscores one of the central themes of this book: human rights advances emerge out of a confluence of popular struggles, state interests, and the workings of the international community. The resistance of Brazilian slaves contributed mightily to the abolition of slavery. The US Indian Civil Rights Act emerged from decades of American Indian activism. The collapse of the Soviet Union resulted from the human rights struggles of Andrei Sakharov, Larisa Bogoraz, and many others, whose actions deprived the reigning system of legitimacy. The examples are legion.

Yet never did activism in and of itself suffice. The Brazilian elite came to understand that their country would never be recognized as progressive and modern if it remained a bastion of slavery. Britain, France, and Russia feared ongoing instability in the Eastern Mediterranean so long as Greek rebels continued their fight for national independence. As a result, the Great Powers intervened and created the first post-Napoleonic, semi-sovereign state. Little did they think that they had sounded the death knell of European empires. Democracy in Korea came out of determined struggle on the part of South Koreans, but also acceptance by the United States—at long last, after its backing of authoritarian rulers—that continued support of a military dictatorship no longer served American interests. The confluence that promoted the founding of nation-states and human rights advances was often fragile and fleeting, but of great import when it occurred.

After 1945, the nation-state model spread to Africa, the Middle East, and Asia.[8] The European and Japanese national empires—those compact nation-states with colonies—found themselves shorn of their overseas possessions. Mass movements, from Zionism to the Congress Party in India to Parmehutu in Rwanda and Uprona in Burundi and many others, drove the effort to establish independent, sovereign nation-states. They reprised on a grander scale Greece in 1830, the Balkan states in 1878, and the nation-states founded after World War I at the Paris Peace Conference.

Anticolonial movements found major support at the UN, an organization whose breadth and depth surpassed any international association that preceded it. Its establishment marked a major departure in international politics. UN staff, not just the Security Council and General Assembly, played a significant role in fostering decolonization, independent nation-states, and human rights around the globe. Anticolonial movements mobilized upon the UN principles found in the Charter, the UDHR, and the later resolutions and covenants that proclaimed self-determination a right of all peoples. As in the past, new sovereign states could come to fruition only by great-power recognition. Often, as in the case of Greece, the Balkan states in 1878, and a host of others in 1919, it was grudgingly given. The UN, in contrast, backed new states with enthusiasm, whatever the hesitations of the colonial powers like France, Great Britain, Belgium, and Portugal, and the United States as well.

In the background of this flurry of new state foundings and human rights proclamations lay nearly two hundred years of intellectual and political ferment, starting with the revolutions of the late eighteenth century. Nation-states and human rights helped foster the creation of a global world in which ideas, people, and movements traveled rapidly across oceans and continents—another sharp contrast to the world of the late eighteenth and early nineteenth centuries. Consider Nelson Mandela, born in Mvezo in Southern Africa to a royal Xhosa family, hearing about the Atlantic Charter some seven thousand miles from Newfoundland (where Churchill and Roosevelt met and signed the document), and then becoming the icon of the South African liberation struggle and a global symbol of social justice. Or Ralph Bunche, born in Detroit, three generations removed from slavery on his mother's side, moving about to Palestine and Africa bearing the flag of the UN and then, as a revered official within the UN, marching with the Reverend Doctor Martin Luther King Jr. in Selma, Alabama (see figure Concl.3). Or Bertha Lutz, born in São Paulo of Swiss and British parents, educated

FIGURE CONCL.3 The Great Freedom March, Montgomery, Alabama, 1965. Reverend Doctor Martin Luther King Jr. led a group of marchers from Selma to Montgomery to fight for black suffrage, one of the most crucial events of the civil rights movement. Ralph Bunche always linked the African-American struggle in the United States with decolonization abroad. Here, he is in the center in the white shirt, next to Doctor King. (© Bruce Davidson/Magnum Photos.)

in Paris, feminist activism taking her all across South and North America and to Paris and London as well, while she also pursued a scientific career in her native Brazil. Even when they remained at home, Mandela, Bunche, and Lutz moved in a global world that they helped create through their international connections and commitments.

The efforts of those like Mandela, Bunche, and Lutz, who advocated a new human rights system for the postwar world, came early to fruition. At a pace fast and furious, a cluster of new declarations, treaties, and judicial proceedings emerged between 1945 and 1952. A lull ensued thereafter, largely because of the Cold War, and then a new surge took off from the mid-1960s onward.

The backdrop to the initial surge was, of course, World War II and the atrocities committed by Nazi Germany and Imperial Japan. The victorious Allies as well as activists from all around the world believed that a peaceful world order would only endure if the individual's rights and dignity were respected. Those who created the new order drew quite deliberately on earlier precedents, notably the declarations and constitutions of the American, French, and Latin American revolutions of the late eighteenth and early nineteenth centuries, those sweeping political movements that for the first time in history claimed to grant rights to all citizens of the nation. But the creators knew they also had to go further and explicitly establish rights for all people, whatever their national citizenship, whatever their race or gender. They also believed that the proclamation of rights had to be backed up by global means of enforcement.

This new world order was not a creation only of liberal, Western states. Both at the founding moment in the immediate postwar period and in the later surge from the 1960s onward, the Soviet Union, its Soviet-bloc allies, and the countries of the Global South played a vital role in pushing forward the international human rights system, however often they violated human rights at home. All the provisions for social and economic rights and self-determination met intense hostility from the United States, Great Britain, France, and other Western countries. They sought to limit human rights to strictly political measures, and argued that developing countries had to demonstrate their "maturity" before they could be granted independence. The Western countries lost these arguments against the force of decolonization and the rapid expansion of UN membership.[9]

Already, the founding Charter included human rights and decolonization as part of the UN's mission. The human rights commitment found expression especially in the UDHR, passed by the General Assembly on 10 December 1948. The negotiations for the UDHR proved to be a long haul. The drafting commission met in countless sessions.[10] At least twice, the deliberations appeared to be at breaking point. The delegates divided over a series of critical issues: the rights of women, religious freedom, social rights, the concept of self-determination. Despite the great difficulties and many drafts, the UDHR passed and remains the foundational document for all human rights endeavors. While primarily political in orientation, the UDHR also contains numerous articles espousing social and economic rights, like the right to social security, an adequate standard of living, and equal pay for equal work.

One day prior to the passage of the UDHR, the UN approved the convention that defined, for the very first time, the crime of genocide and made its perpetrators liable for prosecution.[11] The Genocide Convention built on the Nuremberg and Tokyo tribunals, in which leading figures of Nazi Germany and Imperial Japan were tried for war crimes, crimes against peace, and crimes against humanity. The Nuremberg Tribunal was the more innovative of the two. It established the fundamental human rights principles that individuals, and not just states, can be held responsible for criminal actions. The claims by defendants that they were just "following orders" no longer suffice when the violations against peace and human rights are grave. Crimes against humanity constituted a new doctrine, one that elevated into international law the fundamental principle of personal security against unwarranted and unjust state violence.[12]

These profound innovations were followed by the Fourth Protocols to the Geneva Convention, adopted in 1949; the Refugee Convention of 1951; and the European Convention on Human Rights in 1952. The first of these extends to civilians the protections of the laws of war; the second obliges states to take in political asylum seekers and forbids the forced repatriation of individuals to the country from which they fled. The European Convention and the associated European Court of Human Rights remain, to this day, the strongest regional assertion and enforcer of human rights.[13]

At the end of 1948, when the UN passed the UDHR, the drafters and many others expected that, as a resolution and not a treaty, it would be quickly followed by a single, binding covenant and an international court that would enforce human rights. The political conflicts of the Cold War drastically slowed the process. After the refugee and European conventions, no major human rights treaties or resolutions were brought to the center of international action until the mid-1960s.

However, all through the 1950s and 1960s, in the UN's Third Committee, negotiators were hard at work drafting human rights treaties, which everyone understood as the way to embed in international law the principles espoused in the UDHR. Latin Americans pursued a regional convention, while Europeans brought into practice the provisions of the European Convention. One of the first cases entailed charges against Great Britain for its violent suppression of the movement in Cyprus for union with Greece. The pursuit of a major power helped establish the legitimacy of the court.[14] In the United States, the civil rights movement emerged as a powerful force that faced down the most brutal efforts at its repression. Anticolonial movements in Africa, Asia, and the Middle East racked up one victory after another. The 1950s, in short, were hardly quiescent when it came to human rights and nation-state foundings.

Then came the second surge, beginning in 1966, when the pace of human rights advances accelerated once again. These developments represented not a break with the past, but a quickening and deepening of human rights.[15] We still live in the era of the second surge.

It took years of difficult negotiations, but the UN finally passed, in 1966, the two most important treaties: the Covenant on Civil and Political Rights and the Covenant on Economic, Social and Cultural Rights.[16] Why two? Because it had proven impossible to bring the United States and the Soviet Union together on the principles of the second convention. For the ragingly anticommunist United States, any mention of economic and social rights smacked of socialism and communism. To this day, it still has not ratified the second convention.

From this point on, a series of international conventions have expanded the scope of human rights. The landmark Helsinki Accords in 1975, signed by virtually all European states and the United States, affirmed state sovereignty *and* human rights. Treaties and resolutions protecting women, minorities, and indigenous peoples have entered the canon of international human rights. At the turn of the twenty-first century, the International Criminal Court, envisaged already in the 1940s, was finally established.[17]

Today, the UN identifies nine core human rights conventions, each of which has a monitoring body, as well as ninety-six other conventions, resolutions, and protocols.[18] They include treaties and declarations that establish the rights of minorities and indigenous peoples, refugees and migrants, children and women, and outlaw slavery and racial discrimination. The total of more than one hundred human rights instruments does not even include the Geneva Conventions limiting warfare, or regional treaties and declarations like the African Charter of Human Rights or the European Convention on Human Rights.

Does all the ink spilled on these documents, all the endless hours diplomats and activists spent in dreary negotiating rooms, amount to anything? Any newspaper on any morning of the year publishes articles depicting human rights violations somewhere in the world. At the time of this writing, Muslim Rohingya in Myanmar have been subjected to a genocide, the Chinese government has interned hundreds of thousands of Uighurs for "reeducation," and the Saudi Arabian military, provisioned and supported by the United States, has killed thousands of Yemenis and reduced others to starvation and life-threatening diseases like cholera. Are we really better off because the UN and virtually all nation-states proclaim human rights?

Two advances in the postwar era may help answer these questions. Since 1945 human rights have been extended far beyond propertied white men, as was largely the case in the eighteenth and nineteenth centuries. International human rights now specifically encompass children, asylum seekers, indigenous peoples, the stateless, and, perhaps most broadly, women. In addition, judicial accountability for massive violations of human rights, pioneered at Nuremberg and Tokyo, is now well established. Both developments signal the bracing significance of human rights in global politics, however often they are violated, however partially they are enforced.

လ

"Human rights are women's rights, women's rights are human rights," proclaimed Hillary Clinton to loud, but by no means unanimous, applause at the UN's Fourth World Conference on Women, held in Beijing in September 1995.[19] Clinton was then the First Lady of the United States, and no doubt some who refused to applaud were indicating their

antagonism toward the country. Nonetheless, Clinton's words both captured the moment and have endured as an expression of the signal importance of women's rights in the human rights era.

The UN had previously proclaimed 1975 as "International Women's
Year" and 1976–85 as the "Decade for Women." In the Charter and the
UDHR the UN had recognized the equality of women and men. Yet
little had been done to make those proclamations reality. The UN's
Committee on the Status of Women, established in 1946, met every year
and issued reports. It contributed to development work in the Global
South and collaborated with the ILO and other UN agencies to expand
protective legislation for women in the workplace and other social measures. But the committee occupied a marginal position within the
sprawling UN organization. As if to ensure that minimal status endured,
the UN in 1975—quite ironically, given that this was the UN-proclaimed
International Women's Year—moved the committee out of the New
York headquarters to Geneva, and shifted its bureaucratic location from
the Human Rights Commission to the Centre for Social Development
and Humanitarian Affairs.

The UN, however, had to respond to the global emergence of the
women's movement. During the Decade for Women, the UN convened
three international congresses, in Mexico City in 1975, Copenhagen in
1980, and Nairobi in 1985. These meetings, with thousands of participants, were not easy. Disputes ran along many axes, between the Western
and Soviet-bloc representatives, women from the Global South and
North, radical and moderate feminists.[20] Western participants in particular raised issues of sexuality and women's oppression in the family, and
called for the full-blown legal equality of men and women. Women from
the Global South focused more on issues of economic development and
were sometimes resistant to discussions on the oppression of women
within the family. The Soviet-bloc delegates held to the idea that participation in the paid labor force paved the road to emancipation for women.
They heralded their own achievements in that arena, claiming that wom-
en's liberation had been achieved under socialism, and rejected the concept of gender as a category of analysis to understand women's oppression. They dismissed any effort to think beyond capitalism as the total

explanation for women's lack of rights, positions they expressed again at their own follow-up congress in East Berlin in 1975.[21]

Despite all the conflicts, the Committee on the Status of Women drafted the landmark Convention on the Elimination of All Forms of Discrimination against Women (CEDAW). It was debated and endorsed at the Mexico City congress in 1975, and passed by the General Assembly in 1979. A grand signing ceremony took place at the 1980 congress in Copenhagen. The convention has been signed by almost all members of the UN.

The CEDAW is a wide-ranging document. The rhetoric soars in the introduction as it restates much of the language found in the UDHR regarding the inherent worth and dignity of every human person and the need for equality and justice. Yet discrimination against women persists, the Convention text continues, despite the assertion of the equality of women and men in many UN resolutions and declarations. In the specific articles the CEDAW mixes, not always coherently, provisions for the absolute equality of women with specific protections for women as mothers. The Convention calls on states to eliminate all legal and cultural forms of discrimination against women. In political, economic, and cultural life, women are to be granted the same opportunities as men. They are to have access to adequate healthcare and to receive the same social security as men. Some measures were certainly radical for many countries, such as article 16, which grants women the right to participate equally in family life, including "to decide freely on the number and spacing of their children" and the right "to choose a family name."[22]

The CEDAW is a milestone in the evolution of women's rights. It ranks among the nine "core international human rights instruments," giving it a certain preeminence in rhetoric and fact since it has its own monitoring body (see figure Concl.4). As always, the implementation of its provisions is highly uneven. Nonetheless, the CEDAW establishes an international standard of equality. Moreover, like the League of Nations Mandates Commission and the UN Trusteeship Council, the CEDAW and its monitoring body have opened up avenues of political mobilization, in this case about women's rights. Women around the world can appeal to it for support and redress. Indeed, the International

FIGURE CONCL.4 The Committee on the Elimination of Discrimination against Women addressing journalists at UN Headquarters, 6 February 1998, at the UN Conference on women's rights in 1998. From left to right: Aida Gonzalez (Mexico); Salma Khan (Bangladesh), chairperson of the Committee; Angela King, secretary-general's special adviser on gender issues and advancement of women; and Ayse Feride Acar (Turkey). (UN Photo/Eskinder Debebe.)

Women's Year and the ensuing Decade for Women contributed mightily to the creation of a global women's movement.[23] Despite all the conflicts and debates at the four world congresses, women established contacts and networks that continue to exert influence on women's and gender issues. Many transnational women's groups have fought against the persistent violence that women endure, including in the home and in marriage, and human trafficking. Human rights, once the preserve of propertied white men, are now owned by everyone.

ℰℌ

In November 2011 I sat ten feet away from a war criminal. We were separated by a thick wall of bulletproof glass, but I could feel his presence.

Radovan Karadžić had been indicted by the International Criminal Tribunal for the Former Yugoslavia (ICTY) in The Hague for war crimes, genocide, and crimes against humanity. Serb nationalist troops, operating under his authority, had committed these crimes against Bosnian Muslims during the four years of war that ravaged the one-time country of Yugoslavia. Karadžić hid out—more or less—for ten years, defying the ICTY, until French troops finally caught him and delivered him to the tribunal in The Hague.

Karadžić acted as his own legal defense, and I watched as he, flippant and arrogant, cross-examined a Dutch battalion officer. The Dutchbat (as they were called) soldiers were part of the UN peacekeeping operation in the former Yugoslavia. This particular group was stationed in Srebrenica, one of three supposedly safe cities for Muslims established by the UN. UN peacekeeping, headed by Kofi Annan, later the secretary-general, had left the Dutchbat troops undermanned and underarmed, and unclear about the scope of their mission. Instead of a safe city, Srebrenica turned into a killing field of some eight thousand Muslim men and boys, while the women and girls were sent to concentration camps.

The Dutch officer responded calmly and clearly to Karadžić's interrogation. I could not help but think about the hundreds of thousands of victims in Srebrenica and elsewhere in Bosnia and other parts of the former Yugoslavia, whose killings resulted from the drive to establish an exclusive, expanded Serbian state. Karadžić was a prime agent of that program, emblematic of the worst proclivities of the nation-state.

I also could not help but think about the Dutchbat soldiers. When they returned home to the Netherlands, they were widely reviled by the population and the government. Their fellow citizens accused them of failing to protect Muslims. Their inaction, it was charged, caused one of the worst atrocities in Europe since the end of World War II. As a result of the violations they had witnessed in Srebrenica and the harsh censure hurled at them, the soldiers suffered high rates of alcoholism, divorce, and suicide.[24] Yet if blame lay anywhere aside from Karadžić and his fellow Serb nationalists, it was with the UN, which had left its own peacekeepers exposed and confused about their mission.

Five years later I opened a newspaper to discover that the ICTY had indeed convicted Karadžić of genocide and a host of other crimes. For once, I mused, justice triumphed. As of this writing, Karadžić languishes in prison in The Hague, as does his close collaborator, Ratko Mladić.

The ICTY decision in the Karadžić case and many others, as well as prosecutions by the International Criminal Tribunal for Rwanda (ICTR), signaled a new era of human rights enforcement. Violators of human rights can now be hauled before international tribunals. Most importantly, the ICTY made rape and other acts of sexual violence crimes against humanity, and has convicted thirty-two individuals on that basis.[25] All the international tribunals empaneled by the UN in the 1990s and early 2000s, including, in addition to the ICTY and ICTR, those for Sierra Leone and Cambodia, built on the Nuremberg precedent.[26] Even earlier, beginning in the 1970s, national courts in Greece, Portugal, and Argentina prosecuted former dictators and their multitudinous supporters who were responsible for tortures, arbitrary imprisonments, and extrajudicial killings.[27] The national courts were unprecedented, and were possible only because human rights had become a standard that no one could ignore.

In another landmark development, fifty years after the passage of the UDHR, the Rome Treaty created the International Criminal Court (ICC) for the prosecution of those who had perpetrated genocide, crimes against humanity, and other violations of human rights. Truth and reconciliation commissions, pioneered by Argentina and South Africa, have established a new form of transitional justice.[28] In 2005, the General Assembly unanimously passed the Responsibility to Protect, a resolution that profoundly limits state sovereignty in cases of massive crimes against humanity.

All these developments have faced massive criticisms. The international tribunals have been costly and slow. Justice is always rendered after the fact, after genocides, tortures, and other violations. The bulk of the cases before the ICC have originated in Africa. It is unlikely that any of the Great Powers will be hauled before the ICC. Truth and reconciliation commissions often allow perpetrators their freedom after they express remorse; justice has not been rendered. The gacaca proceedings, forms of communal justice in Rwanda, dispense with due process. Those who are accused have few means of defending themselves. The Responsibility to Protect has been sharply criticized as mere rhetoric that fails to account for the reality of state power and state interests. Only the weak have to worry about international intervention. Without planning for what comes after, greater violence and human rights violations may ensue, as in the case of Libya. Great Powers have nothing to fear, certainly not with the veto authority five of them exercise in the UN Security Council.[29]

Despite all these criticisms, some of them well founded, the new era of accountability has transformed the global political landscape. In 2001, even before the Karadžić case, the ICTY rendered convictions in the "rape trial" of Dragoljub Kunarac, Radomir Kovač, and Zoran Vuković. Along with other Serb nationalists, the three had kept Muslim women in sexual slavery for months, sometimes buying and selling them. Among the victims was a twelve-year-old girl, who was never heard from again. Her mother, in agony, testified at the trial. The presiding judge, Florence Mumba of Zambia, could barely contain her rage as she delivered the sentence. To Kovač she said: "Particularly appalling and deplorable is your treatment of 12-year-old A. B., a helpless little child for whom you showed absolutely no compassion whatsoever, but whom you abused sexually in the same way as the other girls. You finally sold her like an object, in the knowledge that this would almost certainly mean further sexual assaults by other men."[30] Judge Mumba went on to accuse Kovač of having a "morally depraved and corrupt character."[31]

No judicial decision will ever bring the girl back to life or resolve her mother's pain. Nonetheless, it is of utmost significance that Kovač was convicted and served a prison term, even if it was not as lengthy as many wished. Potential *génocidaires* and serial rapists, who use sexual violence as a political tactic to shame and humiliate, to force into submission those whom they categorize as less than human, have to calculate that they might end up in the dock at The Hague, as did Karadžić and Kovač. Perhaps the girl's mother derived some small quantum of relief from the recognition of her ordeal and the assertion, by the decision of the ICTY, of her personhood.

It is impossible to prove that any of these judicial actions have actually prevented other violations of human rights. How can one prove something that did not happen? Nor will the principle of accountability usher in a reign of complete human rights compliance. Like every human rights advance discussed in this book, judicial accountability brings with it new complexities and challenges. How far down the chain of command should perpetrators be prosecuted? Will officials of Russia, China, the United States, or any other Great Power ever be brought before a tribunal? Whatever the limitations of national courts and international tribunals, it is hard to imagine that we would be better off if we lived in a world of complete impunity, if Serb nationalists and other perpetrators of severe human rights violations were allowed to go about their lives freely, never having to account for the atrocities they committed.

The complex of human rights covenants, Geneva Convention limitations on warfare, and international criminal justice—"humanity's law"—is of major significance yet hardly suffices to make human rights reality.[32] Every human rights advance discussed in this book, from slavery abolition to minority protection to democracy in South Korea, has been the product of popular movements. Humanity's law is one girder in the house of human rights, but it is hardly the only load-bearing element in the construction. In the era of the second human rights surge (the period since 1966 and the signing of the two covenants), human rights efforts have also been promoted by the dramatic growth of NGOs.[33] Disillusionment with communism and with the 1960s New Left in general lay at the root of many of these organizations.[34] Amnesty International, founded in 1961, was the pioneer.[35] It was followed in the 1970s by Helsinki Watch, which developed into Human Rights Watch (as mentioned in chapter 8). Hundreds, perhaps thousands, of others have been founded, some local in character, others well funded and with a global reach.

The rather haphazard character of these organizations in the early years has been replaced by a high degree of professionalization. The annual reports produced by Human Rights Watch, for example, are fundamental to any contemporary discussion of local, national, and global politics. Countless community groups have also spearheaded human rights progress, like the Center for the Victims of Torture in Minnesota; and Human Rights Advocates in Berkeley, San Francisco, and Minneapolis-Saint Paul; or grassroots activist groups in Guatemala and in countless other places around the globe that have demanded human rights and whose members have often suffered imprisonment, torture, and killings.[36]

In many places, local groups have spearheaded initiatives to reconcile communities and build peace in the aftermath of massive human rights violations. Sometimes international NGOs have aided their efforts with funds and advisers; at other times local organizers have been on their own. In Burundi, activists have established radio stations that hire Hutus and Tutsis and broadcast programs about those who protected their neighbors during the waves of violence. Others have founded youth centers where young people of all backgrounds meet, play sports, dance, and discuss; learn about AIDS; and receive jobs training. Thousands (literally) of other examples could be cited from conflict zones all around the world. Such efforts are always fragile. The possibility of collapse into communal violence is ever present. Indeed, political conflict in Burundi starting in 2015 resulted, once again, in refugee streams numbering in the hundreds of thousands. The organizers of these grassroots programs often run great risks. But their efforts are critical to the advance of human rights.[37]

Authoritarian systems and individual dictators and warlords are among the supreme violators of human rights. The Cold War also drastically limited the implementation of rights, as we have seen most clearly in the case of Korea. For the United States after 1948, anticommunism trumped every commitment to human rights. From East Asia to Latin America to Africa and the Middle East, the United States supported dictators, some of them as bad as it can get, so long as they proclaimed themselves fighters against communism and allies of the United States. It is a sorry record, one that continues today in post–Cold War variations. The Soviet Union did the same in reverse. It supported every anticolonial struggle, every new postcolonial state, so long as its leaders proclaimed their support for socialism and allied their countries with the Soviet bloc. No beacon of human rights domestically, the Soviet Union displayed little concern when these movements and countries descended into dictatorships and engaged in the worst kinds of violations of human rights.

The limitations, the cracks and fissures in the postwar human rights system, the violations that we see all around us, run deeply and are not simply the result of reprehensible individuals or states. Every chapter of this book has shown the partiality of human rights advances when they have been built around national citizenship. Exclusion as well as inclusion, human rights and their violations, lie in the nature of the beast, the nation-state. The contradictions are blatant and cannot be easily resolved, nor wished away. They are, in fact, irresolvable, an intrinsic part of the human rights system based in nation-state citizenship.

The UN Charter explicitly affirms state sovereignty and the right of self-determination, as do many subsequent declarations and conventions.[38] Both 1966 human rights covenants assert the "right of self-determination" for "all peoples" so they can "freely determine their political status and freely pursue their economic, social and cultural development."[39] The UN Declaration on Principles of International Law concerning Friendly Relations and Co-operation among States (1970) and the Helsinki Final Act (1975) and virtually every other major human rights document assert the same principle.[40] The famed conference of non-aligned nations at Bandung in 1955 wrote self-determination into its final document. The African Charter on Human and Peoples' Rights (1982), by its very title, underscores the understanding of rights as inhering in peoples, not just individuals. Its first eighteen articles concern individual human rights. Article 20 states that "all peoples . . . shall have the unquestionable and inalienable right to self-determination. They shall freely determine their political status and shall pursue their economic and social development according to the policy they have freely chosen."[41]

Self-determination has become enshrined as a fundamental principle of the modern state system. Its Enlightenment origins concerning individual emancipation became transformed into a doctrine of state sovereignty and national emancipation.[42] Self-determination in its modern version is about collectivities—nations—not individuals. It expresses the dilemmas, the limits, the very contradictions of human rights anchored in nation-states. Who, after all, constitutes the self-determining nation? Who has the right to have rights in nation-states that exclude as fast as they include?

The condition of refugees underscores the limitations of human rights when they are based in national citizenship. The fate of those wholly outside the borders of the state is highly tenuous and often deadly.[43] In September 2018, UNHCR counted the staggering number of 68.5 million "forcibly displaced people." Only one-third of them are under UN mandate, 19.9 million in UNHCR camps, 5.4 million Palestinians in UNRWA (UN Relief and Works Administration) settlements. UNRWA was established in 1949 for Palestinian refugees; its mandate has been continually renewed by the General Assembly, making Palestinians the longest-running refugee population in the era of nation-states and human rights. Half of those classified as refugees—that is, under UNHCR or UNRWA—are under the age of eighteen.[44] The UN counts ten million stateless people among the total number of those forcibly displaced. Thirty people are forcibly displaced every minute of the day. Nearly two-thirds of the 68.5 million refugees are categorized as "internally displaced persons" (IDPs).[45] In 2017, the International Displacement Monitoring Centre, an NGO based in Geneva, counted the astounding number of forty million people displaced internally by conflict situations.[46]

These people—refugees, migrants, and IDPs—have all been forced out of their homes by politics and economics. The lives they lead and suffer are the consequence of human-made activities. None of the figures noted above account for the tens of millions more displaced by climate events like typhoons, hurricanes, and earthquakes (though these, too, are at least partly the result of human-induced climate change). Nor do they include the millions of people who have migrated in search of work, like the estimated eleven million undocumented immigrants in the United States and thirty-two million migrant laborers in the Arab states, including an estimated six hundred thousand forced laborers.[47]

With a total world population of 7.6 billion, 68.5 million forcibly displaced people is small in percentage terms, less than 1 percent. Even if the official figures are probably low and we add, say, fifty million migrant workers worldwide for a total of 115 million, the percentage is still small. Yet the numbers are dramatic as manifestations of violent political conflict and the chasm of economic inequality that divides the Global North and South. Moreover, forcibly displaced persons are not evenly distributed across the globe. The majority of IDPs are concentrated in a dozen countries—most, though not all, in the Global South: Congo, Syria, Iraq, Afghanistan, Yemen, Nigeria, Sudan, South Sudan, Turkey, Colombia, Somalia, and Ukraine.[48]

The life situations are devastating for those affected; only a tiny percentage of them have any access to rights despite all the international treaties that grant *everyone*, whether or not they are nation-state citizens, human rights.[49] The lucky few will attain citizenship over time, or at least their children will, if they become officially accepted and ultimately integrated into the population. The vast majority will linger in the netherworld of refugee and migration status despite an array of conventions and resolutions that affirm access to human rights for the stateless.

The tragic, poignant condition of refugees powerfully expresses the problem examined in this book in different cases around the globe. Nation-state citizenship is still fundamental to our ability to exercise rights. We are literally nothing without a state structure around us. Statelessness, as Hannah Arendt wrote, is the worst condition imaginable, just short of physical annihilation. Yet citizenship is always exclusive as well as inclusive, even if the state defines citizenship internally in the broadest way possible. So long as rights are fundamentally linked to the nation-state, they will always be limiting.

In the twenty-first century the stream of human rights politics runs far more deeply and broadly than ever before. Skeptics abound.[50] Some charge that human rights are mere veneers that enable states to protect themselves while they carry out all sorts of inhumane acts. Others condemn human rights as mere rhetoric or evidence of Western neo-imperialism. Even human rights stalwarts like Aryeh Neier and Michael Ignatieff evince some disappointment and seem to yearn for the 1990s when the human rights surge seemed unstoppable.[51]

Indeed, all around us, as I write these lines, we see a tidal wave of right-wing populist and extreme nationalist movements in the United States and Europe. Authoritarian dictators around the globe firm up their power and hold on to their offices for years on end. Some crisis situations, as in Syria, go on with no resolution in sight while the population endures bombardments, displacements, and malnutrition, the utter shattering of their society. Wars rage elsewhere as well, and civilians, perhaps more than ever, bear the brunt of their furies. Since the passage of the Genocide Convention in 1948, genocides have taken place in Burundi and Rwanda (as we have seen), Guatemala, the former Yugoslavia, Darfur in Sudan, among Yazidis in Iraq and Rohingya in Myanmar. The Chinese government has launched a vast "reeducation" campaign of Uighur, placing tens of thousands of them in detention. Much of the world still lives under dictatorial regimes and in conditions of extreme inequality. On a global scale, democracy seems to be in retreat. And we are witnessing today the largest refugee crisis in history.

But perhaps it is too early to sound the death knell of the human rights era. After all, who could have predicted, in the early eighteenth century, the abolition of slavery? In the early nineteenth century, the triumph of the idea of human rights? Or in late 1961, the Helsinki Final Act, the fall of the Berlin Wall, and the collapse of communism?

As this book has tried to demonstrate, human rights have never proceeded in a straight line. They are complex and move in crooked paths. A future in which human rights reign supreme and we all live in peace and fellowship is a chimera. Utopian sentiments are only good insofar as they project the possibility of a better life upon humane principles. Without those hopes, we stagnate in the present without any path forward.

The very term "human rights" has moved into the center of politics at all levels—local, national, and international. It provides a powerful motivating force for people to demand lives of liberty and security. From the mothers of the disappeared in Argentina to Soviet dissidents, anti-apartheid activists in South Africa, and women all around the globe—all of them have adopted the rhetoric of human rights to rally support and make their claims in the streets, in the halls of governance, and on the floor of the UN General Assembly. The meaning of human rights has expanded over two and one-half centuries, and now includes social and economic as well as political rights.

Amid all these developments, the nation-state remains. It has shown its mettle and commands power and loyalty. It will not disappear anytime in the foreseeable future. In the best of circumstances, the nation-state is our protector if we live within the charmed circle of rights-bearing citizens. It is also our greatest threat, the powerful violator of human rights and the exclusion-enforcing institution that drives out, removes, forcibly assimilates, and kills those denied the right to have rights within its borders.[52]

Since the 1940s, human rights have been proclaimed for everyone regardless of citizenship status. Human rights protections have moved—in part—to the international plane. The UDHR, the Genocide Convention, international tribunals, the ICC—all the measures and conventions and resolutions discussed above infringe on the absolute sovereignty of the nation-state. Thankfully so. Anything that moves the conception and enforcement of human rights to the international level moves us beyond the nation-state as the sole enforcer (and violator) of rights, and that is progress.

The nation-state remains; so do our identities as individuals of particular nationalities, ethnicities, religions (or the lack thereof), and genders. The Enlightenment fiction of an abstract individual, stripped of all markers, is just that—a fiction. A system of human rights built on that understanding will always be flawed and easily subject to attack by the heralds of an exclusive, supposedly timeless culture of nation or race or of the essential differences between men and women. Yet diversity of all sorts is the intractable reality of human existence. How we live with that difference is the critical issue. Those who somehow differ from a dominant group may be subordinated, driven out, or killed, or they may be recognized as fellow humans and accorded the same rights as everyone else—without being required to dispense with their identities.[53]

For all the partial advances, for all the contradictions, all the sheer opposition—human rights remain our best hope for the future. Their advocates sometimes espouse utopian aspirations. A restrained perspective is more appropriate and effective. Human rights will never be implemented in the all-embracing fashion of declarations like the UDHR; they will always face opponents, some quite strong. Yet human rights provide a powerful affirmation of the human spirit. They require that people be respected and afforded recognition no matter what their specific gender, nationality, or race. They demand that all people have access to the basic necessities of life, and have the freedom to express themselves, to work and build and create as they wish, to join with others as they desire, and to be free of the scourge of violence and forced displacement. Those *are* our fundamental human rights. We should demand nothing less from the worlds we inhabit.

NOTES

Notes to Introduction

1. I take this story from the Amnesty International website: "I Welcome: Protecting the Rights of Refugees and Asylum-Seekers," n.d., accessed 13 August 2018, https://www.amnesty usa.org/campaigns/refugee-and-migrant-rights/, and "Help Release 15-Year-Old Astrid and Her Father," n.d., accessed 13 August 2018, https://act.amnestyusa.org/page/21189/action/1.

2. Figure from the United Nations High Commission for Refugees, "Figures at a Glance," n.d., accessed 13 August 2018, http://www.unhcr.org/en-us/figures-at-a-glance.html.

3. Hannah Arendt, *The Origins of Totalitarianism* (1951; Cleveland: Meridian, 1958), 296. Arendt's formulation, "the right to have rights," is uncannily close to Fichte's: "The one true right that belongs to the human being as such [is]: the right to be able to acquire rights." See Johann Gottlieb Fichte, *Foundations of Natural Right, according to the Principles of the Wissenschaftslehre*, ed. Frederick Neuhouser, trans. Michael Baur (1796; Cambridge: Cambridge University Press, 2000), 333. Arendt makes no reference to Fichte's formulation, nor do any of the major Arendt scholars.

The German original: "Dies allein is das eigentliche Menschenrecht, das den [dem, editor] Menschen, als Menschen, zukommt; die Möglichkeit sich Rechte zu erwerben." Johann Gottlieb Fichte, *Grundlage des Naturrechts nach Principien der Wissenschaftslehre* (1796), in *J. G. Fichte: Gesamtausgabe der Bayerischen Akademie der Wissenschaften*, ed. Reinhard Lauth and Hans Gliwitzky, pt. 1, vol. 4, *Werke 1797–1798* (Stuttgart: Friedrich Frommann Verlag, 1970), 163.

4. I do not, however, share the withering criticisms of some recent authors, who tell us that human rights are on the wane; have altogether failed; are utopian in character and therefore undermine the real and necessary world of politics, which has to be about limited goals; divert attention from more critical social issues, like inequality; or are Western-based and therefore necessarily imperialist in character. See, for example, Samuel Moyn, *Not Enough: Human Rights in an Unequal World* (Cambridge: Belknap Press of Harvard University Press, 2018), and *The Last Utopia: Human Rights in History* (Cambridge: Belknap Press of Harvard University Press, 2010); Eric A. Posner, *The Twilight of Human Rights Law* (Oxford: Oxford University Press, 2014); and Stephen Hopgood, *The Endtimes of Human Rights* (Ithaca: Cornell University Press, 2013). For a very effective challenge to such critiques, see Kathryn Sikkink, *Evidence for Hope: Making Human Rights Work in the 21st Century* (Princeton: Princeton University Press, 2017), and Beth A. Simmons, *Mobilizing for Human Rights: International Law in Domestic Politics* (Cambridge: Cambridge University Press, 2009). See also the pioneering work of Lynn Hunt, *Inventing Human Rights: A History* (New York: Norton, 2007). On the French debates, see Justine Lacroix

and Jean-Yves Pranchère, *Le procès des droits de l'homme: Généalogie du scepticisme démocratique* (Paris: Seuil, 2016), which is highly critical of the francophone opponents of human rights. Lacroix and Pranchère's position is very similar to my own.

5. See Christian Reus-Smit, *Individual Rights and the Making of the International System* (Cambridge: Cambridge University Press, 2013), 210–11, who writes similarly. For two significant works on related themes, though neither addresses directly human rights, see Philipp Ther, *The Dark Side of Nation-States: Ethnic Cleansing in Modern Europe*, trans. Charlotte Kreutzmüller (2011; New York: Berghahn, 2014), and Michael Mann, *The Dark Side of Democracy: Explaining Ethnic Cleansing* (New York: Cambridge University Press, 2005).

6. See David Weissbrodt, *The Human Rights of Non-Citizens* (Oxford: Oxford University Press, 2008).

7. Amid a huge literature on citizenship and rights, I have found especially compelling Ayten Gündoğdu, *Rightlessness in an Age of Rights* (New York: Oxford University Press, 2015); Margaret R. Somers, *Genealogies of Citizenship: Markets, Statelessness, and the Right to Have Rights* (Cambridge: Cambridge University Press, 2008); and Seyla Benhabib, *The Rights of Others: Aliens, Residents, and Citizens* (Cambridge: Cambridge University Press, 2004). All three authors work in conversation with Hannah Arendt. On the long and complex history of citizenship, see Frederick Cooper, *Citizenship, Inequality, and Difference: Historical Perspectives* (Princeton: Princeton University Press, 2018). Cooper emphasizes the diverse meanings of citizenship, in the present as well as historically. For one of the classic statements, see T. H. Marshall, "Citizenship and Social Class" (1950), in *Class, Citizenship, and Social Development: Essays by T. H. Marshall*, introduction by Seymour Martin Lipset (Garden City: Doubleday, 1964), 65–122.

8. See Steve J. Stern and Scott Straus, "Introduction: Embracing Paradox: Human Rights in the Global Age," in *The Human Rights Paradox: Universality and its Discontents*, ed. Stern and Straus (Madison: University of Wisconsin Press, 2014), 3–28. Also on the complexity of human rights, see Stefan-Ludwig Hoffmann, "Introduction: Genealogies of Human Rights," in *Human Rights in the Twentieth Century*, ed. Hoffmann (2010; Cambridge: Cambridge University Press, 2011), 1–26.

9. Isaiah Berlin's famed distinction between negative and positive liberty applies here. See "Two Concepts of Liberty" (1958), in *Four Essays on Liberty* (Oxford: Oxford University Press, 1969), 118–72.

10. On the varieties of liberal thought, see Helena Rosenblatt, *The Lost History of Liberalism* (Princeton: Princeton University Press, 2018). For arguments about the socialist contribution to a broadened conception of human rights, see Lacroix and Pranchère, *Procès des droits de l'homme*, and Gregory Claeys, "Socialism and the Language of Human Rights: The Origins and Implications of Economic Rights," in *Revisiting the Origins of Human Rights*, ed. Pamela Slotte and Miia Halme-Tuomisaari (Cambridge: Cambridge University Press, 2015), 206–36. See also Hunt, *Inventing Human Rights*.

11. For the text of the constitution, see "Guatemala's Constitution of 1985 with Amendments through 1993," Constitute Project, 17 January 2018, https://www.constituteproject.org/constitution/Guatemala_1993.pdf.

12. See Martha C. Nussbaum, *Creating Capabilities: The Human Development Approach* (Cambridge: Belknap Press of Harvard University Press, 2011), 18–20; Amartya Sen,

Development as Freedom (New York: Knopf, 1999), and "Elements of a Theory of Human Rights," *Philosophy and Public Affairs* 32:4 (2004): 315–56, esp. 330–38, 345–48. See also James Griffin, *On Human Rights* (New York: Oxford University Press, 2008), 33; 51; 305, n. 4; generally 176–87. For a powerful defense of human rights as solely political in nature, see Aryeh Neier, *The International Human Rights Movement: A History* (Princeton: Princeton University Press, 2012). For an important study that criticizes human rights for neglecting rampant inequality, see Moyn, *Not Enough*.

13. On the creation of the global world, see especially Jürgen Osterhammel, *The Transformation of the World: A Global History of the Nineteenth Century*, trans. Patrick Camiller (2009; Princeton: Princeton University Press, 2014), and C. A. Bayly, *The Birth of the Modern World, 1780–1914: Global Connections and Comparisons* (Malden: Blackwell, 2004).

14. J.G.A. Pocock, *The Machiavellian Moment: Florentine Political Thought and the Atlantic Republican Tradition* (Princeton: Princeton University Press, 1975).

15. Hobbes might seem an odd choice here given his overwhelming emphasis on the all-powerful state, but see Richard P. Hiskes, "A Very Promising Species: From Hobbes to the Human Rights to Water," in S. Stern and Straus, *Human Rights Paradox*, 224–45.

16. On law in the Russian Empire, see Jane Burbank, "An Imperial Rights Regime: Law and Citizenship in the Russian Empire," *Kritika* 7:3 (2006): 397–431. On Ottoman and Islamic property law, see Colin Imber, "The Law of the Land," in *The Ottoman World*, ed. Christine Woodhead (Oxford: Routledge, 2012), 41–56; Roger Owen, ed., *New Perspectives on Property and Land in the Middle East* (Cambridge: Center for Middle Eastern Studies of Harvard University, 2000), esp. Owen, "Introduction," vii–xxiv, Huri İslamoğlu, "Property as a Contested Domain," 3–62, and Denise Jorgens, "A Comparative Examination of the Provisions of the Ottoman Land Code and Khedive Sa'id's Law of 1858," 93–119; Huri İslamoğlu, "Politics of Administering Property: Law and Statistics in the Nineteenth-Century Ottoman Empire," in *Constituting Modernity: Private Property in East and West*, ed. İslamoğlu (London: I. B. Tauris, 2004), 276–319; and Martha Mundy and Richard Saumarez Smith, *Governing Property, Making the Modern State: Law, Administration and Production in Ottoman Syria* (London: I. B. Tauris, 2007). I thank Lev Weitz for pointing me to these sources on Ottoman and Islamic property law.

17. Stated most powerfully by Moyn, *Last Utopia*, and Jan Eckel, *Die Ambivalenz des Guten: Menschenrechte in der internationalen Politik seit den 1949er* (Göttingen: Vandenhoeck and Ruprecht, 2014). See my critique, "Samuel Moyn and the New History of Human Rights," *European Journal of Political Theory* 12:1 (2013): 84–93.

18. See Griffin, *On Human Rights*: "The two terms ['human rights' and 'natural rights'] come from the same continuous tradition" (9). See also Lacroix and Pranchère, *Procès des droits de l'homme*, who argue similarly, and Dan Edelstein, *On the Spirit of Rights* (Chicago: University of Chicago Press, 2019), who reaches back into the early modern period for the origins of human rights. There is also a linguistic conundrum here. In English there is some distinction between the rights of man and human rights. But not in French, German, or Spanish, where the very same words or phrases mean both. *Droits humaines*, a relatively recent linguistic innovation in French, does not seem to have much currency in the francophone world.

19. William Lloyd Garrison said he was a "HUMAN RIGHTS MAN" (emphasis in original) and American feminists used the term prevalently, including in the famed Seneca Falls

Declaration. See Kathryn Kish Sklar, "Human Rights Discourse in Women's Rights Conventions in the United States, 1848–70," in Slotte and Halme-Tuomisaari, *Revisiting the Origins*, 163–88, quotes 183. Frederick Douglass used the phrase in an article, "Reconstruction," in the *Atlantic Monthly* (December 1866), reprinted in *The Life and Writings of Frederick Douglass*, vol. 4, ed. Philip S. Foner (New York: International, 1975), 198–99, 202. For many other nineteenth-century examples of the use of the term "human rights," see Ana Stevenson, "The 'Great Doctrine of Human Rights': Articulation and Authentication in the Nineteenth-Century U.S. Antislavery and Women's Rights Movements," *Humanity* 8:1 (2017): 413–39. See also Bonny Ibhawoh, *Human Rights in Africa* (Cambridge: Cambridge University Press, 2018).

20. As Osterhammel, *Transformation of the World*, and Bayly, *Birth of the Modern World*, both note, this was also the period of great global transformations around the world, marked by the creation of a truly global empire by Great Britain, crises in the Ottoman and Chinese empires, and the extension of Russian power southward and eastward.

Some scholars would contest the very notion of diffusion. But it seems clear to me that the *political* initiative regarding nation-states and human rights originates in the West. Bayly and Osterhammel offer an effective middle ground, critiquing a notion of one-way diffusion from the West to the rest of the world, but not denying the predominant role of the West.

21. On the latter point, see Eric D. Weitz, "Self-Determination: How a German Enlightenment Idea Became the Slogan of National Liberation and a Human Right," *American Historical Review* 120:2 (2015): 462–96. Amartya Sen has written about Indian traditions, going back millennia, of rational disputation, toleration, and pluralism. These characteristics may not exactly constitute human rights, but they are most definitely the values associated with human rights. See *The Argumentative Indian: Writings on Indian History, Culture and Identity* (New York: Farrar, Straus, and Giroux, 2005). See also Ibhawoh, *Human Rights in Africa*, on the way some African traditions were consonant with modern human rights ideas.

A number of the leading individuals, like Charles Malik of Lebanon and Wellington Koo of China, are sometimes disparaged because they were Western educated. But I think that too easily dismisses their biographies and thought. For a counterview, one that draws especially on the Latin American role in the drafting of the founding documents of the UN, see Sikkink, *Evidence for Hope*, as well as Johannes Morsink, *The Universal Declaration of Human Rights: Origins, Drafting, and Intent* (Philadelphia: University of Pennsylvania Press, 1999).

22. For an effective elaboration of the concept of natural rights, see Charles Beitz, *The Idea of Human Rights* (Oxford: Oxford University Press, 2009), 50–72. But he then goes on to argue that human rights have no necessary foundation in natural rights. For an important book that comes to the opposite conclusion—i.e., natural rights as part of the deep tradition of human rights—see Griffin, *On Human Rights*, 30–32, which draws on Brian Tierney, *The Idea of Natural Rights: Studies on Natural Rights, Natural Law and Church Law, 1150–1625* (Atlanta: Scholars Press, 1997). See Edelstein, *Spirit of Rights*, on the varied early modern intellectual sources of human rights.

23. For a succinct statement amid a huge literature, see Sen, "Theory of Human Rights," 338–42.

24. Fichte makes that argument in a compelling fashion in *Foundations of Natural Right*. A far more rigorous statement, one that virtually compels action from people, can be found in

Thomas Pogge, *World Poverty and Human Rights: Cosmopolitan Responsibilities and Reforms*, 2nd ed. (Cambridge: Polity, 2008).

25. For important recent studies of empires, see Krishan Kumar, *Visions of Empire: How Five Imperial Regimes Shaped the World* (Princeton: Princeton University Press, 2017), and Jane Burbank and Frederick Cooper, *Empires in World History: Power and the Politics of Difference* (Princeton: Princeton University Press, 2010).

26. Three classic works on nationalism and the nation-state are: Ernest Gellner, *Nations and Nationalism* (Oxford: Blackwell, 1983); Benedict Anderson, *Imagined Communities: Reflections on the Origins and Spread of Nationalism* (London: Verso, 1983); and Elie Kedourie, *Nationalism*, 4th ed. (1960; Oxford: Blackwell, 1993).

27. On these local loyalties, see Bayly, *Birth of the Modern World*, 64–71, 199–243.

Chapter 1: Empires and Rulers

1. For the East Asian example, see Jürgen Osterhammel, *Unfabling the East: The Enlightenment's Encounter with Asia*, trans. Robert Savage (1998; Princeton: Princeton University Press, 2018).

2. On these nineteenth-century developments, see the magisterial works of Jürgen Osterhammel, *The Transformation of the World: A Global History of the Nineteenth Century*, trans. Patrick Camiller (2009; Princeton: Princeton University Press, 2014); and C. A. Bayly, *The Birth of the Modern World, 1780–1914: Global Connections and Comparisons* (Malden: Blackwell, 2004); along with the powerful article by Sebastian Conrad, "Enlightenment in Global History: A Historiographical Critique," *American Historical Review* 117:4 (2012): 999–1027. Bayly emphasizes the growing uniformity of social practices and political and economic developments around the world, as well as the greater complexity of societies. Osterhammel is more attuned to difference. In regard to state power, Bayly's formulation is insightful: "[States] had to trench into areas of society that had formerly been autonomous" (7).

3. James E. De Kay, *Sketches of Turkey in 1831 and 1832* (New York: Harper, 1833), 330.

4. Ibid., 260.

5. Ibid.

6. Ibid., 261–62.

7. The example of the eyeglasses is from Georg Heinrich von Langsdorff, *Voyages and Travels in Various Parts of the World during the Years 1803, 1804, 1805, 1806, and 1807* (Carlisle: George Philips, 1817), 204. Langsdorff was a German physician and scientist who was employed in Russian service; his book is dedicated to Tsar Alexander I.

8. Harold Nicolson, *The Congress of Vienna: A Study in Allied Unity: 1812–1822* (New York: Harcourt, Brace, 1946), 126–33, 158–63. But for an effective argument that the sociability surrounding the Congress is key to understanding the diplomacy, see Brian E. Vick, *The Congress of Vienna: Power and Politics after Napoleon* (Cambridge: Harvard University Press, 2014).

9. For one example, see Varnhagen von Ense, in *Der Wiener Kongreß: In Schilderungen von Zeitgenossen*, ed. Karl Soll (Berlin: Allstein, n.d.), 16–20.

10. Richard Bright, *Travels from Vienna through Lower Hungary; with Some Remarks on the State of Vienna during the Congress, in the Year 1814* (Edinburgh: Archibald Constable, 1818), 14–16.

11. Jeremy Waldron, following Ernst Bloch, writes about "walking upright," and quotes Immanuel Kant: "Be no man's lackey. . . . Do not let others tread with impunity on your rights. . . . Bowing and scraping before a human being seems in any case unworthy of . . . human [dignity]." See Waldron, "Dignity, Rights, and Responsibilities," *Arizona State Law Review* 43:4 (2011): 1107–36, quote 1127. I thank León Castellanos-Jankiewicz for pointing me toward Waldron's writings on dignity.

12. *The Complete Journal of Townsend Harris: First American Consul General and Minister to Japan*, ed. Mario Emilio Cosenza (Garden City, NY: Doubleday for the Japan Society, 1930), 1 May 1856, 133–34.

13. Quote from Horace Webster, the founding president of the Free Academy, in "Our History," The City College of New York, n.d., accessed 16 February 2019, https://www.ccny.cuny.edu/about/history. Only beginning in 1951 were women able to enroll in all units of the College.

14. Harris, *Complete Journal*, 24 May 1856, 153.

15. Ibid., 7 December 1857, 474–75.

16. Ibid., 12 December 1857, 484–86.

17. Ibid., 8 June 1857, 373.

18. Quoted in Nicolson, *Congress of Vienna*, 39.

19. Vere Monro, *A Summer Ramble in Syria, with a Tatar Trip from Aleppo to Stamboul* (London: R. Bentley, 1835), vol. 1, 263–64.

20. Ibid., 302.

21. Bayard Taylor, *A Visit to India, China, and Japan in the Year 1853* (New York: Putnam, 1855), 268, 269.

22. Ibid., 269–70

23. Ibid., 270.

24. Osterhammel, *Transformation of the World*, 198–99.

25. Jan de Vries, *The Industrious Revolution: Consumer Behavior and the Household Economy, 1650 to the Present* (Cambridge: Cambridge University Press, 2008); Bayly, *Birth of the Modern World*, 49–64.

26. Kenneth Pomeranz, *The Great Divergence: China, Europe, and the Making of the Modern World Economy* (Princeton: Princeton University Press, 2000). The literature is vast. For a comprehensive discussion replete with statistics, see Angus Maddison, *Contours of the World Economy, 1–2030 AD* (Oxford: Oxford University Press, 2007), 69–182.

27. Osterhammel, *Transformation of the World*, 167–240.

28. Ibid., 170–84.

29. Friedrich Engels, *The Condition of the Working Class in England*, trans. and ed. W. O. Henderson and W. H. Chaloner (1845; Stanford: Stanford University Press, 1968), 171–72, 184–85, 201–2.

30. Taylor, *Visit to India*, 36.

31. Ibid.

32. On slavery in the Ottoman Empire, see William Gervase Clarence-Smith, *Islam and the Abolition of Slavery* (Oxford: Oxford University Press, 2006); Ehud R. Toledano, *Slavery and Abolition in the Ottoman Middle East* (Seattle: University of Washington Press, 1998); Y. Hakan Erdem, *Slavery in the Ottoman Empire and Its Demise, 1800–1909* (Houndmills: Macmillan, 1996);

and Bernard Lewis, *Race and Slavery in the Middle East: An Historical Inquiry* (Oxford: Oxford University Press, 1990).

33. Clarence-Smith, *Islam and the Abolition*, 10.

34. John Leyden and Hugh Murray, *Historical Account of Discoveries and Travels in Africa* (Edinburgh: A. Constable, 1817), vol. 2, 496–97. The two authors compiled their book from earlier travel accounts. They never actually journeyed to Africa.

35. See the traveler accounts in James C. Fletcher and D. P. Kidder, *Brazil and the Brazilians Portrayed in Historical and Descriptive Sketches* (London: Low and Marston, 1866), 124, 131–32; Thomas Ewbank, *Life in Brazil; or, A Journal to the Land of Cocoa and Palms* (New York: Harper and Brothers, 1856), 436–41; as well as Gilberto Freyre, *Brazil: An Interpretation* (New York: Knopf, 1945), 47, who mentions numerous traveler accounts.

36. Ewbank, *Life in Brazil*, 115.

37. Ibid., 115–16.

38. Ibid., 118. Such accounts render highly suspect that myth of Brazilian slavery as more humane than that of the United States, as we shall see in more detail in chapter 4. See Freyre, *Brazil: An Interpretation*, 49, for one such classic claim.

39. Orlando Patterson, *Slavery and Social Death: A Comparative Study* (Cambridge: Harvard University Press, 1982).

40. Calculated from the detailed figures provided below. For some figures on the period prior to 1800, see Osterhammel, *Transformation of the World*, 129, and James Belich, *Replenishing the Earth: The Settler Revolution and the Rise of the Anglo World, 1783–1939* (Oxford: Oxford University Press, 2009), 26.

41. For a comprehensive study of migrations in world history, see Dirk Hoerder, *Cultures in Contact: World Migrations in the Second Millennium* (Durham: Duke University Press, 2002). On the evolution of scholarly approaches, see ibid., 8–21, and Patrick Manning, *Migration in World History*, 2nd ed. (New York: Routledge, 2013), 191–205.

42. Angus Maddison, *The World Economy*, vol. 1, *A Millennial Perspective* (Paris: Organisation for Economic Co-operation and Development, 2006), 30, 412–13, 538. Massimo Livi-Bacci, *A Concise History of World Population*, trans. Carl Ipsen (Cambridge: Blackwell, 1992), 31, provides world population figures of 771 million in 1750, 954 million in 1800, 1.241 billion in 1850, and 1.634 billion in 1900. The population in Western Europe in 1820 amounted to 114.571 million, and in China 381 million. The Chinese comprised fully one-third of the global population.

43. Osterhammel, *Transformation of the World*, 154.

44. Ibid., 156.

45. Calculated from David Eltis and David Richardson, *Atlas of the Transatlantic Slave Trade* (New Haven: Yale University Press, 2010), 4–5. For best estimates on the total number of slaves in the Islamic world, see Clarence-Smith, *Islam and the Abolition*, 11–16.

46. David Northrup, *Indentured Labor in the Age of Imperialism, 1834–1922* (Cambridge: Cambridge University Press, 1995), 159–60, and "Migration from Africa, Asia, and the South Pacific," in *The Oxford History of the British Empire*, vol. 3, ed. Wm. Roger Louis and Andrew Porter (Oxford: Oxford University Press, 1999), 88–100, figures 89.

47. Northrup, "Migration from Africa," 91. Indentured laborers often lived and worked in conditions little better than slavery. But they were at least legally free. Osterhammel,

Transformation of the World, 157–64, argues strongly for the distinctions between slavery and indentured labor, as does Northrup, *Indentured Labor*.

48. Sunil S. Amrith, *Migration and Diaspora in Modern Asia* (Cambridge: Cambridge University Press, 2011), 5–7 and passim.

49. Kemal H. Karpat, *Ottoman Population, 1830–1914: Demographic and Social Characteristics* (Madison: University of Wisconsin Press, 1985), 60–77, figures 66–69, 75. Additional emigrations continued well into the twentieth century. In 1951–52, 152,000 Turks were forced to emigrate from Bulgaria to Turkey. Ibid., 75.

50. Northrup, "Migration from Africa," 94.

51. Osterhammel, *Transformation of the World*, 145–46.

52. Chinese figures from ibid., 133–39, 145. The death toll estimates for the Taiping Rebellion range from ten to sixty-six million. Ibid., 349.

53. Northrup, "Migration from Africa," 95–96, and Amrith, *Migration and Diaspora*, 18–19. The best estimates are that fully 80 percent of Chinese migrants and probably 25 percent of European migrants returned at some point during their lives to their home countries and regions. See also Osterhammel, *Transformation of the World*, 163. Idaho's population at one point was 30 percent Chinese!

54. See Osterhammel's discussion in *Transformation of the World*, 322–91; Mohamed Adhikari, ed., *Genocide on Settler Frontiers: When Hunter-Gatherers and Commercial Stock Farmers Clash* (Cape Town: University of Cape Town Press, 2014); and A. Dirk Moses, ed., *Empire, Colony, Genocide: Conquest, Occupation, and Subaltern Resistance in World History* (New York: Berghahn, 2008).

55. For an excellent analysis, see John C. Weaver, *The Great Land Rush and the Making of the Modern World, 1650–1900* (Montreal: McGill-Queen's University Press, 2003).

56. For trenchant comments on this process, see Osterhammel, *Transformation of the World*, 324; Bayly, *Birth of the Modern World*, 436, 437; and multiple works by Patrick Wolfe, including *Traces of History: Elementary Structures of Race* (London: Verso, 2016); "Structure and Event: Settler Colonialism, Time, and the Question of Genocide," in Moses, *Empire, Colony, Genocide*, 102–32; and "Settler Colonialism and the Elimination of the Native," *Journal of Genocide Research* 8:4 (2006): 347–409.

57. As Eric Hobsbawm noted long ago in *The Age of Revolution, 1789–1848* (Cleveland: World Publishing, 1962). For an excellent modern-day application of that insight, see Sven Beckert, *Empire of Cotton: A Global History* (New York: Knopf, 2014). For an interesting analysis of the British debates on indentured labor, see Jonathan S. Connolly, "Indentured Labour Migration and the Meaning of Emancipation: Free Trade, Race, and Labour in British Public Debate, 1838–1860," *Past and Present* 238 (2018): 85–119.

58. For a global perspective, see Osterhammel, *Transformation of the World*, 241–321.

59. Figures from ibid., 251–54, and Belich, *Replenishing the Earth*, 1–3.

60. See S. Conrad, "Enlightenment in Global History," and the classic study by Jürgen Habermas, *The Structural Transformation of the Public Sphere: An Inquiry into a Category of Bourgeois Society*, trans. Thomas Burger and Frederick Lawrence (1962; Cambridge: MIT Press, 1989).

61. On Humboldt, see the magnificent biography by Andrea Wulf, *The Invention of Nature: Alexander von Humboldt's World* (New York: Knopf, 2016).

62. See Lisbeth Koerner, *Linnaeus: Nature and Nation* (Cambridge: Harvard University Press, 1999).

63. De Kay, *Sketches of Turkey*, 75, 76.

64. Monro, *Summer Ramble*, vol. 1, 110–21, quote 111.

65. C. S. Sonnini, *Travels in Greece and Turkey, Undertaken by Order of Louis XVI, and with the Authority of the Ottoman Court*, trans. from French, 2 vols. (London: T. N. Longman, 1801), vol. 1, 5–6.

66. Harris, *Complete Journal*, 20 February 1856, 64–65.

67. Taylor, *Visit to India*, 354.

68. Leyden and Murray, *Historical Account*, vol. 1, 39.

69. De Kay, *Sketches of Turkey*, 123.

70. See, for example, Monro, *Summer Ramble*, vol. 1, 88–89, and Langsdorff, *Voyages and Travels*, 189, 221.

71. See Louis Menand, *The Metaphysical Club* (New York: Farrar, Straus, and Giroux, 2001), and Edward Lurie, *Louis Agassiz: A Life in Science* (Chicago: University of Chicago Press, 1960).

72. The archive is housed in the Peabody Museum at Harvard. Photographic archives were a staple of nineteenth- and early twentieth-century racial-anthropological research. For other examples, see Eugen Fischer, *Die Rehobother Bastards und das Bastardierungsproblem beim Menschen: Anthropologische und ethnographische Studien am Rehobother Bastardvolk in Deutsch-Südwest-Afrika* (Jena: Fischer, 1913), and the collection of early twentieth-century photos from Rwanda and Burundi of the German Colonial Society, in the database of the University Library in Frankfurt, at http://www.ub.bildarchiv-dkg.uni-frankfurt.de/Bildprojekt/frames/hauptframe.html.

73. See *Brazil through the Eyes of William James: Letters, Diaries, and Drawings, 1865–1866*, ed. Maria Helena P. T. Machado (Cambridge: David Rockefeller Center for Latin American Studies, Harvard University Press, 2006). See also Robert D. Richardson, *William James: In the Maelstrom of American Modernism. A Biography* (New York: Houghton Mifflin, 2006), 65–74; Menand, *Metaphysical Club*, 97–148.

74. James to Henry James Sr. and Mary Robertson Walsh James, 21 April 1865, and James to Alice James, 31 August 1865, both in James, *Brazil through the Eyes*, 53–56, quote 54, and 69–75, quote 72–73.

75. James to Henry James Sr. and Mary Robertson Walsh James, 21 October 1865, in ibid., 79–82, quote 80.

76. William James, "Brazilian Diary," in ibid., 87–92, quote 90.

77. Ibid., quote 92.

78. Eltis and Richardson, *Atlas*, 84.

79. This paragraph and what follows is based on Nile Green, *The Love of Strangers: What Six Muslim Students Learned in Jane Austen's London* (Princeton: Princeton University Press, 2016). Also interesting is Rifaʻa Rafiʻ al-Tahtawi, *An Imam in Paris: Account of a Stay in France by an Egyptian Cleric (1826–1831)*, trans. Daniel L. Newman (London: Saqi, 2004).

80. N. Green, *Love of Strangers*, 19–20.

81. Ibid., 62–71.

82. Ibid., 121–28, 138–40, 157–59.

83. Ibid., 202–16, 301.

84. Ibid., 170–76, 261–65.

85. Ibid., 90, 202–16, 301. Until 1837, Persian was the administrative language of the East India Company. It hired Indian-language teachers both abroad and in Britain to teach its employees and administrators. Not satisfied with the results and facing unexpected resistance from a stodgy Oxbridge, it founded two of its own colleges in Britain that showcased the study of Urdu and Persian.

86. "Article 1 of the Final Act of the Congress of Vienna," in Augustus Oakes and R. B. Mowat, eds., *The Great European Treaties of the Nineteenth Century* (Oxford: Clarendon, 1918), 38; and "Annex IX, Article XVI to the Final Act of the Congress of Vienna," in Wikisource contributors, "Final Act of the Congress of Vienna/Act IX," Wikisource, version ID 7000214 (accessed 14 December 2016), https://en.wikisource.org/wiki/Final_Act_of_the_Congress_of_Vienna/Act_IX. Generally, see Max J. Kohler, "Jewish Rights at International Congresses," in *The American Jewish Year Book 5678 (1917–18)*, ed. Samson D. Oppenheim (Philadelphia: Jewish Publication Society of America, 1917), 106–60. The Vienna Treaty also mandated religious toleration in Belgium.

87. Vick, *Congress of Vienna*, goes a little overboard in arguing that the Congress recognized and affirmed nationality. On the great influence of the US founding document, see David Armitage, *The Declaration of Independence: A Global History* (Cambridge: Harvard University Press, 2007).

88. Laurent Dubois, *Avengers of the New World: The Story of the Haitian Revolution* (Cambridge: Belknap Press of Harvard University Press, 2004); David Brion Davis, *The Problem of Slavery in the Age of Emancipation* (New York: Knopf, 2014), 45–82.

89. "Annex XV to the Final Act of the Congress of Vienna," in Wikisource contributors, "Final Act of the Congress of Vienna/Act XV," Wikisource, version ID 4276542, accessed 14 December 2016, https://en.wikisource.org/wiki/Final_Act_of_the_Congress_of_Vienna/Act_XV. See Vick, *Congress of Vienna*, 204, 208–11, and Nicolson, *Congress of Vienna*, 209–14. Vick argues as well that racist sentiments were rarely expressed at the Congress.

90. The literature on abolitionism is vast. See multiple works by David Brion Davis, including *Slavery in the Age of Emancipation* and *The Problem of Slavery in the Age of Revolution* (Ithaca: Cornell University Press, 1975); Seymour Drescher, *Abolition: A History of Slavery and Antislavery* (Cambridge: Cambridge University Press, 2009); Adam Hochschild, *Bury the Chains: Prophets and Rebels in the Fight to Free an Empire's Slaves* (Boston: Houghton Mifflin, 2005); and Rebecca Scott, *Slave Emancipation in Cuba: The Transition to Free Labor, 1860–1899* (Pittsburgh: University of Pittsburgh Press, 2000). Clarence-Smith, *Islam and the Abolition*, demonstrates the diverse influences that led to abolition in the Islamic world, including Western pressure as well as Muslim traditions. Modern scholarship on slavery and its abolition begins with Eric Williams, *Capitalism and Slavery* (Chapel Hill: University of North Carolina Press, 1944).

91. William Blake, "Jerusalem ['And Did Those Feet in Ancient Time']," Poetry Foundation, n.d., accessed 7 October 2018, https://www.poetryfoundation.org/poems-and-poets/poems/detail/54684. See also Tony Benn, ed., *Writings on the Wall: A Radical and Socialist Anthology, 1215–1984* (London: Faber and Faber, 1984). There are no apostrophes—no "England's"—in Blake's original writing. See the facsimile at [William Blake], "Preface," Wikimedia.org, n.d., accessed 7 October 2018, https://upload.wikimedia.org/wikipedia/commons/1/17/Milton_preface.jpg.

92. Bayly, *Birth of the Modern World*, 148–55, and Osterhammel, *Transformation of the World*, 547–51, provide good summaries.

93. Taylor, *Visit to India*, 273.

94. Ibid., 272.

95. Sonnini, *Travels in Greece and Turkey*, vol. 1, xxv, 12–13. Sonnini undertook these travels in 1777–78. He was known as a naturalist, and, indeed, the greatest part of his writing is about flora and fauna.

96. Quoted in Roderic H. Davison, *Reform in the Ottoman Empire* (Princeton: Princeton University Press, 1963), 90.

97. And described by M. Şükrü Hanioğlu, *A Brief History of the Late Ottoman Empire* (Princeton: Princeton University Press, 2008), 72–73.

98. Isabella L. Bird, *Unbeaten Tracks in Japan: An Account of Travels on Horseback in the Interior, Including Visits to the Aborigines of Yezo and the Shrines of Nikkô and Isé*, 2 vols. (New York: G. P. Putnam's Sons, 1881), vol. 1, 42, 46, 47, quote 42.

99. The reports are available in English. See Kume Kunitake, comp., *The Iwakura Embassy, 1871–73: A True Account of the Ambassador Extraordinary & Plenipotentiary's Journey of Observation through the United States of America and Europe*, ed. Graham Healey and Chushichi Tsuzuki (Chiba: Japan Documents, 2002). I thank Sheldon Garon for the reference.

100. J. W. Spalding, *The Japan Expedition: Japan and around the World. An Account of Three Visits to the Japanese Empire* (New York: Redfield, 1855), 74.

101. Harris, *Complete Journal*, 11 January 1856, 42. Italics in original. This was, of course, the famous King Mongkut, immortalized (and perhaps infantilized) first in the memoir by his son's tutor, Anna Leonowens, and then in the Rogers and Hammerstein Broadway production *The King and I*. The son, Prince Chulalongkorn, would succeed his father and be an even more fervent advocate of modernization.

102. Harris, *Complete Journal*, 13 April 1856, 79, and 15 April 1856, 83.

103. See S. Conrad, "Enlightenment in Global History," and Bayly, *Birth of the Modern World*, 76–80.

Chapter 2: Greece

1. Rhigas Velestinlis, "Hymne patriotique" and "Nouveau statut politique des habitants de la Roumélie, de l'Asie-mineure, des Iles méditerranéennes et de la Moldovalachie," in *Les oeuvres de Rhigas Velestinlis*, ed. Ap. Dascalakis (Paris, 1937), 61–71, quote 65–67; and 73–124, comment on Turks 75, 79.

2. Velestinlis, "Nouveau statut politique," 87.

3. Ibid., 79.

4. Ibid., 81.

5. Ibid., 87.

6. Ibid., 93, 95. In these clauses Velestinlis also outlined the provisions for naturalization. A person could become Greek if he or she has married a Greek, supports (*aider*) Greece even if he lives outside the country, speaks Greek, or adopts a Greek child.

7. Beating Belgium, which also became independent in 1830, by eight months.

8. Generally on the Greek Revolution, see David Brewer, *The Flame of Freedom: The Greek War of Independence, 1821–1833* (London: J. Murray, 2001), and Douglas Dakin, *The Greek Struggle for Independence, 1821–1833* (Berkeley: University of California Press, 1973). Specifically on the Danubian revolt, see Richard Stites, *The Four Horsemen: Riding to Liberty in Post-Napoleonic Europe* (New York: Oxford University Press, 2014), 186–239. Stites specifically connects Greek events to other movements in the broader Mediterranean world and in Russia.

9. Richard Clogg, ed., *The Movement for Greek Independence, 1770–1821: A Collection of Documents* (London: Macmillan, 1976), provides a good sense of Greek society on the eve of the War of Independence.

10. See John S. Koliopoulos, *Brigands with a Cause: Brigandage and Irredentism in Modern Greece, 1821–1912* (Oxford: Clarendon, 1987). For one memoir, see Th. Kolokotronis, *Memoirs from the Greek War of Independence, 1821–1833*, trans. G. Tertzetis (1892; Chicago: Argonaut, 1969). Stites, in *Four Horsemen*, calls the memoir "self-serving and fantasy-laden," but nonethess effective in conveying the life and spirit of brigands (214).

11. See Dakin, *Greek Struggle for Independence*, 41–49, 60.

12. Stites, *Four Horsemen*, 202–3.

13. See the classic study by Miroslav Hroch, *Social Preconditions of National Revival in Europe*, trans. Ben Fowkes (1968; Cambridge: Cambridge University Press, 1985).

14. Richard Clogg, *A Concise History of Greece*, 3rd ed. (Cambridge: Cambridge University Press, 2013), 20–28.

15. George Finlay, *History of the Greek Revolution* (Edinburgh: William Blackwood and Sons, 1861), vol. 1, 278.

16. John L. Comstock, nineteenth-century historian and a former British consul in Petras, *History of the Greek Revolution Compiled from Official Documents of the Greek Government* (1832; Hartford: Silas Andrus and Son, 1853), 153–54.

17. Odysseus Androuzzos to Mehmet Pasha, 15/27 November 1822, and "The Patriot Odysseus," Athens, 10/22 June 1823, in Thomas Gordon, *History of the Greek Revolution* (Edinburgh: William Blackwood, 1832), vol. 1, 466; vol. 2, 40–41.

18. Rodios to Canning, Naples, 11 August 1824, in *British and Foreign State Papers*, vol. 12, 1824–25 (London: J. Harrison and Son, 1826), 899–900. Canning unceremoniously rejected the appeal, which was also connected to a request for a loan from Britain.

19. Peter Mavromichalis, "To the Citizens of the United States of America," by the Messenian Senate at Calamata, Peter Mavromichalis Commander-in-Chief, Calamata, 25 May 1821, quoted in *North American Review* 17:41 (1823): 415–16. I thank Fabian Klose for the reference.

20. On Muhammad 'Ali and Greece, see Khaled Fahmy, *Mehmed Ali: From Ottoman Governor to Ruler of Egypt* (Oxford: Oneworld, 2009), 68–78, and Afaf Lufti Al-Sayyid Marsot, *Egypt in the Reign of Muhammad Ali* (Cambridge: Cambridge University Press, 1984), 205–31.

21. Gordon, *History of the Greek Revolution*, vol. 1, 1.

22. Finlay, *History of the Greek Revolution*, vol. 1, 1, 2.

23. For one semi-recent work that thrills with enthusiasm, see C. M. Woodhouse, *The Philhellenes* (London: Hodder and Stoughton, 1969), 93. Generally on the Philhellenes, see also William St. Clair, *That Greece Might Still Be Free: The Philhellenes in the War of Independence* (London: Oxford University Press, 1972), and Douglas Dakin, *British and American Philhellenes*

during the War of Greek Independence, 1821–1833 (Thessaloniki: N. Nicolaides, 1955). For a broader perspective that covers the Philhellenes in Western Europe and the United States, see Natalie Klein, *"L'humanité, le Christianisme, et la liberté": Die internationale Philhellenische Vereinsbewegung der 1820er Jahre* (Mainz: Philipp von Zabern, 2000).

24. Byron, journal entry, 19 June 1823, in *Byron's Letters and Journals*, ed. Leslie A. Marchand, vol. 11, *1823–24* (London: John Murray, 1981), 29.

25. Byron to Andreas Londos, Missolonghi, 30/18 January 1824, in ibid., 103–4, quote 103.

26. See, for example, Byron to his mother, Catherine Gordon Byron, Prevesa, 12 November 1809, in *Selected Letters of Lord Byron*, ed. Jacques Barzun (New York: Farrar, Straus and Young, 1953), 24–30. All Europeans, including Greeks, used the term "Turks," but it was not the Ottoman name. Until the Turkish Republic was founded under Mustapha Kemal in 1923, "Turk" in the Ottoman realm was a pejorative that suggested a low-class person.

27. Byron to his mother, Patras, 30 July 1810, and Athens, 14 January 1811, and to John Cam Hobhouse, Athens, 18 March 1811, in *Letters and Journals*, vol. 2: *1810–1812* (London: John Murray, 1973), 8–9, 34–35, 43–44.

28. Byron to Mayer, [21 February 1824], in *Letters and Journals*, vol. 11, 118.

29. Byron to John Murray, Messalonghi, 25 February 1824, and Byron to Thomas Moore, Messolonghi, 4 March 1824, in ibid., 123–25 and 125–26.

30. Byron, journal entry, 28 September 1823, in ibid., 32–33.

31. Ibid.

32. Byron to Mavrocordatos, Cefalonia, 1 October 1823, in ibid., 37–39, quotes 38.

33. Quoted in Gary J. Bass, *Freedom's Battle: The Origins of Humanitarian Intervention* (New York: Knopf, 2008), 69.

34. Quotes in order: "Proclamations of the National Assembly at Epidaurus, 16 and 28 April 1826," in *British and Foreign State Papers*, vol. 13, *1825–26* (London: J. Harrison and Son, 1827), 1062–67, quote 1062; British vice-admiral Edward Codrington to Stratford Canning, HMS Asia in the Port of Navarin, 20 October 1827, in *British and Foreign State Papers*, vol. 17, 309; *The Times*, responding to the massacre at Chios, quoted in Bass, *Freedom's Battle*, 71; and Comstock, *History of the Greek Revolution*, 153.

35. See, for example, his account of the seizure of Navarin in August 1821, in Finlay, *History of the Greek Revolution*, vol. 1, 262–64.

36. Ibid., 187.

37. Ibid., 188.

38. Ibid., vol. 2, 237.

39. Ibid., 225.

40. See K. E. Fleming, *Greece: A Jewish History* (Princeton: Princeton University Press, 2008).

41. I thank Yannis Kotsonis for emphasizing to me the point about other minorities. Many of them were slowly assimilated into Greek society, a process of "ethnic simplification," as Kotsonis calls it. For many, though by no means all, their common Christianity eased their assimilation.

42. "Proclamation d'indépendance de l'Assemblée Nationale Hellenique," Epidaure, 27 January 1822, in *British and Foreign State Papers*, vol. 9, *1821–22* (London: J. Harrison and Son, 1829), 629–32, quote 630.

43. Ibid., 630. For another example, see "The Patriot Odysseus, Athens, 10/22 June 1823," in Gordon, *History of the Greek Revolution*, vol. 2, 40–41. In general, however, the brigands had little in the way of formal political ideology. Koliopoulos, *Brigands with a Cause*, supplies virtually no evidence that the brigands were engaged with the ideology of liberty and rights; nor does the memoir by the brigand Kolokotronis, *Memoirs from the Greek War*.

44. For one example: the Greek provisional government sought entry to the European deliberations, only to find its request denied: Provisional Government of Greece, "Déclaration adressée aux Monarques réunis à Vérone, Argos," 29 August 1822, in *British and Foreign State Papers*, vol. 10, *1822–23* (London: J. Harrison and Son, 1828), 1021–22.

45. On the broader history of foreign intervention in Greece, see especially Davide Rodogno, *Against Massacre: Humanitarian Interventions in the Ottoman Empire, 1815–1914* (Princeton: Princeton University Press, 2011), which is more nuanced than Bass, *Freedom's Battle*, and the important collection by Lucien J. Frary and Mara Kozelsky, eds., *Russian-Ottoman Borderlands: The Eastern Question Reconsidered* (Madison: University of Wisconsin Press, 2014). For some of the classic studies, see Paul W. Schroeder, *The Transformation of European Politics, 1763–1848* (Oxford: Clarendon, 1994), 606–21, 637–65; M. S. Anderson, *The Eastern Question, 1774–1923: A Study in International Relations* (London: Macmillan, 1966), 53–87; and Dakin, *Greek Struggle for Independence*. See also Michael N. Barnett, *Empire of Humanity: A History of Humanitarianism* (Ithaca: Cornell University Press, 2011).

46. For one instructive though exaggerated account, see Harris J. Booras, *Hellenic Independence and America's Contribution to the Cause* (Rutland: Tuttle, 1934). See also Bass, *Freedom's Battle*, 88–99.

47. On the emergence of the Russian public sphere in direct connection to the Greek events, see Lucien J. Frary, *Russia and the Making of Modern Greek Identity, 1821–1844* (Oxford: Oxford University Press, 2015).

48. Here I think Bass, *Freedom's Battle*, goes too far when he argues that "Britain repeatedly went against its own realpolitik interests . . . in the name of humanity" (19). Humanitarian concerns were certainly present, as they were in slavery abolition, but they did not completely trump standard diplomatic concerns.

49. For the nineteenth century, see also Rodogno, *Against Massacre*.

50. Stroganoff to the Reis Effendi [the head of the Chancery of the Imperial Council, from 1836 the foreign minister], Buyukdere, 6 and 18 July 1821, in *British and Foreign State Papers*, vol. 8, *1820–21* (London: J. Harrison and Son, 1830), 1251–57, quote 1254.

51. "Mémoire du Cabinet du Russie," 31 May 1824, in *British and Foreign State Papers*, vol. 11, *1823–24* (London: J. Harrison and Son, 1825), 819–27, here 822–23.

52. The Russian foreign minister Count Karl Robert Nesselrode advised his ambassador to Great Britain, Prince Lieven, that Black Sea shipping and the general relations with the Ottoman Empire offered France and Britain profits and other advantages; for Russia, however, access to the straits was a lifeline, an existential issue affecting all of Russia's interests. Nesselrode to Lieven, St. Petersburg, 26 December 1827/6 January 1828, in *British and Foreign State Papers*, vol. 17, 30–40, here 31.

53. Schroeder, *Transformation*, 645.

54. "Manifesto of the Sublime Porte," 9 June 1827, in *British and Foreign State Papers*, vol. 14, *1826–27* (London: J. Harrison and Son, 1828), 1042–48, quote 1045–46.

55. Ibid., 1043, 1046–47.

56. "Proclamation of the Ottoman Porte," 20 December 1827, in *British and Foreign State Papers*, 14: 1052–57, quote 1056.

57. "Firman of the Grand Seignior," 16 August 1821, in *British and Foreign State Papers*, vol. 8, 1290–91, quote 1290. See also a similar statement from Reis Effendi to Viscount Strangford, Constantinople, 2 December 1821, in *British and Foreign State Papers*, vol. 9, 659–61, quote 661. Theophilus Prousis has edited four volumes of Strangford's reports from Istanbul: *Lord Strangford at the Sublime Porte: The Eastern Crisis* (Istanbul: Isis, 2010).

58. Reis Effendi to Russian envoy [Stroganoff], 26 July 1821, in *British and Foreign State Papers*, vol. 8, 1260–67, quote 1262.

59. Ibid., 1263.

60. Ibid.

61. "Firman of the Grand Seignior," 15 August 1821, in *British and Foreign State Papers*, vol. 8, 1287–90.

62. Schroeder, *Transformation*, 638.

63. For the long course of British interests in Greece, see Robert Holland and Diana Markides, *The British and the Hellenes: Struggles for Mastery in the Eastern Mediterranean, 1850–1960* (Oxford: Oxford University Press, 2006).

64. See, for example, ibid., as well as the classic work of M. S. Anderson, *Eastern Question*.

65. Rodogno, *Against Massacre*, 78–80, argues that the Russians deliberately fostered the rumors so Britain would intervene, but not unilaterally and only in cooperation with Russia.

66. See ibid., on Russia's promotion of the story. See also Lucien J. Frary, "Slaves of the Sultan: Russian Ransoming of Christian Captives during the Greek Revolution, 1820–1830," in Frary and Kozelsky, *Russian-Ottoman Borderlands*, 101–30.

67. Duke of Wellington, "Memorandum," 29 January 1826, in Field Marshall Arthur Duke of Wellington, *Despatches, Correspondence, and Memoranda*, vol. 3, *1826–27*, ed. Duke of Wellington [his son] (London: John Murray, 1868), 77–79, quote 79.

68. Lord Bathurst to the lords commissioners of the Admiralty, 8 February 1826, in ibid., 82–83.

69. Duke of Wellington, "Memorandum of conversation with the emperor of Russia," 11 March 1826, in ibid., 179–91, here 183.

70. Canning to Wellington, Foreign Office, 10 February 1826, in ibid., quote 92.

71. George Canning to Stratford Canning, Foreign Office, 10 February 1826, in ibid., 104–7, quote 106.

72. Captain the Hon. Robert Spencer to Sir Harry Neale, Bart., 18 March 1826, HMS Naiad, Gulf of Patras, in ibid., 285–86, quote 285, and Spencer to Ibrahim Pasha, 14 March 1826, HMS Naiad in Gulf of Patras, in ibid., 287–88. Conflicting reports were coming in from British diplomats. Stratford Canning wrote that at least the Porte was not involved in the plan, while Lord Bathurst affirmed the opposite. See Stratford Canning to the Duke of Wellington,

Constantinople, 16 March 1826, in ibid., 196–98, here 198, and Bathurst to Wellington, Downing Street, 17 February 1826, in ibid., 119.

73. "Treaty between Great Britain, France, and Russia," 6 July 1827, in *British and Foreign State Papers*, vol. 14: 632–39, quote 635.

74. "Protocol of the Conference, between the British and Russian Plenipotentiaries," 23 March and 4 April 1826, in *British and Foreign State Papers*, vol. 14, 629–32.

75. Canning to Wellington, Foreign Office, 17 February 1826, in Wellington, *Despatches*, vol. 3, 125. See also, for example, Wellington to Bathurst, Berlin, 17 February 1826, in ibid., 113–16. There was also talk of transporting the entire Greek population of Samos because it was deemed too exposed to Ottoman reprisals. See Count Ferronays to Prince Polignac, Paris, 28 April 1828, in *British and Foreign State Papers*, vol. 17, 67–70.

76. "Protocole de la conférence [of the plenipotentiaries of Great Britain, France, and Russia] tenue au Foreign Office," 22 March 1829, in *British and Foreign State Papers*, vol. 16, *1828–29* (London: James Ridgway, 1832), 1095–99, here 1096. Moreover, Greeks were encouraged to emigrate from Ottoman territory, Muslims from Greece. Ibid., 1097–98. The original draft provision is in the "Protocol of the Conference, between the British and Russian Plenipotentiaries," 23 March and 4 April 1826, in *British and Foreign State Papers*, vol. 14, 629–32.

77. Dakin, *Greek Struggle for Independence*, 87–89.

78. "Constitution provisoire de l'Hellenie," in *British and Foreign State Papers*, vol. 9, 620–29, here 621. Generally, see Nicholas Kaltchas, *Introduction to the Constitutional History of Modern Greece* (New York: Columbia University Press, 1940). I thank Lucien Frary for the reference.

79. "Constitution provisoire de l'Hellenie," 621.

80. Stratford Canning to George Canning, aboard the HMS Revenge, 10 January 1826, in Wellington, *Despatches*, vol. 3, 121–24, quote 122.

81. "Resolution of the third Greek National Congress," Piada, 16/28 April 1826, addressed to Stratford Canning, in Gordon, *History of the Greek Revolution*, vol. 2, 329.

82. From the very beginning, in the Danubian principalities, the Greek rebels carried out atrocities against Muslims. See Stites, *Four Horsemen*, 201–2.

83. For example, "Constitution politique de la Grèce," Trezene, May 1827, in *British and Foreign State Papers*, vol. 15, *1827–28* ([London]: J. Harrison and Son, 1829), 1069–83.

84. Dakin, *Greek Struggle for Independence*, 306–7.

85. Only the 1864 constitution was welcoming to non-Christians.

86. In 1826, George Canning had dispatched Wellington to St. Petersburg to pressure Russia to exercise restraint. The letters and memoranda that ensued indicate Russia's lack of enthusiasm for the Greek cause. See Canning to Wellington, Foreign Office, 10 February 1826, in Wellington, *Despatches*, vol. 3, 85–93; Wellington to Canning, St. Petersburg, 5 March/21 February 1826, in ibid., 148–50, quote 149–50. See also subsequent letters of Wellington's that also report on his meetings with the tsar and convey the same lack of interest for the Greek cause; e.g., "Memorandum of Conversation with the Emperor of Russia," 11 March 1826, in ibid., 179–91.

87. Vice-Admiral Edward Codrington to Stratford Canning, HMS Asia in the Port of Navarin, 20 October 1827, and Rear Admiral Rigny to Count Guilleminot, *Sirene à Navarin*, 20 October 1827, both in *British and Foreign State Papers*, vol. 17, 309.

88. "Circular of the Russian Government to Its Ministers at Foreign Courts, on the Declaration of War against Turkey," 14 and 30 April 1828, in ibid., vol. 15, 1095–98, quote 1096; Nesselrode to Prince de Lieven, St. Petersburg, 14 and 20 February 1828, in ibid., vol. 17, 50–57, esp. 53 and 54.

89. For one example, see Earl of Dudley to the Prince de Lieven, Foreign Office, 6 March 1828, in ibid., 42–48.

90. Articles 5 and 6, "Protocol of Conference between Great Britain, France, and Russia, Relative to the Independence of Greece," London, 3 February 1830, in Augustus Oakes and R. B. Mowat, eds., *The Great European Treaties of the Nineteenth Century* (Oxford: Clarendon, 1918), 120–23, quote 121, and "Protocole de la conférence tenue au Foreign Office," 16 June 1830, in *British and Foreign State Papers*, vol. 18, *1830–31* (London: James Ridgway, 1833), 600–602.

91. "Convention, relative à la souveraineté de la Grèce, entre les Cours de la Grand Bretagne, de France, et de Russie, d'une part, et la Cour de Bavière, de l'autre," London, 7 May 1832, in *British and Foreign State Papers*, vol. 19, 33–41, quote 35–36.

92. See "Les représentands des trois Cours au Comte d'Aberdeen, Constantinople," 27 April 1830, in *British and Foreign State Papers*, vol. 18, 600–605.

93. Richard Clogg, *A Short History of Modern Greece*, 2nd ed. (Cambridge: Cambridge University Press, 1986), 70.

94. Quoted in ibid., 76.

95. Dimitris Glinos, "What Is the National Liberation Front (EAM) and What Does It Want?" (September 1942), in Richard Clogg, ed., *Greece, 1940–1949: Occupation, Resistance, Civil War—A Documentary History* (Houndmills: Palgrave Macmillan, 2002), 76–99, quote 76.

96. On the devastation of Greece under Nazi occupation, see Mark Mazower, *Inside Hitler's Greece: The Experience of Occupation, 1941–44* (New Haven: Yale University Press, 1993). For the decree ordering reprisal executions of Greeks, issued 25 October 1943, see Clogg, *Greece, 1940–1949*, 101.

97. Glinos, "National Liberation Front," quote 86; 1821 invoked 76, 84. Despite being enmeshed in factional conflicts on the left, a moving account of the resistance and subsequent civil war is, Dominique Eudes, *Les Kapétanios: La guerre civile grecque, 1943–1949* (Paris: Fayard, 1970).

98. See the text in Dionysios Solomos, *The Free Besieged and Other Poems*, ed. Peter Mackridge, trans. Peter Thompson (Nottingham: Shoestring, 2000), 11–55. Solomos later also wrote "Hymn to Freedom," adapting Velestinlis's text from the 1790s, to memorialize the Greek War of Independence in the 1820s. The first two stanzas of the hymn have been incorporated into the Greek national anthem since the 1860s. The original is 158 stanzas. Rudyard Kipling's translation of seven of them, including the first two, is available at https://en.wikisource.org/wiki/Hymn_to_Liberty_(Kipling), accessed 7 October 2018.

99. The Theodorakis-Rotas version served as the theme song for the 1969 movie *Z* (Office National pour le Commerce et l'Industrie Cinématographique, dir. Costa-Gavras), which depicted the assassination of the left-wing activist and deputy Grigoris Lambrakis in 1963.

100. The lyrics have been reworked many times and by various individuals, first by Rotas. For some of the history, see Patrick Comerford, "Maria Farantouri's 80 Great Songs and Her Revolutionary Spirit," Patrick Comerford's blog, 1 September 2017, http://www.patrick

comerford.com/2017/09/maria-farantouris-80-great-songs-and.html. The great excitement and enthusiasm at the concert is palpable from the films that exist, which can be viewed at "Theodorakis Farantouri To Yelasto Pedi 1974," YouTube, 8 September 2007, https://www.youtube.com/watch?v=NLgerQJo7zM, and "Mikis Theodorakis—Maria Farantouri 'To Gelasto Paidi,'" YouTube, 1 February 2016, https://www.youtube.com/watch?v=ZhoLsSvm40Q. I have translated the Farantouri version into English from the German subtitles.

101. For one summary, see Christos Lyrintzis, "PASOK in Power: From 'Change' to Disenchantment," in *Greece, 1981–89: The Populist Decade*, ed. Richard Clogg (New York: St. Martin's, 1993), 26–46.

102. Woodhouse, in *Philhellenes*, writes, "a particular strength to the new democracy was the homgeneity of the Greek people" (181). But that masks the reality of population diversity in the country. In general, on the constitutional and political provisions following the 1862 coup, see ibid., 171–72, and Kaltchas, *Constitutional History*, 110–36.

103. Articles 3, 4, 13, and 25 of "The Constitution of Greece," Hellenic Resources Network, n.d., accessed 10 October 2018, http://www.hri.org/docs/syntagma/. But for an argument that the constitution limits individual rights by emphasizing the family and the state, see Keith R. Legg and John M. Roberts, *Modern Greece: A Civilization on the Periphery* (Boulder: Westview, 1997), 113–16.

104. "Greek Citizenship Code," trans. Haris Psarras (n.p.: EUDO-Citizenship Observatory, n.d., accessed 10 October 2018, http://eudo-citizenship.eu/NationalDB/docs/GRE%20Citizenship%20Code%20(as%20of%202010,%20English).pdf.

105. US Bureau of Democracy, Human Rights, and Labor, "International Religious Freedom Report 2006," US Department of State, n.d., accessed 10 October 2018, https://www.state.gov/j/drl/rls/irf/2006/71383.htm. See also Richard Clogg, ed., *Minorities in Greece: Aspects of a Plural Society* (London: Hurst, 2002).

106. "Proclamation adressée aux Grecs par le président de la troisième Assemblée Nationale," Trézène (Damala), 17 May 1827, in *British and Foreign State Papers*, vol. 15, 1067–69, quote 1068. French original: "Des milliers de Musulmans ont disparu du sol sacré de la Patrie. Nous pouvons en anéantir des milliers d'autres, si nous savons nous aimer, et n'avoir tous qu'une volonté, le salut de la Patrie: Concitoyens! le bien de tous aujourd'hui, c'est de délivrer le Pays."

Chapter 3: America

1. Governor Alexander Ramsey to Secretary of War E. M. Stanton, Saint Paul, 21 August 1862, quoted in Charles W. Johnson, "Narrative of the Sixth Regiment," in *Minnesota in the Civil and Indian Wars, 1861–1865*, ed. Board of Commissioners, vol. 1 (St. Paul: Pioneer, 1890), 300–46, quote 310.

2. Ramsey to Stanton, Saint Paul, 21 August 1862, quoted in Board of Commissioners, *Minnesota*, vol. 2, *Official Reports and Correspondence* (St. Paul: Pioneer, 1893), 194–95.

3. Stanton to Maj. Gen. John Pope, Washington, DC, 6 September 1862, quoted in ibid., 225.

4. I have chosen to use "mixed-race" despite its problematic connotations, as it is at least preferable to "half-breeds" and "half-bloods," the terms typically used in the sources.

5. William Watts Folwell, *A History of Minnesota*, 4 vols. (1921–29; St. Paul: Minnesota Historical Society, 1956–69), vol. 1 (1956), 351–53, 359–61, and James Belich, *Replenishing the Earth:*

The Settler Revolution and the Rise of the Anglo World, 1783–1939 (Oxford: Oxford University Press, 2009), 335–36.

6. See Emmanuel Kreike, *Environcide and Total War* (Princeton: Princeton University Press, forthcoming), on the deliberate destruction of the environmental infrastructure in war, with cases drawn from the Americas, Indonesia, and the Netherlands.

7. On this global process, see Patrick Wolfe, *Traces of History: Elementary Structures of Race* (London: Verso, 2016); Wolfe, "Structure and Event: Settler Colonialism, Time, and the Question of Genocide," in *Empire, Colony, Genocide: Conquest, Occupation, and Subaltern Resistance in World History*, ed. A. Dirk Moses (New York: Berghahn, 2008), 102–32; Wolfe, "Settler Colonialism and the Elimination of the Native," *Journal of Genocide Research* 8:4 (2006): 387–409; Mohamed Adhikari, ed., *Genocide on Settler Frontiers: When Hunter-Gatherers and Stock Farmers Clash* (Cape Town: University of Cape Town Press, 2014); Belich, *Replenishing the Earth*; and Mark Levene, *Genocide in the Age of the Nation-State*, vol. 2, *The Rise of the West and the Coming of Genocide* (London: I. B. Taurus, 2005).

8. The Dakota are members of the much larger Sioux Nation, which also includes the Lakota, who live farther west. In the 1870s, a decade after the Dakota-US War in Minnesota, the Lakota and other tribes fought the United States in the Great Sioux War, with battles ranging over Montana, Wyoming, and the Dakota territories. The defeat of the US Army led by George Armstrong Custer at Little Big Horn was one battle in the larger war.

9. On the Dakota, see especially Gwen Westerman and Bruce White, *Mni Sota Makoce: The Land of the Dakota* (St. Paul: Minnesota Historical Society, 2012).

10. Good depictions of the first encounters from the late seventeenth to the early nineteenth centuries are in Westerman and White, *Mni Sota Makoce*, as well as the early histories by Edward D. Neill, *History of the Minnesota Valley, including the Explorers and Pioneers of Minnesota* (Minneapolis: North Star, 1882), 141–50; Folwell, *History of Minnesota*, vol. 1; Theodore C. Blegen, *Minnesota: A History of the State* (Minneapolis: University of Minnesota Press, 1963); and William E. Lass, *Minnesota: A History*, 2nd ed. (New York: Norton, 1998).

11. See Gary Clayton Anderson, *Kinsmen of Another Kind: Dakota-White Relations in the Upper Mississippi Valley, 1650–1862* (Lincoln: University of Nebraska Press, 1984).

12. Neill, *History of the Minnesota Valley*, 74–75.

13. On the treaties, see Westerman and White, *Mni Sota Makoce*, 133–95, and Folwell, *History of Minnesota*, vol. 1, 266–326. In total, twelve treaties were signed between the Dakota and the US government.

14. "Vast domain" was a common term, used also by Supreme Court Justice Henry Baldwin in *Cherokee Nation v. State of Georgia*, 30 U.S. (5 Pet.) 1, 32 (1831).

15. For an excellent example of the linguistic differences between Dakota and English, which gave rise to many misunderstandings beyond the outright deceit practiced by traders, see Westerman and White, *Mni Sota Makoce*, 173–79. The authors provide three versions of the 1851 Treaty of Traverse des Sioux.

16. On the early missionaries, see Folwell, *History of Minnesota*, vol. 1, 170–212, and generally, David A. Hollinger, *Protestants Abroad: How American Missionaries Tried to Change the World but Changed America* (Princeton: Princeton University Press, 2017).

17. Folwell, *History of Minnesota*, vol. 1, 352–53.

18. Ibid., 354.

19. Quoted in ibid., 355.

20. Figures from ibid., 58–59.

21. "Big Eagle's Account" (1894), in *Through Dakota Eyes: Narrative Accounts of the Minnesota Indian War of 1862*, ed. Gary Clayton Anderson and Alan R. Woolworth (St. Paul: Minnesota Historical Society, 1988), 21–27, quote 23. For a counterstory by an Indian who had converted and embraced Christianity, see "Narrative of Paul Mazakootemane" (1869), trans. Rev. S. R. Riggs, in *Collections of the Minnesota Historical Society*, vol. 3, *1870–1880* (St. Paul: Minnesota Historical Society, 1880), 82–90.

22. The Ojibway, farther north, were more isolated in the dense and watery Northern woods, and therefore not yet subject to the same degree of pressure as the Dakota, even though they, too, had signed treaties—eleven in all—that ceded land and placed them on reservations.

23. "Big Eagle's Account," 24.

24. Ibid.

25. Folwell, *History of Minnesota*, vol. 2 (1961), 225–41.

26. Charles S. Bryant, *A History of the Great Massacre by the Sioux Indians, in Minnesota, including the Personal Narratives of Many Who Escaped* (Cincinnati: R. W. Carroll, 1868), 179–81; Folwell, *History of Minnesota*, vol. 2, 217–22, figures 222; Louis H. Roddis, *The Indian Wars of Minnesota* (Cedar Rapids: Torch, 1956), 54; and Gregory F. Michno, *Dakota Dawn: The Decisive First Week of the Sioux Uprising, August 17–24, 1862* (New York: Savas Beatie, 2011), 17.

27. "Big Eagle's Account," 24.

28. "Wabasha's Statement" (1868), in G. Anderson and Woolworth, *Through Dakota Eyes*, 27–31, here 29.

29. Folwell, *History of Minnesota*, vol. 2, 216–18, quote 217–18.

30. "Little Crow's Speech" (1862), in G. Anderson and Woolworth, *Through Dakota Eyes*, 39–42, quote 41–42. The speech is cited in all accounts. The text of the speech dates from an interview with Little Crow's son, fifteen years after the event.

31. See, for example, "Big Eagle's Account," 25–26.

32. See the accounts, some written soon after the events, others decades later, in G. Anderson and Woolworth, *Through Dakota Eyes*, 129–45.

33. "Paul Mazakutemani's Statement" (1880), in G. Anderson and Woolworth, *Through Dakota Eyes*, 195–98, quote 196.

34. Quoted in Isaac V. D. Heard, *History of the Sioux War and Massacres of 1862 and 1863* (New York: Harper and Brothers, 1863), 156–57. Heard was a prominent attorney and prosecutor in Minnesota, who served as one of the judges in the Sioux trials. His book was the first history of the uprising.

35. Quoted in ibid., 159.

36. Roddis, *Indian Wars*, 63–64. This story also appears in all accounts of the war.

37. Examples in ibid., 79–83.

38. The first quote is from John G. Nicolay, "The Sioux War" (1863), in *Lincoln's Secretary Goes West: Two Reports by John G. Nicolay on Frontier Indian Troubles 1862*, ed. Theodore C. Blegen (La Crosse: Sumac, 1965), 45–69, quote 63. Nicolay was sent by Lincoln to negotiate a

treaty with the Ojibway. The rebellion broke out while he was on his way to Minnnesota. The second quote is from Pope to Major General Halleck, St. Paul, 23 September 1862, in Board of Commissioners, *Minnesota*, vol. 2, 238–39, quote 239.

39. Folwell, *History of Minnesota*, vol. 2, 124.

40. Nicolay, "Sioux War," 45.

41. "Esther Wakeman's Reminiscences" (published by her daughter in 1960), in G. Anderson and Woolworth, *Through Dakota Eyes*, 53–55, quote 55.

42. Many of the testimonies in *Through Dakota Eyes* convey the great fear.

43. See, for example, "Big Eagle's Account," 55–56.

44. Folwell, *History of Minnesota*, vol. 2, 148.

45. Ibid.

46. See the classic book by Richard White, *The Middle Ground: Indians, Empires, and Republic in the Great Lakes Region, 1650–1815* (Cambridge: Cambridge University Press, 1991).

47. "Samuel J. Brown's Recollections," (1897), in G. Anderson and Woolworth, *Through Dakota Eyes*, 70–71.

48. Lincoln to Ramsey, Washington, DC, 27 August 1862, quoted in C. Johnson, "Narrative of the Sixth Regiment," 310.

49. Roddis, *Indian Wars*. For narrative accounts of the fighting, see G. Anderson and Woolworth, *Through Dakota Eyes*, 157–65.

50. Roddis, *Indian Wars*, 193.

51. Sibley to his wife, 20 October 1862, quoted in ibid., 158.

52. Nicolay to Stanton, St. Paul, 27 August 1862, in Board of Commissioners, *Minnesota*, vol. 2, 202.

53. Scott W. Berg, *38 Nooses: Lincoln, Little Crow, and the Beginning of the Frontier's End* (New York: Pantheon, 2012), 97, 163.

54. Pope to Sibley, St. Paul, 28 September 1862, in Board of Commissioners, *Minnesota*, vol. 2, 257.

55. On the militias, see Roddis, *Indian Wars*, 188–92.

56. See Wolfe, *Traces of History*, "Structure and Event", and "Settler Colonialism"; Adhikari, *Genocide on Settler Frontiers*; Belich, *Replenishing the Earth*; and Levene, *Rise of the West*.

57. Pope to Sibley, St. Paul, 17 September 1862, in Board of Commissioners, *Minnesota*, vol. 2, 233–34, and 28 September 1862, in Roddis, *Indian Wars*, 140–41.

58. Roddis, *Indian Wars*, 142–45.

59. Ibid., 132–33.

60. Quoted in General C. C. Andrews, "Narrative of the Third Regiment," in Board of Commissioners, *Minnesota*, vol. 1, 147–97, quote 159.

61. The figure of one thousand comes from Henry H. Sibley, "Reminiscences of the Early Days of Minnesota," in *Collections of the Minnesota Historical Society*, vol. 3, *1870–1880*, 242–82, here 242. More conservative numbers are given by G. Anderson, *Kinsmen of Another Kind*, 261, who cites 500 Indian warriors. Berg, *38 Nooses*, 173, writes that 93 white soldiers and between 400 and 600 white settlers had been killed, and only a few dozen Indians. Indian agent Galbraith counted 644 whites and 93 soldiers killed—Folwell, *History of Minnesota*, vol. 2, 392. The number of Indians killed has "never been ascertained." Ibid., 393. The Indian death toll would rise

substantially in the coming months and years due to the brutal conditions of internment and other excesses they suffered in the aftermath of the war, and raids by the US Army.

62. Sibley to Ramsey, St. Peter, 24 August 1862, in Board of Commissioners, *Minnesota*, vol. 2, 198–99.

63. Roddis, *Indian Wars*, 147–49.

64. Westerman and White, *Mni Sota Makoce*, 194–95.

65. For examples, see Bryant, *History of the Great Massacre*, 251–56. See also Folwell, *History of Minnesota*, vol. 2, 190–211.

66. George A. Morse, "Report from December 1862," in Bryant, *History of the Great Massacre*, 253–54.

67. Roddis, *Indian Wars*, 156.

68. Ramsey to Lincoln, Saint Paul, 10 November 1862, quoted in ibid., 161. See also the account of the trials in Chas. E. Flandrau, "The Indian War of 1862–1864, and the Following Campaigns in Minnesota," in Board of Commissioners, *Minnesota*, vol. 1, 726–53, here 746–49.

69. The sense of alarm among civilian and military officials is palpable in various communiqués. See, for example, Pope to Lincoln, St. Paul, 24 November 1862, and Sibley to Brigadier General Elliott, St. Paul, 6 December 1862 and 8 December 1862, in Board of Commissioners, *Minnesota*, vol. 2, 290–91.

70. For an eyewitness account published by the St. Paul press, see Heard, *History of the Sioux War*, 272–95.

71. Roddis, *Indian Wars*, 168. His wife and remaining children were later ransomed.

72. Sibley to Lincoln, St. Paul, 27 December 1862, in Board of Commissioners, *Minnesota*, vol. 2, 292.

73. Lincoln to Sibley, 6 December 1862, quoted in ibid., 163.

74. From the *Stillwater Messenger*, 12 November 1862, quoted in Berg, *38 Nooses*, 207–8.

75. Benjamin Madley, *An American Genocide: The United States and the California Indian Catastrophe, 1846–1873* (New Haven: Yale University Press, 2016).

76. Roddis, *Indian Wars*, 194–95.

77. Michno, *Dakota Dawn*, 397; Roddis, *Indian Wars*, 194–98; and Bryant, *History of the Great Massacre*, 255.

78. Westerman and White, *Mni Sota Makoce*, 201–3; Doane Robinson, *A History of the Dakota or Sioux Indians* (1904; Minneapolis: Ross and Haines, 1974), 388–93; Folwell, *History of Minnesota*, vol. 2, 261–64; Anderson, *Kinsmen of Another Kind*, 276–80.

79. Westerman and White, *Mni Sota Makoce*, 194–95.

80. See the extraordinary collection of letters in Clifford Canku and Michael Simon, ed. and trans., *The Dakota Prisoner of War Letters* (St. Paul: Minnesota Historical Society, 2013).

81. Ruban His Sacred Nest to Riggs, April full moon 1864 [22 April 1864], in ibid., 35–37.

82. Robert Hopkins to Riggs, 24 October 1864, in ibid., 73–77, quote 77.

83. See Westerman and White, *Mni Sota Makoce*.

84. Roddis, *Indian Wars*, 230–33.

85. Ibid., 218–20. For other examples, see ibid., 246–56; Willima H. Houlton, "Narrative of the Eighth Regiment," and Eugene M. Wilson, "Narrative of the First Regiment of Mounted Rangers," in Board of Commissioners, *Minnesota*, vol. 1, 386–415, here 386–94, and vol. 1, 519–42,

here 520–24, as well as other accounts in this volume, and "Report of Col. Robert N. McLaren, Second Minnesota Cavalry," 29 July 1864, in ibid., vol. 2, 543–44.

86. They included the Episcopal bishop Henry Benjamin Whipple, who defended the Indians in an 1863 paper, "An Appeal for the Red Man"; Riggs, who had lived among the Sioux for years, and had learned Dakota and given it written form; another missionary, Father Ravoux; and former Indian agent Joseph R. Brown, who had married the daughter of a friendly Dakota chief (and was himself mixed race).

87. For one description of the interplay between allotments and forest devastation as individual Ojibway dealt with lumber merchants, see Edmund Jefferson Danziger Jr., *The Chippewas of Lake Superior* (Norman: University of Oklahoma Press, 1978), 96–104.

88. An examination of the names of Minnesota military veterans who died between 1860 and 1910, served during the Civil War years, and were buried in Minnesota confirms the point about their geographic origins. See "Minnesota Veterans Graves Registration," Minnesota Historical Society, n.d., accessed 8 October 2018, http://www.mnhs.org/people/veteransgraves.

89. See Theodore C. Blegen, ed., *Land of Their Choice: The Immigrants Write Home* (Minneapolis: University of Minnesota Press 1955), 419–22

90. See the letters in ibid., 425–30.

91. On the role of individual states in adopting an array of discriminatory measures that deprived Indians of political and civil rights and segregated them from white society, see Deborah A. Rosen, *American Indians and State Law: Sovereignty, Race, and Citizenship, 1790–1880* (Lincoln: University of Nebraska Press, 2007). For the case of the dispossession of the Cherokee and others by state governments, see Tim Alan Garrison, *The Legal Ideology of Removal: The Southern Judiciary and the Sovereignty of Native American Nations* (Athens: University of Georgia Press, 2002).

92. See Stephen L. Pevar, *The Rights of Indians and Tribes*, 4th ed. (New York: Oxford University Press, 2012), 5–15, and N. Bruce Duthu, *American Indians and the Law* (New York: Viking, 2008), who follow slightly different chronologies but agree on the essentials. For a good summary, see Duthu, *American Indians and the Law*, xv–xix.

93. The "unique conjuncture of rights—individual and collective—," writes David E. Wilkins, "distinguishes Indians from the rest of the American populace." David E. Wilkins, *American Indian Sovereignty and the US Supreme Court: The Masking of Justice* (Austin: University of Texas Press, 1997), 24.

94. Rev. S. R. Riggs, "The Dakota Mission" (1865), in *Collections of the Minnesota Historical Society*, vol. 3, 114–28, quote 119.

95. Bryant, *History of the Great Massacre*, 184.

96. Ibid., 179–80.

97. Preface to *Collections of the Minnesota Historical Society*, vol. 3, iv.

98. For a few other examples, see Madley, *American Genocide*, about the Yuki in California; Adhikari, *Genocide on Settler Frontiers*, with many predominantly Southern African and Australian cases; and Karl Jacoby, " 'The Broad Platform of Extermination': Nature and Violence in the Nineteenth Century North American Borderlands," *Journal of Genocide Research* 10:2 (2008): 249–67, about the Apaches in the Southwest United States.

99. See Vine Deloria Jr. and David E. Wilkins, *Tribes, Treaties, and Constitutional Tribulations* (Austin: University of Texas Press, 1999), 72.

100. Ibid., 72–73.

101. Ibid., 73, 75.

102. Rev. S. R. Riggs, "Memoir of Hon. Jas. W. Lynd," in *Collections of the Minnesota Historical Society*, vol. 3, 107–14.

103. On the complex legal history involving American Indians, I draw especially on the writings of David E. Wilkins, including *Hollow Justice: A History of Indigenous Claims in the United States* (New Haven: Yale University Press, 2013); Wilkins and K. Tsianina Lomawaima, *Uneven Ground: American Indian Sovereignty and Federal Law* (Norman: University of Oklahoma Press, 2001); Deloria and Wilkins, *Tribes, Treaties, and Constitutional Tribulations*; and Wilkins, *American Indian Sovereignty*; as well as Pevar, *Rights of Indians and Tribes*; Frank Pommersheim, *Broken Landscape: Indians, Indian Tribes, and the Constitution* (New York: Oxford University Press, 2009); Duthu, *American Indians and the Law*; Blue Clark, *Lone Wolf v. Hitchcock: Treaty Rights and Indian Law at the End of the Nineteenth Century* (Lincoln: University of Nebraska Press, 1994); and Petra T. Shattuck and Jill Norgren, *Partial Justice: Federal Indian Law in a Liberal Constitutional System* (New York: Berg, 1991). For the longer history, see Robert A. Williams Jr., *The American Indian in Western Legal Thought: The Discourses of Conquest* (New York: Oxford University Press, 1990).

104. Wilkins and Deloria, *Tribes, Treaties, and Constitutional Tribulations*, 25. The constitutional provision is in article 1, section 8.

105. Ibid., 26.

106. *Johnson and Graham's Lessee v. William M'Intosh*, 21 U.S. (8 Wheat.) 543 (1823).

107. *Id.*, at 586.

108. *Id.*, at 587.

109. *Id.*, at 588.

110. *Id.*, at 589.

111. *Id.*, at 591–92.

112. *Id.*, at 592.

113. *Id.*, at 591.

114. *The Cherokee Nation v. The State of Georgia*, 30 U.S. (5 Pet.) 1, 16 (1831).

115. *Id.*

116. *Id.*, at 17.

117. Marshall's reasoning was not accepted by all the justices, either those concurring or those dissenting. Justice William Johnson, while concurring, could not see how the Indian tribes could be designated as states. Their status as tribes made them an "anomaly unknown to the books that treat of states." The laws of nations would "regard them as nothing more than wandering hordes, held together only by ties of blood and habit, and having neither laws or government beyond what is required in a savage state." *Id.*, at 27–28. Justice Henry Baldwin went further. Without the trappings of civilization, most notably a state with all that entailed regarding laws and bounded territory, Indians could not be considered sovereign. Civilization and sovereignty ran together, in his (and many others') views. See *id.*, at 38 and 40.

118. *Id.*, at 53 and 54.

119. *Id.*, at 77.

120. *Id.*, at 78.

121. *Samuel A. Worcester v. The State of Georgia*, 31 U.S. (6 Pet.) 515 (1832).

122. *Id.*, at 543.

123. *Id.*, at 543–44.

124. *Id.*, at 544–45.

125. *Id.*, at 552, 554.

126. *Id.*, at 561.

127. Pommersheim, *Broken Landscape*, 92. The author refers here in particular to *Johnson's Lessee v. M'Intosh*, but the point can be generalized.

128. Pevar, *Rights of Indians and Tribes*, 81–84.

129. Shattuck and Norgren, *Partial Justice*, 116.

130. See Frances Prucha, *American Indian Policy in Crisis: Christian Reformers and the Indian, 1865–1900* (Norman: University of Oklahoma Press, 1976); Prucha, *Americanizing the American Indians: Writings by the "Friends of the Indian," 1880–1900* (Cambridge: Harvard University Press, 1973); and Shattuck and Norgren, *Partial Justice*, 78–102.

131. Quoted in Shattuck and Norgren, *Partial Justice*, 98.

132. Quoted in ibid., 102.

133. Wilkins, *Hollow Justice*, 38. See also David A. Chang, *The Color of the Land: Race, Nation, and the Politics of Landownership in Oklahoma, 1832–1929* (Chapel Hill: University of North Carolina Press, 2010), on the complex interactions among Indians, whites, and blacks around property, especially during the allotment period.

134. Rosen, *American Indians and State Law*, 136–42.

135. Ibid., 149–50.

136. John R. Wunder, *"Retained by the People": A History of American Indians and the Bill of Rights* (New York: Oxford University Press, 1994), 50–51.

137. Pevar, *Rights of Indians and Tribes*, 11.

138. Wilkins, *American Indian Sovereignty*, 166.

139. Quoted in Pevar, *Rights of Indians and Tribes*, 12.

140. All told, more than four hundred treaties have been concluded between the United States and Indian tribes.

141. Roddis, *Indian Wars*, 298.

142. Wilkins, *Hollow Justice*, xv–xvi, 151–63.

143. See Shattuck and Norgren, *Partial Justice*, 164–89, and Wunder, *Retained by the People*, 135–41, 149–53. The act did not implement the Bill of Rights in total because of fears that some of the provisions would interfere with Indians' religious practices and with self-government on the reservations.

144. For one example, see Elvira Pulitano, ed., *Indigenous Rights in the Age of the UN Declaration* (Cambridge: Cambridge University Press, 2012).

145. UN General Assembly (UNGA), Resolution 61/295, Declaration on the Rights of Indigenous Peoples, A/61/L.67 and Add. 1 (13 September 2007), http://www.un.org/esa/socdev/unpfii/documents/DRIPS_en.pdf.

146. See Wenona T. Singel, "Indian Tribes and Human Rights Accountability," *San Diego Law Review* 49 (2012): 567–625, and Duthu, *American Indians and the Law*, 137–63. See also Kirsten Matoy Carlson, "Jurisdiction and Human Rights Accountability in Indian Country,"

Michigan State University Law Review 355 (2013): 355–401. For a defense of tribal sovereignty against a "one-size-fits-all approach to civil liberties," see Angela R. Riley, "(Tribal) Sovereignty and Illiberalism," *California Law Review* 95 (2007): 799–848, quote 847.

Chapter 4: Brazil

1. Georg Heinrich von Langsdorff, *Voyages and Travels in Various Parts of the World during the Years 1803, 1804, 1805, 1806, and 1807* (Carlisle: George Philips, 1817), 62.

2. Stefan Zweig, *Brazil: Land of the Future*, trans. Andrew St. James (New York: Viking, 1941), 3. For a recent, lyrical evocation of Brazil's enchanting power, see Kenneth Maxwell, "First Encounters," in *Naked Tropics: Essays on Empire and Other Rogues* (New York: Routledge, 2003), 1–10.

3. Zweig, *Brazil*, 7–8.

4. Ibid., 8.

5. See William James, *Brazil through the Eyes of William James: Letters, Diaries, and Drawings, 1865–1866*, ed. Maria Helena P. T. Machado (Cambridge: David Rockefeller Center for Latin American Studies, Harvard University Press, 2006).

6. Calculated from David Eltis and David Richardson, *Atlas of the Transatlantic Slave Trade* (New Haven: Yale University Press, 2010), 203.

7. Ibid., 204.

8. The classic statement along these lines is by Gilberto Freyre, *The Masters and the Slaves: A Study in the Development of Brazilian Civilization*, trans. Samuel Putnam (1932; New York: Knopf, 1946). See also Freyre, *Brazil: An Interpretation* (New York: Knopf, 1945), where he writes, "the slave on Brazilian plantations was generally well treated" (49), and "it was possible for men of exceptional talent, no matter how socially inferior their origin, to rise to the highest positions in the Brazilian aristocratic and monarchical system" (51). Frank Tannenbaum, in *Slave and Citizen: The Negro in the Americas* (New York: Knopf, 1946), drew on Freyre and also postulated that Brazil had a mild form of slavery, a position that prevailed for the following ten years or so.

9. Orlando Patterson, *Slavery and Social Death: A Comparative Study* (Cambridge: Harvard University Press, 1985).

10. Excerpt from Agostinho Marques Perdigão Malheiro, *Escravidão no Brasil: Ensaio histórico-juridico-social*, 2 vols., 2nd ed. (1866; São Paulo: Edicoes Cultura, 1944), in Robert Edgar Conrad, ed., *Children of God's Fire: A Documentary History of Black Slavery in Brazil* (Princeton: Princeton University Press, 1983), 237–44, quote 237, italics in original. Sidney Chalhoub cites these same sentences in "The Politics of Silence: Race and Citizenship in Nineteenth-Century Brazil," *Slavery and Abolition* 27:1 (2006): 71–85, here 76.

11. On Brazilian slavery and its society and polity in general, I draw especially on Lilia Moritz Schwarcz and Heloisa Maria Murgel Starling, *Brazil: A Biography* (2015; London: Allen Lane, 2018); Emilia Viotti da Costa, *The Brazilian Empire: Myths and Histories* (Chapel Hill: University of North Carolina Press, 2000); Herbert S. Klein and Francisco Vidal Luna, *Slavery in Brazil* (Cambridge: Cambridge University Press, 2010); Stuart B. Schwartz, *Sugar Plantations in the Formation of Brazilian Society: Bahia, 1550–1835* (Cambridge: Cambridge University Press, 1985); Robert Edgar Conrad, *The Destruction of Brazilian Slavery, 1850–1888*, 2nd ed. (1972; Malabar:

Krieger, 1993); and some of the essays in Maxwell, *Naked Tropics*. For the state of the historiography as of the 1990s, see Stuart B. Schwartz, *Slaves, Peasants, and Rebels: Reconsidering Brazilian Historiography* (Urbana: University of Illinois Press, 1992), 1–38. H. Klein and Luna, in *Slavery in Brazil*, offer a more recent synthesis of the historiography.

12. For the Rio example, see Mary C. Karasch, *Slave Life in Rio de Janeiro, 1808–1850* (Princeton: Princeton University Press, 1987), 92–184.

13. David Brion Davis, *Inhuman Bondage: The Rise and Fall of Slavery in the New World* (New York: Oxford University Press, 2006), 104.

14. Ibid., 324.

15. Figure from Costa, *Brazilian Empire*, 128. For more detail, see Thomas W. Merrick and Douglas H. Graham, *Population and Economic Development in Brazil, 1800 to the Present* (Baltimore: Johns Hopkins University Press, 1979), 26–39. The first comprehensive census was taken only in 1872.

16. Figures from Merrick and Graham, *Economic Development in Brazil*, 49–52; on manumission, 53–55; and generally on the demographics of slavery, 49–79. Of the African-descended populaton, one-quarter was enslaved, three-quarters free.

17. R. Conrad, *Destruction of Brazilian Slavery*, 3.

18. See the classic work by Sidney Mintz, *Sweetness and Power: The Place of Sugar in Modern History* (New York: Viking, 1985).

19. Davis, *Inhuman Bondage*, 119.

20. Karasch, *Slave Life*, 21–25. On the strong ties between Brazil, particularly the Southeast, and Angola, see Roquinaldo Ferreira, *Cross-Cutural Exchange in the Atlantic World: Angola and Brazil in the Era of the Slave Trade* (Cambridge: Cambridge University Press, 2012), and Ferreira, "Atlantic Microhistories: Mobility, Personal Ties, and Slaving in the Black Atlantic World (Angola and Brazil)," in *Cultures of the Lusophone Black Atlantic*, ed. Nancy Priscilla Naro, Roger Sansi-Roca, and David H. Treece (New York: Palgrave Macmillan, 2007), 99–128. Ferreira shows that while originating in the slave trade, the ties between the two regions were multidimensional and transformative of both places. In Brazil's Northeast the links were strongest with the area from Senegambia to the Bight of Benin.

21. For a weighing of the evidence with the conclusion that, in economic terms, only Africans could supply the necessary labor force, see H. Klein and Luna, *Slavery in Brazil*, 13–17.

22. Excerpt from Count Pedro de Almeida to King João V, 1719, in R. Conrad, *Children of God's Fire*, 394–97, quote 396–97.

23. Ibid.

24. An adviser to King João VI, quoted in ibid., 359.

25. Quoted in ibid., 241.

26. Here and below I draw on the extraordinary work by João José Reis, *Slave Rebellion in Brazil: The Muslim Uprising of 1835 in Bahia*, trans. Arthur Brakel (1986; Baltimore: Johns Hopkins University Press, 1993). Generally on slave resistance, see H. Klein and Luna, *Slavery in Brazil*, 189–211, and Schwartz, *Slaves, Peasants, and Rebels*, 103–36.

27. Testimony of Dr. Joseph Cliffe, 1848–49, and of Augustino, 1849, before the British Parliament Select Committee on the Slave Trade, in R. Conrad, *Children of God's Fire*, 28–37 and 37–39, 34–35, on mortality rates. Cliffe was American-born but spent many years in Brazil and

was an ex–slave trader at the time of his testimony. Augustino was seized as a young boy and transported on a slave ship.

28. Testimony of William Page before the American consul in Rio de Janeiro, 1845, in ibid., 39–42.

29. Excerpt from Thomas Nelson, *Remarks on the Slavery and Slave Trade of the Brazils* (London: J. Hlachard and Son, 1848), in ibid., 43–48, quote 43–44.

30. See Jenny S. Martinez, *The Slave Trade and the Origins of International Human Rights Law* (New York: Oxford University Press, 2014).

31. Excerpt from Robert Walsh, *Notices of Brazil in 1828 and 1829*, 2 vols. (London: Frederick Westley and A. H. Davis, 1830), in R. Conrad, *Children of God's Fire*, 48–52, quote 49. See also the excerpts from Braz Hermenegildo do Amaral and Jean-Bapiste Debret, "Valongo, a Notorious Slave Market," in *The Rio de Janeiro Reader: History, Culture, Politics*, ed. Daryle Williams, Amy Chazkel, and Paulo Knauss (Durham: Duke University Press, 2016), 41–44. For an important scholarly study, Karasch, *Slave Life*, 29–54.

32. On the character of labor on the sugar plantations, see Schwartz, *Sugar Plantations*, and *Slaves, Peasants, and Rebels*, 39–63; on the coffee plantations, the classic work of Stanley J. Stein, *Vassouras: A Brazilian Coffee Country, 1850–1900. The Role of Planter and Slave in a Plantation Society* (1958; Princeton: Princeton University Press, 1985). Schwartz emphasizes that slaveholders' economic rationality could, at times, mitigate the worst brutalities of slavery. On urban slave labor, see Karasch, *Slave Life*, 185–213.

33. See Sidney Chalhoub, "The Precariousness of Freedom in a Slave Society: Brazil in the Nineteenth Century," *International Review of Social History* 56:3 (2011): 405–39.

34. Ibid., 409.

35. Excerpts from the criminal code (1830), in R. Conrad, *Children of God's Fire*, 253.

36. The specifics here from the reports of H. Augustus Copwer, British consul in Recife, to the Earl of Aberdeen, 1843 and 1846, and Francisco Peixoto de Lacerda Werneck's handbook for plantation management (1847), in ibid., 71–76 and 77–79.

37. Excerpt from F. A. Brandão Júnior, *A escravatura no Brazil precedida d'um artigo sobre a agricultura a colonisação no Maranhão* (Brussels: H. Thiry-Vern Buggenhoudt, 1865), in ibid., 96–99, quote 99.

38. Excerpt from the medical thesis of Dr. David Gomes Jardim, 1847, in ibid., 91–96, quote 93.

39. See excerpts from the court case in ibid., 273–81.

40. Merrick and Graham, *Economic Development in Brazil*, 56–57.

41. Speech by Cristiano Benedito Ottoni, Minas Gerais, 1871, quoted in R. Conrad, *Children of God's Fire*, 99–100.

42. On literacy, see Reis, *Slave Rebellion in Brazil*, 104–8; percentage from R. Conrad, *Destruction of Brazilian Slavery*, x.

43. See Schwartz, *Sugar Plantations*.

44. For some examples, Reis, *Slave Rebellion in Brazil*, 40, 47, 56, 121, 122.

45. Ibid., 120–23.

46. For a few examples, ibid., 48.

47. Quoted in ibid., 192.

48. Quote and comment in ibid., 199–200.

49. Ibid., 199–204.

50. Ibid., 205–30.

51. João Saldanha da Gama, governor of Bahia, quoted in ibid., 42.

52. Schwartz, *Slaves, Peasants, and Rebels*, 106–7, lists thirty-five just for Bahia between 1614 and 1826. On the flight of urban slaves, see Karasch, *Slave Life*, 302–34.

53. Schwartz, *Slaves, Peasants, and Rebels*, 122–28, and Schwarcz and Starling, *Brazil*, 96–99.

54. Schwartz, *Slaves, Peasants, and Rebels*.

55. Excerpt from Arthur Ramos, "O auto dos quilombos," *Revista do Instituto Arqueológico, Historico e Geográfico Pernambucano* 37 (1941–42), quoted in R. Conrad, *Children of God's Fire*, 377–79, quote 378. On Palmares and two other quilombos, see Schwartz, *Slaves, Peasants, and Rebels*, 103–36. Generally, see H. Klein and Luna, *Slavery in Brazil*, 194–99.

56. Reis, *Slave Rebellion in Brazil*, 41.

57. Ibid., 42–44, 104–5.

58. Excerpt from police report, Rio de Janeiro, 1876, in R. Conrad, *Children of God's Fire*, 384–86, quote 384–85. Another report described maroon communities that supported themselves by mining, the output of which they traded for food, ammunition, and provisions. When the police attempted to destroy another community, they were met with blacks who were "well-armed and supplied with ammunition," who were able to hold off the authorities for hours, but not ultimately. About two hundred slaves lived in the community, the authorities reported. Report of president of Maranhão, 1853, in ibid., 386–89, quote 388.

59. Antônio de Castro Alves, "Voice of Africa," in *The Major Abolitionist Poems*, ed. and trans. Amy A. Peterson (New York: Garland, 1990), 2–20, quote 3.

60. Ibid., 7–9

61. This is a huge theme, of course, in Atlantic world history. I have benefitted especially from Jeremy Adelman, *Sovereignty and Revolution in the Iberian Atlantic* (Princeton: Princeton University Press, 2006).

62. Thomas E. Skidmore, *Brazil: Five Centuries of Change*, 2nd ed. (New York: Oxford University Press, 2010), 44.

63. On Brazil in the nineteenth century, see especially Costa, *Brazilian Empire*, 22–23, for a compelling summary of her views. She emphasizes more the aristocratic character and the clientelist system of Brazil, less its liberalism.

64. See the exaggerated but insightful work of Arno Mayer, *The Persistence of the Old Regime: Europe to the Great War* (New York: Pantheon, 1981).

65. Costa, *Brazilian Empire*, 59–60.

66. On the many meanings of liberalism, see Helena Rosenblatt, *The Lost History of Liberalism* (Princeton: Princeton University Press, 2018).

67. For a bristling statement along these lines, Costa, *Brazilian Empire*, 75–76.

68. Thomas Ewbank, *Life in Brazil; or, a Journal to the Land of Cocoa and Palms* (New York: Harper and Brothers, 1856), 184–85.

69. I am compressing here a very large and contested literature, and drawing on the chapter "Race and Nation: An Intellectual History" in my book *A Century of Genocide: Utopias of Race and Nation*, edition with new preface (2003; Princeton: Princeton University Press, 2015), 16–52. Among those who would argue differently, that a concept of race already existed in the ancient

world, are Benjamin Isaac, *The Invention of Racism in Classical Antiquity* (Princeton: Princeton University Press, 2004), and David M. Goldenberg, *The Curse of Ham: Race and Slavery in Early Judaism, Christianity, and Islam* (Princeton: Princeton University Press, 2003). The broader and classic statement, that capitalism created race, is to be found in Eric Williams, *Capitalism and Slavery* (Chapel Hill: University of North Carolina Press, 1944). An incisive recent study is Patrick Wolfe, *Traces of History: Elementary Structures of Race* (London: Verso, 2016). Wolfe demonstrates the variety of racial constructions, distinguishing especially between territorial dispossession of indigenous peoples and the commodification of the body, as in slavery.

70. For a scathing contemporary critique of the Catholic Church and its support for slavery, see L. Anselmo da Fonseca, *A escravidão, o clero e o abolicionismo* (Bahia: Imprensa Economica, 1887). I thank Daniela Traldi for help with this and other Portuguese-language sources.

71. Excerpt from José Veríssimo, *A educação nacional*, 2nd ed. (1906), in R. Conrad, *Children of God's Fire*, 221–25, quote 225.

72. Excerpt from João Dunshee de Abranches, *O captiveiro (memorias)*, in ibid., 225–29, quote 226–28.

73. Antônio de Castro Alves, "Tragedy at Sea: The Slave Ship," in Peterson, *Major Abolitionist Poems*, 11–23, quote 23.

74. See R. Conrad, *Destruction of Brazilian Slavery*, 108–31.

75. See Leslie Bethell and José Murilo de Carvalho, eds., *Joaquim Nabuco, British Abolitionists, and the End of Slavery in Brazil: Correspondence 1880–1905* (London: Institute for the Study of the Americas, University of London, 2009). Among many works on the British abolitionist movement, Adam Hochschild, *Bury the Chains: Prophets and Rebels in the Fight to Free an Empire's Slaves* (Boston: Houghton Mifflin, 2005), makes for compelling reading.

76. Joaquim Nabuco, *Abolitionism: The Brazilian Antislavery Struggle* (1883), trans. and ed. Robert Conrad (Urbana: University of Illinois Press, 1977), 9–10.

77. Ibid., 10, 19. See also the first great Brazilian abolitionist statement, by Brazil's first prime minister, José Bonifacio de Andrada e Silva, in 1823, excerpts in R. Conrad, *Children of God's Fire*, 418–27.

78. Nabuco, *Abolitionism*, 19–21, quotes 19–20.

79. Ibid., 98–103. Another abolitionist, L. Anselmo da Fonseca, in his *Escravidão*, was more hostile, even racist, toward blacks. But that did not stop him from opposing slavery.

80. Nabuco, *Abolitionism*, 98.

81. Ibid., 24.

82. Ibid.

83. Nabuco to Allen, Rio de Janeiro, 5 June 1881, in Bethell and Carvalho, *Joaquim Nabuco*, 46.

84. Nabuco, *Abolitionism*, 22.

85. Ibid., 83.

86. See also Nabuco's correspondence with the British abolitionist Catherine Impey, London, 24 November 1882, in Bethell and Carvalho, *Joaquim Nabuco*, 73–74.

87. R. Conrad, *Destruction of Brazilian Slavery*, 112–16.

88. Ibid., 181.

89. For the refutation of the second part of Eric Williams's argument that slavery was ended when it was no longer profitable, see Seymour Drescher, *Econocide: British Slavery in the Era of*

Abolition (Pittsburgh: University of Pittsburgh Press, 1977), and *Abolition: A History of Slavery and Antislavery* (Cambridge: Cambridge University Press, 2009). However, the case of Brazil seems rather different.

90. See Costa, *Brazilian Empire*, 152–55.

91. Ibid.

92. Skidmore, *Brazil*, 61.

93. Earl of Derby to George Buckley Mathew, Foreign Office, 21 July 1876; Mathew to Earl of Derby, Rio de Janeiro, 4 September 1876; and Mathew to Messrs. Johnstone and Co., Rio de Janeiro, 17 August 1876, in *British and Foreign State Papers*, vol. 67, *1875–76* (London: William Ridgway, 1883), 343–45.

94. Correspondence between Mathew and other consuls and with the Earl of Deby, in ibid., 346–47.

95. Two early histories of the abolitionist movement, with interesting details regarding tactics and strategy, are Evaristo de Moraes, *A campanha abolicionista, 1879–1888* (Rio de Janeiro: Editora Leite Ribeiro, 1924), and Osorio Duque-Estrada, *A abolição (esboço histórico) 1831–1888* (Rio de Janeiro: Livraria Editora Leite Ribeiro e Maurillo, 1918).

96. R. Conrad, *Destruction of Brazilian Slavery*, 124–37.

97. Sidney Chalhoub, "The Politics of Ambiguity: Conditional Manumission, Labor Contracts, and Slave Emancipation in Brazil (1850s–1888)," *International Review of Social History* 60:1 (2015): 161–91, here 164.

98. R. Conrad, *Destruction of Brazilian Slavery*, 186.

99. Davis, *Inhuman Bondage*, 326–27.

100. Text of the law in R. Conrad, *Children of God's Fire*, 480–81.

101. Quoted in R. Conrad, *Destruction of Brazilian Slavery*, 205.

102. Ibid.

103. On the fundamental significance of slavery abolition to the emergence of a universal concept of humanity, see Fabian Klose, "'A War of Justice and Humanity': Abolition and Establishing Humanity as a Universal Norm," in *Humanity: A History of European Concepts in Practice from the Sixteenth Century to the Present*, ed. Klose and Mirjam Thulin (Göttingen: Vandenhoek and Ruprecht, 2016), 168–86. On abolition as a human rights movement, see Bonny Ibhawoh, *Human Rights in Africa* (Cambridge: Cambridge University Press, 2018), 55–89.

104. For a bracing comparative study of post-emancipation, see Rebecca J. Scott, *Degrees of Freedom: Louisiana and Cuba after Slavery* (Cambridge: Belknap Press of Harvard University Press, 2005). Scott demonstrates the possibilities for cross-racial cooperation in Cuba versus the strict color-line segregation established in Louisiana. She writes that the issue of white supremacy was not merely one of prejudice or "psychosocial pathology . . . but white supremacy as an organized structure constraining the public voice and civic standing of those whom it labeled inferior" (258). After slavery "various possibilities were open—ranging from an inclusive citizenship that would transcend color to an exclusionary social order that would constrain public and political rights" (258). See also Frederick Cooper, Thomas C. Holt, and Rebecca J. Scott, *Beyond Slavery: Explorations of Race, Labor, and Citizenship in Postemancipation Societies* (Chapel Hill: University of North Carolina Press, 2000).

105. "Decree on Naturalization of Foreigners, 15 December 1889," in *British and Foreign State Papers*, vol. 81, *1888–1889* (London: Her Majesty's Stationery Office, n.d.), 233–34.

106. For the emphasis on continuity, see especially Costa, *Brazilian Empire*.

107. See José Verissimo, *A educação nacional*, 2nd ed. (Rio de Janeiro: Livraria Francisco Alves, 1906).

108. On the difficult and imprecise transition from slavery to freedom, see especially Chaloub, "Politics of Ambiguity"; H. Klein and Luna, *Slavery in Brazil*, 295–319; Rebecca J. Scott, ed., *Abolition of Slavery and the Aftermath of Emancipaton in Brazil* (Durham: Duke University Press, 1988); and, generally, Cooper, Holt, and Scott, *Beyond Slavery*.

109. Figures from Chaloub, "Politics of Silence," 84. The essays by Cooper, Holt, and Scott in *Beyond Slavery*, though not about Brazil, demonstrate the highly contested and problematic character of the integration of ex-slaves after emancipation.

110. See Lilia Moritz Schwarcz, *The Spectacle of the Races: Scientists, Institutions, and the Race Question in Brazil, 1870–1930*, trans. Leland Guyer (1993; New York: Hill and Wang, 1999); Thomas E. Skidmore, "Racial Ideas and Social Policy in Brazil, 1870–1940," in *The Idea of Race in Latin America, 1870–1940*, ed. Richard Graham (Austin: University of Texas Press, 1990), 7–36; and Skidmore, *Black into White: Race and Nationality in Brazilian Thought* (New York: Oxford University Press, 1974).

111. Jean Baptiste de Lacerda, "The *Metis*, or Half-Breeds, of Brazil," in *Papers on Inter-Racial Problems Communicated to the First Universal Races Congress, Held at the University of London, July 26–29 1911*, ed. G. Spiller (London: P. S. King and Son, 1911), 377–82.

112. Ibid., 382.

113. For example, Verissimo, *Educação nacional*.

114. On immigration policies, see Anthony W. Marx, *Making Race and Nation: A Comparison of the United States, South Africa, and Brazil* (Cambridge: Cambridge University Press, 1998), 162–63.

115. Oscar Niemeyer, "The Curves of Life: An Interview with Oscar Niemeyer," by Niklas Maak, in *Oscar Niemeyer: A Legend of Modernism*, ed. Paul Andreas and Ingeborg Flagge (Basel: Birkhäuser, 2003), 21–26, here 21. See also the comment by the Rio urban planner Augusto Ivan Pinheiro in Michael Kimmelman, "The Last of the Moderns," *New York Times Magazine*, 15 May 2005, http://www.nytimes.com/2005/05/15/magazine/the-last-of-the-moderns.html.

116. Oscar Niemeyer, *The Curves of Time: The Memoirs of Oscar Niemeyer*, trans. Izabel Murat Burbridge (London: Pahidon, 2000), frontmatter.

117. Niemeyer, quoted in David Underwood, *Oscar Niemeyer and the Architecture of Brazil* (New York: Rizzoli, 1994), 115.

118. Niemeyer, interview by Niklas Maak, 25.

119. Preamble to the Constitution of the Federative Republic of Brazil, accessed 9 October 2018, http://livraria.camara.leg.br/direito-e-justica/constitution-of-the-federative-republic-of-brazil.html.

120. Brazilian Constitution, ch. II, art. 7, xviii, and ch. III, art. 12, i and ii.

121. Figures from A. Marx, *Making Race and Nation*, 171–72, 254, and Skidmore, *Brazil*, 189.

122. See the World Bank figures at "GINI Index (World Bank Estimate)," World Bank, n.d., accessed 15 May 2018, https://data.worldbank.org/indicator/SI.POV.GINI/, and the the CIA's

inequality list (based on the same GINI index used by the World Bank) at "Country Comparison: Distribution of Family Income—GINI Index," CIA, 1995–2017, accessed 15 May 2018, https://www.cia.gov/library/publications/the-world-factbook/rankorder/2172rank.html.

123. Skidmore, *Brazil*, 199.

124. Along with A. Marx, *Making Race and Nation*, for other important comparative studies of race, see Wolfe, *Traces of History*, and George M. Fredrickson, *Racism: A Short History* (Princeton: Princeton University Press, 2003), though the latter addresses the United States, South Africa, and Nazi Germany, the three states that have had legally enshrined racism, not Brazil.

125. Brazilian Institute of Geography and Statistics, "What Color Are You?" in *The Brazil Reader: History, Culture, Politics*, ed. Robert M. Levine and John J. Crocitti (Durham: Duke University Press, 1999), 386–90.

126. Wolfe, *Traces of History*, 113–14, citing the study by Marvin Harris and Conrad Kotak, "The Structural Significance of Brazilian Categories," *Sociologica* 25 (1963): 203n.

Chapter 5: Armenians and Jews

1. Catholicos Khrimian to Bismarck, 27 June 1878, and "Projet de réglement organique pour l'Arménie turque," submitted by the Delegation of Armenians of Turkey to Bismarck, 27 June 1878, both in Politisches Archiv des Auswärtigen Amts (hereafter PAAA)/R12868. Khrimian had been patriarch but was forced out of this more exalted position in 1873 by the Ottoman government.

2. Kann and C. Netter to Bismarck, Berlin, 12 June 1878, with accompanying memorandum from the Comité central de l'Alliance Israélite universelle and twenty-three other organizations and individuals to the president (Bismarck) and members of the European Congress in Berlin, 9 June 1878, PAAA/R12867. I have been unable to locate Kann's first name.

3. On the Rothschilds' efforts to secure Jewish emancipation at the time of the Vienna Congress, see Niall Ferguson, *The House of Rothschild: Money's Prophets, 1798–1848* (New York: Viking, 1998), 172–77.

4. But see Abigail Green, *Moses Montefiore: Jewish Liberator, Imperial Hero* (Cambridge: Belknap Press of Harvard University Press, 2010), who argues convincingly that Montefiore pioneered public activism on behalf of Jews. The same can be said of Crémieux, the founder, in 1860, of the Alliance Israélite universelle. Still, the organizing in 1878 was far more extensive.

5. For another discussion that joins together Armenians and Jews, though in the latter case focused on the Jews of Baghdad, see Elie Kedourie, " 'Minorities,' " in *The Chatham House Version and Other Middle-Eastern Studies* (1970; Chicago: Ivan R. Dee, 2004), 286–316.

6. This observation regarding the many appeals to Bismarck and the Congress is based on reviewing the hundreds of petitions and other communiqués in numerous files of the German Foreign Office (PAAA).

7. Text of Vienna Treaty in Augustus Oakes and R. B. Mowat, eds., *The Great European Treaties of the Nineteenth Century* (Oxford: Clarendon, 1918), quotes art. 16 (44) and art. 36 (57).

8. See Eric D. Weitz, "From the Vienna to the Paris System: International Politics and the Entangled Histories of Human Rights, Forced Deportations, and Civilizing Missions," *American Historical Review* 113:5 (2008): 1313–43.

9. On the important and usually neglected history of the terminology of "minority" and "majority," see Kai Struve, " 'Nationale Minderheit'—Begriffsgeschichtliches zu Gleichheit und Differenz," *Leipziger Beiträge zur Jüdischen Geschichte und Kultur* 2 (2004): 233–58, and Erwin Viefhaus, *Die Minderheitenfrage und die Entstehung der Minderheitenschutzverträge auf der Pariser Friedenskonferenz 1919* (Würzburg: Holzner, 1960), 8–19, 28–34, 39–53.

10. On the slew of "questions" and "problems" that enveloped Europe in the nineteenth century, clearly a result of nation-state formation, political revolution, and the Industrial Revolution, see Holly Case, *The Age of Questions: Or, A First Attempt at an Aggregate History of the Eastern, Social, Woman, American, Jewish, Polish, Bullion, Tuberculosis, and Many Other Questions over the Nineteenth Century, and Beyond* (Princeton: Princeton University Press, 2018).

11. William E. Gladstone, *Bulgarian Horrors and the Question of the East* (London: John Murray, 1876), 11–12. Gladstone's writing was part of the nineteenth-century surge of humanitarian intervention. See Fabian Klose, ed., *The Emergence of Humanitarian Intervention: Ideas and Practice from the Nineteenth Century to the Present* (Cambridge: Cambridge University Press, 2016); Davide Rodogno, *Against Massacre: Humanitarian Interventions in the Ottoman Empire, 1815–1914* (Princeton: Princeton University Press, 2011); and Gary J. Bass, *Freedom's Battle: The Origins of Humanitarian Intervention* (New York: Knopf, 2008).

12. Gladstone, *Bulgarian Horrors*, 12–13. For a sharp rejoinder to Gladstone by a fellow member of parliament, see H. A. Munro Butler-Johnstone, *Bulgarian Horrors and the Question of the East: A Letter Addressed to the Right Hon. W. E. Gladstone, M.P.* (London: William Ridgway, 1876). Butler-Johnstone wrote that the Muslims of the Ottoman Empire "bear favourable comparison with any people under the sun" (10).

13. Details of the proposal are in Delegation of Armenians of Turkey to Bismarck, 27 June 1878; "Projet de réglement organique pour l'Arménie turque," PAAA/R12868, and Delegation of Armenians of Turkey to Bismarck, 3 July 1878, and accompanying memo, "Quelques indications sur les reforms à introduire dans l'admnistration de l'Arménie," PAAA/R12869, no. 42.

14. See the important books by Carole Fink, *Defending the Rights of Others: The Great Powers, the Jews, and International Minority Protection, 1878–1938* (Cambridge: Cambridge University Press, 2004), and Fritz Stern, *Gold and Iron: Bismarck, Bleichröder, and the Building of the German Empire* (New York: Knopf, 1977), 351–93.

15. See, for example, "Petition of the Roumanian Jews to the Chamber of Deputies" (1872), in Max J. Kohler and Simon Wolf, *Jewish Disabilities in the Balkan States: American Contributions toward Their Removal, with Particular Reference to the Congress of Berlin* (Philadelphia: Publications of the American Jewish Historical Society, 1916), 98–101.

16. N. M. Gelber, "Jüdische Probleme beim Berliner Kongreß 1878," in *Deutsches Judentum: Aufstieg und Krise. Gestalten, Ideen, Werke*, ed. Robert Weltsch (Stuttgart: Deutsche Verlags-Anstalt, 1963), 216–52, here 225.

17. See, for example, the letter sent by the representative of the Swiss Jewish community, L. Dreyfuss Neumann to Bismarck, 2 July 1878, PAAA/R12869, no. 43, as well as by the Berlin Jewish community in Gelber, "Jüdische Probleme," 226.

18. Gelber, "Jüdische Probleme," 237, and Kohler and Wolf, *Jewish Disabilities*, 49–53.

19. For details on the complicated story, see F. Stern, *Gold and Iron*, 351–93.

20. Quoted in Gelber, "Jüdische Probleme," 226, n. 15.

21. Rististch [Ristić] to Bismarck, 3 July 1878, PAAA/R12869, no. 47. Ristić admitted that one archaic law remained, which banned Jews from permanent residence in Belgrade, but promised that it would be stricken from the books as soon as peace had been concluded.

22. Kann and Netter to Bismarck, Berlin, 12 June 1878, with accompanying memorandum, PAAA/R12867.

23. See Kohler and Wolf, *Jewish Disabilities*, 41–42.

24. Memo of 11 June 1878 from various Jewish organizations, drafted by Netter and Kann of the Alliance Israélite, quoted in Gelber, "Jüdische Probleme," 236.

25. Telegram, Delegation of Muslims of Roumeli to Bismarck, 3 July 1878, PAAA/R12869, no. 51.

26. Telegram, unclear provenance but likely the same or another delegation of Muslims of Roumeli to Bismarck, 4 July 1878, PAAA/R12869. Also printed as introduction to *Appel des Musulmans opprimés au Congrès de Berlin: Leur situation en Europe et en Asie depuis le Traité de San-Stéfano* (Constantinople, 1878), iii–iv, in PAAA/R12869, which contains petitions for compensation for losses sustained during the conflict. Many petitions for restitution are also in PAAA/R12869 and R12870. See also the similar "Petition addressed to the Congress of Berlin," submitted by Cherif Bey, Rifaat Effendi, Hassan Bey, Enim Bey, Rechid Bey, Ahmad Pacha, and Kassin Bey, 24 June 1878, PAAA/R12868, no. 20.

27. I. Rististch [Jovan Ristić], Minister of Foreign Affairs of Serbia, to Prince Bismarck, 12/24 June 1878, PAAA/R12868, no. 21. See also "Mémoire sur les actes de cruauté de barbarie commis par l'armée turque pendant la guerre *serbo-turque*," Belgrade, 12 December 1876, PAAA/R12868.

28. "Données explicatives destinés à accompagner la Carte indiquant les revendications territoriales de la Serbie," 12/24 June 1878, PAAA/R12868, p. 20, and "Notice statistiques sur la Péninsula des Balcans," PAAA/R12868, p. 5 [accompanies memo of minister of foreign affairs].

29. "Mémoire sur les actes de cruauté de barbarie commis par l'armée turque pendant la guerre *serbo-turque*," Belgrade, 12 December 1876, PAAA/R12868, p. 1. Similarly, see telegram, representatives of the Kazas of Pristina, 13/25 June 1878, PAAA/R12868, no. 27.

30. Telegram, notables of Uskuip to Excellence Délegue de l'Allemagne, 24 June 1878, PAAA/R12868, no. 25. See, in addition, notables of Scutari to plenipotentiaries of the Powers meeting at the Congress of Berlin, 3/15 June 1878, PAAA/R12869, no. 48. See also the booklet *Appel des Musulmans opprimés*, in PAAA/R12869, which contains six petitions signed by Muslims and Christians together; telegram, delegation of Muslim inhabitants of Crete to Bismarck, 2 July 1878, PAAA/R12869, no. 44; and telegram, delegation of Muslims of Roumeli to Bismarck, 3 July 1878, PAAA/R12869, no. 51.

31. Technically, Bulgaria was defined as an "autonomous tributary Principality" to the Ottoman sultan, but for all intents and purposes it became independent. See art. 1 of the Berlin Treaty in Oakes and Mowat, *Great European Treaties*, 332.

32. Arts. 5, 27, 35, and 44, in Oakes and Mowat, *Great European Treaties*, 335–36, 345–46, 350, and 354.

33. Arts. 12, 30, and 39, in ibid., 339, 348, and 352. This provision was not applied to Romania.

34. Art. 61, in ibid., 358. The treaty also accepted the Armenain demand that all persons "without distinction of religion" shall be allowed to give evidence at trials. Art. 62, in ibid., 359.

35. See Simon Vratzian, "The Armenian Question and the Birth of the Revolution," *Armenian Review* 3:3 (1950), http://asbarez.com/144618/the-armenian-revolution-and-the-armenian-revolutionary-federation/. Vratzian notes that upon his return to Istanbul, Catholicos Khrimian apparently called on Armenians to take up arms in self-defense. I thank Taner Akçam for the reference.

36. Gelber, "Jüdische Probleme," 248. F. Stern, *Gold and Iron*, 373–93, takes a much more moderate view, seeing the victory as highly tenuous and largely the result of Bleichröder's efforts.

37. On the depressing dénoument in Romania, see F. Stern, *Gold and Iron*, 380–93.

38. Stephan H. Astourian, "The Silence of the Land: Agrarian Relations, Ethnicity, and Power," in *A Question of Genocide: Armenians and Turks at the End of the Ottoman Empire*, ed. Fatma Müge Göçek, Norman M. Naimark, and Ronald G. Suny (New York: Oxford University Press, 2011), 55–81, and Elke Hartmann, "The Central State in the Borderlands: Eastern Anatolia in the Late Nineteenth Century," in *Shatterzone of Empires: Coexistence and Violence in the German, Habsburg, Russian, and Ottoman Borderlands*, ed. Omer Bartov and Eric D. Weitz (Bloomington: Indiana University Press, 2013), 172–90.

39. For American efforts, see Peter Balakian, *The Burning Tigris: The Armenian Genocide and America's Response* (New York: HarperCollins, 2003).

40. Figure from Fink, *Defending the Rights of Others*, 45.

41. US Secretary of State John Hay, in 1902, protested to the Romanian government against its treatment of Jews, "in the name of humanity." Quoted in Kohler and Wolf, *Jewish Disabilities*, 80. American Jews were thrilled with his action. See Oscar S. Straus's letter to Hay and President Roosevelt, in ibid., 82

42. See Kemal H. Karpat, *Ottoman Population 1830–1914: Demographic and Social Characteristics* (Madison: University of Wisconsin Press, 1985), 60–77.

43. For an analysis of the modern character of subsequent deportations, see Fikret Adanir and Hilmar Kaiser, "Migration, Deportation, and Nation-Building: The Case of the Ottoman Empire," in *Migrations et migrants dans une perspective historique: Permanences et innovations*, ed. René Leboutte (Brussels: PIE–Peter Lang, 2000), 273–92.

I thank Peter Holquist for first pointing out to me the existence and importance of the Russian-Ottoman agreements. See also his chapter, "To Count, to Extract, and to Exterminate: Population Statistics and Population Politics in Late Imperial and Soviet Russia," in *A State of Nations: Empire and Nation-Making in the Age of Lenin and Stalin*, ed. Ronald Grigor Suny and Terry Martin (New York: Oxford University Press, 2001), 111–44.

44. See Eric D. Weitz, "Germany and the Young Turks: Revolutionaries into Statesmen," in Göçek, Naimark, and Suny, *Question of Genocide*, 175–98.

45. See George F. Kennan, *The Other Balkan Wars: A 1913 Carnegie Endowment Inquiry in Retrospect* (Washington: Carnegie Endowment for International Peace, 1993).

46. Stephen Ladas, *The Exchange of Minorities: Bulgaria, Greece, and Turkey* (New York: Macmillan, 1932), 15–16, 18.

47. Karpat, *Ottoman Population*, 60–77.

48. See Mark Mazower, *Salonica, City of Ghosts: Christians, Muslims and Jews, 1430–1950* (New York: HarperCollins, 2004).

49. See Louis Marshall, President, American Jewish Committee to President Taft, 14 January 1913, quoted in Kohler and Wolf, *Jewish Disabilities*, 84–86; Acting Secretary of State J. B. Moore to Cyrus Adler, 24 July 1913, 30 July 1913, 6 August 1913, and 9 August 1913, in ibid., 89–92; and British Foreign Secretary Edward Grey, in ibid., 93–94.

50. For World War I as a war among peoples, see George L. Mosse, *Fallen Soldiers: Reshaping the Memory of the World Wars* (New York: Oxford University Press, 1990).

51. On the Young Turks from their origins to 1908, see the standard works of M. Şükrü Hanioğlu, *The Young Turks in Opposition* (New York: Oxford University Press, 1995), and *Preparation for a Revolution: The Young Turks, 1902–1908* (Oxford: Oxford University Press, 2001).

52. See Erik Jan Zürcher, "The Young Turks: Children of the Borderlands?" *International Journal of Turkish Studies* 9:1–2 (2003): 275–85.

53. On the popular response to the Young Turk Revolution, see Michelle U. Campos, *Ottoman Brothers: Muslims, Christians, and Jews in Early Twentieth-Century Palestine* (Stanford: Stanford University Press, 2011). For a strong argument regarding the Young Turks' commitment to the empire rather than to nationalism, see Ronald Grigor Suny, *"They Can Live in the Desert but Nowhere Else": A History of the Armenian Genocide* (Princeton: Princeton University Press, 2015).

54. See Hans-Lukas Kieser, *Talaat Pasha: Father of Modern Turkey, Architect of Genocide* (Princeton: Princeton University Press, 2018). I take the term "national empire" from a conversation with Mustafa Aksakal of Georgetown University. More generally on the longevity of empires into the modern period, see Jane Burbank and Frederick Cooper, *Empires in World History: Power and the Politics of Difference* (Princeton: Princeton University Press, 2010).

55. The major historian of the Young Turks writes of the "tremendous ideological power and extraordinary dynamism that the new gospel of Turkism lent to the Young Turk movement." See M. Şükrü Hanioğlu, "Turkism and the Young Turks, 1889–1908," in *Turkey: Beyond Nationalism towards Post-Nationalist Identities*, ed. Hans-Lukas Kieser (London: I. B. Tauris, 2006), 3–19, quote 13. See also Hanioğlu, *Atatürk: An Intellectual Biography* (Princeton: Princeton University Press, 2011). This dynamism applied to the economy as well. A number of Young Turk ideologues drew on the national economy ideas of Friedrich List. See Uğur Ümit Üngör and Mehmet Polatel, *Confiscation and Destruction: The Young Turk Seizure of Armenian Property* (London: Continuum, 2011), 27–37.

56. See especially Mustafa Aksakal, *The Ottoman Road to War in 1914: The Ottoman Empire and the First World War* (Cambridge: Cambridge University Press, 2008).

57. For the most important recent accounts, see Suny, *Live in the Desert*; Taner Akçam, *The Young Turks' Crime against Humanity: The Armenian Genocide and Ethnic Cleansing in the Ottoman Empire* (Princeton: Princeton University Press, 2012); and Raymond Kévorkian, *The Armenian Genocide: A Complete History* (2006; London: I. B. Tauris, 2011).

58. As quoted in Neurath to Bethmann Hollweg, Pera, 5 November 1915, Nr. 654, PAAA/R13799/nn.

59. "Bericht von Dr. Jäckh über Konstantinopel und Dardanellen," 17 October 1915, PAAA/R13750/17–18 (of report). The original of the quote: "Talaat freilich machte keinen Hehl daraus, dass er die Vernichtung des armenischen Volkes als eine politische Erleichterung begrüsse."

60. Quoted in Ulrich Trumpener, *Germany and the Ottoman Empire, 1914–1918* (Princeton: Princeton University Press, 1968), 127.

61. See Weitz, "Vienna to the Paris System."

62. Commission of Inquiry, "Preliminary Survey," in US Department of State, *Papers Relating to the Foreign Relations of the United States, 1919: The Paris Peace Conference*, vol. 1 (Washington: Government Printing Office, 1942), 17–21, here 18–20. See also Manley O. Hudson, "The Protection of Minorities and Natives in Transferred Territories," in *What Really Happened at Paris: The Story of the Peace Conference, 1918–19*, ed. Edward Mandell House and Charles Seymour (New York: C. Scribner's Sons, 1921), 204–30.

63. The commitment to establishing states based on homogeneous populations is also evident in the Inquiry's call for maps that were based on "racial boundary lines." See Commission of Inquiry, "Preliminary Survey," 20.

64. On the history of the concept, see Eric D. Weitz, "Self-Determination: How a German Enlightenment Idea Became the Slogan of National Liberation and a Human Right," *American Historical Review* 120:2 (2015): 462–96.

65. Both sentiments, fear and hope, come across clearly in various memos written by the Western Jewish organizations to the Allied governments. See, for example, Alliance Israélite to minister of foreign affairs, Paris, 16 July 1918, in Alliance Israélite universelle, *La question juive devant la conférence de la paix* (Paris: Siège de la Société, 1918), 5–8, and Alliance Israélite universelle, "Appeal to Humanity," in ibid., 46–48, in which the Alliance warns that the pogroms were so severe that they threatened the "extermination" of Jews (47); Board of Deputies of British Jews, Joint Foreign Committee of the Board of Deputies of British Jews, and Anglo-Jewish Association, *The Peace Conference: Paris, 1919. Report of the Delegation of the Jews of the British Empire on the Treaties of Versailles, Saint-Germain-en-Laye and Neuilly and the Annexed Minorities Treaties* (London, 1920); and memorandum, Joint Foreign Committee to Balfour, 2 December 1918, in Board of Deputies of British Jews, *Peace Conference*, 72–76.

66. Leo Motzkin, "Les revendications nationales des Juifs," in Comité des délégations juives auprès de la Conférence de la Paix, *Les droits nationaux des Juifs en Europe orientale* (Paris: Beresniak et Fils, 1919), 7–20, quote 14–15. See also Léon Reich, "Avant-propos," in ibid., 3–4. An early but still useful history is Nathan Feinberg, *La question des minorités à la Conférence de la Paix de 1919–1920 et l'action juive en faveur de la protection internationale des minorités* (Paris: Librairie Arthur Rousseau, 1929), which was sponsored by the successor organization, the Conseil pour les droits des minorités juives.

67. For the most thorough analysis, see Jonathan Schneer, *The Balfour Declaration: The Origins of the Arab-Israeli Conflict* (New York: Random House, 2010).

68. See Fink, *Defending the Rights of Others*, 193–264. Fink's overall assessments are, I think, too negative. She cites diplomatic and popular resentment over Jewish triumphs at the Peace Conference, a rising tide of antisemitism, and the sharp divisions among Jews. Yet, as she well describes, there were numerous moments during the negotiations of late winter and spring 1919 when minority protection would have been abandoned altogether but for the constant lobbying of Jewish representatives, especially Lucien Wolf and Louis Marshall (despite their mutual antipathy). The leading American delegates—Julian Mack, Louis Marshall, and Cyrus Adler—had excellent access to Wilson's major adviser, David Miller, and his assistant, O. Manley Hudson. The head of the American Committee of Experts, A. C. Coolidge, also played a critical role. Both Miller and Coolidge were fully supportive of minority protection.

69. For example, A. C. Coolidge, the head of the American Committee of Experts, the successor to the Committee of Inquiry, quoted in David Hunter Miller, *My Diary at the Conference of Paris* (n.p.: author, 1924), vol. 7, 366–67, quoted in Oscar I. Janowsky, *The Jews and Minority Rights (1898–1919)* (New York: Columbia University Press, 1933); "International Protection of Human Rights," *Survey*, 29 November 1919, in "Jewish Rights at Peace Conferences," Kohler Papers, Center for Jewish History (hereafter CJH), box 15, folder 11; and Julian W. Mack, Louis Marshall, and Stephen S. Wise, "Memorial to the President Concerning the Status of Jews in Eastern Europe," 1 March 1919, in American Jewish Congress, "Memorials Submitted to President Wilson Conerning the Status of the Jews of Eastern Europe, and in Palestine, by Representatives of the American Jewish Congress on March 2, 1919" (brochure), 8, CJH.

70. A concise statement of this sort is in David Hunter Miller, "The Making of the League of Nations," in House and Seymour, *What Really Happened at Paris*, 398–424. See also "Memorandum of the Committee of the Jewish Delegations at the Paris Peace Conference," submitted 10 May 1919, in Jacob Robinson et al., *Were the Minorities Treaties a Failure?* ed. Institute of Jewish Affairs of the American Jewish Congress and the World Jewish Congress (New York: Antin, 1943), 319–25. For a full account of the development of the minority treaties, see Fink, *Defending the Rights of Others*, 133–264.

71. On the explicit definition of "civilization" developed by international lawyers just before World War I, see Gerrit W. Gong, *The Standard of "Civilization" in International Society* (New York: Oxford University Pess, 1984), 24–53, and Martti Koskenniemi, *The Gentle Civilizer of Nations: The Rise and Fall of International Law, 1870–1960* (Cambridge: Cambridge University Press, 2002), 71–78.

72. See, for example, the memorandum of Polish prime minister Ignace Jan Paderewski to the Allied leaders, 15 June 1919, in US Department of State, *Papers Relating to the Foreign Relations of the United States, 1919: The Paris Peace Conference*, vol. 6 (Washington: Government Printing Office, 1946), 535–40, and Clemenceau's response, the covering letter to Paderewski accompanying the Polish Treaty, June 1919 [no further date], in ibid., 629–34.

73. Janowsky, *Jews and Minority Rights*, 380–83, and table in Janowsky, *Nationalities and National Minorities with Special Reference to East-Central Europe* (New York: Macmillan, 1945), 171–72. Janowsky does not mention Iraq. See also Viefhaus, *Minderheitenfrage*, who provides an excruciatingly detailed account of the drafting of all the treaties, agreements, and declarations related to minority issues.

74. Peace Treaty of Versailles, art. 93, text available at http://net.lib.byu.edu/~rdh7/wwi /versa/versa2.html, accessed 9 October 2018.

75. For details on the workings of the Minorities Commission, see, Susan Pedersen, *The Guardians: The League of Nations and the Crisis of Empire* (Oxford: Oxford University Press, 2015); Natasha Wheatley, "Mandatory Interpretation: Legal Hermeneutics and the New International Order in Arab and Jewish Petitions to the League of Nations," *Past and Present* 227 (2015): 205–48; and Fink, *Defending the Rights of Others*; as well as the older accounts by Julius Stone, *International Guarantee of Minority Rights: Procedure of the Council of the League of Nations in Theory and Practice* (London: Oxford University Press, 1932); Robinson et al., *Minority Treaties a Failure?*; Viefhaus, *Minderheitenfrage*; and Ernst Flachbarth, *System des internationalen Minderheitenrechtes* (Budapest: R. Gergely, 1937).

76. Alliance Israélite universelle, "Declaration of Alliance Israélite sur les dispositions of the Polish Treaty," Paris, 9 July 1919, in *Question juive*, 37–39, quote 37.

77. Board of Deputies of British Jews, "Peace Conference," 34. For more recent arguments that the Jewish role has been much exaggerated, see David Engel, "Perceptions of Power: Poland and World Jewry," *Jahrbuch des Simon-Dubnow-Instituts* 1 (2002): 17–28, and Fink, *Defending the Rights of Others*. Mark Levene emphasizes the role of British Jewry, and, in particular, Lucien Wolf, in the formulation of the minorities treaties, in *War, Jews, and the New Europe: The Diplomacy of Lucien Wolf, 1914–1919* (Oxford: Oxford University Press, 1992).

78. For one later critique of Lausanne as a violation of the spirit of Paris, see J. Robinson et al., *Minorities Treaties a Failure?*, 57. On the policies of ethnic cleansing and partition generally in this period, see Laura Robson, *States of Separation: Transfer, Partition, and the Making of the Modern Middle East* (Berkeley: University of California Press, 2017).

79. Flachbarth, *System des internationalen Minderheitenrechtes*, 81–82, and Roland Huntford, *Fridtjof Nansen and the Unmixing of Greeks and Turks in 1924*, Nansen Memorial Lecture 1998 (Oslo: Norwegian Academy of Sciences, 1999).

80. Venizelos was the towering figure in Greek politics for almost two generations. There is no good biography in English, French, Italian, or German, and one is left with older hagiographies in which Venizelos is portrayed by British or American Philhellenes as the great reviver of Hellenism in the modern world—e.g., in Herbert Adams Gibbons, *Venizelos* (Boston: Houghton Mifflin, 1920). For a brief, colorful portrait of Venizelos, see Margaret MacMillan, *Paris 1919: Six Months that Changed the World* (New York: Random House, 2003), 347–65, 429–37. More recent scholarship on Venizelos is evident in Paschalis M. Kitromilides, ed., *Eleftherios Venizelos: The Trials of Statesmanship* (Edinburgh: Edinburgh University Press, 2006), but even this volume cannot always manage to avoid idealized treatments of its hero. For one statement of his views, see Eleutherios Venizelos, *Greece before the Peace Congress of 1919: A Memorandum Dealing with the Rights of Greece* (New York: Oxford University Press for the American-Hellenic Society, 1919).

81. Viefhaus, *Minderheitenfrage*, 214–15.

82. "Convention Concerning the Exchange of Greek and Turkish Populations," art. 1, in *The Treaties of Peace, 1919–1923*, vol. 2 (New York: Carnegie Endowment for International Peace, 1924), 1036.

83. On the treaty provisions and their impact, see Flachbarth, *System des internationalen Minderheitenrechtes*, 348–59; Renée Hirschon, ed., *Crossing the Aegean: An Appraisal of the 1923 Compulsory Population Exchange between Greece and Turkey* (New York: Berghahn, 2003); and Dzovinar Kévonian, *Réfugiés et diplomatie humanitaire: Les acteurs européens et la scène proche-orientale pendant l'entre-deux-guerres* (Paris: Broché, 2004), 71, 109–29. As Kévonian writes, although the Lausanne Treaty defined the communities subject to the exchange by religion (Orthodox Christians or Muslims), it really signified a conception of the nation characterized by homogeneity in which religion blended into nation or race (71, 135–36). On the background to Lausanne, see Michael Llewellyn Smith, *Ionian Visions: Greece in Asia Minor, 1919–1922* (New York: St. Martin's, 1973).

84. For some of the criticisms, see Kévonian, *Réfugiés et diplomatie humanitaire*, 122–24, 252–61.

85. Ministère des affaires étrangères, France, *Documents diplomatiques: Conférence de Lausanne*, vol. 1, *21 novembre 1922–1 février 1923* (Paris: Imprimerie nationale, 1923), meeting of 13 December 1922, 170–78, quote 175. Curzon disingenuously claimed that Greece had nothing to do with proposing the exchange.

86. Ibid., meeting of 27 January 1923, 307–17, quote 311.

87. Ibid., 310.

88. I thank Stephen Blake for pointing out to me Curzon's plan for Bengal.

89. Figures in Renée Hirschon, "The Consequences of the Lausanne Convention: An Overview," in *Crossing the Aegean*, 13–20, here 14–15. On the movement of Muslims since the 1860s, see Karpat, *Ottoman Population*, and Justin McCarthy, *Death and Exile: The Ethnic Cleansing of Ottoman Muslims, 1821–1922* (Princeton: Darwin, 1995).

90. See Richard G. Hovannisian, *Armenia on the Road to Independence, 1918* (Berkeley: University of California Press, 1967), and Hovannisian, *The Republic of Armenia*, 4 vols. (Berkeley: University of California Press, 1971–96).

91. See Balakian, *Burning Tigris*.

92. *Winona Independent*, 13 October 1915, and *Minneapolis Journal*, 25 September 1915. I thank Lou Ann Matossian for providing me copies of these articles.

93. See Hovannisian, *Republic of Armenia*, vol. 1, 157–60.

94. For a good summary of the events, see Simon Payaslian, *The History of Armenia: From the Origins to the Present* (New York: Palgrave Macmillan, 2007), 145–70.

95. Hovannisian, *Republic of Armenia*, vol. 1, 126–33.

96. James W. Gerard, "Why America Should Accept Mandate for Armenia," *New York Times*, 6 July 1919, in American Committee for the Independence of Armenia and Armenian National Union of America, *America as Mandatary for Armenia*, brochure (New York, 1919), 3–10, quotes 3, 5, 9, 10.

97. Vahan Cardashian, "Should America Accept a Mandate for Armenia?" in ibid., 25–36, here 30. For other examples, see "Armenia," *New York Times*, 16 February 1919, in ibid., 18–19, and Hovannisian, *Republic of Armenia*, vol. 1, 261–76.

98. Cardashian, "Mandate for Armenia," 30.

99. See *The Armenian Question Before the Peace Conference: A Memorandum Presented Officially by the Representatives of Armenia to the Peace Conference at Versailles, on February 26th, 1919* (n.p., n.d.).

100. Ibid., 12. More details in Hovannisian, *Republic of Armenia*, vol. 1, 309–12.

101. "Armenian Question Before the Peace Conference," 26.

102. Ibid., 29.

103. Ernst Neissner, "Bericht über meine Reise in die Türkei," n.d. [February 1918], PAAA/R13200/69–93, quote 83.

104. Erik Jan Zürcher's pathbreaking argument about the continuity between the CUP and the Kemalists is now widely accepted. See Zürcher, *The Unionist Factor: The Role of the Committee of Union and Progress in the Turkish National Movement, 1905–1926* (Leiden: Brill, 1984). See also Hanioğlu, *Atatürk*.

105. Erik Jan Zürcher, *Turkey: A Modern History*, 3rd ed. (London: I. B. Tauris, 2004), 164. Some sources give an even lower figure, 70–75 percent Muslim, in pre-war Anatolia.

106. On the very complex legal issues, see especially Taner Akçam and Ümit Kurt, *The Spirit of the Laws: The Plunder of Wealth in the Armenian Genocide* (New York: Berghahn, 2015). See also Üngör and Polatel, *Confiscation and Destruction*.

107. Akçam and Kurt, *Spirit of the Laws*, 20–22 and passim. The Lausanne population exchange opened up even more lands for expropriation. A subsequent treaty between Greece and Turkey in 1929 left it up to each state to provide compensation, replacing the League of Nations' compensation commissions. Little was done under either system, so one can speak of the forced expropriation of Christians in Turkey and of Muslims in Greece.

108. See ibid., and Üngör and Polatel, *Confiscation and Destruction*, 85–92.

109. Zürcher, *Turkey*, 200.

110. See Speros Vryonis, *Mechanism of Catastrophe: The Turkish Pogrom of September 6–7, 1955, and the Destruction of the Greek Community of Istanbul* (New York: Greekworks, 2005). Only in 1986 were the laws of abandoned properties abolished. See Üngör and Polatel, *Confiscation and Destruction*, 57.

111. Üngör and Polatel, *Confiscation and Destruction*, 56.

112. On one of the earlier resettlements, prior to the genocide, see Vizekonsul von Zitkovszky to Grafen Aehrenthal, Monastir, 14 October 1910, A18643, PAAA/R13797/1–4, here 3. On related policies, see Adanir and Kaiser, "Migration, Deportation, and Nation-Building." On the deportation of Greeks, which began in 1913, see Akçam, *Young Turks' Crime against Humanity*.

113. Çağlar Keyder, "Class and State in the Transformation of Modern Turkey," in *State and Ideology in the Middle East and Pakistan*, ed. Fred Halliday and Hamza Alavi (Basingstoke: Macmillan Education, 1988), 191–221, here 199, and Keyder, *State and Class in Turkey: A Study in Capitalist Development* (London: Verso, 1987), 81. See also M. Şükrü Hanioğlu, *A Brief History of the Late Ottoman Empire* (Princeton: Princeton University Press, 2008), 190–91; Zürcher, *Turkey*, 125–27; and Carter Vaughn Findley, *Turkey, Islam, Nationalism, and Modernity: A History, 1789–2007* (New Haven: Yale University Press, 2010), 229, and generally 226–33.

Both Ottoman and foreign observers recognized that the removals of the Christian commercial class gravely weakened the empire's economy. For some examples, Ernst Neissner, "Bericht über meine Reise in die Türkei," n.d. [February 1918], PAAA/R13200/69–93; Kühlmann to Bethmann Hollweg, Pera, 16 February 1917, no. 112, PAAA/R13820/nn; Auskunftsstelle für Deutsch-Türkische Wirtschaftsfragen to Legationsrat Dr. von Rosenberg, AA, 2 August 1916, PAAA/R13197/10–72 (of file), especially 47–48, 62–63, 66–67, 71; Professor Dr. Dettweiler, "Deutschland und die Türkei," Constantinople, 24 April 1924, in PAAA/R78485/L016398–406.

114. Bernard Lewis, *The Emergence of Modern Turkey*, 2nd ed. (1961; Oxford: Oxford University Press, 1968), 459–60, 466–68, 472–74; Keyder, "Transformation of Modern Turkey," 204–5; Ayhan Aktar, "Economic Nationalism in Turkey: The Formative Years, 1912–1925," *Boğazici Journal: Review of Social, Economic and Administrative Studies* 10:1–2 (1996): 263–90; Zürcher, *Unionist Factor*; and Rifat B. Bali, "The Politics of Turkification during the Single Party Period," in Kieser, *Turkey*, 47–48. On the labor policies of foreign companies, which favored Christians, see Donald Quataert, *The Ottoman Empire, 1700–1922* (Cambridge: Cambridge University Press, 2005), 184–86.

115. Keyder, *State and Class in Turkey*, 82.

116. See Dery Bayir, *Minorities and Nationalism in Turkish Law* (Farnham: Ashgate, 2013), 19–63; on the Lausanne Treaty, 88–94.

117. On all these measures, see Lerna Ekmekçioğlu, *Recovering Armenia: The Limits of Belonging in Post-Genocide Turkey* (Stanford: Stanford University Press, 2016), and "Republic of Paradox: The League of Nations Minority Regime and the New Turkey's Step-Citizens," *International Journal of Middle East Studies* 46:3 (2014): 657–79, who refreshingly analyzes together the policies of discrimination and assimilation. See also Corinna Görgü Guttstadt, "Depriving Non-Muslims of Citizenship as Part of the Turkification Policy in the Early Years of the Turkish Republic: The Case of Turkish Jews and Its Consequences during the Holocaust," in Kieser, *Turkey*, 50–56, here 52–55; Üngör and Polatel, *Confiscation and Destruction*, 59; Bayir, *Minorities and Nationalism*, 95–142, 149; Murat Ergin, " 'Is the Turk a White Man?': Towards a Theoretical Framework for Race in the Making of Turkishness," *Middle Eastern Studies* 44:6 (2008): 827–50; Soner Çagaptay, *Islam, Secularism, and Nationalism in Modern Turkey: Who Is a Turk?* (London: Routledge, 2006); and Mesut Yeğen, "Citizenship and Ethnicity in Turkey," *Middle Eastern Studies* 40:6 (2004): 51–66. The laws and decrees were porous, however. Some Europeans, including Jews, were granted citizenship. See Çagaptay, *Islam, Secularism, and Nationalism*, 69–81. See also Hanioğlu, *Atatürk*, 160–98, for a discussion of some of the wilder elements of Kemalist racial theories in the 1930s.

118. Bali, "Politics of Turkification," 43–49.

119. Quoted in ibid., 46.

120. Ibid., and Hans-Lukas Kieser, introduction to *Turkey*, vii–xvii, quote ix.

121. Hans-Lukas Kieser, "An Ethno-Nationalist Revolutionary and Theorist of Kemalism: Dr. Mahmut Esat Bozkurt (1892–1943)," in *Turkey*, 20–27.

122. See William W. Hagen, "Before the 'Final Solution': Toward a Comparative Analysis of Political Anti-Semitism in Interwar Germany and Poland," *Journal of Modern History* 68:2 (1996): 351–81.

123. See Martin Dean, *Robbing the Jews: The Confiscation of Jewish Property in the Holocaust, 1933–1945* (Cambridge: Cambridge University Press, 2008); Martin Dean, Constantin Goschler, and Philipp Ther, eds., *Robbery and Restitution: The Conflict over Jewish Property in Europe* (New York: Berghahn, 2007); and Götz Aly, *Hitlers Volksstaat: Raub, Rassenkrieg und Nationalsozialismus* (Frankfurt am Main: Fischer, 2005).

124. On integration, see Norbert Frei, *Vergangenheitspolitik: Die Anfänge der Bundesrepublik und die NS-Vergangenheit* (Munich: Beck, 1996).

125. On the restitution and reparations process, see Dean, Goschler, and Ther, *Robbery and Restitution*; Tobias Winstel, *Verhandelte Gerechtigkeit: Rückerstattung und Enschädigung für jüdische NS-Opfer in Bayern und Westdeutschland* (Munich: Oldenbourg, 2006); and Constantin Goschler, *Wiedergutmachung: Westdeutschland und die Verfolgten des Nationalsozialismus (1945–1954)* (Munich: Oldenbourg, 1992). Generally on the topic, see John Torpey, *Making Whole What Has Been Smashed: On Reparations Politics* (Cambridge: Harvard University Press, 2006), and Elazar Barkan, *The Guilt of Nations: Restitution and Negotiating Historical Injustices* (New York: Norton, 2000).

126. Jan T. Gross, *Fear: Anti-Semitism in Poland after Auschwitz. An Essay in Historical Interpretation* (Princeton: Princeton University Press, 2006), 39–51, 245–61.

Chapter 6: Namibia

1. Quoted in Gesine Krüger, *Kriegsbewältigung und Geschichtsbewußtsein: Realität, Deutung und Verarbeitung des deutschen Kolonialkriegs in Namibia 1904 bis 1907* (Göttingen: Vandenhoeck and Ruprecht, 1999), 45. Anticolonial activists in the 1950s adopted the name Namibia from the Namib Desert along the Atlantic coast. In Khoi, "Namib" means "the barren plains behind the dunes." See Gerhard Pool, *Samuel Maharero* (Windhoek: Gamsberg Macmillan, 1991), xii. A United Nations resolution in 1968 formally renamed German Southwest Africa as Namibia. Although "Namibia" is anachronistic for the period under discussion here, it has the advantage of familiarity, so I use Namibia and Southwest Africa interchangeably.

2. Quoted in Isabel V. Hull, *Absolute Destruction: Military Culture and the Practices of War in Imperial Germany* (Ithaca: Cornell University Press, 2005), 7. "Windhuk" is the older spelling; I use the contemporary "Windhoek."

3. Technically, it was at first a German protectorate (*Schutzgebiet*), but both Germans and the natives treated it as a colony from the beginning, and that is the terminology I use here.

4. For a careful weighing of the always incomplete statistics, see Hull, *Absolute Destruction*, 88–90.

5. On the latter point, see Jennifer Pitts, *A Turn to Empire: The Rise of Imperial Liberalism in Britain and France* (Princeton: Princeton University Press, 2005), and Uday S. Mehta, *Liberalism and Empire: A Study in Nineteenth-Century British Liberal Thought* (Chicago: University of Chicago Press, 1999).

6. W. E. Burghardt Du Bois, *The Souls of Black Folk: Essays and Sketches* (1903; New York: Fawcett, 1961), 23. See also Patrick Wolfe, *Traces of History: Elementary Structures of Race* (London: Verso, 2016); Marilyn Lake and Henry Reynolds, *Drawing the Global Colour Line: White Men's Countries and the International Challenge of Racial Equality* (Cambridge: Cambridge University Press, 2008); and George M. Fredrickson, *Racism: A Short History* (Princeton: Princeton University Press, 2003). Wolfe is especially strong on the various constructions of race.

7. On settler colonialism, see Caroline Elkins and Susan Pedersen, eds., *Settler Colonialism in the Twentieth Century: Projects, Practices, Legacies* (New York: Routledge, 2005).

8. For the term, see Gary Wilder, *The French Imperial Nation-State: Negritude and Colonial Humanism between the Two World Wars* (Chicago: University of Chicago Press, 2005).

9. Quoted in Krüger, *Kriegsbewältigung und Geschichtsbewußtsein*, 35.

10. On the Herero, see especially Dag Henrichsen, *Herrschaft und Alltag im vorkolonialen Zentralnamibia: Das Herero- und Damaraland im 19. Jahrhundert* (Basel: Basler Afrika Bibliographien, 2011), and Krüger, *Kriegsbewältigung und Geschichtsbewußtsein*, 33–45. Henrichsen convincingly argues that the Herero became pastoralists largely in the nineteenth century in the context of emergent merchant capitalism in Southern Africa. On the Witbooi Nama, see Wilhelm J. G. Möhlig, ed., *Die Witbooi in Südwestafrika während des 19. Jahrhunderts: Quellentexte von Johannes Olpp, Hendrik Witbooi jun. und Carl Berger* (Cologne: Rüdiger Köppe, 2007). Generally, see J. S. Malan, *Peoples of Namibia* (Pretoria: Rhino, 1995), and the older studies of Carl Hugo Linsingen Hahn, Heinrich Vedder, and L. Fourie, *The Native Tribes of South West Africa* (1928; New York: Barnes and Noble, 1966), and Heinrch Vedder, *South West Africa in Early Times: Being the Story of South West Africa up to the Date of Maharero's Death in 1890*, ed. and trans. Cyril G. Hall

(London: Oxford University Press, 1938). But note the very critical comments on Vedder in Brigitte Lau, " 'Thank God the Germans Came': Vedder and Namibian Historiography," in *History and Historiography: Four Essays in Reprint* (Windoek: Discourse/MSOP, 1995), 1–16, and Henrichsen, *Herrschaft und Alltag*, 301–12.

11. For more on the missionaries, see Adam A. Blackler, "Heathens, 'Hottentots,' and *Heimat*: Colonial Encounters and German Identity in Southwest Africa, 1842–1915" (unpublished PhD thesis, University of Minnesota, 2017).

12. As a result, we have as documentary records the written correspondence of people like Samuel Maharero, Hendrik Witbooi, and a number of others. On Witbooi, see Adam A. Blackler, "From Boondoggle to Settlement Colony: Hendrik Wittbooi and the Evolution of Germany's Imperial Project in Southwest Africa, 1884–1894," *Central European History* 50:4 (2017): 449–70. For one good source, see Gustav Menzel, *"Widerstand und Gottesfurcht": Hendrik Witbooi—Eine Biographie in zeitgenössischen Quellen* (Cologne: Rüdiger Köppe, 2000), as well as Pool, *Samuel Maharero*. See also Krüger, *Kriegsbewältigung und Geschichtsbewußtsein*, 39–41, who shows that by the latter third of the nineteenth century, many of the Herero leaders were sending their children to mission schools, where they became christianized. Governor Leutwein wrote that Witbooi had "two souls": one Christian and moral, the other a "barborous, fanatical Hottentot soul," which emerged again in his last rebellion (that is, during the Namibian War). See Theodor Leutwein, *Elf Jahre Gouverneur in Deutsch-Südwestafrika* (Berlin: Ernst Siegfried Mittler und Sohn, 1907), 305.

13. Scholars have long debated the reason for Bismarck's colonial turn. For two of the older important studies, see Woodruff D. Smith, *The German Colonial Empire* (Chapel Hill: University of North Carolina Press, 1978), and Hans-Ulrich Wehler, *Bismarck und der Imperialismus* (Cologne: Kiepenheuer and Witsch, 1969). Wehler's social imperialism argument, that the colonial empire was merely a diversion tactic of Bismarck's with the goal of national integration and the weakening of socialism, holds little sway today.

14. See especially Stig Förster, Wolfgang J. Mommsen, and Ronald Robinson, eds., *Bismarck, Europe, and Africa: The Berlin Africa Conference 1884–1885 and the Onset of Partition* (Oxford: Oxford University Press, 1988).

15. See, for example, Birthe Kundrus, *Moderne Imperialisten: Das Kaiserreich im Spiegel seiner Kolonien* (Cologne: Böhlau, 2003); Kundrus, ed., *Phantasiereiche: Zur Kulturgeschichte des deutschen Kolonialismus* (Frankfurt am Main: Campus, 2003); Sara Friedrichsmeyer, Sarah Lennox, and Susanna Zantop, eds., *The Imperialist Imagination: German Colonialism and Its Legacies* (Ann Arbor: University of Michigan Press, 1998); and John Noyes, *Colonial Space: Spatiality in the Discourse of German Southwest Africa, 1884–1915* (Philadelphia: Harwood Academic, 1992).

16. Rohrbach to his brother Fritz, 6 February 1906, Bundesarchiv Koblenz (hereafter BAK)/ NL1408/69. Rohrbach had first come to Southwest in 1903, before the Namibian War, when he was appointed to head the Settlement Commission, an agency designed to investigate economic conditions and to encourage Germans to emigrate to the colony. During the Namibian War, he was delegated again to Southwest, this time as head of the Compensation Commission. See also Clara Rohrbach to her parents and sister, Windhoek, 15 November 1905, BAK/NL1408/68. For other optimistic and even lyrical homages to life in the colony, see the nineteen-page report by assistant physician and deputy district chief Jodtka on his journey through the Okavango,

17 May–6 July 1902, Bundesarchiv Berlin Lichterfelde, Reichskolonialamt (hereafter RKA)/ R1001/2084 (film 205)/7–16, and the unsigned article "Die Kalaharibuschleute," *Kölnische Volks-zeitung*, 21 January 1903, RKA/R1001/2084 (film 205)/38–40.

17. Quoted in Blackler, "Heathens, 'Hottentots,' and *Heimat*," 215.

18. Quoted in Krüger, *Kriegsbewältigung und Geschichtsbewußtsein*, 76.

19. Figure from ibid., 69.

20. Jan-Bart Gewald and Jeremy Silvester, eds., *"Words Cannot Be Found": German Colonial Rule in Namibia. An Annotated Reprint of the 1918 Blue Book* (Leiden: Brill, 2003), 71–73. In 1918, after German control had been overthrown, British officers conducted interviews with Africans in the colony. As an official "investigation into German crimes in Southwest Africa," the *Blue Book*, as it was called, formed part of the rationale for the expropriation of German colonies by the Allies at the Paris Peace Conference in 1919. The *Blue Book* has often been disparaged as a politically motivated document. But the testimonies and other information gathered by the British constitute an invaluable historical source. The historians Jan-Bart Gewald and Jeremy Silvester republished the book in an excellent critical edition with a striking introduction concerning the history of the *Blue Book*; notably, the attempt by South African authorities in the 1920s to gather up all the copies and burn them.

21. Among many sources on the impact of the rinderpest, see Jan-Bart Gewald, *Herero Heroes: A Socio-Political History of the Herero of Namibia, 1890–1923* (Oxford: James Currey, 1999), 110–40.

22. Witbooi to Leutwein, Naukluft, 4 May 1894, in *The Hendrik Witbooi Papers*, 2nd ed., trans. Annemarie Heywood and Eben Maasdorp, ed. Brigitte Lau (Windhoek: National Archives of Namibia, 1995), 150–52, quote 151. This letter is only one among an extensive correspondence between Witbooi and Leutwein, each threatening the other with war, each claiming to want to uphold the peace.

23. Prussia, Grosser Generalstab, Kriegsgeschichtliche Abteilung, *Die Kämpfe der deutschen Truppen in Südwestafrika. Auf Grund amtlichen Materials*, three-volume ed. (Berlin: Ernst Sieg-fried Mittler und Sohn, 1906), vol. 1, 3.

24. Ibid., 4, 6.

25. See Gewald, *Herero Heroes*, 29–60, 81–100, and Krüger, *Kriegsbewältigung und Geschichts-bewußtsein*, 40–41.

26. Gewald, *Herero Heroes*, 101–7, and Krüger, *Kriegsbewältigung und Geschichtsbewußtsein*, 42–43.

27. See Gewald and Silvester, *"Words Cannot Be Found,"* esp. 83–97, 159–68.

28. Testimony of Adam Pienaar, in ibid., 160–61.

29. Krüger, *Kriegsbewältigung und Geschichtsbewußtsein*, 59.

30. The German general staff also thought that the impulse to rebellion came from younger men, often leaders and the sons of tribal elders. See Prussia, Grosser Generalstab, *Kämpfe der deutschen Truppen*, vol. 1, 24.

31. Quoted in Horst Drechsler, *Südwestafrika unter deutscher Kolonialherrschaft: Der Kampf der Herero und Nama gegen den deutschen Imperialismus (1884–1915)* (Berlin: Akademie, 1966), 166.

32. The military historians claimed that the rebellion became a revolt of all Herero because they feared being punished for the actions of a few. But this is only partly correct. See Prussia, Grosser Generalstab, *Kämpfe der deutschen Truppen*, vol. 1, 24.

33. The older accounts of the war remain valuable. See Drechsler, *Südwestafrika*; Helmut Bley, *Kolonialherrschaft und Sozialstruktur in Deutsch-Südwestafrica 1894–1914* (Hamburg: Leibniz-Verlag, 1968); and Jon Bridgman, *The Revolt of the Hereros* (Berkeley: University of California Press, 1981). Among the important more recent publications are Krüger, *Kriegsbewältigung und Geschichtsbewußtsein*; Gewald, *Herero Heroes*; Jürgen Zimmerer, *Deutsche Herrschaft über Afrikaner: Staatlicher Machtanspruch und Wirklichkeit im kolonialen Namibia* (Münster: Lit, 2002); Zimmerer and Joachim Zeller, eds., *Völkermord in Deutsch-Südwestafrika: Der Kolonialkrieg (1904–1908) in Namibia und seine Folgen* (Berlin: Ch. Links, 2003); and Hull, *Absolute Destruction*.

34. Quoted in Drechsler, *Südwestafrika*, 180.

35. Quoted in Krüger, *Kriegsbewältigung und Geschichtsbewußtsein*, 55. A longer quote is in Gewald, *Herero Heroes*, 167–68.

36. See Hull, *Absolute Destruction*, 5–69.

37. Prussia, Grosser Generalstab, *Kämpfe der deutschen Truppen*, vol. 3, 151–52.

38. Testimony of Jan Kubas in Gewald and Silvester, *"Words Cannot Be Found,"* 117. See also the testimony of Manuel Timbu, in ibid., 115–16, quote 116, and the army's own description of the privations and gruesome deaths suffered by the Herero: Prussia, Grosser Generalstab, *Kämpfe der deutschen Truppen*, vol. 3, 202–11.

39. Ludwig von Estorff, *Wanderungen und Kämpfe in Südwestafrika, Ostafrika und Südafrika, 1894–1910* (Wiesbaden: Wiesbaden Kurier Verlag und Druckerei, n.d.), 117. For another example, see Hull, *Absolute Destruction*, 47, quoting Viktor Franke's diary.

40. Quoted in Hull, *Absolute Destruction*, 56.

41. Krüger, *Kriegsbewältigung und Geschichtsbewußtsein*, 53.

42. For the second order, see Hull, *Absolute Destruction*, 68; text of the order in Lau, *Hendrik Witbooi Papers*, 220.

43. On the correspondence between Leutwein and Witbooi, see Lau, *Hendrik Witbooi Papers*, 189–94.

44. Witbooi to Leutwein, 14 November 1904, in ibid., 193–94, quote 193.

45. Witbooi to Schmidt, Tsumis, received 26 July 1905, in ibid., 195.

46. See Gewald, *Herero Heroes*, 195, quoting the missionary Elger. See also the testimony of Africans in Gewald and Silvester, *"Words Cannot Be Found,"* 169–80, 196–206.

47. Krüger, *Kriegsbewältigung und Geschichtsbewußtsein*, 116–22.

48. Testimony of Fritz Isaac, in Gewald and Silvester, *"Words Cannot Be Found,"* 173.

49. Drechsler, *Südwestafrika*, 251.

50. See the testimony of the Nama Franz Lambert, in Gewald and Silvester, *"Words Cannot Be Found,"* 173, as well as Drechsler, *Südwestafrika*, 211–14, and Zimmerer, *Deutsche Herrschaft*, 42–56.

51. See Benjamin Madley, *An American Genocide: The United States and the California Indian Catastrophe, 1846–1873* (New Haven: Yale University Press, 2016), and Adam Hochschild, *King Leopold's Ghost: A Story of Greed, Terror, and Heroism in Colonial Africa* (Boston: Houghton Mifflin, 1999).

52. The best assessment, with an excellent guide to the substantial literature, is Thomas Kühne, "Colonialism and the Holocaust: Continuities, Causations, and Complexities," *Journal*

of Genocide Research 15:3 (2013): 339–62. Jürgen Zimmerer set off the debate. See his various articles in *Von Windhuk nach Auschwitz? Beiträge zum Verhältnis von Kolonialismus und Holocaust* (Münster: Lit-Verlag, 2011).

53. This is Hull's argument in *Absolute Destruction*.

54. Quoted in Bley, *Kolonialherrschaft und Sozialstruktur*, 204. The German original: "*Die Nation als solche vernichtet werden muß*."

55. As the official military history paraphrased Trotha's views: Prussia, Grosser Generalstab, *Kämpfe der deutschen Truppen*, vol. 3, 212.

56. Quoted in Krüger, *Kriegsbewältigung und Geschichtsbewußtsein*, 65.

57. Quoted in ibid., 66.

58. Quoted in ibid., 167.

59. Kaiserliches Gouvernement (in Vertretung von Trotha) to Kolonial-Abteilung Auswärtiges Amt, Windhuk, 15 October 1904, no. 975, RKA/R1001/1139 (film 110)/232–47/4 (of report).

60. Ibid., 4–5, quote 5 (of report).

61. Ibid., 6–7 (of report).

62. See, for example, the comments by Chief of the General Staff von Schlieffen to Chancellor Bülow, quoted in Drechsler, *Südwestafrika*, 192–94.

63. Prussia, Grosser Generalstab, *Kämpfe der deutschen Truppen*, vol. 3, 211.

64. See, for example, "Bericht über die Besprechungen Seiner Exzellenz des Herren Staatssekretär Dernburg mit den Referenten des Gouvernements," Windhuk, 12 August 1908, RKA/R1001/2086 (film 205)/22–48, especially 22–23; Paul Rohrbach in his draft report with much detail on the destruction of white farms, 16 August 1904, RKA/R1001/1139 (film 110)/87–159 (hereafter Rohrbach report), here 65–67 (of report); and Leutwein, *Elf Jahre Gouverneur*, 524–25, though the latter, since his dismissal, was no longer a force to be reckoned with. In the historical literature, see especially Zimmerer, *Deutsche Herrschaft*, and Bley, *Kolonialherrschaft und Sozialstruktur*, 149–279.

65. Rohrbach report, 16 August 1904, 64–67 (of report).

66. Quoted in Krüger, *Kriegsbewältigung und Geschichtsbewußtsein*, 164, citing Drechsler, *Südwestafrika*, 166. See also the earlier, shorter (thirty-three pages), untitled draft of Rohrbach's report, 2 May 1904, RKA/R1001/1139 (film 110)/23, 24 (of report), and Rohrbach to his parents, Okahandja, 2 September 1904, BAK/NL1408/67, and Rohrbach to his brother Fritz, Windhuk, 3 February 1906, BAK/NL1408/69.

67. Moritz Julius Bonn, quoted in Krüger, *Kriegsbewältigung und Geschichtsbewußtsein*, 66, from *Frankfurter Zeitung*, 14 September 1909. Bonn was a social reformer, a member of the Verein für Sozialpolitik.

68. Still, there were strong disagreements about the character of future development. Governor Lindequist, for example, advocated small German farms and limited state involvement, while Rohrbach argued for large ranches and a more active role for the state. See the account in Daniel Joseph Walther, *Creating Germans Abroad: Cultural Policies and National Identity in Namibia* (Athens: Ohio University Press, 2002), 1–27.

69. See, for example, Rohrbach report, 16 August 1904, 64 (of report), and "Bericht über die Besprechungen Seiner Exzellenz des Herren Staatssekretärs Dernburg mit den Referenten des

Gouvernements," Windhuk, 12 August 1908, RKA/R1001/2086 (film 205)/22–48, quote 22–23. Not all the officials were keen on Dernburg's proposals. They warned that if the Herero were able to increase their herds, a new security danger would emerge, and worried about the practicality of imposing taxes.

70. Some of these measures had been implemented earlier. An initial ban on interracial marriages, for example, had been issued in 1905. The 1907 decrees were more far-reaching and systematic.

71. Rohrbach report, 16 August 1904, 49 (of report).

72. Ibid., 45–47 (of report).

73. [Unclear sender] to Lindequist, Berlin, 19 May 1904, RKA/1001/1139 (film 110)/36.

74. See the documents in National Archives of Namibia (hereafter NAN)/BRE 14/B.10.n. See also Lora Wildenthal, *German Women for Empire, 1884–1945* (Durham: Duke University Press, 2001). The Kolonial-Frauenschule in Bad Weilbach educated no more than a dozen women per year to take up positions in the colonies. They were instructed in household and farm labor and economies. See, for example, *Jahres-Bericht der Gesellschaft mit beschränkter Haftung Kolonial-Frauenschule für das Geschäftsjahr 1912/1913 über die Kolonial-Frauenschule in Bad Weilbach* (Cassel: Casseler Verlagsanstalt, 1913), in NAN/BRE 14/B.10.g.

75. See Rohrbach report, 2 May 1904, 21 (of report). See also letters in BAK/NL/1408/67. It took weeks on horseback to reach the farms where he needed to assess damages. On this issue he was supported by Trotha, despite their many disagreements. See Kaiserliches Gouvernement (in Vertretung von Trotha) to Kolonial-Abteilung Auswärtiges Amt, Windhuk, 15 October 1904, no. 975, RKA/R1001/1139 (film 110)/11–12 (of report).

76. See two documents of unclear provenance, one to State Secretary Dernburg, Berlin, 30 July 1909, RKA/1001/2231 (film 217)/62–65.

77. Kaiserlicher Gouverneur (Schuckmann) to Reichskolonialamt, Windhuk, 5 May 1909, J. Nr. 11509, RKA/1001/2231 (film 217)/60–61. Apparently, such measures had already been approved by the Reich Colonial Office, but in restricted amounts, and Schuckmann was now requesting an additional appropriation of one hundred thousand marks.

78. Kaiserlicher Gouverneur (im Auftrag Hosenberg) to Kaiserliche Bezirksamt Reheboth, Windhuk, 14 November 1910, J. Nr. 24874, NAN/BRE 26/E.1.l/113–14. Even the Reheboth Bastar needed the permission of the governor to possess cattle and horses. German farmers were warned not to simply grant such animals to the natives: Kaiserliches Bezirksamt to Polizeistation, Reheboth, 12 July 1913, NAN/BRE 26/E.1.e/6. For one example of a farmer requesting permission to sell a cow to his "native Hottentot, Jacob Stewe," see Kaiserliche Bezirksamt Reheboth, NAN/BRE 22/E.1.c/29.

79. For a collection of petitions by Africans to the authorities requesting ownership of animals, see NAN/DOK 25/E.1.e.

80. Statement taken by Polizeisergeant Kubeth, signed with three "X's" by van Wyk, Cabiras, 22 May 1909, NAN/BRE 26/E.1.l/97.

81. Kaiserlicher Gouverneur to Kasierliche Distriktsamt Reheboth, Windhuk, 9 June 1909, J. Nr. 11983, NAN/BRE 26/E.1.l/98.

82. Kaiserlicher Gouverneur (im Auftrag Hosenberg) to Kaiserliche Bezirksamt Reheboth, Windhuk, 14 November 1910, J. Nr. 24874, NAN/BRE 26/E.1.l/113–14.

83. Kaiserlicher Gouverneur (Lindequist), Windhuk, 18 August 1907, J. No. 20762, NAN/ BRE 27/E.2.a, Bd. 1/12vs.

84. Ibid., 7vs–7rs.

85. For some examples: Kaiserlicher Gouverneur (?Kalte) to Regierungs Finanz[amt] Reheboth, Windhuk, 24 June 1913, J. Nr. 13717, NAN/BRE 22/E.1.c/23; Kaiserliches Bezirksamt, Windhuk, 30 September 1913, J. Nr. 2866, NAN BRE 22/E.1.c/27; Polizeistation to Bezirksamt Keetmanshoop, 3 December 1912, J. Nr. 677, with reply from Polizei Sergeant Aunzberg, NAN/ BKE 13/E.2.b/7, and correspondence between Kaiserliches Bezirksamt Keetmanshoop and various police stations, 14 December 1912 and 28 January 1913, NAN/BKE 13/E.2.b/7RS.

86. Distrikt Okahandja to Kaiserliches Gouvernement Windhuk, Farm Okonjete, 31 January 1914, J. No. 3287, NAN/DOK 27/E.2.f/17–18.

87. See, for example, the documents in NAN/BRE 27/E.2.b, Bd. 2; NAN/DOK 27/E.2.f; and NAN/DOK 29/E.4.d., Bd. 7. For just one typical example, Kaiserlicher Gouverneur (Hintrager), Windhuk, 21 July 1909, J. Nr. 17420, NAN/BRE 26/E.1.m/2, and Kaiserlicher Gouverneur to Kaiserliche Distriktsamt Reheboth, Windhuk, 12 November 1909, J. Nr. 27141, NAN/ BRE 26/E.1.m/7.

88. "Protocol," Windhuk, 6 March 1913, NAN/DOK 29/E.4.d, Bd. 7/17–19.

89. See, for example, Kaiserliches Distriktamt Gobabis to Kaiserliche Gouvernement, 9 November 1909, J. Nr. 2812, NAN/BRE26/E.1.g.1/7.

90. Ibid.

91. See Lynn Hunt, *Inventing Human Rights: A History* (New York: Norton, 2007). Voltaire had written one of the great tracts against torture and delivered a riveting satire of it in *Candide*.

92. For many such incidents in the Okahandja region, see NAN/DOK/E.4da, Bde. 1 and 2. See also Zimmerer, *Deutsche Herrschaft*, 199–211.

93. Colonial Secretary Dernburg to colonial governors, Berlin, 12 July 1907, NAN/ DOK/E.4.b/10.

94. Kaiserliches Gouvernement (Lindequist) to Kaiserliches Distriktsamt Okahandja, Windhuk, 22 December 1905, J. Nr. 15665, NAN/DOK29/E.4.b/3.

95. Kaiserlicher Gouverneur (Hintrager) to Kaiserliche Distriktsamt Okahandja, 2 February 1912, J. Nr. 1516, NAN/DOK 29/E.4.a, Bd. 1/25.

96. Kaiserlicher Gouverneur [presumably], n.d., NAN/ DOK 29/E.4.a, Bd. 1/31.

97. Ibid.

98. Kaiserlicher Gouverneur (Seitz) to Kaiserliche Bezirksamt Reheboth, Windhuk, 14 August 1913, J. Nr. 14837, quoting Landesrat, NAN/BRE 27/E.2.a, Bd. 1/69.

99. For the order demanding complete information on the imposition of judgments against natives, see Kaiserlicher Gouverneur to Kaiserliche Distriktsamt Okahandja, Winduk, 21 August 1911, J. Nr. 20905, NAN/DOK 29/E.4.a, Bd. 1/24.

100. "Protocol," Okahandja, 8 January 1913, NAN/DOK 30/E.4.i, Bd 2/nn. For other examples: Kaiserlicher Gouverneur (Hintrager) to Kaiserliche Distriktsamt Okahandja, 28 June 1912, NAN/DOK 29/E.4.a, Bd. 1/28–29; Strafbuch Nr. 152, Omaruru, 26 October 1912, NAN/ BOM 1/E.4.C/4; Protocols, Okahandja, 28 April 1913 and 1 August 1914, NAN/DOK 30/E.4.i, Bd. 2/nn; and Strafbuch Nr. 37, Okorusu, 8 September 1914, NAN/BOM 1/E.4.C/nn.

101. "Protocol," Okahandja, 4 January 1913, NAN/DOK/E.4.i, Bd. 2/nn.

102. Strafbuch Nr. 152, Omaruru, 26 October 1912, NAN/BOM 1/E.4.C/4.

103. Strafbuch Nr. 37, Okorusu, 8 September 1914, NAN/BOM 1/E.4.C/[no page number].

104. Strafbuch Nr. 13/14, Okombahe, 21 November 1914, NAN/BOM 1/E.4.C/[no page number].

105. Clara Rohrbach to her parents and sister, Windhuk, 24 July 1905, BAK/NL1408/68.

106. Clara Rohrbach to her parents and sister, Windhuk, 15 November 1905, BAK/NL1408/68.

107. Generally on this point, see Sebastian Conrad, *Deutsche Kolonialgeschichte* (Munich: C. H. Beck, 2008), 70–75.

108. See generally, on the directives regarding labor contracts, Kaiserlicher Gouverneur (Lindequist), Windhuk, 18 August 1907, NAN/BRE 27/E.2.a, Bd. 1/1–15, and on their violations, 5RS; Kaiserlicher Gouverneur to Kaiserliche Bezirks- bzw. Distriktsamte, Windhuk, 18 January 1908, RKA/R1001/2235 (film 217)/49; and Kaiserliches Bezirksamt to Herrn Gouverneur, Reheboth, 21 October 1912, NAN/BRE 27/E.2.a, Bd. 1/43–44. See also Zimmerer, *Deutsche Herrschaft*, 176–211.

109. Kaiserlicher Gouverneur (Lindequist), Windhuk, 18 August 1907, NAN/BRE 27/E.2.a, Bd. 1/13rs–15vs.

110. On these issues, see Dieter Gosewinkel, *Einbürgern und Ausschließen: Die Nationalisierung des Staatsangehörigkeit vom Deutschen Bund bis zur Bundesrepublik Deutschland* (Göttingen: Vandenhoeck and Ruprecht, 2001).

111. See Blackler, "Heathens, 'Hottentots,' and *Heimat*," 193–95.

112. Ibid., 193–95, 255–57, quotes 194. I have slightly altered the translation.

113. Trotha threatened to "settle accounts" with the Reheboth Bastar, as noted earlier. Kaiserliches Gouvernement (in Vertretung von Trotha) to Kolonial-Abteilung Auswärtiges Amt, Windhuk, 15 October 1904, RKA/R1001/1139 (film 110)/232–47/4–7, quote 5 (of report). For a study on the dangers of race mixing by an anthropologist who had a long, illustrious career into the Nazi years, see Eugen Fischer, *Die Rehobother Bastards und das Bastardierungsproblem beim Menschen: Anthropolgische und ethnographische Studien am Rehobother Bastardvolk in Deutsch-Südwest-Afrika* (Jena: Fischer, 1913).

114. The mixed sentiments regarding the Herero come through clearly in the army's official history. See Prussia, Grosser Generalstab, *Kämpfe der deutschen Truppen*, vol. 2, esp. 69, 89, 129. George Steinmetz's contention that the Germans viewed the Herero as unyieldingly debased is, I believe, one-sided. See Steinmetz, *The Devil's Handwriting: Precoloniality and the German Colonial State in Qingdao, Samoa, and Southwest Africa* (Chicago: University of Chicago Press, 2007).

115. See Hahn, Vedder, and Fourie, *Native Tribes*, and Vedder, *South West Africa*.

116. Kaiserliches Gouvernement (in Vertretung Tecklenburg) to Distriktskommando Reheboth, Windhoek, 20 November 1902, NAN/BRE 14/B.10.e/4. For more on the Boers, see Blackler, "Heathens, 'Hottentots,' and *Heimat*," 228–40.

117. Kaiserliches Gouvernement (in Vertretung Estorff) to Kaiserliche Distrikt Reheboth, Windhoek, 9 September 1902, J. Nr. 6237, NAN/BRE 14/B.10.e/9RS.

118. Kaiserliches Gouvernement (in Vertretung Tecklenburg) to Distriktskommando Reheboth, Windhoek, 20 November 1902, NAN/BRE 14/B.10.e/4RS.

119. Kaiserlicher Gouverneur (in Vertretung Estorff), "Bedingungen für die Ansiedlung holländischer Afrikaner in Deutsch-Südwestafrika," Windhoek, 13 November 1902, NAN/BRE 14/B.10.e/5–6.

120. Kaiserlicher Gouverneur to Kaiserliche Bezirksamt (in Vertretung Hintrager), Windhuk, 7 June 1910, NAN/BRE 14/B.10.a/1.

121. Kaiserliches Gouvernement (Lindequist) to Kaiserliche Distriktsamt Reheboth, Windhuk, 20 December 1905, J. Nr. 16325, NAN/BRE 14/B.10.m/5.

122. Rohrbach report, 16 August 1904, 45 (of report).

123. See the descriptions of the ceremony in Gewald, *Herero Heroes*, 274–82, and Krüger, *Kriegsbewältigung und Geschichtsbewußtsein*, 203–16.

124. See Gewald, *Herero Heroes*, 192–230, and Krüger, *Kriegsbewältigung und Geschichtsbewußtsein*, 163–82.

125. Adam Ewing, *The Age of Garvey: How a Jamaican Activist Created a Mass Movement and Changed Global Black Politics* (Princeton: Princeton University Press, 2014), 91–95. On the militarization of Herero society in the nineteenth century, which accompanied the trade for horses and guns, see Henrichsen, *Herrschaft und Alltag*.

126. See John Torpey, *Making Whole What Has Been Smashed: On Reparations Politics* (Cambridge: Harvard University Press, 2006).

127. Quoted in Heike Büchter, "'Nicht länger ohne uns!': Muss Deutschland für seine Kolonialverbrechen Entschädigung zahlen?" *Die Zeit*, 11 January 2018, 19.

Chapter 7: Korea

1. Percival Lowell, *Choson: The Land of the Morning Calm. A Sketch of Korea* (Boston: Ticknor, 1886), 11.

2. The number of settlers was 170,000 in 1910; 583,428 in 1935; 700,000 civilians and 300,000 army personnel in 1945. See Jun Uchida, *Brokers of Empire: Japanese Settler Colonialism in Korea, 1876–1945* (Cambridge: Harvard University Asia Center, 2011), 3, 10. In 1935, Japanese settlers constituted 30 percent of the population of Seoul and Pusan (ibid., n. 18). Michael E. Robinson, *Korea's Twentieth-Century Odyssey* (Honolulu: University of Hawai'i Press, 2007), 37, cites a figure of 752,830 Japanese, 3 percent of the overall population, in Korea in 1942.

3. On Allied repatriation policies at the end of World War II, see Lori Watt, *When Empire Comes Home: Repatriation and Reintegration in Postwar Japan* (Cambridge: Harvard University Asia Center, 2009).

4. An excellent example of Japanese claims to have brought profound economic and social progress to Korea and Manchuria is Bank of Chosen, *Pictorial Chosen and Manchuria: Compiled in Commemoration of the Decennial of the Bank of Chosen* (Seoul, 1919). Both the text and the many photographs are most interesting.

5. For background on Korean history, I have relied on M. Robinson, *Korea's Twentieth-Century Odyssey*; Bruce Cumings, *Korea's Place in the Sun: A Modern History*, updated ed. (1997; New York: Norton, 2005); Kang Man-gil, *A History of Contemporary Korea*, trans. John B.

Duncan (1984; Folkestone: Global Oriental, 2005); and Ki-baik Lee, *New History of Korea*, trans. Edward W. Wagner and Edward J. Schultz (Cambridge: Harvard-Yenching Institute and Harvard University Press, 1984).

For a depiction of the rather convoluted and contrived genealogy that preserved the dynasty in the nineteenth century, see James Scarth Gale, *History of the Korean People*, 2nd new ed., ed. Richard Rutt (1927; Seoul: Royal Asiatic Society by Seoul Computer Press, 1983), 302–20.

6. For some examples of reform efforts, see Peter H. Lee, ed., *Sourcebook of Korean Civilization*, vol. 2, *From the Seventeenth Century to the Modern Period* (New York: Columbia University Press, 1996), 296–304.

7. Lowell, *Chosön*, 158.

8. For an important account by one of the most prominent missionaries, see James Scarth Gale, *Korea in Transition* (New York: Educational Department, Board of Foreign Missions of the Presbyterian Church in the USA, 1909), 17.

9. For one study that does recognize the connection, see Sheldon M. Garon, *Molding Japanese Minds: The State in Everyday Life* (Princeton: Princeton University Press, 1997).

10. Hong Ŭlsu, quoted in Hildi Kang, *Under the Black Umbrella: Voices from Colonial Korea, 1910–1945* (Ithaca: Cornell University Press, 2001), 24–36, quote 27.

11. Ibid., 29.

12. Ibid., 31.

13. Ibid.

14. Population figures from Jan Lahmeyer, "Korea: Historical Demographical Data of the Whole Country before 1950," Populstat, 8 February 2001, last modified 26 December 2001, http://www.populstat.info/Asia/koreaco.htm, and Phillip Connor, "6 Facts about South Korea's Growing Christian Population," Pew Research Center, 12 August 2014, http://www.pewresearch.org/fact-tank/2014/08/12/6-facts-about-christianity-in-south-korea/.

15. See Gale, *History of the Korean People*, including editor Richard Rutt's biography of Gale, 1–92.

16. On American missionaries in general, see the important work of David A. Hollinger, *Protestants Abroad: How American Missionaries Tried to Change the World but Changed America* (Princeton: Princeton University Press, 2017).

17. "Kume Kunitake's Assessment of European Wealth and Power," in Wm. Theodore de Bary, Carol Gluck, and Arthur E. Tiedemann, eds., *Sources of Japanese Tradition*, 2nd ed., vol. 2, *1600–2000* (1958; New York: Columbia University Press, 2005), 679–80, quote 679.

18. Even prior to the Restoration in 1868, a few Japanese delegations had gone abroad to the United States and Europe, and some ambitious reformers were learning English as well as Dutch. See the very interesting memoir, Fukuzawa Yukichi, *The Autobiography of Fukuzawa Yukichi*, trans. Eiichi Kiyooka (Tokyo: Hokuseido, 1934). I thank Sheldon Garon for pointing me to this source.

19. For one important discussion, see Cemil Aydin, *The Politics of Anti-Westernism: Visions of World Order in Pan-Islamic and Pan-Asian Thought* (New York: Columbia University Press, 2007), 71–92. The British reporter Angus Hamilton published his book, *Korea* (New York: C. Scribner's Sons, 1904), the very same week that the Russo-Japanese War broke out. He acutely

described the Russian and Japanese conflict for supremacy in East Asia and depicted Korea as rather hapless and its position between the two powers as hopeless.

20. I thank Michael Gordin for making this point to me.

21. For a fine literary rendition of the poverty Koreans endured and the hopes for a better life in Japan, see Min Jin Lee, *Pachinko* (New York: Grand Central, 2017). For oral histories of Korean immigrants to the United States, who late in life recalled with admiration Japanese rule, see, for example, the testimony of Yi Sangdo, in H. Kang, *Under the Black Umbrella*, 10–11.

22. For recent, nuanced studies on the impact of Japanese colonialism, see Uchida, *Brokers of Empire*; Hong Yung Lee, Yong Chool Ha, and Clark W. Sorensen, eds., *Colonial Rule and Social Change in Korea, 1919–1945* (Seattle: Center for Korea Studies and University of Washington Press, 2013); Andre Schmid, *Korea between Empires, 1895–1919* (New York: Columbia University Press, 2002); and Gi-Wook Shin and Michael Robinson, eds., *Cultural Modernity in Korea* (Cambridge: Harvard University Asia Center and Harvard University Press, 1999). For two classic works, see Peter Duus, *The Abacus and the Sword: The Japanese Penetration of Korea, 1895–1910* (Berkeley: University of California Press, 1995), and Ramon H. Myers and Mark R. Peattie, eds., *The Japanese Colonial Empire, 1895–1945* (Princeton: Princeton University Press, 1984).

23. P. Lee, *Sourcebook of Korean Civilization*, 430. Other estimates go as high as over two million participants.

24. Self-determination was hardly an American invention. In the World War I era, Lenin was the first prominent figure to use the term publicly. The Bolshevik influence is generally slighted by those who concentrate on Wilson's enunciation of the term. See, for example, Erez Manela, *The Wilsonian Moment: Self-Determination and the International Origins of Anticolonial Nationalism* (New York: Oxford University Press, 2007), and Aydin, *Politics of Anti-Westernism*, 127–60. For a different view, see Eric D. Weitz, "Self-Determination: How a German Enlightenment Idea Became the Slogan of National Liberation and a Human Right," *American Historical Review* 120:2 (2015): 462–96.

25. Son Pyŏnghŭi, et al., "Declaration of Independence" (1919), in P. Lee, *Sourcebook of Korean Civilization*, 432–34, quote 432.

26. See David Armitage, *The Declaration of Independence: A Global History* (Cambridge: Harvard University Press, 2007).

27. Son Pyŏnghŭi, et al., "Declaration of Independence," 434.

28. On the cultural dimensions of Korean nationalism, see Michael Edson Robinson, *Cultural Nationalism in Colonial Korea, 1920–1925* (Seattle: University of Washington Press, 1988).

29. As in previous chapters, I adopt the term "imperial nation-state" from Gary Wilder, *The French Imperial Nation-State: Negritude and Colonial Humanism between the Two World Wars* (Chicago: University of Chicago Press, 2005).

30. I thank Sheldon Garon for the information and explanation here, as well as for many other informative conversations on Japanese and Korean history.

31. On the complexities and confusions of Japanese policies toward Koreans in Manchuria, see Barbara J. Brooks, "Peopling the Japanese Empire: The Koreans in Manchuria and the Rhetoric of Inclusion," in *Japan's Competing Modernities: Issues in Culture and Democracy, 1900–1930*, ed. Sharon A. Minichiello (Honolulu: University of Hawai'i Press, 1998), 25–44. However, Japanese settlers in Korea resented any advances Koreans made and any forms of representation

they had. Settlers had come to dominate, not to accept Koreans as equals. See Uchida, *Brokers of Empire*.

32. Uchida, *Brokers of Empire*, 83–85.

33. Kang Pyŏngju, in H. Kang, *Under the Black Umbrella*, 49–60, quote 55.

34. U'Ch'an'gu, in ibid., 47–48.

35. For example, Yang Sŏngdŏk, in ibid., 70–71.

36. A major theme in M. J. Lee, *Pachinko*.

37. Uchida, *Brokers of Empire*, 41–43.

38. Quoted in ibid., 76.

39. Ibid., 307–54.

40. The numbers vary greatly, and will probably never be exactly known. M. Robinson, *Korea's Twentieth-Century Odyssey*, cites one hundred to two hundred thousand women in total, most of them Korean.

41. See the testimony of Pak Sŏngp'il, in H. Kang, *Under the Black Umbrella*, 65–66, who claims that the Japanese requisitioned 70 percent of the rice crop. But this figure is probably exaggerated.

42. A fine literary depiction of the chaos in Manchuria as the Japanese withdrew is in Haruki Murakami, *The Wind-Up Bird Chronicle*, trans. Jay Rubin (New York: Knopf, 1997).

43. On the varied reactions to the defeat, see Lori Watt, "Embracing Defeat in Seoul: Rethinking Decolonization in Korea, 1945," *Journal of Asian Studies* 74:1 (2015): 153–74. On the repatriation policies, L. Watt, *When Empire Comes Home*.

44. Cumings, *Korea's Place in the Sun*, 186–87.

45. For Rhee's biography, see Young Ick Lew, *The Making of the First Korean President: Syngman Rhee's Quest for Independence, 1875–1948* (Honolulu: University of Hawai'i Press, 2014). For a hagiographic, but nonetheless interesting, treatment by one of Rhee's key American advisers in the 1940s and 1950s, see Robert T. Oliver, *Syngman Rhee: The Man Behind the Myth* (New York: Dodd Mead, 1954).

46. See Young Ick Lew et al., eds., *The Syngman Rhee Correspondence in English, 1904–1948*, 8 vols. (Seoul: Institute for Modern Korean Studies, Yonsei University, 2009), esp. vols. 2 and 3.

47. For example, P. K. Yoon to Rhee, Portland, Oregon YMCA, 17 August 1913, and Chi Pum Hong to Rhee, Honolulu, 29 May 1912, in Lew et al., *Syngman Rhee Correspondence*, vol. 2, 90–92, 60.

48. Francesca Rhee to Rhee, Washington, 26 November 1945, in ibid., vol. 3, 462–63, quote 462.

49. Francesca Rhee to Rhee, Washington, 28 November 1945, in ibid., 462–64.

50. Series of letters from US occupation officers to Rhee, 25–29 December 1945, in ibid., 489–93.

51. Note also the role slated for Christians, native Koreans as well as missionaries, in the reeducation campaign directed at the North during the Korean War. See Charles K. Armstrong, *Tyranny of the Weak: North Korea and the World, 1950–1992* (Ithaca: Cornell University Press, 2013), 38–41.

52. I am drawing here on Carter J. Eckert, *Park Chung Hee and Modern Korea: The Roots of Militarism* (Cambridge: Belknap Press of Harvard University Press, 2016), 295–300.

53. Ibid., 107–45.

54. Ibid., 295–300.

55. Ibid., 131–35.

56. Quoted in ibid., 126.

57. Quoted in ibid., 146.

58. Quoted in ibid., 180.

59. Quoted in ibid., 181.

60. Park Chung Hee, *The Country, the Revolution and I*, ed. Leon Sinder (Seoul, 1963), 52–53.

61. Ibid., 53.

62. On total-war thinking, see Eckert, *Park Chung Hee*, 210–33.

63. Park, *Country, the Revolution and I*, 14.

64. Yi Hangno, "Three Memorials," in P. Lee, *Sourcebook of Korean Civilization*, 328–29.

65. Park, *Country, the Revolution and I*, 13.

66. Ibid., 16.

67. Ibid., 57.

68. Quoted in Eckert, *Park Chung Hee*, 234.

69. Ibid. See also Park Chung Hee, "Results of Efforts Not a Miracle: Impressions of Visit of West Germany" (December 1964), in *Major Speeches by Korea's Park Chung Hee*, ed. Shin Bum Shik (Seoul: Hollym, 1970), 19–27.

70. Park Chung Hee, *Korea Reborn: A Model for Development* (Englewood Cliffs: Prentice-Hall, 1979), 21.

71. Ibid., 65.

72. ibid., 76–82.

73. For example, Park Chung Hee, "In Defense of Freedom" (May 1965), in *Major Speeches*, 34–40.

74. For this history I draw especially on Dae-Sook Suh, *The Korean Communist Movement, 1918–1948* (Princeton: Princeton University Press, 1967), and Robert A. Scalapino and Chong-Sik Lee, *Communism in Korea*, 2 vols. (Berkeley: University of California Press, 1972).

75. For just one example, "Directives of the Communist International" (1928), in *Documents of Korean Communism, 1918–1948*, ed. Dae-Sook Suh (Princeton: Princeton University Press, 1970), 149.

76. Figures from Scalapino and Lee, *Communism in Korea*, vol. 1, 4–5, 138.

77. Ibid., 139.

78. On this period, see ibid., 66–136, and "Dissolution Declaration of the Japanese Bureau of the Korean Communist Party and the Japanese Section of the Korean Communist Youth Association" (1931), in Suh, *Documents of Korean Communism*, 401–3.

79. Suh, *Korean Communist Movement*, 67.

80. Ibid., 74.

81. "Manifesto of the Korean Communist Party" (1921), in Suh, *Documents of Korean Communism*, 25–29, quote 27. See also "Political Programs" (1929), in ibid., 156–67. In one listing of revolutionary goals in the program, "complete national independence" is given second rank, following only the "overthrow of Japanese imperialism" (158).

82. "Platform and Manifesto of the North China Korean Youth Federation," in ibid., 412–16, quote 412.

83. "Programs and Platforms of the North China Korean Independence League" (1942), in ibid., 417–21, quote 420. Amid various programmatic statements and demands translated into English, this is one of only two documents that deploy the term "human rights." See also "Action Platform of the Korean Communist Party" (1945), in ibid., 489–93, quote 493. Aside from the point about human rights, similar demands are evident in "Slogans of the Korean Communist Party" (1925) and "Platform of Action of the Communist Party of Korea" (1934), in ibid., 140–41 and 326–50.

84. "To the Laborers, Farmers, and Working Masses on the Occasion of the Establishment of *Nodong Kegŭp-sa* [laboring class group]" (1932), in ibid., 404–11, quotes 404.

85. See Suh, *Korean Communist Movement*, 132–41.

86. Ibid., 281. For more on the guerrilla movement, see M. Kang, *History of Contemporary Korea*, 23–97.

87. Scalapino and Lee, *Communism in Korea*, vol. 1, 202.

88. See the account in ibid., 224–27.

89. Charles K. Armstrong, *Tyranny of the Weak*, 20. Earlier figures, based on US intelligence estimates, were higher.

90. Suh, *Korean Communist Movement*, 317. Generally on this period and the Soviet backing of Kim, see also Scalapino and Lee, *Communism in Korea*, vol. 1, 313–81.

91. "Slogans of the Korean Communist Party," 140.

92. See especially, Charles K. Armstrong, *The North Korean Revolution, 1945–1950* (Ithaca: Cornell University Press, 2003). For communist goals, see "Reports by Kim Il-sŏng and by Kim Tu-bong" (1946), "Declaration of the North Korean Workers' Party" (1946), and "The Coalition of Three Democratic Political Parties in South Korea" (1946), in Suh, *Documents of Korean Communism*, 494–96, 497–98, 499–503.

93. "Constitution of the Democratic People's Republic of Korea," in Scalapino and Lee, *Communism in Korea*, vol. 2, 1319–30.

94. For this view, see Armstrong, *Tyranny of the Weak*, and M. Robinson, *Korea's Twentieth-Century Odyssey*, 114–15. The classic critical, though contested, work is Bruce Cumings, *Origins of the Korean War*, 2 vols. (Princeton: Princeton University Press, 1981 and 1990), with some updating in Cumings, *Korea's Place in the Sun*.

95. See Armstrong, *Tyranny of the Weak*, 10–51, and Cumings, *Korea's Place in the Sun*, 237–98. On the civilian victims of anticommunist violence in South Korea, which continued long after the end of the war, see Su-kyoung Hwang, *Korea's Grievous War* (Philadelphia: University of Pennsylvania Press, 2016).

96. Kim Il-sŏng, *On Juche: In Our Revolution* (Pyongyang: Foreign Languages Publishing, 1975).

97. Quote from a 1968 National Youth Mobilization Conference, in Scalapino and Lee, *Communism in Korea*, vol. 2, 705.

98. Ibid., 706.

99. "Poet laureate" is Cumings's phrase, in *Korea's Place in the Sun*, 373.

100. Kim Chi Ha, "The Story of a Sound" (1972), in *The Middle Hour: Selected Poems of Kim Chi Ha*, trans. David R. McCann (Stanfordville: Human Rights Publishing, 1980), 33–43, quotes 35, 38.

101. Ibid., 39.

102. Ibid., 42.

103. For one effective description and analysis, see George E. Ogle, *South Korea: Dissent within the Economic Miracle* (London: Zed, 1990). Ogle is a Protestant missionary and labor activist.

104. Kim Chi Ha, "The Road to Seoul," in *Middle Hour*, 16.

105. Figures from Cumings, *Korea's Place in the Sun*, 349.

106. For harrowing accounts of the army's brutality, see Henry Scott-Stokes and Lee Jai Eui, eds., *The Kwangju Uprising: Eyewitness Press Accounts of Korea's Tiananmen* (Armonk: M. E. Sharpe, 2000).

107. See Kim Dae Jung's foreword in Scott-Stokes and Lee, *Kwangju Uprising*, xiii–xv, in which he lauds the movement for its commitment to human rights and non-violence. By 2000, the date of publication, Kim was president of the Republic of Korea.

108. See Kim Chi Ha, "A Declaration of Conscience: To All Who Cherish Truth and Justice" (1975), in *Middle Hour*, 78–87, and Kim Dae Jung, *Prison Writings*, trans. Choi Sung-il and David R. McCann (Berkeley: University of California Press, 1987).

109. Cumings, *Korea's Place in the Sun*, 443, on the varying statistics.

110. The preference of guns for butter went back decades. See Armstrong, *Tyranny of the Weak*, 134.

111. Gale, *Korea in Transition*, 131. William Elliot Griffis, in *Corea: The Hermit Nation*, 6th ed. (New York: Charles Scribner's Sons, 1897), also described it as the "little pivot country of the Far East" (viii). So did Korean communists some twenty-five years later. "Korea, with her geographical position, historical relations, and strategic advantages, has always been . . . the pivot on which the Far Eastern problem revolves . . . [and] the fuse that ignites the fire of international arms." See "The Asiatic Revolutionary Movement and Imperialism" (1922), in Suh, *Documents of Korean Communism*, 91–105, quote 104.

Chapter 8: The Soviet Union

1. J. V. Stalin, "The National Question and the Soviet Constitution" (1936), in Stalin, *Marxism and the National Question: Selected Writings and Speeches* (New York: International, 1942), 217–22.

2. Ibid., 218.

3. Ronald Grigor Suny has a most interesting discusssion of the Georgian background in "Stalin: From Koba to Commissar" (unpublished MS, 2017), as well as Stephen Kotkin, *Stalin*, vol. 1, *Paradoxes of Power, 1878–1928* (New York: Penguin, 2014), 1–55. I thank Ron Suny for allowing me to read and cite his manuscript biography of Stalin.

4. For the following I draw on my article, "Self-Determination: How a German Enlightenment Idea Became the Slogan of National Liberation and a Human Right," *American Historical Review* 120:2 (2015): 462–96.

5. Self-determination, for example, does not appear at all in *Capital*, and only once in its drafts, whether in the *Grundrisse* or in later economic manuscripts. See Karl Marx, "Economic Manuscripts of 1861–1863: Capital," in Marx and Friedrich Engels, *Collected Works* (hereafter MECW) (London: Lawrence and Wishart, 1975–2004), vol. 34 (1994), 435. Original in Marx,

"Ökonomische Manuskripte 1863–1867: Das Kapital," in *Marx-Engels Gesamtausgabe* (Berlin: Dietz, 1972–), II, vol. 4.1 (1988), 101–2.

6. See Roman Rosdolsky, *Engels and the "Nonhistoric" Peoples: The National Question in the Revolution of 1848*, trans. John-Paul Himka (n.p.: Critique, 1987).

7. Friedrich Engels, "For Poland," published in *Der Volksstaat*, 24 March 1875, in MECW, vol. 24 (1989), 57, and in Karl Marx and Friedrich Engels, *Werke* (hereafter MEW) (Berlin: Dietz, 1957–68), vol. 18 (1962), 574. See also Marx to Hermann Jung, 20 November 1865, in MEW, vol. 31 (1965), 486–87, and in MECW, vol. 42 (1987), 200, in which he calls for self-determination for Poland to be included in the program of the International, and to Jung in "Letters to the Editor of *L'echo de Verviers*," 20 February 1866, in MECW, vol. 20 (1985), 399, and "Briefe an das *Echo des Verviers*," 15 February 1866, in MEW, vol. 16 (1962), 518. Shortly before his death, Engels had come around to the point that Czechs were worthy of self-determination. See Engels to Czech Social Democrats, August 1893, in MECW, vol. 27 (1990), 403.

8. Otto Bauer, *Die Nationalitätenfrage und die Sozialdemokratie*, 2nd ed. (1924, original 1907), in Bauer, *Werkausgabe* (Vienna: Europa, 1975), vol. 1, 332, 368.

9. See Robert C. Tucker, *Stalin as Revolutionary, 1879–1929: A Study in History and Personality* (New York: Norton, 1973), 104–5, 155–56.

10. Suny, "Stalin," chapter "The Expert."

11. J. V. Stalin, *Marxism and the National Question* (1913), in *Works*, vol. 2, 1907–1913 (Moscow: Progress, 1953), 300–381, quote 307. See also Bauer, *Nationalitätenfrage und die Sozialdemokratie*, 332. Lenin had written about self-determination earlier, as in "Critical Remarks on the National Question" (1913), in V. I. Lenin, *Collected Works* (Moscow: Progress, 1964), vol. 20, *December 1913 to August 1914*, 17–51, esp. 22, 45–46. But see, especially, "The Right of Nations to Self-Determination" (1914), in ibid., 393–454, and "The Socialist Revolution and the Right of Nations to Self-Determination," in *Collected Works*, vol. 22, 143–56.

12. Stalin, *Marxism and the National Question* (1913), 307.

13. Stalin, "Deviations on the National Question" (1930), in *Selected Writings and Speeches*, 208–9.

14. Ibid., 212.

15. Bauer, *Nationalitätenfrage und die Sozialdemokratie*, 332.

16. Yuri Slezkine, "The USSR as a Communal Apartment, or How a Socialist State Promoted Ethnic Particularism," *Slavic Review* 52:2 (1994): 414–52, quote 432.

17. On these policies, see Francine Hirsch, *Empire of Nations: Ethnographic Knowledge and the Making of the Soviet Union* (Ithaca: Cornell University Press, 2005); Terry Martin, *The Affirmative Action Empire: Nations and Nationalism in the Soviet Union, 1923–1939* (Ithaca: Cornell University Press, 2001); Terry Martin and Ronald Grigor Suny, eds., *A State of Nations: Empire and Nation-Making in the Age of Lenin and Stalin* (New York: Oxford University Press, 2001); Yuri Slezkine, "N. Ia. Marr and the National Origins of Soviet Ethnogenetics," *Slavic Review* 55:4 (1996): 826–62; and Y. Slezkine, "USSR as a Communal Apartment."

18. See Yuri Slezkine, *Arctic Mirrors: Russia and the Small Peoples of the North* (Ithaca: Cornell University Press, 1994).

19. Stephen Kotkin, *Magnetic Mountain: Stalinism as a Civilization* (Berkeley: University of California Press, 1995), 198–237.

20. On the importance of the 1936 constitution as a transitional moment, see Amir Weiner, *Making Sense of War: The Second World War and the Fate of the Bolshevik Revolution* (Princeton: Princeton University Press, 2001).

21. For the following I draw on my article, "Racial Politics without the Concept of Race: Reevaluating Soviet Ethnic and National Purges," *Slavic Review* 61:1 (2002): 1–29, and book, *A Century of Genocide: Utopias of Race and Nation*, edition with new preface (2003; Princeton: Princeton University Press, 2015), 53–101.

22. Examples from Martin, *Affirmative Action Empire*.

23. Norman M. Naimark, *Fires of Hatred: Ethnic Cleansing in Twentieth-Century Europe* (Cambridge: Harvard University Press, 2001), 89–92.

24. For descriptions of the various deportations, see Naimark, *Fires of Hatred*, 85–107; J. Otto Pohl, *Ethnic Cleansing in the USSR, 1937–1949* (Westport: Greenwood, 1999); Amir Weiner, "Nature, Nurture, and Memory in a Socialist Utopia: Delineating the Soviet Socio-ethnic Body in the Age of Socialism," *American Historical Review* 104:4 (1999): 1114–55; Jean-Jacques Marie, *Les peuples déportés d'Union soviétique* (Brussels: Éditions Complexe, 1995); N. F. Bugai, "K voprosu o deportatsii narodov SSSR v 30-40-kh godakh," *Istoriia SSSR* 6 (1989): 135–44; and the older but still useful work by Aleksandr M. Nekrich, *The Punished Peoples: The Deportation and Fate of Soviet Minorities at the End of the Second World War*, trans. George Saunders (New York: Norton, 1978), as well as the documents published by N. F. Bugai in "'Pogruzheny v eshelony i otpraveleny k mestam poselenii . . .': L. Beriia-I. Stalinu," *Istoriia SSR* 1 (1991): 143–60, and "20-40-e gody: Tragediia narodov," *Vostok* 2 (1992): 122–39.

25. Terry Martin, "The Origins of Soviet Ethnic Cleansing," *Journal of Modern History* 70:4 (1998): 813–61, here 839.

26. See Michael Gelb, "An Early Soviet Ethnic Deportation: The Far-Eastern Koreans," *Russian Review* 54 (1995): 389–412, and N. F. Bugai, "Vyselenie sovetskikh koreitsev s dal'nego vostoka," *Voprosy Istorii* 5 (1994): 141–48.

27. See Bugai, "Pogruzheny v eshelony"; Pohl, *Ethnic Cleansing*; Nekrich, *Punished Peoples*; and Nicolas Werth, "Un état contre son peuple: Violences, répressions, terreurs en Union sovietique," in *Le livre noir du communisme: Crimes, terreur et répression*, ed. Stéphan Courtois (Paris: Robert Laffont, 1997), 49–295, here 241, 242.

28. Bugai, "K voprosu o deportatsii," 141–42.

29. Ibid., 135, 137, and Bugai, "20-40-e gody," 122.

30. Nicolas Werth, "Logiques de violence dans l'URSS stalinienne," in *Stalinisme et nazisme: Histoire et mémoire comparées*, ed. Henry Ruosso (Brussels: Éditions Complexe, 1999), 99–128, here 122.

31. Werth, "Logiques de violence," 121–22. On the high proportion of children and elderly on the transports, see Bugai, "K voprosu o deportatsii," 140.

32. On Soviet actions, see Naimark, *Fires of Hatred*, 96–99, 101–4, and Nekrich, *Punished Peoples*, 34–35, 59–60.

33. See Werth, "État contre son peuple," 269–76.

34. Weiner, *Making Sense of War*, 198; Werth, "État contre son peuple," 276; and Ronald Grigor Suny, *The Soviet Experiment: Russia, the USSR, and the Successor States* (New York: Oxford University Press, 1998), 374.

35. For more on the Soviets and self-determination, see various writings of Bill Bowring, including "The Soviets and the Right to Self-Determination of the Colonized: Contradictions of Soviet Diplomacy and Foreign Policy in the Era of Decolonization," in *The Battle for International Law in the Decolonization Era*, ed. Jochen von Bernstorff and Philipp Dann (Oxford: Oxford University Press, forthcoming).

36. Andrei Gromyko, quoted in Howard M. Sachar, et al., eds., *The Rise of Israel: A Documentary Record from the Nineteenth Century to 1948* (New York: Garland, 1987), vol. 37, 42.

37. Ibid., 43.

38. Ibid., 43, 45.

39. Once the UN was founded, the key places where the debates on human rights unfolded were the Committee on Social, Humanitarian and Cultural Affairs (as it is now known), more commonly called the Third Committee; its subsidiary bodies, the Commission on Human Rights (now the Human Rights Council) and the various drafting committees; and the General Assembly. In general, see Roger Normand and Sarah Zaidi, *Human Rights at the UN: The Political History of Universal Justice* (Bloomington: Indiana University Press, 2008).

40. UN Charter, 26 June 1946, http://www.un.org/en/sections/un-charter/un-charter-full-text/. The trusteeship system is elaborated in arts. 73-91. On Bunche's role in the formation of the UN, see Brian Urquhart, *Ralph Bunche: An American Life* (New York: Norton, 1993), 111-38.

41. For representative statements at the debates on whether or not to include self-determination in the human rights covenants, see UNGA, Official Records: Third Committee, Social, Humanitarian and Cultural Questions (hereafter, UN, Third Committee), sixth session (1951-52), 358th meeting (30 November 1951), 69; 359th meeting (4 December 1951), 74; 362nd meeting (8 December 1951), 93, 95; 365th meeting (11 December 1951), 108; and 366th meeting (12 December 1951), 115, 116, 117.

42. Ibid., 365th meeting (11 December 1951), 110.

43. UNGA, Official Records, Sixth Session, Plenary Meetings (1951-52), 374th meeting (4 February 1952), 509-10.

44. UN, Third Committee, sixth session (1951-52), 394th meeting (19 January 1952), 280.

45. On the relationship between civil rights struggles and US foreign policy, see Carol Anderson, *Eyes Off the Prize: The United Nations and the African-American Struggle for Human Rights, 1944-1955* (Cambridge: Cambridge University Press, 2003), and Mary L. Dudziak, *Cold War Civil Rights: Race and the Image of American Democracy* (Princeton: Princeton University Press, 2002).

46. UN, Third Committee, sixth session (1951-52), 361st meeting (7 December 1951), 84.

47. Ibid., 373rd meeting (5 February 1952), 515. See also Jay Winter and Antoine Prost, *René Cassin and Human Rights: From the Great War to the Universal Declaration* (Cambridge: Cambridge University Press, 2013), and Mary Ann Glendon, *A World Made New: Eleanor Roosevelt and the Universal Declaration of Human Rights* (New York: Random House, 2001).

48. UNGA, Official Records: Plenary Meetings (hereafter UNGA, Plenary), pt. 1, fifteenth session (1960), vol. 2, 947th meeting (14 December 1960), 1283.

49. For a recent study that emphasizes the role of the Global South in creating the international human rights system, see Steven L. B. Jensen, *The Making of International Human Rights:*

The 1960s, Decolonization and the Reconstruction of Global Values (Cambridge: Cambridge University Press, 2016).

50. For a few highlights of the debate in 1951–52, see the comments by Dehousse, the Belgian representative; Eleanor Roosevelt for the United States; and Hajek, the Czech delegate, in UNGA, Official Records, Sixth Session, Plenary Meetings (1951–52), 374th Meeting (4 February 1952), 504, 505, 510.

51. UNGA, Plenary, pt. 1, fifteenth session (1960), vol. 1, 869th meeting (23 September 1960), 61.

52. Ibid., 73–74.

53. Ibid., 76.

54. Ibid., vol. 2, 984. For other representative statements, see ibid., 997–98, 1034, 1102.

55. For some highlights of this debate, see the British representative, Ormsby-Gore; the US delegate, Wadsworth; and a host of voices from the Soviet bloc and the Global South, in ibid., 925th meeting (28 November 1960), 984; 926th meeting (28 November 1960), 997–98; 929th meeting (30 November 1960), 1034; 933rd meeting (2 December 1960), 1102; and 947th meeting (14 December 1960), 1283–84. For the vote count, see ibid., 947th meeting (14 December 1960), 1273–74. For the text of the resolution, see UNGA, Resolution 1514 (XV), Declaration on the Granting of Independence to Colonial Countries and Peoples, A/RES/1514 (XV) (14 December 1960), http://www.un.org/en/decolonization/declaration.shtml.

56. Ornes-Coiscou, UNGA, Plenary, twenty-first session (1966), vol. 3 (contd.), 1495th meeting (16 December 1966), 12.

57. See, for example, the words of the Chilean representative, Figueroa, in UNGA, Plenary, sixth session (1951–52), 374th meeting (4 February 1952), 502–3.

58. UNGA, Plenary, twenty-first session (1966), vol. 3 (contd.), 1496th meeting (16 December 1966), 6. The Czech resolution against the use of force and in favor of self-determination passed ninety-eight to two with eight abstentions. Ibid., 1482nd meeting (30 November 1966), 17.

59. UNGA, Plenary, twenty-first session (1966), vol. 3 (contd.), 1495th meeting (16 December 1966), 7.

60. Edward Kline, preface to Valery Chalidze, *The Soviet Human Rights Movement: A Memoir* (New York: Jacob Blaustein Institute for the Advancement of Human Rights of the American Jewish Committee, 1984), vii–xii, quotes ix.

61. Ludmilla Alexeyeva, *Soviet Dissent: Contemporary Movements for National, Religious, and Human Rights* (Middletown: Wesleyan University Press, 1985), 7.

62. For a good, early collection in English, see Michael Meerson-Aksenov and Boris Shragin, eds., *The Political, Social and Religious Thought of Russian "Samizdat": An Anthology*, trans. Nickolas Lupinin (Belmont: Nordland, 1977). An exhibit catalog with many insightful essays and striking images covering the entire Soviet bloc is Wolfgang Eichwede, ed., *Samizdat: Alternative Kultur in Zentral- und Osteuropa: Die 6oer bis 8oer Jahre* (Bremen: Edition Temmen, 1980).

63. I thank Rajan Menon and Benjamin Nathans for bibliographic help on the Soviet dissident and human rights movements.

64. See Jennifer Amos, "Embracing and Contesting: The Soviet Union and the Universal Declaration of Human Rights, 1948–1958," in *Human Rights in the Twentieth Century*, ed. Stefan-Ludwig Hoffmann (2010; Cambridge: Cambridge University Press, 2011), 147–65. Divisions

existed within the Soviet state: the Foreign Ministry was less supportive of the UDHR; the Procuracy (the state prosecutor), more of an advocate.

65. See the account in William Taubman, *Khrushchev: The Man and His Era* (New York: Norton, 2003), 270–89. Khrushchev knew that the speech would not stay secret for long (283).

66. See the important article by Benjamin Nathans, "The Dictatorship of Reason: Aleksandr Vol'pin and the Idea of Rights under 'Developed Socialism,'" *Slavic Review* 66:4 (2007): 630–63, as well as Nathans, "Soviet Rights-Talk in the Post-Stalin Era," in Hoffmann, *Human Rights*, 166–90.

67. Nathans, "Dictatorship of Reason," 642, and Nathans, "Die Entzauberung des Sozialismus: Sowjetische Dissidenten, Menschenrechte und die neue globale Moralität," in *Moral für die Welt? Menschenrechtspolitik in den 1970er Jahren*, ed. Jan Eckel and Samuel Moyn (Göttingen: Vandenhoeck and Ruprecht, 2012), 100–119.

68. Quoted in Nathans, "Dictatorship of Reason," 655.

69. Vladimir Bukovsky, quoted in Joshua Rubenstein, *Soviet Dissidents: Their Struggle for Human Rights* (Boston: Beacon, 1985), 36. For an interesting study of the motivating power of ethics in the dissident and human rights movements, see Philip Boobbyer, *Conscience, Dissent and Reform in Soviet Russia* (London: Routledge, 2005).

70. The writings of Sakharov and Chalidze make very clear the commitment to socialist legality. See, for example, Chalidze, *Soviet Human Rights Movement*, and *To Defend These Rights: Human Rights and the Soviet Union*, trans. Guy Daniels (New York: Random House, 1974).

71. Nathans, "Dictatorship of Reason," 660–61.

72. On the founding of the committee, see Rubenstein, *Soviet Dissidents*, 131–34. The Initiative Group for the Defense of Human Rights, established in 1969, was the first such organization in the USSR.

73. For histories of the Soviet dissident and human rights movement, I have relied on Nathans, "Entzauberung des Sozialismus" and "Soviet Rights-Talk"; Aryeh Neier, *The International Human Rights Movement: A History* (Princeton: Princeton University Press, 2012), 138–60; Alexeyeva, *Soviet Dissent*; Rubenstein *Soviet Dissidents*. Older but still valuable studies include Rudolf L. Tökés, ed., *Dissent in the USSR: Politics, Ideology, and People* (Baltimore: Johns Hopkins University Press, 1975), and Peter Reddaway, ed. and trans., *Uncensored Russia: Protest and Dissent in the Soviet Union. The Unoffical Moscow Journal "A Chronicle of Current Events"* (New York: American Heritage, 1972).

74. Chalidze, *Soviet Human Rights Movement*, 22, and Neier, *International Human Rights Movement*, 204–32.

75. See Sarah B. Snyder, *Human Rights Activism and the End of the Cold War: A Transnational History of the Helsinki Network* (Cambridge: Cambridge University Press, 2011), and Daniel C. Thomas, *The Helsinki Effect: International Norms, Human Rights, and the Demise of Communism* (Princeton: Princeton University Press, 2001).

76. Organization for Security and Co-operation in Europe, Helsinki Final Act (1975), 1a: VII, https://www.osce.org/helsinki-final-act?download=true.

77. On the latter point, see Alexeyeva, *Soviet Dissent*, 335–36.

78. Ibid., 336.

79. See Rubenstein, *Soviet Dissidents*, 213–50, and Alexeyeva, *Soviet Dissent*, 335–49, 367–73.

80. See Snyder, *Human Rights Activism*, and Alexeyeva, *Soviet Dissent*, 318–86.

81. Nathans, "Entzauberung des Sozialismus."

82. Alexeyeva, *Soviet Dissent*, 382–83.

83. Ibid., 345.

84. Snyder, *Human Rights Activism*, 38–52.

85. Ibid.

86. See Peter Slezkine, "From Helsinki to Human Rights Watch: How an American Cold War Monitoring Group Became an International Human Rights Institution," *Humanity* 5:3 (2014): 345–70.

87. Thomas, *Helsinki Effect*, 138–48, 189–94, 196–99. There was also a meeting in Vienna in 1986–89.

88. Andrei Sakharov, "Progress, Coexistence, and Intellectual Freedom" (1968), in *Sakharov Speaks*, ed. Harrison E. Salisbury (New York: Vintage, 1974), 55–114, quote 58.

89. Ibid., 60–62.

90. Ibid., 88.

91. Ibid., 70.

92. See Neier, *International Human Rights Movement*.

93. For Sakharov's condemnation of racism and nationalism, "Progress, Coexistence, and Intellectual Freedom," 78.

94. Andrei Sakharov, "Memorandum" (1971), in *Sakharov Speaks*, 135–50, quote 142.

95. Andrei Sakharov, "Postscript to Memorandum" (1972), in *Sakharov Speaks*, 151–58, here 153.

96. Andrei Sakharov, "Open Letter to Anatoly Aleksandrov, President of the USSR Academy of Sciences" (1980), in *On Sakharov*, ed. Alexander Babyonyshev, trans. Guy Daniels (New York: Knopf, 1982), 212–22, quote 215. See also Sakharov, "The Responsibility of Scientists" (1981), in ibid., 205–11.

97. On psychiatric investigations of dissidents and internment in mental hospitals, see Sidney Bloch and Peter Reddaway, *Soviet Psychiatric Abuse: The Shadow over World Psychiatry* (London: Gollancz, 1984), and Zhores A. Medvedev and Roy A. Medvedev, *A Question of Madness* (London: Macmillan, 1971), both with harrowing stories.

98. For one of the more radical positions, see Andrei Amalrik, *Notes of a Revolutionary*, trans. Guy Daniels (New York: Knopf, 1982).

99. See Rubenstein, *Soviet Dissidents*, 153–85, and Alexeyeva, *Soviet Dissent*, 175–98.

100. For example, Sahkahrov, "Progress, Coexistence, and Intellectual Freedom," 129, and "Memorandum," 149.

101. Chalidze, *To Defend These Rights*, 149.

102. Valery Chalidze, *Glasnost and Social and Economic Rights* (New York: Freedom House, 1988), 11–30.

103. Ibid.

104. Ibid., 6–7.

105. See Nathans, "Soviet Rights-Talk," and "Dictatorship of Reason."

Chapter 9: Palestine and Israel

1. Palestine Royal Commission, *Report: Presented by the Secretary of State for the Colonies to Parliament by Command of His Majesty, July, 1937* (London: His Majesty's Stationery Office, 1937), quotes 390.

2. See Bashir Bashir and Amos Goldberg, eds., *The Holocaust and the Nakba: A New Grammar of Trauma and History* (New York: Columbia University Press, 2019).

3. For the most detailed treatment, see Jonathan Schneer, *The Balfour Declaration: The Origins of the Arab-Israeli Conflict* (New York: Random House, 2010).

4. Arthur Balfour, quoted in "Memorandum Submitted to the Palestine Royal Commission on Behalf of the Jewish Agency for Palestine" (London: Jewish Agency for Palestine, 1936), in *The Rise of Israel: A Documentary Record from the Nineteenth Century to 1948*, ed. Howard M. Sachar, et al. (New York: Garland, 1987), vol. 23, 1–288, here 13. Hereafter cited as Jewish Agency Memorandum 1936.

5. Earl Peel, in 106 Parl. Deb. H.L. (5th ser.) (1909–2005) col. 607 (20 July 1937), reprinted in Sachar et al., *Rise of Israel*, vol. 25: 604–15, quote 607 (original pagination).

6. Jewish Agency Memorandum 1936, 34.

7. Ibid.

8. Quoted in League of Nations, Permanent Mandates Commission, *Minutes of the Thirty-Second (Extraordinary) Session Devoted to Palestine, 30 July to 18 August 1937* (Geneva: Series of League of Nations Publications, 18 August 1937) (hereafter PMC Minutes 1937), reprinted in Sachar et al., *Rise of Israel*, vol. 25, 16 (original pagination).

9. For one example, see the "Memorandum by Lacy Baggallay," Foreign Office, 21 March 1938, in Sachar et al., *Rise of Israel*, vol. 32, 1–35. Baggallay provides a long histsorical account of the rise of Islam, and argues against the terminology of a nation or race for Arabs.

10. Golda Meir, from *Sunday Times* (London), 15 June 1969, 12, quoted in Rashid Khalidi, *Palestinian Identity: The Construction of Modern National Consciousness* (New York: Columbia University Press, 1997), 147.

11. For a recent, insightful biography, see Anita Shapira, *Ben-Gurion: Father of Modern Israel* (New Haven: Yale University Press, 2014).

12. See Rashid Khalidi, *The Iron Cage: The Story of the Palestinian Struggle for Statehood* (Boston: Beacon, 2006); Khalidi, *Palestinian Identity*; and Gudrun Krämer, *A History of Palestine: From the Ottoman Conquest to the Founding of the State of Israel*, trans. Graham Harman and Krämer (Princeton: Princeton University Press, 2008). For a history that roots a distinctive Palestinian consciousness as far back as the 1830s, see Baruch Kimmerling and Joel S. Migdal, *The Palestinian People: A History* (Cambridge: Harvard University Press, 2003).

13. See William W. Hagen, "Before the 'Final Solution': Toward a Comparative Analysis of Political Anti-Semitism in Interwar Germany and Poland," *Journal of Modern History* 68:2 (1996): 351–81.

14. As proclaimed already in 1919 in a statement by the General Syrian Congress, "Our Objections to Zionism and Western Imperialism" (1919), in *The Middle East and Islamic World Reader*, ed. Marvin Gettleman and Stuart Schaar (New York: Grove, 2003), 171–73, quote 173.

15. Basheer M. Nafi, *Arabism, Islamism and the Palestine Question, 1908–1941: A Political History* (Reading: Ithaca, 1998), 90–95; Krämer, *History of Palestine*, 216–25; and Kimmerling and Migdal, *Palestinian People*, 89–91.

16. See Weldon C. Matthews, *Confronting an Empire, Constructing a Nation: Arab Nationalists and Popular Politics in Mandate Palestine* (London: I. B. Tauris, 2006).

17. Specifically on the way the mandate system and its provisions for petitions encouraged the development of Palestinian identity, see Natasha Wheatley, "The Mandate System as a Style of Reasoning: International Jurisdiction and the Parceling of Imperial Sovereignty in Petitions from Palestine," in *The Routledge Handbook of the History of the Middle East Mandates*, ed. Cyrus Schayegh and Andrew Arsan (New York: Routledge, 2015), 106–22, and Wheatley, "Mandatory Interpretation: Legal Hermeneutics and the New International Order in Arab and Jewish Petitions to the League of Nations," *Past and Present* 227 (2015): 205–48. For the argument that the mandatory officials consistently denied Palestinians any avenues of representation, which they had indeed possessed under the Ottomans, see Khalidi, *Iron Cage*. Generally on the workings of the PMC, see Susan Pedersen, *The Guardians: The League of Nations and the Crisis of Empire* (New York: Oxford University Press, 2015); Michael D. Callahan, *A Sacred Trust: The League of Nations and Africa, 1929–1946* (Brighton: Sussex Academic, 2004); and Callahan, *Mandates and Empire: The League of Nations and Africa, 1914–1931* (Brighton: Sussex Academic, 1999).

18. For one account of the Arab Revolt that also situates it in the larger politics of the region, including Iraq, Syria, and Egypt, see Nafi, *Arabism*, 191–328.

19. William Ormsby-Gore, 326 Parl. Deb. H.C. (5th ser.) (1909–81) cols. 2242, 2247 (21 July 1937), reprinted in Sachar et al., *Rise of Israel*, vol. 25.

20. William Ormsby-Gore, in PMC Minutes 1937, 26 (original pagination). See also Ormsby-Gore, 326 Parl. Deb. H.C. (5th ser.) (1909–81) col. 2249 (21 July 1937), reprinted in Sachar et al., *Rise of Israel*, vol. 25.

21. William Ormsby-Gore, 326 Parl. Deb. H.C. (5th ser.) (1909–81) col. 2250 (21 July 1937), reprinted in Sachar et al., *Rise of Israel*, vol. 25.

22. The policies of population transfer, resettlement, and partition were widely accepted by the imperial powers in the interwar period. See Laura Robson, *States of Separation: Transfer, Partition, and the Making of the Modern Middle East* (Berkeley: University of California Press, 2017).

23. William Ormsby-Gore, in PMC Minutes 1937, 17.

24. Ibid.

25. For just one withering critique, see the comments of Archibald Sinclair in 326 Parl. Deb. H.C. (5th ser.) (1909–81) col. 2269 (21 July 1937), reprinted in Sachar et al., *Rise of Israel*, vol. 25.

26. PMC Minutes 1937, 230.

27. Wheatley, "Mandate System" and "Mandatory Interpretation."

28. Benny Morris, *1948: A History of the First Arab-Israeli War* (New Haven: Yale University Press, 2008), 18–19.

29. Chaim Weizmann, "Faith in the Future of the Jewish Nation," speech to the Zionist Congress, 11 August 1937, in Sachar et al., *Rise of Israel*, vol. 25, 436–43, quote 440–41. See also Weizmann to Ormsby-Gore, 4 July 1937, in ibid., 332–40.

30. Weizmann, "Faith in the Future," 442.

31. See Shapira, *Ben-Gurion*, 105–13.

32. Weizmann to Jan Smuts, 29 September 1937, in Sachar et al., *Rise of Israel*, vol. 25, 450–59, quote 457.

33. David Ben-Gurion to his son Amos Ben-Gurion, 27 July 1937, in ibid., 361–72, quote 371. For other comments of Ben-Gurion's from the 1930s, see Benny Morris, *The Birth of the Palestinian Refugee Problem, 1947–1949* (Cambridge: Cambridge University Press, 1987), 24–25.

Ben-Gurion did at times argue against transfers, but it is hard to take these comments very seriously given his many comments in support of the policies and his actions as prime minister. See, for example, his long memorandum on Zionist policies, 15 October 1941, in Sachar et al., *Rise of Israel*, vol. 31, 13–39, here 27–29. The British authorities seized this document from Ben-Gurion as he was entering the country.

34. Ben-Gurion at meeting of the Jewish Agency Executive, 12 June 1938, quoted in Ilan Pappe, *The Ethnic Cleansing of Palestine* (Oxford: Oneworld, 2006), xi, and in Morris, *Birth*, 27.

35. Quoted in Morris, *Birth*, 27, from Weitz's diary. For another example, see the comments of Avraham Menahem Ussishkin, the head of the Jewish National Fund, in ibid., 26.

36. Yet to suggest, as Pappe does in *Ethnic Cleansing*, a direct and absolutely consistent line from the talk of transfer to its implementation is to simplify the history, to make Zionist leaders the sole progenitors of political developments, and to place History itself on a predetermined course.

37. See Shapira, *Ben-Gurion*, 83, who states that the Zionist leadership considered it "unwise to engage with the Arab question."

38. Judah L. Magnes, "A Solution Through Force?" (17 July 1946), in *Towards Union in Palestine: Essays on Zionism and Jewish-Arab Cooperation*, ed. Martin Buber et al. (Jerusalem: Ihud, 1947), 14–21, quote 14.

39. Moshe Smelansky, "Citrus Growers Have Learnt to Cooperate," and Gabriel Baer, "Jewish and Arab Workers: Divided or United?" in Buber, *Towards Union in Palestine*, 57–65 and 76–83.

40. "Well Meant but Dangerous," *Ba'ayoth* [Hebrew monthly of Ihud] (May 1944), in ibid., 98.

41. "A New Start" (unsigned, 2 May 1946), in ibid., 12–13.

42. *Jewish Chronicle*, 3 January 1919, quoted in Jewish Agency Memorandum 1936, 70–71.

43. Ibid., 71–72.

44. See Morris, *Birth*, 36–41.

45. Ben-Gurion at meeting of the Jewish Agency Executive, American Section, 13 May 1947, quoted in Sachar et al., *Rise of Israel*, vol. 37, 32.

46. Ibid.

47. Ibid., 33.

48. See British notes on Ben-Gurion's testimony before UNSCOP, in ibid., 53–54.

49. Quoted in Morris, *Birth*, 28.

50. Ben-Gurion, "Memorandum on Zionist Policy," 15 October 1941, in Sachar et al., *Rise of Israel*, vol. 31, 13–39, here 22.

51. "Displaced Persons in Germany: Letter from President Truman to General Eisenhower transmitting report of Earl G. Harrison," 31 August 1945 (released to the press 29 September 1945), in Sachar et al., *Rise of Israel*, vol. 35, 44–53, quote 50.

52. Acheson to Truman, 6 October 1945, in ibid., 56–57. Generally on Truman's unsteady position on Palestine, see John B. Judis, *Genesis: Truman, American Jews, and the Origins of the Arab/Israeli Conflict* (New York: Farrar, Straus and Giroux, 2014).

53. For just one example, Lord Halifax (the British ambassador to the United States) to Foreign Office, 4 October 1945, in Sachar et al., *Rise of Israel*, vol. 35, 58–59.

54. Attlee to Truman, 16 September 1945, in ibid., 41–43.

55. "Report of the Anglo-American Committee of Enquiry regarding the Problems of European Jewry and Palestine," 20 April 1946, in ibid., 136–218, especially the recommendations, 1–10

(original pagination). The report did recommend the immediate immigration of one hundred thousand Jews and called for an end to "racialist" criteria for land purchases, both key demands of Zionists.

56. "Minutes of Zionist Executive Meeting, London," 29 April 1946, in ibid., 229–32, quotes 231, 230.

57. "Meeting of British Cabinet Defence Committee," 24 April 1946, in ibid., 225–27.

58. High commissioner to colonial secretary, 4 June 1946, in ibid., 269–74, quotes 269–70.

59. "Memorandum by Colonial Secretary Hall," 8 July 1946, in ibid., 290–95, quotes 294, 295. The Joint Chiefs concurred, raising dire scenarios of Arab distrust of Britain and advancing Russian interests, Arab rebellion, and Jewish terrorism, reminding all concerned of the vital strategic asset of oil. See "Memorandum by Joint Chiefs," 10 July 1946, in ibid., 296–98.

60. For just two examples: "Memorandum by the Secretary of State for Foreign Affairs [Bevin]," 14 January 1947, and "Memorandum by the Secretary of State for the Colonies [Creech-Jones]," 16 January 1947, both in ibid., vol. 36, 64–71 and 72–76.

61. "Minutes of Meeting Held at the Colonial Office," 29 January 1947, in ibid., 80–94.

62. Ibid., 82.

63. Ibid.

64. Ibid., 82–83.

65. Ibid., 83.

66. Ibid., 84.

67. Ibid., 86.

68. Ibid., 89.

69. Bevin in the House of Commons, 25 February 1947, quoted in ibid., 158.

70. "Minutes of Meeting at Colonial Office," 13 February 1947, in ibid., 118–29, quotes 119, 120–21.

71. "Constitutional Proposals Put Forward by the Arab States Delegations to the Palestinian Conference," 30 September 1946, in ibid., 14–16.

72. Arab Higher Committee for Palestine, *The Palestine Arab Case: A Statement by the Arab Higher Committee* (Cairo: Costa Tsoumas, 1947), 68.

73. Ibid., 3.

74. Ibid., 3–4, 8, 9–11, 18–19, 46. The other betrayals, standard in Arab claims, were the contention that the Hussein-McMahon correspondence included Palestine in the proposed independent Arab state, and the Sykes-Picot Agreement.

75. Ibid., 32, 67.

76. Ibid., 12.

77. Ibid., 13.

78. On Bunche, see Brian Urquhart, *Ralph Bunche: An American Life* (New York: Norton, 1993). Urquhart, who also had a long and illustrious career at the UN, was later Bunche's assistant.

79. See Urquhart, *Ralph Bunche*, 139–98.

80. "Partition Resolution," in Sachar et al., *Rise of Israel*, vol. 37, 170.

81. "Ben-Gurion Speech at Meeting of Executive Committee of General Federation of Jewish Labour in Palestine," 3 December 1947, English summary of Hebrew document, in Israel State Archives, *Political and Diplomatic Documents, December 1947–May 1948: Companion Volume*, ed. Gedalia Yogev (Jerusalem: Government Printer, 1979), 3–4.

82. Ben-Gurion to Agricultural Centre, 4 December 1947, English summary of Hebrew document, in ibid., 4.

83. See Shertok to chairman of United Nations Palestine Commission, New York, 20 January 1948, in ibid., 196–99.

84. The majority of documents in Israel State Archives, *Political and Diplomatic Documents, December 1947–May 1948: Main Volume*, ed. Gedalia Yogev (Jerusalem: Government Printer, 1979), are along these lines. One excellent example is the memorandum of a consultation of Jewish Agency staff and advisers, Washington, 3 February 1948, 294–97.

85. See Judis, *Genesis*, 320–53.

86. Gromyko in the "Official Records of the First Special Session of the UN General Assembly," reprinted in Sachar et al., *Rise of Israel*, vol. 37, 42.

87. In many ways, Benny Morris's original account, *The Birth of the Palestinian Refugee Problem*, first published in 1987, remains the most important work, even though his argumentation sometimes runs against his own evidence. Morris was still trying to save the Zionist leadership from total condemnation by denying, at least for the initial phase of 1947–48, any coordinated acts to promote Arab flight. Then he reduces matters to the supposed logic of "military necessity." Or he argues that the Zionist and Israeli leaderships were merely opportunist—that is, as Arabs fled, they made little effort to convince them to stay. For representative comments, see Morris, *Birth*, 59–64, 87–93, 128–31, 155. Much of the dispute around whether there existed a central plan concerns military "Plan D." The text of the plan was first published by Walid Khalid in the 1950s.

88. Ibid., 197–98.

89. Shapira, *Ben-Gurion*, 170–71, states that there is only one instance when Ben-Gurion gave direct orders to expel Arabs, and that was in regard to Lydda (Lod).

90. For a rich and moving description of one case, see Alon Confino, "Miracles and Snow in Palestine and Israel: Tantura, a History of 1948," *Israel Studies* 17:2 (2012): 25–61, and Confino, "The Warm Sand of the Coast of Tantura: History and Memory in Israel after 1948," *History and Memory* 27:1 (2015): 43–82.

91. Morris relates the events in *Birth*, 224–34.

92. Morris's term in ibid., 179.

93. See Tom Segev, *1949: The First Israelis* (New York: Free Press, 1986).

94. See Shapira, *Ben-Gurion*, 179–81, for a succinct analysis.

95. Morris, *Birth*, 261–62.

96. Ibid., 280.

97. Quoted in ibid., 280.

98. Quoted in ibid., 261.

99. Quoted in ibid., 283.

100. Quoted in Ibid., 257.

101. Figures from Kimmerling and Midgal, *Palestinian People*, 135.

102. Onn and Ben-Tzvi both quoted in Segev, *1949*, 47n and 46–47.

103. See Arnon Yehuda Degani, "The Decline and Fall of the Israeli Military Government, 1948–1968: A Case of Settler-Colonial Consolidation?" *Settler Colonial Studies* 5:1 (2015): 84–99, and Degani, "From Republic to Empire: Israel and the Palestinians after 1948," in *The Routledge Handbook of Settler Colonialism*, ed. Edward Cavanagh and Lorenzo Veracini (London: Routledge, 2017), 353–67. I thank Dirk Moses for pointing me toward these and other sources.

104. Shira Robinson, *Citizen Strangers: Palestinians and the Birth of Israel's Liberal Settler State* (Stanford: Stanford University Press, 2013), 33–38.

105. See Leena Dallasheh, "Troubled Waters: Citizenship and Colonial Zionism in Nazareth," *International Journal of Middle East Studies* 47:3 (2015): 467–87.

106. Leena Dallasheh, "Persevering through Colonial Transition: Nazareth's Palestinian Residents after 1948," *Journal of Palestine Studies* 45:2 (2016): 8–23, here 10.

107. On all these measures, see Amal Jamal, *Arab Minority Nationalism in Israel: The Politics of Indigeneity* (London: Routledge, 2011), 108–31; Kimmerling and Migdal, *Palestinian People*, 170–78; and S. Robinson, *Citizen Strangers*, 46–49.

108. See S. Robinson, *Citizen Strangers*, 113–93.

109. Quoted in Degani, "Decline and Fall," 91.

110. Ibid.

111. Adalah: The Legal Center for Arab Minority Rights in Israel, *The Democratic Constitution*, draft (Shafa'amr: Adalah, 20 March 2007), https://www.adalah.org/uploads/oldfiles/Public /files/democratic_constitution-english.pdf; Mada al-Carmel: Arab Center for Applied Social Research, *The Haifa Declaration* (n.p., 15 May 2007), 15, http://mada-research.org/en /files/2007/09/haifaenglish.pdf; and National Committee for the Heads of the Arab Local Authorities in Israel, *The Future Vision of the Palestinian Arabs in Israel*, ed. Ghaida Rinawie-Zoabi, trans. Abed Al Rahman Kelani (Nazareth: author, 2006), https://www.adalah.org/uploads/old files/newsletter/eng/dec06/tasawor-mostaqbali.pdf. For a trenchant analysis, see Jamal, *Arab Minority Nationalism*, 161–87, as well as Bashir Bashir, "The Strength and Weaknesses of Integrative Solutions for the Israeli-Palestinian Conflict," *Middle East Journal* 70:4 (2016): 560–78.

112. Mada al-Carmel, *Haifa Declaration*, 15.

113. Ibid.

114. Ibid., 16.

115. "Israeli Law Declares the Country the 'Nation-State' of the Jewish People," *New York Times*, 19 July 2018.

116. Mada al-Carmel, *Haifa Declaration*, 17.

Chapter 10: Rwanda and Burundi

1. *Le Manifeste des Bahutu* (n.p., 24 March 1957), http://jkanya.free.fr/manifesteba hutu240357.pdf. On the *Statement of Views* (*Mise au point*), see Innocent Nsengimana, *Rwanda: La marche vers l'indépendance (1952–1962): Une contribution à l'histoire du Rwanda contemporain* (Lille: Editions Sources du Nil, 2012), 35–37.

2. *Manifeste des Bahutu*, quotes 1–2, 4, 8.

3. For background on the history of Rwanda and Burundi, I have relied on René Lemarchand, *The Dynamics of Violence in Central Africa* (Philadelphia: University of Pennsylvania Press,

2009), *Burundi: Ethnocide as Discourse and Practice* (Cambridge: Cambridge University Press, 1994), and *Rwanda and Burundi* (New York: Praeger, 1970); as well as Jean-Pierre Chrétien and Marcel Kabanda, *Rwanda: Racisme et génocide. L'idéologie hamitique* (Paris: Belin, 2013); Nigel Watt, *Burundi: Biography of a Small African Country*, 2nd ed. (London: Hurst, 2012); Catharine Newbury, *The Cohesion of Oppression: Clientship and Ethnicity in Rwanda, 1860–1960* (New York: Columbia University Press, 1988); David Newbury, *The Land Beyond the Mists: Essays in Identity and Authority in Precolonial Congo and Rwanda* (Athens: Ohio University Press, 2009); and Mahmood Mamdani, *When Victims Become Killers: Colonialism, Nativism, and the Genocide in Rwanda* (Princeton: Princeton University Press, 2001).

4. See the extraordinary collection of colonial photographs from Rwanda and Burundi, all taken as evidence of racial differentiation among the population, of the German Colonial Society, in the database of the University Library in Frankfurt, at http://www.ub.bildarchiv-dkg .uni-frankfurt.de/Bildprojekt/frames/hauptframe.html.

For one rather typical anthropological depiction of the population, see the publication by l'Office de l'information et des relations publiques pour le Congo belge et le Ruanda-Urundi, *Le Ruanda-Urundi* (Brussels, 1959), which includes contributions by many scholars.

5. See Lemarchand's discussion of the myth, in *Dynamics of Violence*, 54–68, as well as Chrétien and Kabanda, *Rwanda*. For the longer history, see David M. Goldenberg, *The Curse of Ham: Race and Slavery in Early Judaism, Christianity, and Islam* (Princeton: Princeton University Press, 2003).

6. C. Newbury, *Cohesion of Oppression*, studiously avoids the term "race." But she provides an important analysis of the transformation of social relations and the intensification of oppression from 1860 to 1960, not all of it a result of Belgian domination.

7. L'Office de l'information et des relations publiques pour le Congo belge et le Ruanda-Urundi, *Ruanda-Urundi*, 29. The volume lists quite a number of scholarly contributors, but does not say who authored which chapter. Vansina may well have written the passages I cite below.

8. Ibid., 30.

9. Only Patrice Lumumba comes close in stature, but he was Congolese.

10. Nsengimana, *Rwanda*, 25–32, and Lemarchand, *Rwanda and Burundi*, 106–11.

11. See Lemarchand, *Rwanda and Burundi*, 111–17.

12. Lemarchand, *Dynamics of Violence*, 31.

13. On the fluidity of peoples and cultures across the large region of the Rift Valley, see especially D. Newbury, *Land Beyond the Mists*.

14. Lemarchand, *Dynamics of Violence*, 13–21.

15. For a particularly critical take on the founding, see Mark Mazower, *No Enchanted Palace: The End of Empire and the Origins of the United Nations* (Princeton: Princeton University Press, 2009).

16. See various documents of the United Nations Association of the United States, San Francisco Chapter, Hoover Institution Archives, boxes 1–5, 7, 9–10.

17. In general on human rights, anticolonial movements, and the UN, see Bonny Ibhawoh, *Human Rights in Africa* (Cambridge: Cambridge University Press, 2018); Jennifer Johnson, *The Battle for Algeria: Sovereignty, Health Care, and Humanitarianism* (Philadelphia: University of Pennsylvania Press, 2016); Fabian Klose, *Human Rights in the Shadow of Colonial Violence: The Wars of Indendence in Kenya and Algeria*, trans. Dona Geyer (2009; Philadelphia: University of

Pennsylvania Press, 2013); Bradley R. Simpson, "Self-Determination, Human Rights, and the End of Empire in the 1970s," *Humanity* 4:2 (2013): 239–60; Talbot C. Imlay, "International Socialism and Decolonization during the 1950s: Competing Rights and the Postcolonial Order," *American Historical Review* 118:4 (2013): 1105–32; Roland Burke, *Decolonization and the Evolution of Human Rights* (Philadelphia: University of Pennsylvania Press, 2010); and Geoffrey Robinson, *"If You Leave Us Here, We Will Die": How Genocide Was Stopped in East Timor* (Princeton: Princeton University Press, 2010).

18. For one statement along these lines, see Ralph J. Bunche, *Peace and the United Nations*, Tenth Montague Burton Lecture on International Relations (Leeds: University of Leeds, 1952), 7.

19. See, for example, the text of the charge given to the secretary-general's special representative in Ruanda-Urundi, 25 June 1962, special representative of SG, United Nations Archives (hereafter UNA)/S-0279-0019-04.

20. See ibid.

21. UN General Assembly (hereafter UNGA), Resolution 1514 (XV), Declaration on the Granting of Independence to Colonial Countries and Peoples, A/RES/1514 (XV), ¶¶ 2, 3, and 5 (14 December 1960), https://documents-dds-ny.un.org/doc/RESOLUTION/GEN /NR0/152/88/IMG/NR015288.pdf?OpenElement.

22. UNGA, Resolution 1579 (XV), Question of the Future of Ruanda-Urundi, A/RES/1579 (XV), ¶11 (20 December 1960), https://documents-dds-ny.un.org/doc/RESOLUTION /GEN/NR0/153/53/IMG/NR015353.pdf?OpenElement.

23. Ibid.; UNGA, Resolution 1580 (XV), Question of the Mwami, A/RES/1580 (XV) (20 December 1960), https://documents-dds-ny.un.org/doc/RESOLUTION/GEN/NR0/153/54 /IMG/NR015354.pdf?OpenElement; and UNGA, Resolution 1605 (XV), Question of the Future of Ruanda-Urundi, A/RES/1605 (XV) (21 April 1961), https://documents-dds-ny.un.org/doc /RESOLUTION/GEN/NR0/198/20/IMG/NR019820.pdf?OpenElement.

24. Spaak at UNGA, sixteenth session, Fourth Committee, A/C.4/530 (30 January 1962), UN Office for Special Political Affairs, UNA/S-0201-0033-01.

25. Ibid., 9

26. Rahnema at the UNGA, sixteenth session, Fourth Committee, A/C.4/525 (23 January 1962), UNA/S-0201-0033-01.

27. Ibid., quote 4.

28. Ibid., quotes 5–6.

29. Ibid., 7.

30. Rahnema, UNA/S-0201-0033-01,18.

31. Louis Rwagasore, "Le Burundi a choisi une vrai révolution!" *La dépêche du Ruanda-Urundi* (Usumbura, 8 January 1960), in *Paroles et écrits de Louis Rwagasore, leader de l'Indépendance du Burundi*, ed. Christine Deslaurier, trans. Domitien Nizigiyimana (Bujumbura and Paris: Éditions Iwacu and Éditions Karthala, 2012), 132–37, both quotes 133.

32. See Christine Deslaurier, "Introduction: La pensée de Louis Rwagasore à travers ses mots," in Rwagasore, *Paroles et écrits*, 8–39, and Deslaurier, "Rwagasore *for Ever*? Des usages contemporaines d'un héros consensuel au Burundi," *Vingtième siècle* 118 (2013): 15–30.

33. Louis Rwagasore, "A bâtons rompus avec L. Rwagasore," *Temps nouveaux d'Afrique* (Usumbura, 20 November 1955), in *Paroles et écrits*, 48–53, quote 51.

34. Louis Rwagasore, "'Mise au point et prise de position' de Louis Rwagasore sur les coopératives," *La dépêche du Ruanda-Urundi* (Usumbura, 26 July 1958), in ibid., 88–95, quote 95.

35. Louis Rwagasore, "Discours prononcé par Louis Rwagasore pour l'ouverture de la Copico (Coopérative indigène de consommation)" (Usumbura, 4 September 1958), in ibid., 96–101, quote 99.

36. Louis Rwagasore, "Rapport destiné au gouvernement de la République arabe unie" (Brussels, 11 June 1958), in ibid., 80–87.

37. On Belgium's political, economic, and media campaign against Rwagasore, see Augustin Mariro, *Burundi 1965: La 1ère crise ethnique. Genèse et contexte géopolitique* (Paris: L'Harmattan, 2005), 68–103.

38. Rwagasore, "Ouverture de la Copico," 97.

39. For example, Louis Rwagasore, "Discours du prince Rwagasore lors de son investiture comme chef du Buyenzi-Sud (territoire de Ngozi)" (Rango, 21 February 1959), in *Paroles et écrits*, and "Ouverture de la Copico," 115–17.

40. Louis Rwagasore, "Lettre adressé à Monseiur Maus par le prince Louis Rwagasore," *La dépêche du Ruanda-Urundi* (Usumbura, 4 December 1959), in *Paroles et écrits*, 118–23, quote 121. Maus was a Belgian colonist who organized a Hutu party and attacked the Tutsis for exploiting the Hutus. He committed suicide when independence came.

41. Rwagasore, "Vrai Révolution!" both quotes 135.

42. Louis Rwagasore, "Exposé du prince Louis Rwagasore à la Chambre de commerce et d'industrie du Burundi (CCIB)" (Usumbura, 25 August 1960), in *Paroles et écrits*, 162–83, quote 173.

43. See Mariro, *Burundi 1965*, 107–29, and Lemarchand, *Burundi*, 53–57.

44. Mariro, *Burundi 1965*, 195. Mariro calls it the "the ethnicization of politics," but I think racial is more appropriate here.

45. Marin to Amachree and Protich, 23 May 1962, cable 516, under-secretary-general for special political affairs (hereafter USGSPA), UNA/S-0238-0006-08.

46. Taghi Nasr to Turner, Usumbura, 30 August 1962, telegram UNREB 175, USGSPA, UNA/S-0238-0006-01.

47. Jamieson (UNHCR director of operations) to High Commission for Refugees, Geneva, 28 November 1963, no. ZY362, UNA/S-0279-0019-06.

48. Obrdlik to Marin, Usumbura, 31 May 1962, cable UNCRU 93, USGSPA, UNA/S-0238-0006-08.

49. For example, David Blickenstaff to Nasr, Kigali, 13 August 1962, UNA/S-0279-0019-06, on the difficulties of creating even an economic union between the two countries.

50. See telegrams sent by Bunche to Dorsinville with the text of messages circulated by both governments to missions of the member states of the UN, 31 January 1964 and 6 February 1964, UNA/S-0238-0006-10; National Assembly Burundi to prime minister Burundi, 24 January 1964, and "Protestation du parlement du Burundi contre l'attitude du Rwanda," 27 January 1964, UNA/S-0238-0006-11.

51. Republique rwandaise, Ministère des affaires étrangères, "Toute la verité sur le terrorisme 'Inzenzi,'" February 1964, submitted to His Excellency Mr. U Thant, secretary-general of the UN at New York, USGSPA, UNA/S-0238-0002-11, 2. See also "Message du Président Kayibanda

à l'occasion du 28 Janvier 1964, 3e anniversaire de la démocratie au Rwanda," secretary-general of the UN at New York, USGSPA, UNA/S-0238-0002-11.

52. Republique rwandaise, Ministère des affaires étrangères, "Terrorisme 'Inzenzi,'" quotes 2–3, 5.

53. Lucas to Bunche, in which Lucas specifically mentions the strong reaction in the European and American press, 31 January 1964, UNA/0238-0006-11; René Mabeu (director-general of UNESCO) to U Thant, 27 January 1964, and Bunche to Lucas, 3 February 1964, UNA/S-0238-0006-10.

54. Lucas to Bunche, Bujumbura, 26 January 1964, UNA/S-0238-0006-11.

55. Telegram [unclear provenance] to Janecek, received UN New York 3 February 1964, UNA/S-0238-0002-09; Marlin to Urrutia, telegram, HCR/269, n.d., probably September 1964, USGSPA, UNA/S-0238-0003-02. For recent scholarly estimates, see the conclusion to this chapter.

56. See various documents in USGSPA, UNA/S-0238/0006/10.

57. Marlin to Urrutia, telegram, HCR/269, n.d., probably September 1964, quote 4.

58. See the leaflet in UNA/S-0238-0006-10, presumably March 1964.

59. A. J. Lucas to Bunche, 6 March 1964, UNA/S-0238-0006-10.

60. "1964 Programme—New Projects," proposal submitted by UNHCR in support of ILO program, General Assembly, Executive Committee of the High Commissioner's Programme, annex 4, eleventh session, A/AC.96/240, 28 April 1964, USGSPA, UNA/S-0238-0003-03.

61. Marlin to Urrutia, telegram, HCR/269, n.d., probably September 1964; Urquhart to Osorio-Tafall, 15 September 1964, cable 3088, USGSPA, UNA/S-0238-0003-02; and Press Service, Office of Public Information, press release REF/467, 22 May 1964, USGSPA, UNA/S-0238-0003-03.

62. Jaeger/Goge to Bunche and Schnyder, UNHCR, 2 October 1964, cable T-323, USGSPA, UNA/S-0238-0003-02.

63. "1964 Programme—New Projects," A/AC.96/240, 28 April, 1964.

64. Ibid.

65. For example, Schnyder to 38th floor, UNHCR, New York, HC 360 for Urrutia, 18 December 1964, UNA/S-0238-0004-04. See also Osorio-Tafall to Bunche, Leopoldville, 7 September 1964, UN USGSPA, UNA/S-0238-0004-04. For a positive assessment, UN Press Services, Office of Public Information, press release REF 483, 22 December 1964, UNA/S-0238-0004-04. For an acute analysis of the intermingling of the refugee crisis and political mobilizations, see Lemarchand, *Dynamics of Violence*.

66. As is evident from numerous communications in the UNHCR Archive (Geneva) on Rwanda and Burundi, as in: Jaerger to HICOMREF [UNHCR] New York, 17 January 1966 (received), HCRNY/16; Hordijk to Jamieson and Jaeger, 6 February 1967 (received), HCRBUJ/24; and Cuénod to UNHCR Bujumbura, Geneva, 9 May 1968, 6/6/BUR.

67. Schnyder to 38th floor, UNHCR New York, HC 360 for Urrutia, 18 December 1964, USGSPA, UNA/S-0238-0004-04.

68. Lucas to Bunche, Bujumbura, 8 February 1964, UNA/S-0238-0006-10. In general, this file indicates the UN's concern with refugees on humanitarian grounds, but also its understanding of the entwining of political issues with the refugees.

69. Lucas to Bunche, Bujumbura, 7 February 1964, UNA/S-0238-0006-10.

70. Ibid.

71. *Le Monde*, 4 February 1964, in UNA/S-0238-0006-10.

72. Osorio-Tafall to Bunche, Leopoldville, 7 September 1964, USGSPA, UNA/S-0238-0004-04.

73. Ibid.

74. On these events, see Lemarchand, *Burundi*, 58–75.

75. Figures from N. Watt, *Burundi*, 36. For a more complete history, see Jean-Pierre Chrétien and Jean-François Dupaquier, *Burundi 1972: Au bord des génocides* (Paris: Editions Karthala, 2007), as well as Lemarchand, *Burundi*, 76–105, who puts the number of refugees at 150,000 (104).

76. Judi Rever, *In Praise of Blood: The Crimes of the Rwandan Patriotic Front* (Toronto: Random House, 2018), places the responsibility squarely on Kagame and the RPF.

77. Meghan Foster Lynch, "Civilian Agency in Times of Crisis: Lessons from Burundi," in *The Human Rights Paradox: Universality and Its Discontents*, ed. Steve J. Stern and Scott Straus (Madison: University of Wisconsin Press, 2014), 81–103, 85 for figure of three hundred thousand, and Lemarchand, *Burundi*. For harrowing personal stories from both Hutus and Tutsis, see N. Watt, *Burundi*, 50–57.

78. Timothy Paul Longman, *Proxy Targets: Civilians in the War in Burundi* (New York: Human Rights Watch, 1998), 1.

79. For some major works on the Rwandan Genocide, see Lee Ann Fujii, *Killing Neighbors: Webs of Violence in Rwanda* (Ithaca: Cornell University Press, 2009); Scott Straus, *The Order of Genocide: Race, Power, and War in Rwanda* (Ithaca: Cornell University Press, 2006); Mamdani, *When Victims Become Killers*; Alison Des Forges, *"Leave None to Tell the Story": Genocide in Rwanda* (New York: Human Rights Watch, 1999); Philip Gourevitch, *We Wish to Inform You that Tomorrow We Will Be Killed with Our Families: Stories from Rwanda* (New York: Farrar, Straus, and Giroux, 1999); as well as the interesting analysis of Hollie Nyseth Brehm, "Subnational Determinants of Killing in Rwanda," *Criminology* 55:1 (2017): 5–31.

80. See his moving memoir, Roméo Dallaire with Brent Beardsley, *Shake Hands with the Devil: The Failure of Humanity in Rwanda* (Toronto: Random House, 2003).

81. See especially Rever, *In Praise of Blood*.

82. See Scott Straus, *Making and Unmaking Nations: War, Leadership, and Genocide in Modern Africa* (Ithaca: Cornell University Press, 2015); Gérard Prunier, *Africa's World War: Congo, the Rwandan Genocide, and the Making of a Continental Catastrophe* (Oxford: Oxford University Press, 2009); and Lemarchand, *Dynamics of Violence*.

83. Human Rights Watch, "Burundi: Events of 2017," World Report 2018, Human Rights Watch, n.d., accessed 16 October 2018, https://www.hrw.org/world-report/2018/country-chapters/burundi.

84. Both quotes from interviews conducted by the aid worker Nigel Watt, in *Burundi*, 37.

85. Ibid., 38.

86. One of Fujii's interviewees, quoted in *Webs of Violence*, 92. Generally, see ibid., 76–127.

87. Quoted in Lynch, "Civilian Agency," 91.

88. Straus, *Order of Genocide*, emphasizes the deep penetration of the state in Rwanda, one of the factors that made the genocide so extensive.

89. Mamdani, *When Victims Become Killers*, goes too far in assigning virtually all the blame to Belgium.

90. See the personal testimonies regarding 1972 in N. Watt, *Burundi*, 99–106. On the silences, see Chrétien and Dupaquier, *Burundi 1972*, 465–78.

91. Chrétien and Dupaquier, *Burundi 1972*, 471.

Notes to Conclusion

1. Nelson Mandela, *Long Walk to Freedom: The Autobiography of Nelson Mandela* (Boston: Little, Brown, 1994), 83.

2. "Atlantic Charter" (14 August 1941), Yale Law School, Lillian Goldman Law Library, n.d., accessed 16 October 2018, http://avalon.law.yale.edu/wwii/atlantic.asp.

3. Mandela, *Long Walk to Freedom*, 83–84.

4. Ibid. I first read of Mandela's reaction to the Atlantic Charter in Elizabeth Borgwardt, *A New Deal for the World: America's Vision for Human Rights* (Cambridge: Harvard University Press, 2005). On the impact of the Atlantic Charter generally on anticolonial movements, see Fabian Klose, *Human Rights in the Shadow of Colonial Violence: The Wars of Independence in Kenya and Algeria*, trans. Dona Geyer (2009; Philadelphia: University of Pennsylvania Press, 2013).

5. Ralphe Bunche, "Informal Lecture Delivered by Dr. Ralph Bunche on 'Palestine,'" 16 June 1949, UCLA Library, Ralph J. Bunche Papers, box 98, folder 3.

6. I thank Daniela Traldi for pointing me toward Lutz. See Traldi, "A Transnational History of Brazilian Feminism: Bertha Lutz and the International Woman Suffrage Alliance" (unpublished MA thesis, London School of Economics and Political Science, 2015), and Traldi, "Women's Rights Pioneers: Latin Americans at the Birth of the United Nations" (doctoral student paper, Graduate Center of the City University of New York, 2017), the latter also about Minerva Bernardino, the Dominican Republic's representative at the San Franciso Conference. See also Kathryn Sikkink, *Evidence for Hope: Making Human Rights Work in the 21st Century* (Princeton: Princeton University Press, 2017). The text of the UN Charter is at http://www.un.org/en/sections/un-charter/un-charter-full-text.

7. Many streams of thought contributed to the making of human rights. On the sometimes neglected conservative role, see Marco Duranti, *The Conservative Human Rights Revolution: European Identity, Transnational Politics, and the Origins of the European Convention* (New York: Oxford University Press, 2017), and Samuel Moyn, *Christian Human Rights* (Philadelphia: University of Pennsylvania Press, 2015).

8. For the effort to remake the French empire with equitable stature for Africans, see Frederick Cooper, *Citizenship between Empire and Nation: Remaking France and French Africa, 1945–1960* (Princeton: Princeton University Press, 2014). However, that effort ultimately failed, resulting in a myriad of francophone nation-states in Africa.

9. On the role of the Global South in creating the international human rights system, see Steven L. B. Jensen, *The Making of International Human Rights: The 1960s, Decolonization and the Reconstruction of Global Values* (Cambridge: Cambridge University Press, 2016).

10. For the most extensive discussion of the drafting, see Johannes Morsink, *The Universal Declaration of Human Rights: Origins, Drafting, and Intent* (Philadelphia: University of Pennsylvania Press, 1999). Also important are Jay Winter and Antoine Prost, *René Cassin and Human Rights: From the Great War to the Universal Declaration* (Cambridge: Cambridge University

Press, 2013), and Mary Ann Glendon, *A World Made New: Eleanor Roosevelt and the Universal Declaration of Human Rights* (New York: Random House, 2001).

11. For the most rounded and thoughtful discussion of the concept of genocide and its progenitor, Raphael Lemkin, see A. Dirk Moses, "Empire, Colony, Genocide: Keywords and the Philosophy of History," in *Empire, Colony, Genocide: Conquest, Occupation, and Subaltern Resistance in World History*, ed. Moses (New York: Berghahn, 2008), 3–54.

12. For the history of the concept, see Peter Holquist, "'Crimes against Humanity': Genealogy of a Concept (1815–1945)" (unpublished MS, 2015). I thank Peter Holquist for letting me read and cite his unpublished paper.

13. On the Fourth Protocols and their connection to human rights, see William I. Hitchcock, "Human Rights and the Laws of War: The Geneva Conventions of 1949," in *The Human Rights Revolution: An International History*, ed. Akira Iriye, Petra Goedde, and Hitchcock (Oxford: Oxford University Press, 2012), 93–112. For a notable interpretation of the European Convention, see Duranti, *Conservative Human Rights Revolution*.

14. See A. W. Brian Simpson, *Human Rights and the End of Empire: Britain and the Genesis of the European Convention* (Oxford: Oxford University Press, 2001). Generally on the Cyprus issue, see a number of books published in the series Minnesota Mediterranean and East European Monographs, ed. Theofanis G. Stavrou: William Mallinson, *Partition through Foreign Aggression: The Case of Turkey in Cyprus* (Minneapolis: Modern Greek Studies, 2010), 15–27; Van Coufoudakis, *International Aggression and Violations of Human Rights: The Case of Turkey in Cyprus* (Minneapolis: Modern Greek Studies, 2008), 15–18; and Stella Soulioti, *Fettered Independence: Cyprus, 1878–1964* (Minneapolis: Modern Greek Studies, 2006).

15. For different views that emphasize discontinuity, see Stefan-Ludwig Hoffmann, "Human Rights and History," *Past & Present* 232 (2016): 279–310, and Samuel Moyn, *The Last Utopia: Human Rights in History* (Cambridge: Belknap Press of Harvard University Press, 2010).

16. International Covenant on Civil and Political Rights, 19 December 1966, 999 U.N.T.S. 14668, https://treaties.un.org/doc/publication/unts/volume%20999/volume-999-i-14668-english.pdf; International Covenant on Economic, Social and Cultural Rights, 16 December 1966, 993 U.N.T.S. 14531, https://treaties.un.org/doc/Treaties/1976/01/19760103%2009-57%20PM/Ch_IV_03.pdf.

17. The founding document is the Rome Statute of the International Criminal Court, 17 July 1998, 2187 U.N.T.S. 38544, http://legal.un.org/icc/statute/99_corr/cstatute.htm.

18. "The Core International Human Rights Instruments and Their Monitoring Bodies," UN Human Rights, Office of the High Commissioner, n.d., accessed 18 May 2018, http://www.ohchr.org/EN/ProfessionalInterest/Pages/CoreInstruments.aspx. Ninety-six is my count based on "Universal Human Rights Instruments," UN Human Rights, Office of the High Commissioner, n.d., accessed 18 May 2018, http://www.ohchr.org/EN/ProfessionalInterest/Pages/UniversalHumanRightsInstruments.aspx.

19. Excerpts of the speech are widely available, including at hpa kythuat, "Hillary Clinton Women's Rights Are Human Rights," YouTube, 11 June 2013, https://www.youtube.com/watch?v=BAhKz3y7mJk.

20. See Jean Quataert, *Advocating Dignity: Human Rights Mobilizations in Global Politics* (Philadelphia: University of Pennsylvania Press, 2009), 149–81, and Celia Donert, "Wessen

Utopie? Frauenrechte und Staatssozialismus im Internationalen Jahr der Frau 1975," in *Moral für die Welt? Menschenrechtspolitik in den 1970er Jahren*, ed. Jan Eckel and Samuel Moyn (Göttingen: Vanenhoeck and Ruprecht, 2012), 367–93.

21. See Donert, "Wessen Utopie?" and Nationales Organisationsbüro der DDR für den Weltkongreß im Internationalen Jahr der Frau, ed., *Dokumente des Weltkongresses im Internationalen Jahr der Frau in Berlin, 20.-24. Oktober 1975* (Dresden: Graphischer Großbetrieb Völkerfreundschaft, 1975).

22. Convention on the Elimination of All Forms of Discrimination against Women, 1249 U.N.T.S. (18 December 1979), p. 13, http://www.un.org/womenwatch/daw/cedaw/text/econvention.htm.

23. See J. Quataert, *Advocating Dignity*, 149–81.

24. I learned this from a lecture by a Dutch psychiatrist who works with Dutchbat veterans. His presentation took place at the annual meeting of the International Association of Genocide Scholars, June 2001.

25. "In Numbers," UN ICTY, last updated September 2016, http://www.icty.org/en/features/crimes-sexual-violence/in-numbers.

26. On the tribunals, see David Scheffer, *All the Missing Souls: A Personal History of the War Crimes Tribunals* (Princeton: Princeton University Press, 2012).

27. See Kathryn Sikkink, *The Justice Cascade: How Human Rights Prosecutions Are Changing World Politics* (New York: Norton, 2011).

28. See Priscilla Hayner, *Unspeakable Truths: Confronting State Terror and Atrocity* (New York: Routledge, 2001).

29. For a scathing criticism of the Responsibility to Protect, see Rajan Menon, *The Conceit of Humanitarian Intervention* (New York: Oxford University Press, 2016). See also Michael Geyer, "Humanitarianism and Human Rights: A Troubled Rapport," in *The Emergence of Humanitarian Intervention: Ideas and Practice from the Nineteenth Century to the Present*, ed. Fabian Klose (Cambridge: Cambridge University Press, 2016), 31–55.

30. I relate these events in my book, *A Century of Genocide: Utopias of Race and Nation*, edition with new preface (2003; Princeton: Princeton University Press, 2015), 227–29. For the quote, "Judgement of Trial Chamber II in the Kunarac, Kovac and Vukovic Case," ICTY press release, 22 February 2001, http://www.icty.org/en/press/judgement-trial-chamber-ii-kunarac-kovac-and-vukovic-case.

31. "Judgement of Trial Chamber II."

32. See Ruti Teitel, *Humanity's Law* (New York: Oxford University Press, 2011), although she goes overboard in her enthusiasms and expectations for what the new era of human rights law can accomplish. See also Teitel, *Globalizing Transitional Justice: Contemporary Essays* (New York: Oxford University Press, 2014), in which she emphasizes the new prevalence of judicial mechanisms and constitutions in the transition from dictatorial to democratic regimes. Teitel's confidence in the law is echoed by many others, including Jürgen Habermas, *The Divided West*, ed. and trans. Ciaran Cronin (Cambridge: Polity, 2006), 15, 116, and David Held, "Laws of States, Laws of Peoples: Three Models of Sovereignty," *Legal Theory* 8:1 (2002): 1–44. On humanitarianism as distinct from human rights, see Michael N. Barnett, *Empire of Humanity: A History of Humanitarianism* (Ithaca: Cornell University Press, 2011).

33. On these developments, see Jan Eckel, *Die Ambivalenz des Guten: Menschenrechte in der internationalen Politik seit den 1940er* (Göttingen: Vandenhoeck and Ruprecht, 2014); Aryeh Neier, *The International Human Rights Movement: A History* (Princeton: Princeton University Press, 2012); Stefan-Ludwig Hoffmann, ed. *Human Rights in the Twentieth Century* (2010; Cambridge: Cambridge University Press, 2011); and Moyn, *Last Utopia*.

34. Moyn, *Last Utopia*.

35. See especially Eckel, *Ambivalenz des Guten*.

36. See the website of the Center for Victims of Torture, https://www.cvt.org; the papers of Human Rights Advocates in the University of California-Berkeley Bancroft Library, Manuscripts Collection; and on Guatemala, Victoria Sanford, *Buried Secrets: Truth and Human Rights in Guatemala* (New York: Palgrave Macmillan, 2003).

37. These examples from Nigel Watt, *Burundi: Biography of a Small African Country*, 2nd ed. (London: Hurst, 2012), 117–64.

38. On the history of the concept, see Eric D. Weitz, "Self-Determination: How a German Enlightenment Idea Became the Slogan of National Liberation and a Human Right," *American Historical Review* 120:2 (2015): 462–96.

39. Article 1 of both the International Covenant on Civil and Political Rights, 19 December 1966, 999 U.N.T.S. 14668, https://treaties.un.org/doc/publication/unts/volume%20999/volume-999-i-14668-english.pdf, and the International Covenant on Economic, Social and Cultural Rights, 16 December 1966, 993 U.N.T.S. 14531, https://treaties.un.org/doc/Treaties/1976/01/19760103%2009-57%20PM/Ch_IV_03.pdf. See also UNGA, Resolution 637 (VII), The Right of Peoples and Nations to Self-Determination, A/RES/637 (VII), 16 December 1952, http://www.worldlii.org/int/other/UNGARsn/1952/148.pdf, and UNGA, Resolution 1514 (XV), Declaration on the Granting of Independence to Colonial Countries and Peoples, A/RES/1514 (XV), 14 December 1960, https://www.ohchr.org/EN/ProfessionalInterest/Pages/Independence.aspx.

40. UNGA, Resolution 2625 (XXV), Declaration on Principles of International Law concerning Friendly Relations and Co-operation among States in accordance with the Charter of the United Nations, A/RES/25/2625, 24 October 1970, http://www.un-documents.net/a25r2625.htm, and The Final Act of the Conference on Security and Cooperation in Europe (Helsinki Declaration), 14 I.L.M. 1292, 1 August 1975, http://www1.umn.edu/humanrts/osce/basics/finact75.htm. Self-determination is mentioned numerous times in both documents.

41. African Charter on Human and Peoples' Rights, OAU Doc. CAB/LEG/67/3 rev. 5 (27 June 1981), 21 I.L.M. 58 (1982), http://www1.umn.edu/humanrts/instree/z1afchar.htm.

42. Weitz, "Self-Determination."

43. For two important histories of refugees and migrants, see Philipp Ther, *Die Außenseiter: Flucht, Flüchtlinge und Integration im modernen Europa* (Berlin: Suhrkamp, 2017), and Howard Adelman and Elazar Barkan, *No Return, No Refuge: Rites and Rights in Minority Repatriation* (New York: Columbia University Press, 2011).

44. "Figures at a Glance," UNHCR, n.d., accessed 25 September 2018, http://www.unhcr.org/en-us/figures-at-a-glance.html. On the highly precarious situation of child migrants, see Jacqueline Bhabha, *Child Migration and Human Rights in a Global Age* (Princeton: Princeton University Press, 2015).

45. "Figures at a Glance."

46. Internal Displacement Monitoring Centre, "2017 Internal Displacement Figures by Country," Global Internal Displacement Database, 31 December 2017, http://www.internal -displacement.org/database/displacement-data.

47. Figures for the Arab states from "Labour Migration," ILO, n.d., accessed 21 February 2019, http://www.ilo.org/beirut/areasofwork/labour-migration/lang--en/index.htm; US figures from Jens Manuel Krogstad, Jeffrey S. Passel, and D'Vera Cohn, "5 Facts about Illegal Immigration in the U.S.," Pew Research Center, 28 November 2018, http://www.pewresearch.org /fact-tank/2017/04/27/5-facts-about-illegal-immigration-in-the-u-s/.

48. "World Population Clock Live," The World Counts, n.d. (updated continuously), accessed 25 October 2017, http://www.theworldcounts.com/counters/shocking_environmental _facts_and_statistics/world_population_clock_live; Internal Displacement Monitoring Centre, Global Internal Displacement Database, http://www.internal-displacement.org/database/.

49. See David Weissbrodt, *The Human Rights of Non-Citizens* (Oxford: Oxford University Press, 2008).

50. For some examples: Samuel Moyn, *Not Enough: Human Rights in an Unequal World* (Cambridge: Belknap Press of Harvard University Press, 2018), and *Last Utopia*; Eric A. Posner, *The Twilight of Human Rights Law* (Oxford: Oxford University Press, 2014); Stephen Hopgood, *The Endtimes of Human Rights* (Ithaca: Cornell University Press, 2013); David Kennedy, *The Dark Sides of Virtue: Reassessing International Humanitarianism* (Princeton: Princeton University Press, 2004); and David Rieff, *A Bed for the Night: Humanitarianism in Crisis* (New York: Simon and Schuster, 2002).

51. See Michael Ignatieff, "The Destruction of Syria and the Crisis of Universal Values," Kelman Seminar, Harvard Law School, 7 March 2016, http://www.michaelignatieff.ca, and "The Refugee Crisis in Europe: How Did It Happen? What Do We Do Now?" Central European University, 21 January 2016, https://www.youtube.com/watch?v=AbO-3M5dwSE, and Neier, *International Human Rights Movement*.

52. For a similar comment, see Christian Reus-Smit, *Individual Rights and the Making of the International System* (Cambridge: Cambridge University Press, 2013), 210–11.

53. In my thinking about these issues I have benefited from reading Jeremy Waldron, "What Is Cosmopolitan?" *Journal of Political Philosophy* 8:2 (2000): 227–43; Seyla Benhabib, *Another Cosmopolitanism* (New York: Oxford University Press, 2006), and Benhabib, *The Rights of Others: Aliens, Residents, and Citizens* (Cambridge: Cambridge University Press, 2004). See also Waldron's discussion of dignity and the evolution of the concept from hierarchy to equality, in *Dignity, Rank, and Rights* (New York: Oxford University Press, 2012). I thank León Castellanos-Jankiewicz and Graziella Romeo for pointing me to these discussions. I take it as a given that identities are always culturally constructed and never fixed and timeless. But they do have particular characteristics at any moment in time.

BIBLIOGRAPHY OF PRIMARY SOURCES

Archives

Bundesarchiv (Germany) Koblenz
Bundesarchiv (Germany) Lichterfelde
Center for Jewish History, New York
Hoover Institution Archives, Stanford
Minnesota Historical Society, Saint Paul
National Archives of Namibia, Windhoek
Politisches Archiv des Auswärtigen Amts, Berlin
United Nations Archive, New York
United Nations High Commission for Refugees Archive, Geneva

Libraries

New York Society Library
Princeton University Library
Staatsbibliothek Berlin
Universitätsbibliothek Frankfurt am Main, Bildarchiv
University of California Berkeley, Bancroft Library
University of California Los Angeles, Special Collections, Charles E. Young Research Library
University of Minnesota Library

Published State Papers

Belgium, L'Office de l'information et des rélations publiques pour le Congo belge et le Ruanda-Urundi. *Le Ruanda-Urundi*. Brussels, 1959.

Cherokee Nation v. State of Georgia. 30 U.S. (5 Pet.) 1, 32 (1831). https://scholar.google.com/scholar_case?case?64815241009036119.

Constitution of Greece. 1988. http://www.hri.org/docs/syntagma/.

Constitution of the Federative Republic of Brazil. 1988. http://livraria.camara.leg.br/direito-e-justica/constitution-of-the-federative-republic-of-brazil.html.

France, Ministère des affaires étrangères. *Documents diplomatiques: Conférence de Lausanne.* Vol. 1, *21 novembre 1922—1er février 1923*. Paris: Imprimerie nationale, 1923.

Greek Citizenship Code. 2004. http://eudo-citizenship.eu/admin/?p=file&appl=currentCitizen
shipLaws&f=GRE%20Citizenship%20Code%20%28as%20of%202010%2C%20English
%29.pdf.

International Criminal Tribunal for the Former Yugoslavia. Documents relating to the trial of
Dragoljub Kunarac, Radomir Kovač, and Zoran Vuković. www.icty.org.

Israel, State Archives. *Political and Diplomatic Documents, December 1947–May 1948*. Edited by
Gedalia Yogev. 2 vols. Jerusalem: Government Printer, 1979.

Johnson & Graham's Lessee v. M'Intosh [21 U.S. (8 Wheat.) 543 (1823)]. The Oyez Project at
IIT Chicago-Kent College of Law. https://www.oyez.org/cases/1789-1850/21us543.

Minnesota, Board of Commissioners, ed. *Minnesota in the Civil and Indian Wars, 1861–1865*. 2
vols. St. Paul: Pioneer, 1890–93.

Minnesota Historical Society. *Collections of the Minnesota Historical Society*. Vol. 3, *1870–1880*.
St. Paul: Minnesota Historical Society, 1880.

Nationales Organisationsbüro der DDR für den Weltkongreß im Internationalen Jahr der Frau,
ed. *Dokumente des Weltkongresses im Internationalen Jahr der Frau in Berlin, 20.–24. Oktober
1975*. Dresden: Graphischer Großbetrieb Völkerfreundschaft, 1975.

Organization for Security and Cooperation in Europe. Conference on Security and Cooperation in Europe Final Act [Helsinki Final Act]. Helsinki, 1975. https://www.osce.org
/helsinki-final-act?download=true.

Prussia, Grosser Generalstab, Kriegsgeschichtliche Abteilung. *Die Kämpfe der deutschen Truppen in Südwestafrika. Auf Grund amtlichen Materials*, three-volume ed. Berlin: Ernst Siegfried
Mittler und Sohn, 1906.

United Kingdom, Foreign Office. *British and Foreign State Papers*. Vols. 8–10 (1820–23), 12–15
(1824–28). London: J. Harrison and Son, 1825–30.

———. *British and Foreign State Papers*. Vols. 16–19 (1824–32). London: James Ridgway,
1832–33.

———. *British and Foreign State Papers*. Vol. 67 (1875–76). London: William Ridgway, 1883.

———. *British and Foreign State Papers*. Vol. 81 (1888–89). London: Her Majesty's Stationery
Office, n.d..

———. *Documents on British Foreign Policy 1919–1939*. First Series. Vol. 6. London: Her Majesty's
Stationery Office, 1956.

United Kingdom, Palestine Royal Commission. *Report: Presented by the Secretary of State for the
Colonies to Parliament by Command of His Majesty, July, 1937*. London: His Majesty's Stationery Office, 1937.

United Nations. Charter. 26 June 1946. http://www.un.org/en/sections/un-charter/un
-charter-full-text/.

United Nations General Assembly. Convention on the Elimination of All Forms of Discrimination against Women. 18 December 1979. 1249 U.N.T.S. http://www.un.org/womenwatch
/daw/cedaw/text/econvention.htm.

———. International Covenant on Civil and Political Rights. 19 December 1966. 999 U.N.T.S.
14668. https://treaties.un.org/doc/publication/unts/volume%20999/volume-999-i-14668
-english.pdf.

———. International Covenant on Economic, Social and Cultural Rights. 16 December 1966.
993 U.N.T.S. 14531. http://www.ohchr.org/EN/ProfessionalInterest/Pages/CESCR.aspx.

———. Official Records. Sixth Session (1951–52). Plenary Meetings.

———. Official Records. Sixth Session (1951–52). Third Committee. Social, Humanitarian and Cultural Questions.

———. Official Records. Fifteenth Session (1960). Plenary Meetings. Part I, vols. 2 and 3.

———. Official Records. Twenty-First Session (1966). Plenary Meetings. Vol. 3 (continued).

———. Resolution 1514. Declaration on the Granting of Independence to Colonial Countries and Peoples. A/RES/1514 (XV). 14 December 1960. https://documents-dds-ny.un.org/doc /RESOLUTION/GEN/NR0/152/88/IMG/NR015288.pdf?OpenElement.

———. Resolution 1579. Question of the Future of Ruanda-Urundi. A/RES/1579 (XV). 20 December 1960. https://documents-dds-ny.un.org/doc/RESOLUTION/GEN /NR0/153/53/IMG/NR015353.pdf?OpenElement.

———. Resolution 1580. Question of Mwami. A/RES/1580 (XV). 20 December 1960. https:// documents-dds-ny.un.org/doc/RESOLUTION/GEN/NR0/153/54/IMG/NR015354 .pdf?OpenElement.

———. Resolution 1605. Question of the Future of Ruanda-Urundi. A/RES/1605 (XV). 21 April 1961. https://documents-dds-ny.un.org/doc/RESOLUTION/GEN/NR0/198/20 /IMG/NR019820.pdf?OpenElement.

———. Universal Declaration of Human Rights, 10 December 1948. http://www.un.org/en /universal-declaration-human-rights/.

United States, Department of State. Papers Relating to the Foreign Relations of the United States, 1919: The Paris Peace Conference. Vols. 1, 6, and 7. Washington: Government Printing Office, 1942–46.

———. "Greece: International Religious Freedom Report 2006." https://www.state.gov/j/drl/ rls/irf/2006/71383.htm.

Vienna Congress. Final Act, 1815. "Final Act of the Congress of Vienna/Act XV." Wikisource. Version ID 4276542. Accessed 14 December 2016. https://en.wikisource.org/wiki/Final_Act _of_the_Congress_of_Vienna/Act_XV.

Wellington, Duke of (Arthur Wellesley). Despatches, Correspondence, and Memoranda. Vol. 3, 1826–27, ed. Duke of Wellington [his son]. London: John Murray, 1868.

Worcester v. Georgia [31 U.S. (6 Pet.) 515 (1832)]. The Oyez Project at IIT Chicago-Kent College of Law. Accessed 22 January 2019. https://www.oyez.org/cases/1789-1850/31us515.

Other Published Political Sources

Adalah: The Legal Center for Arab Minority Rights in Israel. The Democratic Constitution, draft (Shafa'amr: Adalah, 20 March 2007). https://www.adalah.org/uploads/oldfiles/Public/files /democratic_constitution-english.pdf.

Alliance Israélite universelle. La question juive devant la conférence de la paix. Paris: Siège de la Société, 1918.

Amalrik, Andrei. Notes of a Revolutionary. Translated by Guy Daniels. New York: Knopf, 1982.

American Committee for the Independence of Armenia and Armenian National Union of America. America as Mandatary for Armenia. Brochure. New York, 1919.

Anderson, Gary Clayton, and Alan R. Woolworth, eds. *Through Dakota Eyes: Narrative Accounts of the Minnesota Indian War of 1862*. St. Paul: Minnesota Historical Society, 1988.

Arab Higher Committee for Palestine. *The Palestine Arab Case: A Statement by the Arab Higher Committee*. Cairo: Costa Tsoumas, 1947.

"The Armenian Question Before the Peace Conference: A Memorandum Presented Officially by the Representatives of Armenia to the Peace Conference at Versailles, on February 26th, 1919." n.p., n.d.

Babyonyshev, Alexander, ed. *On Sakharov*. Translated by Guy Daniels. New York: Knopf, 1982.

Bank of Chosen. *Pictorial Chosen and Manchuria: Compiled in Commemoration of the Decennial of the Bank of Chosen*. Seoul, 1919.

Bauer, Otto. *Die Nationalitätenfrage und die Sozialdemokratie*. 2nd ed. 1924, original 1907. In Bauer, *Werkausgabe*, vol. 1. Vienna: Europa, 1975.

Benn, Tony, ed. *Writings on the Wall: A Radical and Socialist Anthology, 1215–1984*. London: Faber and Faber, 1984.

Blegen, Theodore C., ed. *Land of Their Choice: The Immigrants Write Home*. Minneapolis: University of Minnesota Press, 1955.

———, ed. *Lincoln's Secretary Goes West: Two Reports by John G. Nicolay on Frontier Indian Troubles 1862*. La Crosse: Sumac, 1965.

Board of Deputies of British Jews, Joint Foreign Committee of the Board of Deputies of British Jews, and the Anglo-Jewish Association. *The Peace Conference: Paris, 1919. Report of the Delegation of the Jews of the British Empire on the Treaties of Versailles, Saint-Germain-en-Laye and Neuilly and the Annexed Minorities Treaties*. London, 1920.

Buber, Martin, et al., eds. *Towards Union in Palestine: Essays on Zionism and Jewish-Arab Cooperation*. Jerusalem: Ihud, 1947.

Bugai, N. F. "20-40-e gody: Tragediia narodov." *Vostok* 2 (1992): 122–39.

———. " 'Pogruzheny v eshelony i otpravleny k mestam poselenii . . .': L. Beriia-I. Stalinu." *Istoriia SSR* 1 (1991): 143–60.

Bunche, Ralph J. "Peace and the United Nations." Tenth Montague Burton Lecture on International Relations. Leeds: University of Leeds, 1952.

Butler-Johnstone, H. A. Munro. *Bulgarian Horrors and the Question of the East: A Letter Addressed to the Right Hon. W. E. Gladstone, M.P.* London: William Ridgway, 1876.

Canku, Clifford, and Michael Simon, eds. and trans. *The Dakota Prisoner of War Letters*. St. Paul: Minnesota Historical Society, 2013.

Carnegie Endowment for International Peace. *The Treaties of Peace, 1919–1923*. 2 vols. New York: Carnegie Endowment for International Peace, 1924.

Chalidze, Valery. *Glasnost and Social and Economic Rights*. New York: Freedom House, 1988.

———. *The Soviet Human Rights Movement: A Memoir*. New York: Jacob Blaustein Institute for the Advancement of Human Rights of the American Jewish Committee, 1984.

———. *To Defend These Rights: Human Rights and the Soviet Union*. Translated by Guy Daniels. New York: Random House, 1974.

Clogg, Richard, ed. *Greece 1940–1949: Occupation, Resistance, Civil War—A Documentary History*. Houndmills: Palgrave Macmillan, 2002.

————, ed. *The Movement for Greek Independence, 1770–1821: A Collection of Documents*. London: Macmillan, 1976.

Comité des délégations juives auprès de la Conférence de la Paix. *Les droits nationaux des Juifs en Europe orientale*. Paris: Beresniak et Fils, 1919.

Comstock, John L. *History of the Greek Revolution Compiled from Official Documents of the Greek Government*. 1832. Hartford: Silas Andrus and Son, 1853.

Conrad, Robert Edgar, ed. *Children of God's Fire: A Documentary History of Black Slavery in Brazil*. Princeton: Princeton University Press, 1983.

Dallaire, Roméo, with Brent Beardsley. *Shake Hands with the Devil: The Failure of Humanity in Rwanda*. Toronto: Random House, 2003.

De Bary, Wm. Theodore, Carol Gluck, and Arthur E. Tiedemann, eds. *Sources of Japanese Tradition*. 2nd ed. Vol. 2, *1600–2000*. 1958. New York: Columbia University Press, 2005.

Douglass, Frederick. *The Life and Writings of Frederick Douglass*. Vol. 4. Edited by Philip S. Foner. New York: International, 1975.

Du Bois, W. E. Burghardt. *The Souls of Black Folk: Essays and Sketches*. 1903. New York: Fawcett, 1961.

Duque-Estrada, Osorio. *A abolição (esboço histórico) 1831–1888*. Rio de Janeiro: Livraria Editora Leite Ribeiro e Maurillo, 1918.

Eichwede, Wolfgang, ed. *Samizdat: Alternative Kultur in Zentral- und Osteuropa: Die 6oer bis 8oer Jahre*. Bremen: Edition Temmen, 1980.

Engels, Friedrich. *The Condition of the Working Class in England*. Translated and edited by W. O. Henderson and W. H. Chaloner. 1845. Stanford: Stanford University Press, 1968.

Estorff, Ludwig von. *Wanderungen und Kämpfe in Südwestafrika, Ostafrika und Südafrika, 1894–1910*. Wiesbaden: Wiesbaden Kurier Verlag und Druckerei, n.d.

Fichte, Johann Gottlieb. *Foundations of Natural Right, according to the Principles of the Wissenschaftslehre*. 1796. Edited by Frederick Neuhouser. Translated by Michael Baur. Cambridge: Cambridge University Press, 2000.

————. *Grundlage des Naturrechts nach Principien der Wissenschaftslehre*. 1796. In *J. G. Fichte: Gesamtausgabe der Bayerischen Akademie der Wissenschaften*. Edited by Reinhard Lauth and Hans Gliwitzky. Part 1. Vol. 4, *Werke 1797–1798*. Stuttgart: Friedrich Frommann, 1970.

Finlay, George. *History of the Greek Revolution*. 2 vols. Edinburgh: William Blackwood and Sons, 1861.

Fischer, Eugen. *Die Rehobother Bastards und das Bastardierungsproblem beim Menschen: Anthropologische und ethnographische Studien am Rehobother Bastardvolk in Deutsch-Südwest-Afrika*. Jena: Fischer, 1913.

Fonesca, L. Anselmo da. *A escravidão, o clero e o abolicionismo*. Bahia: Imprensa Economica, 1887.

Fukuzawa, Yukichi. *The Autobiography of Fukuzawa Yukichi*. Translated by Eiichi Kiyooka. Tokyo: Hokuseido, 1934.

Gettelman, Marvin, and Stuart Schaar, eds. *The Middle East and Islamic World Reader*. New York: Grove, 2003.

Gewald, Jan-Bart, and Jeremy Silvester, eds. *"Words Cannot Be Found": German Colonial Rule in Namibia. An Annotated Reprint of the 1918 Blue Book*. Leiden: Brill, 2003.

Gladstone, William E. *Bulgarian Horrors and the Question of the East*. London: John Murray, 1876.

Gordon, Thomas. *History of the Greek Revolution*. 2 vols. Edinburgh: William Blackwood, 1832.

Heard, Isaac V. D. *History of the Sioux War and Massacres of 1862 and 1863*. New York: Harper and Brothers, 1863.

Hook, Sidney, Vladimir Bukovsky, and Paul Hollander. *Soviet Hypocrisy and Western Gullibility*. n.p.: Ethics and Public Policy Center, 1987.

House, Edward Mandell, and Charles Seymour, eds. *What Really Happened at Paris: The Story of the Peace Conference, 1918–19*. New York: C. Scribner's Sons, 1921.

Human Rights Watch. "Burundi: Events of 2017." World Report 2018. Human Rights Watch. Accessed 16 October 2018. https://www.hrw.org/world-report/2018/country-chapters /burundi.

———. "The Rwandan Patriotic Front." Reports 1999. Human Rights Watch. https://www.hrw .org/reports/1999/rwanda/Geno15-8-03.htm.

Hutu Manifesto. *La Manifeste des Bahutu*. n.p., 24 March 1957. http://jkanya.free.fr/manifeste bahutu240357.pdf.

Kang, Hildi, ed. *Under the Black Umbrella: Voices from Colonial Korea, 1910–1945*. Ithaca: Cornell University Press, 2001.

Kennan, George F. *The Other Balkan Wars: A 1913 Carnegie Endowment Inquiry in Retrospect*. Washington: Carnegie Endowment for International Peace, 1993.

Kim, Dae Jung. *Prison Writings*. Translated by Choi Sung-il and David R. McCann. Berkeley: University of California Press, 1987.

Kim, Il-sŏng. *On Juche: In Our Revolution*. Pyongyang: Foreign Languages Publishing House, 1975.

Kohler, Max J., and Simon Wolf. *Jewish Disabilities in the Balkan States: American Contributions toward Their Removal, with Particular Reference to the Congress of Berlin*. Philadelphia: Publications of the American Jewish Historical Society, 1916.

Lacerda, Jean Baptiste de. "The *Metis*, or Half-Breeds, of Brazil." In *Papers on Inter-Racial Problems Communicated to the First Universal Races Congress, held at the University of London, July 26–29 1911*. Edited by G. Spiller. London: P. S. King and Son, 1911.

Lee, Peter H., ed. *Sourcebook of Korean Civilization*. Vol. 2, *From the Seventeenth Century to the Modern Period*. New York: Columbia University Press, 1996.

Lenin, V. I. "Critical Remarks on the National Question" (1913). In *Collected Works*, vol. 20, *December 1913 to August 1914*, 17–51. Moscow: Progress, 1964.

———. "The Right of Nations to Self-Determination" (1914). In *Collected Works*, vol. 20, *December 1913 to August 1914*, 393–454. Moscow: Progress, 1964.

———. "The Socialist Revolution and the Right of Nations to Self-Determination" (1916). In *Collected Works*, vol. 22, *December 1915 to July 1916*, 143–56. Moscow: Progress, 1964.

Leutwein, Theodor. *Elf Jahre Gouverneur in Deutsch Südwestafrika*. Berlin: Ernst Siegfried Mittler und Sohn, 1907.

Levine, Robert M., and John J. Crocitti, eds. *The Brazil Reader: History, Culture, Politics*. Durham: Duke University Press, 1999.

Longman, Timothy Paul. *Proxy Targets: Civilians in the War in Burundi*. New York: Human Rights Watch, 1998.

Mada al-Carmel: Arab Center for Applied Social Research. *The Haifa Declaration*. n.p., 15 May 2007. http://mada-research.org/en/files/2007/09/haifaenglish.pdf.

Marx, Karl, and Friedrich Engels. *Collected Works.* Vols. 20, 24, 27, 34, 42. London: Lawrence and Wishart, 1985–94.

———. *Marx-Engels Gesamtausgabe.* Pt. II. Vol. 4.1. Berlin: Dietz, 1988.

———. *Werke.* Vols. 18 and 31. Berlin: Dietz, 1962–65.

Masaryk, Thomas G. *The New Europe (the Slav Standpoint).* Edited by W. Preston Warren and William B. Weist. 1918. Lewisburg: Bucknell University Press, 1972.

Medvedev, Zhores A., and Roy A. Medvedev. *A Question of Madness.* London: Macmillan, 1971.

Meerson-Aksenov, Michael, and Boris Shragin, eds. *The Political, Social and Religious Thought of Russian "Samizdat": An Anthology.* Translated by Nickolas Lupinin. Belmont: Nordland, 1977.

Menzel, Gustav. *"Widerstand und Gottesfurcht": Hendrik Witbooi—Eine Biographie in zeitgenössischen Quellen.* Cologne: Rüdiger Köppe, 2000.

Möhlig, Wilhelm J. G., ed. *Die Witbooi in Südwestafrika während des 19. Jahrhunderts: Quellentexte von Johannes Olpp, Hendrik Witbooi jun. und Carl Berger.* Cologne: Rüdiger Köppe, 2007.

Moraes, Evaristo de. *A campanha abolicionista, 1879–1888.* Rio de Janeiro: Editora Leite Ribeiro, 1924.

Nabuco, Joaquim. *Abolitionism: The Brazilian Antislavery Struggle.* 1883. Translated and edited by Robert Conrad. Urbana: University of Illinois Press, 1977.

———. *Joaquim Nabuco, British Abolitionists, and the End of Slavery in Brazil: Correspondence 1880–1905.* Edited by Leslie Bethell and José Murilo de Carvalho. London: Institute for the Study of the Americas, University of London, 2009.

National Committee for the Heads of the Arab Local Authorities in Israel. *The Future Vision of the Palestinian Arabs in Israel.* Edited by Ghaida Rinawie-Zoabi. Translated by Abel Al Rahman Kelani. Nazareth: author, 2006. https://www.adalah.org/uploads/oldfiles/newsletter/eng/dec06/tasawor-mostaqbali.pdf.

Oakes, Augustus, and R. B. Mowat. *The Great European Treaties of the Nineteenth Century.* Oxford: Clarendon, 1918.

Park, Chung Hee. *The Country, the Revolution and I.* Edited by Leon Sinder. Seoul, 1963.

———. *Korea Reborn: A Model for Development.* Englewood Cliffs: Prentice-Hall, 1979.

———. *Major Speeches by Korea's Park Chung Hee.* Edited by Shin Bum Shik. Seoul: Hollym, 1970.

Prucha, Frances, ed. *Americanizing the American Indians: Writings by the "Friends of the Indian," 1880–1900.* Cambridge: Harvard University Press, 1973.

Reddaway, Peter, ed. and trans. *Uncensored Russia: Protest and Dissent in the Soviet Union. The Unofficial Moscow Journal "A Chronology of Current Events."* New York: American Heritage, 1972.

Rhee, Syngman. *The Syngman Rhee Correspondence in English, 1904–1948.* 8 vols. Edited by Young Ick Lew, et al. Seoul: Institute for Modern Korean Studies, Yonsei University, 2009.

Rwagasore, Louis. *Paroles et écrits de Louis Rwagasore, leader de l'Indépendance du Burundi.* Edited by Christine Deslaurier. Translated by Domitien Nizigiyimana. Bujumbura and Paris: Éditions Iwacu and Éditions Karthala, 2012.

Sachar, Howard M., et al., eds. *The Rise of Israel: A Documentary Record from the Nineteenth Century to 1948.* Vols. 23, 25, 31, 32, 35, 36, 37. New York: Garland, 1987.

Sakharov, Andrei. *Sakharov Speaks.* Edited by Harrison E. Salisbury. New York: Vintage, 1974.

Scott-Stokes, Henry, and Lee Jai Eui, eds. *The Kwangju Uprising: Eyewitness Press Accounts of Korea's Tiananmen.* Armonk: M. E. Sharpe, 2000.

Sibley, Henry H. "Reminiscences of the Early Days of Minnesota." In *Collections of the Minnesota Historical Society*, vol. 3, *1870–1880*, 242–82. Saint Paul: Minnesota Historical Society, 1880.

Soll, Karl, ed. *Der Wiener Kongreß: In Schilderungen von Zeitgenossen*. Berlin: Allstein, n.d.

Stalin, J. V. *Marxism and the National Question* (1913). In *Works*, vol. 2, *1907–1913*, 300–381. Moscow: Progress, 1953.

———. *Marxism and the National Question: Selected Writings and Speeches*. New York: International, 1942.

Strangford, Viscount Percy Smythe. *Lord Strangford at the Sublime Porte: The Eastern Crisis*. 4 vols. Edited by Theophilus C. Prousis. Istanbul: Isis, 2010.

Suh, Dae-Sook, ed. *Documents of Korean Communism, 1918–1948*. Princeton: Princeton University Press, 1970.

Velestinlis, Rhigas. *Les oeuvres de Rhigas Velestinlis*. Edited by Ap. Dascalakis. Paris, 1937.

Venizelos, Eleutherios. *Greece before the Peace Congress of 1919: A Memorandum Dealing with the Rights of Greece*. New York: Oxford University Press for the American-Hellenic Society, 1919.

Verissimo, José. *A educação nacional*. 2nd ed. Rio de Janeiro: Livraria Francisco Alves, 1906.

Williams, Daryle, Amy Chazkel, and Paulo Knauss, eds. *The Rio de Janeiro Reader: History, Culture, Politics*. Durham: Duke University Press, 2016.

Witbooi, Hendrik. *The Hendrik Witbooi Papers*. 2nd ed. Translated by Annemarie Heywood and Eben Maasdorp. Edited by Brigitte Lau. Windhoek: National Archives of Namibia, 1995.

Travel Accounts

Bird, Isabella L. *Unbeaten Tracks in Japan: An Account of Travels on Horseback in the Interior, Including Visits to the Aborigines of Yezo and the Shrines of Nikkô and Isé*. 2 vols. New York: G. P. Putnam's Sons, 1881.

Bright, Richard. *Travels from Vienna through Lower Hungary; with Some Remarks on the State of Vienna during the Congress, in the Year 1814*. Edinburgh: Archibald Constable, 1818.

De Kay, James E. *Sketches of Turkey in 1831 and 1832*. New York: Harper, 1833.

Ewbank, Thomas. *Life in Brazil; or, A Journal to the Land of Cocoa and Palms*. New York: Harper and Brothers, 1856.

Fletcher, James C., and D. P. Kidder. *Brazil and the Brazilians Portrayed in Historical and Descriptive Sketches*. London: Low and Marston, 1866.

Gale, James Scarth. *Korea in Transition*. New York: Educational Department, Board of Foreign Missions of the Presbyterian Church in the USA, 1909.

Griffis, William Elliot. *Corea: The Hermit Nation*. 6th ed. New York: Charles Scribner's Sons, 1897.

Hamilton, Angus. *Korea*. New York: C. Scribner's Sons, 1904.

Harris, Townsend. *The Complete Journal of Townsend Harris: First American Consul General and Minister to Japan*. Edited by Mario Emilio Cosenza. Garden City: Doubleday for the Japan Society, 1930.

James, William. *Brazil through the Eyes of William James: Letters, Diaries, and Drawings, 1865–1866*. Edited by Maria Helena P. T. Machado. Cambridge: David Rockefeller Center for Latin American Studies, Harvard University Press, 2006.

Kolokotronis, Th. *Memoirs from the Greek War of Independence, 1821–1833*. Translated by G. Tertzetis. 1892. Chicago: Argonaut, 1969.

Kunitake, Kume, comp. *The Iwakura Embassy, 1871–73: A True Account of the Ambassador Extraordinary & Plenipotentiary's Journey of Observation through the United States of America and Europe*. Edited by Graham Healey and Chushichi Tsuzuki. Chiba: Japan Documents, 2002.

Langsdorff, Georg Heinrich von. *Voyages and Travels in Various Parts of the World during the Years 1803, 1804, 1805, 1806, and 1807*. Carlisle: George Philips, 1817.

Leyden, John, and Hugh Murray. *Historical Account of Discoveries and Travels in Africa*. 2 vols. Edinburgh: A. Constable, 1817.

Lowell, Percival. *Chosön: The Land of the Morning Calm. A Sketch of Korea*. Boston: Ticknor, 1886.

Monro, Vere. *A Summer Ramble in Syria, with a Tatar Trip from Aleppo to Stamboul*. 2 vols. London: R. Bentley, 1835.

Sonnini, C. S. *Travels in Greece and Turkey, Undertaken by Order of Louis XVI, and with the Authority of the Ottoman Court*. 2 vols. Translated from French. London: T. N. Longman, 1801.

Spalding, J. W. *The Japan Expedition: Japan and around the World. An Account of Three Visits to the Japanese Empire*. New York: Redfield, 1855.

Tahtawi, Rifa'a Rafi' al-. *An Imam in Paris: Account of a Stay in France by an Egyptian Cleric (1826–1831)*. Translated by Daniel L. Newman. London: Saqi, 2004.

Taylor, Bayard. *A Visit to India, China, and Japan in the Year 1853*. New York: Putnam, 1855.

Art, Music, Architecture, and Literature

Blake, William. "Jerusalem ['And Did Those Feet in Ancient Time']" (1808). Poetry Foundation. https://www.poetryfoundation.org/poems-and-poets/poems/detail/54684.

Byron, George Gordon. *Byron's Letters and Journals*. Edited by Leslie A. Marchand. London: John Murray, 1981.

———. *Selected Letters of Lord Byron*. Edited by Jacques Barzun. New York: Farrar, Straus and Young, 1953.

Farantouri, Maria. "The Laughing Boy." In Pieter Hendriks, "Theodorakis Farantouri To Yelasto Pedi 1974," YouTube, 8 September 2007, https://www.youtube.com/watch?v=NLgerQJo7zM. And in Mikis Theodorakis, "Mikis Theodorakis–Maria Farantouri 'To gelasto paidi,'" YouTube, 1 February 2016, https://www.youtube.com/watch?v=ZhoLsSvm40Q.

Kim, Chi Ha. *The Middle Hour: Selected Poems of Kim Chi Ha*. Translated by David R. McCann. Stanfordville: Human Rights Publishing, 1980.

Lee, Min Jin. *Pachinko*. New York: Grand Central, 2017.

Murakami, Haruki. *The Wind-Up Bird Chronicle*. Translated by Jay Rubin. New York: Knopf, 1997.

Niemeyer, Oscar. "The Curves of Life: An Interview with Oscar Niemeyer." By Niklas Maak. In *Oscar Niemeyer: A Legend of Modernism*, edited by Paul Andreas and Ingeborg Flagge, 21–26. Basel: Birkhäuser, 2003.

———. *The Curves of Time: The Memoirs of Oscar Niemeyer*. Translated by Izabel Murat Burbridge. London: Pahidon, 2000.

Peterson, Amy A., ed. and trans. *The Major Abolitionist Poems*. New York: Garland, 1990.

Rotas, Vassilis. "The Laughing Boy." In Pieter Hendriks, "Theodorakis Farantouri To Yelasto Pedi 1974," YouTube, 8 September 2007, https://www.youtube.com/watch?v=NLgerQJo7zM. And in Mikis Theodorakis, "Mikis Theodorakis–Maria Farantouri 'To gelasto paidi,'" YouTube, 1 February 2016 https://www.youtube.com/watch?v=ZhoLsSvm40Q.

Solomos, Dionysios. *The Free Besieged and Other Poems*. Edited by Peter Mackridge. Translated by Peter Thompson. Nottingham: Shoestring, 2000.

———. "Hymn to Freedom" (1918). Translated by Rudyard Kipling. In Wikisource contributors, "Hymn to Liberty (Kipling)," Wikisource, version ID 6145610, https://en.wikisource.org/wiki/Hymn_to_Liberty_(Kipling).

INDEX

A page number in italics refers to a figure or map, or to its caption.

HUMAN RIGHTS AND CRIMES AGAINST HUMANITY

Eric D. Weitz, Series Editor